Austria

M. Hertlein/MICHELIN

"Land of mountains, land on the river,
Land of fields, land of cathedrals,
Land of hammers, rich in outlook!
You are the native home of great sons,
A people uniquely gifted for the beautiful,
Much applauded Austria."

Austrian National Anthem
(Translation of original text by Paula von Preradoviæ)

38 Clarendon Road - WATFORD Herts WD1 1SX - U.K.
Tel. (01923) 415 000
www.michelin-travel.com
TheGreenGuide-uk@uk.michelin.com

Manufacture française des pneumatiques Michelin
Société en commandite par actions au capital de 2 000 000 000 de francs
Place des Carmes-Déchaux – 63000 Clermont-Ferrand (France)
R.C.S. Clermont-Fd B 855 200 507

Dépôt légal mars 2001 – ISBN 2-06-000886-7 – ISSN 0763-1383

Printed in France 02-01/3.1

Compogravure : MAURY Imprimeur S.A., Malesherbes
Impression et brochage : AUBIN, Ligugé.

Cover design : Carré Noir, Paris 17e

THE GREEN GUIDE: The Spirit of Discovery

The exhilaration of new horizons, the fun of seeing the world, the excitement of discovery: this is what we seek to share with you. To help you make the most of your travel experience, we offer first-hand knowledge and turn a discerning eye on places to visit.
This wealth of information gives you the expertise to plan your own enriching adventure. With THE GREEN GUIDE showing you the way, you can explore new destinations with confidence or rediscover old ones.
Leisure time spent with THE GREEN GUIDE is also a time for refreshing your spirit, enjoying yourself, and taking advantage of our selection of fine restaurants, hotels and other places for relaxing.
So turn the page and open a window on the world. Join THE GREEN GUIDE in the spirit of discovery.

Contents

Introduction

Sights

J.-D. Sudres/DIAF

Austrian customs: a masked "Perchten" (pre-Epiphany processions)

Y. Travert/DIAF

Goldenes Dachl, Innsbruck

Practical information

Pratt-Pries/DIAF

Traditional East Tyrolean costume

S. Grandadam/HOA-QUI

Vienna - Coffee time

Maps and plans

COMPANION PUBLICATIONS

Michelin map 926 Österreich
– a road map with tourist information, at a scale of 1:400 000, with an index of place names and maps of the Salzburg and Vienna conurbations

... and for getting to Austria:

Michelin map 987 Deutschland, Österreich, Benelux, Ceská Republika
– a road map with tourist information, at a scale of 1: 1 000 000

Michelin map 970 Europe
– a road map with tourist information, at a scale of 1: 3 000 000, with an index of place names

Michelin road atlas Europe
Spiral-bound, with an index of place names, more than 40 states, 73 city and conurbation maps, including Salzburg and Vienna

LIST OF MAPS AND PLANS

Local maps

Route cross sections

Town plans

Site maps and ground plans

Other maps

Using this guide

For a fascinating adventure, use The Green Guide to be well informed and well prepared to set off in search of fun and novelty on your holiday.

- The summary maps on the following pages are designed to assist you in planning your trip: the **Map of principal sights** identifies major sights and attractions and the **Map of touring programmes** proposes regional driving itineraries for exploring some of Austria's most beautiful regions.
- We recommend that you read the **Introduction** before setting out on your trip. The background on history, the arts and traditional culture will make your visit more meaningful.
- The main towns and attractions are presented in alphabetical order in the **Sights** section ; original place names have been used throughout. The clock symbol ⓥ refers you to the **Admission times and charges** section at the end of the guide, listed in the same order as in the Sights section. The detailed **Index** helps you find references to subjects covered in the guide.
- A new feature of this guide is the **blue pages** which list hotels and restaurants for the major towns in Austria as well as other suggestions for an evening on the town and entertainment.
- The **Practical information** section offers more useful addresses for planning your trip, seeking accommodation, indulging in outdoor activities and more; opening hours and admission prices for monuments, museums and other tourist attractions; festival and carnival dates etc.

Let us hear from you. We are interested in your reaction to our guide, in any ideas you have to offer or good addresses you would like to share. Send your comments to Michelin Tyre PLC, Michelin Travel Publications, 38 Clarendon Road, Watford, Herts WD1 1SX, U.K. or *thegreenguide-uk@uk.michelin.com.*

M. Hertlein/MICHELIN

Key

	Sight	Seaside Resort	Winter Sports Resort	Spa
Worth a journey	★★★			
Worth a detour	★★			
Interesting	★			

Tourism

- Admission Times and Charges listed at the end of the guide
- Sightseeing route with departure point indicated
- Ecclesiastical building
- Synagogue – Mosque
- Building (with main entrance)
- Statue, small building
- Wayside cross
- Fountain
- Fortified walls – Tower – Gate
- Visit if time permits
- AZ B Map co-ordinates locating sights
- Tourist information
- Historic house, castle – Ruins
- Dam – Factory or power station
- Fort – Cave
- Prehistoric site
- Viewing table – View
- Miscellaneous sight

Recreation

- Racecourse
- Skating rink
- Outdoor, indoor swimming pool
- Marina, moorings
- Mountain refuge hut
- Overhead cable-car
- Tourist or steam railway
- Waymarked footpath
- Outdoor leisure park/centre
- Theme/Amusement park
- Wildlife/Safari park, zoo
- Gardens, park, arboretum
- Aviary, bird sanctuary

Additional symbols

- Motorway (unclassified)
- Junction: complete, limited
- Pedestrian street
- Unsuitable for traffic, street subject to restrictions
- Steps – Footpath
- Railway – Coach station
- Funicular – Rack-railway
- Tram – Metro, Underground
- Bert (R.)... Main shopping street
- Post office – Telephone centre
- Covered market
- Barracks
- Swing bridge
- Quarry – Mine
- B F Ferry (river and lake crossings)
- Ferry services: Passengers and cars
- Foot passengers only
- ③ Access route number common to MICHELIN maps and town plans

Abbreviations and special symbols

G	Police (Gendarmerie)
J	Law courts (Justizgebäude)
L	Provincial capital (Landeshauptstadt)
L	Provincial government (Landhaus)
M	Museum (Museum)
POL.	Police (Polizei)
R	Town hall (Rathaus)
T	Theatre (Theater)
U	University (Universität)
P	Park and Ride
20	National road with right of way (Vorfahrtsberechtigte Bundesstraße)
128	Other federal roads (Sonstige Bundesstraße)

NB: The German letter ß (eszett) has been used throughout this guide.

Principal sights

The names of towns and sights described in the guide appear in black on the maps. See the index for the page number.

The main winter sports resorts and spas are classified according to range of facilities offerred.

Worth a journey ★★★

Worth a detour ★★

Interesting ★

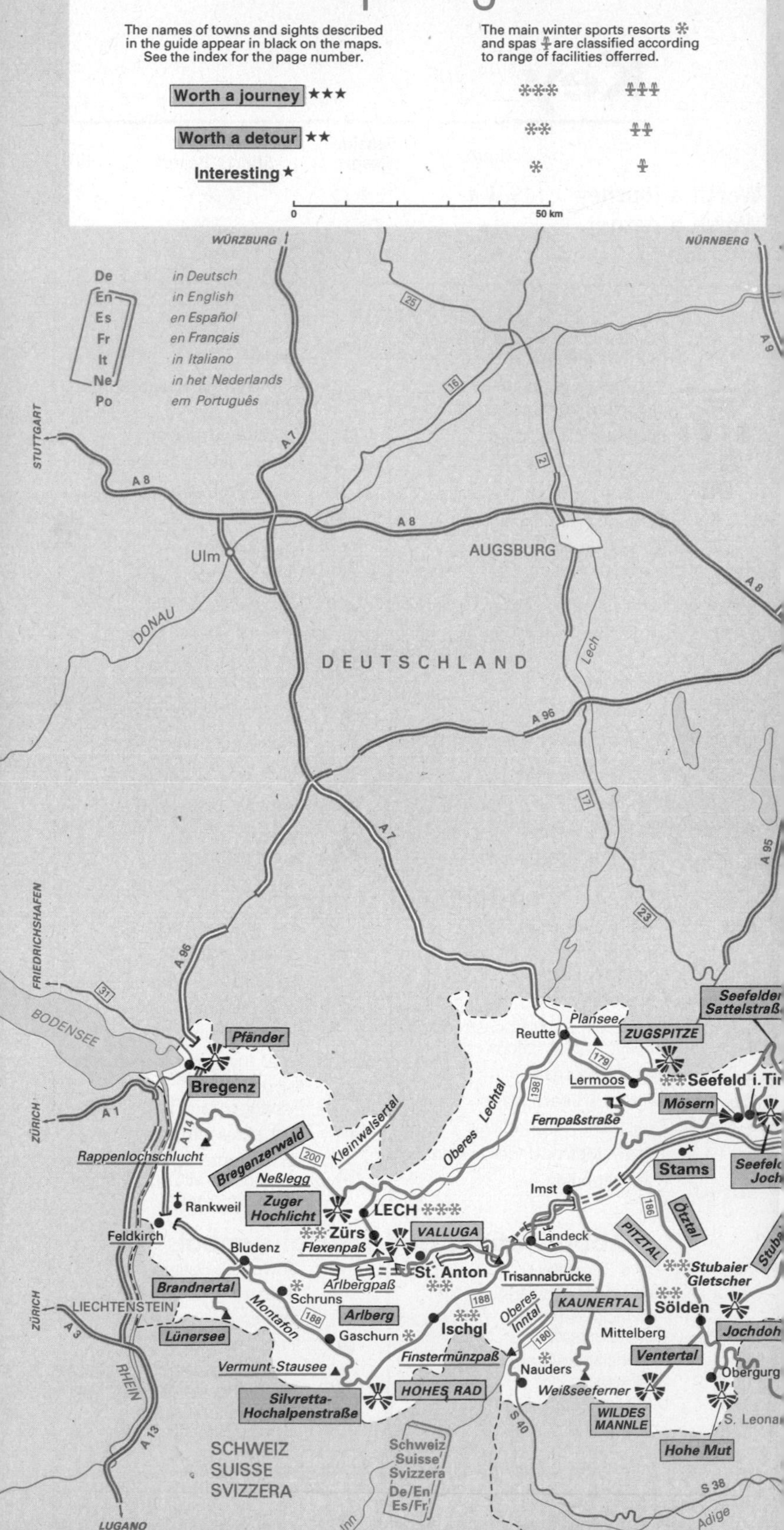

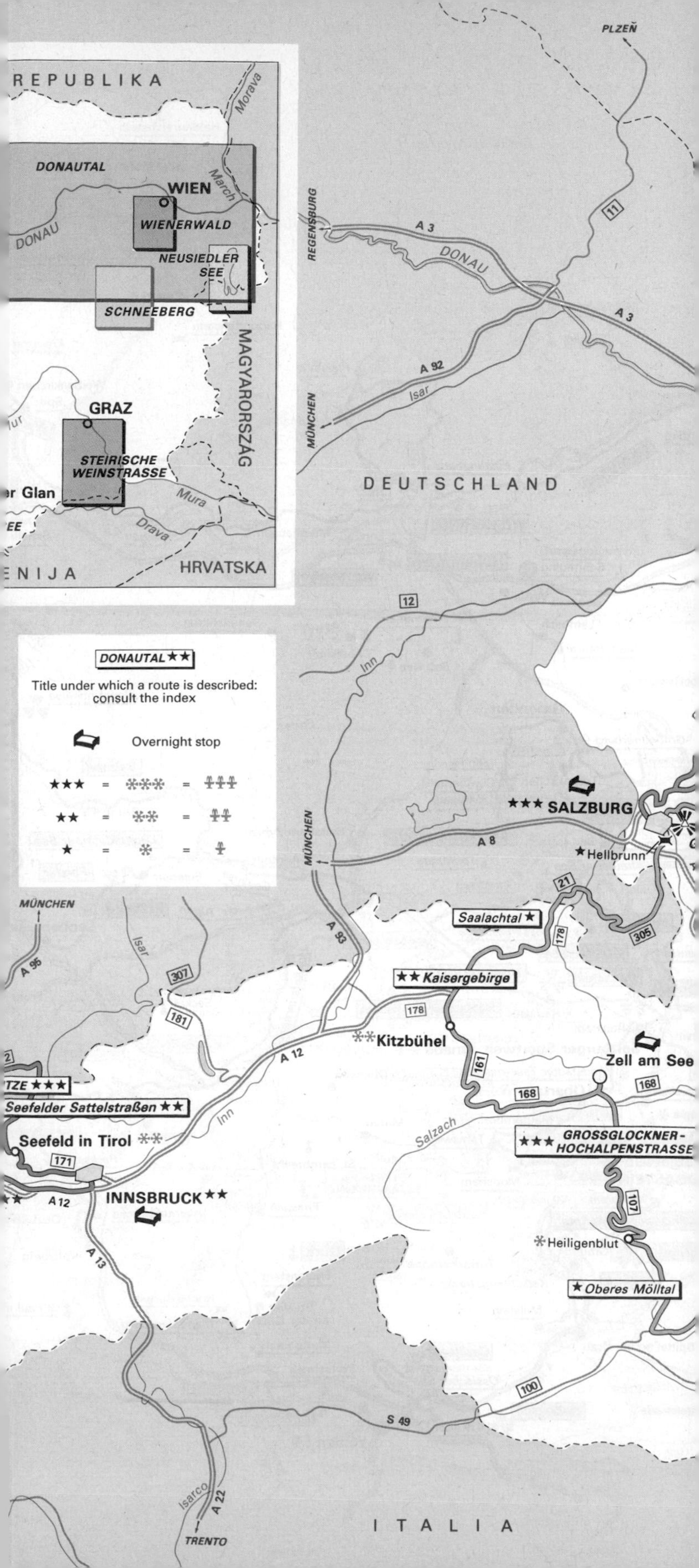

REPUBLIKA
Morava
DONAUTAL
WIEN
March
DONAU
WIENERWALD
NEUSIEDLER SEE
SCHNEEBERG
MAGYARORSZÁG
GRAZ
STEIRISCHE WEINSTRASSE
Mura
Drava
HRVATSKA
PLZEŇ
REGENSBURG
A 3
DONAU
11
A 92
Isar
MÜNCHEN
DEUTSCHLAND
12
Inn
DONAUTAL ★★
Title under which a route is described: consult the index
Overnight stop
★★★ = ✻✻✻ = ‡‡‡
★★ = ✻✻ = ‡‡
★ = ✻ = ‡
★★★ SALZBURG
A 8
★Hellbrunn
21
Saalachtal ★
178
305
★★ Kaisergebirge
MÜNCHEN
A 93
A 95
307
181
178
✻✻Kitzbühel
A 12
161
Zell am See
168
168
Seefelder Sattelstraßen ★★
Seefeld in Tirol ✻✻
171
Inn
Salzach
★★★ GROSSGLOCKNER-HOCHALPENSTRASSE
INNSBRUCK★★
A 12
A 13
107
✻Heiligenblut
★ Oberes Mölltal
100
S 49
Isarco
A 22
TRENTO
ITALIA

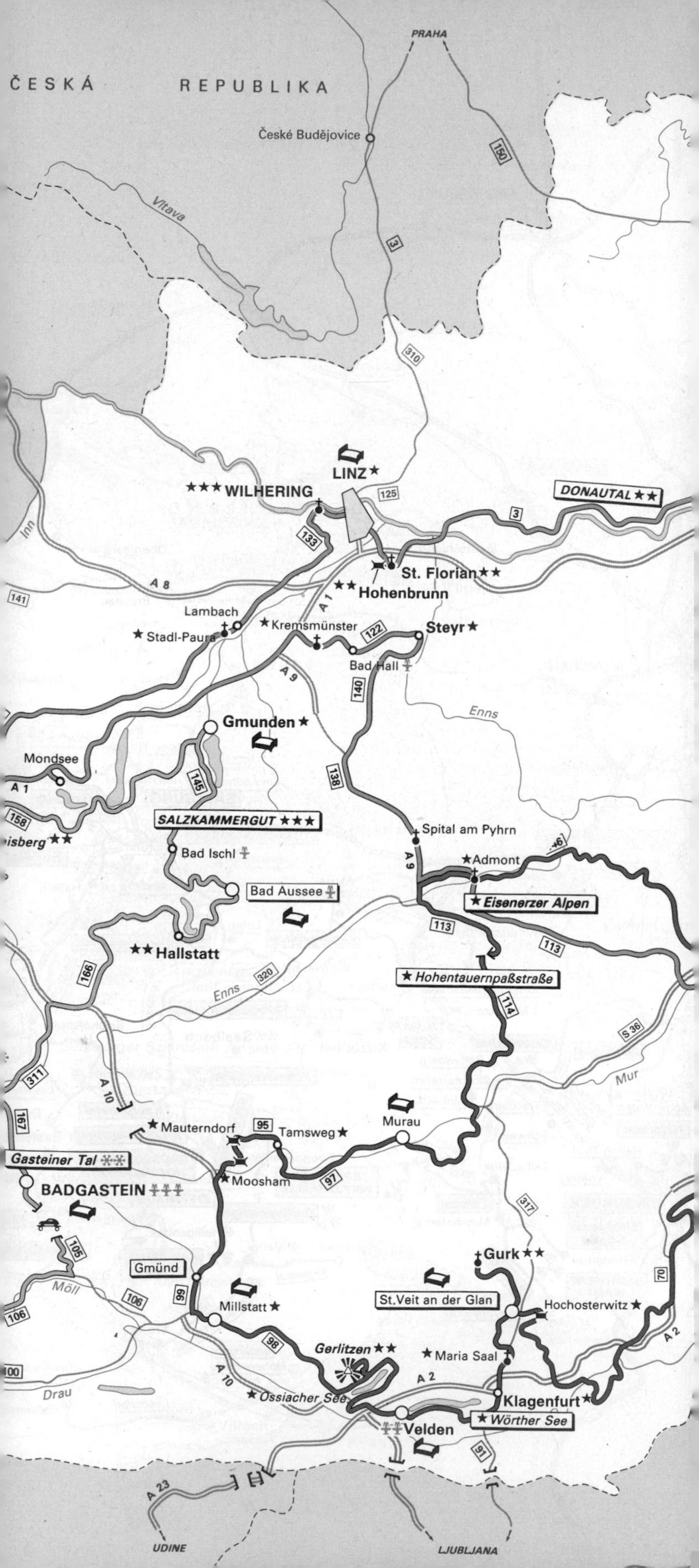

PRAHA
ČESKÁ REPUBLIKA
České Budějovice
Vltava
150
3
310
LINZ ★
★★★ WILHERING
125
DONAUTAL ★★
3
133
Inn
St. Florian ★★
★★ Hohenbrunn
A 8
141
Lambach
★ Kremsmünster
★ Stadl-Paura
122
Steyr ★
A 1
A 9
Bad Hall
140
Enns
Gmunden ★
Mondsee
A 1
145
138
158
SALZKAMMERGUT ★★★
isberg ★★
Spital am Pyhrn
Bad Ischl
★ Admont
A 9
146
Bad Aussee
★ Eisenerzer Alpen
113
113
★★ Hallstatt
★ Hohentauernpaßstraße
166
320
Enns
114
S 36
311
Mur
A 10
167
★ Mauterndorf
95
Tamsweg ★
Murau
Gasteiner Tal
BADGASTEIN
★ Moosham
97
317
105
Gurk ★★
Gmünd
Möll
106
99
106
Millstatt ★
St. Veit an der Glan
Hochosterwitz ★
70
98
Gerlitzen ★★
★ Maria Saal
A 2
100
A 10
A 2
Drau
★ Ossiacher See
Klagenfurt ★
★ Wörther See
Velden
91
A 23
UDINE
LJUBLJANA

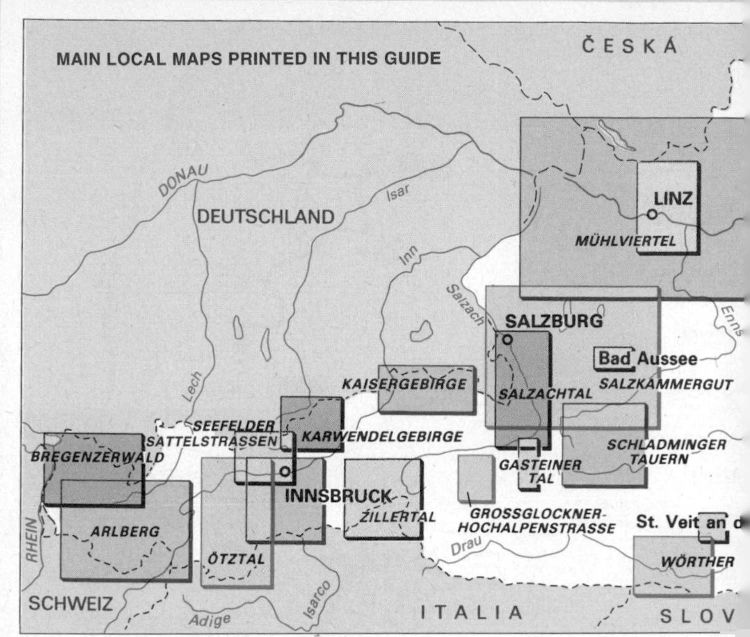

Vorarlberg - Tyrol: 550km - 342 miles - 4 days, including 1 day in Innsbruck.

Hohe Tauern - Salzkammergut: 750km - 466 miles 6 days, including 1 day in Salzburg.

Austrian Baroque: 1 150km - 715 miles - 8 days, including 1 day in Salzburg and 2 days in Vienna (Wien).

Styria - Carinthia: 1 200km - 747 miles - 8 days, including 1 day in Graz.

Vienna (Wien) and surrounding area: 300km - 186 miles 4 days, including 2 days in Vienna (Wien).

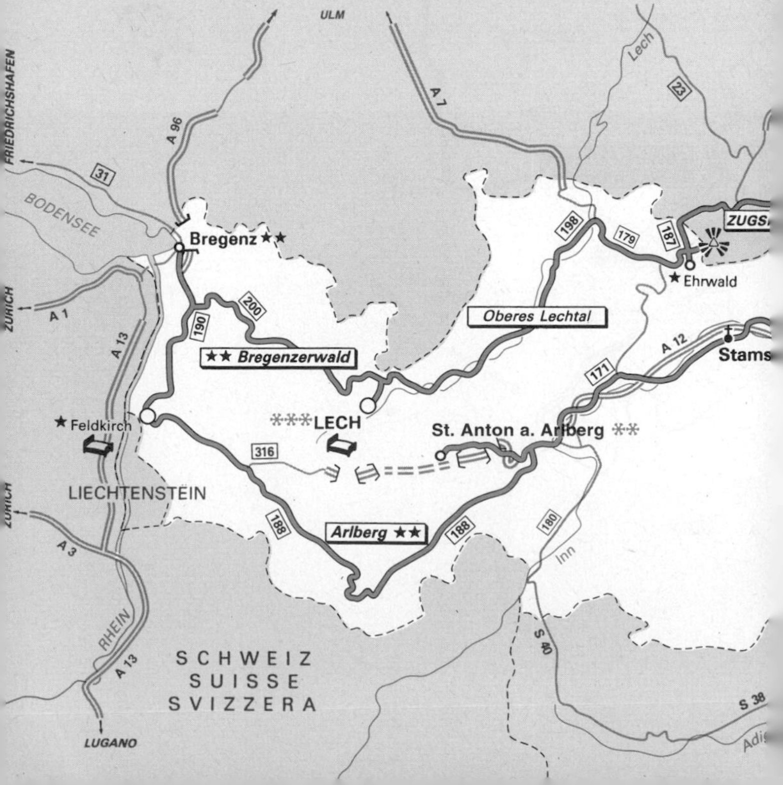

ULM
FRIEDRICHSHAFEN
A 96
A 7
Lech
23
31
BODENSEE
Bregenz ★★
198
179
187
ZUGS
★ Ehrwald
ZURICH
A 1
200
190
A 13
Oberes Lechtal
★★ Bregenzerwald
A 12
Stams
171
★ Feldkirch
✻✻✻ LECH
St. Anton a. Arlberg ✻✻
316
LIECHTENSTEIN
ZURICH
A 3
188
Arlberg ★★
188
180
Inn
RHEIN
A 13
SCHWEIZ
SUISSE
SVIZZERA
S 40
S 38
LUGANO
Adi

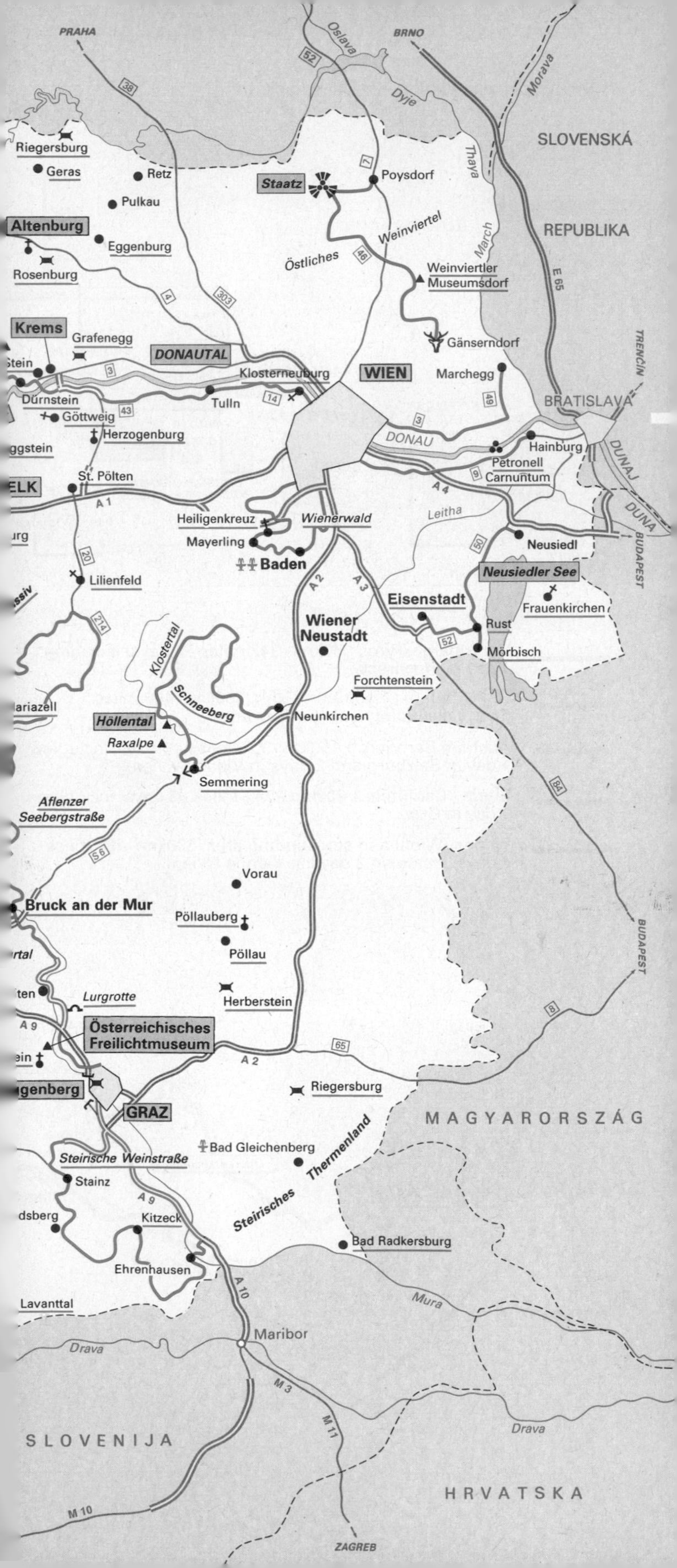

PRAHA
BRNO
Oslava
Dyje
Morava
Thaya
SLOVENSKÁ
REPUBLIKA
Riegersburg
Geras
Retz
Pulkau
Staatz
Poysdorf
Altenburg
Eggenburg
Rosenburg
Weinviertel
Östliches
March
Weinviertler Museumsdorf
E 65
Krems
Grafenegg
DONAUTAL
Gänserndorf
TRENČÍN
Stein
Klosterneuburg
WIEN
Marchegg
Dürnstein
Tulln
Göttweig
Herzogenburg
BRATISLAVA
DONAU
Hainburg
Petronell Carnuntum
DUNAJ
St. Pölten
A 1
A 4
Leitha
DUNA
Heiligenkreuz
Wienerwald
Mayerling
Baden
Neusiedl
BUDAPEST
Lilienfeld
Neusiedler See
A 2
A 3
Eisenstadt
Frauenkirchen
Rust
Wiener Neustadt
Mörbisch
Klostertal
Forchtenstein
Schneeberg
Neunkirchen
Höllental
Raxalpe
Semmering
Aflenzer Seebergstraße
Vorau
Bruck an der Mur
Pöllauberg
Pöllau
BUDAPEST
Lurgrotte
Herberstein
A 9
Österreichisches Freilichtmuseum
A 2
Riegersburg
GRAZ
MAGYARORSZÁG
Bad Gleichenberg
Steirisches Thermenland
Steirische Weinstraße
Stainz
A 9
Kitzeck
Bad Radkersburg
Ehrenhausen
A 10
Mura
Lavanttal
Maribor
Drava
M 3
M 11
Drava
SLOVENIJA
HRVATSKA
M 10
ZAGREB

Touring programmes

Traunkirchen in the Salzkammergut

Introduction

Description of the country

At the heart of the Alps, Austria covers an area of 84 000km²/32 430sq mi, stretching for 580km/360mi from Switzerland to Hungary. For a distance of 2 600km/1 600mi, it shares a border with Germany, the Czech and Slovak republics, Hungary, Slovenia, Italy, Switzerland and Liechtenstein.
The River Danube, which acts as a catchment for virtually all the rivers of Austria, flows west-east for 360km/224mi across the Danube plain, a vast uplands abutting the foothills of the Bohemian mountains to the north and encompassing the mountainous Wachau region. This is the historical heart of Austria. Two thirds of the country is covered by the Alpine chain, beginning with the eastern end of the Alps in the south. To the east, Austria runs into the Puszta, or Hungarian plain.

AN ALPINE COUNTRY

The Austrian Alps are divided from north to south into three chains: the Northern Limestone Alps, the High or Central Alps, and the Southern Limestone Alps, separated from each other by the great furrows which form the valleys of the Inn, the Salzach and the Enns in the north; and the Drava and the Mur in the south.

The Northern Limestone Alps – These overflow to a large extent into Bavaria and spread out west to east into the massifs of Rätikon, Lechtal, Karwendel, Kaisergebirge, Steinernes Meer, Tennengebirge, Dachstein, the Alps of Ennstal, Eisenerz, Hochschwab and Schneeberg, where the dark green forests stand out against the grey limestone cliffs. The highest point is the Parseierspitze at 3 038m/9 967ft.

Transverse valleys – The Limestone Alps are far from forming an unbroken barrier, difficult to cross, in fact the Northern Limestone Alps are divided into distinct massifs by transverse valleys, along which the waters of the Lech, Ache (the Alz in Bavaria), Saalach and Enns flow towards the Danube plateau. Tourists with cars can easily cross or go round these massifs, while the resulting cliffs provide plenty of potential for exploration by mountaineers.

Karst plateaux – The Alps east of the Ache have a characteristic outline: the Dachstein, the Hochschwab and the Raxalpe rise sharply to summits of more than 2 000m/6 500ft. The porous nature of their limestone rocks makes these barren plateaux into stony deserts, scored here and there with narrow furrows, between which rise small sharp crests formed by watercourses through the limestone. Here, the flow of the water is almost entirely subterranean and results in the formation of numerous caves, the most well known being those of the Dachstein.

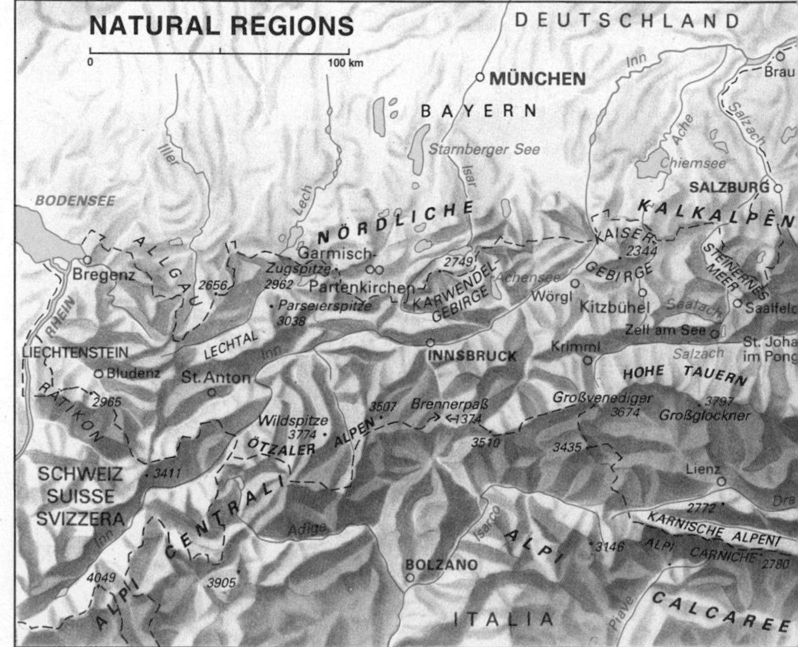

The climb by cable-car to the Krippenstein or the Raxalpe will reveal all the characteristic features of this karstic landscape.

Long river valleys – The Northern Limestone Alps are bounded to the south by a deep cleft, separating them from the High Alps. This cleft is divided into valleys, each with its own river, the Inn (between Landeck and Wörgl), the Salzach (between Krimml and St. Johann im Pongaa), and the Enns (between Radstadt and Hieflan). The presence of this major break in the landscape has been of great benefit to east-west communications, making it possible to drive along the chain for its entire length.

The High or Central Alps – The High Alps, mostly of crystalline rock, appear as a succession of ridges topped by glaciers, comprising (west to east): the Ötztal Alps (Wildspitze, 3 774m/12 382ft), the Hohe Tauern (Großvenediger, 3 674m/12 054ft – and Großglockner, 3 797m/12 458ft) with their dazzling glaciers, and the Niedere Tauern. The line of the crests hardly drops below 3 000m/10 000ft for a distance of more than 250km/150mi; mountain passes are rare, making the barrier no easy matter to cross. The Brenner pass (1 375m/4 510ft), the medieval route to Venice, links the valleys of the Inn and the Adige. The Großglockner road and the Felbertauern tunnel enable tourists to cross the imposing massif of the Hohe Tauern. To the south of the High Alps, the furrows of the Drava, Mur and Mürz rivers play a role that is comparable to the great valleys of the north and form the natural link between Vienna and Venice or Milan.

Nationalpark Hohe Tauern – Some of the eastern slopes of the Großglockner and part of the Schobergruppe massif have been designated a national park, with the aim of conserving the varied landscapes, rich flora and wildlife of the area. The extensive network of signposted footpaths gives access to areas of virtually virgin landscape as well as to those parts of the park where a traditional mountain economy and culture still flourish.

The Southern Limestone Alps – The Carnic Alps and the Karawanken are Austrian on their northern slopes only, following Austria's cession, under the terms of the St-Germain-en-Laye Peace Treaty in 1919, of the southern part of the Tyrol to Italy and the Julian Alps to then Yugoslavia.

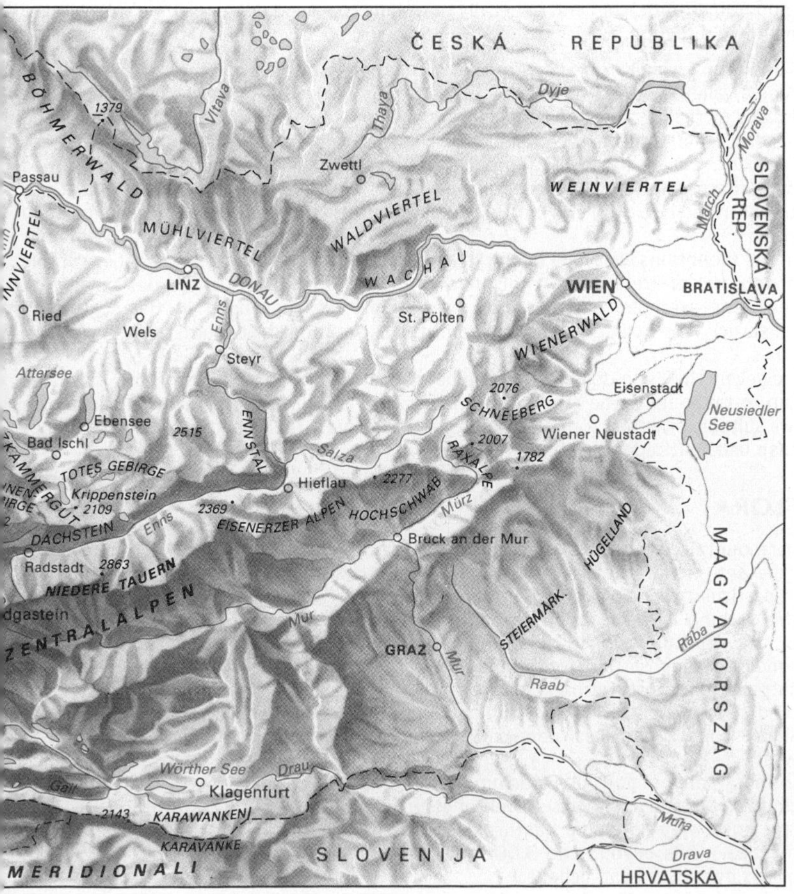

The work of the Alpine glaciers

About 10 000 years ago, the Alpine glaciers advanced northwards, extending over the Bavarian plateau almost as far as the site of modern Munich. These solid rivers of ice were immensely thick; the glacier which occupied the Inn Valley reached a maximum depth of 1 700m/nearly 6 000ft.

The action of the glaciers led to a substantial remodelling of the relief of the Alpine valleys. They scooped out natural amphitheatres known as cirques, like the one closing off the Brandnertal, scoured valleys into a U-shaped section (like the steep-sided Saalach Valley north of Saalfelden), and created hanging valleys (one of the best examples being the one above the Achensee) – funnel-shaped basins with steep cliff walls often featuring spectacular waterfalls where they join the main valley.

Glaciers tended not to follow the existing continuous slope of a valley but to carve out a series of well-defined steps, as evident in the Karawanken, which are natural sites for modern hydroelectric installations. The reservoirs often lie amid breathtaking mountain scenery, as in the case of the Glockner-Kaprun hydroelectric installation, one of the most impressive in Austria.

Carrying along a mass of rocky debris, which when deposited is known as a moraine, the glaciers added an extra, complex layer to the landscape of the pre-alpine plateau. The terminal moraines, semicircular in shape, created natural dams behind which water accumulated to form the lakes of the Bavarian plateau and of the northern Salzkammergut.

Mountain climate

In contrast to weather in the valleys, the mountain climate varies considerably according to difference in altitude, physical relief or exposure to sunshine.

Winds – At the end of morning, the warm expanded air of the valleys creeps up the natural corridors to the heights, causing the formation of clouds round the summits. These clouds are a sign of settled fine weather. However, visitors should nonetheless not leave it until too late in the morning to climb up to viewpoints. Getting on for 5pm the valley breeze drops, and coolness suddenly sets in; it is now the turn of the mountain breeze, cold and generally stronger, to sweep down into the valley in the opposite direction.

The Föhn – This warm autumn wind is most strongly felt north of the Alps, in the Alpine valleys of the Rhine, the Inn (especially in the Ötztal) and the Salzach. It is caused by the passage of a deep depression along the north slope of the Alps. Having shed its moisture on the Italian slope of the range, where storms and rain are frequent, the air drawn in by the depression spills over the crest-line and, warmed by compression as it loses altitude (1°C per 100m or about 34°F per 330ft), is transformed into a dry and burning gale, while the atmosphere becomes wonderfully clear.

In the mountains everyone is on the alert. Torrents are in spate, avalanches rumble and the risk of fire is great. Local inhabitants live in such a state of nervous exhaustion that, for example, examinations are sometimes suspended in the schools in Innsbruck. The Föhn can even be submitted as a mitigating circumstance in criminal trials.

However, the Föhn does have some beneficial effects. It melts the snow, so flocks can be taken up to the Alpine pastures early in the spring. In certain valleys, which are suitably oriented, it makes it possible to cultivate maize and fruit trees at higher than usual altitudes.

FLORA

In mountain areas the pattern of vegetation is not only influenced by soil type and climate but also strongly linked to altitude and aspect. Tree species in particular tend to succeed one another in clearly defined vertical stages, though this staging is much modified by human influences as well as by the orientation of the particular slope. Northern, ie south-facing, sunny slopes offer the best conditions for settlement and agriculture and have therefore been the most subject to deforestation. Southern, ie north-facing, slopes by contrast have tended to keep their trees, which flourish in the prevailing wetter and more shady conditions. This pattern is seen at its best in valleys running east-west.

In most parts of the Alps, farming is practiced up to about the 1 500m/5 000ft contour; beyond this there is a belt of conifer forest. At around 2 200m/7 000ft, the trees give way to alpine pastures with their rich mixture of grasses, herbs and myrtles, while beyond the 3 000m/10 000ft level bare rock prevails, relieved in places by mosses and lichens.

Trees

The Alpine forests consist mainly of conifers, four of which are characterized below. There are many different species of pine, all of which have their needles grouped in bunches of two to five, while their cones have hard, coarse scales.

Spruce (Fichte) – This is the typical tree of north-facing slopes. It has a pointed outline and drooping branches, while its reddish bark (hence its German name of *Rottanne* means red fir) becomes deeply fissured with age. It has sharp needles and its downward-hanging cones fall in one piece from the tree.

Larch (Lärche) – The only European conifer to lose its needles in winter, the larch, is the characteristic tree of sunny south-facing slopes. Its delicate light-green foliage casts a relatively light shade, favouring the growth of a rich grass and herb layer. The small cones are carried upright on the twigs.

M. Janvier/MICHELIN

Austrian Pine

Austrian pine (Schwarzkiefer) – A tree of medium height, the Austrian pine has a dense crown, dark green foliage and a pale and darkly fissured bark. Its needles grow in pairs. It is undemanding in terms of soil and climate, and therefore tolerates the harsh extremes of the continental climate. It is frequently used in reclamation work in difficult conditions (eg on thin limestone soils).

Stone pine (Zirbel) – This pine is easily recognized by its upward-curving branches which give it the look of a candelabra. It grows right up to the tree line, often tortured into fantastic shapes by the wind. Its bluish-green needles grow in clusters of five. The dense wood of this pine is much appreciated by woodcarvers and makers of rustic furniture.

Alpine flora

The name "Alpine" is normally used to describe plants which grow above the tree line. Because of the short growing season (June to August) they flower early, while the disproportionate development and colouring of the flower is a result of exposure to intense ultraviolet light. Resistance to drought is often important (woolly leaf surfaces, thick leaves for water storage). Flowering plants found in the Austrian Alps include the Alpine Rose, Gentian, Primrose, Globe Flower and Cyclamen, Martagon Lily, Alpine Aster, Carline Thistle and on the edges of the snow-fields Soldanellae. Rocky areas are home to Edelweiss, Saxifraga, Alpine Poppy and Glacier Crowfoot.

FAUNA

Austria has a rich and varied animal life. The most interesting fauna are to be found around the shores of the Neusiedler See, a paradise for waterfowl and waders *(see illustration under entry)*, of which the area can boast over 250 species: kingfishers, river terns, spoonbills, herons, bitterns, snipes and hoopoes. Storks are also regular visitors here. On the lakes of the Salzkammergut and Upper Austria, swans add a fairy-tale element to the scene.

The Danube is home to 60 of the 80 species of fish to be found in Austria, including eels, perch and catfish.

Various kinds of deer, wild boar, badgers and foxes common to Central Europe make their home in Austria's forests, while the fields and woodlands are a playground for rabbits and hares.

Alpine fauna

Visitors never fail to succumb to the charms of Austria's cutest Alpine resident, the grey-brown **marmot**, which can be up to 60cm/24in long and which lives on slopes exposed to the sun. Unfortunately, being of a somewhat shy disposition, it only rarely grants lucky ramblers a public audience. The **blue hare** is equally cautious, and has the added advantage of a coat which changes colour from brown to white with the seasons, helping it to blend in better with its surroundings.

Herds of nimble **chamois** are to be seen principally in the Limestone Alps. **Alpine ibex**, equally agile and also very strong, live from the tree line up to an altitude of 3 500m/11 483ft. Red deer are common throughout Austria. The snow-mouse makes its home above the forest line, while the Alpine salamander prefers the shores of mountain lakes.

Typical Alpine bird life includes the snow-partridge, the Alpine jackdaw, the griffon vulture and the capercaillie, which is more rare a sight, tending to keep to lower-lying areas, as does the blackcock. On the whole, and especially during the mating season, these birds are more likely to be heard than seen. King of them all, however, is surely the **golden eagle**, a truly majestic bird with a wingspan of 2m/7ft, which sadly rather seldom makes an appearance.

Edelweiss
Leontopodium alpinum
July to September

Stemless Trumpet Gentian
Gentiana acaulis
May to August

Alpine Sea Holly
Eryngium alpinum
July and August

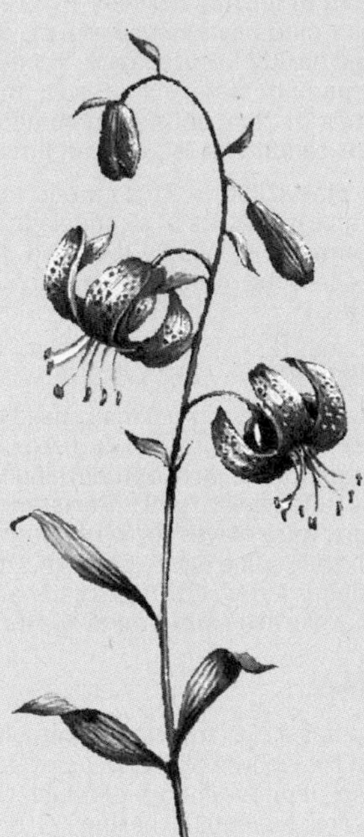

Martagon Lily
Lilium martagon
June to August

Orange Lily
Lilium bulbiferum
June and July

Alpenrose
Rhododendron ferrugineum
July and August

M. Janvier/MICHELIN

Historical table and notes

The main events since the rise of the Habsburgs.

The Habsburgs

1273-1291	**Rudolf I**, founder of the Habsburg dynasty, is elected by the German princes to succeed the Babenbergs, defeats Ottokar and divides Austria and Styria between his sons.
1335	Carinthia and Carniola are annexed to the Habsburg territory.
1358-1365	Reign of **Rudolf IV**. The Tyrol is annexed to Austria (1363).
1440-1493	Friedrich III, Duke of Styria, inaugurates a policy of political succession and intermarriage which raises the Habsburgs to the highest rank in the west. His son Maximilian is the first to benefit from this.

Expansion of the Habsburg Empire

1493-1519	By his marriage to the daughter of Charles the Bold, **Maximilian I**, Emperor of the Holy Roman Empire, gains possession of most of the Burgundian states (Low Countries, Franche-Comté). He marries his eldest son, Philip the Handsome, to the Infanta of Spain. Their son, Charles V, inherits the whole of their possessions.
1519-1556	Reign of **Emperor Charles V**. Vienna is besieged by the Turks (1529).
1556	Abdication of Charles V and partition of the Empire. Charles' brother, Ferdinand I, becomes Emperor and head of the Austrian branch of the House of Habsburg. He founds the Austrian Monarchy and also reigns over Bohemia and Hungary. Charles' son, Philip II, is given Spain and Portugal, Sicily, Naples and northern Italy, the Low Countries and Burgundy.
1618-1648	Thirty Years War begins as a religious conflict and ends up as a Europe-wide power struggle.

Consolidation of the Austrian Empire

1657-1705	Reign of Leopold I. Vienna is again besieged by the Turks (1683). The Hungarian monarchy falls to the Habsburgs (1687).
18C	Throughout this century, Austrian policy is overshadowed by three great problems: the Succession to the Empire; the territorial threat from the Turks, the Piedmontese and the French; the unified administration of very different countries.
1713	To ensure his daughter's succession to the imperial crown in the absence of male heirs, Charles VI sacrifices territorial rights to the great European countries and promulgates the Pragmatic Sanction. When the king dies, Maria Theresa has to defy its signatories in order to keep her empire. War of the Austrian Succession (1740-48). Seven Years War (1756-63).
1740-1790	Reign of **Maria Theresa** (1740-65). With the help of able ministers, she becomes popular for her financial and administrative reforms. Reign of **Joseph II** (1765-90) who, in the authoritarian manner of enlightened despotism, continues the work of reorganization begun by his mother.
1781	Abolition of serfdom.
1786	Secularization: Dissolution of 738 houses of contemplative orders in favour of the parishes under Joseph II.
1792-1835	Reign of **Franz II**. In 1805 Austria receives the territory of the archbishops of Salzburg as compensation for the losses of territory suffered by her under the Treaty of Pressburg. Franz II renounces the title of Head of the Holy Roman Empire and adopts that of Emperor of Austria under the name of **Franz I** in 1806.
1809	Austrian policy, particularly foreign policy, is directed by Chancellor **Metternich** who works for revenge against France. Rebellion of the Tyrol is led by Andreas Hofer against the Franco-Bavarian alliance.

Maria Theresa

Trouble and downfall of the monarchy

1814-1815 — **Congress of Vienna** to redraw the map of Europe. Austria recovers Lombardy and Venetia, lost in her wars with France, and takes a leading position in the Germanic Confederation of which Metternich is the mastermind.

1848-49 — March Revolution in Vienna. Fall of Metternich, Hungarian rebellion is suppressed with the help of Russia.

1848-1916 — Reign of **Franz Joseph**.

1866 — War between Austria and Prussia. Austria is defeated at Sadowa (Königgrätz, Bohemia), gives up her intervention in German politics and casts her eyes upon the Balkans.

1867 — Creation of the dual Austro-Hungarian monarchy, with common foreign, defence and economic policies.

1914 — Outbreak of the First World War (1914-18), provoked by the assassination of the Crown Prince Franz Ferdinand at Sarajevo in Bosnia and Austria's subsequent attack on Serbia.

1916-1918 — Reign of **Karl I**. Collapse of the Austro-Hungarian monarchy after defeat in the First World War.

The Republic

1919 — Treaty of St Germain-en-Laye (drawing up of new national boundaries). Cession of South Tyrol to Italy. A plebiscite (1920) determines that southern Carinthia should remain in Austria and not be ceded to then Yugoslavia.

Women are given the vote.

1920 — Passing of federal constitution.

1933 — Chancellor **Engelbert Dollfuß** inaugurates an authoritarian regime, hostile both to the Social Democrats and to the Nazis.

1934 — Social Democratic Party banned. Suppression of Nazi putsch. Assassination of Chancellor Dollfuß. His successor Schuschnigg seeks to avoid war with Germany at all costs.

1938 — Hitler annexes Austria to the German Reich as the Ostmark, or Eastern March of the Greater German Reich; the annexation **(Anschluß)** is approved by a referendum.

1939-45	Second World War.
1943	In the Moscow Declaration the four Allied Nations undertake to restore Austria's independence after the war and restore the frontiers of 1 January 1938.
1945	The Russians occupy Vienna on 11 April. On 27 April a new government is formed under the premiership of Karl Renner. Austria and Vienna are divided into four occupied zones.
1949-66	Coalition government formed by the "People's Party" (ÖVP) and Social Democrats (SPÖ).
15 May 1955	**Staatsvertrag**, treaty between the occupying powers and Austria. Withdrawal of occupying troops.
26 October 1955	Austria declares its neutrality.
1956	Austria is accepted onto the Council of Europe.
1970-83	Social democrats form a government on their own under Chancellor Bruno Kreisky, for the first time with an absolute majority in Parliament.
1983-2000	Government is once again a coalition of the SPÖ and ÖVP.
1989	Austria applies for membership of the European Community.
	Death of Zita of Bourbon-Parma, last Empress of Austria and Queen of Hungary, in exile since 1919.
1 January 1995	Austria becomes a member of the European Union.
1998	Austria is admitted as a member of the European Monetary Union.
2000-	Coalition government formed by the ÖVP and the Austrian Freedom (or Liberal) Party (FPÖ).

MILESTONES IN AUSTRIAN HISTORY

The Eastern March - The Romans arrived in the Danube Valley at an early date. All along the river there arose a defensive system of forts and castles, of which Carnuntum (Petronell), capital of the province of Pannonia, was the hub. The mixing of peoples which occurred in Europe following the Celtic occupation had its greatest effect in Austria.
After defeating the Avar tribes, who lived in the area that is now Hungary, Charlemagne (747-814) reinforced the defensive system of his empire by forming, on the banks of the Danube, the Eastern March - Ostmark or Ostarrîchi - whose name became Österreich in German and finally Austria in English.
This Eastern March was granted to the Babenberg family by Emperor Otto I, son of Heinrich I, Duke of Saxony and successor to the Germanic branch of the Carolingian dynasty.

The House of Babenberg (976-1246) - This family brought unity to a country wrestling with opposing influences and cleverly preserved it through the quarrels of the Papacy and the Empire which set popes against emperors. They chose as residences Pöchlarn, Melk, Tulln, the Leopoldsberg and finally Vienna. It is to them that we owe the foundation of abbeys such as Kremsmünster, St. Florian, Melk, Göttweig and Klosterneuburg.
Under Heinrich II Jasomirgott, Austria was elevated to the rank of a hereditary duchy. The last of the Babenbergs, Frederick the Warrior, was killed while fighting the Magyars.

Bohemian intervention (1246-78) - The vacancy left by Frederick aroused the envy of the kings of Bohemia and Hungary. Ottokar of Bohemia got the better of his rival and imposed his rule on the former possessions of the Babenbergs, but ended by finding an opponent in Rudolf of Habsburg, who had been chosen by the prince-electors to succeed the Babenbergs.

Rudolf the founder - Rudolf I, who was crowned in 1273, immediately attacked Ottokar, occupied Vienna and won the victory of Marchfeld in 1278. The opening phase had begun of what was to be the remarkable destiny of the House of Habsburg.

A.E.I.O.U.

Austria Est Imperare Orbi Universo - "Austria shall rule the world". The meteoric career of the Habsburg dynasty *(see genealogical tree)* in less than three centuries was such that it could adopt this proud motto. To the political wisdom of those Habsburg representatives wearing the imperial crown was added great diplomatic skill.

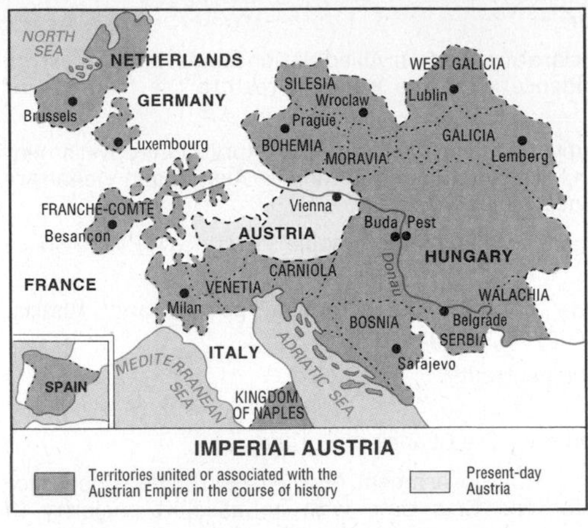

A clever marriage policy brought Austria, in the 16C, more territory than the most fortunate of wars: Maximilian I, a prince who was a friend of the arts *(see INNSBRUCK)*, acquired the Franche-Comté and the Low Countries by his marriage to Mary of Burgundy, daughter of Charles the Bold; his son, Philip the Handsome, married Joan the Mad, Queen of Castile, the child of this union being **Charles V**.

As Holy Roman Emperor, King of Spain, possessor of Naples, Sicily and Sardinia and territories in the two Americas, Emperor Charles V, the successor of the Habsburgs through his father, was the most powerful sovereign in Europe. However, this vast empire remained united for only a short time beneath a single crown. On the abdication of Charles V, the territories were divided between Charles' son, Philip II, and his brother, Ferdinand I, who reigned over the Habsburg's German possessions and Bohemia and Hungary.

Maria Theresa "the Great" (1740-80) – During her reign, Charles VI's daughter managed to win the respect she deserved from Europe's other monarchs largely due to her strength of character and perseverance in pushing forward policy. Maria Theresa can justly be considered a forerunner of "enlightened despotism".

The Empress enjoyed huge popularity among her subjects. She lived unostentatiously, dividing her time between the Hofburg and Schönbrunn, among her immediate family. She bore her husband Francis, Duke of Lorraine, a total of 16 children and took great care to see that her daughters were well married: Maria Antonia became Queen of France (as Marie-Antoinette); Maria Karolina Queen of Naples; Maria Amalia Duchess of Parma; and Maria Christina Governor of the Netherlands.

The struggle with revolutionary France and Napoleon (1792-1815) – For the 23 years during which revolutionary, then Imperial, France was at war with the rest of Europe, Austria was, together with England, her most determined opponent.

It was France which declared war on Franz II, Emperor of Austria and Germany, on 20 April 1792. The war went badly for the Austrians; they came under threat at Leoben in 1797, after Napoleon's daring campaign in north Italy, and were beaten at Marengo and Hohenlinden in 1800.

The accession of Napoleon to the Imperial French throne in 1804 dealt a heavy blow to the Habsburg monarchy. Napoleon I opened his reign with the victories of Ulm and Austerlitz (1805) and forced Franz II to sue for peace and renounce the crown of the Holy Roman Empire. In 1809 the defeat of the French on the battlefields of Essling and Aspern and the successes of the Tyrolese partisans under the leadership of **Andreas Hofer** brought new hope to the Austrians; but the victory of Napoleon at Wagram was followed by the **Treaty of Vienna**, a humiliation for Austria which had to relinquish Carniola, Carinthia, Trieste, Rijeka (or Fiume) and Galicia. In 1810 the victor married Marie-Louise, daughter of the vanquished Emperor. Metternich however refused to accept humiliation and after the Russian campaign of 1812 threw all the forces of Austria against Napoleon. In 1814 the Austrian troops under Schwarzenberg entered Paris. The **Congress of Vienna** consolidated not only the triumph of Metternich, who was virtually directing the politics of all Europe, but renewed the power of the Habsburgs.

The century of Franz Joseph – Franz Joseph's reign of 68 years (1848-1916), one of the longest in history, ranks as a particular milestone in Austria's history, despite the collapse of the Habsburg monarchy two years after his death, largely due to the monarch's personality and the profound social, economic and political changes he made during his reign.

Few monarchs have had to face so many political difficulties: the revolution of 1848, on his accession to the throne, marked by a terrible revolt of the Hungarians, which was checked by aggressive Russian intervention; the compromise *(Ausgleich)* of 1867 which created a dual Austro-Hungarian government; disastrous wars in Italy against Napoleon III in 1859 and against Prussia in 1866. There were also family misfortunes: death of the Emperor's brother, Emperor Maximilian of Mexico, shot in 1867; death of his only son, Crown Prince Rudolf, at Mayerling *(see entry)* in 1889;

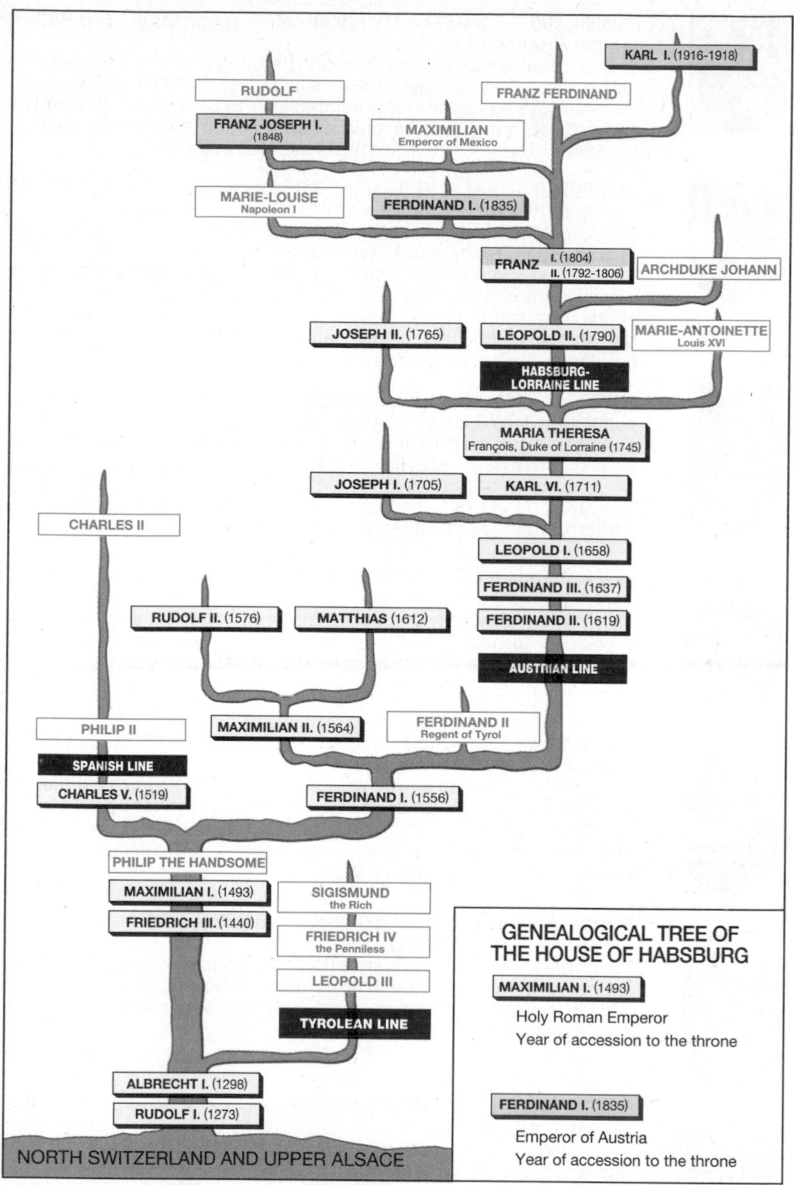

assassination of his wife, Empress Elisabeth (the beautiful Sissi) at Geneva in 1898; assassination of his nephew, Archduke Franz Ferdinand *(see ARTSTETTEN)* at Sarajevo in 1914.

Yet his reign resulted in economic prosperity and a relatively easy going way of life, reflected in the middle class of the period, and by an artistic and cultural revival and development of town planning of which, in Vienna, the layout of the Ring was typical.

THE REPUBLIC OF AUSTRIA

Since 1920, when it adopted a federal constitution similar to that of Switzerland, the Republic of Austria has been a Federal State consisting of nine autonomous provinces.

The Austrian provinces (Bundesländer) – The population of each province *(Land)* elects the members of their **Provincial Diet** every five or six years. The number varies between 36 and 56 in proportion to the size of the population of the province. Only the Diet of Vienna has 100 members.

The diet elects the members of the **Provincial Government** *(Landtag)* on the basis of proportional representation. This government is the administrative organ of the *Land;* it has to have the confidence of the diet, and takes its decisions on a majority vote.

BURGENLAND - 3 965km²/1 531sq mi - population 270 880 - capital: Eisenstadt
This German-speaking province on the border of Hungary became part of Austria under the St Germain Treaty of 1919 and has been the republic's easternmost province since 1921. It is predominantly agricultural, and boasts a unique lake on the edge of the Central European steppes in the form of the Neusiedler See.

CARINTHIA (Kärnten) - 9 533km²/3 681sq mi - population 547 798 - capital: Klagenfurt
The "province of lakes" features about 200 smaller lakes in addition to the four main ones (Wörther, Ossiacher, Millstätter and Weißensee) and numerous charming bathing resorts. This southern province has the only considerable national minority in Austria (4% of the inhabitants speak Slovene). In 1920 a plebiscite was held in the southern districts being claimed by then Yugoslavia, which decided in favour of Austria.

LOWER AUSTRIA (Niederösterreich) - 19 174km²/7 403sq mi - population 1 473 813 - capital: St. Pölten
Considered the historical cradle of the Austrian nation, this is the largest Austrian province and also the most prosperous and extensive agricultural region (arable fields, market gardens, vineyards). It is rich in natural resources (eg oil) and boasts thriving industry, mainly concentrated in the south Viennese basin.

UPPER AUSTRIA (Oberösterreich) - 11 980km²/4 625sq mi - population 1 333 480 - capital: Linz
This region between the Salzkammergut and Bohemia is highly developed agriculturally and industrially. Tourism is of great importance in the lake district of the Salzkammergut.

SALZBURG - 7 154 km²/2 763sq mi - population 482 365 - capital: Salzburg
The former domains of the prince-archbishops of Salzburg did not become part of Austria until 1805. Their economy was based on salt. The Salzburg Festival, together with the province's spas (Badgastein and Bad Hofgastein) and well-equipped ski resorts, attract thousands of tourists every year.

STYRIA (Steiermark) - 16 388km²/6 327sq mi - population 1 184 720 - capital: Graz
The "green province" of Austria (half its surface is covered by forest) is one of the oldest industrial regions in Europe, with important timber and steel industries, stock-breeding and, most importantly for Austria, mining.

TYROL (Tirol) - 12 648km²/4 883sq mi - population 631 410 - capital: Innsbruck
Although 35% of its area is given over to agriculture, the Tyrol is an important industrial area and vital axis for European traffic. It is world-famous as a tourist destination, generating more revenue in this category than any other Austrian province. Since the south Tyrol was ceded to Italy, the east Tyrol is separated from the rest of the province.

VORARLBERG - 2 601km²/1 004sq mi - population 331 472 - capital: Bregenz
Smallest of the federal provinces, this "Ländle" (little country) has a thriving textile and tourism industry and is a major producer of hydroelectric power. Local inhabitants speak a dialect called Alemannisch, related to Swiss and Swabian German.

VIENNA (Wien) - 415 km²/160sq mi - population 1 539 848
The services and ministries of the Federal Government and of the *Land* (District) of Vienna have their headquarters in the capital, as do a number of international organizations.

Federal organization - The **Federal Assembly** *(Bundestag)* consists of the members of the National Council and of the Federal Council, who share the legislative power.
The **National Council** *(Nationalrat)* has 183 members elected for four years by universal suffrage (proportional representation, 4% restrictive clause), by men and women over 19 years of age. It is convoked or dissolved by the Federal President.

The **Federal Council** *(Bundesrat)* is formed by 63 representatives elected by the provincial diets. Its role is to safeguard the rights of the provinces in the administrative and legislative fields *vis-à-vis* the Federation. On the federal level, it has the right to propose laws and its approval is necessary for international agreements and treaties.
The **Federal President** *(Bundespräsident)* or President of the Republic, elected by the people for six years, holds executive power together with the Federal Government. Along with representing the Republic abroad the President appoints the Chancellor and senior civil servants, and promulgates the laws.
The **Federal Government** *(Bundesregierung)* is made up of a Chancellor, a Vice-Chancellor, Ministers and Secretaries of State, appointed by the Federal President on the advice of the Chancellor.

Economic activity

Austria has a total population of some 8 million. About a third of the inhabitants live in the five cities, Vienna, Graz, Linz, Salzburg and Innsbruck, which have a population of more than 100 000. Austria has a population density of 93 people per km^2 - one of the lowest in Europe (population density of the UK: 227 people per km^2). 98% of Austrians speak German as their first language, and there are six recognised ethnic minorities: Slovenians, Croatians, Hungarians, Czechs, Slovakians and Romany gipsies. 78% of Austrians are Roman Catholic.
Austria has been a member of the European Union since January 1995. It has been implementing the Schengen Agreement since 1998 and has belonged to the group of countries introducing the single European currency since 1 January 1999.

AGRICULTURE, FORESTRY AND THE TIMBER INDUSTRY

Although vast areas of mountainous land in Austria are not suitable for cultivation, with the result that there is a steady fall in farming jobs available, **agriculture** continues nonetheless to make an important contribution to the Austrian economy, providing for almost 100% of national food requirements. With a payroll of 159 000, around 5% of Austria's workforce is employed in agriculture and forestry. In 1997, there were still 252 000 going concerns in agriculture and forestry, 51% of which were smaller than 10ha/25 acres, and just 2.6% of which were larger than 100ha/247 acres.
Forests are one of Austria's richest natural resources. They are made up mainly of coniferous trees and cover about 47% of the country's total surface area - a statistic surpassed elsewhere in Europe only by Sweden and Finland. In 1997, over 14.7 million m^3/9 700acft of timber were felled. Agriculture and forestry represent about 3% of gross domestic product.

NATURAL RESOURCES AND INDUSTRY

The break-up of the Austro-Hungrian Empire in 1919 transformed Austria into a rump, cut off from its traditional markets and part of its raw material sources. The situation was exacerbated by the fact that Austrian industry had been developed during the 19C purely to meet the needs of its own huge empire and had not been geared to compete in international markets.
However, Austria is now one of the wealthiest countries in the EU, measured by gross domestic product, and ranks as a highly developed industrial power with a significant services industry sector.

Energy sources

As a mountainous country with numerous rivers, Austria is first and foremost a producer of **hydroelectric power**. Most of its domestic energy requirements are provided for by the output from some 1 300 hydroelectric power stations. The power stations along the Danube alone generate a quarter of the state electricity production.
Oil, another of the natural resources which have been developed since 1938, still plays a role in the Austrian economy, with production at 1 million tons in 1997. The wells, which supply only a fraction of the country's needs however, are mostly located around Matzen, Aderklaa and Zistersdorf in Lower Austria; the oil is refined at Schwechat on the edge of the Vienna conurbation.
The construction of a pipeline leading off to Vienna from the great transalpine Trieste-Ingolstadt oil pipeline (TAL) in 1970 has allowed the refinery at Schwechat, with a capacity of nearly 10 million tons, to work to full production and also supply 26% of the total Austrian industrial, automobile and domestic oil requirements.
Natural gas from Austria's oilfields is highly prized by the country's industrial concerns. Production reached about 1.5 billion m^3/53 billion cu ft in 1997. To meet national demand, 5.9 billion m^3/208 billion cu ft was imported, mainly from Russia.

Mining and heavy industry

Austria is a country with a long tradition in mining and heavy industry; in the Tyrol especially, deposits of gold, silver and copper were mined intensively up to the 17C. Salt mining and the mining of non-ferrous minerals are still carried on, in particular in the production of **magnesite**. Austria is among the most important producers in the world of this mineral, which is used in the fireproof linings for blast furnaces and smelting ovens and also in construction work. So far as building resources are concerned, Austria is self-sufficient in cement.

Of key importance to **heavy industry** in Austria is production in the metallurgical basin in Styria where the well-known Iron Mountain, the Erzberg, is situated. The biggest opencast mine in Europe, it supplies the blast furnaces of Donawitz which produce steel sections and those of Linz producing sheet metal. Domestic iron ore production reached about 2 million tons in 1997.

The relative lack of iron ore and, above all, of scrap iron for the smelting ovens has stimulated research. Austrian engineers have perfected the "Linz-Donawitz" (after the steel centres of these names in Upper Austria and Styria), or steel-blasting, technique *(L.-D.-Verfahren)*, enabling them to process up to 300t of raw iron ore into steel in 20min. This technique has been licensed worldwide and is now used in about 60% of raw steel production. The technique of processing metallurgical powders developed in Austria (Plansee works near Reutte) has also won global acclaim.

Salt mining

Salt mining is now only of minor importance. Nonetheless, since prehistoric times the precious mineral has played such a part in the civilization of the eastern Alps that tourists can hardly overlook the various enterprises still being worked in the Salzburg area. Moreover, the salt waters of numerous spa resorts such as Bad Aussee, Bad Ischl and Hall in Tirol still play an important part in the treatment of a variety of illnesses. Place names often include the syllable *Salz* or *Hall* – synonymous terms, meaning salt, salt works. Tours through the mine galleries still attract tourists. The miners stick faithfully to their traditional vocabulary – the greeting *"Glück auf!"* (Hope you come up again!) is still heard – and they still have their dress uniform and recount the old legends about the underground world with its gnomes and goblins.

Melting mountains – Except in the natural springs *(Solequellen)* of Bad Reichenhall, the mineral deposits in the Austrian Alps consist of a mixture, called *Haselgebirge*, of salt, clay and gypsum. The miners begin by making a pit in the bed, which they flood and keep supplied regularly with fresh water. This water dissolves the rock on the spot and so, being saturated with salt (27%), sinks to the bottom of the basin, from which it can be pumped, while impurities are left behind. Modern methods of extraction involve the drilling of boreholes and the dissolving of the deposit by the injection of hot water. The brine *(Sole)* is brought to the surface and pumped into the vats of the salt factories *(Sudhütten)*, for the production of domestic or industrial salt.

The first pipelines – By the 17C much of the woodland around the salt mines had disappeared, burnt up as fuel in the furnaces. This, coupled with the remoteness of many of the mines, led to attempts by the authorities to site the centres of salt production closer to the market for the product. This involved the construction of impressive lengths of pipeline made of timber, lead or cast iron, to bring the brine down from the mountains to the lowlands. The longest of these **Soleleitungen** ran 79km/49mi from Bad Reichenhall to Rosenheim in Bavaria and was in use from 1810 to 1958. Pumping stations *(Brunnhäuser)* kept up a constant flow of brine, over hill and dale. To prevent too sudden a drop, the aqueducts included long mountainside sections, as in the water-conduits *(bisses)* of the Swiss Valais. The footpaths *(Soleleitungswege)* which followed them made splendid corniche routes; such is the mine road from Hallstatt to Bad Ischl, clinging to the mountainside above the lake of Hallstatt.

When the salt had been refined it was sent on by water – on the Inn below Hall in Tirol and the Lower Traun – or in carts. Many salt roads *(Salzstraßen)* in Austria, one of the best known being the Ellbögener Straße *(see INNSBRUCK: Tour of the Mittelgebirge)*, recall memories of this traffic, so fruitful for the country's economy and the public treasury.

SALT-MINING IN THE SALZBURG REGION

Other major economic activities

Austria's most important industry sectors, and those most able to compete internationally, are the machine building and steel industries, chemicals and textiles (centre of man-made fibre production at Lenzing in Upper Austria), and engine and gear manufacture. More than 850 000 engines are produced annually, and about 90% of all engines and gears produced is exported. Austria also has international standing in the production of electronic components such as microchips and integrated circuits (it produces components for Airbus and high-speed trains). In general, Austrian industry is strongly oriented to exportation, with about two-thirds of its foreign trade being conducted with fellow European Union member countries (and about one-third with Germany alone). Nonetheless, its highest export growth rates are currently being achieved with countries outside the European Union. A further main focus of national production is the foodstuffs and luxury food industry (3.5% of GDP), which principally caters for domestic consumption. Factories are concentrated regionally around Vienna and also in Upper and Lower Austria, where they can reach a production value, or number of factories and employees, ratio of up to about two-thirds.
The largest proportion of gross domestic product, over 60%, however is generated by the services industry, with a substantial contribution being made by tourism.

TOURISM

Austria is a tourist destination par excellence, offering magnificent scenery, major historical monuments, a wide range of leisure opportunities in both summer and winter, and an outstanding tourist infrastructure. Tourism is extremely important to the Austrian economy both in terms of job creation and as a source of revenue which makes an invaluable contribution to the country's balance of payments. In 1997, it brought in takings of nearly 135 billion Austrian schillings. Traditionally, the Tyrol attracts most visitors from home and abroad, followed by Salzburg and Carinthia.
In 1998, the number of foreign visitors to Austria was 81 900 000, the majority of whom were German.

Traditional Austria

Religious belief

Austria is a country steeped in tradition, where old customs are kept very much alive, particularly in rural communities. A religious faith which is deeply rooted in Austria's people has left its mark on town and countryside alike.
Roofed crosses *(Wiesenkreuze)*, set up at the roadside or in the middle of a field, are thus very much a feature of Austria's rural landscape, being particularly prevalent in the Tyrol. A common sight in Carinthia is a post *(Bildstock)* with a little roof protecting a faceted pole decorated with paintings of biblical scenes. Crucifixes are also frequently on display inside Austrian homes, in the *Herrgottswinkel* (God's corner) – in the Tyrol these are to be found in virtually every house, including guesthouses and inns.
Religious figures are also a common subject for the paintings to be found on many an Austrian façade *(Lüftlmalerei)*: St Florian features particularly prominently in these in his role as protector against fire. Another popular figure is St George, the dragon slayer. From time to time, visitors will come across a church containing an enormous painting of St Christopher, such as that in Imst. These arose in response to the popular belief that looking at the image of this saint would protect the viewer from a violent death for another day. The figure of St John of Nepomuk is often to be found adorning bridges and fountains, of which he is the patron saint (having been martyred by being thrown off a bridge in Prague).

A custom for all seasons

See Calendar of events.

The year begins with processions of masked "Perchten" accompanying St Nicholas through the villages during the "bitter nights" leading up to Epiphany on 6 January. The costumed figures representing good and evil spirits can be beautiful or ugly – the latter are usually clad with shaggy fur and wearing scary horned masks – and are supposed to banish the cold and dark of winter and bring fertility and blessings for the coming year. The feast of the Epiphany itself brings Christmas celebrations to a close by commemorating the journey of the Three Kings guided by the Star of

Bethlehem (children's carol singing and processions, *Sternsingen* and *Dreikönigsritte;* in some places local people parade in giant head-dresses decorated with bells, *Glöcklerläufe).* Carnival time, or **Fasching** (*Fasnacht* in western Austria), is ushered in as early as January in Vienna with the start of the ball season. Elsewhere, Fasching is celebrated with traditional carnival parades, to which a colourful note is added by the masks handed down from generation to generation. Some of the most famous of these parades include: those in the Tyrol, at Imst *(Imster Schemen)* and Telfs *(Schleicherlaufen);* the Bad Aussee carnival with its original and colourful *Trommelweiber* and *Flinserln;* and the *Fetzenfasching* in Ebensee.
Palm Sunday is marked by the blessing of the "palm branches" - generally willow catkins or box. This is closely followed by May Day celebrations (1 May), complete with maypole *(Maibaum),* climbing competitions *(Maibaumkraxeln)* and dancing. The feast of Corpus Christi sees more processions, which vary according to the particular traditions of the region: carrying 8-10m/25-30ft wooden poles wound around with garlands of fresh flowers *(Prangstangen)* in Bischofshofen and Zederhaus (24 June); laying down a carpet of flowers *(Blumenteppich)* in Deutschlandsberg; processions on horseback, as in Brixental in Tirol, or on water, as in Traunkirchen and Hallstatt. In August, Murau and Krakaudorf (Styria) are the scene of *Samsonumzüge:* parades involving a giant 5m/16ft figure of Samson carried by one man - this show of strength was believed in the 17C and 18C to protect the religious procession. In August and September many communities celebrate the consecration of their local church (Kirtag) with a fair. Autumn is the time for Harvest Festival *(Erntedankfest)* season, and when livestock is brought down from the mountain pastures to its winter quarters.
The feast of St Hubert is celebrated on 3 November (church services, parades on horseback etc), and that of St Leonard (patron saint of livestock) on 6 November. The feast of St Martin, with torchlit processions, brightens up the darker months. The periods of Advent and Christmas make December full of events, from the feast of St Nicholas (6 December), with the *Nikolospiel* parade in Bad Mitterndorf, through to the crib scenes on show, even in people's private homes in the Tyrol (eg Thaur).

Traditional costumes

Although traditional local costumes are rarely worn every day any more, they occasionally make an appearance on religious festivals and local fête days, much to the admiration of onlookers.
The velvet corsages of the women of Bad Ischl, the embroidered silk blouses of those from the Wachau, the colourful beribboned bodices of the Montafon, the finely pleated costumes of the Bregenzerwald and the lace aprons of the Burgenland are all evidence of a rich tradition of local folklore. Men wear leather or *Loden* wool breeches (tight at the knee) or shorts (which are less restrictive for the brisk movements of Tyrolean dancing), wide braces with a decorated chest panel and short, collarless jackets. The shape of the hat indicates the region its wearer comes from.
The traditional *dirndl* (pleated skirt, pastel coloured apron, full white blouse with short puffed sleeves and a buttoned or laced bodice) and the *Steirer Anzug* ("Alpine dinner jacket", consisting of grey or brown *Loden* breeches embroidered in green, white socks and a long flared coat with green embroidery and gilt buttons) are not that common a sight these days. However, they are the original inspiration behind the so-called "traditional Austrian look", so popular with tourists, in which modern styles are combined with traditional decorative features and natural materials such as linen, cotton, felt and heavy woollen *Loden.*

Rural scenery

The distinctive fences woven from laths which were once the most common style delimiting fields in the Salzburg, Tennengau and Pinzgau regions are becoming more rare. But it is still not unusual to see farmers piling hay at harvest time onto special drying racks made of metal wire or wooden stakes, to keep it off the damp ground while it is drying.
In the Carinthian Alps cereals are grown on the sunny slopes up to a height of 1 500m/4 500ft, but the harvest often has to be gathered early on account of frost. The sheaves are spread out on wooden dryers with horizontal struts, sometimes covered, so the grain is able to ripen.

Urban settlement

In Styria, Carinthia and the Danubian countryside the most interesting examples of urban development are often those based on a main road. When a town was first developed the old road was widened to form a sort of esplanade, known as the *Anger* (green). When all the land on each side of the *Anger* was built over, the resulting form was known as a *Straßenplatz* (street-square). These street-squares, shaped like spindles or regular oblong rectangles, form the heart of the town, approached by the once fortified gateways. Monuments to municipal dignity are generally to be found there: the *Pestsäule* (Plague Column) like the one set up in Vienna at the end of the 17C; also fountains etc.

House built around a square courtyard in the Mühlviertel (Upper Austria)

Traditional Austrian houses

House in the Bregenzerwald (Vorarlberg)

Tyrolean country chalet

Rural estate in Lower Austria

Food and drink

Austrian cooking has drawn on the culinary traditions of the different peoples incorporated in the old Empire: German, Italian, Hungarian, Serb and Czech.

Austrian cooking – Soup is served first, followed by the main dish, almost always consisting of meat, fried in breadcrumbs or boiled, accompanied by salad and stewed fruit (such as bilberries: *Preiselbeeren*).
Dumplings *(Knödel)* made of liver or flour may be served instead of vegetables, as in Bavaria. Middle Eastern influences can be detected in the liberal use of spices in many Austrian dishes.

Meat – The most famous dish *(Wiener Schnitzel)* is fillet of veal, fried in egg and breadcrumbs, normally served with potato salad. Goulash is a highly flavoured stew of Hungarian origin, spiced with red pepper or paprika and garnished with tomatoes, onions and potatoes. In Graz and Styria duck or chicken, fried in egg and breadcrumbs, is delicious. Game of all kinds is widely available in season.

Dessert – There is a great variety of Austrian sweets. The most famous, the Sacher cake *(Sachertorte)*, invented by Prince Metternich's chef, has a subtle and delicate flavour; it is a large, rich chocolate cake covered with chocolate icing above a thin layer of apricot jam; the original recipe remains a secret (but see p 379 for a version of it!). Other favourites include a jam tart *(Linzertorte)*, consisting of pastry made with almonds, filled with apricot or raspberry jam and covered with a pastry lattice; a turnover *(Strudel)* filled with apples, cherries or cream cheese and currants; plum or apricot fritters; and a sweet soufflé *(Salzburger Nockerl)*.

Schreiber/ÖSTERREICH WERBUNG

Sachertorte

Austrian Wine – Vineyards cover about 58 000ha/143 000 acres in Lower Austria, in the Weinviertel, on the slopes near Vienna, and in the Burgenland and Styria. White wine (81%) is much more popular than red. Annual production is of the order of 2.8 million hectolitres/62 million gallons, of which more than a third is exported.

White wines – There are many well-known Austrian white vintages: Grüner Veltliner (Valteline), Müller-Thurgau, Welschriesling etc. Most vintages yield pleasant table wines which are often light and sparkling. New wine, made that year, is drunk in the typical wine shops called *Heurige* in Vienna and *Buschenschenken* in Styria. The district of Wachau in the Danube Valley produces wines with a delicate bouquet (Spitz, Dürnstein, Weißenkirchen, Krems, Langenlois). Grinzing, the most famous of Vienna's suburban wine villages, makes a pleasant sparkling wine, whilst Gumpoldskirchen, to the south, a stronger wine altogether.

Red wines – The red wines, especially the Blauer Portugieser and the Blaufränkischer, are of high quality. In Lower Austria the best-known wines are those from Bad Vöslau, south of Vienna, from Retz (the Retz wine is known as *Spezi*, ie a special), from Haugsdorf and from Matzen, in the Weinviertel. In the Burgenland the wines of Pöttelsdorf, Oggau and particularly Rust, and in Styria those of Leibnitz, have a great reputation.

Decoding an Austrian menu

Backhendl	Fried chicken in breadcrumbs
Baunzerl	White bread roll
Buchteln	Sweet dumplings cooked in milk and sugar
Blunzen	Black pudding
Erdäpfel	Potato
Faschiertes	Mince, meat balls
Fisolen	Green beans
Frittaten	Pancakes cut into strips and put in soups
Gansljunges	Dish made out of goose giblets
Geselchtes	Salted or smoked meats
Golatschen	Small, usually square, filled pastry
G'spritzter	Wine mixed with soda water
G'spritzter Obi	Apple juice mixed with soda water
Häuptlsalat	Lettuce
Hasenjunges	Jointed hare
Heuriger	Young wine (less than a year old) or the inn where you get it from
Hupfauf	Tyrolean dessert
Indian gefüllt	Stuffed baby turkey
Jungfernbraten	Roast loin of pork with caraway seeds
Kaiserfleisch	Cured pork spare ribs
Kaiserschmarren	Dessert made with eggs and raisins
Karfiol	Cauliflower
Kohlsprossen	Brussels sprouts
Kracherl	Fruit-flavoured soft drink
Kren, Apfelkren	Horseradish, horseradish sauce with apples
Kukuruz	Sweetcorn
Marillen	Apricots
Nockerln	Dumplings
Obi	Apple juice
Palatschinken	Thin pancake filled with apricot jam or chocolate sauce
Paradeiser	Tomatoes
Powidl	Plum jam
Quargel	A type of cheese
Ribisel	Blackcurrants
Risibisi	Rice and peas
Schill	Perch
Schlagobers	Whipped cream
Schmankerl	Hot sweet pudding
Schöberl	Little biscuits (similar to croutons), put in soups
Schwämme, Schwammerln	Mushrooms
Seidel Lichtes	Small lager
Steirisches Schöpsernes	Styrian mutton dish
Strudel	Thin pastry roll with various fillings
Tafelspitz	Boiled beef and vegetable stew
Topfen	Type of cream cheese *(Quark)*

Art

ABC OF ARCHITECTURE

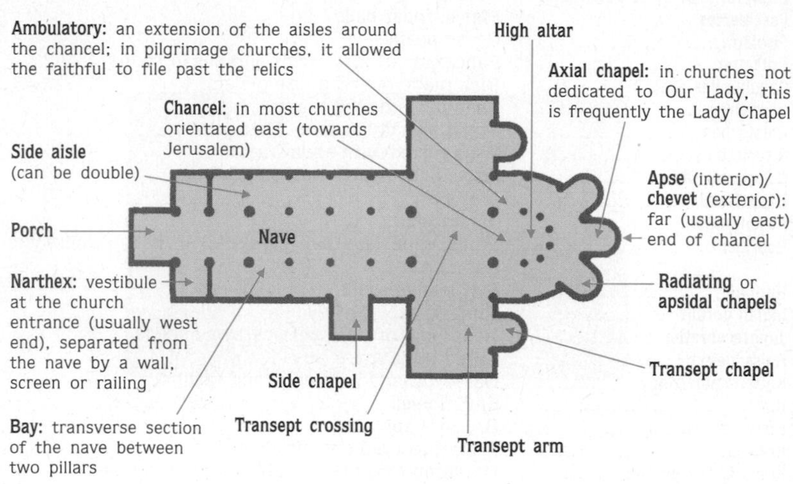

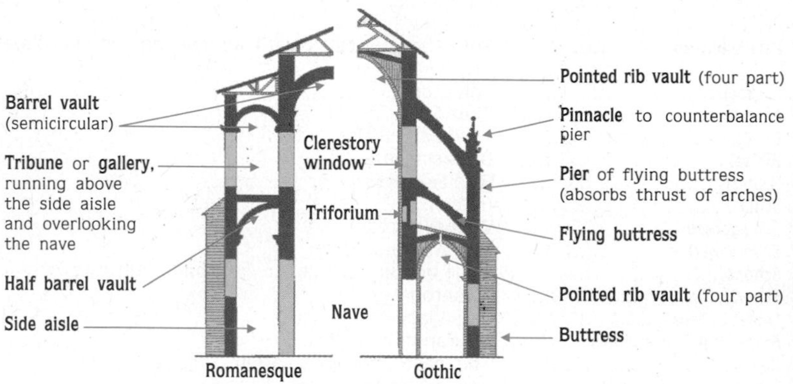

Riesentor (west door) of Stephansdom, Vienna (1230-40)

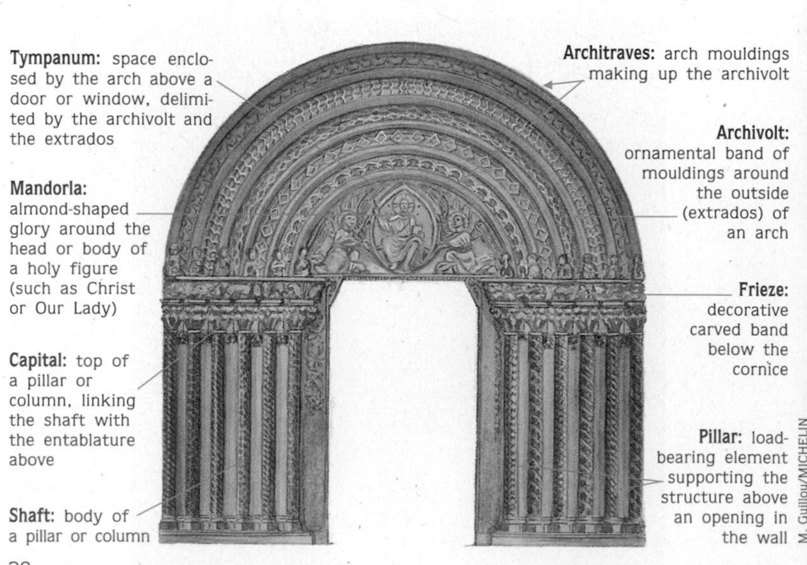

Chancel of Wilhering Abbey Church (1734-48)

Melk Abbey Church (1702-36)

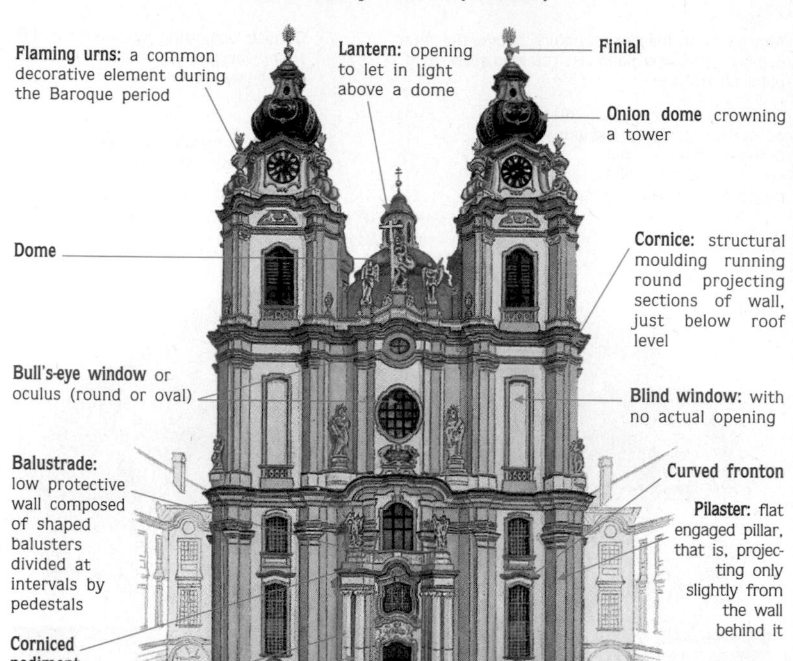

Oberes Belvedere, Vienna (1722)

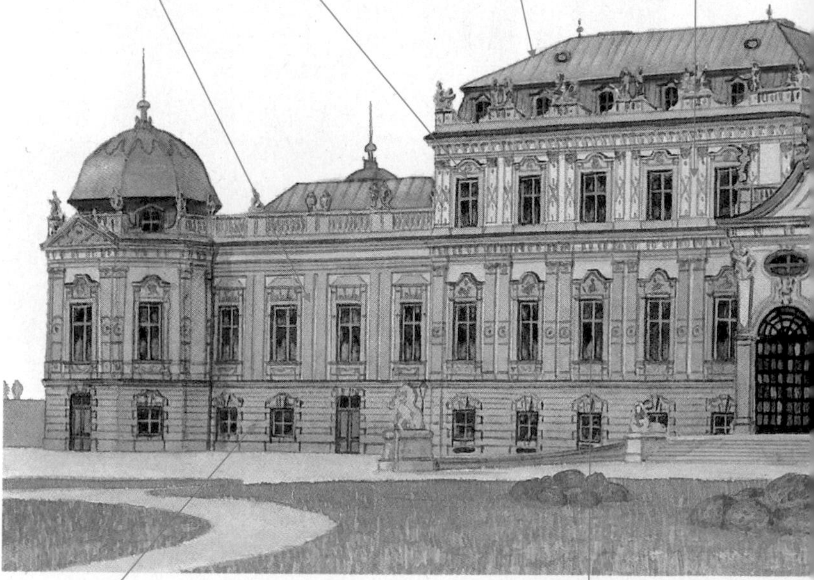

Mansard roof: with a double slope, the lower of which is steeper

Pier: segment of wall between two windows at the same level

Piano nobile: principal storey in a house, usually the first floor; houses formal reception and dining rooms

Attic storey: built above the wall cornice as a crowning feature of the façade

Socle: lowest storey which offers the possibility of compensating for uneven ground

Axis: row of tall windows along the building's façade

Burg Rappottenstein (12C-16C)

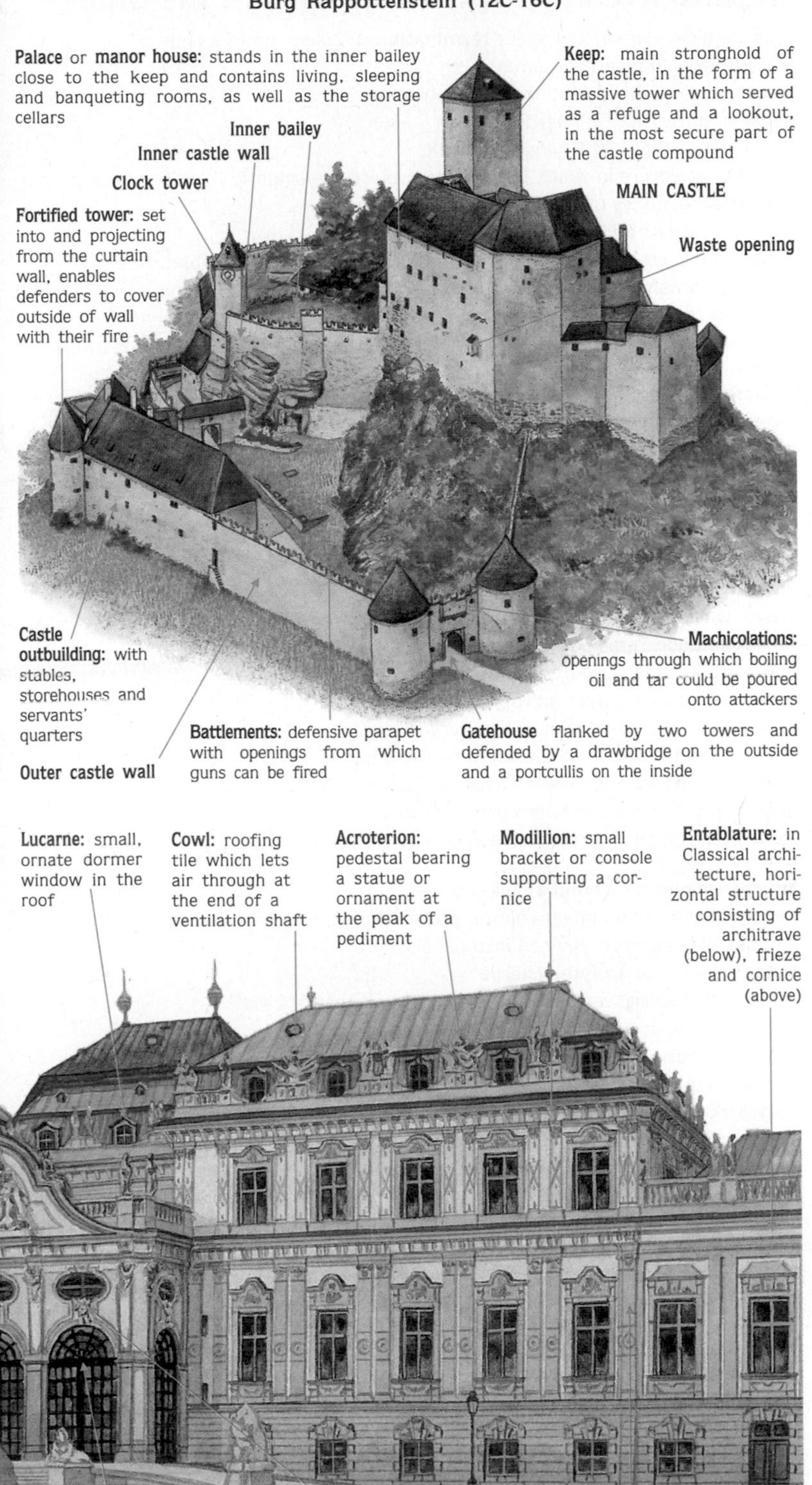

Portico: colonnaded porch marking the main entrance to a building

Mascaron: ornamental sculpted face, either human or part-human, usually caricatured

Pilaster: engaged pillar with a capital and base

M. Guillou/MICHELIN

ART AND ARCHITECTURAL TERMS USED IN THE GUIDE

Apse: semicircular vaulted space terminating the east end of a church
Archivolt: moulding around an arch
Baldaquin: altar canopy supported on columns
Barbican: outwork of a fortified place
Barrel vault: simple, half-cylindrical vault
Bas-relief: sculpture in which the figures project only slightly from the background
Blind arcading: series of arches attached to a wall
Bond: pattern of brick or stonework
Capital: moulded or carved top of a column supporting the entablature
Cartouche: ornamental panel with inscription or coat of arms (Baroque)
Champlevé (enamel): enamelling with relief design in metal
Chapter-house: building attached to religious house used for meetings of monks or clergy
Chiaroscuro: treatment of areas of light and dark in a work of art
Ciborium: lidded vessel used to hold Communion wafers
Corbel: stone bracket
Cupola: small dome
Curtain wall: stretch of castle wall between two towers
Entablature: projecting upper part of building supporting the roof
Flamboyant: final phase of French Gothic style (15C) with flame-like forms
Fleuron: small floral ornament
Fresco: watercolour wall painting on plaster
Grisaille: monochrome painting in shades of grey
Hall-church: Germanic church in which aisles are of the same height as the nave
Lantern: windowed turret on top of a dome
Lintel: horizontal beam over a door or window
Narthex: rectangular vestibule between the porch and nave of a church
Oriel: bay window corbelled out from an upper floor level
Ossuary: place where the bones of the dead are stored
Pendentive: triangular section of vaulting rising from the angle of two walls to support a dome
Peristyle: colonnade around a building
Pilaster: shallow rectangular column projecting from a wall
Predella: altar platform divided into panels
Putto/i: painted or sculpted cherub
Quadripartite vaulting: vault divided into four quarters or cells
Reredos: screen to the rear of an altar
Reticulated: patterned like a net
Rib: projecting band separating the cells of a vault
Saddleback roof: roof with a ridge between two gables, suggesting a saddle shape
Scotia: concave moulding
Sgraffito: decoration made by scratching through a layer of plaster or glaze to reveal the colour of the surface beneath
Shingle: wooden tile
Stucco or stuccowork: decorative plasterwork
Torus: convex moulding
Transept: wing or arm of a church at right angles to the nave
Triptych: set of three panels or pictures, often folding and used as an altarpiece
Trompe-l'œil: use of techniques such as perspective, or the combination of sculptures and painted figures, to deceive the viewer into seeing three dimensions where there are only two
Tympanum: space between the lintel and arch of a doorway
Volute: spiral scroll on an Ionic capital

EVOLUTION OF AUSTRIAN ART

Over the course of the centuries Austria has been a meeting place for very varied cultures and its artistic achievement has often reflected these external influences which provided some of its best sources of inspiration. At certain periods, however, a style developed which was appropriate to the nation's aspirations, particularly in the 18C, under the enlightened rule of the Habsburgs, when Austrian Baroque blossomed so vigorously that previous achievements were relegated to second place.

The Roman occupation has left traces at Carnuntum (Petronell), in the Danube Valley, downstream from Vienna, which was then called Vindobona, in Enns (Lauriacum) where St Florian was martyred and especially in Carinthia, at Teurnia (near Spittal) and Magdalensberg overlooking St. Veit an der Glan, but also in the Tyrol at Aguntum (near Lienz).

Markowitsch/ÖSTERREICH WERBUNG

Gurk Cathedral

Romanesque

From the 12C onwards church building flourished in Austria as in all Christian Europe. The main centres of the Romanesque style were the Episcopal seats of Salzburg, Passau and Brixen. The style was also promoted by the foundation of many Benedictine, Cistercian and Augustinian convents and monasteries, such as those at Melk, Göttweig, Klosterneuburg, Zwettl, Seckau and Heiligenkreuz, or the transformation of those already in existence. The best preserved buildings from this period are the cathedrals of Gurk and Seckau, but the cloisters at Millstatt and the great door of the Stephansdom in Vienna are particularly impressive examples of Austrian Romanesque art.

Mural paintings developed most extensively in the Archbishopric of Salzburg (interior decoration of the cathedral of Gurk). Salzburg was already an art centre, while Vienna as yet had no bishop. The frescoes at Lambach Abbey, dating from 1090 and completely restored in 1967, are of considerable interest.

Gothic

In the 14C and 15C the Gothic style invaded Austria. The Cistercians drew inspiration from the French pointed arch and the Franciscans kept to their traditional Italian architecture.

Most Gothic churches are of the **hall-church** *(Hallenkirche)* type with nave and aisles of equal height, as in Vienna in the Augustinerkirche, the Minoritenkirche, and the church of Maria am Gestade. The Stephansdom too is of this type (particularly the chancel); this, the most characteristic building of the Gothic period in Austria, was begun in 1304 by architects who were in touch with their contemporaries in Regensburg and Strasbourg.

Until the 16C there was a preference for sectional vaulting where decorative ribs form a pattern of groined or star vaulting in which richness of design contrasts boldly with the bare walls. This **Late Gothic** *(Spätgotik)* developed into a style of long straight lines – the exact opposite of the ornamental opulence of the Flamboyant Gothic to be seen in France at this period.

Paired naves were the fashion in the Alps, especially in the Tyrol: two naves at Feldkirch, four at Schwaz.

The great Gothic altarpieces, which were a synthesis of all the plastic arts – architecture, sculpture, painting – have, for the most part, sadly suffered extensive and often wilful damage over the centuries. Two are of exceptional quality: Kefermarkt, which was restored at the instigation of the writer Adalbert Stifter, and especially St. Wolfgang, painted and carved in 1481 by a Tyrolese, **Michael Pacher**, the greatest Late Gothic artist.

Trumler/ÖSTERREICH WERBUNG

Kefermarkt Altarpiece

A few 15C secular buildings have fortunately been preserved, such as the Kornmesserhaus at Bruck an der Mur and Goldenes Dachl at Innsbruck. The decorative elements adorning the façades of these buildings herald the Renaissance.

The Renaissance

Examples of the architectural heritage of a Renaissance inspired by Italian models are few and far between in Austria (arcaded courtyards at Schloß Schallaburg near Melk, Schloß Porcia in Spittal an der Drau and at the Landhaus in Graz). A notable exception is Salzburg, which the prince-archbishops dreamed of making into a second Rome. Although Austria did not close its ears to the great outpouring of new ideas, enthusiastically supported by Emperor Maximilian I (1493-1519), the Gothic tradition continued to dominate in the 16C. Even Maximilian's tomb at Innsbruck, which is regarded as a typical product of the German Renaissance, is still clearly influenced by the famous Gothic tombs of the dukes of Burgundy in Dijon, surrounded by bronze figures of the Emperor's forebears.

Baroque (17C-18C)

The revolution in the arts which took place in Italy at the end of the 16C derives its name from the Portuguese word *"barroco"* meaning something irregularly shaped (originally used of pearls). It affected all aspects of art – architecture, painting, sculpture – and also literature and music, giving rise to some outstanding masterpieces.

In Austria, the Baroque gave the country its richest artistic period since the Gothic. There are various reasons why this new direction in art found such fertile ground in Austria. In essence a religious art, it accorded perfectly with the mood of mystical rejoicing which followed the Council of Trent. It enjoyed the favour of the Habsburgs, ardent supporters of the Counter Reformation, and benefited from the euphoria which followed the defeat of the Turks at the gates of Vienna in 1683, when the whole country was seized by a passion for building – at last the danger that had overshadowed the lives of generations of Austrians was no more and they could get on with their lives and work in peace. Another factor in the triumph of the Baroque style and its rapid spread throughout the country was the Austrian love of show, of dramatic effects, of elegance and colour and *joie de vivre*.

The churches, monasteries and palaces of the Baroque can only be understood fully in relation to the new liturgical and festive music which emerged ever more strongly in the years after 1600, in which a dominant melodic line supplanted the older and more complex vocal polyphony. It followed that virtuosi, solo instrumentalists as well as singers, came to occupy pride of place in choirs and chapels. The pomp and circumstance of the new liturgies (in the wake of the Council of Trent, 1545-63) were backed by the rich and powerful sounds of ever more sophisticated church organs.

Austrian Baroque architecture – Austrian Baroque needs to be understood as an essentially local phenomenon, the expression of an authentically Austrian sensibility, and not as an import. With its irregular outlines, abundance of forms and richness of ornament, the Baroque is above all a style of movement. Its dynamism results from colour (the use of both bright and delicate colours, the contrast of black, white and gilt), line (curves and undulations), the exuberant treatment of features like pediments, cornices, balustrades, statues and a delight in unexpected effects of angle and perspective.

The great Baroque abbeys – St. Florian, Melk, Altenburg, Kremsmünster, Göttweig... these great abbeys are manifestations of Austrian Baroque at its peak, surpassing in their magnificence any secular buildings of the period. Often prominently sited, these "monuments of militant Catholicism" (Nikolaus Pevsner) draw together bold terraces, elegant entrance pavilions, inner and outer courtyards and main wings of imposing dimensions into harmonious compositions of unparalleled splendour. The scale and lavishness of ornamentation of these vast structures give rise to a certain duality of feeling; places of worship, they are also temples dedicated to art, to which the Baroque assigned a key role in celebrating the splendours of God's creation.

Baroque churches and abbeys

Churches – All over Austria stand graceful onion-domed churches, their elegant exteriors giving away little of the delights within. It is only once inside the church door that the Baroque, that love of exuberant decoration capable of transforming the most modest of structures, bursts into full and glorious voice.

Many such churches are in fact Gothic (Rattenberg, Mariazell) or even Romanesque (Rein, Stams) buildings, remodelled in the Baroque style in the course of the 17C and 18C by local masons working alongside famous sculptors, painters and decorators. The rigours of the Reformation and its separation of soul and body were overcome by these artists, who knew how to stir the soul by appealing to the senses. A particularly fine example of Baroque religious architecture in Austria is the unique Dreifaltigkeitskirche at Stadl-Paura, every aspect of which symbolises the Trinity.

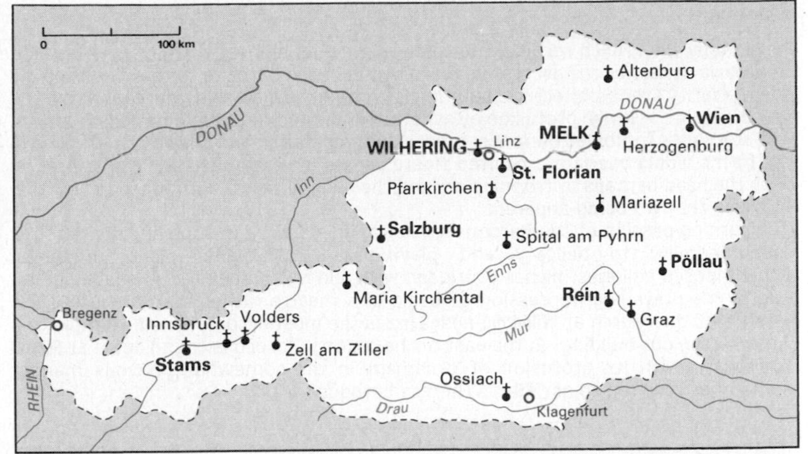

Secular buildings – Their façades alive with colour and movement, palace and town house alike were treated as stage sets for the urban theatre by local masters as well as by Italian architects like dell'Allio or the Carlones. In the 17C, sumptuous residences took shape on the edge of towns like Graz (Schloß Eggenberg) and Salzburg (Schloß Hellbrunn) as well as Vienna (the Belvedere – early 18C).

Great Baroque architects – Contributing to the triumph of Baroque in Austria were a number of local figures. Although they succeeded in creating a truly national style, they were by no means immune to foreign influences; Italy in particular excited their admiration, and those who had not actually received their architectural training there undertook at least one tour in Italy.

After a stay in Italy and study of French architecture, **Johann Bernhard Fischer von Erlach** (1656-1723) created a monumental, national style based on his own interpretation of foreign (particularly Italian) influences. The Dreifaltigkeitskirche at Salzburg is one of the prototypes of this style. Many of the most beautiful buildings in Vienna bear the stamp of his genius: the Nationalbibliothek (then the Imperial Library), the Palais Schwarzenberg and winter palace belonging to Prince Eugene. Most of these buildings were completed after his death by his son, Joseph Emmanuel (1693-1742), who also built the indoor riding school (Winterreitschule) in the Hofburg.

Johann Lukas von Hildebrandt (1668-1745) settled in Vienna after a period of study in Italy and worked with Fischer von Erlach. In Vienna he designed the two palaces at the Belvedere, the Peterskirche with its oval cupola, the Piaristenkirche and the Palais Kinsky, and in Salzburg Schloß Mirabell. His considerable body of work had a significant influence on the artists of his generation.

The Tyrolean architect **Jakob Prandtauer** (1660-1726) had a masterly touch in relating massive structures to their landscape setting. Thus, while his church interiors are conventional or even somewhat heavy, his staircase at St. Florian and the two pavilions and great bastion at Melk, overlooking the Danube and forming an impressive ensemble, are achievements of a very high order. The monastery at Melk, jewel of Austrian Baroque, was to be completed by Prandtauer's son-in-law, **Josef Munggenast** (1680-1741), who later went on to work at Dürnstein, Altenburg and Geras. Prandtauer did not restrict his talents to religious architecture alone, however – he was responsible for a number of beautiful secular buildings as well, such as Schloß Hohenbrunn.

Baroque painting and sculpture – Baroque architecture is unimaginable without its natural complements of painting and sculpture, which, together with artists' stuccowork creations, breathe joyful life into the spaces created by the architect. Church walls disappear beneath elaborate altarpieces, myriad saints and angels people the ceilings and an army of statues puts to flight their Gothic predecessors, now deemed crude and unsophisticated. Palaces and abbeys are endowed with huge stairways, while cheerfully coloured and stuccoed façades lend a theatrical air to both village street and town square.

Great painters and sculptors devoted their talent to the decoration of palaces and churches. Among them were **Johann Michael Rottmayr**, Fischer von Erlach's preferred collaborator and the precursor of a specifically Austrian pictorial style, **Balthasar Permoser** whose famous marble of the Apotheosis of Prince Eugene graces the museum of Baroque art in Vienna, **Daniel Gran** who executed the painting of the Nationalbibliothek in Vienna, **Paul Troger**, master of Austrian ceiling paintings, **Martin Johann Schmidt** ("Kremser Schmidt") whose altarpieces are to be found all over Lower Austria, **Bartolomäus Altomonte** who decorated the splendid library at Admont, and his uncle **Martin Altomonte** whose airy frescoes and altar paintings grace Wilhering. It is however with **Franz Anton Maulbertsch** that Austrian painting of this period attains its peak. **Georg Raphael Donner**, sometimes referred to flatteringly as the "Austrian Michelangelo", is best-known for the fine fountain in the Neuer Markt in Vienna.

Rococo

Inspired by the French rocaille, this style reached its highest form of development in Bavaria. It carries the decorative refinements of the Baroque to their limit, giving them priority over architecture: painting in *trompe-l'œil*, marble, stucco, bronze and wood are used in lavish profusion by artists who allowed their imaginations free rein. The stuccoists combined garlands, medallions, vegetation and shell work. Often two art forms would overlap: a painted figure passes indistinguishably into sculpture, with the head perhaps in *trompe-l'œil* and the body in relief, without the transition between the two being apparent.

The burning passion of the Baroque gives way to a delight in sophisticated effects, monumentality to delicacy and playfulness. Baldaquins, sham draperies, superimposed galleries, niches overladen with gilding and painted in pastel shades add to the prevailing impression of being in a theatre rather than a church. The interior of the church at **Wilhering** near Linz is the most accomplished example of a Rococo religious building. In the east of the country Rococo is found again at **Schloß Schönbrunn**, with its profusion of ornament in the somewhat precious manner sometimes referred to as "Maria-Theresa Baroque".

M. Hertlein/MICHELIN

Schloß Schönbrunn seen from the gardens

19C

Neo-Classicism – After the excesses of Rococo came the triumph of neo-Classicism, inspired by Greece and Rome, a cold style characterized by the columns and pediments of Classical antiquity. This tendency, which had little in common with the Austrian and even less with the Viennese character, was patronized by certain German rulers, including Ludwig I of Bavaria who transformed Munich. Vienna saw the construction of a number of buildings of great sobriety like the Technische Hochschule, the Schottenstift and the Münze (Mint). The equestrian statue of Joseph II in the Hofburg by **Franz Anton Zauner** is a typical example of neo-Classical sculpture.

Biedermeier (early 19C) – Biedermeier is the name given to the style which dominated the "Vormärz" (Pre-March), the period between the Congress of Vienna in 1814 and the insurrections of March 1848, the "Year of Revolutions". It is an essentially middle-class style, reflecting the prosperity and settled way of life of this increasingly important section of society.

Comfortable furniture – The cosy interiors inhabited by the rising Vienna bourgeoisie were furnished with simple yet elegant pieces, frequently fashioned in pleasingly light-coloured woods, their design reflecting new ideas of function and comfort. The discretion and modesty of this utterly unpretentious style eventually fell out of fashion, later (c 1900) earning it the unflattering title of "Biedermeier" (a combination of *"bieder"*, meaning solid or worthy, and "Meyer", the commonest German surname), a name originally applied to one of a pair of characters invented by German author Joseph Viktor von Scheffel in 1848. The Kaiserliches Hofmobiliendepot (national furniture collection) in Vienna has an important collection of Biedermeier furniture and other objects.

Realistic painting – Austrian painting, and Viennese painting in particular, developed in a remarkable way during this period. **Georg Ferdinand Waldmüller** showed himself to be a master of light and colour in his rendering of landscape, while Friedrich Gauermann captured the atmosphere of the age with great accuracy and left many fine drawings of outstanding quality. The art of watercolour was popular during this period. **Rudolf von Alt** was the greatest master in this medium, becoming honorary president of the Vienna Secession at an advanced age.

Historicism (late 19C) – Between 1840 and 1880, on Emperor Franz Joseph's orders, Vienna's encircling fortifications were pulled down and work begun on replacing them with the great processional way known as the Ringstraße, or "Ring". The buildings along the new boulevard were designed according to the dictates of **Historicism**, an eclectic movement in fashion at the time and drawing on a great variety of past styles for its inspriation: Florentine Renaissance (Museum für angewandte Kunst by Heinrich von Ferstel), Greek Classical (Parlament by Theophil Hansen), Flemish Gothic (Rathaus by Friedrich Schmidt), and French Gothic (Votivkirche also by Heinrich von Ferstel).
Having triumphed in the capital, Historicism went on to leave its mark on the other cities of the Empire. Towards the end of the 19C, however, opposition to this uncreative and backward-looking style began to grow in Vienna, culminating in open revolt by a number of artists who joined forces to found the famous Secession in 1897.

Late-19C painting and sculpture – Sculpture flourished during this period, not least because of the abundance of public commissions. These included the martial statues of Prince Eugene and Archduke Karl (by **Anton Fernkorn**) in Vienna's Heldenplatz and the moving monument to Andreas Hofer (by Natter) on the Bergisel in Innsbruck.
The late 19C was a turning point for Austrian painting. The great tradition of Realism continued in the work of landscape painters like **Emil Jakob Schindler**. However, the highly original talent of artists such as **Anton Romako**, although still influenced by Romanticism, increasingly addressed the subject matter taken up by later painters, like decline, decay and death.

Jugendstil (early 20C)

In the final years of the 19C, a radical new artistic movement known as the Jugendstil swept through all the German-speaking countries, with its epicentre in Munich. It took its name from the widely read magazine *Jugend* (Youth), published between 1896 and 1940, which contained illustrations by artists.
In Vienna, the movement was headed by two exceptionally talented figures, the painter **Gustav Klimt** and the architect **Otto Wagner**. Its influence was felt in the provinces too, albeit in a more subdued form, and there are good examples of Jugendstil buildings in places like Wels or Graz.
Jugendstil drawing and painting are characterised by a love of flat surfaces, curvilinear forms and floral decoration. The movement was paralleled in other countries; **Art Nouveau** in France, Modern Style in Britain (whose Charles Rennie Mackintosh was much admired by his Viennese contemporaries), and in Italy, where it was known as "Stile Liberty".

The Secession – On 25 May 1897 a small group of friends led by Gustav Klimt founded the **Association of Austrian Artists**, the **Vienna Secession**. The following year the architect Joseph Maria Olbrich built an exhibition hall – the Secession – in the Karlsplatz. Completed in only six months, this building remains one of the purest expressions of Jugendstil aspirations, even though contemporaries nicknamed it the "Golden Cabbage" because of its dome of gilded laurel leaves. Its façade proclaims the slogan "Der Zeit ihre Kunst – der Kunst ihre Freiheit" (To each age its art, to art its liberty). Olbrich's Secession building was home to numerous exhibitions of contemporary, progressive art, many of them international in scope. It became a focus of opposition to the values represented by historicism, academic art and the tendency towards pastiche that had characterised artistic life in Vienna during construction of the Ring-

M. Hertlein/MICHELIN

"To each age its art": the Secession building with a temporary installation as part of an exhibition

straße. For the artists of the Secession art was above all a matter of personal expression, requiring sincerity and a quest for truth as well as a rejection of prevailing social and aesthetic conventions.

Gustav Klimt (1862-1918) – Painter and interior designer Gustav Klimt was one of the leading exponents of the Jugendstil and in many ways the typical Secession artist, whose elegant and subtle works are world-renowned. Early in his career he put his academic training behind him and abandoned all attempts at naturalism in favour of rich and subtle decorative effects carried out on a two-dimensional surface free of the constraints of perspective. His sinuous line, his original use of colour (especially greens and gold), his stylised foliage, his cult of the sensual and the delicacy of his female portraits provoked a revolution in Viennese artistic circles. Symbolism was an additional influence in the work of this major figure, the forerunner of what was later known as **"Viennese Expressionism"**, represented by painters like Egon Schiele and Oskar Kokoschka.

Otto Wagner (1841-1918) – Wagner was the dominant architectural figure of the whole of the Jugendstil period. Born in Biedermeier times and educated in the most classical tradition, he rose to become Professor at the Academy of Fine Arts and Imperial Architectural Adviser for Vienna. For more than 20 years his career was one of conventional success; he designed a number of buildings in neo-Renaissance style along the Ring for example. But then, at the age of 50, Wagner broke decisively with his past, joining the Secession in 1899. His uncompromisingly contemporary views on architecture had already been published in his *Modern Architecture* of 1895, still a standard reference text. Wagner favoured the use of glass and steel, a rational approach to spatial design and the omission of superfluous ornament. His finest works include the pavilions for the Karlsplatz underground railway station (1894) in Vienna, the Postsparkasse (1906) near the Ring and the Steinhof Church (1907).

Wiener Werkstätten (Vienna Workshops) – Founded in 1903 by the banker Waerndorfer, the architect Josef Hoffmann and the artist **Kolo Moser**, one of the most gifted members of the Secession movement, the Wiener Werkstätten were intended to make good art accessible to all and to put both artist and craftsman on a firm professional footing. A wide range of products was made adopting Jugendstil tenets, from household utensils, furniture and wallpaper to fashion garments and jewellery. Though expensive, these products were a great commercial success, much in demand among the wealthier strata of society. Beauty of form and the use of high quality materials were considered to be more important than functionality. Financial problems led to the workshops' closure in 1932. Together with Klimt's paintings, the output of the Wiener Werkstätten marks the high point of Austrian Jugendstil and enjoys enduring acclaim.

Josef Hoffmann (1870-1956) – This highly versatile figure was one of Otto Wagner's most talented students. As well as designing buildings, he was also responsible for their interior design, furniture and fittings. He was strongly influenced by the work of Scottish architect and designer Charles Rennie Mackintosh, founder of the Glasgow School of Art Nouveau. Hoffmann co-founded the Wiener Werkstätten in 1903 and worked closely with them until 1931. One of the results of this fruitful collaboration is the magnificent **Palais Stoclet** in the suburbs of Brussels, his greatest achievement and one in which he applied his aesthetic principles with awesome single-mindedness. Built regardless of cost between 1905 and 1911, this palatial residence is a complete work of art. Both Klimt and Moser contributed to its decoration.

Museum für angewandte Kunst, Wien – G. Zugmann

Tea service by Josef Hoffmann
(Österreichisches Museum für angewandte Kunst, Vienna)

As well as designing material for a sizeable private clientele, Hoffmann also received a considerable number of commissions from Vienna city council, for whom he produced several blocks of flats for rental in the years 1923-25.

Adolf Loos (1870-1933) – Educated by the Benedictine monks of Melk, this innovatory architect called himself a stonemason, though he was considered by Le Corbusier to be the forerunner of architectural Modernism. An admirer of the sober Classicism of Palladio, Loos made a violent attack on the Historicist architecture of Vienna's Ring in 1898, in the pages of the Secessionist journal *Ver Sacrum*. He was soon to break with the architects of the Secession, however, accusing them of "gratuitous ornamentalism". Following a period of residence in the USA (1893-96) and influenced by the Chicago School, he built a number of villas, blocks of flats and cafés in Vienna, adopting the principles of a purely functional architectural style. In addition he designed sculpture and furniture. His work reached maturity in the Golman and Salatsch store (1909) and in his controversial Michaeler Platz building (1908) which attracted bitter criticism because of its total lack of ornament. Loos has gone down in history as one of the high priests of 20C functionalism. His ideas were taken up and developed by architects the world over. He was a particularly strong influence on artists of the International style.

Music

See WIEN: "Vienna, capital of music"

Middle Ages

9C Musical culture flourished in the monasteries where Gregorian chant was sung. The earliest examples of written music in Austria are the Lamentations from the abbey at St. Florian and the Codex Millenarius Minor from Kremsmünster.

12C and 13C The Germanic troubadours known as the **Minnesänger** celebrated the joys and sorrows of courtly love at the court of the Babenbergs in Vienna as well as at St. Veit an der Glan in Carinthia, drawing their inspiration from the Volkslied (folksong), the authentic expression of popular feeling. The most famous were: Reinmar von Hagenau and his pupil Walther von der Vogelweide, Hermann von Salzburg and Neidhart von Reuenthal.

14C and 15C The burgher-class **Meistersinger** (Mastersingers), organized into guilds, continued the aristocratic *Minnesang* tradition, setting strict rules and testing achievement by means of competitions.

Renaissance

This was the age of polyphony, pioneered in Austria by the Tyrolean Oskar von Wolkenstein, who worked at the Court at Salzburg, then developed throughout the Empire in the work of a number of musicians belonging to the Franco-Flemish School.

The 17C

1619 The accession to the Imperial throne of Archduke Ferdinand of Styria marked the beginning of the supremacy of Italian music in Austria, notably in opera and oratorio. A long line of Italian masters directed the music of the Court Chapel, the last of their number being none other than Mozart's great rival, **Antonio Salieri** (1750-1825).

Gluck and the reforming of the opera

Vienna was the setting for the reform of opera, thanks to the German composer, Gluck.

1714-1787 **Christoph Willibald Gluck** considered opera as an indivisible work of art, both musical and dramatic; he sought, above all, natural effects, truth, simplicity and a faithful expression of feeling.

1754 Gluck is named Kapellmeister of the Opera at the Imperial Court of Maria Theresa.

1774 Two of his operas are performed for the first time in Paris: *Iphigenia in Aulis* and *Orpheus and Euridice*. The enthusiasm of the Gluckists clashed with the Piccinnists (traditionalists).

The Viennese Classics

This was the age of Haydn, Mozart, Beethoven and Schubert, all Viennese by birth or adoption. Their primarily instrumental work dominated the musical world for almost a century and made Vienna its uncontested capital.

1732-1809 **Joseph Haydn**

Conductor and composer attached to the service of Prince Esterházy at Eisenstadt for 30 years, Haydn was the creator of the string quartet and laid down the laws of the classical symphony.

1756-91 **Wolfgang Amadeus Mozart**

Mozart brought every form of musical expression to perfection, owing to his exceptional fluency in composition and constantly renewed inspiration. His dramatic genius produced great operas of enduring appeal: *The Marriage of Figaro, Don Giovanni, Così fan Tutte* and *The Magic Flute (for details of Mozart's life and work see SALZBURG).*

ROGER VIOLLET

Ludwig van Beethoven

1770-1827 **Ludwig van Beethoven**

Heir to Haydn and Mozart, Beethoven had a Romantic conception of music. He was much affected by the ideas of the French Revolution and felt himself to be the bearer of a message for the whole of mankind.

1805 First performance of his only opera *Fidelio* at the theatre "An der Wien".

1824 The Ninth or Choral Symphony concluding with the *Ode to Joy* (fourth movement) with words by Friedrich Schiller. In 1972, this Ode to Joy was adopted as the European anthem.

Romanticism

1797-1828 **Franz Schubert**

Blessed with a great sensibility, Schubert was an outstanding improviser, who rediscovered in the Lieder the old popular themes of the Middle Ages. His Lieder, of which he wrote more than 600, even more than his symphonies, masses, impromptus and compositions of chamber music, made him secure as the leading lyrical composer of the 19C.

The Viennese waltz and operetta

1820 In Vienna, a musical genre, the **waltz**, which had its origins in popular triple-time dance, was triumphant. Adopted first in the inns and then in the theatres on the outskirts of the city, the waltz scored such success that it appeared at the Imperial Court.

Two men, **Joseph Lanner** (1801-43) and **Johann Strauss** (1804-49), helped to give this musical form such an enviable place that the waltz known everywhere as the "Viennese Waltz" enjoyed worldwide popularity. The Strauss sons, Joseph and Johann, carried the waltz to a high degree of technical perfection, taking it further and further from its origins to make it a symphonic form.

With the performance at the Carltheater in 1858 of Offenbach's *Die Verlobung bei der Laterne*, Vienna's enthusiasm for **operetta** knew no bounds. Encouraged by Offenbach, **Johann Strauss the Younger** (1825-99) enjoyed equal success with his *Fledermaus* and *Gipsy Baron*. For many years the operetta, that child of the waltz, carried all before it with compositions by **Franz von Suppè** (1819-95), **Franz Lehár** (1870-1948, *The Merry Widow, The Land of Smiles*), **Ralph Benatzky** (1884-1957, *White Horse Inn*) and **Robert Stolz** (1880-1975, *Spring in the Prater*).

Symphonic renewal

1824-1896 **Anton Bruckner** ranks among the most significant composers of church music, producing nine great symphonies, numerous mass settings and the *Te Deum*. He spent many years as organist of St. Florian and at Linz Cathedral before his appointment as professor at the Vienna Conservatory.

1833-1897 Of German origin but settled in Vienna, **Johannes Brahms** composed a large body of work of a lyrical nature, inestimable in its impact (1868, *A German Requiem*).

1842 Founding of the Vienna Philharmonic Orchestra playing under the guidance of illustrious conductors (Richard Strauss, Wilhelm Furtwängler) chosen by the players themselves.

ROGER VIOLLET

Johannes Brahms

1860-1903 **Hugo Wolf**, a tormented spirit who eventually became insane, composed fine Lieder in his lucid periods, based for the most part on the poems of Goethe, Mörike and Eichendorff.

1860-1911 **Gustav Mahler**, a disciple of Bruckner, was the last of the great Romantic composers. An inspired conductor, he composed many Lieder as well as his nine symphonies. He helped to set in motion the revolutionary changes in music at the turn of the century.

20C

From 1903 onwards the "New Viennese School" led by Schönberg is a major influence in the evolution of modern music as seen in the work of composers such as Ernst Krenek and Pierre Boulez.

1864-1949 The German composer/conductor **Richard Strauss** carried on the Classical/Romantic Austrian tradition, composing symphonic poems and operas. He was one of the founders of the Salzburg Festival.

1874-1951 **Arnold Schönberg**, whose early works clearly reflect the influence of Wagner and Mahler, revolutionized music by rejecting the tonal system which had prevailed for 300 years.
Together with his followers **Anton von Webern** (1883-1945) and **Alban Berg** (1885-1935) he introduced a new method of atonal composition, based on the concept of series. This is known as dodecaphony, or in its more advanced form, as serial composition. His change of style did not meet instant approval with the public, however – the première of his first chamber symphony provoked a riot!
Having pursued his study of atonality in Berlin, Schönberg was exiled from Germany under the Nazis, and settled in the United States, where he finally adopted US citizenship.

1894-1981 The conductor **Karl Böhm** helped to stage two operas composed by his friend Richard Strauss. His fame rests on his seminal interpretations of the works of the great German composers.

1908-1989 The conductor **Herbert von Karajan** brought classical music to a wide audience by his mastery of audio-visual techniques. For many years he presided over the destinies of the Salzburg Festival as well as directing both the Vienna Philharmonic and Berlin Philharmonic.

1947 Salzburg première of the opera *Danton's Death* by **Gottfried von Einem** (b 1918).

1958 *"Die Reihe"* ensemble founded by **Friedrich Cerha** (b 1926).

1996 Death of **Gottfried von Einem** *(see above)* who had for a long time played an important part in Austrian cultural life.

Stephansdom and Haas-Haus, Vienna

Bartl/Österreich Werbung

Sights

Stift ADMONT★

Steiermark

Michelin map 926 fold 22 – Alt 641m/2 103ft

The Benedictine Abbey of Admont was founded in the 11C by St Emma of Gurk *(see GURK)* and Gebhard, Archbishop of Salzburg. The spires of its church are framed by the summits of the Haller Mauern and the Großer Buchstein, the northern pillar of the Gesäuse. Matching them in the west, are the towers of Frauenberg *(see EISENERZER ALPEN)*. There is a particularly good view looking towards Admont from the Hieflau road as it runs along the Gesäuse.
The abbey buildings were completely reconstructed after a fire in 1865. Fortunately the library was spared by the flames and still has its valuable archives.

★★ **Stiftsbibliothek (Abbey Library)** ⊙ – The abbey library's magnificent state room stretches for 70m/230ft, on either side of a central rotunda beneath a domed ceiling. The seven ceiling frescoes by Bartolomäus Altomonte (1702-83), which depict an allegory of Theology and the various Arts and Sciences, together with the two floors of bookcases and the upper gallery with its intricate wrought-iron balustrade, constitute a splendid Rococo ensemble of 1776, a worthy setting for the treasures the library contains. Note in particular the famous statues of the "Four Last Things" – Death, Judgement, Heaven and Hell – by **Joseph Stammel** (1695-1765), who revived the art of woodcarving, neglected in Styria since the end of the Gothic period, to its former glory in his work, most of which was donated to the abbey. The manuscripts and printed texts on display under glass are a selection from the library's collection of 1 400 manuscripts and 150 000 volumes, making this the largest abbey library in the world. The display is regularly rotated and follows a specific theme.

Trumler/ÖSTERREICH WERBUNG

Admont Abbey Library

Museums ⊙ – *Closed for restoration until May 2002.* The **art history section** displays a small but very fine selection of the abbey's treasures, including a portable altar dating from 1375 and valuable monstrances. Particularly remarkable are the ceremonial vestments and paraments, products of the Admont School of Embroidery which flourished in the 17C.
The **scientific collection** was assembled from the early 19C onwards as teaching material for the school attached to the monastery.

AFLENZER SEEBERGSTRASSE★

Steiermark

Michelin map 926 fold 23

This is the last really mountainous pass road in the Austrian Alps on the approaches to Vienna. The Aflenzer Seeberg (alt 1 253m/4 111ft) or Seeberg pass makes communication easy between the Mariazell basin and the industrialized valleys of the Mur and the Mürz. The views of the imposing limestone ridges of the Hochschwab massif and the crossing of the Aflenz basin are pleasant sections on this run.

FROM BRUCK AN DER MUR TO MARIAZELL *61km/38mi*

★ **Bruck an der Mur** - *See BRUCK AN DER MUR.*

Start out from Bruck an der Mur northwards on the road to Vienna.

Leaving the industrial landscape of the Lower Mürz at Kapfenberg, the road winds its way through the narrow Thörlbach Valley, where a few wire mills and nail factories are still operative. The picturesque setting of the Thörl gateway marks the exit from this first defile.

Thörl - This little settlement, lying in a rocky cleft, began as a fortification barring the entrance to the Aflenz basin. Exactly in line with the valley, the ruins of the stronghold of Schachenstein stand on their steep-sided spur. The castle was built in 1464 and was the summer residence of the Abbot of St Lambrecht. Beside the road, to the south, an oratory shelters a Calvary dating from 1530.

Of the gateway *(Törlein)* from which the village gets its name there remain, on the mountainside, an 18C building through which the roadway passed under an arch, still in existence, and a semicircular tower with an adjacent chapel dedicated to St Barbara. This spot has acquired a reputation as a good starting point for hikes in the Hochschwab massif.

Aflenz-Kurort - Aflenz is a medium altitude, climatic health resort, in a quiet location and very popular. In winter the chair lift to the Bürgeralm takes the skiers to the sunny Schönleiten plateau, while in summer it serves the mountaineers aiming for the Hochschwab massif. The **church**, which is squat and rustic, belongs to the final phase of Gothic architecture in Austria. The tower has been fortified since the end of the 15C. The remarkable south door has a design of little columns and string-courses superimposed on multilobed archwork. The figure below the keystone, dating from around 1900, is presumably a representation of the architect responsible for the renovation. The most striking features of the interior, which has no pillars, are the rib vaulting which merges into the side walls without any visible support, and the statues of the 12 Apostles. The altars date from the second half of the 18C, while to the left of the choir the impressive wooden cross is Romanesque (1135).

From Aflenz to Au the **road**★ runs along the upper slopes of the last foothills of the Hochschwab. The houses with their wooden galleries are typical of the area. At **Seewiesen**, whose 14C Gothic church stands on a small hill, the final climb begins. To the west the Seetal, with its evenly inclined slopes, is headed by the great blocks of the Hochschwab massif, including the Aflenzer Staritzen and the Mitteralm.

Brandhof - This hunting lodge was created by Archduke Johann. He was secretly married here to Anna Plochl, the postmaster's daughter, on 18 February 1829 *(see Bad AUSSEE).*

On the northern side of the pass the road first clings to the slopes and then runs along the valley floor. The climb to Mariazell offers fine views of the famous pilgrimage church in its wonderful setting.

★ **Mariazell** - *See MARIAZELL.*

Stift ALTENBURG★★

Niederösterreich

Michelin map 926 fold 11

Founded in 1144, this Benedictine abbey fell victim to many an assault because of its frontier location. It was sacked in 1645, and its reconstruction was begun by a mere handful of monks who undertook to raise it from its ruins. The abbey complex was completed in the Late Baroque style and is the masterpiece of **Paul Troger**, who besides painting altar panels here, was responsible for the decoration of nine cupolas. Much damage was inflicted on the abbey in both World wars, though subsequent restoration work has gone a long way to recreate its original splendour.

Stiftskirche (Abbey church) - This is interesting in terms of both its architecture and its interior decoration. The architect responsible for the transformation of what had once been a Gothic church was Joseph Munggenast, the son-in-law and pupil of Prandtauer. The work was completed between 1730 and 1733.

Altenburg Abbey - Frescoes in the "Krypta" (detail)

The **west front**, decorated with statues (St Benedict, angels) is surmounted by a graceful onion dome. It forms part of a group of buildings framing the prelates' courtyard.
The **interior**, adorned with marble, stucco and frescoes, is of noble proportions. The nave is roofed by an oval dome decorated by Paul Troger with **frescoes** whose central theme is the struggle between good and evil. The same artist painted the Assumption above the high altar as well as a number of pictures on the side altars. The stuccowork is from the workshop of **Franz Joseph Holzinger** of St. Florian. The **organ** of 1773 is remarkable for the elegance of its case with delicately gilded woodwork.

Stiftsgebäude (Abbey buildings) ⏱ - Despite the effects of destruction and restoration, this is one of the liveliest as well as one of the most complete groupings of Baroque buildings.

Library - The decoration of the vestibule is by Johann Jakob Zeiler. The library takes the form of a broad nave articulated by majestic columns between which, in place of lateral chapels, rise the shelves of books. The three domes above the room are painted, like those of the church, with **frescoes** by Paul Troger on the theme of Human and Divine Wisdom.
It is at Altenburg more than anywhere else that one can appreciate the Baroque concept of the library as the temple of the spirit, treated with the same architectural magnificence as the temple of God. The Benedictine motto "Ora et Labora" (Pray and Work) draws a parallel between God and Spirit and opens the way for the joyful Baroque play of symmetries and intersections.

"Krypta" - With its cradle vault lit by lunettes, this vast luminous space has no equal among the abbeys of Austria. Its decor, consisting of warmly coloured frescoes painted by some of Troger's pupils, deals breezily with death, mixing macabre elements among its abundance of floral and geometric motifs.

Sala terrena - Painted all over with frescoes of limitless pictorial inventiveness, these four rooms are the epitome of Baroque extravagance but also evoke the charm and humour equally characteristic of the style. The theme of the first three rooms is water, the element which is the source of life and of purity. The fourth, or "Chinese", room is a timeless vision of the Far East.

Main staircase - Of the utmost refinement and sumptuosity, this leads to the **imperial apartments.** Here, all the decorative techniques employed come together to create an atmosphere of aristocratic solemnity - gilded capitals punctuating the play of colours of the stucco and artificial marblework, gleaming marquetry...
It is also possible to see parts of the medieval abbey (cloister, monks' quarters, founders' chapel etc) which were buried under the Baroque buildings and have only recently been excavated.

ARLBERGGEBIET★★

Vorarlberg und Tirol

Michelin map 926 folds 28 and 29 or 218 folds 5, 6 and 7

Between the Upper Rhine and the Inn corridor, the mountainous region of the Arlberg, with which may be grouped the Lechtal Alps and the massifs of the Verwall, the Rätikon and the Silvretta, was for a long time a formidable obstacle to communications.
The road to the Arlberg pass, which was made fit for wheeled traffic in 1825, and especially the railway tunnel, 10km/6mi long, completed in 1884, provide a reliable link between the Vorarlberg and the Tyrol.
The **Arlberg road tunnel**, 14km/9mi long, was opened in 1978, providing an all-year-round link between the two regions.

Cradle of Alpine skiing – The teaching of Alpine skiing began at the foot of the Arlberg. In 1901 the Ski-Club Arlberg was founded and a native of Stuben, **Hannes Schneider** (1890-1955), under the direction of Victor Sohm, began to create a technique of movement on the fast slopes of the region, adapting styles imported from Scandinavia.
Schneider, with the great British sportsman **Sir Arnold Lunn** (1888-1974) – who in 1922 introduced slalom gates, thereby creating the Alpine slalom race, and who also in 1930 induced the Fédération Internationale de Ski to recognize competition in downhill as well as slalom skiing – founded the **Arlberg-Kandahar Cup** in 1928, a tradition which continues today in the form of the Arlberg Alpine World Cup races.

Why Kandahar?

The first downhill race on skis was organised at Montana in Switzerland on 6 January 1911 by Sir Arnold Lunn, who promoted competitive Alpine skiing.
The race was sponsored by Lord Roberts of Kandahar (1832-1914), a British Field Marshal who took his title from the name of a town in Afghanistan which was captured by the Indian army during a military campaign, and his name was therefore adopted for the Kandahar skiing club founded by Lunn in 1924. As this club was joint promoter with the Arlberg skiing club of the skiing championships held at Arlberg from 1928 onwards, which grew into the great international event, this exotic title has been perpetuated.
Skiers who are named five times among the first three in the downhill, slalom or combined event are awarded the Kandahar diamond. Karl Schranz of Austria has gained this honour twice in his career.

★ARLBERG PASS

1 From Bludenz to Landeck *68km/42mi*

Bludenz – This town, favourably located at the meeting point of five valleys (Walgau, Brandnertal, Montafon, Klostertal and Großwalsertal), has developed into the economic centre of the Vorarlberg uplands (chocolate and textile industries) and is an ideal departure point for excursions into the local area. The picturesque pedestrian zone in the old town, at the foot of the St. Laurentius Church tower, has some very inviting vaulted passages just begging to be explored.

If you choose the quieter old road via Innerbraz, Dalaas, Wald and Klösterle to go up to the Arlberg pass, and not the Arlberg tunnel road, you can drive at a leisurely pace and enjoy the view of the surrounding mountains.

Between Bludenz and Langen the road climbs through the **Klostertal**, a valley which takes its name from the house built in the Middle Ages by the Hospitallers of St John of Jerusalem, to provide help for travellers at a place now called the Klösterle (little monastery).
On leaving Bludenz, the craggy outcrop of the Roggelskopf (2 284m/7 494ft) comes into view. After Dalaas, a fresh panorama opens out with the steep wooded slopes of the Batzigg (1 833m/6 014ft) in the foreground and the Rohnspitze peak (2 455m/8 055ft) in the background.
Between **Langen**, where the monumental entrance to the **Arlberg tunnel road** opens, and St. Christoph on the other side of the pass, the landscape is severe in character. Ravines cut into the thinly turfed slopes. The electricity pylons stand on concrete bases with spurs to break avalanches.

The Brotherhood of St. Christoph

Crossing the Arlberg pass used to be a major hurdle for travellers. Many risked, or even lost, their lives due to storms, severe cold or the hazards of the route. For this reason, Heinrich the Foundling from Kempten had an emergency shelter and chapel built just below the pass in 1386. This was the "hospice" in which travellers could seek refuge. Heinrich founded the brotherhood for the upkeep of the hospice, its charitable works to be funded by donations. Even royalty joined the association and its patrons came from as far afield as Prague, Magdeburg and Strasbourg. The Reformation heralded the decline of the brotherhood and it was finally disbanded under Emperor Joseph II. However, it was reinstated by the Tyrolean bishopric in 1961 and now has more than 11 000 members globally, whose donations go towards helping those in need all over the world.

Stuben – This tiny village lying at an altitude of 1 407m/4 616ft below the pass consists of little more than a few hotels and is probably the most peaceful holiday resort in the Arlberg region. It gets its name from a room *(Stube)* where travellers could warm themselves and get some rest before making their final climb to the summit. Skiers can travel directly from here to the St. Anton ski slopes. Zürs is easily reached by car. Three chair-lifts give access up the Albonagrat ridge, which towers over Stuben (difference in altitude: 1 000m/3 280ft). There are also some exciting possibilities for off-piste skiing, as the mountainside boasts vast snowfields with no sudden drops.

★ **Albonagrat** – *Accessible to skiers from Stuben.* Take the Albona I and II chair-lifts, which lead up to the Maroj Sattel (2 323m/7 621ft). Interesting **panorama**★ of the Verwall range to the south and the Arlberg pass to the north, with Zürs and the Widderstein in the background.

Ski down the Albonagrat-Sonnleiten piste and take the chair-lift up to the Albonagrat ridge (2 400m/7 874ft)). There is a far-reaching **panorama**★ over the Monafon and Arlberg regions.

High above, to the left above the resort, the tunnel galleries of the Flexen pass road can be seen. The road from Stuben winds tortuously up the cliff-face and reaches the junction with the access road to the Flexen pass (turn-off to Lech: *see route* 2 *below*). Another lengthy climb brings you to the rather desolate Arlberg ridge (*Arle* means "mountain pine" in the local dialect) at the entrance to St. Christoph, and the pass itself at 1 793m/5 882ft.

St. Christoph am Arlberg – Since 1386 there has been a hospice below the pass on the Tyrolean slope of the Arlberg, which is the seat of the charitable Brotherhood of St Christoph. The hospice was gutted by a fire in 1957 but has been rebuilt as a hospice-hotel and the **Brotherhood Chapel** has likewise been rebuilt nearby. A small settlement has grown up around the hospice, which has acted as a mountain annexe of St. Anton since the very early days of skiing.

On leaving St. Christoph the imposing Sulzbergkopf peak (2 853m/9 360ft) comes into view straight ahead. This is part of the Verwall mountain range stretching away to the right of the Arlberg road.

★★ **St. Anton am Arlberg** – *See ST. ANTON AM ARLBERG.*

Stanzertal – After St. Anton, the road follows the **Valley of the Rosanna**, also known as the Stanzertal. The pale

limestone escarpments of the Lechtal Alps to the north and the dark rocks of the Hoher Riffler range to the south emphasise the impressive nature of the landscape. Meadows dotted with little barns, and villages remarkable for the beauty of their settings also contribute to the charm of the scene. The resorts of **St. Jakob**, **Pettneu**, **Schnann** and **Flirsch**, through which the road leads one after the other, are most attractive in spite of their tourist infrastructure. After Flirsch the valley narrows and the road runs between wooded slopes. Shortly after **Strengen**, the last resort in the Stanzertal, the Trisanna bridge comes into sight to the right, level with the tributary of the Rosanna and Trisanna.

★ **Trisannabrücke** – Since 1884, a metal bridge has carried the railway high (86m/282ft) above the torrent close to the medieval stronghold of Wiesberg. The bridge, which is light and slender, in no way spoils the romantic setting.
In the **Sanna Valley**, formed by the junction of the Trisanna and the Rosanna, the valley floor opens out once more. The high-lying villages occupy mountainside terraces from which the forest has been banished. At Landeck, the river flows into the Inn.

Landeck – This town at the junction of the Arlberg road and Inn Valley lies at the foot of an imposing **castle** (13C-18C), which now houses the museum of local history. The **Liebfrauenkirche** (15C-16C) at the foot of the castle is one of the most harmonious Gothic church buildings in the Tyrol. The tracery decoration in its windows and ribbed vault are typical of the Late Gothic style. The highlight of the church's interior fittings is the Late Gothic hinged "Schrofenstein" altarpiece in the chancel, representing the Adoration of the Magi. This work dates from the beginning of the 16C, although the paintings on the side panels and at its top are more recent. On the unusually high predella, King Oswald the saint is depicted enthroned holding his sceptre and votive vessel, with the donors kneeling on either side of him. These lifelike, coloured statuettes bear the features of Praxedis of Wolkenstein and of Oswald of Schroffenstein, whose ruined castle can still be seen on the mountainside north of Landeck (the original sculptures are displayed on the south chancel wall).

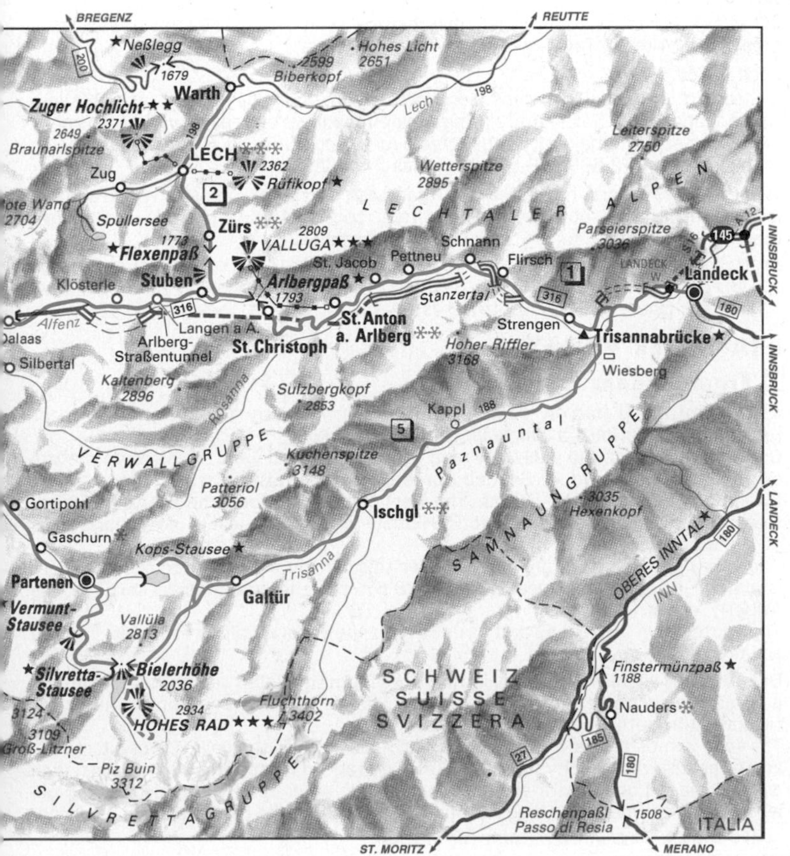

★THE FLEXEN PASS

2 From the Arlberg road to Warth *17km/11mi*

The galleries of the Flexen pass road seen from Stuben

Between Lech and Warth the road is generally blocked by snow from November to May.

The Flexen pass road, built in 1900, which serves the ski resorts of Zürs and Lech, is open all winter owing to the defensive works against avalanches. It branches off the Arlberg pass road in a long smooth bend. At the end of the bend there is a wide-ranging **panorama** across the Kloster Valley, with the Rätikon peaks, characterised by the Zimba summit and the tip of the Schesaplana glacier, etched on the distant skyline. In order to protect the **ascent**★ to the pass from avalanches, a series of tunnels and galleries had to be built along a 600m/656yd stretch of the road.

After crossing the pass at 1 773m/5 816ft the road brings you to Zürs.

✻✻ **Zürs** – *See ZÜRS.*

After two stretches of tunnel, just before Lech, the valley narrows into a breathtaking rocky ravine only a few metres wide.

✻✻✻ **Lech** – *See LECH.*

On leaving Lech, the road runs along halfway up the valley sides through a less rugged landscape. Softly undulating Alpine meadows alternate with steep rocky cliffs, dotted with majestic spruce trees. At the entrance to Warth, the imposing Biberkopf peak (2 599m/8 527ft) comes into view.

Warth – This resort, more peaceful than Lech and Zürs, offers a wide range of leisure facilities in both summer (hiking, tours of the summit) and winter (downhill and cross-country skiing, snowboarding).

From Warth you can choose between either continuing to Lake Constance through the Bregenzerwald region (see BREGENZERWALD) or crossing the upper Lech Valley (see Oberes LECHTAL) towards Reutte.

BRANDNER VALLEY

3 From Bludenz to the Lünersee

15km/9mi along narrow roads, climbing continuously from Brand onwards (gradient 1 in 8), plus a 2hr walk there and back.

On leaving Bludenz the well-built road offers an overall view of the town, before climbing through a wood. Beyond Bürserberg, recognisable from some way off by the onion dome of its church, the view opens out along the Brandner Valley towards the Schesaplana summit (2 965m/9 728ft), to the left of the dark mass of the Mottakopf.

The valley gets increasingly narrow after this. Through a gorge to the left there is a **view**★ of the Zimba peak (2 643m/8 672ft), the "mini-Matterhorn" of the Arlberg region.

The route down into the Brand basin reveals the resort's picturesque **site**★ to full advantage.

Brand – This village founded by immigrants from the Valais region has grown into a popular resort offering a wide range of leisure pursuits and opportunities for relaxation in both winter and summer.

The road climbs to the foot of the **cirque**★★ closing off the valley, a great natural amphitheatre whose rocky sides rise like a barricade in front of the Schesaplana, then on to a rugged gorge with scree-covered slopes. After the Schattenlagant refuge, where tourists who are pushed for time can turn back, the road reaches a dead end.

Leave the car at the lower cable-car station.

★★ **Lünersee** – *2hr there and back, including 10min by cable-car.*
The **cable-car** ⊙ brings tourists to the lake shore next to the Douglas-Hütte chalet. In its original state, the Lünersee was the largest mountain lake of the eastern Alps, set in a ring of jagged rocky crests. In 1958 the water level was raised 27m/90ft by a dam, creating a reservoir of 78 million m³/2 754 million cu ft, which feeds the Lünersee and Rodund (near Tschagguns) power stations more than 1 000m/3 280ft lower down.

★MONTAFON

4 From Bludenz to Partenen – *See MONTAFON.*

★★SILVRETTA ALPINE ROAD

5 From Partenen to Landeck – *See SILVRETTASTRASSE.*

Schloß-Museum ARTSTETTEN★★

Niederösterreich

Michelin map 926 fold 10 – 18km/12mi west of Melk
Local map see DONAUTAL

The origins of Artstetten go back to a fortified residence erected here in the 13C. Close to the Danube, and thus on the classic invasion route into the heart of Europe, this early building was much exposed to the hazards of war. The characteristic silhouette of the present castle dates only from 1912 when its pitched roofs were replaced by the present bulbous structures. Terrible fires laid waste both castle and village in 1730 and again in 1760; nevertheless, the south front dates back to 1750 and most of the rest of the building to 1691-98.
Artstetten entered the mainstream of history when, in 1823, it became the property of the Imperial family. Its effective owner at that time was Emperor Franz I. The castle subsequently belonged to various members of the Imperial family before passing in 1861 into the ownership of Archduke Karl Ludwig, brother of emperors Franz Joseph and Maximilian. As his summer residence for many years, Artstetten was much altered and rebuilt by the Archduke; it was he who landscaped the park, giving it its present appearance. In 1866, the unfortunate Archduke Maximilian became the owner, albeit briefly; the following year, as Emperor of Mexico, he was executed by a revolutionary firing squad. In 1890 it was the turn of Karl Ludwig's son, the heir to the Imperial throne, Archduke Franz Ferdinand, to become master of the castle. Artstetten was the final residence of Franz Ferdinand and Duchess Sophie of Hohenberg before their assassination at Sarajevo in 1914; the castle still belongs to their direct descendants.

ARCHDUKE FRANZ FERDINAND

Heir to the throne – The tragic death of Crown Prince Rudolf at Mayerling meant that Archduke Karl Ludwig became heir to the Imperial throne. His utter lack of interest in politics made it hard to imagine that he could ever succeed his brother, Franz Joseph. In the event, however, it was Karl Ludwig's able son, Franz Ferdinand, effectively heir already for a number of years having been entrusted with a number of official Imperial missions, who officially became next in line to the ageing Emperor in 1896, when his father died.

Franz Ferdinand was born in 1863 in Graz and later inherited a fortune from the last duke of Modena. In his youth there seemed to be no prospect of his ever succeeding to the throne and he therefore embarked on a military career early on.

In the service of the Empire – As a young lieutenant of 19, Franz Ferdinand trained for his chosen profession as a soldier with his regiment at Enns, where he spent five years. Later he commanded a regiment of hussars in Hungary for two years. Perceptive and far-sighted, he played the leading part in giving Austria an effective navy, and was rewarded with promotion to the rank of admiral in 1902. He was an accomplished horseman and an excellent shot, as well as a connoisseur and patron of the arts. He was also an indefatigable traveller, obtaining the Emperor's permission to make a tour of the world lasting almost a year, in the course of which he visited the USA, Japan, India and China, returning home with many new ideas and filled with reforming zeal.
As anxious to preserve the dynasty as the uncompromising Franz Joseph but of much more flexible mind, Franz Ferdinand strove to overcome Austria-Hungary's perennial political crises by accommodating the rising tide of nationalism among the Emperor's Slav subjects, a project doomed to failure because of the inflexibility of the Empire's privileged nations, the Germans and Hungarians.

Schloß Artstetten

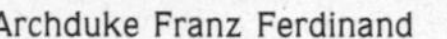

Archduke Franz Ferdinand

Schloß Artstetten

Sophie, Duchess of Hohenberg

A dynamic personality – A complex and forceful man, Franz Ferdinand enjoyed a happy family life. The two-year struggle for his right to marry the woman of his choice won him the respect of the Austrian people; although she was from an old aristocratic family, Sophie Chotek was not regarded as a suitable partner for an archduke and heir to the throne, as custom demanded that he should marry only a princess from a ruling dynasty. Franz Ferdinand overcame all obstacles, including the resistance of the Emperor, and Countess Chotek was made Duchess of Hohenberg on 1 July 1900, her wedding day. Three children were born of the marriage, who were exiled from Bohemia in 1921 and their property seized, but they subsequently found refuge in Vienna and at Artstetten. During the Second World War they were deported to Dachau, an experience they nevertheless survived.

Assassination at Sarajevo – On Sunday 28 June 1914, the Archduke and Duchess Sophie were on an official visit to Bosnia. In spite of the tense political situation in the recently annexed province, they were welcomed in the capital, Sarajevo, by an enthusiastic crowd. As the Austrian party drove through the streets, a grenade was thrown at the Archduke's car; rolling off the folded-back hood, it exploded underneath the following vehicle, injuring a number of officers and onlookers. The Archduke ordered his chauffeur to carry on to the town hall, where speeches of welcome were made. Ordered by her husband to return to the Governor's residence, Duchess Sophie insisted on staying at his side. Spurning the advice of anxious officials to wait until troops had cleared the streets, Franz Ferdinand set off again. A mistake on the part of his driver meant that the archducal car was halted for a few moments directly in front of one of the seven conspirators, the Bosnian student Gavrilo Princip. Seizing his opportunity, Princip fired two shots at almost point-blank range, killing both the Archduke and his wife. He was 51 years old, she 46. Both Princip and his fellow-conspirator who had thrown the grenade were arrested; they were condemned to 20 years imprisonment but died in gaol of tuberculosis.

The consequences of Sarajevo – The European powers had entrusted the administration of Bosnia-Herzegovina to Austria in 1878. In 1908 the province was annexed outright by the Empire in an attempt to counter "Yugoslav" agitation in both Bosnia and Croatia. The Serbian government had long stood in the way of Austrian ambitions in the Balkans; given the apparent involvement of Serbian officers in the Archduke's assassination, the time seemed ripe to bring Belgrade to heel, though the old Emperor counselled caution.

On 23 July 1914 an Austrian ultimatum was presented to Serbia and, although its basic conditions were accepted, the interlocking pattern of alliances meant that the international situation deteriorated rapidly. Russia let it be known that she supported Serbia and, after the Austrian attack on 28 July, there was no turning back; Russia mobilized on 30 July, Germany and France on 1 August and by 2 August the First World War had begun.

★★ ERZHERZOG-FRANZ-FERDINAND-MUSEUM ⌚

An important but relatively little-known chapter of history is presented in the museum under the heading "For Heart and Crown". The castle's rooms contain various objects once in the possession of the Imperial family – personal effects, photos, furniture, weapons – associated with events leading to the outbreak of war in 1914. Though the tragic figure of Archduke Rudolf looms large, it is above all Archduke Franz Ferdinand who features in these displays, his character, his life and his manifold activities emerging in a sharper focus.

Bad AUSSEE✝

Steiermark

Population 5 040

Michelin map 926 fold 21 – Local map see SALZKAMMERGUT

Alt 659m/2 162ft

Bad Aussee is the capital of the Styrian Salzkammergut, a region which is still deeply influenced by tradition. It is built at the confluence of two upper branches of the Traun and enjoys a peaked mountain setting. Cutting into the Bad Aussee basin, the Dachstein and the Totes Gebirge throw out a series of well defined bastions, framing picturesque lakes: the Altausseer See and the Grundlsee.
Bad Aussee, which makes equal industrial and medical use of the salt marshes and sodium-sulphate waters brought from the mines of Altaussee, offers an exceptional choice of walks and excursions.

The people's prince – If Bad Ischl owed its fortune to Franz Joseph, the great man of Bad Aussee was **Archduke Johann**. The prince's controversial romance with Anna Plochl, the daughter of the local postmaster, and his almost clandestine marriage at Brandhof in 1829 filled the romantic chronicles of the period, confirming the popularity of the "Prince of Styria".
At Bad Aussee itself, it will therefore be no surprise to find the prince's statue in the municipal gardens (Kurpark), the medallion of the couple on the bridge over the Grundlseer Traun (Erzherzog-Johann-Brücke) and souvenirs of the Plochl family preserved in the former post office (Alte Pferdepost), no 37 Meranplatz.

Chlumeckyplatz – This square in the centre of the town, containing a fountain and a plague column, is a pleasant place for a stroll. Also on the square is the Kammerhof, once the office of the salt mine regulators and an impressive testimony to Late Gothic and Renaissance architecture with its marble doorway and window surrounds dating from 1536, its cartouches with cable mouldings (1624) and its coat of arms featuring the Imperial eagle above the main entrance. This historic mansion now houses the local museum, the **Ausseer Kammerhofmuseum** ⏱.
The Hoferhaus, nearby, which in the 16C was the home of the director of the mines, has preserved mural paintings of the period. Seen on the outside are St Sebastian, St Anne's Family Group, St Florian; inside are Samson and Delilah and a hunting scene.

EXCURSIONS

★ **Grundlsee** – *5km/3mi to the Grundlsee resort; 10km/6mi to the Gössl fork. Leave Bad Aussee on the Grundlseer Straße.*
At Seeklause (a landing-stage at the head of the lake) there is a **view**★★ over the vast stretch of water that is the Grundlsee, overlooked from the left by the Backenstein promontory. The road skirts the foot of this after passing through the resort of **Grundlsee.**
From the resort in its picturesque setting there is an open view across to the snow-capped summits of the Totes Gebirge.

Turn back at the end of the lake, at the Gössl fork.

Further interest will be added to this **trip**★★ if it includes a visit *(about 3hr there and back after leaving Bad Aussee)* to the hamlet of Gössl, from where a 20min walk will bring you to the rugged beauty of the **Toplitzsee**★. The views from the lake can be seen only by taking the **motorboat excursion** ⏱. Beyond the final isthmus lies the little **Kammersee** hemmed in between the walls of the Totes Gebirge.

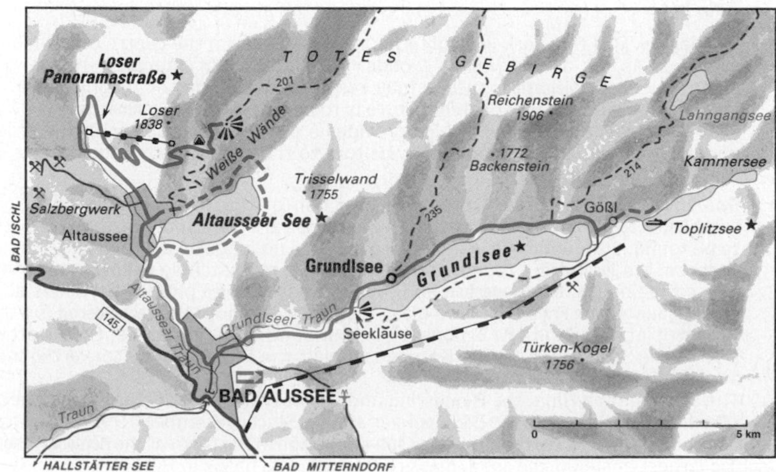

★ **Altausseer See** - *5km/3mi to the north.*
The road ends at the widely dispersed climatic resort of **Altaussee**, from which it is possible to walk round the lake *(max 2hr)*, or undertake the popular tour of the nearby salt mines **(Salzbergwerk)** ⊙, which were used by the Germans as a place of safety for art collections during the Second World War. Among them was the splendid polyptych, *Adoration of the Mystic Lamb*, now back in St-Baaf Cathedral at Ghent.

★ **Loser Panoramastraße** - *13km/8mi - about 1hr. Leave Altaussee to the north and follow the "Loser Panoramastraße" signs: toll point after 3.4km/2mi.*
This delightful scenic road climbs to an altitude of 1 600m/5 250ft.
From the mountain restaurant (Bergrestaurant) car park at the top there is an extensive view over Altaussee Lake, the sheer "Weiße Wände" ("White Walls") cliffs and, in the distance to the south, the Dachstein range and the Hunerkogel. The car park is the starting point for a number of waymarked footpaths.

BAD

See under proper name

BADEN ✦✦

Niederösterreich

Population 23 900

Michelin map 926 fold 25 - Local map see WIENERWALD - Alt 228m/748ft

The highly reputed spa town of Baden lies in a delightful setting on the edge of the rolling hills of the Vienna Woods, in the midst of vineyards and meadows. Elegant villas and Biedermeier architecture add to the town's charms. Baden has much to offer the visitor, from the restorative atmosphere of a well equipped, modern spa resort, to the beauty of the town itself and of the surrounding area, not forgetting the wide range of leisure facilities and entertainment, culminating in the annual summer operetta festival.

Spa resort - The healing properties of Baden's hot-water springs were appreciated already in the Roman era; Emperor Marcus Aurelius mentioned the "Aquae Pannoniae lying 18 000 double paces south of Vindobona" (Vienna). Nowadays, the spa's 15 mineral springs yield more than 4 million l/880 000gal per day, and the spring waters reach a natural temperature of 36°C/97°F. The spa waters are used in the treatment of rheumatic complaints, and for improving the circulation, connective tissues and blood vessels. The spa had its heyday in the Biedermeier period, when Emperor Franz I spent every summer here from 1803 to 1834.

Famous visitors - Musicians in particular seem to have been attracted to this idyllic spot; Wolfgang Amadeus Mozart, who wrote his "Ave Verum" here, Franz Schubert and above all **Ludwig van Beethoven**, who visited Baden no fewer than 15 times and composed part of his Missa Solemnis and his Ninth Symphony here. These famous musicians were followed by the great names of waltz and operetta composition: Strauss, Lanner, Millöcker and Zeller. From 1813 to 1834, Baden was the summer residence of the Imperial court, and the "guest lists" of the spa from 1805 onwards read like a Gotha family tree. One illustrious guest, Emperor Napoleon I, was particularly impressed by the Helenental (a river valley) to the west of town.

SIGHTS

★ **Kurpark** - This fine park lies only a short distance from the centre of town and stretches as far as the Vienna woods. At the edge of the park stands the cream-coloured **Spielcasino**, successfully restored to its former magnificence. A good example of Jugendstil architecture is to be found in the **Sommerarena** (1906) with its movable glass roof, which provides a pretty backdrop for the summer operetta festival. In the afternoons, visitors to the spa can listen to concerts at the music pavilion.

★ **Spa town architecture** - During the first half of the 19C, numerous thermal establishments were built in Baden in the Classical style. Some of these are still to be found, although for the most part they are no longer used for their original purpose: the **Josefsbad**, a round, domed building in eye-catching yellow now serves as a coffee house; the **Frauenbad** (in Frauengasse) with its pillared portico is now an art gallery; the **Franzensbad** is a glass-making workshop; the **Leopoldsbad** (on the Brusattiplatz), built in 1812, houses the tourist information office. On the other side of the Schwechat Joseph Kornhäusel built the **Sauerhof**, now converted into a hotel.
The Kaiser-Franz-Ring, the Rainerring and the Breyerstraße feature a number of **villas** in the neo-Classical or Biedermeier styles. Since December 1999 Baden has been able to boast a further top-class spa attraction in the form of the **Römerthermen**, the largest unsupported span, glass-roofed thermal baths in Europe.

Rathaus – This impressive town hall was constructed in 1815 by Joseph Kornhäusel, who is responsible for several other elegant buildings in town. The central block is adorned with Ionic columns and a triangular gable. In front of the Rathaus stands the richly decorated **Dreifaltigkeitssäule** (Trinity Column) by Giovanni Stanetti, erected in 1714-18 after a plague.

M. Hertlein/MICHELIN

Dreifaltigkeitssäule and Rathaus

Beethoven-Gedenkstätte ⌚ – *Rathausgasse 10.* The great composer wrote part of the Missa Solemnis and completed his Ninth Symphony while staying here between 1821 and 1823. There is a small exhibition on his life and work, as part of which the composer's bedroom and study can be viewed.

Kaiserhaus – *Hauptplatz 17.* Emperor Franz I spent the summer in this house for 30 years. Austria's last emperor, Karl I, also came here in 1917-18.

Stadtpfarrkirche St. Stephan – All that remains of the original Romanesque building are the two stumps of towers, between which a Gothic-looking tower with a Baroque dome was added in 1697. Inside there is a dodecahedral font dating from the 14C and an altarpiece by Paul Troger depicting the *Stoning of St Stephen.*

Doblhoff Park – The main attraction in this park is the **Rosarium**★ covering 9ha/3.6 acres and displaying 25 000 roses of 600 different varieties. In June the Badener Rosentage attract innumerable flower-lovers.

BRAUNAU

Oberösterreich

Population 18 000

Michelin map 926 folds 6 and 7 – Alt 352m/1 155ft

This frontier town, the birthplace of **Adolf Hitler**, has had a civic charter since 1260. It was not until 1779 that the town, together with the Bavarian bank of the River Inn, became part of Austria. A bridge over the Inn connects Braunau with Simbach in Bavaria. The picturesque town centre and the suburb towards Salzburg with its numerous Gothic town houses, which survived the great fire of 1874, testify to the former wealth of Braunau, earned through the salt trade and a number of civic privileges. Vestiges of the town's original three rings of fortifications can be seen.

SIGHTS

Altstadt – The focal feature of the old town is the Stadtplatz, an elongated square which is surrounded by groups of houses dating from a wide variety of architectural periods. Particularly interesting examples of these are the **Glockengießerhaus** *(Johann-Fischer-Gasse 18)*, built in 1385, which still has its original bell-foundry workshop, and, not far off, the **Herzogsburg**, which now houses the regional museum.

Pfarrkirche St. Stephan – A square tower in several sections, the third highest in Austria (96m/315ft), abuts on the chancel which was built at the end of the 15C in the Gothic style. Built in 1906, the **high altar** is a late and rather droll example of the neo-Gothic style. The reredos echoes in some ways the authentic Gothic altar by Michael Pacher at St. Wolfgang. The side chapels contain evidence of the old patronage of the guilds, for example the remarkable **Bäckeraltar**, donated by the bakers' guild before 1490. The chapel nearest to the chancel in the south aisle contains the tomb of a bishop of Passau who died in 1485.

BREGENZ★★

Ⓛ Vorarlberg

Population 29 000

Michelin map 926 fold 14 or 216 fold 11

Local map see BREGENZERWALD – Alt 398m/1 306ft

Hotels and Restaurants: see The Red Guide Deutschland

Bregenz is the administrative capital of the Vorarlberg. It draws a considerable tourist trade from its position on the shore of Lake Constance (the "Bodensee" to German speakers), at the point where the "Swabian Sea" touches the mountains. Bregenz remains popular with sun-seeking holiday-makers, who are drawn especially to the Bregenz Festival *(see Calendar of events)*, as well as to the lakeside with its wide variety of water sports facilities and splendid views.

Winsquer/BREGENZER FESTSPIELE

Lakeside theatre, Bregenz

LOWER TOWN (INNENSTADT)

Lake Shore (ABY) – The main shopping streets (pedestrian zone) cluster at the foot of the former fortified city (Oberstadt or Altstadt) of the counts of Bregenz and Montfort.

In the Middle Ages the waters of the "Bodan", as the French-speaking Swiss call it, still lapped against the base of the little lakeside chapel (Seekapelle – **BY**). Insulated from road traffic by the railway, the shady quays and flowerbeds of the lake shore stretch from the Seeanlagen to the passenger port. A walk along the landscaped harbour breakwater is particularly pleasant.

The **view★** (**BY**) from the end extends to the last hills of Upper Swabia with the island of Lindau in the foreground, with its twin belfries. To the west the Strandweg serves the beach and the festival area *(Festspiel- und Kongreßhaus)* (**AY**) where every summer there are lavish open-air productions of operas.

★ **Vorarlberger Landesmuseum** ⓥ (**BY**) – The collections are particularly well displayed in the prehistory and Roman departments on the first floor.

The second floor houses local folk costumes and examples of popular religious art. Note the portative organ dating from the beginning of the 16C.

On the third floor is a display of lapidary specimens (9C ornamental plaque with interlaced motifs from Lauterach) and Romanesque and Gothic works of religious art taken from the richest churches in the province. Among these exhibits is a crucifix from the former abbey church at Mehrerau, dating from the beginning of the 16C.

On the same floor are works of mythological or religious inspiration and portraits *(Duke of Wellington)* by **Angelika Kauffmann** (1741-1807), considered a native of the Vorarlberg because of her connection with the Bregenzerwald.

She lived in Rome and Venice, as well as spending 15 years in England. She was a founding member of the Royal Academy in 1768 and a follower of Reynolds.
Close to the Landesmuseum is the **Kunsthaus Bregenz** built in 1997 on the Karl-Tizian-Platz, whose façade of etched glass makes a bold statement. It is the work of the Swiss architect Peter Zumthor, who has created here what is probably the most modern building in Austria to display contemporary art.

UPPER TOWN (OBERSTADT) AND CHURCH QUARTER

With its silent squares and deserted streets, this small enclosed town is restful when the season is in full swing on the lake shore.
It can be reached by car via the Kirchstraße, the Thalbachgasse and the Amtstorstraße, on the left. Walkers will prefer to stroll up the direct way from the central crossroads of the Leutbühel by the paved ramp of the Maurachgasse as far as the Martinstor, an old fortified gateway.

Martinsturm ⏲ (**BY**) - This 13C tower took on its present appearance, crowned by a heavy bulbous dome, between 1599 and 1602. The chapel arranged in the base of the tower contains a massive Late Gothic altar canopy and an important series of 14C mural paintings, fairly well preserved.
The skylights in the attic provide pretty **glimpses**★ of the remains of the wall and the roofs of the old town, the lake and belfries of Lindau and, in the distance, the Appenzell Alps.

Pfarrkirche St. Gallus (**BZ**) - The church faces the fortified town across the Thalbach ravine.

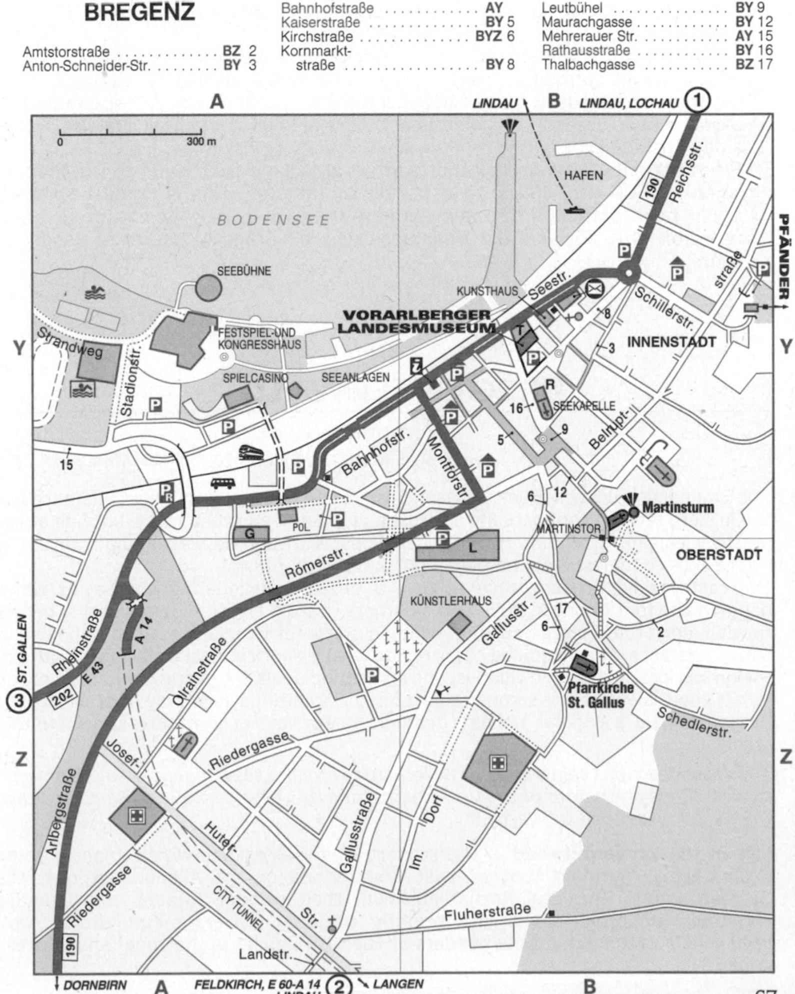

The building is fronted by a porch-belfry. Built of sandstone in the 15C, the porch-belfry is surmounted by a scalloped Baroque gable. The church has a single 18C Baroque nave, decorated with the relative restraint which appears in the Vorarlberg churches when compared with Tyrolean and Bavarian churches of the same period.
The walnut stalls, which are in valuable marquetry, were made in about 1740 for the nearby abbey of Mehrerau and have rounded backs decorated with effigies of saints.

EXCURSION

★★ **Pfänder** - *Summer mists make it advisable to do this excursion either in the early morning or in the evening before sunset.*

Leave Bregenz on ① and the lakeside road to Lindau.

Turn right towards the village of **Lochau**. Directly after the church at Lochau turn right onto the steep and twisting by-road to Pfänder, which when it passes over open ground gives many lovely views of the lake and of Lindau. After about 6km/4mi there is a fee-paying car park *(about 15min walk from here to the Pfänder summit)*. If you carry straight on along the road for another half a mile or so you reach a plateau with the Pfänder mountain refuge *(car parking facilities)*. Alternatively, it is possible to travel up from Bregenz with the **Pfänderbahn cable-car** ⌚, which takes you up to the top station on this same plateau *(for the lower station, see town plan)*.
From the plateau of the Pfänder mountain hut, there is a **panorama** to the south *(viewing table)*, from left to right of the Allgäu Alps, seemingly propped up against the sharply serrated chalk cliffs (Kanisfluh) of the Bregenzerwald, the snow-covered Schesaplana, the great furrow of the Rhine and, lastly, the Altmann and the Säntis, which are both situated in Switzerland. When visibility is good, one can even see the snow-capped Tödi peak (alt 3 620m/11 877ft) in the Glarus Alps.
To the north of the plateau is the entrance to the **Alpenwildpark** game reserve. A 30min circuit introduces visitors to Alpine fauna such as moufflons, ibex, marmots and red deer, housed in generous enclosures. The circuit also takes you past the eagle observation point where there are **bird of prey flight displays** ⌚ twice a day in summer.
From opposite the mountain hut a small woodland path leads to the Pfänder summit (1 064m/3 491ft) in a matter of minutes. This is home to a directional radio station. From the summit there is a view of the great sheet of water that forms Lake Constance and of Bregenz stretching along its shore.

BREGENZERWALD★★

Vorarlberg

Michelin map 926 folds 14, 15 and 27

The Bregenzerwald, which lies between Bregenz on the shores of Lake Constance and the Arlberg range, is not actually a forest as its name might suggest, but one of the most varied natural regions of the eastern Alps, with landscapes ranging from softly rolling hills to majestic Alpine peaks (alt 2 600m/8 500ft).
The fast-flowing Bregenzerach follows a broadly meandering course, at times hugging the foot of sheer cliffs and at others cutting through open valleys, before flowing along the bottom of a long, winding gorge far from any road and finally into Lake Constance. The unspoiled countryside with its agricultural tradition still intact, the typical local houses and villages, and last but not least the partly Alemannic, partly Valais population with its strong regard for the traditional local way of life make the Bregenzerwald a popular holiday destination for lovers of nature and mountain scenery.

The route described below and on the local map crosses the Bregenzerwald from east to west. For a pretty tour of the Vorarlberg, take the Arlbergstraße to Rauz, and then the Flexen pass road to Warth.

Life in the Bregenzerwald - The scenery of the Bregenzerwald region to some extent brings to mind that of east Switzerland or the Allgäu, just over the German border. The local farmsteads with their wooden façades and verandas and their windows decked with brightly coloured flowers might almost have been constructed by the same builders as the farmhouses in the upper and western Allgäu.

In the **Hochtannberg** mountain villages of Schröcken and Warth, around the source of the Bregenzerach and in Damüls, which were all settled by immigrants from the Valais (Walser) in the 13C and 14C, as were the Brandnertal *(see ARLBERGGEBIET 3)*, the Kleinwalsertal and the Großes Walsertal east of Feldkirch, the visitor will come across wooden houses with exposed beams which could have come straight from the upper valley of the Rhône. The remaining 19 villages in the Bregenzerwald were settled by the Alemanni from the 10C. The beautiful traditional costumes worn by the women of the Bregenzerwald are among the oldest and least altered in the German-speaking world. Although they are worn only for special occasions in everyday modern life, they are nonetheless frequently in evidence, being worn to church on Sundays or for major festivals. The remarkable variety of traditional headdresses, which reflect the marital status of the wearer or her current activity (going to church, travelling etc), reminds us that Bregenzerwald costumes were influenced by the Spanish early on.

Tourismusbüro Bezau

Traditional costumes from the Bregenzerwald

★ HOCHTANNBERGSTRASSE

From Warth to Dornbirn *65km/40mi*

The road between Warth and Schröcken may be closed for several days at a time between November and March because of risk of avalanches.

This run crosses the Hochtannberg pass and goes through the upper gorge of the Bregenzerach, following the twists and turns of the torrent. The crossing of the Bödele pass lends a mountainous character to the final leg of the trip and gives magnificent views of the Rhine Valley. Between Warth and Neßlegg the road runs through Hochtannberg pastureland.

Hochtannbergpaß – At the pass the Hochtannberg road reaches its highest point at an altitude of 1 675m/5 495ft. This section is overlooked by the Widderstein, an imposing peak of the Vorarlberg. According to local tradition, its rocks scraped the sides of Noah's ark.

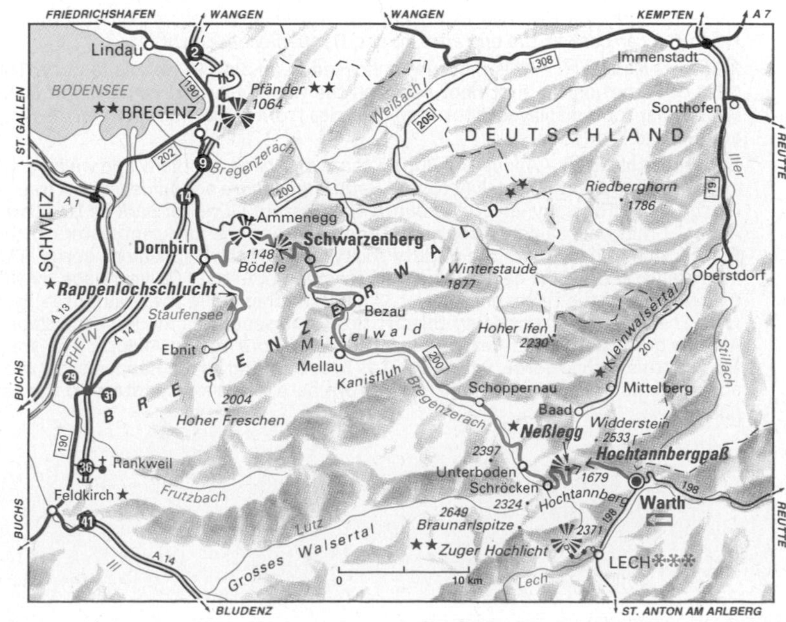

★ **Neßlegg** – The viewpoint by the Hotel Widderstein, at the spot where the road leaves the heart of the Hochtannberg to plunge into the wooded Schröcken tunnel, offers an overall **view**★ of the cirque closing the upper valley of the Bregenzerach. From left to right you can see the Mohnenfluh, the Braunarlspitz and its snowfields, the Hochberg, the Schadonapaß gap and the Hochkünzelspitze.
From Neßlegg to Schröcken a steep and winding descent through woods gives a few glimpses of the village of **Schröcken**, clustering round its church tower.
Downstream from the splendidly engineered Hochtannberg bridge appears the hamlet of **Unterboden**, a typical specimen of Valaisian settlement. The sunken sections which follow run through the upper gorges of the Bregenzerach, within view of the Künzelspitzen escarpments.
Between Schoppernau and the resort of **Mellau** the varied structure of the Kanisfluh is revealed to view; its north face forms particularly steep cliffs. Continuing along the road, there is a succession of idyllic landscapes.
Further on, the wide valleys with their increasingly important fruit-growing enterprises are graced by the villages of **Bezau** and Schwarzenberg.

Schwarzenberg – The **village square**★ displays flower-decked houses (eg Gasthof Hirschen), whose dark walls contrast with the bright roughcast of the church. The latter, which was rebuilt in 1757, has a roomy and well lit nave, characteristic of the local Bregenzerwald School. **Angelika Kauffmann** (1741-1807), the famous artist and herself the daughter of a painter, executed, at the age of 16, the medallions representing the Apostles and Jesus' disciples, and in 1801, the picture on the high altar. You can see the bust of this local celebrity (born at Chur but whose father was a native of Schwarzenberg) against the north wall of the nave. More of her works can be seen in the Vorarlberger Landesmuseum in Bregenz and the Heimatmuseum in Schwarzenberg.
Crossing the Bödele ridge gives clear **views**★ to the east of the open basin of the Bregenzerwald and the crests of the Allgäu Alps marking the German border. In the foreground lies the long ridge of the Winterstaude. On the Rhine slope, after a long run through forest, the **panorama**★ opens out near **Ammenegg** (Gasthaus Sonnblick). From north to southwest can be seen, in clear weather, Lake Constance, the Appenzell Alps (Säntis and Altmann) and the minor range of the Alvier.

Dornbirn – The economic capital and the most populous city of the Vorarlberg (42 400 inhabitants) attracts businesspeople from all over Central Europe to its annual trade fairs in spring and autumn. The town centre is the pedestrian zone around the market square. The Rotes Haus (Red House), next to the neo-Classical parish church of St. Martin (1839-40), is a well-restored 17C half-timbered building which, with its triangular gables, is a good example of the traditional Rhine Valley construction method.

Vorarlberger Naturschau ⓥ – *Marktstraße.* More than 100 oil paintings by museum founder Siegfried Fussenegger (1894-1966) depict the countryside and mountain scenery of the Vorarlberg region, while vivid dioramas illustrate local flora and fauna.

Leave Dornbirn on the road towards Ebnit/Gütle. After about 3.5km/2mi you reach the car park at the entrance to the Rappenlochschlucht.

Rolls-Royce-Museum ⓥ – This museum is housed in an old 19C textile factory. The "Hall of Fame" on the first floor contains the world's largest collection of Rolls Royce Phantoms displayed in rotation (vehicles from the period between the First and Second World Wars).

★ **Rappenlochschlucht** ⓥ – *About 1hr 30min there and back for the whole walk as far as the road to Ebnit. From July to mid September there are guided walks free of charge every Thursday: meeting point is the Gasthof Gütle car park at 10.30am.*
About 20min walk along the footpath running beside the turbulent waters of the Ebniter Ach brings you to the mighty rocky cliffs of the Rappenloch gorge. The impressive 72m/236ft-deep ravine was formed about 10 000 years ago by the melt-waters of the retreating glacier. A little further on is the Staufensee dam wall. The marl basin containing this artificial lake separates the Rappenloch and Alploch gorges. The path leads along the lake shore to the Alploch. The walk through this second gorge, which is not as breathtaking as the Rappenloch, takes about 20min as far as the Ebnit road. From here, retrace your steps to the car park.

BRUCK AN DER MUR★

Steiermark

Population 15 090

Michelin map 926 fold 23 – Alt 481m/1 578ft

Bruck lies at the confluence of the Mur and the Mürz, in the beautiful setting of the Upper Swabian massif. It is overlooked by the ruins of the old fortress of Landskron. Bruck is favoured by its situation astride important communication routes and by its proximity to the steelworks at Leoben. It is a busy industrial town, whose iron-processing factories carry memories of the rich ironmasters and traders in metal of the past. The town's main sights are in the main square (Koloman-Wallisch-Platz) and its nearby streets.

SIGHTS

★★ **Eiserner Brunnen** (**A**) – The wrought-iron well-head was made in 1626 by a local artisan, Hans Prasser, and is considered the finest example of Styrian wrought ironwork. The forged portion stands on a stone base and is remarkably elegant in execution, particularly the canopy, which has Renaissance motifs.

★ **Kornmesserhaus** (**B**) – In spite of remodelling and restoration, this fine building, erected by a rich merchant, Pankraz Kornmeß, at the close of the 15C, still has its original appearance. The main façade onto the main square has a series of arcades whose decorative arches are adorned with the early rosettes characteristic of Late Gothic. The loggia which forms part of the first floor already shows the influence of the Italian Renaissance.

Old Houses – There are still a good many 15C and 16C houses with arcaded courtyards. The **Rathaus** (**A R** – town hall) has a court with three storeys of arcades. The **Flößmeisterhaus** *(no 5)* (**B B**), a house adorned with a paired window of the Renaissance period, at the entrance to the Herzog-Ernst-Gasse, also has an interesting inner courtyard.

Pfarrkirche (**A**) – In the chancel, to the left, is a finely forged wrought-iron **sacristy door**★. Like the finely wrought door knocker it is believed to date from the beginning of the 16C and to come from the Kornmesserhaus.
In the north side chapel is a fine late-18C **altar of the Holy Cross** showing Christ on the Cross, between the Virgin Mary and St John.

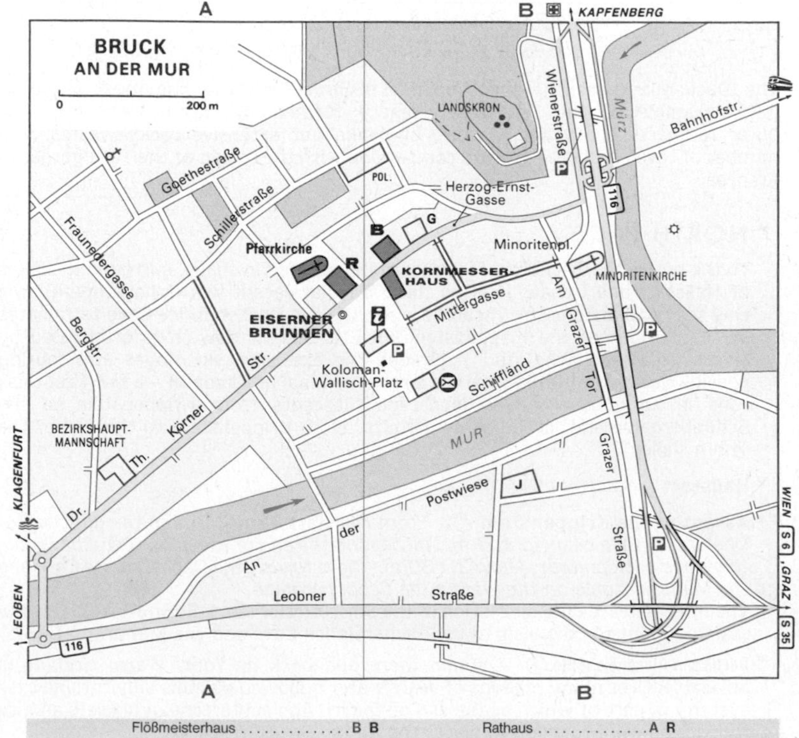

Flößmeisterhaus .... B B   Rathaus .... A R

CHRISTKINDL

Oberösterreich

Michelin map 926 fold 22 – 3km/2mi west of Steyr.

The village of Christkindl (the name means Christ Child) with its charming pilgrims' chapel is associated with a quaint tradition every Christmas season.

"Christkindl-Post" – The Austrian Post Office sets up a special post office at Christkindl from the end of November to 6 January every year, from which Christmas goodwill messages can be sent all over the world (a reply is sent to letters written by children to the Christ Child, if the return postage is enclosed). Over Christmas 1999, there were more than 2 200 000 letters and cards processed in Christkindl from all over the world.

Österr. Post AG

Pfarr- und Wallfahrtskirche – The Baroque central structure, dedicated to the Infant Christ, was begun c 1702 by Giovanni Battista Carlone and completed after 1708 by Jakob Prandtauer. Four semicircular chapels stand round a great cupola with a fresco by Johann Carl Reslfeld (1710) depicting the Assumption of the Virgin. The miraculous effigy itself is a wax figure of the Christ Child, only 10cm/4in high, kept above the tabernacle which is shaped like a globe. In 1720 the altar was adorned with 35 gilded statuettes of angels arranged around the trunk of the "Christ tree" in which the effigy used to be kept. The gilded Rococo pulpit (1751) is also a magnificent piece of work.

Krippenschau – *The crib display is housed in the old working quarters of the presbytery and is open to visitors from the beginning of Advent to 6 January.*

Mechanical crib – This was made over a period of 40 years (1899-1939). It has nearly 300 figures, a large proportion of which can move, being operated by a system of cogs and chains.

Pöttmesser crib – This crib, made in 1930-34, is one of the largest of its kind in the world, with 778 figures and a surface area of 58m^2/624sq ft.

DACHSTEIN★★

Salzburg, Steiermark und Oberösterreich

Michelin map 926 folds 20 and 21 – Local map see SALZKAMMERGUT

The Dachstein massif (highest point 2 995m/9 826ft) is the most characteristic example of the limestone scenery formed by the eastern Alps. Its outer ramparts guard not a world of peaks but extensive rocky wastes. The number of caves found here bears comparison with the region of the Tarn gorges in France.

★ NORTH FACE

To the north, the Dachstein foothills, more rounded in shape, surround the lakes of Hallstatt and Gosau. It is on this side that recent works have opened the way for popular tourism. A cable-car serving the Dachstein Ice Cave terminates at the summit of the Krippenstein with its superb view. It is often used by skiers in winter, who find – besides the extensive ski slopes and touring possibilities of the plateau, served by the terminal of Gjaidalm – a few first class runs in an unusually wild landscape (descents from Krippenstein to the Schönbergalpe and, if the snow permits, from Krippenstein to the end of the Traun Valley).

★★ **Hallstatt** – *See HALLSTATT.*

★★ **Ascent of the Krippenstein** ⌚ – *From Hallstatt 4km/2.5mi in the direction of Obertraun; then bear right 2km/1mi beyond the end of the lake, then 2hr 30min there and back on foot. Allow 2hr 30min more to visit the Dachstein Ice Cave and the Mammuthöhle on the way to the Schönbergalpe.*
The intermediate **cable-car** station of the **Schönbergalpe** (alt 1 345m/4 413ft) is the starting point for the visit to the Dachstein Ice Cave and the Mammoth Cave.

★ **Dachstein-Rieseneishöhle** ⌚ – *30min there and back on foot. Warm clothing is advisable.* Over many millions of years water hollowed out this labyrinthine cave system, in part of which at the end of the Ice Age subterranean glaciers and ice mountains were formed. In places the ice is 25m/82ft thick.

The Ice Cave, which is well equipped with lamps placed behind ice draperies and hanging icicles, is toured along a circular route. "King Arthur's Cathedral" and the "Great Ice Chapel" are among the features of this underground expedition.

Mammuthöhle ⊙ – *30min there and back on foot. 1km/0.5mi walk through the cave.* Some 50km/31mi of this vast subterranean network have already been explored. In the "Midnight Cathedral" impressions are shown of the parts of the cave lying deep inside the mountain. A visit to the Mammuthöhle brings home how small and insignificant people are.

★★ **Krippenstein** – *From the cable-car station (hotel), 30min on foot there and back.* A chapel stands at the top (alt 2 109m/6 919ft) of this rounded height with a **general view**★★ of the high Dachstein plateau, from which emerge the mossy heads of the final peak and also three patches of snow, the largest being a small glacier, the Hallstätter Gletscher. To get a **bird's-eye view**★★ of the lake at Hallstatt to the north, walk a little further to the Pioneers' Cross (Pionierkreuz). The path is marked by signs *(allow an extra 30min)* at the beginning of the Krippenstein road.

Koppenbrüllerhöhle ⊙ – *From Gasthaus Koppenrast in Obertraun, 1km/0.5mi. Guided tour: 1hr.* The cave, in a wooded defile of the Traun, is the only cavern in the Dachstein still in the process of natural enlargement. Flowing through it is a torrent, which swells in times of flood, fills the lower chambers and gushes from the cave mouth with a roar which echoes the length of the valley, to cascade down into the Traun.
Man-made galleries lead from the cave mouth to a great cleft, the Hannakluft, running in a dead straight line, where the underground waters may be seen swirling by. The Bocksee (Goat Lake) terminates the visit.

★★★ **Gosauseen** – *See GOSAUSEEN.*

★★ SOUTH FACE

The towering bulk of the Dachstein massif, with its sheer rock faces rising to a height of 1 000m/3 280ft, drops steeply down to the Alpine pastures of Ramsau. The majestic serenity of the Dachstein and the welcoming tranquillity of the mountain plateaux of Ramsau combine to form a highly original and charming landscape. The pastures, bright with Alpine flowers, the larch forests and the rocky cliffs create their own individual palette of colour, and make a particularly beautiful scene in the light of sunrise and sunset.

P. Mertz/VIENNASLIDE

South face of the Dachstein

FROM EBEN IM PONGAU TO GRÖBMING

62km/39mi, not counting the detour to Stoderzinken

✲ **Filzmoos** - Alt 1 057m/3 468ft. This attractive holiday resort occupies a pretty **site**★ tucked against the western foothills of the Dachstein massif. Towering above the village is the distinctive outline of the **Bischofsmütze** (Bishop's Mitre), a 2 454m/8 049ft tower of rock which dominates the surrounding countryside. In the winter, Filzmoos offers a small ski slope, spread over the Roßbrand massif (1 050-1 600m/3 445-5 249ft) and the Dachstein foothills (1 050-1 645m/ 3 445-5 397ft). The ski pass is valid also for the other ski resorts which constitute the **Salzburger Sportwelt Amadé**★★ *(see separate listing)*, the nearest of which are at Flachau and Altenmarkt, about 15km/9mi away. For cross-country skiers there is a well laid, 14km/8.6mi long track at 1 600m/5 249ft, leading from the mountain station of the Papageno cable-car to the Radstädter Hütte (refuge).

In the summer, Filzmoos is the perfect departure point for walks in the surrounding mountains. An excursion to the **Gerzkopf**★★ summit (1 729m/ 5 673ft, *4hr there and back on foot from Schattbach*) is particularly recommended. From the summit there is a similar panorama to that from the Roßbrand peak.

★★ **Roßbrand** - Alt 1 770m/5 807ft. After taking the Papageno cable-car, follow the ridge footpath west to the summit *(about 2hr there and back, easy going)*. There is a magnificent **panorama**★★ mainly of the Dachstein range, the Schladminger Tauern (Hochgolling, Höchstein), the Ankogel range, the Hohe Tauern (Großglockner, Großvenediger) and the Hochkönig. A panoramic telescope makes it possible to pick out the most famous of the 150 peaks that can be seen from here.

Carry on towards Ramsau. After 12km/7.5mi, turn left and then take a small toll road to the right up to the foot of the Hunerkogel.

★★★ **Hunerkogel** - Alt 2 700m/8 856ft. *Take the* **Dachstein-Südwandbahn** ⏲ *(also known as the Gletscherbahn Ramsau) to the top, allow at least 1hr there and back.*
From the end of the toll road (alt 1 700m/5 576ft), the Hunerkogel can be seen looming like some impregnable fortress. The ascent of the sheer rock face by cable-car is spectacular.
From the upper station, there is a good view south of the Schladminger Tauern range and Hochgolling peak. The view takes in the mighty cliffs of the nearby summits of the Hoher Dachstein and the Koppenkarstein. To the north, the softer slopes of the Dachstein and Salzkammergut glaciers form a contrasting scene. From the other side of the panoramic restaurant there is a breathtaking **view**★★★ of the successive folds of the Austrian Alps stretching away into the distance, including such peaks as those of Sportwelt Amadé, the Gasteinertal and the Hohe Tauern (Großglockner, Großvenediger).
The Dachstein glacier is equipped with about 10km/6mi of cross-country ski tracks and two downhill ski slopes (one for beginners and one for proficient skiers) with a drop of 400m/1 312ft.

✲ **Ramsau am Dachstein** - Alt 1 150m/3 772ft. At the beginning of the 20C, Ramsau was better known by the name of Ahorntal (Sycamore Valley). The houses of the resort, which is well integrated into the local landscape, occupy a sunnily exposed mountain plateau and offer numerous possibilities for accommodation (capacity about 6 700, mainly in bed and breakfasts, guesthouses and family hotels). Ramsau is an oasis of peace and quiet and a ramblers' paradise in every season. In winter there are still 70km/44mi of footpaths open to walkers. The **cross-country ski tracks**★★★ cover over 150km/90mi between altitudes of 1 000-1 750m/3 281-5 740ft and include a wide range of levels of difficulty. There are also 40km/25mi of skating tracks. The nearby Dachstein glacier also offers cross-country ski tracks at an altitude of 2 700m/8 858ft against a magnificent backdrop of mountain peaks.
The possibilities for downhill skiing in Ramsau are somewhat limited, but not far off are the **Schladminger Tauern**★★ *(see separate listing)*, which more than amply compensate.
From Ramsau take the small mountain road towards Weißenbach, which cuts through some delightful **scenery**★. Level with Aich, at the foot of the Schladminger Tauern, the road leads onto E 651. Keen walkers can at this point make a detour up to Stoderzinken.

★★ **Walk up to Stoderzinken** - Alt 2 048m/6 718ft. *45min driving time and 2hr 15min on foot there and back.*
Follow E 651 to Gröbming and then the small, 12km/7.5mi long road signposted "Stoderzinken Alpenstraße" which has a regular gradient of 1 in 11. Toll after 2km/1mi.

At the end of the road climb to the Steiner hut and from there take the untaxing footpath *(30min)* to a pretty little chapel, the **Friedenskircherl**, which seems to be hanging on the very edge of an abyss. There is a remarkable **view★** of the Schladminger Tauern range (with the ski slopes of Haus, Schladming and Hochwurzen in the foreground).
Turn back for a short distance, then take a challenging footpath *(at least 1hr)* up to the Stoderzinken summit. It is recommended to wear proper climbing boots, particularly in damp weather, as the path is rocky and can be slippery. From the top, there is a marvellous **panorama★★** of the better-known peaks around Schladming and of the magnificently forested slopes of the Dachstein.
For those energetic enough to walk on, it is possible to climb from here to the Brünner hut. Otherwise, turn back and return the way you came.

DONAUTAL★★

DANUBE VALLEY – Oberösterreich and Niederösterreich

Michelin map 926 folds 6 to 13

The Danube is the longest river in Central Europe (2 826km/1 756mi) and the second longest in Europe, after the Volga (3 895km/2 292mi). It flows through or skirts 10 states, and four capital cities have been built on its banks, bearing witness to its international importance.
The Danube is Austrian for only 360km/224mi from Achleiten, below Passau, to Hainburg, at the gates of Bratislava, that is, for one-eighth of its course. It is a vital artery for the economy of the country. This section of the river, wholly navigable, is used by shipping which serves Vienna, the capital, Linz, a great industrial town, and indirectly the industrial centres of Steyr and St. Pölten. Although the waters of the river are not always the colour of which *The Blue Danube* sings, especially when water levels are high, the river's banks, particularly between Grein and Krems, boast idyllic scenery which will captivate most visitors. Old fortified castles, over which the ghost of a Burgrave still watches, gracious Renaissance palaces with charming arcaded courts, and beautiful fortified churches and abbeys grace the banks of this much-sung river.

Engineering works – For more than two centuries engineering has been going on to improve the navigability and usefulness of the Austrian stretch of the Danube. The deepening of the river bed near Vienna has allowed several of the arms of the river to be drained and thus removed the danger of flooding.
Austria has the following hydroelectric installations in operation: Jochenstein on the German frontier, Aschach, Ottensheim-Wilhering, Abwinden-Asten, Ybbs-Persenbeug, Wallsee-Mitterkirchen, Melk, Altenwörth, Greifenstein and Wien-Freudenau, which went into operation in 1998 as the largest river power station in a city with over a million inhabitants. Altenwörth is the largest of these civil engineering projects, with an annual power output of almost 2 milliard kWh. The power stations along the Danube produce a total of about 12 billion kWh per year, accounting for about a quarter of Austria's national annual electricity output.

1 FROM PASSAU (IN GERMANY) TO LINZ *86km/55mi*

From Passau to Aschach, the route proposed below runs southeastwards along the south bank of the river. From the north bank rise the granite heights of the Mühlviertel. In this section of its course the Danube crosses an area formerly filled by glaciers. With the melting of the glaciers, gravel plains formed along the valleys, while the hills were colonized by coniferous forest and grassland.

★★ **Passau** – The "town of three rivers" (the Danube, Inn and Ilz flow into one another at the east end of town) lies at the foot of the formidable Oberhaus fortress to the north and the Baroque pilgrimage church of Mariahilf to the south, from both of which there are very good views of the town. The well-preserved old town of Passau occupies a tongue of land between the Danube and the Inn, its picturesque streets clustered around the cathedral of St. Stephan. *For a more detailed description see The Green Guide Germany.*

Leave Passau by crossing the Inn and taking the road towards Linz.

The river can be seen flowing along to the left of the road, wide and majestic, between wooded, rocky slopes. The road, running along the valley floor, follows every curve of the river. At Obernzell, which can be seen on the German shore, the river opens out into a magnificent lake. This is the reservoir of the Jochenstein dam on the Danube.

Jochenstein-Kraftwerk – The Jochenstein power station, with an annual production of 1 600 million kWh, was a joint Austro-Bavarian project.
From Engelhartszell to Wesenufer the valley narrows. The clifftop road, running above the first stretches of water created by the Aschach dam, gives some fine views; from time to time the outline of a castle can be seen. A little after **Wesenufer**,

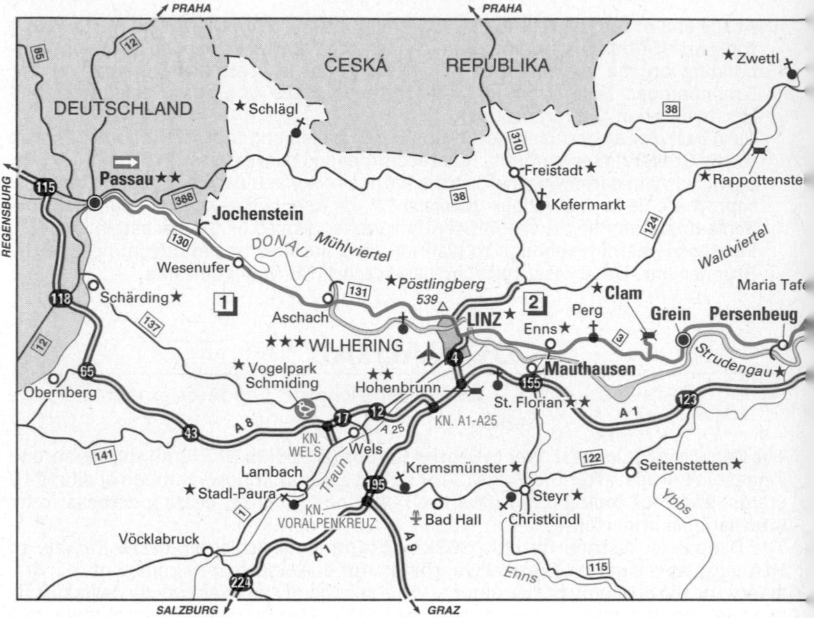

a pretty village with flowered balconies, the road leaves the shore of the Danube, which flows on in wide, sunken loops further north. The road climbs in a wooded gorge and reaches the picturesque Aschach Valley, which it leaves on reaching the alluvial plain, to cross the Danube below the **Aschach-Kraftwerk**, one of the largest power stations of its kind in Europe.
Beyond Ottensheim and its dam, the road follows the inside bank of the bend in the river to Linz.

2 FROM LINZ TO GREIN *72km/45mi*

★ **Linz** - *See LINZ.*

Below Linz the valley opens out into a wide basin filled by the alluvial soil of the river and its tributaries, the Traun and the Enns. Cereals, sugarbeet and fruit trees flourish on this fertile soil. To the north lie the slopes and wooded ridges of the Mühlviertel and further on the Waldviertel.

Leave Linz to the southeast via St.-Peterstraße towards Grein.

The road goes through the impressive industrial zone of Linz with its steelworks and nitrogen plant and crosses the Danube at the Steyregg bridge. A little after Steyregg, there is a last view of Linz before the road cuts across a plateau to return to the Danube plain at St. Georgen.

Take the turn towards the camp (Lager) at Mauthausen.

Mauthausen - *See MAUTHAUSEN.*

From Mauthausen to Dornach the road crosses a vast cultivated plain (sugarbeet, maize and wheat) which gradually gives way to a more wooded landscape.

Near Saxen turn right towards Burg Clam.

★ **Burg Clam** ⌚ - Dominated by its central tower, the castle's silhouette rises romantically from its leafy surroundings. The rock on which it stands has been fortified since 1149. The residential part of the castle focuses on the charmingly irregular arcaded **courtyard**★ of 1581.
The castle houses an unusually complete pharmacy whose fittings date from 1603. There are fine examples of Vienna and Meissen ware in the porcelain room and, in the dining room, some rare Louis XVI armchairs. Among the family memorabilia of the castle's owners is the breastplate worn by Karl von Clam-Martinic at the battle of Leipzig in 1813 as well as the uniform he wore while escorting Napoleon to Elba. There are also souvenirs brought back by Heinrich von Clam-Martinic who accompanied Archduke Franz Ferdinand on a world tour in 1892-93.

Return to the Danube road.

Below Dornach the road hugs the north bank of the river. Its waters, already held back by the dam at Ybbs-Persenbeug *(below)*, are hemmed in by rocky, wooded slopes. The approach to Grein is particularly pretty.

Grein - This charming summer holiday resort is dominated by the hills of the Mühlviertel. The pretty, enclosed town square (Stadtplatz) is surrounded by turreted houses. The church contains an altarpiece by Bartolomäus Altomonte on

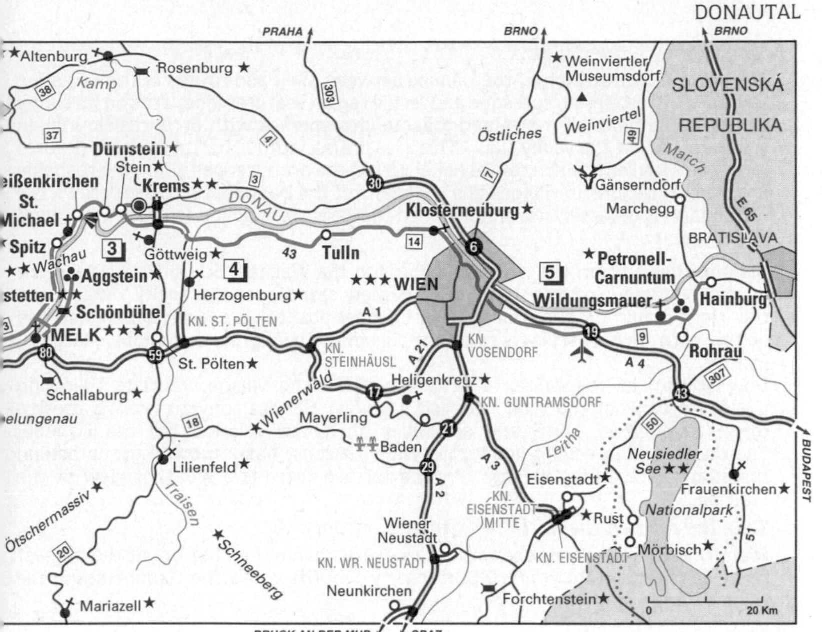

the 18C high altar. Grein is very proud of the little **Rokoko-Theater** ⏲ housed in the town hall. Entirely made of wood, it was built by the townspeople at the end of the 18C and is in use every summer and autumn.

Greinburg Castle, still in the ownership of the house of Saxe-Coburg-Gotha, has four wings joined by corner turrets, whose simplicity is in stark contrast to the elegance of the Renaissance inner **courtyard**★, with three tiers of arcades. A fountain, an old cistern and a Virginia creeper, hanging over the arches of the ground floor arcade, make a romantic picture. Within the generous spaces of the interior is an interesting local navigation museum, the **Schiffahrtsmuseum** ⏲, with numerous models of bridges, landing-stages and locks as well as works of art evoking the life of the great river in this part of Austria.

3 FROM GREIN TO KREMS *95km/59mi*

Between Grein and Krems stretches the most picturesque section of the Danube Valley in Austria. It is hollowed out of the granite of the Waldviertel, which forms the last foothills of the Bohemian massif.

Grein - *Description under* 2 *above.*

From Grein to Ybbs, the **Strudengau**★, sunken between the high wooded cliffs which overlook it from a height of over 400m/1 300ft, often silent and shrouded in mist, provides a heroic and romantic setting. The castle ruins of Burg Struden, clinging to their rock, and then those of Burg Sarmingstein, catch the eye. The river embraces willow-covered islands, then expands into a splendid lake, formed by the Ybbs-Persenbeug dam, whose power station has an annual output of 1 358 million kWh. The locks built to allow the passage of barges are particularly interesting.

Persenbeug - The last Austrian emperor, Karl I, was born in this castle on a rock by the Danube in 1887.

Between Persenbeug, which stands at the head of a fertile plain formed by a meander in the Danube, and Melk, the valley was the scene of certain episodes in the Nibelungen epic. It was here, in the **Nibelungengau**, that Gunther and Hagen undertook their rides through the forest; it is here that they gathered their knights to go to Attila's court at the invitation of Kriemhild who had married the King of the Huns to avenge the murder of her first husband, Siegfried.

In a splendid **site**★ on a hillock to the left is the pilgrimage church of **Maria Taferl**, whose main façade facing the Danube was designed to be seen from a distance. Begun in 1660, it did not receive its finishing touches until 50 years later, from Jakob Prandtauer, who completed the dome.

★★ **Artstetten Castle and Museum** - *See Schloß-Museum ARTSTETTEN.*

In the 10C the Babenbergs, who began the extraordinary expansion of the Austrian monarchy, settled at Pöchlarn on the south bank of the river. It was they who founded the nearby abbey at Melk, whose fine Baroque façade comes into view at Ebersdorf.

Take the bridge over the Danube to Melk.

★★★ **Melk Abbey** - *See MELK.*

The 35km/22mi stretch of the Danube between Melk and Krems is known as the **Wachau**★★. This very picturesque and fertile region features vineyards on its sunny slopes, while fields of maize and tobacco interspersed with orchards flourish in the loamy soil of the valley floor. This area is also famous for its apricots (known locally as *Marillen*), which can be bought from the producers all along the roadside in summer. Delightful villages line the banks of the Danube, fortresses crown the clifftops and characteristic onion-domed church towers can be seen dotted around the landscape.

Schönbühel - From the main road through the Wachau, **Schloß Schönbühel**, built at the beginning of the 19C, can be seen standing on a rocky outcrop on the right bank of the Danube. Its pepper-pot towers and bulbous-domed belfry, with rows of fruit trees on the hills in the background, make a charming picture.

Downstream of the castle, a little way from the village, tourists following the south bank of the river can visit a former Servite convent (now a presbytery), founded in 1666 and also built on a cliff overlooking the Danube. The **church**, whose ceiling is adorned with frescoes, has a moving group behind the altar representing a Pietà. From a terrace there is a pleasant view of the Wachau.

Take the road on the north bank towards Krems.

From Grimsing onwards the famous vineyards begin. Further on, at the highest point on the opposite shore, 300m/nearly 1 000ft above the Danube stand the ruins of Aggstein.

★ **Burgruine Aggstein** - Its exceptional **site**★ and colossal size made this 12C fortress one of Austria's finest strongholds in its heyday. It was frequently the object of disputes and suffered extensive damage on several occasions, including in 1529 at the hands of the Turks. Anna of Polheim had the fortifications reinforced in 1606, but the fortress fell into ruins from the 18C. The proud remains of its towers and defensive walls are still an impressive sight for modern visitors. A steep path *(2hr on foot there and back)* leads from Aggstein hamlet up to the castle gate. The tip of the spur on which the castle stands gives a fine view of the surrounding countryside.

Schloß Schönbühel

At **Willendorf** a very primitive earthenware statue dating from about 25 000 years ago, known as the "Willendorf Venus", was found in 1906. It is now kept in Vienna at the Naturhistorisches Museum.

★ **Spitz** – From the main road, the little town of Spitz lies half-hidden behind a curtain of fruit trees. It lies at the foot of a terraced vineyard known as the "Tausendeimerberg", because in a good year it produces 1 000 "Eimer" of wine (56 000l/12 300gal). Only the squat shape of the parish church rises above the house roofs, and above, the ruins of the castle of Hinterhaus stand out against the wooded mountain slope. Spitz has fine old town houses, with arcades and balconies. The Schloßgasse with its arcades is one of its most picturesque streets and leads to the 17C castle.
The **Pfarrkirche** ⌚, a Gothic building of the 15C, has a chancel out of line with the nave; the elegant chancel has network vaulting. The organ loft is adorned with statues of Christ and the 12 Apostles (c 1420). The altarpiece (1799) by Kremser Schmidt over the Baroque altar shows the martyrdom of St Maurice.

St. Michael – This fortified church on the north bank of the Danube was built c 1500 in the Gothic style. The original building dated from the 10C, making this one of the oldest parishes in the Danube Valley. The decorative Renaissance battlements on the church tower were added in 1544 following a fire.

Weißenkirchen – This wine-growing village lies tucked between the Danube and the hills of the hinterland. Above the narrow winding streets and fine old houses adorned with oriels rises the imposing outline of the Gothic fortified church (15C-16C).

Wachaumuseum ⌚ – The museum is housed in the Teisenhoferhof, a 16C fortified farm which has a charming arcaded courtyard and a covered gallery decorated with garlands of flowers and sheaves of maize whose golden colour stands out boldly from the white-washed masonry. Inside, there is an interesting display of works by Wachau painters (artists active at the turn of the 19C-20C).

★ **Dürnstein** – *See DÜRNSTEIN.*

The countryside becomes flatter on the approach to the towns of Stein and Krems.

★★ **Krems und Stein** – *See KREMS und STEIN.*

Partaj/BILDAGENTUR BUENOS DIAS

4 FROM KREMS TO VIENNA *83km/52mi*

★★ **Krems und Stein** - *See KREMS und STEIN.*

Cross the Danube on the great steel bridge at Stein, west of Krems.

A little after Mautern on the right, crowning a wooded hill, stands the impressive Benedictine abbey of Göttweig. Near the river are alluvial terraces on which vines and fruit trees grow, and then meadows and fields of cereals. The road runs near the river, which is divided into a number of branches at this point.

Tulln - *See TULLN.*

At Greifenstein, near the Vienna Woods, the valley narrows, and the road squeezes a passage between the river and high wooded hills.

★ **Klosterneuburg** - *See KLOSTERNEUBURG.*

The road then enters the suburbs of Vienna.

★★★ **Vienna** - *See WIEN.*

5 FROM VIENNA TO HAINBURG *84km/52mi*

The suggested route follows the south bank of the river as it flows through a very wide stretch of valley.

★★★ **Vienna** - *See WIEN.*

Leave Vienna on road no 9 to go through Schwechat, which is famous for its breweries.

Before skirting the buildings of the international airport of Vienna at Schwechat, one sees indistinctly on the left the outlines of the Island of Lobau where Napoleon's forces recovered their strength in 1809, after the unexpected victories of the Austrians at Eßling and Aspern.

Wildungsmauer - In spite of restorations and additions (including a 19C porch and tower), the little church of St. Nikolaus has kept its essentially Romanesque character. It originated in a fortified building of about 1200.

Petronell-Carnuntum - *See PETRONELL-CARNUNTUM.*

Between Bad Deutsch-Altenburg and Hainburg a range of hills comes into view, on the far bank of the Danube and its tributary the March/Morava in Slovakia; these are the Little Carpathians, the last outrunners of the great circle of mountains encircling the Hungarian plain.

Hainburg - Still with its ring of walls and fortified gateways below the remains of its castle, Hainburg had an important strategic role in the Middle Ages on the highway linking Vienna and Bratislava. The hundredfold increase in traffic between Austria and Slovakia since 1989 has brought the town renewed importance and prosperity.

DÜRNSTEIN★

Niederösterreich

Population 1 002

Michelin map 926 fold 11 - Local map see DONAUTAL - Alt 209m/686ft

The little fortified town of Dürnstein stands at the foot of a ridge on which terraced vineyards are cultivated, producing well-known wines. Crowned by the ruins of a fortress and still girded by its walls, it lies on a rocky ridge overlooking the Danube, forming one of the most famous scenes in the Wachau. The modern road to the Wachau avoids the old town by passing through a tunnel underneath it.

Richard the Lionheart held prisoner - It is said that during the 3rd Crusade, Richard the Lionheart, King of England, had a furious altercation with the Duke of Austria, Leopold V. At the attack against Acre in Palestine, Richard is supposed to have removed the Duke's banner from a tower, thus insulting the Duke's honour.
By chance, Richard was shipwrecked in the Adriatic on his way back to his kingdom and had to cross the land of his rival. Though disguised as a merchant, he was recognized at an inn near Vienna, arrested and handed over to Leopold, who shut him up in the fortress at Dürnstein.
In the spring of 1193, as Richard was languishing in gaol, his attention was caught by some familiar, indeed some of his own favourite, airs being played by a minstrel outside the castle walls. This turned out to be the faithful **Blondel**, who was looking for his sovereign lord. Unfortunately, Blondel's discovery of where his master was being held prisoner was to no avail, as Richard was transferred and held prisoner for nearly a year longer at the Imperial Castle of Trifels in the Rhineland Palatinate, before being granted his liberty at the price of an enormous ransom.

SIGHTS

Baroque church tower, Dürnstein

Hauptstraße - This, the main street, runs through the town from end to end and is bounded in the east by an old fortified gateway. It is most pleasing with its old houses, some of them 16C, featuring bracketed turrets, oriels and flower-filled balconies.
The wrought-iron signs of several inns - where it is a pleasure to taste the famous *Heuriger* (current year's wine) of the Wachau - will recall the story of Richard the Lionheart's imprisonment and the touching story of the faithful Blondel.

Pfarrkirche ⊙ - The former Augustine canons' monastery was founded in the 15C and rebuilt between 1720 and 1725 in the Baroque style. In the courtyard surrounded by old monastic buildings, one can admire the magnificent doorway decorated with carved columns and statues of the Church Fathers.
The magnificently decorated Baroque **tower*** of the church was designed by Matthias Steinl and Josef Munggenast. The interior is adorned with restrained stucco; rows of curved balconies run round the nave. The woodwork of the chancel, the pulpit and the high altar forms a harmonious whole. The side chapels house paintings by Kremser Schmidt. The sacristy, also adorned with delicate stucco, shows valuable marquetry. The cloister has been altered by restorations. From the balustraded terrace at the foot of the tower of the façade, remarkable for its height and its decoration, there is a pleasant view of the Danube Valley.

Castle Ruins - *45min on foot there and back*. The ruins *(Burgruine)* are reached by a path which begins on the level of the ramparts east of the town and climbs among rocks. From the ruins there is a remarkable **view** of Dürnstein and the valley.

Schloß EGGENBERG**

Steiermark

Michelin map 926 folds 36 and 37 - 3.5km/2mi west of Graz

A long avenue lined with lawns leads to the palace of the Princes of Eggenberg, its façade only coming into view as one comes closer. The palace grounds have become natural parkland, where peacocks, game birds and wild sheep roam.

Residence of a high-ranking dignitary - Between 1625 and 1635 a princely residence for Johann Ulrich von Eggenberg was constructed round a medieval core. Von Eggenberg had been promoted to the rank of Prince of the Empire in 1623 and in the reign of Ferdinand II he was appointed to one of the most important posts, Statthalter (Governor) of Inner Austria. The building work was entrusted to the Italian architect **Pietro de Pomis**, who had demonstrated his skills a few years earlier with his work on Ferdinand's mausoleum in Graz.

Plan - In some aspects the palace is similar to the Escorial near Madrid - huge buildings, arranged on a square ground plan and separated by corner towers, enclosing three inner courtyards and a majestic chapel. The three tiers of arches in the main courtyard are articulated by engaged columns.

Architectural theme - The exceptional originality of Schloß Eggenberg derives from the fact that the whole building is an elaborately detailed allegory of the universe. The castle teems with images and symbols of the cosmos, and the initial impression is one of identification with the four elements: the earth which supports it, the air which

surrounds it, the water in the moats encircling it and the fire of its red roofs above it. The four towers stand for the four cardinal points of the compass, and mark the perimeter of a strikingly symbolical structure containing 365 windows for every day of the year, a suite of 24 state rooms for every hour of the day and night, and 52 windows letting light into these rooms and symbolizing the 52 Sundays of the year.

TOUR

★★★ **State Apartments (Prunkräume)** – *2nd floor.* The many notable guests who have occupied these apartments include **Emperor Leopold I** who came to Eggenberg in 1673 to celebrate his marriage to Claudia Felizitas von Tirol.
The decoration of the 24 **state rooms** was carried out in the 17C and 18C in the Baroque style. The rich profusion of stuccowork and painting is set off by the sparkle of the chandeliers. There are also interesting mid-18C murals by **Johann Baptist Raunacher** in some rooms. This suite of drawing rooms and bedrooms, interspersed with a number of Chinese and Japanese cabinets which were very fashionable at the time, compose a residence of considerable charm. It is interesting to note that, although these apartments were decorated with festivities in mind, their huge dimensions do not impose the cold atmosphere that might be expected.
The spacious reception room, known as the **Room of the Planets** (Planetensaal), is the central pivot of a suite of 24 rooms, arranged in a symmetrical fashion. The walls and ceiling are decorated with paintings (completed in 1685) by the Styrian artist Hans Adam Weißenkircher. The stuccowork is by Alessandro Serenio.
During the summer, the Eggenberg Concerts take place here in addition to official receptions.

Abteilung für Vor- und Frühgeschichte ⓥ - The Styrian antiques collection is housed on the ground floor of the south wing.

★★ **Strettweg Votive Chariot** - The centrepiece of the collection is a bronze chariot made 2 700 years ago in the 7C BC, a moving example of the work of the Hallstatt period (early Iron Age). It was found in a tumulus at Strettweg, near Judenburg. Its votive role is inferred from a female figure standing in the middle of the chariot and bearing a round vessel as if making an offering. The chariot is surrounded by soldiers on horseback and on foot, and the artist has captured them performing the swirling movements of a ritual dance. Other treasures, urns and various objects which were unearthed at the same burial mound are also on display in this room.

Coin and Antique Cabinet - This had its origin in the private collection of Archduke Johann and is the second largest of its kind in Austria. It is mainly devoted to the coins and economic history of Styria.

EGGENBURG★

Niederösterreich

Population 3 625

Michelin map 926 fold 11 - Alt 325m/1 066ft

The town of Eggenburg features some beautiful medieval and Renaissance architecture and can still boast a town wall preserved almost in its entirety with three towers (the Holturm, the Wahrsagerturm and the Kanzlerturm). The **historic town centre** is also well preserved.

SIGHTS

Hauptplatz - The considerable size of the main square becomes evident when one imagines it without the "Grätzl", the structure in its centre, and is an indication of the importance of market towns in past centuries. This is further underlined by the **pillory** (Pranger) and Adlerbrunnen (Eagle Fountain) from the 16C, the Mariensäule (Mary column) from the 17C, and the Trinity plague column erected in 1715. Outstanding among the old houses that line the square and add to its charm is the Gemaltes Haus, a sgraffito house dating from 1547 with images from the Old Testament, based on woodcuts by Burgkmair.

As one strolls through the old town, there is everywhere evidence of the mastery of the Eggenburg masons in their working of the pale local sandstone.

Pfarrkirche St. Stephan ⓥ - Two Romanesque towers, in solid, square-cut masonry (1180), dominate the east end of the parish church. The chancel dates from the mid 14C, and the nave from the 15C. The Late Gothic hall-church with ribbed vaulting, deeply incised clustered piers and beautiful tracery windows contains some rich fittings: interesting stone pulpit (1515); delicately chased pillars (1505); and a Baroque councillors' seat with inlaid strapwork (1710). Alongside the church is the **charnel house** first mentioned in 1299, approached down some steps *(switch on the light)*. It is a macabre reminder of the transience of human existence.

R. Chéret/MICHELIN

Pillory, Eggenburg

★ **Krahuletz-Museum** ⓥ - This collection from primeval and ancient times is of international standing and was assembled by Johann Krahuletz of Eggenburg, who had also recognized the geological importance of the Waldviertel. Cleverly presented, the informative display includes a **landscape model**★ showing the transformation from the "Eggenburg-on-Sea" of 20 million years ago via the primeval Danube of 11 million years ago to the present.

Österreichisches Motorradmuseum ⓥ - Austria's largest motorcycle collection, with 300 examples of a wide variety of makes covering 100 years of motorcycling history, is displayed in a disused factory. A must for motorbike enthusiasts.

"Ausg'steckt Is"

In the "Preßhaus", at the front of the wine cellar building, the grapes are pressed; the resulting must being stored in barrels for fermentation in the tunnel-like cellar at the rear of the building. The Preßhaus, however, is not only used for pressing the grapes but also as a wine parlour when the wine-grower (called Weinhauer in Austria) has a branch, usually of pine or fir, displayed above the door to indicate that he is serving his own wines, together with cold, home-produced food such as "Blunzn" (blood sausage), Geselchtes (smoked pork) and Speck (bacon). As a rule this happens for 6 to 8 weeks in the year. If the weather is fine one can sit outside in the shade of the walnut trees, which are an essential feature of the Kellergasse.

EXCURSION

Stoitzendorf – *4km/2.5mi east of Eggenburg on road no 303. Follow the signs for"Kellergasse".* Stoitzendorf's **Kellergasse** is a really unspoilt example of the roads to be found in Austrian wine-growing areas just outside the villages, lined with rows of small, mostly single-storey "Preßhäuser" where the grapes are pressed. Here in the western wine-growing area these buildings are embedded in the soft loam soil.

Pulkau – *8km/5mi northeast of Eggenburg.* Pulkau is a large wine-producing township not far from the Czech border, in a hilly region which lends itself to the cultivation of vines. The highest ridges are marked by dark Norway spruce forests and the town itself has the added interest of two unusual churches.

Pfarrkirche – The parish church crowns a hill to the north of town. It is flanked on the east by a Romanesque tower. Its most distinguishing feature is the simplicity of the main building. The north chapel has a few traces of early 14C frescoes; the south chapel is decorated with foliated capitals.
In the middle of the graveyard stands an unusual 13C **charnel house** (Karner) with a Romanesque stepped doorway.

Heilig-Blut-Kirche – This church is an unfinished Gothic building which contains a fine carved and painted wooden **altarpiece**★, above the high altar, made by artists of the Danube School at the beginning of the 16C. The figures of Christ, St Sebastian and St Bartholomew occupy the central panel, while the side panels depict scenes from the Passion.

EISENERZ

Steiermark

Population 7 800

Michelin map 926 fold 23 – Alt 694m/2 277ft

Eisenerz is an old mining town clustered at the foot of the mighty stepped pyramid of the Erzberg (Ore Mountain), whose man-made silhouette is particularly impressive in the late afternoon, when it positively glows in iridescent tones of pink and ochre. Since the year 712, some 222 million tonnes of ore have been dug out of this mountain, which is still Austria's sole source of ore, providing a third of the Austrian steel industry's needs.
In recent times, the numbers employed in the mining operations has sunk to a couple of hundred, so that diversification towards exploitation of the area's undoubted tourist attractions has changed the way of life. Its advantages include the splendid situation between the Leopoldsteiner See and the towering Polster mountain, the old houses which bear witness to the town's turbulent history, and the Erzberg itself, which is understandably a big draw for tourists.

★★ **Erzberg** – It is only in the last 200 years that the Erzberg has acquired its present aspect with **opencast mines** ⊙ and rows of associated stopes. During the Middle Ages, mining was carried out in small tunnels or isolated quarries, but at the beginning of the 19C this practice gave way to a more organized system of shafts and tunnels. In 1870 the engineers began the changeover from underground extraction to opencast mining. Today, as much ore is extracted in one day as was produced in a whole year during the 16C – approximately 10 000t. Great stopes, each 12-24m/39-79ft deep, now form a huge stairway in the sky above Eisenerz, leading to the summit of the Erzberg at 1 465m/4 806ft.

W. Geiersperger/BILDAGENTUR BUENOS DIAS

Erzberg, Styria

When mining below ground ceased in 1986, the disused workings were opened to the public as a **Schaubergwerk** (exhibition mine), one of the attractions being an audio-visual simulation of blasting. Another unforgettable experience is the trip on the **Hauly**, an 860hp truck with a viewing platform which takes you above ground through many of the 42 stopes, from which there is a fine **view**★ of the town, the landscape, and the blue lake which has formed at the foot of the mountain.

Altstadt - Only a few of the old houses belonging to the Radmeister, the owners of the 19 smelting plants in Innerberg, as Eisenerz used to be known, have survived. But there are still numerous old houses to be seen, dating from the 16C to the 18C. They are to be found surrounding the Bergmannplatz, where stand the old Gewerkenhof (hall of the miners' guild), Marktskanzlei (local council offices) and Traidkasten (granary), as well as the 16C **Altes Rathaus** in its centre; and also in the Lindmoserstraße, Dr.-Karl-Renner-Straße (no 4 is the Haus zum Heiligen Geist) and Krumpentalerstraße.

★ **St. Oswald** ⏲ - *Climb the steps up to the church.* This is the most important fortified church in Styria, a major work of the Admont masons' guild begun in 1470 under Emperor Friedrich III and completed in 1518. It was fortified on orders from the Emperor in 1532 due to the threat of invasion by the Turks, acquiring the encircling wall, the fortified tower and the massive barbican on the north side which still stand today.
The tympanum above the north porch has an Expulsion from the Garden of Eden in which Adam is shown as a miner. There are other reminders of mining in the interior, in the artificial stone of the **organ loft** and a wooden figure in 16C miner's dress above the second gallery on the north side.

Stadtmuseum ⏲ - *Kammerhof, Schulstraße 1.* This museum vividly presents the art and culture of those associated with the world of mining, as well as the techniques of mining ore.

Schichtturm - Built in 1581 by the Radmeister, this Renaissance tower on the southern slopes of the valley has a bell cast from the metal of Turkish cannons. It summoned the miners to their shifts, and was also used as a fire alarm. Now it is rung to signal noon.

Gesteins-Lehrpfad - This geological trail (400m/440yd) leads along a stream, the Trofengbach, from the valley station of the Erzberg cable-car into the town, and covers in visual terms 200 million years of geological evolution.

EISENERZER ALPEN★

Steiermark

Michelin map 926 folds 22 and 23

The Eisenerz Alps, which include the astonishing Erzberg, on which the industrial power of the former Austrian Empire was based, join up in the northwest with the limestone Ennstal Alps, whose impressive walls line the Gesäuse gGorge.
A pass linking the Enns and Mur valleys, the Präbichl, rises to an altitude of 1 200m/3 940ft. Between Hieflau and Leoben the road passes through a ruggedly picturesque landscape.

1 GESÄUSE GORGE

★ From Liezen to Hieflau *44km/27mi*

The **Gesäuse gorge** takes its name from the noise made by the waters of the Enns rushing over their rocky bed. The autumn colour of its trees makes a splendid spectacle.
Between Liezen and Admont the road winds along the Enns Valley. Soon the two onion domes of Frauenberg Church on its hill come into view in the foreground. Further east in the background rise the Großer Buchstein and the Hochtor, two summits enclosing the Gesäuse gorge; its rocky entrance can be seen a few kilometres after Admont.

From the touring route, follow the signposts on the left for Frauenberg.

Frauenberg - The pilgrimage church was rebuilt by the abbots of Admont in the late 17C, in an Italianate Baroque style; the two eastern towers were added in 1702. Its interior has a remarkable unity of style. The stucco decoration matches in its luxuriance the rich gilding which adorns the dark-stained wood of the altars and pulpit.
The Calvary terrace offers a fine **view**★ of Admont and the slender steeples of its abbey church enclosed in a ring of peaks (Haller Mauern, Reichenstein and Hochtor).

★ **Admont** - *See ADMONT.*

The best **view of the Gesäuse**★★ comes after Admont *(road no 146 at kilometre 93.2, by the bus stop and the turn-off for Weng)*, when the magnificent rock faces of the Hochtor (summit: 2 369m/7 770ft) come into sight.

Haindlkarbrücke - *Shortly before the turning for the Haindlkar hut.* This bridge over a small tributary of the Enns offers a close-up **view**★ of the formidable walls of the Hochtor, which attract numerous enthusiastic climbers.

Gstatterboden - At the only place where the defile widens out is the starting point for the popular climbing tours in the Gesäuse massif, rated by Viennese climbers as among the best mountaineering areas.
Downstream, the gorge is less wild, but the waters of the Enns, dammed close to the Kummerbrücke, offer a constantly changing picture, one moment dark green, the next moment pale.

Hieflau - The village has a wooded setting where the valley widens, at the foot of a south-facing slope.

2 DIE STEIRISCHE EISENSTRASSE (THE STYRIAN IRON ROAD)

★ From Hieflau to Leoben *50km/31mi*

Hieflau - *See 1 above.*

From Hieflau to Eisenerz the Erzbach Valley has beautiful, winding gorges and offers fine panoramas of the Tamischbachturm. When you reach the basin of Eisenerz, with a view of the **Erzberg**★★, make a small detour to see the Leopoldsteiner See.

★★ **Leopoldsteiner See** - This small lake with its deep green waters lies in one of the finest settings in Styria, at the foot of the rock cliffs of the Seemauer in the Hochschwab range.

Eisenerz - *See EISENERZ.*

From Eisenerz, the well-engineered road leads up to the **Präbichl pass** (alt 1 232m/4 041ft). To the northwest the rocky summit of the Pfaffenstein dominates the landscape. To enjoy a general view of the Erzberg take the chair-lift up the Polster.

★★ **Polster** - *About 1hr 30min there and back from the Präbichl, including 30min by* **chair-lift** ⏲ *and 30min on foot.* From the summit (alt 1 910m/6 266ft) crowned with a Calvary, there is a **view** of the Erzberg, standing out, in all its red-brown mass, against the greens of the Alpine pastures and woods, while to the north can be seen the separate sharp rock crests (Griesmauer) of the Hochschwab.

The descent from the Präbichl to Vordernberg passes through a pleasant landscape of Alpine pastures.

Vordernberg – This market town has many **historical sites associated with iron-working**★ which bear witness to the days when the iron industry flourished here. At one time there were 14 smelting plants, and even Archduke Johann acquired one in 1822. The popular prince did much to further the interests of Vordernberg and the development of ore mining. He was also the instigator of the scheme to set up the first mining college, originally opened in 1840 in Vordernberg, but moved in 1848 to Leoben.
The numerous fascinating **monuments** and **museums of technical interest** have been restored and fitted out with loving care and expert knowledge. The **Informationszentrum der Steirischen Eisenstraße** ⓥ (Styrian Iron Road Information Centre) can also provide information on the Erzberg railway which runs from Vordernberg over the Präbichl to Eisenerz, going both round and through the Erzberg.

Leoben – *See LEOBEN.*

EISENSTADT★

L Burgenland

Population 10 150

Michelin map 926 fold 25 – Alt 181m/594ft

Eisenstadt has developed on the south slope of the Leithagebirge, where the forests resemble a huge park. It is at this point that the great Central European Plain begins. The mild climate makes it possible to grow vines, peaches, apricots and almonds.
The proximity of Vienna has checked the economic expansion of the town, which, however, is still the most important market in the region for wine. Since 1925 the political and administrative role of Eisenstadt, as capital of the Burgenland, has somewhat revived the city. Neusiedler See, nearby, also attracts tourists to the area.

Haydn's town – Everything here reminds one of the brilliant composer. For 30 years **Joseph Haydn** (1732-1809) was in the service of Prince Miklós József Esterházy, living sometimes at Eisenstadt, sometimes at the Esterháza palace in Hungary. He had been appointed assistant conductor in 1761. His job included conducting the orchestra and directing the chorus, composing music and tending to administrative work (music librarian, supervisor of instruments and chief of musical personnel). In 1766 he was promoted to musical director. Having an orchestra and a theatre at his disposal, Haydn worked without respite and achieved growing fame.
For Haydn's birthplace at Rohrau see PETRONELL-CARNUNTUM: Excursions.
Eisenstadt cherishes memories of the man who was to Mozart, 24 years his junior, a mentor, a model and a friend.

Trumler/ÖSTERREICH WERBUNG

Joseph Haydn

SIGHTS

★ **Schloß Esterházy** ⓥ **(A)** – Eisenstadt was one of the favourite residences of this noble Magyar family, who largely contributed to the establishment of the Habsburgs' rule in Hungary. One of its princes, Miklós II, even refused the Hungarian crown which Napoleon I offered to him in 1809, preferring to continue his support of the Habsburgs.
Wishing to have a residence fit for his rank, Prince Pál Esterházy commissioned the Italian architect Carlo M Carlone. On the site of a medieval fortress Carlone built, between 1663 and 1672, a great quadrilateral around the court of honour. Each of the four corner towers, at that time, was crowned by an onion dome.

EISENSTADT

Bürgerspitalgasse .... B 3
Domplatz .... B 4
Esterházyplatz .... A 6
Franz-Schubert-Platz .... B 7
Freiheitsplatz .... B 9
Ing.-Julius-Raab-Str. .... B 10
Johann-Permayer-Str. .... B 12
Josef-Hyrtl-Platz .... B 13
Leopold-Kunschak-Str. .... A 15
Matthias-Markhl-Gasse .... B 16
St.-Antoni-Straße .... B 18
Unterbergstraße .... A 19

Burgenländisches Landesmuseum .... A M2
Österreichisches Jüdisches Museum★ .... A M1
Rathaus .... B R

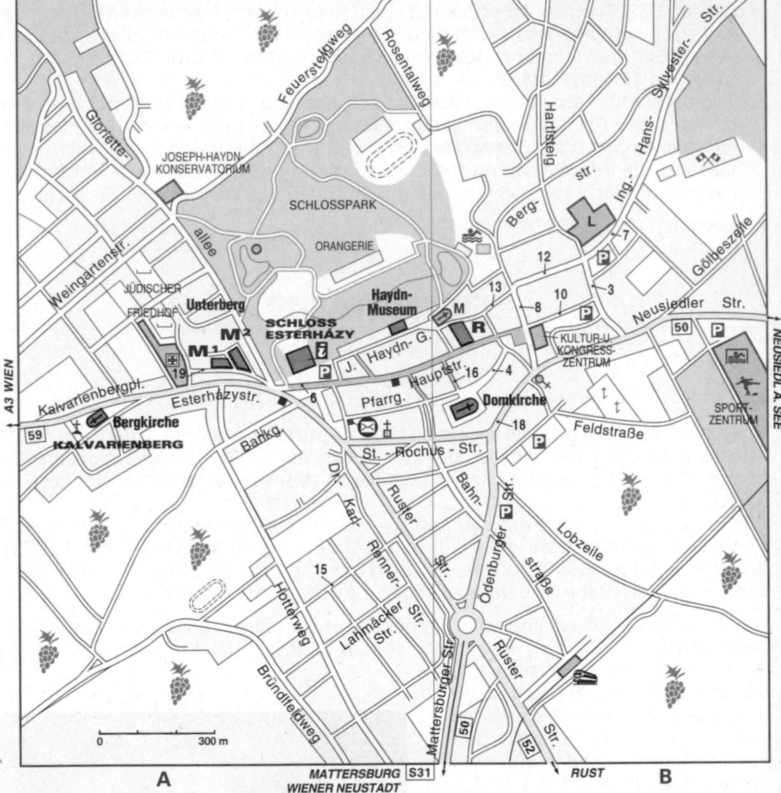

Between 1797 and 1805 the French architect Moreau modified the building in the taste of that day. The façade to the park was given a portico in the neo-Classical style with Corinthian columns, and the entrance gateway in the main façade was surmounted by a terrace, supported by Tuscan columns. Terracotta busts, representing Hungarian tribal and military leaders at the time of the 9C occupation adorn this façade, which is surmounted by an onion-domed tower. On the far side of the forecourt are the former royal stables, built in 1743.

The palace now houses local administrative offices, but the Haydn Room and the Esterházy-Museum are open to visitors.

Interior – The tour of the palace passes through numerous rooms recalling the princely Esterházy family, many of them magnificently furnished. But the highlight is without any doubt the **Haydnsaal★**, the great hall of state which was decorated at the end of the 17C with stucco, *grisailles* of Hungarian kings and frescoes with scenes from Greek mythology. In the 18C the marble floor was replaced with parquet for the sake of better acoustics. It was here that Haydn conducted the court orchestra almost every evening.

Haydn-Museum ⓥ (A) – In Haydngasse, a quiet little street, at no 21 is the modest house in which the composer lived from 1766 to 1778. A covered passage leads to a charming little courtyard, full of flowers. A small **museum** contains interesting mementoes of the life and work of the great musician.

Level with the Franziskanerkirche turn right and follow the Hauptstraße to the town hall.

Rathaus (**B R**) – The town hall was built in the mid 17C in the Renaissance style. It features a highly original façade, with three oriel windows, scrolled gables and a round-arched doorway with diamond-cut stonework.

Domkirche (**B**) – This Late Gothic hall-church from the 15C and 16C is dedicated to St Martin, patron saint of the Burgenland. A charming pulpit and the choir, complete with organ, remain of the original Late Baroque interior decoration. Note the beautiful relief of the Mount of Olives, dating from before 1500.

"Court Jews"

As Christians were forbidden by medieval statutes to handle interest on loans, in the 17C and 18C some Jews came to play a crucial role in financial dealings. A consequence of this was that the Habsburg rulers appointed "court Jews", who enjoyed a special status and unrestricted freedom to trade. One of these was Samuel Oppenheimer, a banker from Speyer, Germany, who financed Prince Eugen of Savoy's campaigns against the Turks, after Karl von Lothringen had brought him to Vienna. Another was his son-in-law Samson Wertheimer, who worked for Leopold I, Joseph I and Karl VI. But this freedom to trade was a privilege reserved for a few, while insecurity and oppression remained the lot of the rest of the Jewish community.

Take the Pfarrgasse onto the Esterházystraße and go past the castle.

Unterberg, the Old Jewish Quarter (A) – Eisenstadt has evidence of a thriving Jewish community dating back to 1296. When Emperor Leopold I expelled the Jews from Vienna in 1671, many of them sought refuge in Eisenstadt. Thus, in the Unterberg district to the west of the castle, in an area delimited by the Museumsgasse, the Wolfgasse, the Unterberggasse and the Wertheimergasse, a Jewish quarter grew up, which is in a remarkably good state of preservation. This ancient ghetto, where the iron chains used to keep the peace on the Sabbath are still to be seen, was particularly famous for its rabbinical college.

★ **Österreichisches Jüdisches Museum** ⏲ **(A M¹)** – *Unterberggasse 6*. The museum is installed in a charming old house which belonged to Samson Wertheimer. There is also a fine synagogue, which escaped destruction by the Nazis. They are well worth a visit, as is the nearby Jewish cemetery *(at the end of the Wertheimergasse)*.

Burgenländisches Landesmuseum ⏲ **(A M²)** – *Museumsgasse 5*. The regional museum, located in two interconnecting, picturesque old houses, is devoted to the ethnological and cultural history of the region, and hence also to the ethnic minorities that still go to make up the population.

Return to Esterházystraße and from there head west to Kalvarienbergplatz.

★ **Kalvarienberg and Bergkirche** ⏲ **(A)** – The artificial hill known as the Kalvarienberg was constructed in the early 18C to provide the setting for 24 **Stations of the Cross**★, made of 260 wooden and 60 stone figures, sculpted in a realistic folk style, which portray the story of the Passion with dramatic intensity and Baroque flair. The last Station of the Cross is at the top of the Kalvarienberg, from where there is a fine view over the town.
Inside the **Bergkirche**, which was completed in 1722, the **Haydn-Mausoleum** is the last resting place of the composer's remains, after some vicissitudes – the skull was removed and only restored in 1954.

EXCURSION

Raiding – *46km/29mi – about 2hr. Leave Eisenstadt, south, on the Bundesstraße 59 A, then on the 331. Leaving Weppersdorf bear left towards Lackenbach to Raiding.*

Liszts Geburtshaus ⏲ – This small house where **Franz Liszt** was born in 1811 was the home which went with his father's job as bailiff to the estate of the princes of Esterházy. Photos and documents are on display. The old church organ on which Liszt used to play is also here.

Höhlen EISRIESENWELT★

Salzburg

Michelin map 926 fold 20 – 6km/4mi northeast of Werfen
Local map see SALZACHTAL

Opening at a height of 1 641m/5 384ft on the western cliffs of the Hochkogel (Tennengebirge), about 1 000m/3 280ft above the Salzach Valley, the **caves** of the World of the Ice Giants, with over 40km/25mi of galleries, are among the world's largest subterranean features. They are especially famous for the fairy like ice decor which goes back for about 1km/0.5mi and adorns the caves near the entrance. The sections of the caves open to the public are covered by some 30 000 m³/more than 1 million cu ft of ground ice, which is up to 20m/65ft thick.
The many and varied ice formations have developed as a result of the fact that the temperature of the rock drops below zero during the winter, so that water from melting snow dripping in through cracks in the rock freezes. Even in summer temperatures in the caves are generally below zero, with the result that the ice formations are preserved all year round.

TOUR ⏲

The route described leaves from road 159 in **Werfen**.

The journey up the **approach roads★★** would be worthwhile for the views alone. Visitors should allow at least 3hr (there and back) for the trip up to and round the caves. Warm clothing, sturdy shoes and gloves are advisable inside the caves, even during summer.

Access – The ascent is made in the following stages:

1. 5km/3mi of unsurfaced mountain road rising at a gradient of 1 in 6 which can be travelled either in your own car, or on the special **bus** ⏲ (Eisriesenweltlinie) which starts from the Hauptplatz in Werfen. There is a car park at 1 000m/3 280ft.
2. 15min on foot from the end of the road to the lower station of the cable-car. The path overlooks the Salzach Valley and Hohenwerfen Fortress *(see SALZACHTAL)*.
3. 3min in the **cable-car** ⏲ to the "Dr.-Oedl-Haus" mountain inn (1 575m/5 168ft).
4. 15min walk along a path cut into the mountainside, which has spectacular **views** of the valley, the Hagengebirge, the Hochkönig and the Gasteiner Tauern, to the vast entrance to the caves at 1 641m/5 384ft.

Guided tour of the caves – *About 1hr 15min.*
By the light of acetylene and magnesium lamps visitors enter the ice world of the caves, climbing up many steps to the Posselt-Halle gallery (named after the first explorer to enter the cave in 1879), as high (30m/100ft) as it is wide. The "Hrymr Hall" with its Hrymr Mountain and "Niflheimr" with Frigg's Veil are both examples of fantastic ice architecture enhanced by clever lighting. At the back of the "Óethinn Gallery" is a throne-like ice formation called Ásgarethr (the home of the gods, called "Asenheim" in German). Then visitors reach the "Cathedral" of Alexander von Mörk, named after the man who founded speleology in Salzburg and whose ashes were brought back to these caves after he perished in the First World War, in accordance with his final wishes. The Ice Palace 800m/2 625ft from the entrance marks the end of this underworld tour and is the turn-back point for tours. On the way back to the entrance, visitors pass the "Ice Gate" at 1 775m/5 824ft, and 134m/440ft above the cave entrance, the highest point of the cave complex.

What's in a name...

The origin of many of the names of the galleries in the Eisriesenwelt subterranean complex is Old Norse mythology, as featured in the Old Icelandic saga "Edda": **Óethinn** is the father of the gods, **Frigg** is his wife and at the same time goddess of fertility, **Hrymr** is an ice giant. **Ásgarethr** is the home of the Æsir gods, who are at war with the Vanir, and **Niflheimr** is the world of shadows in the frozen north that existed before this world was created.

ENNS★

Oberösterreich

Population 11 100

Michelin map 926 fold 9 – 20km/12mi east of Linz – Alt 281m/922ft

Enns, built on the left bank of the River Enns, near its confluence with the Danube, is the oldest town in Upper Austria. The Romans, in fact, chose this site for a camp; the city, Lauriacum, that developed later was big enough to become the capital of the Roman province of Noricum. It was there that St Florian, the patron saint of Upper Austria, suffered martyrdom under Diocletian at the beginning of the 4C.

SIGHTS

Altstadt – The imposing town houses in the old town of Enns are all essentially Gothic in style, and many feature Late Gothic or Renaissance arcaded courtyards (Hauptplatz 5, 7, 10 and 14, Wiener Straße 4, 8 and 9). The **Stadtmuseum Lauriacum** (Hauptplatz 19, **Z M**), formerly the town mint, is located in one of these arcaded houses and contains a number of interesting archeological exhibits dating from Roman times. There are some very picturesque façades around the Hauptplatz, and at Mauthausnerstraße 5 and Linzer Straße 4 and 20.

Stadtturm (**Z**) – In the centre of the Hauptplatz stands the town's best-known landmark in the form of a 60m/197ft high tower. Construction of this was begun by the townspeople in 1564, prior to obtaining building permission from the

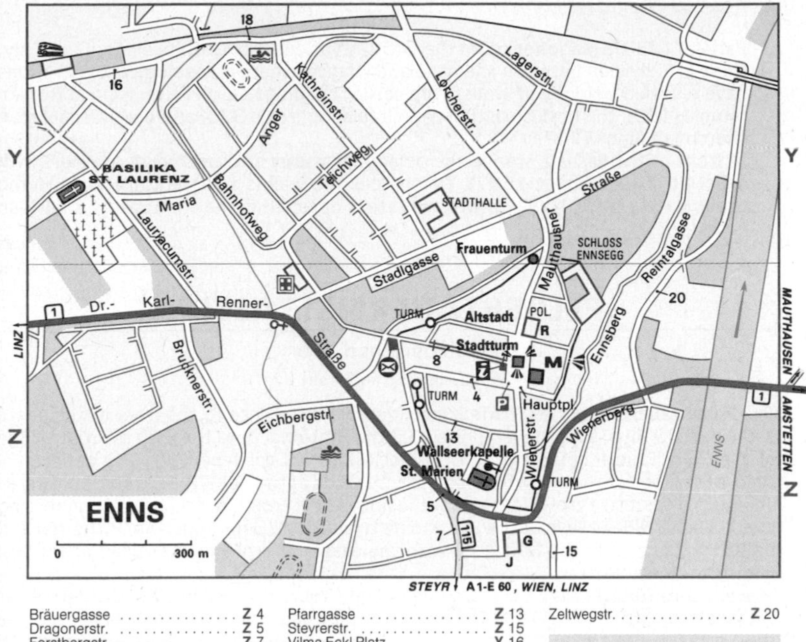

Bräuergasse	Z 4	Pfarrgasse	Z 13	Zeltwegstr.	Z 20
Dragonerstr.	Z 5	Steyrerstr.	Z 15		
Forstbergstr.	Z 7	Vilma-Eckl-Platz	Y 16	Stadtmuseum Lauriacum	Z M
Linzerstr.	Z 8	Westbahnstr.	Y 18		

Emperor. This was granted by Maximilian II in 1565 and the tower was finished in 1568. Designed as a belfry and watchtower, it combines Late Gothic and Renaissance styles. The south side of the tower is adorned with the Imperial eagle and the Habsburg coat of arms; 157 steps lead up to the gallery, crowned with an elegantly curved domed roof. From here, there is a marvellous **view**★ looking down on the town and even, given good visibility, as far as the foothills of the Alps.

Stadtbefestigung (Z) - The town's fortifications, built in 1193-94, have to a large extent survived (ramparts, moats, defensive walls, six watchtowers, including the Pfaffenturm, the Bäckerturm and the Frauenturm). To finance the construction of its defence system, Enns was awarded part of the ransom money England had had to pay Austria for the release of its monarch Richard the Lionheart from the fortress at Dürnstein.

Frauenturm (YZ) - On the top floor is the former chapel of the Knights of St John of Jerusalem with frescoes dating from between 1320 and 1360. In the 14C, the Knights of St John here ran one of the many pilgrims' hospices along the European pilgrimage route from Danzig to Santiago de Compostela.
The key to the Frauenturm can be obtained from the tourist office in Mauthausner Straße 7.

★ **Pfarrkirche St. Marien** ⏲ (Z) - In the south of the old town stands one of the oldest Mendicant Order churches in Austria. It was built by the Minorites in 1276-77, and the chancel was added in the early 14C. This is a good example of the evolution of methods for heightening and lengthening churches prevalent in Gothic religious building. The nave was converted into a double aisled hall-church in the second half of the 15C. The only ornamentation is the beautifully carved keystones. The austere architecture of the Mendicant Orders forms a striking contrast to the richly ornate cathedrals built during the Middle Ages. Three Gothic arches lead into the **Wallseerkapelle**.

Wallseerkapelle (Z) - The Wallseers came to Austria with the Habsburgs and were for many years the ruling family in Enns. This chapel was added to the church in the 14C. It too is a double aisled hall-church, with a triple-aisled chancel equal in width to the nave. This original architectonic device is only found in one other place in Austria besides here. Slim columns and ribs lend the interior a sense of fragility. A remarkable painting from 1625 depicts the *Lorcher Bishops*, a view of the town with local religious dignitaries. The seated Madonna dates from the 13C, and the chancel from the 15C.

★ **Basilika St. Laurenz** ⏲ (Y) - The basilica, which stands on the site of the ancient Roman town of Lauriacum, was built between 1285 and 1290. After the Gothic vaulting collapsed, an Early Baroque cross-ribbed vault was built in 1628. Among the more interesting features of the interior decor are the tabernacle (1480), a

Pietà of 1430, a Madonna from the 14C and various Late Gothic reliefs. Curiously, there is a division between the nave and chancel where archeological excavations have revealed vestiges of walls from earlier buildings on this site: a Gallo-Roman temple (180), the first Christian church (bishop's see, 370) and early Carolingian church buildings (740).
In front of the basilica stands the octagonal **ossuary** or **charnel house** *(Karner)* with a Gothic chapel (about 1507). On the outside wall is a remarkable Ecce Homo group dating from 1690, in which Pilate is depicted in the costume of a Turkish Grand Vizier.

FELBERTAUERNSTRASSE★

Salzburg und Tirol

Michelin map 926 fold 32

The Felbertauern road has made a considerable difference to the lives of residents in the eastern Alps: a high level tunnel, 5.2km/3mi long, goes through the main ridge of the Hohe Tauern between the Großglockner and Großvenediger. The panoramic road leads through the peaceful Alpine countryside of the Hohe Tauern National Park, linking the eastern Tyrol (Lienz) with the northern Tyrol (Innsbruck) and connecting the beautiful wide valleys of the Isel and its tributaries (Defereggental, Virgental and Kalsertal), as well as the Mittersill with the eastern Tyrol and the valley of the Isel with that of the Puster.
Travellers to Austria may take, on one circular tour, the well-known Großglockner *(passable in summer only)* and the Felbertauern road which will enable them to see the Großvenediger snows.

Tauern Valley

FROM LIENZ TO THE FELBERTAUERN TUNNEL *41km/25mi*

Lienz - *See LIENZ.*

From Lienz follow the road up the long, wooded valley of the Isel, where the houses and villages are concentrated half way up the valley slopes.

✲ **Matrei in Osttirol** - *See MATREI IN OSTTIROL.*

Directly behind Matrei is Schloß Weißenstein, once the outpost of the Salzburg archbishops on the southern slopes of the Tauern.
The road now continues along the wooded slope through the **Tauern Valley**★★. In the foreground the Unterer Steiner waterfall marks the mouth of the Proßegg gorge, through which the road soon passes to come to an open valley overlooked by the hanging glacier of the Kristallkopf.
It is possible at this point to continue north directly via the Felbertauern tunnel *(see below; a toll is charged through the tunnel)* or to make an intermediate stop to explore the Großvenediger mountain range.

★★ EXCURSIONS IN THE GROSSVENEDIGER MASSIF

Take a small mountain road to the left of the road leading to the Felbertauern-tunnel (toll), and follow it along the valley floor to the Matreier Tauernhaus (alt 1 512m/4 961ft), a mountain hotel.
Allow at least 2hr there and back for a brief visit, or (better) a whole day to include some sightseeing on foot.

Many beautiful hiking and Alpine routes are located in this massif.

★★ **Walk to Innergschlöß** - *2hr there and back on foot. It is possible to make the trip in horse-drawn transport (1hr 30min there and back).* It takes 45min to get to Außergschlöß (alt 1 695m/5 561ft). The romantic scenery surrounding the chalet in the midst of boulders and larches almost pales into insignificance at the sight of the majestic Großvenediger with its cowl of glaciers (alt 3 674m/12 054ft), which rises up at the right-hand end of a chain of mountains. An almost flat trail leads to the unusual chapel of Außergschlöß, canopied by a mighty rock face, to Innergschlöß *(inn)*, and into the domain of the experienced hiker and the mountaineer.

★ **Bergbahn Venedigerblick (mountain railway)** - Alt 2 000m/6 550ft. *15min ascent.* **View**★ over the Großvenediger and the Tauern Valley.
Hikers with plenty of stamina will reach the magnificent Drei-Seen-Weg trail from the mountain station of the chair-lift. Less agile visitors should content themselves with the walk to the Zirbenkreuz (cross).

★★ **Drei-Seen Circuit** - You should climb at least up to the Meßeling pass *(3hr 15min there and back and a 563m/1 847ft difference in altitude).* The entire circuit is described below *(5hr 15min on foot). Climbing boots are recommended.*

First of all follow the pleasant trail along the Meßelingbach which is well marked in red and white. After 45min you will reach the Grüner See, or Green Lake, which lies in a magnificent **setting**★★ of Alpine pastures, and which looks out over the glaciers of the Großvenediger in the west and the threatening rocky sides of the Teufelsspitze peak in the east.
The higher you climb, the greener the surface of the lake sparkles. After a further 15min you will reach the Schwarzer See, or Black Lake, and can walk along its left bank, followed by the Grauer See, or Grey Lake, 30min later. Continue towards St. Pöltner Hütte mountain lodge. After 10min you will reach the Meßelingscharte (alt 2 563m/8 409ft), which already boasts a remarkable **view**★★.
Fit hikers with a good head for heights and who are wearing sturdy footwear can climb up to the Meßel-

Y. Bontoux
View of the Großvenediger from the Grüner See

ingkogel (alt 2 694m/8 838ft – *45min there and back*). Enjoy a unique **panorama**★★★ over the three lakes from the peak, with the Großglockner (in the background), the Tauerntal Valley and the huge glaciers of the Großvenediger. Lower down it is possible to pick out the Wildensee and Löbensee lakes.
Continue from the Meßelingscharte along the mountainside towards **St. Pöltner Hütte** mountain lodge (*50min on foot*). After 20min you will be able easily to climb up the Alte Tauern with the aid of the rope fixed to the wall. The view from the peak, with the beautiful gentian meadows, looks out across the Tauernsee and Langsee lakes, over which tower the Hochgasse and Höndl. Then climb down to the mountain lodge (alt 2 481m/8 140ft) at the foot of the peaked Tauernkogel. Turn back to the bottom of the valley towards Außergschlöß. In just under an hour you will reach a small bridge over the Tauernbach above the Zirbenkreuz.
Anyone who is feeling tired can turn back to the car park at this point. We recommend that hikers with more stamina should climb up to Außergschlöß (*allow a good 30min for the climb*). The trail through magnificent larch forest is rewarded at the end with a **view**★★ over the Tauern Valley and a waterfall which comes from Dichtensee Lake.

★ **Hike to the Zirbelkreuz** – *1hr 45min on foot, 600m/1 970ft difference in altitude down the mountain*. From the mountain station of the Venedigerblickbahn railway, the trail leads along the mountainside and finally climbs up to a bridge and then to the cross. It is possible to return to the car park at this point. We recommend however that hikers with more stamina should climb up to Außergschlöß (*see above*). This hike can be combined with the hike to Innergeschlöß.

After exploring the Großvenediger massif, drive back to the main road and go through the tunnel.

FROM THE FELBERTAUERN TUNNEL TO MITTERSILL

16km/10mi

On the north face of the Tauern the road emerges from the tunnel into the upper Amertal, a rugged, more or less deserted, high altitude valley.

9km/6mi after the exit from the tunnel turn left towards Hintersee. After 500m/550yd park the car to the right of the road, to visit the Schößwend gorge.

★ **Schößwendklamm** – *15min on foot there and back*. From the other side of the road a path leads down to the Felberbach and across the river. It then leads along the river bank giving a good **view**★ of the interesting sculptural forms that the crystal-clear water has carved out of the rock face.

Drive on for 3km/2mi to the end of the road.

★ **Hintersee** – This mountain lake surrounded by spruce forest lies in the upper Felber Valley, at the foot of a magnificent high mountain range, from which a number of waterfalls cascade down from a great height. To the south lies the Tauernkogel massif (alt 2 989m/9 806ft). Several information panels explain the geology of the area. It is possible to walk round the lake.

Turn back to Bundesstraße 108.

This stretch of road leads through Alpine meadows to **Mittersill**, a holiday resort and important road junction in the upper Salzach Valley (Oberpinzgau), from where roads lead off to the Thurn (*north*) and Gerloß (*west*) passes.

FELDKIRCH★★

Vorarlberg

Population 29 000

Michelin map 926 fold 27 – Local map see BREGENZERWALD

Alt 459m/1 506ft

Feldkirch is the gateway to Austria for travellers coming from the west. Situated on the busy road to the Arlberg pass, the little fortified town nestles at the foot of Schattenburg Castle, at the mouth of the last ravine of the River Ill, but is cut off from the plain of the Rhine by the Ardetzenberg ridge.
It has preserved the symmetry of its medieval plan and the old-world charm of arcaded squares.

The "Intellectual" Town – Feldkirch's numerous educational establishments earned it the name the "intellectual" town, or "Studierstädtle". Since the Middle Ages Feldkirch has had a "Latin school"; the academic tradition is maintained by the present grammar school, for pupils who aim at higher education, and a school for teachers.
Moreover, as the constitution of the Vorarlberg did not systematically centralize all provincial administration at Bregenz, Feldkirch was able officially to remain a capital of lawyers' clerks and finance.

★ OLD TOWN

The triangular plan of the town dates from the 13C. It is sited in a basin and at the hub of a network of roads. Between the new town (Neustadt), to the northeast, which has become, with its hotels, the centre of tourist life, and the suburb (Vorstadt) round the Churertor gateway in the northwest, the Marktplatz district remains the nucleus of the town.
The Hirschgraben (Stags' Ditch) constitutes the most recognizable traces of the old town walls.
The late 15C **Katzenturm** (Cats' Tower) (**A**) owes its name to its defence cannon decorated with lions' heads which became known as "the cats". It is also called the Fat Tower (Dicker Turm). Beside it is a small square, surrounded by picturesque houses with steep pitched roofs.
The **Churertor** (**B**) is distinguished by its stepped gable.

Marktplatz - This long, rectangular area, lined with arcades on its long sides, has retained the charm and tranquillity of a bygone age. Here and there an inn with a painted façade, a corner tower with a bulbous dome, or a Gothic oriel window catches the eye. To the south the view is bounded by the plain belfry and façade of the Johanniskirche. This is the former church of the monastery of the Hospitallers of St John of Jerusalem, who were entrusted with the protection of the Arlberg pass.

ADDITIONAL SIGHTS

Domkirche St. Nikolaus ⓥ - The cathedral church has the double nave, dear to Austrian architects of the 15C, and the net vaulting characteristic of Late Gothic religious architecture. Over the right side altar is a **Descent from the Cross**★ painted in 1521 by Wolf Huber, an artist of the Danube School who was born at Feldkirch and who is regarded as one of the great precursors of German landscape painting.
The pulpit is surmounted by a high canopy in wrought iron (originally a Gothic tabernacle).

Schattenburg - *The castle is approached by car up the Burggasse, a steep slope, or on foot by the Schloßsteig steps.*

In spite of the refitting of the interior as a museum and a restaurant, this castle has, on the whole, kept its former arrangement and the defensive nature of its keep, planted on the top of a rock. The original dwelling or "Palas" is also a tower - recognizable by its tall, conical roof - with walls more than 4m/12ft thick. The advanced defences, guarding the present approach bridge, and the ruined round tower nearby, were built about 1500, when gunpowder was already in use.
Before crossing the bridge there is a **view** of the Rhine Valley in the distance, overlooked by the Hoher Kasten (Alpstein massif, in the Appenzell district). The inner courtyard of the castle (café) is picturesque, with tiers of wooden galleries and vast roofs.

FELDKIRCH

Ardetzenbergtunnel . 2
Bahnhofstraße 3
Burggasse 4
Domplatz 5
Fidelisstraße 7
Ganahlstraße 8
Herrengasse 9
Johannitergasse 10
Kreuzgasse 12
Leonhards-Platz 13
Montfortgasse 15
Neustadt 16
Schillerstraße 17
Schloßgraben 19
Schloßsteig 20
Schmiedgasse 22
Vorstadt 23
Wichnergasse 26
Zeughausgasse 30

Churertor . . . . B
Katzenturm . . . . . . A

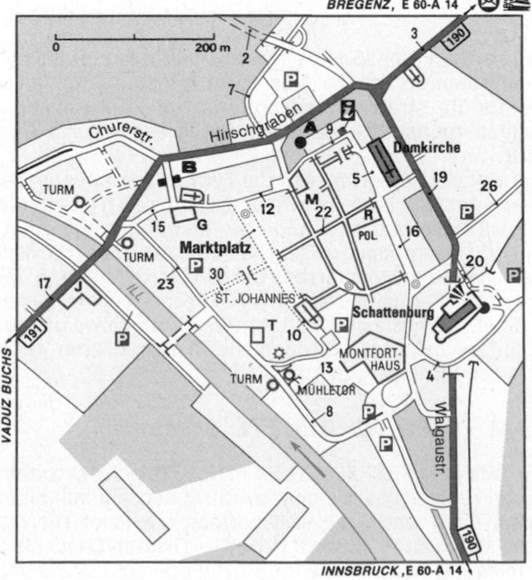

Heimatmuseum ⊙ – This local museum houses well displayed collections of religious art (especially in the former chapel), noble and bourgeois furnishings of the Gothic period, traditional peasant furniture, arms and armour, and coins and records of Old Feldkirch. It is pleasant, during the tour, to look at the changing views of Feldkirch through the windows.

EXCURSION

Rankweil – *19km/12mi there and back. Leave Feldkirch on the road to Bregenz.*
The pilgrimage church at Rankweil overlooks an idyllic stretch of countryside, the Austrian Rhine Valley, whose numerous orchards have earned it the nickname of the "Garden of the Vorarlberg".

Liebfrauenkirche or Burgkirche – *Senior citizens or physically disabled people can reach the church by car up a ramp leading off to the northeast from the ring-road around the castle rock.*
This place of worship dedicated to the Virgin Mary was built perched on a steep-sided rock by the Bishop of Chur in the 8C. It was also used as a parish church. After it had been destroyed during uprisings in 1445, it was rebuilt at the end of the 15C and this time fortified by the addition of a ring of defence works, a cylindrical keep and a rampart walk, giving it quite a forbidding character. In 1986 the church was raised to the status of basilica minor.
The **Gnadenkapelle**, or Chapel of Miracles, was built at the same time as the side aisle adjoining it (1658) and houses the church's most precious treasure, a beautiful Late Gothic statue (c 1460) of the Virgin Mary, attributed to the Swabian School. To the right of the Gnadenkapelle stands the so-called "Miracle-working" or Silver Cross, on the front of which hangs the figure of Christ crucified, a Romanesque work dating from the 13C. It also features three reliefs depicting the Entry of Christ into Jerusalem, the Angel Announcing Christ's Resurrection to the Women at the Tomb, and the Ascension of Christ.
A door beneath the gallery leads to the old **rampart walk**★ (Wehrgang), from where there is a marvellous **view**★ of the Rhine plain, ringed by the Vorarlberg and Swiss mountains. To the west and southwest lies the barrier of the Alpstein (Appenzeller Alps) with the Altmann summit (2 436m/7 992ft), the Wildhaussattel, the jagged Churfirsten and the Alvier group. On the Austrian side, beyond the Ill gap at Feldkirch, the Drei Schwestern (Three Sisters) mark the frontier with Liechtenstein. Through the opening made by a small valley, the Schesaplana summit (alt 2 965m/9 728ft) in the Rätikon range can be seen.
From the church, leave Rankweil on the Satteins road, which twists and turns along the valley floor beneath a mountain range. After a short run, the **view** opens out over the Bludenz basin and the Rätikon mountain range.

Bear right at the entrance to the village of Satteins in order to join Bundesstraße 1 which returns to Feldkirch.

FERNPASSSTRASSE★

Tirol

Michelin map 926 folds 16 and 29

The road to the Fernpaß is varied and picturesque; it is the most hilly section of the earlier route across the Alps from Augsburg to Venice, which was known in the 15C for its strategic and commercial importance, but which is nowadays principally a tourist link between the great resorts of the Bavarian Alps and Innsbruck.
This road is of vital importance to the Tyrol, since it opens the way to the upper valleys of the Lech and the Loisach, which are cut off from the Inn Valley by the barrier formed by the Lechtal Alps and the Miemingergebirge. To reach these isolated, high-lying valleys, grouped under the name **Außerfern** (the district "beyond the Fern"), follow the road from Mötz, across the plateau of Mieming. In Nassereith, to the south of the pass, the Fernpaßstraße (B 179) proper begins, a magnificent stretch of road leading down from the pass to Lermoos, with views of the Wetterstein range with the Zugspitze, and finally through the Zwischentoren Valley whose most dramatic feature is the Ehrenberg defile.

FROM TELFS TO REUTTE *64km/40mi*

From **Telfs** *(see SEEFELDER SATTELSTRASSEN)* to the threshold of Holzleiten the road runs across the gentle, fairly densely inhabited slopes of the Mieming plateau, from which the well defined crests of the Miemingergebirge rise up (Hochplattig, alt 2 758m/9 048ft – Griesspitzen, alt 2 759m/9 052ft). Near Obermieming views of the Inn Valley open out to the left with the snow-capped peaks of the Samnaungruppe in the distance. Stop briefly at Gasthof "Fernblick" (inn), shortly after Fronhausen, to appreciate the view of Locherboden pilgrimage church overlooking the Inn Valley.

Driving down towards **Nassereith** from the **Holzleitner Sattel** (alt 1 126m/3 694ft) through thin larch wood cover, there is a series of delightful **views★** of countryside dotted with villages against a backdrop of the Mieminger mountains to the right, and the Bigerbach Valley stretching off to the southwest as far as Imst *(see Oberes INNTAL)* to the left.

After several stretches of tunnel the road passes Nassereith service area and shortly afterwards reaches "Schloß Fernsteinsee" hotel on the left.

Fernstein - Traffic through this easily defended site was once guarded by a fortified bridgehead, Schloß Fernstein (now part of the hotel). To the right of the road, below the car park, lies the idyllic **Fernsteinsee★**, a lake of shimmering green water in which both the darker green tones of the surrounding conifers and the paler green of the meadows are reflected.

Fernpaß - Alt 1 209m/3 967ft. The pass breaches a crest between Fernstein and Biberwier. The road winds up the south slope in a series of hairpin bends, through a landscape of rugged, isolated gorges and cirques belonging to the Loreakopf range. About 1km/0.5mi beyond the pass itself, the road reaches the viewing point at "Zugspitzblick" restaurant *(car park)*. The **panorama★** stretches, from left to right, from the Zugspitze in the Wetterstein range, across the distinctive Sonnenspitze peak (2 414m/7 920ft) and the adjacent summits of the Wampeter Schrofen (2 520m/8 268ft) and Marienberg (2 561m/8 403ft), to the Wannig (2 493m/8 180ft). At the foot of the viewing point lies the **Blindsee★**, a long and picturesque lake.

The Blindsee is an ideal spot for a refreshing swim or lakeside walk. Access to the lake is on the way down from the Fernpaß, to the north on the left of the road (before the information point).

Follow the road along the north slope of the Fernpaß towards Biberwier.

At the Biberwier junction, the waters of the **Weißensee** can be seen to the right. The road from Biberwier to Lermoos, skirting the Lermoos-Ehrwald basin, offers fine **views★★** of the Wetterstein and the Mieminger range.

★ **Ehrwald** - This resort lies at the west foot of the sheer Zugspitze slopes. Among the variety of local walks, mountain tours and day trips on offer here, the most popular excursion is the ascent of Germany's highest peak, the Zugspitze, by way of the Tiroler Zugspitzbahn cable-car.

★★★ **Ascent to the Zugspitze** ⏲ - *Allow about 1hr, including 10min for the ride in the Tiroler Zugspitzbahn cable-car, which can take 100 passengers at a time.*

The 4.5km/3mi-long road leads through forests of larch and beech from Ehrwald to Obermoos and the valley station of the Tiroler Zugspitzbahn cable-car. It is possible to walk back along this stretch on a pretty forest footpath *(1hr)*. Even for those not going to the top of the Zugspitze this makes a pleasant outing on foot or by car.

★★★ **Zugspitze summit** - The upper station of the cable-car, coming from Ehrwald/Obermoos, lies on Austrian territory on the western peak of the Zugspitze summit (alt 2 964m/9 724ft).

The **panorama** to the south reveals the glacier summits of the Hohe Tauern (Großglockner and Großvenediger), the Tyrolean High Alps (Alps of the Zillertal, Stubai and Ötztal), the Ortler and the Bernina, towering over the forward bastions of the Kaisergebirge, the Dachstein and the Karwendel. Nearer, to the east, the mountains of the Arlberg (Silvretta and Rätikon) make way for a view of the Säntis in the Appenzell Alps. In the foreground can be seen the Allgäu and Ammergau mountains, part of the Bavarian Alps. To the north are the hazy Bavarian lowlands with the shimmering waters of the Ammersee and the Starnberger See.

During the skiing season the Zugspitzbahn cable-car offers experienced winter sports enthusiasts first-class ski runs, such as the great Alpine run of nearly 23km/14mi (Gatterlabfahrt) which takes them from the top of the Zugspitze back to Ehrwald *(guide recommended)*.

★ **Lermoos** - Leermoos occupies an exceptional **site★★** at the edge of a basin in the upper Loisach Valley, surrounded by the Northern Limestone Alps. It would be hard to find a better point from which to admire this group of peaks, dominated by the Zugspitze in the Wetterstein range and the fine pyramidal Sonnenspitze

M. Hertlein/MICHELIN

View of the Mieminger range

summit in the Mieminger range. Lermoos, besides being an excellently equipped winter sports resort, is therefore one of the best places for mountain views in Austria.

Pfarrkirche zur hl. Katharina – This church is a fine example of the southern German Baroque style. The ceiling and cupola are decorated with *trompe-l'œil* paintings by Italian artist Giuseppe Gru from 1784. The Rococo statues of St George and St John of Nepomuk, and the gilded splendour of the pulpit are of particularly high quality.

Maria Opferung – *At the exit from Lermoos, heading towards Reutte, on a hill to the left of the road, see illustration p 1.*

This tiny church, which is reached up a Stations of the Cross, was built in the 17C. There is a splendid **view**★★ of Lermoos and the Mieminger mountains from the vantage point of the hill.

To cross from the Loisach basin into that of the Lech, follow the valley named Zwischentoren ("between gates") in memory of the fortifications which once barred the road to the Fernstein and the Ehrenberg defile. The crossing of the watershed near Lähn passes virtually unnoticed (no natural features as evidence of it), and then the narrow bottleneck of the Ehrenberg defile shortly after Heiterwang is all that has to be negotiated before the road emerges into the Reutte basin.

Ehrenberger Klause – The old road on the floor of this ravine was barred by a gate, now dilapidated but formerly part of the fortifications of the Ehrenberg Fortress, which, from the 16C to the 18C, was the key to the Tyrol against invading Bavarians, Swedes or Frenchmen. The ruins, cleared of vegetation, are visible on the wooded hillside to the left of the road. As Ehrenberg was also the seat of the administrative and judicial authorities, its name was used until 1850 to identify the present Außerfern district.

Before reaching Reutte, it is worth taking a short detour to the Plansee *(about 20km/12mi there and back)*.

★ **Plansee** – Initially the road runs vertiginously above a wooded ravine, and then runs along the lake shore for a 6km/4mi stretch. At the northeast tip of the lake, at "Am Plansee", there is a hotel-restaurant and various kiosks. From here the view stretches southwest through the small strait separating the Plansee from the Heiterwanger See, as far as the Thaneller peak (2 341m/7 680ft).

It is possible to continue into Germany from here via the Ammersattel pass, to Linderhof and Oberammergau.

Driving back along the lakeside road towards Reutte reveals the best perspective of the Plansee against its backdrop of mountain peaks. On arriving in Reutte, there is a fine view to the west of the Tannheimer range with the Gehrenspitze (2 164m/7 100ft) to the far right and the Lechtaler Alps in the background to the left.

Reutte – *See Oberes LECHTAL.*

Burg FORCHTENSTEIN★

Burgenland

Michelin map 926 fold 25

23km/14mi southeast of Wiener Neustadt, access via Mattersburg

The fortress of Forchtenstein, dominated by its massive 50m/164ft high keep, the oldest surviving part of the original construction, overlooks charming scenery from its site on a bluff in the Rosaliengebirge foothills.

The fortress was built at the beginning of the 14C by the counts of Mattersdorf, who had arrived from Spain in the 13C, and took on its present appearance in the 17C. The Esterházy family, owners of Forchtenstein since 1622, had the ring of bastions built because of the threat of Turkish invasion, and the living quarters converted into function rooms. After the early 18C the family moved to Schloß Eisenstadt and Forchtenstein was subsequently used as the family treasury, arsenal and archive.

TOUR ⊙

As part of the tour of the fortress, visitors view the **Fürstlich Esterházysche Sammlungen**★, the extensive family collections which are particularly rich in 17C and 18C works. The majority of the items collected at Forchtenstein can still be seen in this setting, making the fortress with its 20 000 exhibits one of Europe's largest private collections open to the public.

Highlights of the collections include the treasury (art and precious objects, clocks and automata, silverware, chinoiseries, porcelain and library), an impressive testament to the Esterházys passion for collecting things, with a number of magnificent and for the time very exotic items; the picture gallery (family portraits and battle scenes); and the arsenal (Esterházy arms and armour, trophies from the wars against the French and the Prussians, and the "Turkish booty" from the field campaigns of Prince Paul Esterházy (1652-1713).

Follow the road further uphill from the fortress for about 4km/2.5mi to reach the Rosalienkapelle (1670), a chapel dedicated to Rosalia, curer of plagues, from where there is a good view as far as Eisenstadt and the Neusiedler See with the fortress of Forchtenstein in the foreground.

The legend of Rosalia

Legend has it that a certain Giletus was the first lord of Forchtenstein. While he was away from home fighting in a war, his lady Rosalia imposed a harsh regime of discipline on the household. Upon his return, Giletus was informed of his wife's misdoings by his confidants. He described them to his wife as if they had taken place elsewhere and asked her what her judgement would be on such a merciless mistress. Rosalia recommended a punishment to fit the crime and in accordance with this was thrown into the fortress dungeon, where she ended her days. Her restless spirit is said to have haunted the fortress until Giletus had the Rosalienkapelle built to appease it.

FREISTADT★

Oberösterreich

Population 8 000

Michelin map 926 fold 9 – Local map see LINZ: Excursions

Alt 560m/1 837ft

Freistadt, a former stronghold on the ancient salt route which led from the Alpine countries towards Bohemia, stands in the wild countryside of the Mühlviertel, a granite plateau covered with pasture and forest with wide horizons spreading towards the Danube and the frontier of the Czech Republic.

The extensive, largely intact **town fortifications**★, including a stretch of double town wall, towers and gateways, were built in two stages, in around 1300 and 1400. They add a great deal to the charm of the town. With its main square, narrow streets and picturesque houses, Freistadt is an idyllic place to visit.

SIGHTS

★ **Hauptplatz** – This main square is rectangular and well proportioned. To the southwest stands the tower of the parish church, surmounted by a bulbous dome and a small lantern, while opposite rises the castle tower. The houses lining the Hauptplatz are for the most part fronted by porches or arcades; their façades, adorned with delicate stucco and painted in pastel shades, add a lively note to the scene. To the west, almost facing the carved fountain dedicated to the Virgin Mary, stands the **Rathaus** (**R**) and to the right of it at no 3, an old house with a

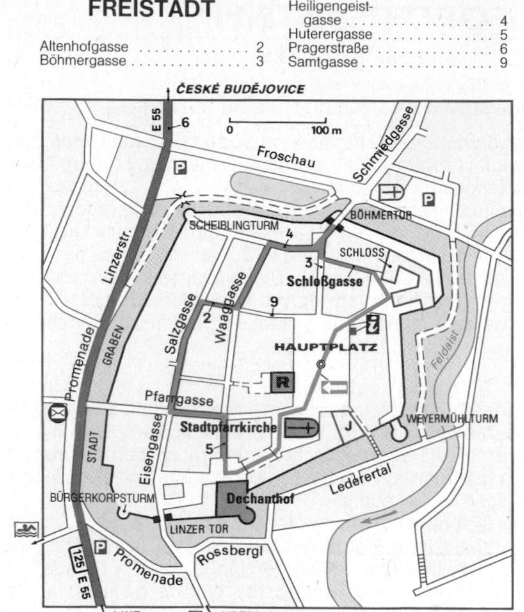

projecting porch and a small tower surmounted by an onion dome. Although not the most spectacular building on the Hauptplatz, the former Rathaus at no 21 is executed in a wonderfully pure Italian Renaissance style. It should also be viewed from the other side, by the moat. Cross the Hauptplatz and make for the castle (Schloß). On three sides the **courtyard** is overlooked by an amusing balcony with a lean-to roof. The **Schloßgasse**, a quaint and picturesque alley with flower-decked balconies and passages, ends in the Böhmergasse which leads to the Böhmertor, a former fortified gateway. Back in the old town the Waaggasse and the Salzgasse contain houses with oriel windows *(Erker)*.

After glancing at the **Dechanthof** (Deanery), built in the early 18C, make for the parish church *(right)* before coming back to the Hauptplatz.

Stadtpfarrkirche – The first thing that strikes the eye is the elegant tower on the north side of the body of the church, a characteristic feature on the town's skyline. It was transformed into the Baroque style by Johann Michael Prunner in 1735. The four wrought-iron balconies of the tower room are particularly noticeable. The church itself is Gothic and dates back to the 13C. The triple-aisled chancel, however, was not built until 1483, and is crowned with a network of ribbed vaulting. The **organ case**, adorned with statues, was built by Leonhard Freund from Passau between 1701 and 1705.

FRIESACH★

Kärnten

Population 7 070

Michelin map 926 fold 36 – Alt 637m/2 090ft

The oldest town in Carinthia is particularly appealing with its three ruined castles, six churches and well-preserved fortifications. This concentration of historical monuments can be explained by the strategic importance of the town, which belonged to the archbishopric of Salzburg from 960 to 1803. It guarded the pass between the Mur Valley and Klagenfurt and was thus a key point along the trade route between Vienna and Venice. It is not hard to imagine the eventful history of such an exposed bastion, which was besieged and set alight on numerous occasions.

SIGHTS

Stadtbefestigung – The fortifications, which include the only water-filled town moat in the German-speaking world, surround the town centre with an 820m/0.5mi-long battlemented wall. This is executed in fine undressed masonry and stands 11m/36ft high and about 1.5m/5ft wide. Of the original 11 defence towers, three remain.

★ **Stadtbrunnen** – This fountain, the work of Italian sculptors in 1563, stands on the Hauptplatz, surrounded by beautiful old houses. It was originally placed in the courtyard of Keutschach's Schloß Tanzenberg, but was brought to Friesach in 1802. The octagonal fountain basin is adorned with a frieze on which scenes from Ancient Greek mythology are depicted. The bowls above are supported by atlantes and putti. The crowning glory of the fountain, a small **bronze group** dating from 1520, is thought to be the creation of either Peter Vischer the Younger of Nuremberg or his brother Hans.

Dominikanerklosterkirche St. Nikolaus von Myra – Friesach monastery, dating from 1217, was the first foundation of the Dominican Order in a German-speaking country. The church, the largest in Carinthia, is a triple-aisled basilica supported by pillars, characterized by an overriding simplicity of style entirely in keeping with the rules of the Mendicant Order. The church contains an interesting life-size statue of the Virgin Mary in sandstone, a fine early-14C work. The larger than life-size Crucifix on a pillar on the north side of the nave dates from 1300. The Late Gothic altar dedicated to St John, made in 1510, is probably the work of a local sculptor.

Deutschordenskirche St. Blasius – The Knights of the Teutonic Order settled in Friesach from 1203 and built this church on the site of an earlier 12C building, from which the frescoes (late 12C) in the west transept come. The church owes its collection of remarkably varied and high quality Gothic woodcarvings to the Order's Commander, Graf von Pettenegg, a keen collector of such work. Note among others the magnificent **high altar** from 1515, a work from St. Veit for the Heiligengestadekirche on Ossiach Lake, and the Late Gothic Frankfurt altarpiece. The nave contains funerary plaques of members of the Order, most of whom came from Bad Mergentheim in Germany, where the Order had its headquarters until 1809.

Petersberg – *20min on foot there and back from the Hauptplatz.* Construction of the fortress which stands proudly on a hilltop to the west of the old town was begun in 1077 under Archbishop Gebhard. However, all that remains of the once grand, sumptuously furnished great hall is one or two windows. The imposing, 30m/98ft high, Romanesque keep now houses the **Stadtmuseum** ⊙, in which the history of Friesach and the surrounding area is related. On the third floor is the old castle chapel, which has preserved some of its original Romanesque painted decoration.
The old inner bailey hosts open-air theatre productions during the summer.

FROHNLEITEN

Steiermark

Population 6 644

Michelin map 926 fold 23 – Alt 438m/1 437ft

Halfway between Bruck an der Mur to the north and the provincial capital Graz to the south, the market town of Frohnleiten is known as "the pearl of the Mur Valley", with its old town centre and impressive outline.
The most attractive **view**★ over the old town is from the riverside, near the bridge over the Mur, the pleasantly wooded setting acting as a foil to Frohnleiten's characteristic red-brown roofscape. Numerous well signposted paths encourage the visitor to walk in the peace of the countryside, while at nearby Murhof there is an 18-hole golf course to be enjoyed by casual as well as serious players.

SIGHTS

Hauptplatz – With its fine trees and many bright flowers, the enchanting main square today gives little hint of the town's troubled past. It suffered serious fires in 1528 and 1559 as well as floods in 1537, 1569 and 1572; a thunderbolt in 1763 ignited a blaze which left hardly a single house intact. It seems a miracle that the medieval, partly fortified town centre has been preserved.

St. Georgskirche – This interesting church is in the hamlet of **Adriach** *(1.5km/1mi west).* The original unvaulted Romanesque building dates from 1050; between 1280 and 1290 it acquired a Gothic chancel, a chapel dedicated to St Joseph and a sacristy. The chapel of St Anne dates from 1500, and that of St Aloysius from 1750. The **interior** is mostly Baroque, with a pulpit of 1720, an altarpiece, a *Martyrdom of St George* and four ceiling frescoes in the nave by **Joseph Adam von Mölck** (1774).
The church's organ was built in 1590 by either Thomas Krueg or Johannes Khever Spichler, both organ builders from the Tyrol.
In the course of the restoration completed in 1987, the foundations of the walls of earlier buildings and a Romanesque crypt were uncovered, and may now be viewed.

GAILBERGSATTELSTRASSE

Kärnten

Michelin map 926 folds 32 and 33 – Between Oberdrauburg and Kötschach

This road links the upper valleys of the Drava (Drau) and the Gail, crossing the pass at 982m/3 222ft.

FROM OBERDRAUBURG TO THE LESACH VALLEY *67km/42mi*

The most attractive part of the route is the stretch of road which climbs the north slope in a series of hairpin bends through the larches.

Laas – The **Filialkirche St. Andreas** is a Late Gothic church (1510-18), with doorways and window frames in local red sandstone. Unfortunately, the extent to which some of the images have been weathered means that they are unrecognisable. The original **vaulting**★★ is particularly beautiful, with a complex and delicate network of groined ribs above the nave continuing into a pretty stellar ribbed vault above the chancel. The inventive creator of this masterpiece was Bartlmä Firtaler, a mason from Innichen in the Pustertal. The fine sacristy doorway with an ogee arch, tabernacle and pulpit base are also all made of local sandstone.

Trumler/ÖSTERREICH WERBUNG

Church vaulting, Kötschach

Kötschach – The small market community of **Kötschach-Mauthen**, set between the Gailtaler and Karnische Alps, is a popular medium-altitude (710m/2 329ft), mountain-air health resort.

The growth of mining in the area brought it prosperity in the 16C, as manifested in the **Pfarrkirche Unsere Liebe Frau** (also known as the "cathedral of the Gailtal"). This church, consecrated in 1485, was totally rebuilt by the architect Bartlmä Firtaler between 1518 and 1527, and embodies the final, exuberantly decorative stage of the Gothic style. It has stunning **traceried rib vaulting**★, with finely executed arabesques swirling gracefully above the body of the church and ending in lilies, roses, acorns and bunches of grapes. The chancel ceiling was decorated with Rococo stucco work and paintings at the end of the 18C. The fresco on the north chancel wall dates from 1499 and depicts the death and assumption into heaven of the Virgin Mary. The "miraculous" statue enclosed in the high altar is a black Madonna.

★ **Lesachtal** – The road follows this charming valley up the course of the Gail, climbing from an altitude of 900m/2 953ft to 1 200m/3 937ft, in between the Carinthian Alps to the left and the Gailtaler Alps to the right. The Lienz Dolomites come into view further up the valley. The valley's position off the beaten tourist track has protected it from being spoiled, so instead of large hotel complexes there are comfortable farmhouses.

St. Lorenzen – This unspoiled village is dominated by the Late Gothic parish church of St. Laurentius. There are some remarkable frescoes in the chancel and on the north wall of the nave (Last Judgement) which date from c 1475. The church is set amid fine painted farmhouses with shallow gable roofs.

Maria Luggau – The name of this Marian pilgrimage site is derived from St Luke the Evangelist, who is a patron saint of the area. The church, another of Bartlmä Firtaler's works, was consecrated in 1536. The Baroque tower dates from 1736. The object of veneration in Maria Luggau is a Late Gothic miraculous image of Our Lady of Sorrows. The sumptuous robes are changed to be in the appropriate liturgical colour throughout the church year. The statue of the Pietà stands on a valuable tabernacle shrine made during the second half of the 18C.

A short steep path leads (from near the baker's) to the picturesque **Luggau water mills**, the remains of 100 mills that used to operate in the Lesach Valley. The five timber constructions, over 200 years old, stand on a masonry base. The water is fed to the water wheels via wooden runnels.

Kartitscher Sattel – This pass is the highest point along the road (1 530m/5 020ft). There is the odd example here and there of the timber constructions for drying hay that were once so common in this region.

GASTEINER TAL**

Salzburg

Michelin map 926 fold 33

The Gasteiner Tal, a long, wide river valley, is one of the most attractive holiday destinations in Austria. It encompasses three main resorts (Dorfgastein at an altitude of 830m/2 723ft, Bad Hofgastein at 860m/2 822ft and Badgastein at 1 000m/3 281ft), having developed into a leading thermal cure centre as early as the 15C. With its exceptional setting amid medium- and high-altitude mountain peaks, it has much to offer both skiers in winter and ramblers in summer.

** **Ski slopes** – The development of the Gasteiner Tal as a winter sports resort began in earnest after the World Ski Championships of 1958, in which the Austrian Toni Sailer won several events. The Alpine ski slopes, which have become second only to the Arlberg among Austria's most extensive and scenic skiing destinations, are spread over five different mountain sides, which can be reached by chair-lifts in two stages: Fulseck (alt 880-2 030m/2 887-6 660ft) above Dorfgastein; Schloßalm (alt 860-2 300m/2 822-7 546ft) above Bad Hofgastein; Stubnerkogel (alt 1 100-2 250m/3 609-7 382ft) and Graukogel (alt 1 100-2 000m/ 3 609-6 562ft) above Badgastein; and Kreuzkogel (alt 1 588-2 690m/5 210-8 825ft) above Sportgastein.

The Gastein-Super-Skischein pass gives access to 52 ski lifts (including half a dozen assorted cable-cars) and 200km/125mi of ski slopes for mainly intermediate abilities. The use of some form of transport, be it car or bus, to get from one place to another is unavoidable as, with the exception of Badgastein and Bad Hofgastein, there is no way of getting from one set of slopes to the other by ski and the possibilities of accommodation are widely dispersed.

Cross-country skiers have 70km/44mi of track at their disposal, covering the whole valley from Dorfgastein as far as Sportgastein.

Thermal cures – The therapeutic effects of the thermal waters of Gastein appear to have been common knowledge for centuries; archeologists have confirmed that the valley was inhabited by Stone Age, Celtic and Roman settlers. The growth in popularity of Badgastein as a spa resort really put on a spurt at the end of the Middle Ages, as people began to travel there from miles away to cure their rheumatic complaints.

After a temporary decline in the 17C and 18C, Badgastein renewed its development in the 19C, finally becoming the most highly sought out spa resort of the age, appreciated by politicians (including German Emperor Wilhelm I, Austrian Emperor Franz Joseph I and Bismarck), artists and writers alike (Franz Schubert, Arthur Schopenhauer).

By the beginning of the 20C, Badgastein had evolved from a somewhat lacklustre Imperial spa town into a thoroughly modern thermal resort, and it has since become the home of a balneological research institute attached to the Austrian Academy of Science, which undertakes scientific analysis of the healing powers of the Gastein springs.

The thermal springs, 17 of them in all, rise on the slopes of the Graukogel massif, and their daily output is 5 million litres (over one million UK gallons) of water at temperatures of up to 47°C/117°F. Visitors can "take the waters" at numerous hotels and guesthouses with their own thermal baths, supplied directly from the springs. The therapeutic effects of the Badgastein springs are due more to the radon, a radioactive noble gas, they contain, than the minerals, of which they contain very few. Depending on the particular treatment, the radon is taken into the body through bathing or inhalation. Since it is not absorbed by the body's tissue, it is soon expelled (in less than 30 minutes after bathing, or about three hours after inhalation). During the brief period it is in the body, radon gives off helium nuclei which give energy to the body and regenerate damaged cells. In this way it helps to soothe chronic complaints such as rheumatism, diseases of the respiratory tract (asthma), veins and circulatory system (coronary thrombosis), skin allergies, hormonal imbalances and problems with the autonomic nervous system.

A further type of thermal treatment or medical cure is available at Badgastein in the Gasteiner Heilstollen, a tunnel in which the temperature is 37.5-41.5°C/99.5-106.7°F. The patients are driven in on a small purpose-built railway and remain lying down to inhale the radon gas. The mild mountain climate in the sheltered valley in which Badgastein lies contributes greatly to the success of such treatments.

The hotels and guesthouses of Bad Hofgastein offer the same cure facilities as Badgastein, since being connected to the Gastein springs in 1828.

FROM LEND TO THE TAUERNTUNNEL

41km/26mi including excursion to Sportgastein

In the summer, we recommend climbing to the Stubnerkogel peak, and in the winter the Kreuzkogel is not to be missed. In order fully to appreciate the magnificent scenery of the Gasteiner Tal, we recommend a stay of several days or more.

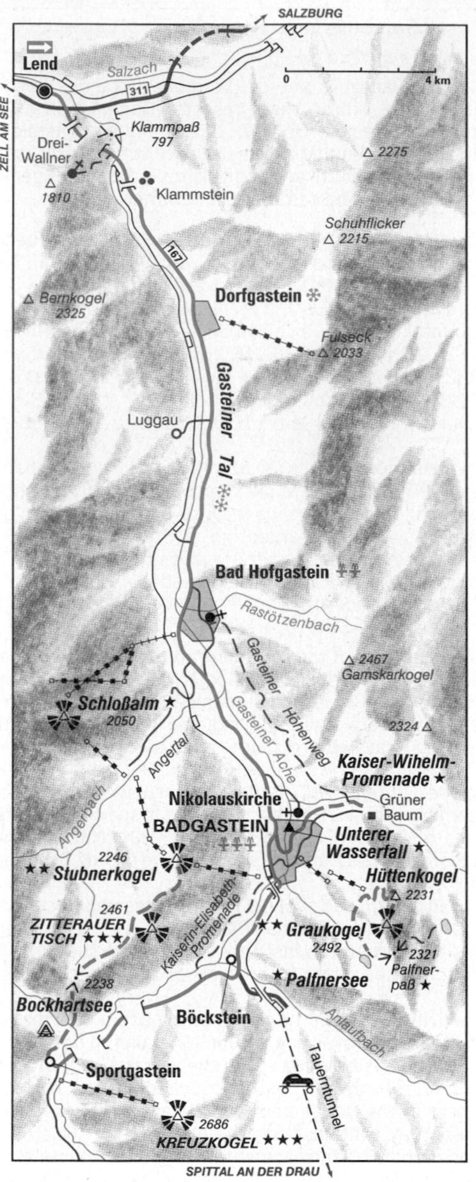

After leaving the industrial town of Lend and the Salzach Valley, the road makes its way over the Klamm pass. The old road *(to the left, with gradients of 1 in 7)*, which runs along the floor of the gorge, can be avoided by taking the tunnel. At the exit to the tunnel stands the Klammstein tower.
Beyond the tunnel, the Gasteiner Tal soon widens out and takes on a less forbidding appearance, with green meadows as far as the eye can see and moderately steep slopes.

Dorfgastein – Alt 830m/2 723ft. This pretty village located on the valley floor does not have to try too hard to convince visitors of the merits of its idyllic setting at the foot of Alpine meadows exposed to the sun, surrounded by beautiful forests. In the summer it offers plenty of fresh air and fun for all the family.
In the winter, it has extensive ski slopes nearby, with a connection to the Großarl ski slopes, overlooked by the Fulseck summit (55km/34mi of slopes). The drop in altitude is over 1 100m/3 609ft on both slopes, and there are good opportunities for off-piste skiing.

Bad Hofgastein – Alt 860m/2 822ft. Bad Hofgastein lies in the broadest, sunniest stretch of the valley. This smart and lively health resort has numerous hotels which offer the same spa facilities as Badgastein. Furthermore, the resort boasts modern, beautifully laid out spa gardens and a swimming pool almost 1 000m/3 300ft long, supplied by the thermal springs.
In winter Bad Hofgastein is an excellent point of departure for exploring the network of cross-country ski tracks in the valley. For those of medium ability, there are tracks along the banks of the Gasteiner Ache towards Badgastein. More proficient cross-country skiers should try the 7km/4mi of track in the Anger Valley. Downhill skiers of intermediate ability can choose from any number of not too steep slopes in the Schloßalm massif. A particularly good ski slope runs from the **Hohe Scharte** (peak is 2 300m/7 546ft) dropping 1 450m/4 757ft to the valley floor, giving marvellous **views**★★ of the Türchlwand, the Hochkönig and the Dachstein peaks.
A further point in favour of the ski slopes at Bad Hofgastein is the fact that they are connected with those at Badgastein (Stubnerkogel) via the Anger Valley.

Pfarrkirche – The parish church, rebuilt in several stages in the 15C and 16C, is a testimony to Bad Hofgastein's wealthy past, in the days when it was regional capital and this was the mother church of the valley. The imposing, Late Gothic body of the church is roofed with stellar and ribbed vaulting. The outside of the church walls and the niches either side of the main doorway are adorned with interesting funerary plaques of wealthy local gold- and silver-mine owners, recalling the town's heyday in the 16C and 17C.

★ **Schloßalm** ⓥ – Alt 2 050m/6 726ft. This is reached by taking the cable-car and then the chair-lift. At the top, there is a good **panorama**★ of the ski slopes, beneath the Maukarspitze and Türchlwand peaks. Further south, the summits of the Stubnerkogel, Ankogel range, Graukogel and Gamskarkogel can be seen. From the second terrace of the restaurant, the view stretches as far as the Dachstein.

‡‡‡ **Badgastein** – Alt 1 013m/3 323ft. Badgastein must rank as one of the most glitteringly beautiful spas and winter sports resorts in Austria. It is located amid spectacular mountain **scenery**★, flanked by the Stubnerkogel to the west and the Graukogel to the east. Its large palace hotels and elegant boutiques are arranged in a horseshoe layout on the slopes of the wooded mouth of a valley. The Gasteiner Ache tumbles down over a rock face, making a waterfall in the centre of the town.
Badgastein has a wide variety of excellent modern leisure facilities: skating rink, thermal swimming baths (one of which is cut into the actual rock face), fitness centres, nine-hole golf course, tennis courts and a casino. With a resident population of 5 600, Badgastein is buzzing with life all year round.
The local ski slopes include some fine runs down the upper section of the Stuberkogel, especially on the slopes of the Anger Valley (Jungeralm, Fleichleiter). At the other end of town, the Graukogel will appeal to lovers of steep slopes.

★ **Unterer Wasserfall der Gasteiner Ache** – After gushing over the edge of a cliff, the river spreads out like a fan and tumbles noisily to the valley floor.
Go down the street past the neo-Gothic Roman Catholic church on the right and turn right into the Kaiser-Wilhelm-Promenade.

★ **Kaiser-Wilhelm-Promenade** – This promenade along the east bank of the Gasteiner Ache gives lovely **views**★ of Bad Hofgastein and its surroundings lower down the valley. It is possible to extend the walk as far as the Grüner Baum hotel *(swimming pool, tennis courts, mini-golf)*, which is about 45min from the point of departure. If pressed for time, turn left off the promenade after the Germania hotel and take the path downhill to the Nikolauskirche.

Nikolauskirche – This plain 15C church, in which religious offices are no longer held, is charming to look at. The Late Gothic stellar vaulting in the nave is supported on a central pillar. Among the vestiges of 15C and 16C frescoes on the walls is a series of scenes of the Last Judgement.

★★ **Stubnerkogel** ⓥ – Alt 2 246m/7 369ft. *Allow 1hr there and back. Ascent is in a chair-lift in two stages. Leave the upper station to the left and climb onto a small rise.*
The **panorama**★★ stretches far to the east to the Graukogel and the Ankogel glacier massif, to the south and the Kreuzkogel, to the west and the Anger Valley with the glaciers of the Hohe Tauern (Großglockner, Hocharn) in the background, and to the north and the lower reaches of the Gasteiner Tal with the Hochkönig rock massif forming a natural barrier.
Turn back to the upper chair-lift station and follow the ridge path as far as it goes.

Böckstein – The tiny parish church built on a hill in 1765 has a polygonal exterior and an elongated oval interior floor plan. The refined, discreet interior decor is an excellent example of the Early Classical style in the Salzburg province.

Tauerntunnel ⓥ – The 8 550m/5.3mi double track railway tunnel runs through the Tauern ridge between Böckstein and Mallnitz. Until the Felbertauern road tunnel was opened this was the only way through the east Alps, east of the Brenner pass, that could guarantee to enable traffic to cross the Alps into the Tauern region, which is particularly difficult to access. Even now, many motorists prefer to use the vehicle transporting railway trucks to the road tunnel.

★★ EXCURSION TO SPORTGASTEIN

Toll road, but which is free of charge to holders of a ski pass. It is not long before the peaceful, wooded, mid-altitude mountain setting gives way to a much harsher, more rugged landscape. The road cuts a way between breathtaking steep rocky cliffs, going through three tunnels and passing numerous avalanche barriers. After 6km/4mi the road reaches Sportgastein (alt 1 588m/5 210ft), a broad plateau set against a majestic **backdrop**★ of rocky peaks and glaciers. This airy outpost of Badgastein has as yet not been the object of any major construction projects. The resort consists essentially of a large car park and a guesthouse.

The altitude guarantees excellent snow cover, much to the delight of cross-country (7km/4mi of tracks) and downhill skiers alike. A modern cable-car leads up to the Kreuzkogel summit, the highest point of the ski slopes, from where there are some exhilarating runs downhill, dropping more than 1 100m/3 600ft, and a highly reputed off-piste run down to the toll point *(details available from the ski slope maintenance team).*

★★★ **Kreuzkogel** - *Ascent by cable-car in two stages.* Even from the level of the mountain station the **view**★★ is already impressive. However, it is well worth taking the 15min walk up to the summit, marked by a cross, from where there is a marvellous **panorama**★★★. Proper mountain boots should be worn, as the snow can be quite deep in places.

To the north, Badgastein can be seen lying deep in the valley, and to the right of it are the chalk massifs of the Tennen range and the Dachstein peak. Two other prominent peaks are those of the Ankogel and the Hochalmspitze. To the south towers a formidable range of peaks on the border of Carinthia. To the west, a further stage by cable-car brings the Hohe Tauern (Schareck, Großglockner and Hocharn) into view.

Travel back down to Böckstein. It is possible to carry on into Carinthia through the Tauerntunnel.

EXPLORING ON FOOT

With its varied terrain suited to walkers of all sorts of abilities, the Gasteiner Tal is one of the **best places in the whole of Austria for a ramble**. There are numerous footpaths throughout the valley, which take walkers through beautiful countryside far from any traffic.

Particularly pretty walks are possible along the **Kaiserin-Elisabeth-Promenade**, from Badgastein to Böckstein, and the **Gasteiner Hohenweg**, which runs down the mountain slope from Badgastein to Bad Hofgastein.

There are many more possibilities open to walkers in the Stubnerkogel, Graukogel, Gamskarkogel and Silberpfennig ranges, from where there are some magnificent panoramas of the surrounding mountain scenery.

It is recommended that walkers obtain a detailed map at a scale of 1:50 000, in order to plan their route.

★★★ **Zitterauer Tisch und Bockhartsee** - *Allow a whole day, including a 4hr 30min walk. Enquire at the tourist office about bus timetables between Sportgastein and Badgastein, so that travelling back to the point of departure during the afternoon will not be a problem.*

Take the cable-car up to the top of the Stubnerkogel. Turn right at the mountain station and follow the waymarked route (red and white flashes and red arrows). In just under 1hr the mountain path reaches the Zitterauer Tisch (2 461m/ 8 074ft). There is a marvellous **view**★★★ of the whole Gasteiner Tal, especially the upper reaches of the valley. To the northeast, the view stretches as far as the Dachstein.

The path drops quickly down to Alpine pastures, before weaving a tortuous route through a bleak and craggy rocky landscape. Another good hour's walk brings you to the Miesbichlscharte (alt 2 238m/7 343ft).

On the way down to the Unterer Bockhartsee there is a good view from a number of points of the glaciers and waterfalls of the Schareck massif as well as of the Hocharn *(to the right)* and the Ankogel *(to the left)*. From the shores of the lake climb up to the hut and then down to Sportgastein. Take the bus back to Badgastein.

★★ **Graukogel** ⌚ - *2hr 30min on foot there and back. Difference in altitude of about 500m/1 640ft. This walk is recommended for good walkers wearing sturdy shoes with non-slip soles.*

Take two chair-lifts, one after the other, up to Tonis Almgasthof (alt 1 982m/6 503ft). A path leads from behind the guesthouse up to the Hüttenkogel summit (alt 2 231m/7 320ft). This is marked by a cross and a viewing table. There is an incredible **panorama**★★ of the Hohe Tauern (Großglockner, Hocharn, Hoher Sonnblick, Schareck) to the west, and the spectacular Reedsee, a lake surrounded by firs and larches lying at the foot of the Tischlerkarkogel and the Hölltorkogel, to the east.

Next follow the path along the ridge (extra care is needed in some of the steeper places) to the **Graukogel**. From the peak there is an even broader **view**★★ as far as the Dachstein. The Palfnersee can be seen glistening immediately below.

Palfnersee

★ **Walk to the Palfnersee** – *1hr 45min on foot there and back.*
This is an untaxing walk through some beautiful countryside. Take the chair-lifts, one after the other, up to the Graukogel. From the mountain station, follow the path past the hut and continue straight on. The mountain footpath gives a good **view**★ of Schareck, Hoher Sonnblick and Hocharn. It leaves the cover of the forest before climbing up to the Palfnersee (alt 2 100m/6 890ft).
It is possible to carry on from here as far as the **Palfner pass**★ (alt 2 321m/7 615ft), from where there is a good all-round view *(allow an extra hour there and back for this).*

Stift GERAS★

Niederösterreich

Michelin map 926 fold 11

The Premonstratensian abbey of Geras, set in a quiet spot far from the main tourist centres, enjoys considerable renown in Lower Austria. It is close to a **nature reserve** (140ha/345 acres) with delightful forest paths enabling the visitor to enjoy the well tended woodlands and visit enclosures where various animals roam freely, mainly fallow deer, roe deer and wild boar.

STIFT (ABBEY) ⌚

The Premonstratensian Canons, an order founded in 1120 at Prémontré, near Laon in northern France, founded a monastery at Geras in 1153. The founder is thought to have been Count Ulrich von Pernegg, who also founded a convent at Pernegg at the same time *(see Excursion below).*
The abbey's buildings retain features from all periods of its existence, but a major proportion of them date from the middle of the 17C, after the monastery had been sacked by Mansfeld's troops coming from Bohemia during the Thirty Years War. In 1736 reconstruction work was entrusted to the architect Joseph Munggenast, after the old gateway and its tower had been pulled down. He was responsible in particular for the "New Building" with its elegant entrance.

Stiftskirche – The basilica still has the basic plan of the Romanesque church, although later given Gothic vaulting and Baroque decoration in their respective periods. The tower was not added until 1655. The main door is decorated with statues (1655) of St Norbert and St Augustine, the two major figures for the Premonstratensian Order. The statue of the **Virgin Mary** on the high altar survived the fire of 1730 undamaged. The frescoes depicting the life of the Virgin Mary are the work of Franz Zoller, a pupil of Paul Troger.

Marmorsaal (**Marble Hall**) – A fine staircase leads up to the summer refectory, designed as a concert hall, on the first floor of the New Building. The almost square hall is well lit and decorated in a most refined style; it also has an air ofsolemnity which distinguishes it from the rest of the abbey buildings. The fireplace is beautifully decorated with stucco in various shades of black, grey and gold; above it hangs a painting of the *Wedding Feast at Cana* by **Paul Troger**. This Baroque master colourist was also responsible for a magnificent **ceiling fresco**★ depicting the miracle of the loaves and fishes, which is still in its original, unrestored state.
In the **Bischofszimmer** (Bishop's Apartments), with their fine tiled stoves, some precious items from the abbey's treasure house are on display.

Art education centre – Since 1970, the east wing of the abbey buildings has housed an art education centre, said to be the greatest centre for creative activities in Europe. About 150 courses are held here every year, covering a wide range of activities (folk art, restoration, ceramics, painting etc).

EXCURSION

Pernegg – *12km/8mi southwest of Geras.* Set in peaceful, unspoilt countryside, Pernegg is home to a Premonstratensian convent for canonesses. The **Pfarr- und Stiftskirche St. Andreas** is dwarfed by the massive, square west tower. The church interior is impressive in size and features a remarkable pulpit dating from 1618 which is a richly ornate example of the Mannerist style.

The convent, which is a daughter house of the abbey at Geras, is also a centre for religious seminars and retreats.

GERLOS-ALPENSTRASSE★

Tirol und Salzburg

Michelin map 926 folds 31 and 32

The Alpine road leading over the Gerlos pass links the Zillertal, a prosperous valley, with the **Oberpinzgau** (Upper Pinzgau), a long basin through which the Upper Salzach flows, taking in many torrents which tumble down from the glaciated summits of the Hohe Tauern (Großvenediger range). A visit to the well-known Krimml falls is worth the trip.

FROM ZELL AM ZILLER TO KRIMML *38km/24mi*

The road is steep and narrow in places. Between the Gerlos pass and Krimml, a toll is payable.

Zell am Ziller – *See ZILLERTAL.*

On leaving Zell am Ziller the road climbs quickly in hairpin bends up the Hainzenberg slope. Soon the pilgrimage chapel of **Maria Rast** (1748) comes into view, partially hidden by trees, at the apex of one of the bends to the right. This guardian of the Zillertal features red onion-domed towers which stand out from the surrounding greenery. After Hainzenberg the road enters the hanging Gerlos Valley. The Gmünd reservoir can be seen to the left of the road.

❄ **Gerlos** – At an altitude of 1 250m/4 101ft, this village tucked in a tributary valley of the Ziller is a favourite destination for skiers in the winter. Excellent ski slopes offer numerous possibilities to downhill skiers, while cross-country skiers are equally well catered for. Summer holidaymakers can choose between rambling and climbing or, if they prefer, water sports on the **Durlaßbodensee**.
Beyond Gerlos the road makes a sweeping bend past the Durlaßboden earth dam amid its greenery. After a hairpin bend, the road runs eastward clinging to the mountainside above the artificial lake which enters the Wildgerlostal to the south. Before reaching the toll point, there is the possibility of driving into the Wildgerlos Valley and going for a mountain hike. The physical effort involved is more than compensated for by the magnificent panorama of the alpine landscape to be had from the Zittau refuge.

★★ **Climb to the Zittauer Hütte** – Alt 2 329m/7 640ft. *The refuge is serviced from mid June to mid October. This taxing walk is recommended only for those who are fit and have stamina; allow at least 6hr for the climb up and down (900m/2 953ft difference in altitude). Proper walking boots are essential, as there are snowfields to be crossed even in summer.*

Shortly before the toll station, turn left and immediately afterwards the first road on the right. Drive on for about 5km/3mi to the end of the road. There are spectacular views of the lake and snow-capped peaks at the end of the Wildgerlos Valley from the narrow road. Leave the car in the car park (fee charged) of the Gasthaus Finkau (alt 1 419m/4 655ft).

The waymarked path leads up through woodland and then across pretty Alpine pastures alongside the Wilder Gerlos, a gushing mountain stream which takes its source from the mountain glacier of the same name. During the lowest third of the route it is possible to leave the main path and take a side one, up relatively steep steps cut into the rock, to the impressive **Leitenkammer ridge**. Heading back from the viewpoint on the ridge, follow the "Zur Trissl-Alm" signs to reach the main path again after a few yards.

The path to the Zittau refuge is a wide and well laid out gravel track up until the final ascent. Simply indicated alternative routes lead upwards across steep, rocky steps, as does the final stretch of the path itself (beyond the lower cable-car station, follow red waymarkings).

On arrival at the Zittau refuge, there is a breathtaking view of the surrounding magnificent **Alpine peaks★★**. The **Unterer Gerlossee** can be seen shimmering blue at the foot of the glittering glaciated cirques at the end of the valley. To the right, above the lake, can be seen (from left to right) the Gabler glacier (3 264m/10 709ft), the Reichenspitze (3 303m/10 837ft, directly to the right behind the glacier), the Hahnenkamm (3 207m/10 522ft) and neighbouring Wildgerlosspitze (3 278m/ 10 755ft), the indentation of the Keeskarscharte wind gap with the pillar-like Sichelkopf peak (2 982m/9 784ft) and at the far right the Weißkarkopf (2 849m/9 348ft).

Retrace your steps to the Gasthof Finkau. Drive back to the Gerlos-Alpenstraße.

After the toll point the road reaches the rugged moorland landscape of the Gerlos plateau. There is a parking area and lookout point at the Filzsteinalpe (1 628m/ 5 341ft). However, a better place to stop and enjoy the view is the panorama car park a little further on to the left of the road, on the steep **descent★** to Krimml. From here there is a superb **view of the Krimml falls★** cascading down several levels in between wooded cliffs, with the Dreiherrnspitze and Hohe Tauern range in the background. After this the road cuts several hairpin bends and crosses a number of bridges to two more panorama car parks on the **Trattenköpfl**, from where there is a closer view of the lower Krimml falls. Further downhill, at the end of the stretch of road subject to toll, there is a car park to the left for those wishing to visit the waterfalls.

M. Hertlein/MICHELIN

Krimml falls

★★★ Krimmler Wasserfälle ⏲

– If coming on Bundesstraße 165 from Neukirchen, leave the car at the exit from Krimml in the signposted car parks near the falls. 3hr taxing walk there and back to see the falls in their entirety.

The Krimmler Ache, which rises from the glacier of that name at more than 3 000m/10 000ft above sea level, cascades in three stages down the wooded cliff sides of the Salzachtalkessel. The falls, among the finest in the Alps, drop 380m/1 250ft in total and are a magnificent sight, especially in the midday sun when the spray glitters in every colour of the rainbow.

Before climbing the path up to the falls, do not miss the opportunity of going to the **viewpoint** at the foot of the lowest fall where the huge volume of water crashes onto a rocky barrier with a thundering cloud of spray before being fed off to the right.

The broad path is well suited to hiking and climbs up beneath the trees in zigzag bends, some of which are quite steep, as far as the top of the fall at 1 465m/4 807ft. Various viewpoints along the way, some branching off the main path bringing you close to the fall itself, make it possible vividly to appreciate the full force of the tremendous torrent. The Schönangerl mountain inn (1 306m/4 285ft, on a terrace at the transition from the middle to top fall) offers the opportunity of fortifying yourself for the final, even steeper part of the climb. The path leads to a plateau above the top of the waterfall where the Krimmler Ache, still a peaceful river at this point, can be seen. *From here, retrace your steps back to the car park.*

Keen walkers might like to take a whole day for this excursion, or even two (with an overnight stay at the Warnsdorfer refuge) by continuing along the course of the Krimmler Ache after viewing the falls, to reach the Krimmler Tauernhaus Alpine guesthouse (1 631m/5 351ft) after about 2hr and the Warnsdorfer Hütte (2 336m/7 664ft) at the foot of the Krimml glacier after about 5hr.

GMÜND

Kärnten

Population 2 700

Michelin map 926 fold 33 – Alt 741m/2 430ft

Gmünd, on the confluence of the Malta and Lieser, once controlled, under the archbishops of Salzburg, the traffic on the main road between Nuremberg and Venice which was then an important route for both strategic and commercial reasons, passing through the Radstädter Tauern mountains and skirting the Katschberg. In 1639, rulership of Gmünd passed into the hands of Count Christoph Lodron, brother of Archbishop Paris Lodron of Salzburg, and remained in possession of this family until 1932.

The town walls have been preserved in their entirety and enclose the medieval town centre, much of the original fabric of which has also been preserved. For this reason, there are many charming discoveries to be made during a stroll through the narrow streets. Gmünd is now home to a thriving artists' community, as the numerous workshops, artists' collectives and galleries indicate.

SIGHTS

Burg – The striking outline of the fortress, or "Gmündner Schloß", built between the 15C and 17C, dominates the little town. Partially destroyed by an earthquake in 1690 and finished off by a fire in 1886, all that now remains of the fortress are ruins. However, considerable efforts have been made over the last few years to transform it into an artists' and cultural centre. A restaurant has already been built and the **keep**, from which there is a good view, is also open to the public.

★ **Stadtbefestigung** – The fortified town walls, featuring battlements in places, date from the 15C and early 16C. Two imposing gateways give access to the town. The **lower gateway** (Unteres Tor) boasts a fine curved gable and a bell turret with an onion dome dating from the 18C. The **upper gateway** (Oberes Tor) is designed as a double gateway; the medieval dungeon can still be seen.

Hauptplatz – This elongated town square contained within the fortified gateways is the heart of the town. Elegant town houses line the square. The solid **Neues Schloß** (near the upper gateway) was built between 1651 and 1654 under Count Christoph Lodron. The building (now a school) has three wings and opens onto a pretty garden, the Porsche-Park, the entrance to which is flanked by the statues of two massive lions originally from the Mirabellgarten in Salzburg.

In **Kirchgasse**, which leads off from the top end of the square, the old prison *(Kirchgasse 56)* contains an informative exhibition on Eva Faschaunerin, the farmer's wife who murdered her husband and who was the last person in Austria to be subjected to torture while being questioned. She was sent to the gallows in 1773.

The street running parallel to the Hauptplatz, **Hintere Gasse**, contains the brewery and the old local authority office where farmers had to deliver their grain tithes, both of which have been successfully restored.

Kirche Maria Himmelfahrt – The Late Gothic church, whose chancel originates from 1399, was consecrated in 1513. On either side of the fine Late Baroque altarpiece stand life-size figures of the Apostles. The pulpit and side altars are Rococo works. There are numerous interesting tomb stones.

Porsche-Automuseum, Gmünd

Porsche Museum

Porsche-Automuseum Helmut Pfeifhofer – This, the only private Porsche museum in Europe, is a reminder that from 1944 to 1950 Gmünd was the sphere of activity of world-famous engineer **Ferdinand Porsche** (d 1998). The first car with the "Porsche" marque, the legendary 356, was made in the Gmünd workshop. Twenty six vehicles are on show, together with several prototypes of military and sports vehicles, as well as actual-size wooden models of the first Porsche car bodies and over 400 model cars.

GMÜND

Niederösterreich

Population 6 934

Michelin map 926 fold 10 – Alt 485m/1 591ft

In the north of the Waldviertel, at the point where the River Lainsitz and the Braunaubach meet, lies this frontier town, part of which was lost to Czechoslovakia after the First World War, including the important rail junction. Gmünd was none the less able to profit from its position, and now has much to offer the visitor: for a start, an enchanting old quarter, peaceful spots beside the Lainsitz and the Blockheide Nature Reserve.

SIGHTS

Stadtplatz – The unusual outline of the **Altes Rathaus** stands out in the centre of the elongated main square. The windows of this Renaissance building from the second half of the 16C are surrounded with tastefully painted sgraffito. The tall gabled tower, rebuilt in 1988, is particularly striking. The Glas- und Steinmuseum at no 34 provides evidence of the glass industry that flourished here at one time.

★ **Houses with sgraffito decoration** – *Stadtplatz 31 and 33.* These Late Gothic gabled houses had blind, battlemented Renaissance façades built onto them in about 1565-70, which are entirely covered in sgraffito work. This incorporates herringbones, tendril arabesques, small diamond patterns and friezes depicting fighting figures in the case of the left-hand house and scenes from classical mythology in the case of the one on the right.

★★ **Blockheide** – To the northeast of the town lies this remarkable nature reserve in terrain reminiscent of Karelia or Sweden, comprising heathland with mighty granite blocks and birch groves. The strange granite formations are 300 to 400 million years old, and have appropriate nicknames such as Pilzstein (mushroom stone), Teufelsbett (devil's bed), and Wackelstein (wobbly stone). Of particular interest are the educational trail on stone dressing and the open-air Geological Museum, displaying every type of rock occurring north of the Danube.

R. Chéret/MICHELIN

House with sgraffito decoration in Weitra

EXCURSIONS

Weitra – *8km/5mi southwest on Bundesstraße 41.* This small town is dominated by its great four-sided **castle** (1590-1606) with gateway tower and battlemented walls. Around the triangular Rathausplatz with its Grätzl (a structure in the middle of a square) there are fine town houses from the 16C to 19C, some of them with sgraffito decoration (no 4 and no 13).

★**Burg Heidenreichstein** ⌚ – *19km/12mi northeast.* This castle was built on a granite bluff in the late 12C and early 13C and altered in the 15C and 16C. It has a four-sided layout with three circular corner towers and a gatehouse with a tower. The 12C keep is 40m/131ft high, and the only entrance is 14m/46ft above the ground. Heidenreichstein is often claimed to be Austria's finest moated castle, and is an impressive sight with the modern town spread out around it. For a long time in the ownership of the princes Palffy, it now belongs to Count Kinsky, who lives here throughout the year. The rooms open to the public contain furniture from the Gothic, Renaissance and Baroque periods.

The sgraffito technique

The name of this technique is derived from the Italian "graffiare", to scratch. It was particularly popular in North Italy at the time of the Renaissance, and spread northwards to areas such as the Waldviertel and neighbouring Bohemia, even to Silesia and Saxony. A coloured undercoat is applied to the rendering and on top of that a thinner coat, which is scratched away before it hardens to give the pattern. Biblical and mythological scenes glorifying the virtues were favourite subjects.

GMUNDEN★

Oberösterreich

Population 12 720

Michelin map 926 fold 21 – Local map see SALZKAMMERGUT

Alt 420m/1 378ft

In Gmunden, a summer resort in the Salzkammergut much sought after by Romantic or Biedermeier artists and poets, visitors will find one of the best equipped lake beaches on the north slope of the Alps. **Lake cruises** ⌚ can be made on the restored paddle steamer *Gisela*, which welcomed Emperor Franz Joseph aboard in 1872. Gmunden has been famous for the manufacture of artistic pottery since the 15C.

SIGHTS

★ **Esplanade** – This walk along the lake shore extends for 2km/1mi – first among flowerbeds, then beneath chestnut trees. It leads from the Rathausplatz (main square), which is marked by the town hall, a Renaissance building with a porcelain tiled clock tower, to the yacht harbour and the beach (Strandbad). In the opposite direction the walk can be pleasantly continued by crossing the river and following it as far as the war memorial (Kriegerdenkmal) or downstream along the River Traun (2km/1mi).

Southwards, the **view**★ takes in the crests of the Erlakogel, which resemble the form of a recumbent woman and are known as the Sleeping Greek ("Schlafende Griechin").

Jezierzanski/ÖSTERREICH WERBUNG

Schloß Ort, Gmunden

★ **Schloß Ort** – Built on a little island linked to the mainland by a wooden bridge, this **Seeschloß** (Lake Castle) is the favourite image of Gmunden. Through the doorway in the onion-domed tower you reach the charming inner courtyard, lined on two sides by arcaded galleries in the style of the 16C.
Archduke Salvator, the nephew of Emperor Franz Joseph, acquired the estate in 1878. Tired of court life, he lived under the assumed name of **Johann Ort** until he disappeared, in conditions which have never been explained, on a cruise off the coast of South America.

★ **Kammerhofmuseum** ⊙ – The museum takes its name from the salt mines administration building in which it is housed and has a wide range of exhibits on the history and way of life of Gmunden and its inhabitants. Since May 2000 it has covered an exhibition on geography and cultural history entitled "From the Big Bang to the Present", which includes an open-air "Millennium Trail" presenting Gmunden and the Traunsee region in the light of the millennium.

EXCURSIONS

★ **Gmundnerberg** – *9km/5mi southwest – Alt 833m/2 733ft. Leave Gmunden by the Esplanade and the Bad Ischl road.*
In **Altmünster** bear right. The road ends in a run along the crest *(after a sanatorium)* which has **views**★ to the south over the whole of the Traunsee basin. The west bank of the lake is mainly flat and populated, the east steeply sloped. The Sleeping Greek *(see above)* can be recognized.

★ **Almtal (Alm Valley)** – *37km/23mi there and back – half a day. Leave Gmunden to the east on B 120 as far as Scharnstein.*

Scharnstein – Strung out along the main road, the village has a Renaissance castle which houses two unusual museums. The building itself dates from 1584, and after many years of neglect has been comprehensively restored. Of particular interest are the painted 16C wooden ceilings.
The exhibits displayed in the 21 rooms of the **Österreichisches Kriminalmuseum** (Austrian Crime Museum) ⊙ trace the fight against crime from medieval instruments of bodily restraint to political violence and contemporary terrorism. Weapons and devices used by wrongdoers are on show, as are the tools of the executioner's trade, notably a guillotine. No one can fail to be affected by such spectacles and the museum is consequently a place more for adults than children.

Konrad Lorenz

Konrad Lorenz (1903-89) is widely regarded as the one of the founders of behavioural science. Soon after finishing his studies in Vienna (medicine and zoology), he devoted himself to the study of the inborn and acquired behavioural patterns of animals, in particular the greylag goose. In 1973, his work was recognized with the award of the Nobel Prize for Medicine, which he shared with Karl von Frisch and Nikolaas Tinbergen.

The extraordinary **Reptilienzoo** (Reptile Zoo) ⓥ occupies the cellars underneath the Museum of Crime. In its glass cages are over 100 poisonous animals from all over the world (snakes, scorpions, giant spiders), just a hair's breadth away from onlookers.

Follow signs towards Grünau im Almtal.

Beyond Grünau the road rises gently through a wooded mountain landscape, particularly attractive in autumn.

★ **Cumberland Wildpark** ⓥ – *In Grünau.* This wildlife park, covering an area of 60ha/148 acres, is set in pleasant wooded mountain countryside. Footpaths run for miles alongside a stream, or skirting some of the numerous lakes, enabling visitors to admire the resident wildlife in a largely natural setting. The wildlife park is a research centre for the **Konrad-Lorenz-Institut**.

Continue up the valley as far as Seehaus.

After the peaceful little village of Habernau the road turns south to the prettily situated **Almsee**★. Beyond the lake, the mountains form a great natural amphitheatre closing off the valley. Signposted footpaths invite the visitor to further exploration of the Almtal.

GOSAUSEEN★★★

Oberösterreich

Michelin map 926 fold 20 – Local map see SALZKAMMERGUT

The Gosau lakes lie amid craggy mountain scenery in the northwest of the Dachstein range, forming one of the unique features of the Austrian Alps. From June to October, they are a popular destination for nature-lovers.

★★★ **Vorderer Gosausee** – Alt 933m/3 061ft. The shores of the lake can be reached from the car park, beyond which the road is closed to traffic. There is an unforgettable **view**★★ of the Hoher Dachstein limestone range (alt 2 995m/9 826ft) with its small glaciers. The play of light on the scene is particularly effective very early or very late in the day, when the glaciers and rock faces are bathed in light while the valley lies in shadow.

A **tour of the lake**★★★ is an absolute must. This easy walk *(allow about 1hr)* gives a marvellous view of the craggy peaks of the Gosau ridge. The mountains and surrounding forest are reflected in the still, clear waters of the lake, making a fairy-tale scene.

Y. Bontoux

Hinterer Gosausee

★★ **Walk to the Hinterer Gosausee** – *From the far (southeast) end of the Vorderer Gosausee, allow 1hr 45min there and back. This walk is recommended for ramblers who are fit.*

The path through the undergrowth soon becomes steeper. On reaching the densely wooded shores of the **Hinterer See**★★ (alt 1 154m/3 786ft), take the right shore as far as the Hinterer-See-Alm.

Keen walkers can continue as far as the **Adamek-Hütte** (alt 2 196m/7 205ft), although it is necessary to be in good physical shape for this. We recommend an early morning departure. Allow 3hr for the climb from Hinterer See (the footpath begins just before the Hinterer-See-Alm). From the Adamek-Hütte it is well worth making a 20min detour to the edge of the Gosau glacier. From the car park, the entire walk takes about 8hr, in other words a day's hard walking, or two days including an overnight stay in the refuge.

Schloß GRAFENEGG★

Niederösterreich

Michelin map 926 fold 11 – 12km/7.5mi east of Krems

Rising out of the flat Tullner Feld plain is Schloß Grafenegg, Austria's most significant example of romanticized historicism. Surrounded by a great park, the castle keep with its gallery and turrets seems like a miraculous vision when seen from the distance.
The castle is based on an earlier building, which probably dated from the 15C and early 16C. A few remnants of this building still survive, for instance the small tower from 1533 on the east wing facing the courtyard.
Graf August Ferdinand Breuner-Enckevoirt was responsible for the appearance of the castle as we see it today. From 1846 to 1853, he took up the challenge of this historicizing re-creation and won through, thanks to the brilliant work of cathedral architect Leopold Ernst. It now belongs to Prince Metternich-Sandór, for whom the restoration of the castle has been his life's work since it suffered so badly during the 10 years of Soviet occupation.
Schloß Grafenegg is well known for its cultural events, which include exhibitions, readings and concerts. The high spot is the "Grafenegger Advent" at the beginning of December, combining Christmas music with a traditional Christmas market.

TOUR ⊙

Crossing the bridge into the castle, decorated with a dragon and lion bearing a coat of arms, we enter the north wing, whose stepped main gable ends in delicate, lace-like tracery. The statue over the doorway shows the person who commissioned the rebuilding with the date 1856.

Rittersaal (Hall of the Knights) – Here Leopold Ernst anticipated the style of the typical buildings on Vienna's Ringstraße, which were to come a good 10 years later. This, the main room on the first floor, suffered particularly from the ravages of the Soviet occupation, so hardly anything remains of the original fittings, although the masterly **coffered ceiling**★ and the chimney-piece which was destroyed post-1945 have been restored.

Schloßkapelle – The chapel was consecrated in 1853, and is a fine example of neo-Gothic architecture with its ribbed vaulting and pendant bosses. The Late Gothic winged altarpiece depicts the Coronation of the Virgin Mary. On the north and south walls, paintings from Late Gothic altarpieces are placed in groups of four, together with 19C figures of Apostles.

Great Salon and Dining Room – Attractive wooden panelling and carved ornaments and figures are features of these rooms. The **coffered ceiling**★ in the Great Salon is particularly appealing, since the ends of the beams have angels and knights bearing coats of arms.
A lasting impression is also left by the generously proportioned stairway, with the figure of a knight and busts of the builder and his architect (inspired by the self-portrait of architect Franz Anton Pilgram in St Stephen's Cathedral in Vienna). No less remarkable are the Yellow Salon and the adjoining bathroom, study and bedroom, the library and the garden room, whose walls and ceilings are covered in exquisite materials, while the fine **Kachelöfen** (tiled stoves) provide a colourful note.

R. Chéret/MICHELIN

Coffered ceiling in the Great Salon, Schloß Grafenegg

EXCURSION

Gobelsburg ⊙ – *10km/6mi northwest in the direction of Langenlois.* The original Renaissance castle was made over in the Baroque style in 1725. The four-sided building with its great hip roof has been the wine-growing estate of the Abbey of Zwettl since 1740. The rooms are decorated with strapwork stucco and in some cases with ceiling frescoes, but it is the **Kachelöfen**★ (tiled stoves) from the second half of the 18C that are particularly impressive. There are tours of the cellars and a visit to the new-wine bar to round off the excursion.

GRAZ★★

L Steiermark

Population 243 400

Michelin map 926 fold 37 – Alt 365m/1 194ft

The capital of Styria is in the valley of the Mur, bounded to the west by the last foothills of the Alps and to the north and east by the Styrian hills. Because of this attractive setting and its extensive parks Graz is sometimes called the Garden City. Austria's second city, Graz is an economic centre and cultural and educational metropolis (50 000 students are enrolled at the three universities here), the hub of an entire region. The city employs some 130 000 people. A variety of industries have set up in the modern suburbs, particularly since the Second World War, including the automobile and shoe industries, mechanical engineering and a leading brewery, to name but a few.

HISTORICAL NOTES

An Imperial city – In 1379 the Leopoldine branch of the Habsburgs chose Graz as their residence. In 1440, the Styrian prince, Friedrich III, who by preference resided in the city, was elected King of Germany, then, in 1452, crowned Holy Roman Emperor. It was he who made Graz an Imperial city and it is from this time that the cathedral dates, as does the "castle" near the Burgtor (though all that remains of it is the Late Gothic double spiral staircase).

A bastion of Christianity – Graz equipped itself with ramparts as early as the 13C as defence against the Turkish invasions in Styria. In 1543 the defences, including the Schloßberg fFortress, were strengthened on the orders of Emperor Ferdinand I by the Italian **Domenico dell'Allio**, who was also architect of the Landhaus. The measures taken to ward off attack were thoroughgoing; a huge arsenal of arms and munitions was built up, the raw material coming from Styria's **"Iron Mountain"** *(see EISENERZ)*. This was then fashioned into sword blades, halberds, breastplates and firearms by a legion of armourers, gunsmiths, blacksmiths and furbishers.

Whenever invasion seemed imminent, the arms were distributed to volunteers chosen from the local population to reinforce the professional troops. The construction of the Zeughaus (Arsenal) next to the Landhaus in 1642 made it possible to bring together arms and munitions which until then had been distributed around the city, in sheds near the city gates, beneath sentry walks or in the cellars of the Landhaus. Following the Habsburg partition of the country in 1564, Graz became the capital of a vast area known as **Inner Austria**, comprising Styria, Carinthia, Gorizia, Carniola and Istria. The splendid court of Archduke Karl II, a true prince of the Renaissance, brought many cultural and artistic benefits to the city.

The Reformation – By 1568 three-quarters of the population had embraced Protestantism. In this year a school and seminary were founded, where the present Paradeishof stands (**CZ 26**), and it was here that the German astronomer Johannes Kepler taught between 1594 and 1598.

In 1571 Archduke Karl II called in the Jesuits to implement the Counter Reformation; they

Rooftops of Graz

founded a college (in the Bürgergasse) and a school (Hofgasse). In 1585 the Archduke founded **Graz University**, which became the intellectual hub of Inner Austria.
However, the city's fortunes took another turn in 1619 when Karl II's son, Archduke Ferdinand II, was elected Holy Roman Emperor. Ferdinand moved the court to Vienna, and Graz, no longer an Imperial residence, lost much of its dynamism.
In the 18C, following the reforms of Maria Theresa, the city had to forgo many of its privileges; later, under Joseph II, the university was downgraded to a grammar school. Graz's days of splendour came to a definite end; this is why the city has so few buildings dating from the Late Baroque period.

A Prince beloved by his people, Archduke Johann – The Habsburg Archduke Johann (1782-1859) enjoyed great personal popularity in Styria and his memory is still honoured today. On settling in Graz, he devoted himself to studies of all kinds, roaming through Styria and Carinthia in the company of naturalists, archeologists and painters.
His romantic marriage to Anna Plochl, a postmaster's daughter from Bad Aussee, together with any number of public enterprises, did nothing to diminish his popularity. He founded model farms, presided over the construction of the railway from Graz to Mürzzuschlag (1844) and promoted the prosperity of the Eisenerz area. In Graz itself, the Technische Hochschule is proof of his progressive spirit, as is the Joanneum Landesmuseum, Austria's oldest museum open to the public, founded in 1811.

★★ OLD TOWN

This is one of the most extensive historic city centres in the German-speaking world. Dominated by the Schloßberg and bordered on the west by the river, its 18C and 19C façades conceal much older buildings with quiet arcaded courtyards – at least 50 of them – some grand, some intimate. The grandest, but not the oldest, is that of the Landhaus. In 1999, Graz Old Town was declared UNESCO world heritage site.

PATRIMONIO MUNDIAL • WORLD HERITAGE • PATRIMOINE MONDIAL

★ **Hauptplatz** (**CZ**) – The heart of Graz, this is the liveliest of squares. The city trams come and go incessantly, disgorging ever more people to join the motley crowd thronging the market stalls. Behind the brightly painted 17C-19C façades are buildings of much older, medieval date, often stretching right back towards the rear of the plot they occupy. At the corner of the Sporgasse stands the arcaded **Haus Luegg** (**CZ A**) with its luxuriant 17C stucco work. The city's oldest pharmacy is at no 4; dating from 1535, it still has some of its original fittings. The **Erzherzog-Johann-Brunnen** (fountain) of 1878 lords it over the square, relegating the statue of the Emperor to a less important site (on the Freiheitsplatz – **DY 10**), a reminder of the affection in which their benefactor was held by the local people. The four female figures gracing the fountain are allegories of the four main rivers flowing through Styria at the time of the monarchy, though the boundary revisions of 1918 left the province with only two of them (the Mur and the Enns).

H. Weisenhofer/ÖSTERREICH WERBUNG

From the pavement in front of the city hall (raised to its present level in 1893) there is a view of the wooded spur of the Schloßberg keeping watch over the city, with, at its far end, the familiar outline of the Uhrturm (Clock Tower), the emblem of Graz.
The Landhaus is reached via the broad and busy **Herrengasse** (**DZ**) with its elegant shops and offices. The **Gemaltes Haus** (painted house, at no 3) was residence of the archdukes until the building of the castle in 1450. The murals on historic (notably Roman) themes date from 1742, when they replaced the original decoration by Pietro de Pomis, architect of the mausoleum.

★★ **Landhaus** (**DZ**) – This, the former seat of the Styrian Diet, is a remarkable Renaissance palace built between 1557 and 1565 by Domenico dell'Allio, the military architect who had just

TRAVELLERS' ADDRESSES

Tourist information

Graz/Steiermark Information, im Landhaus, Herrengasse 16, 8010 Graz. Opening times: June-Sept Mon-Fri 9am-7pm, Sat 9am-6pm, Sun and public holidays 10am-3pm; Oct-May Mon-Fri 9am-6pm, Sat 9am-3pm, Sun and public holidays 10am-3pm; ☎ 03 16/80 75-0.
Graz Information am Hauptbahnhof, Europaplatz 6, 8020 Graz. Opening times: Mon-Fri 9am-6pm (summer only); ☎ 03 16/80 75-0.

Graz also has its own **Web site** at *www.graztourismus.at*

City tours

Tour of Old Town (2hr 30min) - Apr-end Oct daily at 2.30pm, otherwise Sat only at 2.30pm. Meeting point: Graz/Steiermark Information.

Tours of the Schloßberg - Easter-Oct daily 9am-5pm on the hour. Meeting point: at the bell-tower.

Guided tours (in English and German) are available from early April to late October. Departure at 2pm from the Landhausgasse, return at about 7pm.
Fridays: Styrian Castle Route
Saturdays: Piber Lippizaner Stud Farm
Sundays: South Styrian Wine Route

Information and bookings from Graz/Steiermark Information, Herrengasse 16.

Public transport

Tickets are available from ticket machines, advance booking offices and tobacconists (Trafiken), and also from tram and bus drivers.
With the **Stundenkarte** you can use any form of public transport in Graz for 1hr, with the **10-Zonenkarte** you can make 10 journeys within the same zone, and there is also a **24-Stundenkarte** and a **Wochenkarte**, giving travel for 24hr and a week respectively.
Further information on public transport can be obtained from the Graz transport authority (GVB) Zeitkartenbüro (Season ticket office), Hauptplatz 14, ☎ 03 16/8 74 08, or from the Informationsstelle on the Jakominiplatz, ☎ 03 16/88 74 11.

Bicycle hire

Bicycles can be hired from the Hauptbahnhof (☎ 03 16/78 48 326) or Bicycle, Kaiser-Franz-Josefs-Kai 55 and 66 or Rechbauerstraße 57, ☎ 03 16/82 13 57 to explore the city's 75km/47mi of cycle paths.

Inner city parking

Parking is permitted in the **blue zones** for a fee covering a certain time (restricted parking is operated between 9am and 7pm on work days). Parking tickets valid for up to 3hr can be obtained from parking ticket machines. Otherwise you should park in one of the following car parks:
Tiefgarage (underground) Mariahilferplatz; Parkhaus (multi-storey) Griesgasse 10; Tiefgarage Andreas-Hofer-Platz; Tiefgarage Rosarium, Hamerlinggasse; Garage Burgring, Einspinnergasse; Schloßberg-Garage, Sackstraße 29; City-Garage Weitzer, Am Entenplatz.

Post offices

Main post office: **Hauptpostamt**, Neutorgasse 46, Mon-Fri 7am-11pm, Sat 7am-2pm, Sun and public holidays 8am-2pm.
Station post office: **Bahnhofspostamt**, Europaplatz 10, daily, 24hr/24hr.

Shopping

The main shopping street is the Herrengasse, but there are also numerous shops in the pedestrian precincts, such as Sporgasse/Murgasse, the streets around the Hauptplatz, and Schmiedgasse/Stubenberggasse/Hans-Sachs-Gasse.

Markets
Kaiser-Josef-Platz (farm produce), daily 6am-noon.
Lendplatz (farm produce), Mon-Sat 7am-noon.
Karmeliterplatz (flea market), 3rd Sat in the month.

Souvenirs
Craft goods and traditional costume (Trachten): Steirisches Heimatwerk, Herrengasse 10 and Paulustorgasse 4.
Schloßbergkugeln (Schloßberg balls, local speciality chocolates): Konditorei Strehly, Sporgasse 14.
Kernöl (salad oil from pumpkin seeds): farmers' market, Kaiser-Josef-Platz
Styrian wine: Stempfergasse 2.

Entertainment

The **"Bühnen Graz"** (☎ 03 16/80 00, Fax ☎ 03 16/80 08 565, Web site *www.buehnen-graz.com*) association includes five theatres:
The **Opernhaus** at Kaiser-Josef-Platz 10, the **Schauspielhaus** (spoken theatre, 12 premieres every season) on Freiheitsplatz, **Next Liberty** (children's and young people's theatre) at Kaiser-Josef-Platz 10, the **Orpheum** (venue for rock, pop, jazz and cabaret) at Orpheumgasse 8, and in the summer the **Casemates** (open-air theatre) on Schloßberg.

T.i.P. (Theater im Palais), Leonhardstra ße 15, ☎ 03 16/38 91 016, hosts musical and spoken theatre by students from Graz University of Art.

TheatermëRZ, Steinfeldgasse 20, ☎ 03 16/72 01 72. This artists' and authors' theatre can look back on numerous international tours. Its programme focuses on the work of author, director and theatre manager Willi Bernhart: plays, song programmes, children's and young people's theatre.

Theatro, Neubaugasse 6, ☎ 03 16/71 60 27. Independent cultural centre which hosts all kinds of theatre as well as concerts of rock pop and world music.

Casino Graz, Landhausgasse 10, ☎ 03 16/83 25 78. Austria's second largest casino.

Cinemas

Large multiple-screen cinema complexes offering a corresponding variety of films are to be found at **UCI Kinowelt Annenhof** (Annenstraße 29, ☎ 03 16/72 77) and **Cineplexx** (Alte Poststraße 470, ☎ 03 16/29 09).

For films other than current mainstream, try the **Filmzentrum im Rechbauerkino** (Rechbauerstraße 6, ☎ 03 16/83 05 08), **KIZ Kino im Augarten** (Friedrichgasse 24, ☎ 03 16/82 11 86) and **Schubertkino** (Mehlplatz 2, ☎ 03 16/82 90 810).

Eating out

Altsteirische Schmankerlstube (Sackstraße 10, ☎ 03 16/83 32 11); **Franz Schauer's** (Sackstraße 29, 3rd floor, ☎ 03 16/83 45 85); **Kehlberghof** (Kehlbergstraße 83, ☎ 03 16/28 41 25); **Mohrenwirt** (Mariahilfstraße 16, ☎ 03 16/71 20 08); **Landhauskeller** (Schmiedgasse 9, ☎ 03 16/83 02 76); **Pichlmaier** (Petersbergenstraße 9, ☎ 03 16/47 15 97); **Santa Clara** (Abraham-a-Santa-Clara-Gasse 1, entrance Bürgergasse 6, ☎ 03 16/81 18 22); **Stainzerbauer** (Bürgergasse 4, ☎ 03 16/8 15 87 50).

Cafés and bars

Temmel's Kaiserhof (Kaiserfeldgasse 1); **Café Promenade am Burgtor** (Erzherzog-Johann-Allee 1); **Operncafé** (Opernring 22); **Hofbäckerei Edegger-Tax** (Hofgasse 6).
The centre of Graz nightlife (known as the "Bermuda triangle") is the area bordered by the Färberplatz, Glockenspielplatz and Herrengasse. Here there are hostelries and wine parlours to suit every taste. In the university quarter (Leonhardtstraße, Zinzendorfgasse and Schillerplatz) is to be found the young scene.
In the **Gasthaus Keplerkeller** (Stempfergasse 6), you can drink wine and listen to Styrian music, while special beers are available at the **Bierbaron** (Heinrichstraße 56), as well as in the pubs **Eschenlaube** (Glacisstraße 67), and **Schillerhof** (Plüddemanngasse 2). The **Kulturhauskeller** (Elisabethstraße 30) is a pub with music, and the **Café Stockwerk** (Jakominiplatz 18/I) offers jazz. You can also have a drink in one of the many bars in Graz, such as the **Ernst-Fuchs-Bar** in the Hotel Erzherzog Johann (Sackstraße 3-5), the **Fink** (Freiheitsplatz 2), the **Limarutti** (Prokopigasse 4) or the **M1** (Färberplatz 1/III). There is dancing in the **Monte** (Sackstraße 27) and in the **Castello** (Bürgergasse 4). The ambiance of an American bar, complete with live jazz, is recreated in the **Hemingway American Bar** (Klosterwiesgasse 6).

Dates for your diary

Diagonale: March-April, Festival of Austrian film.

Storytime in Graz: at Whitsun, Festival of storytelling and fairy tales. Storytellers from all over the world come to Graz to demonstrate how much fun and excitement story-telling can be.

Classics in the city: in summer, open-air performances of classical music in the Renaissance Lanhaushof with international culinary delights.

Generali Hof Jazz concerts: in summer, open-air performances, free of charge, courtesy of the Graz jazz scene.

Styriarte: July, classical music festival.

Jazz-Sommer: July-August, jazz concerts on the Mariahilfer Platz, free of charge.

AIMS: mid July-end August, festival of classical music by the great composers played by students from the **A**merican **I**nstitute of **M**usical **S**tudies.

La Strada: end July-beginning of August, international festival of puppet and street theatre in the old city.

Styrian Autumn: October, international avant-garde festival of contemporary music, theatre, art exhibitions and readings of literary works.

Mountain and adventure film festival: November, international film competition, with the "Grand Prix Graz" awarded in five different categories.

completed the total reconstruction of the Schloßberg fortress for Emperor Ferdinand I. Today the Landhaus still serves as the meeting place for the Landtag, the Styrian provincial parliament.

The main façade with its round-arched windows above an elegant doorway prepares us for the southern splendour of the courtyard with its three storeys of arcades, flower-bedecked balconies, staircase wells and loggias. The stairway gracing the chapel in the northwest corner of the courtyard was built by another Italian, Bartolomeo di Bosio. The old well-head, the work of local craftsmen, has a fine bronze dais with amoretti and female figures. It was once coloured.

The courtyard forms an enchanting setting for the various performances given here in summer.

A few paces along the Stempfergasse (**DZ 30**) reveal the best view of the façade of the Landhaus, with its middle bay emphasized by a little copper bell-turret. The lower parts of the columns of the twin windows rise from a sculpted ring, a motif much favoured by Domenico dell'Allio. The façade next to the Landhaus is that of the arsenal.

Graz Tourismus

Courtyard of the Landhaus

★★★ **Zeughaus (Arsenal)** ⏲ (**DZ**) – With its portal foreshadowing the appearance of the German Baroque, the real function of this solid-looking building – an arms depot – is betrayed by the statues of Mars and Minerva. In its day it was one of the many arsenals in the world, but it is the only one to have been preserved in its original state with its contents intact.

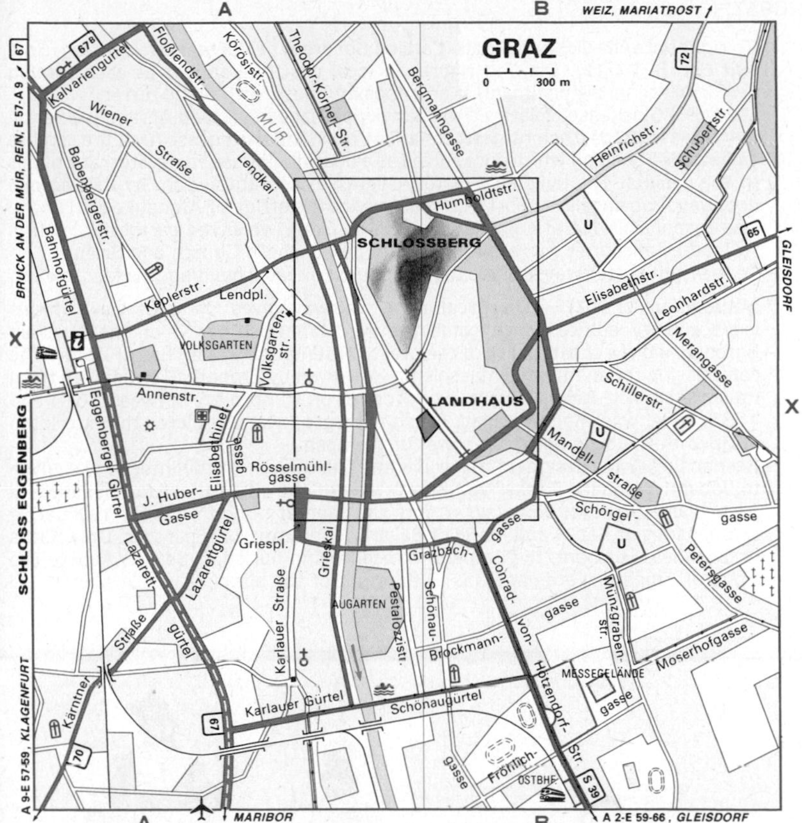

The arsenal was built in 1642. By the beginning of the 18C the Turkish threat had finally disappeared and it was decided to store the standing army's equipment in Vienna. The question of what to do with the now obsolete material at Graz was settled when Maria Theresa allowed the Styrians to keep it here in recognition of the services rendered by the local militias. To enter the arsenal is to leave behind the contemporary bustle of the Herrengasse and to be transported back into the world of four centuries ago; it is as if cavalrymen and foot soldiers could appear at any moment, fresh from being mustered in the courtyard of the Landhaus, to fit themselves out from the array of neatly laid-out material, and set off to harass the Infidel.

The four storeys of the arsenal contain more than 32 000 arms of all imaginable kinds, many to a very high standard of craftsmanship; cold steel, arms on poles and firearms – arquebuses, pistols and muskets with their powder horn – heavy armour for knights and soldiers, breastplates and harnesses for use in battle or jousting. From the top storey of the arsenal the view takes in the Landhaus courtyard and, over the rooftops, the Schloßberg and clock tower.

Stadtpfarrkirche zum Heiligen Blut (DZ) – The original Gothic church building was remodelled in the Baroque taste, then re-Gothicized between 1875 and 1882. Its Baroque **bell-tower**★, the city's finest, was built entirely out of wood in 1780-81 by the architect Josef Stengg and the master carpenter Franz Windisch. It is topped by a three-barred cross, a reminder of its consecration by the Pope.

Inside, on the altar in the south aisle, is an Assumption of the Virgin attributed to Tintoretto. The stained glass of the chancel, the work of the Salzburg artist Albert Birkle in 1953, has an unusual feature; in the left-hand window, the fourth panel from the bottom on the right has Hitler and Mussolini taking part in the flagellation of Christ.

There is an organ concert in the church every Thursday evening in summer.

Go onto the Altstadtpassage (**DZ 3**) *by no 7 Herrengasse.*

The first courtyard has arcaded and vaulted galleries dating from 1648.

A little further on, to the right, are a number of courtyards of which one is reminiscent of the Landhaus.

The passageway comes out onto the **Mehlplatz** (**DZ 22**), flanked by two grand residences with Baroque stucco façades. The Palais Inzaghi to the left (at no 1) was once a music school run by the parents of Robert Stolz, composer of operettas.

Go right onto the **Glockenspielplatz** (Carillon Square – *performances at 11am, 3pm and 6pm* – **DZ 12**). Dancing figures in local costume appear at each carillon performance in the pediment of an imposing house with a bell-turret.

Leave the Glockenspielplatz via the narrow passageway called Abraham-a-Santa-Clara-Gasse (**DZ 2**), then turn left for a view of no 1 Burgergasse (**DZ**), the sombre palazzo-like building which once served as a boarding-house for aristocratic pupils of the Jesuits. The building's history seems to be summed up by its Baroque doorway; two angels support a cartouche with the effigy of Archduke Karl II who was responsible for bringing the Jesuits to Graz, while the cartouche itself is framed by allegories representing the Roman Catholic Church and Science.

To the right, a stairway leads to the city's most unusual building, the Mausoleum.

★★ **Mausoleum** ⌚ (**DZ**) – The great west stairway gives the best view of this extraordinary edifice which combines the Mannerist phase of the Austrian Baroque and the theatricality of the great contemporary churches of Rome. The commission for an Imperial mausoleum was given by Emperor Ferdinand II to an Italian architect, **Pietro de Pomis**, who worked on the project between 1614 and 1633, and it was another Italian, Pietro Valnegro, who completed the exterior in 1636 with the building of the tower of the apse.

Responsibility for designing the exuberant stuccowork of the interior was given to Johann Bernhard Fischer von Erlach, one of the city's most famous men. A particularly fine oval dome surmounts the funerary crypt with the red-marble sarcophagus of Karl II and Maria of Bavaria, the Emperor's parents. Only Karl's Archduchess lies here, the Emperor himself being buried at Seckau Abbey. The tomb of Emperor Ferdinand II is to the right of the altar.

R. Chéret/MICHELIN

Mausoleum, Graz

★ **Domkirche (Cathedral)** (**DZ**) – Before becoming the cathedral in 1786, this vast and luminous edifice served as church to the Imperial court. It was built between 1438 and 1464 by Emperor Friedrich III, whose coat of arms adorns the main entrance. On the southwest corner of the entrance is a series of **frescoes** (1485); as well as including the earliest known depiction of the city, they show the various troubles visited on Graz in the year 1480 (Turks, plague, and swarms of locusts). Inside, the Baroque decor mostly dates from the time when the church was handed over to the Jesuits (1577 onwards).

The church's **interior** has most attractive reticulated vaulting. Of the original decor perhaps the most striking features are the two frescoes of St Christopher (late 15C), discovered in the course of restoration work at the beginning of this century. They recall an old belief according to which one would not die on a day on which one had looked at the saint's image.

The long chancel has a Baroque altar of particularly harmonious design. Near the entrance to the chancel are two magnificent **reliquary chests**★★★. Brought here by the Jesuits, they are works of great sophistication and were once the marriage

chests of Paula di Gonzaga, Duchess of Mantua. Made of ebony and decorated with reliefs in bone and ivory, they date from around 1470 and are in the style of Mantegna. Their subject matter goes back to the *Triumphs* of Petrarch, moral and allegorical poems dealing with the various stages of life from the standpoint of a calm acceptance of death.
The organ with its 5 354 pipes dates from 1978.

Leave the cathedral by the north entrance.

Cross the street by the **Burgtor** (Castle Gate) (**DZ**) and go through the impressive stone gateway commanding the first courtyard of the 15C **castle** (Burg). The left doorway, before the covered way, gives access to the buildings of the provincial government (Landesregierung) and the **Treppenturm**.

★★ **Treppenturm (Staircase Tower)** (**DY B**) – This highly unusual architectural feature with its double stairway (Doppelwendeltreppe) wound around twin axes, is all that chiefly remains of the former residence of Friedrich III. The tower was added in 1499 by his son Maximilian I and is a notable technical achievement in terms of design and the mason's craft.

Freiheitsplatz (**DY 10**) – In the centre of the square stands the statue of Franz II, the last Holy Roman Emperor and elder brother of Archduke Johann. Closing the square is a large red building with a neo-Classical pediment; this is the city residence of the abbots of St Lambrecht. The half relief of the pediment features Freemasons' symbols.
Just before the Sporgasse, on the left, is the old **Hofbäckerei** (Imperial Bakery) with its fine shopfront. Turning right into the Sporgasse, have a look at the Palais Saurau Göss at no 25 with its rusticated Baroque doorway and arcaded doorway; the significance of the Turk brandishing a sword on the gable is a mystery, even to the locals. The Renaissance Zur goldenen Pastete (no 28) is also picturesque.
Follow the bright and busy **Sporgasse** (**CY**) as it winds back to the Hauptplatz. At no 22 is the former Deutschordenshaus (House of the Teutonic Knights); it has an arcaded courtyard in Gothic style. The narrow façade of no 3 is an interesting example of Jugendstil (Art Nouveau).

Turn right onto Sackstraße.

Sackstraße (**CYZ**) – This was once a cul-de-sac (Sack), which was opened by a tower gateway in the 14C whose site is now occupied by the Palais Attems (no 17). The road was lengthened on two occasions in the course of extending the city walls. Because of its proximity to the river, it became the heart of an artisans' district with a great variety of trades: millers, tanners, parchment-makers... After 1650, the oldest part of the street became known as "Lords Blind Alley" because of the aristocratic mansions which can still be seen here.
The Krebsenkeller at no 12 has a **Renaissance courtyard**★ with double windows and arcaded loggias, giving an Italian feel and at the same time an air of secrecy to the ensemble. The former **Palais Herberstein** at no 16, once a grand mansion which now houses the **Neue Galerie** (19C and 20C art), boasts a monumental staircase as evidence of its past splendour.
The **Palais Khuenberg** at no 18 houses the **Stadtmuseum** ⏲ (**M'**). On 18 December 1863 the palace was the birthplace of Archduke Franz Ferdinand *(see ARTSTETTEN)*, who later became heir to the Imperial throne.

Palais Attems (**CY D**) – Opposite the Stadtmuseum, this is without doubt the finest of all the city's Baroque palaces. Its **façades**★★ repay close inspection, with their profuse decoration of pilasters, mouldings and curvilinear window pediments. The palace was built between 1702 and 1716 for Count Attems on a site previously occupied by six town houses.
The nearby city gate was demolished at the same time, having outlived its usefulness.

Dreifaltigkeitskirche (**CY E**) – Built in 1704, the church seems to be watching over its neighbour, the Palais Attems. It reveals its calm and harmonious façade with its scrolled pediment in an almost shy way, notwithstanding the abundance of iconography referring to the Trinity, to which the church is dedicated.
The view from the church door shows the Schloßbergplatz (**CY 29**) from which some 260 steep steps climb up to the Schloßberg itself.

★ **Medieval quarter** – Towards the end of the Middle Ages, a cattle market was held between the river and the ramparts, where the Franziskanerplatz (**CZ 9**) and the Neutorgasse (**CZ**) are now. The strange name (Kälbernes Viertel meaning Calf Town) still used by locals for the area around the Franciscan church recalls these times. In 1620, the area was brought within the ramparts when the city's defences were being strengthened.
The quarter has kept much of its charm, and a stroll through its narrow **streets**★ with their Italian atmosphere is most enjoyable, particularly the pretty Neue-Welt-Gasse (**CZ 23**) and the Franziskanergasse (**CZ 8**), both piled high with the wares of fruiterers and greengrocers.

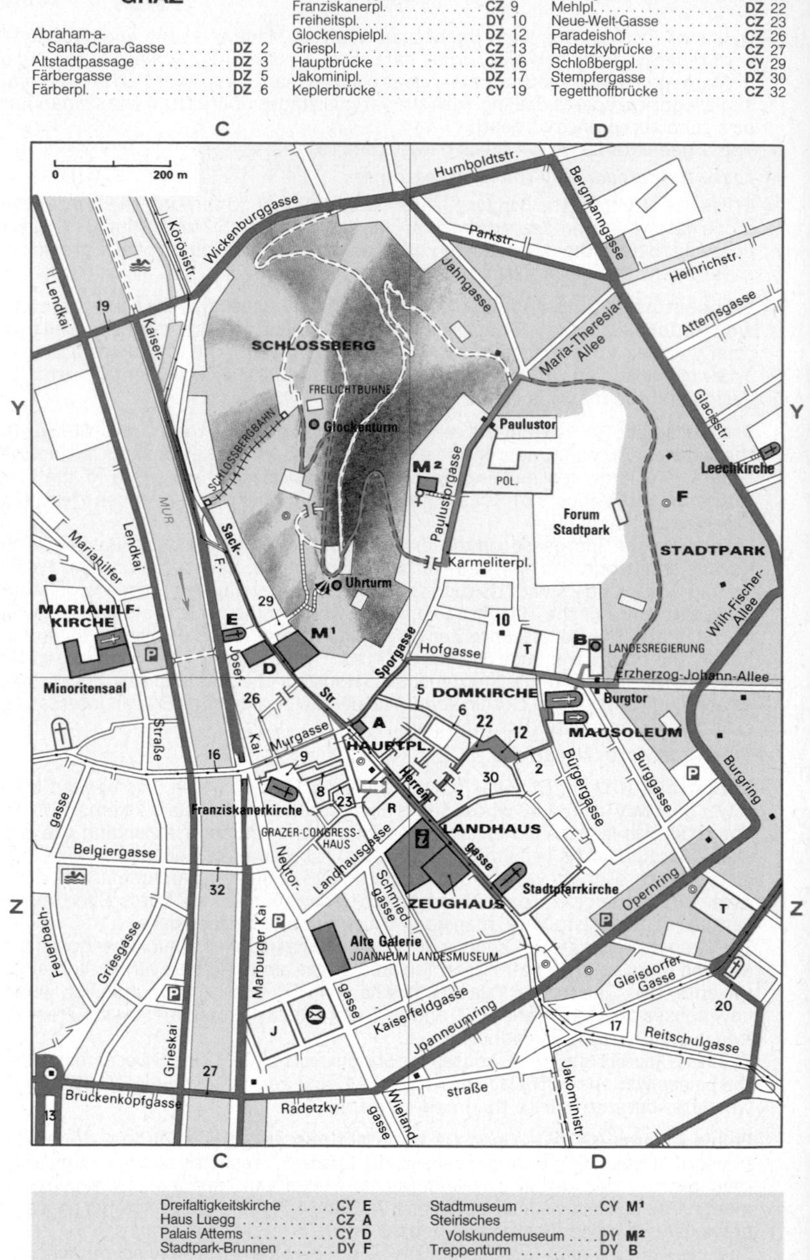

Franziskanerkirche (**CZ**) – Traders set up their stalls against the walls of this church, which was reroofed after the Second World War and given modern glass. It was here in 1240 that the Minorites installed their convent, which passed into the ownership of a closed Franciscan order in the 16C. The oldest part of the church, the Jakobskapelle, dates back to 1330.

★ PARKS

★ **Schloßberg** ⓥ (**CY**) – *Reached by funicular (Schloßbergbahn), from the northern end of the Sackstraße, or via the steps leading from the Schloßbergplatz* (**CY 29**). Overlooking the city from a height of 123m/over 400ft, the impregnable hilltop bristled with redoubts and fortifications right up to the Napoleonic Wars. In 1809 Graz was occupied by French troops led by General MacDonald, though the fortress withstood all assaults. Much to the chagrin of the townsfolk, one of the provisions of the Treaty of Schönbrunn in 1809 involved the dismantling of the Schloßberg. Nevertheless, they succeeded in acquiring, at a considerable price, the **Uhrturm** (Clock Tower) and the **Glockenturm** (Bell-tower) with its four-and-a-half

tonne bell "Lisl", the biggest in town. The rest of the fortress was duly demolished. Later in the 19C the process of converting the Schloßberg into a park was begun. Today it forms a series of pleasantly shaded gardens and terraces. A wide chestnut avenue leads down to the clock tower rising from its massed beds of flowers. The dial is unusual; for a long time it had a single hand, 5.4m/18ft long, which showed the hours. The smaller, minute hand (2.7m/9ft long) was added later, a strange inversion of normal practice.
Go down the steps leading to the Herberstein gardens. From the terrace there are fine **views★★** over the city and the Mur Valley. In the distance to the southwest, beyond the reddish-brown roofs of Graz, can be seen the outlines of the Styrian Prealps.

Climb back up to the clock tower and then go down the first path on the right which leads backs into town to the Karmeliterplatz. Here there is a Trinity Column, erected in 1680 in thanksgiving for relief from the plague.

Go up the Paulustorgasse.

Steirisches Volkskundemuseum ⊙ (**DY M²**) – The museum of local art and traditions forms part of the Joanneum *(below)* and has been housed since 1913 in this former Capuchin monastery. It is devoted to Styrian folk art and traditions, and has some particularly interesting reconstructions of house interiors. *It is currently closed, and the date of reopening was not known at the time of going to press.*
On the rise beyond the museum is one of the "Heimatwerk" shops offering contemporary local crafts.

Paulustor (**DY**) – Together with the Burgtor, this is all that remains of the city walls. Built towards the end of the 16C, it displays the coats of arms, in marble, of Ferdinand II of Austria and of Maria Anna of Bavaria.

★ **Stadtpark** (**DY**) – This is an "English-style" park, laid out informally in the second half of the 19C along the line of the old walls. It runs in a broad band for a distance of 1 200m/0.75mi to the east and southeast of the old city centre. In the middle of the park is the **Forum Stadtpark**, a meeting place of avant-garde artists since 1960. In front of the building stands the **Stadtpark-Brunnen** (**F**), a fountain in a luxuriant setting of fine old trees, shrubs and flowerbeds. The fountain was originally made in 1873 by craftsman Antoine Durenne for the World Exhibition in Vienna. Two similar, but smaller, fountains, made 30 years before their counterpart in Graz, adorn place de la Concorde in Paris.

Go south through the Stadtpark to the Burgtor. Take Hofgasse, then Sporgasse. Turn left into Färbergasse and carry on across Färberplatz and along Prokopigasse. Level with Mehlplatz turn right into Altstadtpassage, which leads into Herrengasse. It is not far from here to Hauptplatz.

ADDITIONAL SIGHTS

★ **Mariahilf-Kirche** (**CY**) – One of the finest of the city's churches, with elegant twin towers and impeccably proportioned Baroque façade, this was the province's most popular place of pilgrimage after Mariazell.
It was begun in 1607-11 by Pietro de Pomis, architect of the Mausoleum and Schloß Eggenberg, who was buried here on his death in 1633. The Late Baroque towers of 1742-44 are the work of Josef Hueber. Renaissance in structure, the interior of the nave gives an overall impression

GEORG MIKES

Mariahilf-Kirche, Graz

of harmony and repose. The door on the left of the façade leads to the cloisters, beyond which is a further courtyard with a little building in the style of the Renaissance, albeit designed as late as the end of the 17C; its first floor is given over entirely to the **Minoritensaal** ⊙, one of the city's concert halls. The charming walnut rostrum of this former ceremonial refectory forms part of the design of the entrance doorway. The building also houses the **Diözesanmuseum** (Diocesan Museum).

Alte Galerie des Steiermärkischen Landesmuseums Joanneum ⊙ (**CDZ**) – The art gallery occupies the ground and second floors of the building. The **medieval art**★ section is particularly interesting, with works by Austrian masters of the 12C to 16C. On the **ground floor**: stained glass, the "Admont Madonna" from 1320, two Admont Pietàs from 1400 and 1420, a Virgin Mary in Glory from 1420, a votive painting of St Lambrecht from 1430, a *Martyrdom of St Thomas à Becket* by Michael Pacher from 1470-80, a large Mariazell altarpiece from 1518-22.

2nd floor: Renaissance, Mannerist and Baroque art: works by Jan Bruegel the Elder, Pieter Brueghel the Younger, Lucas Cranach the Elder, a *Naked Warrior* by Godl/Magt, paintings by Sofonisba Anguissola, Luca Cambiaso, Dosso and Battista Dossi. Austrian and German Baroque artists such as Johann Heinrich Schönfeld, Johann Michael Rottmayr, Josef Stammel, Franz Anton Maulbertsch, Paul Troger and Franz Christoph Janneck. There is also a sizeable collection of Baroque sketches in oil *(bozzetti)*.
The museum also organizes special exhibitions of its graphics collection.

Leechkirche (**DY**) – The university church of Maria am Leech is the oldest religious building in Graz. It was built between 1275 and 1293 by the Teutonic Order and bears a certain resemblance to the Sainte-Chapelle in Paris. The Early Gothic, many layered **west front**★ is crowned by a Virgin and Child on the tympanum, a work in Late Romanesque angular style. The **stained glass**★, which dates from 1330 and depicts various saints and the story of Christ's Passion, is of particular interest.
Excavation work in the church has revealed that this was a burial place in the 9C-8C BC for the Urnfield Culture. This tradition was also followed in the Hallstatt period (7C BC). At the beginning of the 13C a round Romanesque church was built on this site, which was destroyed at an early stage.

EXCURSIONS

★★ **Schloß Eggenberg** (**AX**) – *3.5km/2mi west. See Schloß EGGENBERG.*

★★ **Österreichisches Freilichtmuseum** (**Austrian Open-air Museum**) – *15km/9.5mi northwest via the Bruck-an-der-Mur road* (**AX**). *Leave the motorway at Gratkorn, cross the Mur, turn right after the railway and continue for 3km/2mi. Description under MURTAL.*

★ **Stift Rein** (**AX**) – *15km/9.5 mi northwest.*
Founded in 1129 by monks from the abbey at Ebrach in Germany, Rein is the oldest Cistercian abbey in Austria. Its buildings, dominated by the elegant Baroque tower, stand out against a background of wooded hills, including the 1 000m/3 300ft high Ploschkogel.
The abbey's Cistercian monks played an important cultural and commercial role in the early development of this part of Styria. Devastated by the Turks, it was fortified in the 15C, then remodelled in the Baroque style in the 18C.

★★ **Stiftskirche** ⊙ – It was a master builder from Graz, one Johann Georg Stengg, who presided over the transformation of the old Romanesque abbey church, which now has the rank of minor papal basilica. The alignment of the building was changed for reasons of convenience. A new façade, curvilinear in the extreme, resembles a violin in its subtle play of convex and concave forms. A characteristically Baroque trick is the organ topping the main pediment.
The interior, bathed in light, is a stage as much as a church, a splendid setting for the drama of the Mass, best viewed from the grand balconies swelling out above the side chapels of the nave. *Trompe-l'œil* effects abound in the exuberant and brightly coloured decor, the work of Josef Adam Mölck, contributing further to a theatricality hardly to be expected among the followers of St Bernard.
The painting on the main altar is by Kremser Schmidt.

Wallfahrtskirche Mariatrost – *7km/4mi east via road no 72* (**BX**). Austria has many of these great pilgrimage churches dedicated to the Virgin Mary standing on a prominent site just outside the city limits. Salzburg is proud of the sanctuary of Maria Plain, Linz is overlooked by Pöstlingberg, Klagenfurt venerates Maria Saal. Graz has Mariatrost, strikingly sited in its leafy suburban setting, easily identifiable by its twin towers resembling organ pipes. This was among the most ambitious of Baroque architectural projects, its aim being the exaltation of the Virgin Mary, comforter of humanity. Building began in 1714 under the direction of the architects Stengg, first Andreas, then Johann Georg. Inside, there are murals – much restored – painted between 1733 and 1754 by Lukas von Schramm and Johann Baptist Scheidt, a pulpit by Veit Königer (1730-31), and a fine organ, a work from Vorarlberg dating from 1993.

Schloß GREILLENSTEIN★

Niederösterreich

Michelin map 926 west of fold 11 – 1km/0.5mi north of Fuglau

Greillenstein Castle, with its austere façades and numerous windows, stands in an unspoilt stretch of country in the Waldviertel, to the north of the forests in the valley of the River Kamp.

The huge castle is laid out according to a square ground plan around a main courtyard relieved by a two-tiered arcaded gallery facing south. The Renaissance building was built between 1570 and 1590 on the ruins of an earlier fortress. A tall entrance tower crowned with four corner turrets dominates the castle. As Greillenstein has always been owned by the same family, many of the castle's original interior fittings have been preserved.

TOUR ⊙

The castle's perimeter – a balustrade with obelisks and fine sculptures – dates from the 17C and depicts an entire fable: how a raging lion is transformed into the most gentle of beasts, mirroring the triumph of good over evil. A splendid entrance gateway with rusticated columns and a projecting pediment leads into the attractive inner courtyard.

The courtyard balustrade and the six monumental vases were sculpted in stone after sketches by JB Fischer von Erlach. Standing in the inner courtyard, look up to the roof above the arcades with its Renaissance chimneys dating from 1590, each one different.

Registrar's Office – From the 16C onwards Greillenstein had jurisdiction over an area covering 14 local villages; the main administrative, fiscal and judicial matters were settled at the castle. The filing cabinets and pigeon holes containing contemporary documents have been preserved.

Courtroom – This baronial courtroom has been preserved in its original state, including the bar where the oath was taken. Minor local cases were heard here. In 1634 Ferdinand II also granted Greillenstein the powers of a higher court. Accordingly, serious cases could be heard, but no death sentence was ever passed.

Chapel – The chapel is well lit and roofed with a network of delicate pointed vaulting. The **Renaissance altar**★ is of an elegant and original design; the entablature, supported on four columns of imitation marble framing a painting of the crucifixion, gives the sanctuary an unusual solemnity.

When the Kuefstein family, the owners of Greillenstein Castle, converted from Protestantism to the Catholic faith, they kept the Protestant altar (1603) and placed it to the right of the new altar.

Turkish Room – This room contains a number of souvenirs of a member of the Kuefstein family who was appointed Ambassador to Turkey in 1628. During his two-year stay he succeeded in signing a peace treaty which established a ceasefire lasting 25 years.

Museum Schloß Greillenstein

Schloß Greillenstein

GROSSGLOCKNER-HOCHALPENSTRASSE★★★

Salzburg und Kärnten

Michelin map 926 folds 19 and 32

Like the Iseran pass in France and the Susten pass in Switzerland, the Großglockner route *(1)*, opened in 1935, heralded the age of modern Alpine roads designed specifically for motor traffic. The pass road, so vital to Austrian tourist traffic, is an international route linking Bavaria, the Tyrol and Salzburg with Venice via the Plöckenstraße and Dolomites, attracting 1.2 million users a year.
The promotion of tourism loomed large in the concept of this great highway, notably in the construction of two spurs; the first of these leads to the summit of the Edelweiß-Spitze, the second to the Franz-Josephs-Höhe with its view of the dazzling Pasterze glacier at the foot of the highest peak in the Austrian Alps, the Großglockner mountain itself (alt 3 797m/12 457ft). The first known description of the Großglockner, by the scientist Balthasar Haquet, dates from 1779. Celebrated in myth and legend, the mountain has long attracted crowds of visitors and climbers. The modern road follows in part the course of a much older mule track.

The mountain region around the Großglockner is an integral part of the **Hohe Tauern National Park**, 1 800km²/695sq mi in extent, designated particularly to protect the Alpine flora and fauna.

The Großglockner

FROM ZELL AM SEE TO HEILIGENBLUT *75km/47mi*

The **Großglockner Alpine Highway** *toll road is generally blocked by snow from early November to the beginning of May (the Edelweiß-Spitze and Franz-Josephs-Höhe are often snowed in longer).*

★ **Zell am See** – *See ZELL AM SEE.*

South of Zell am See the road to the Großglockner properly speaking begins at Bruck. It plunges into the **Fuschertal**, a valley whose austere setting and scanty sunshine have not encouraged people to settle there. In the east stand the dark foothills of the Schwarzkopf.
Between Fusch and Ferleiten the route, which is already more hilly, includes a short corniche section above a little wooded gorge, the **Bärenschlucht**. Beyond the gorge one begins to see the summits across the end of the valley, particularly the fine **Sonnenwelleck** group, rocky and jagged, and the Fuscherkarkopf, rounded and snow covered, standing to the right of the gap made by the Untere Pfandlscharte (alt 2 663m/8 737ft).

(1) For more detailed information consult the official map-guide Freytag "GroßglocknerHochalpenstraßen" (in German) at a scale of 1:50 000.

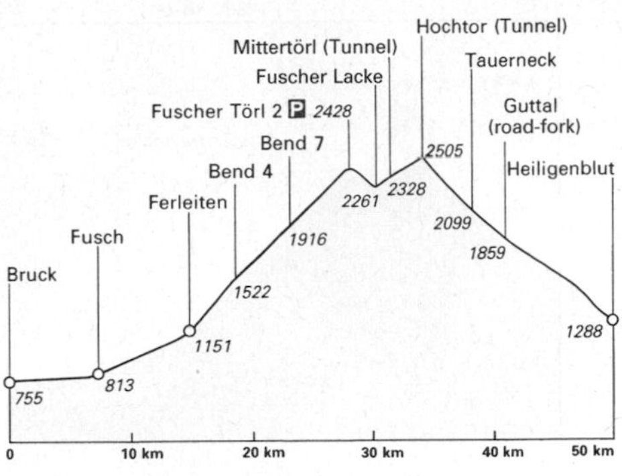

Further upstream the Walcherbach falls tumble down the opposite slope. From **Ferleiten** *(toll point)* to the Fuscher Törl the route continues with several hairpin bends along the east side of the valley. Here it has to climb some 1 300m/4 200ft - and flat sections are few. The first few miles *(hairpin bends nos 1 to 4)* are close to the Großes Wiesbachhorn and its 3 000m/10 000ft companions. Above the Piffkar ravine (alt 1 620m/5 315ft) the **views**★★ are magnificent towards the Sonnenwelleck group and the Fuscherkarkopf, at the foot of which lies a great natural amphitheatre, streaked with waterfalls, the Käfertal. The view from the Hochmais car park (alt 1 850m/6 070ft - *information panel)* is particularly impressive. The last larches disappear and the road continues as a corniche as far as Naßfeld bridges. From here it passes through a rocky wasteland known as the Witches' Kitchen (Hexenküche) and climbs across the basins of Naßfeld. About 2km/1 mi before the pass there is a botanical nature trail at an altitude of about 2 260m/7 415ft and the **Alpine Nature Museum**.

★ **Museum Alpine Naturschau** ⓥ - A botanical nature trial leads to the museum car park. The museum is devoted to Alpine ecology above the tree-line and gives a clear demonstration of the complex interrelations between flora and fauna. Before walking round the museum's various displays, visitors should watch a slide show called "Voyage into the Arctic" *(18min)* on the ground floor, which gives a good introduction to the nature of the Alpine region. The museum is very well designed as an educational exhibition.

★★ **Edelweißspitze** - Alt 2 577m/8 455ft. *No access for coaches. Very steep road.* From the observation tower, the **panorama** is made especially attractive by the heights enclosing the Fuschertal to the west, the Brennkogel across to the Großes Wiesbachhorn. The peak of the Großglockner can be seen just behind the Sonnenwelleck. To the east, the Goldberg group is more conspicuous for its covering of snow than for its height. Due north the Fuschertal gap opens up a view of the Zell Lake, the chalky massifs of the Loferer and the Leoganger Steinberge, and still further to the right, the Steinernes Meer.

★ **Fuscher Törl** - Alt 2 428m/7 964ft. The road builders used this "little gate" (Törlein) to form a panoramic bend. Leave the car in the Fuscher Törl 2 car park. The road between the Fuscher Törl and the Hochtor tunnel passes through a somewhat sinister and stony landscape. As the roadway could not pass directly from the Fusch to the Möll valleys - the passes here being blocked by glaciers - the engineers overcame the difficulty by suspending the road above the Seidelwinkl Valley, one of the branches of the adjacent Rauris Valley. The views are impressive looking east towards the jagged heights of the Goldberg.

Fuscher Lacke - Alt 2 262m/7 422ft. An information centre here contains an informative display on the construction of the Großglockner Alpine road. A path leads round the lake for those wishing to stretch their legs.

Hochtor - The road reaches its highest point (2 505m/8 218ft) at the north end of the tunnel pierced under the pass (alt 2 575m/8 448ft). This is also the boundary between Salzburg and Carinthia. From the south exit there is an open view of the Schober massif.
The winding descent from the Hochtor passes through Alpine pastures within view of the Schober massif, which forms a crown round the Gößnitz Valley.
At the Tauerneck bend the sharp peak of the Großglockner rises behind the Wasserradkopf foothills and there is a view down into the Heiligenblut basin.
From the Guttal ravine, turn right onto the "Glacier Road" (Gletscherstraße) leading to Franz-Josephs-Höhe.
During the holiday season and fine weather there can be delays on the trip up to Franz-Josephs-Höhe, as the capacity of the car parks is exceeded. In this case, visitors will be directed to overflow car parks from where there is a shuttle service to Franz-Josephs-Höhe.

Schöneck - Alt 1 958m/6 424ft. An excellent bird's-eye view of Heiligenblut.

Wunderwelt Glocknerwiesen - Between the inn at Schöneck and the Glocknerhaus lie the Pockhorner Alpine meadows with their wonderful variety of unique plantlife. A nature display and botanical trail give an overview of Alpine flora and insects.

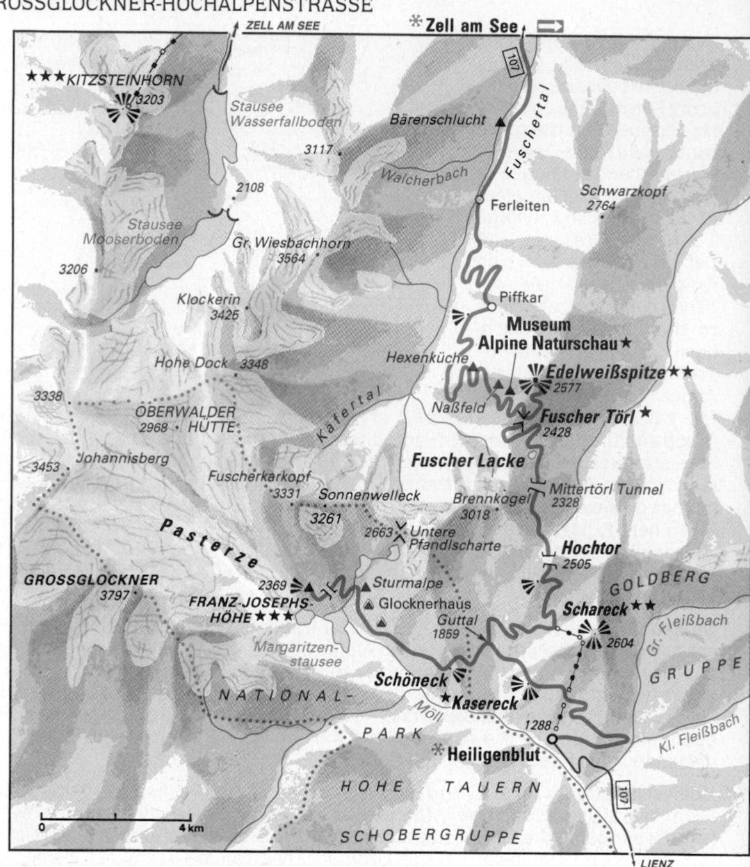

As the Großglockner gets nearer, the **view★★**, soon extending to the tongue of the Pasterze glacier, becomes increasingly impressive. From the Glocknerhaus, the Pasterze glacier path branches off to the left, leading to the Freiwandeck on Franz-Josephs-Höhe itself (3hr) or the Sternzeichenplatz (1hr 30min).

The road leads up to the terrace of the Franz-Josephs-Höhe in another series of hairpin bends in the Sturmalpe combe. The artificial Lake Margaritze is retained below the tongue of the glacier by two dams bedded on a rock bar. The reservoir is part of the Glockner-Kaprun, an impressively vast, hydroelectric scheme *(see KAPRUN)*.

★★★ **Franz-Josephs-Höhe** – In summer the Kaiser Franz-Josephs-Haus is the starting point for hikes and climbing tours in the Großglockner massif.

The "Glacier Road" ends here in a long panoramic terrace, partly hewn in the rock. Go along it, if possible, to the last platform, the Freiwandeck, at an altitude of 2 369m/7 772ft. At the foot of the Großglockner, buttressed by shining ice and sharp ridges, the magnificent 10km/6mi flow of the **Pasterze glacier** ⏲ begins, to which a funicular operates. The tiny figures of tourists can be seen moving around on the glacier far below. Further up, at the foot of the Johannisberg ice cap, a spur has produced the effect of an eddy, creating a semblance of fluidity.

From Freiwandeck the Panoramaweg Kaiserstein, laid out as a botanical trail, leads to the **Swarovski observation point**. The glass tower is equipped with telescopes *(use is free of charge)* so that visitors can get a close-up view of the surrounding mountain scenery.

From Franz-Josephs-Höhe, trace the route to the Guttal fork and turn right there towards Heiligenblut.

Opposite the wooded opening of the Gößnitz Valley there is a cascade.

★ **Kasereck** – Alt 1 913m/6 276ft. Halt on this grassy spur, which has **views** of the Großglockner and the Heiligenblut basin. There is a cheesemaking establishment open to the public.

On the drive down to Heiligenblut note the unusual wooden grain dryers in the form of grilles (known locally as "harps"). The last hairpin bend, curving above the Fleiß Valley, reveals the Sonnblick (alt 3 105m/10 187ft). A little further on there is the famous view of the church of Heiligenblut, a slender stone spike standing out against the background of the far-off Großglockner.

✻ **Heiligenblut** – *See HEILIGENBLUT.*

GURGLER TAL★★

Tirol

Michelin map 926 fold 29 – Local map see ÖTZTAL

The Gurgl valley, which branches off the **upper valley of the Ötz**★★ *(see ÖTZTAL)*, must number among the most remarkable holiday destinations in the Austrian Tyrol. Its exceptionally beautiful **setting**★★ makes it a favourite location for ramblers and hikers.

Accommodation (primarily hotels and guesthouses in the upper comfort quality range) is to be found in Obergurgl-Hochgurgl: **Obergurgl**✻ (alt 1 793-1 930m/5 883-6 332ft), which is particularly pretty with its **view**★ of the 20 surrounding mountains all above 3 000m/10 000ft, such as Hohe Wilde or Hangerer; and the popular winter sports resort **Hochgurgl**✻ (alt 2 150m/7 054ft), Austria's highest-lying village with a church and a winter sports area up to 3 080m/10 105ft.

Ski slopes – These cover 110km/68mi of pistes of varying degrees of difficulty at altitudes ranging from 1 800m/5 906ft to 3 082m/10 112ft. They are equipped with 23 ski lifts. The high altitude guarantees snow cover from November to May. There are 12km/7.5mi of cross-country ski runs.

★★ **Hohe Mut** ⏲ – Alt 2 653m/8 704ft. *Allow 1hr there and back. Take the chair-lift up in two stages.*

There is a splendid **panorama**★★ of the Rotmoosferner and Gaisbergferner glaciers to the southeast and of the Manigenbach to the west.

Listed below are several easy walks, which can be combined to make up a pleasant day's outing.

★★ **Walk from the Hohe Mut to the Schönwieshütte** – *400m/1 300ft drop in altitude.* Those in a hurry can walk straight to the Schönwies refuge in about 1hr. It is preferable, however, to follow along the foot of the cliff to the foot of the **Rotmoosferner glacier**★★ and then carry on along the banks of the Gebirgsbach in the valley floor. The path leads through a majestic, captivating **Alpine setting**, dominated by the Liebenerspitze (alt 3 400m/11 155ft) and Seelenkogel (alt 3 470m/11 385ft) summits. From the refuge there is a view of the Gampleskogel peak.

Those who do not wish to take the chair-lift to the top of the Hohe Mut can reach the refuge in about 1hr along a wide footpath from Obergurgl.

★ **Around the Schönwieshütte** – *Allow 1hr 30min there and back.* Two easy detours are recommended from the refuge. Go towards the Langtalereckhütte as far as the so-called **Gurgler Alm** (alt 2 252m/7 388ft), from where there is a **view**★ of the three glaciers higher up with the Schalfkogel (alt 3 540m/11 614ft) in centre picture.

Return the way you came and turn left shortly before the refuge towards the Schönwieskopf (alt 2 324m/7 625ft). From the summit, a wide **panorama**★ stretches away over the valley.

★ **Walk from the Schönwieshütte through the Zirbenwald to Obergurgl** – *1hr 15min on foot, dropping 330m/1 080ft in altitude. This is a pleasant walk through pretty countryside, with numerous inviting benches along the route.*

From the refuge take a wide footpath towards Obergurgl. Shortly after setting out turn left and take a steep path downhill, waymarked in blue. Next, the path leads past the impressive **Rotmoos waterfall**★. Take the left fork, following a path which leads into the woods and along the valley floor. It is not unusual to catch sight of chamois in this area. There is a good view of Obergurgl and Hochgurgl at the end of the path.

GURK★★

Kärnten

Michelin map 926 fold 35

A convent is believed to have been founded here originally by Countess Hemma of Friesach-Zeltschach in 1043. However, Gebhard Archbishop of Salzburg dissolved this in 1072 and made Gurk the seat of his newly founded suffragan diocese in Carinthia. Due to the Investiture Controversy, a cathedral chapter was not established here until 1123. The Augustinian canons remained in this secluded valley in north Carinthia until 1787, when the diocese was transferred to Klagenfurt. The convent has been run by Salvatorians since 1932.

The cathedral, Austria's most important Romanesque building, remained almost forgotten until the mid 19C, when a Prussian curator brought it once more into the public eye.

R. Chéret/MICHELIN

CATHEDRAL (DOM)

The High Romanesque cathedral was built between 1140 and 1200 under Prince-Bishop Roman I, Councillor to Frederick Barbarossa. Baroque gemel windows - the much smaller round-arched Romanesque windows can now only be seen on the interior of the north tower - and onion domes were added to both towers in 1680.

After looking at the relatively plain façade and the old charnel house to the right of it, skirt the south side, going through the graveyard, to admire the limestone masonry, stained faint reddish brown by age and the iron framework, and elegant round arched frieze of the nave. The transept frieze additionally features fine interlacing. The influence of Lombard craftsmen is evident in the exterior decoration of the east end with its three apsidal chapels. The middle chapel is adorned with a beautifully crafted **lion-basilica relief★** dating from 1175, above the stepped and splayed axial window.

Return to the front porch.

Porches - The exterior wall of the porch was built in the Gothic period, but inside there is some stained glass dating from 1340, which has been heavily restored, along with Gothic **frescoes★** from the same period. The mural paintings on the north wall depict scenes from the Old and those on the south from the New Testament.
The pillars, arches and capitals of the Romanesque **west door★★** (c 1200) with its fine stepped splaying are richly decorated with foliage motifs. The carved and painted medallions in the upper third of the door panels date from 1220.

Interior ⏲ - It is immediately evident upon entering that many styles have contributed to this building: the Romanesque triple-nave pillared basilica is surmounted by Gothic net vaulting, the frescoes are from the Gothic and Renaissance periods, while the furnishings are predominantly Baroque.
The main and subsidiary apses are closed off by altarpieces. Before studying the furnishings and decor of the church more closely, turn and look at the architecture of the narrow vestibule (Innere Vorhalle): the semicircular engaged pilasters have fine Romanesque capitals with palm branches and foliage.

(1) Hemma reliquary, containing a ring and a pendant thought to have belonged to the saint: a fine testimony to the goldsmith's craft, in the form of a tree, covered with precious stones (1955).

(2) Samson doorway: the **tympanum★** shows Samson slaying the lion. This is fine piece of Romanesque sculpture (1200) was once part of the transept doorway.

(3) and **(8)**: **Carved panels★** (16C) vividly depicting scenes from the life of St Hemma, commissioned before 1508.

(4) A gigantic wall painting of St Christopher (1250). The doorway to the left with its richly decorated ogee arch was built in 1445. The small oratorium above it was added by Probst von Thurn in 1678.

(5) High Altar★★ (1626-32), entirely decorated in gold, with full-size, strikingly realistic figures (72 statues, 82 angels' heads), and the four Evangelists at pedestal level with the Church Fathers above them. The central focus is the Madonna in Glory floating up to the Trinity. This whole work filling the entire breadth and height of the apse is a masterpiece by Michael Hönel from Pirna in Saxony, created between 1626 and 1632.
During Lent the altar is shrouded by a **Fastentuch★** ⏲ (Lenten veil, 1458). This custom was abolished almost everywhere at the end of the Middle Ages. The exquisitely beautiful veil at Gurk is 9m/30ft square, and is entirely covered with

99 scenes from the Old and New Testaments. It was completed in 1458 by Master Konrad of Friesach and is the oldest and largest Lenten veil in Carinthia. *(The Lenten veil can be seen as part of a guided tour.)*

(**6**) **Choir stalls** (1680): these richly and decoratively carved stalls are the work of local craftsmen. Each separate place, crowned with the head of a cherub, is decorated with charming painted floral motifs.

(**7**) Gothic murals (c 1390): these were uncovered at the beginning of the 20C and illustrate the conversion of St Paul and Christ enthroned as Judge of the World, surrounded by the Twenty Four Elders of the Apocalypse as narrated by St John the Divine. The donors can be seen at the foot of Christ's throne with their nine children.

(**8**) See (**3**) above.

(**9**) Altar of the Holy Cross (1741), with a **Pietà**★ cast in lead by Georg Raphael Donner, his last work. The artist has created a well-rounded and very affecting work, using material, form and expression to their best advantage.

(**10**) **Baroque pulpit**★ (1740), one of the most inspired works of the Counter Reformation, designed by Giuseppe and Antonio Galli Bibiena who had already earned themselves a high reputation in Vienna as set designers. The iconography is fully in keeping with the ideas of the Counter Reformation, taking as its subject the triumph of the Church and of Truth. Allegories of the Church, Faith and Hope adorn the sounding board, from which a heretic is in the process of falling to his doom. The lead reliefs around the body of the pulpit are the work of Georg Raphael Donner.

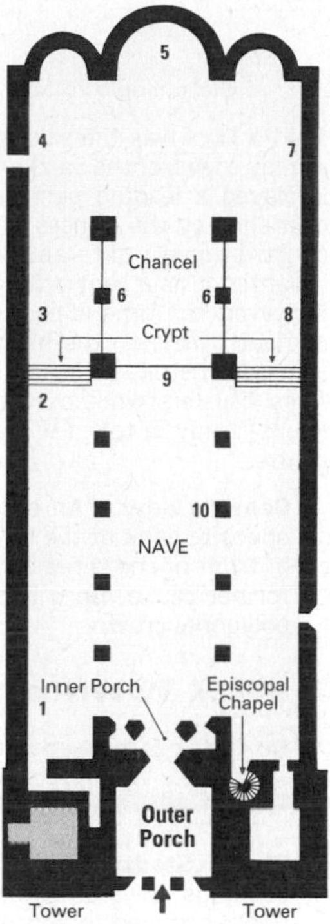

★★ **Crypt** – *(Can only be visited as part of a guided tour.)* A subdued half-light greets visitors to the crypt, which was completed in 1174. This masterpiece of the Romanesque style in the east Alps reflects both Lombard and Rhenish influence. It is supported on 96 single and two pairs of twin marble pillars which seem to form a mysterious underground forest, sheltering the stone sarcophagus of St Hemma, patron of Carinthia. The relics of the saint, who died in 1045 and was sanctified in 1938, were kept in the crypt from 1174. The present tomb of St Hemma was made in 1720-21 of red marble. It rests on three Romanesque support pillars with marble heads. The sculpture group at the top by Antonio Corradini is arrestingly delicate. Note in particular the finely executed face of the Allegory of Faith seen through its veil (right-hand statue).

Episcopal Chapel – *(Can only be visited as part of a guided tour.)* The chapel is built into the gallery behind the façade and displays an impressive series of Romanesque **murals**★★ dating from c 1260 and preserved in their original state. The lively angular style is combined with generous composition and line. The general theme, which gives the key to the symbolic meaning of the various scenes, will be found in the Latin inscription over the altar niche: "Here shines in splendour the throne of the great King and of the Lamb." The throne is a symbol for the Virgin Mary by reference to the throne of her predecessor, King Solomon, and is here shown opposite the Transfiguration of Christ. The vaults of the chapel, one depicting the Garden of Eden, the other a celestial Jerusalem, show an admirable adaptation of ornament to architecture.

The round window on the west wall features stained glass that is contemporary with the frescoes and depicts the Descent from the Cross. This is Austria's earliest stained glass in the angular style.

Before leaving Gurk look at the large group of 15C and 17C priory buildings once occupied by the cathedral canons.

EXCURSION

Straßburg – This small town within sight of Gurk is dominated by its **castle**, once the episcopal palace. The bishops of Gurk had a residence built here as early as 1147, which they used until 1780, adding and renewing parts of it substantially over the centuries. The present castle predominantly bears the stamp of the Baroque and is grouped around a charming courtyard on two levels. Inside the castle is a fine collection on **folklore** which gives a detailed insight into peasant life in Carinthia, and a museum on **hunting**.

HALL IN TIROL★

Tirol

Population 12 620

Michelin map 926 fold 30 – Local map see INNSBRUCK – Alt 581m/1 906ft

Hall in Tirol was the salt town of the Inn Valley. During the Middle Ages, like the mining towns of the Salzkammergut in Upper Austria or the archbishops in Salzburg, it played a leading part in the economic life of the country and was especially cherished by the princes of the Tyrol. From 1303 onwards these granted it liberal constitutional rights and, by comparison with their austere court at Innsbruck, regarded it as a centre for pleasure and amusement.
However, the time is past when Hall marked the starting point of a large volume of river traffic on the Inn and the end of their journey upstream for the rafts of logs which stoked the salt boilers. Hall is still wrapped in the charm of the Middle Ages. This erstwhile mint town, with its picturesque old town centre, nonetheless keeps firmly in touch with the present; it is a highly active cultural and economic centre.

★ **General view** – An excellent general view of the town may be had from the opposite bank of the Inn *(under the motorway and up the minor road to Tulfes).* In front of the three belfries of the Upper Town can be seen the remains of the former castle, Burg Hasegg, and the **Münzerturm** (Mint Tower) with its curious polygonal crown.

★ UPPER TOWN (OBERE STADT)

No traffic is allowed in the Upper Town on Saturday mornings.

Start from the Unterer Stadtplatz (**24**)*, an open space formed by the road from Innsbruck to Vienna. Take the Langer Graben up to the Oberer Stadtplatz.*

Oberer Stadtplatz – This irregular open space is surrounded by interesting buildings. Several picturesque streets, lined with façades with oriels on several floors grouped together behind grilles, also radiate from the square.

★ **Stadtpfarrkirche (A)** – The parish church was built at the end of the 13C, but by the early 14C it was already in need of enlargement. The chancel dates from this period. During 1420 to 1437, Hanns Sewer, the master builder from Hall, began an ambitious project to extend the building. He faced a hard task, however, as the church, like the rest of the town, stands on an enormous conical pile of debris, which drops sheer away from the south side of the church. As a result, it was only possible to extend the building to the north, which accounts for the asymmetry which strikes visitors entering the generously proportioned hall-church with its triple nave.
In the 17C and 18C, the influence of the Baroque made itself felt on the church **interior**, which boasts ceiling paintings by Joseph Adam von Mölck (1752) and a high altar adorned with a painting by Quellini, a pupil of Rubens. The **Waldaufkapelle** (late 15C) in the north transept houses a Late Gothic figure of the Virgin Mary from the circle of Michael Pacher, as well as numerous sumptuously decorated reliquaries.

HALL IN TIROL

Agramsgasse	2
Eugenstraße	3
Guarinonigasse	4
Krippgasse	5
Langer Graben	7
Milserstraße	8
Rosengasse	13
Salvatorgasse	14
Scheidensteinstraße	15
Schulgasse	16
Schweighofferstiege	17
Speckbacherstraße	18
Stiftsplatz	20
Unterer Stadtplatz	24
Wallpachgasse	25

Rathaus	R
Stadtpfarrkirche	A

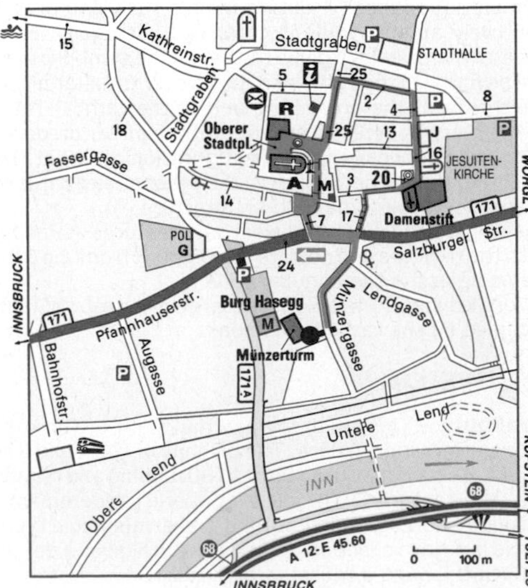

Rathaus (R) – The town hall is distinguished by its large hipped roof. Once the town fortress – note the tin-clad wall – it consists of two main parts: that to the east has a great stone doorway, which dates from the Renaissance; that to the west is the royal residence, which was donated to the town by Duke Leopold IV in 1406. The council chamber is particularly handsome, with a beamed ceiling dating from 1451.

Walk up the Wallpachgasse (**25**) for a clear view of the Bettelwurfkette mountains (Karwendel massif).

*Follow the Agramgasse (**2**), the Quarinongasse (**12**) and the Schulgasse (**16**) to the Stiftsplatz.*

Stiftsplatz (20) – Contrasting with the fantasy of the medieval town, the classical arrangement of this square is entirely harmonious, bounded as it is on the east by the sober façades of the former college and church of the Jesuits (transformed into a concert hall), and on the south by those of the Damenstift (former convent for noble ladies).

Damenstift – Archduchess Magdalena, the sister of Archduke Ferdinand II, founded this ladies' abbey in 1567-69. The stuccowork and main doorway date from 1691. The **west front**★ with its four full-length fluted pilasters is a fine example of the transition from the Renaissance to the Baroque style.

*Return to the Unterer Stadtplatz via the Eugenstraße (**3**) and the Schweigerhofstiege steps (**17**) to the left. Follow the Münzergasse to Burg Hasegg.*

Burg Hasegg ⏲ – Dominated by its famous tower, the castle originated as a strong point controlling river traffic. It took on its historical importance in 1567, when the rulers of Tyrol transferred their mint here. The most famous coin produced in Hall was the **Haller Silbertaler** (silver dollar), accepted all over Europe until the early 19C. In 1975 the **mint** started production again and regularly produces commemorative coins; it is open to the public.

Also in the castle is the **Stadtmuseum** ⏲ with a rich collection of exhibits on the history of the town.

From the top of the **Münzerturm** *(200 steps)* there is a splendid view of the town and the impressive mountain range to the north with the Bettelwurf peak (alt 2 726m/8 944ft).

Return to the Unterer Stadtplatz.

HALLSTATT★★

Oberösterreich

Population 1 130

Michelin map 926 fold 21 – Local map see SALZKAMMERGUT

Alt 511m/1 677ft

The village of Hallstatt clings to the steep slope of a foothill of the Dachstein and takes its name from the **lake**★★, the Hallstätter See, into whose dark waters the slope dips. Hallstatt provides a picture of romantic Austria with streets so narrow and so steep that it has become customary for the popular Corpus Christi procession to take place on the lake in boats.

In 1998 the region around Hallstatt (the Dachstein range an central Salzkammergut) was declared a UNESCO world heritage site.

PATRIMONIO MUNDIAL · WORLD HERITAGE · PATRIMOINE MONDIAL

A cradle of civilization – The salt mines in the neighbouring mountains have been exploited since the Neolithic Era. Although mining began in 3000 BC on a local scale, during the first millennium BC it developed into a European enterprise; there is proof that the salt was distributed by the trade routes as far as the Baltic in the north and the Mediterranean in the south. It was their iron and bronze tools that enabled the miners of Hallstatt to become masters of the art of salt extraction. So many traces of salt mining have been found in the vicinity of Hallstatt (excavation of 2 000 graves) that the name has been given to the **Hallstatt Period** (1000-500 BC), which was marked by the development of iron metallurgy and Celtic immigration into Gaul. Hallstatt artefacts are displayed in the local prehistoric museum, **Prähistorisches Museum** ⏲, in the Natural History Museum in Vienna and in the collection of antiquities at Schloß Eggenberg near Graz.

The salt mines, **Salzbergwerk** ⏲, are the oldest in the world. The Celts began extracting salt from this mountain over 3 000 years ago. The salt mines are still being worked and the galleries may be visited to gain an insight into modern salt-mining technology and the history of this industry. *(Allow 3hr for this excursion taking the funicular from Lahn.)*

H.A. Jahn/VIENNASLIDE

Hallstatt

SIGHTS

Leave the car on one of the **viewing terraces**★ constructed above the town at the halfway point on the underground one-way bypass (the north-south terrace is open air; the south-north terrace is covered). Go down the steps marked "Abgang zur Stadt" and turn left into the pretty street leading up to the church (Kirchenweg).

Pfarrkirche – In the romantic **setting**★★ of its churchyard bordering the lake, this massive building of the late 15C is flanked by a squat tower whose peculiar roof, with its overhanging eaves, suggests some Chinese building, in contrast with the pointed steeple of the Protestant church built on the lakeshore in the 19C.
Inside, the hall-type nave and chancel are double, with star vaulting, bearing witness to the taste for twin naves which became fashionable in the mountain districts of Austria at the end of the Gothic period. The large **altarpiece**★ on the high altar, presented by a rich *Salzfertiger* (salt merchant), represents the Virgin between St Barbara and St Catherine *(centre panel)*. It was painted between 1505 and 1515.

St. Michaelskapelle – *North of the church, beyond the tiny cemetery.* The lower storey of this Gothic church houses the parish charnel house, in use since 1600 as the cemetery is so small. Of the 1 200 skulls contained here, 700 are inscribed with the date of death, the age, the profession etc of their previous occupants and painted with motifs such as roses, laurel, ivy or oak leaves.

Return and go down the Kirchenweg; turn right after the covered passage.

Heimatmuseum ⓥ – The local museum is in a picturesque house abutting on the rock and contains collections of folklore and history.

Return to the lower town in order to take a walk along the lakeshore; and then to the car by way of the Kirchenweg and the stairs leading to the viewpoint terraces.

HEILIGENBLUT※

Kärnten

Population 1 260

Michelin map 926 fold 32 – Local map see GROSSGLOCKNER HOCHALPENSTRASSE – Alt 1 288m/4 226ft

Heiligenblut, at the foot of the south slope of the Großglockner, is a return to the bustle of civilization for the tourist who has just traversed the lonely upper mountains.
The **site**★ of the church is picturesque; the slim building with its steeple in silhouette against the Großglockner.

※ **Ski slopes** – These stretch between the Schareck, Gjaidtroghöhe and Viehbühel peaks at altitudes from 1 300m/4 265ft to 2 912m/9 554ft. Keen skiers will find 14 ski lifts and 55km/34mi of pistes with a variety of descents, well laid out through the rugged, treeless mountain landscape. In spite of the high altitude, snow conditions can begin to deteriorate from as early as March.

★ **Church** ⏲ – The church was built on a fine site amid magnificent scenery in the 15C by the monks of Admont, to perpetuate their devotion to a relic of the Holy Blood (Heiliges Blut). The twin-aisled crypt contains the tomb of Briccius, an officer of the Imperial Court of Byzantium, who is said to have brought the precious substance there in the 10C. The chancel, built in 1430, and the nave, completed in 1483, are both roofed in the Late Gothic tradition with network and star vaulting. The side galleries of the nave were necessary to accommodate the numerous pilgrims.
Particularly outstanding examples among the church's furnishings include the great **altarpiece**★ on the high altar (1520), attributed to the school of Michael Pacher, and the ornately sculpted Gothic canopy (1496) carved in pale sandstone. Opposite the church is the Hohe Tauern national park **information point** with an interesting little exhibition on the "Großglockner adventure".

★★ **Schareck** ⏲ – Alt 2 604m/8 543ft. *Cable-car ascent in two stages, then 10min on foot to the summit (marked by a cross).*
From the Schareck there is an impressive **panorama**★★ encompassing 40 peaks towering to 3 000m/10 000ft, with the pyramidal Schildberg and the Großglockner range to the west, and to the east the Gjaidtrog, the highest point of the ski slopes, with the Hocharn to its left.

Stift HEILIGENKREUZ★

Niederösterreich

Michelin map 926 fold 25 – Local map see WIENERWALD

The abbey of Heiligenkreuz was founded by the Babenberg Margrave Leopold III, known as the Holy, who wanted to create here a burial place for his dynasty. At the instigation of his son, Otto von Freising, who had joined the Cistercian Order, he brought 12 monks from Morimond, a daughter foundation of Cîteaux *(see below)* in France, who laid the foundation stone on 11 September 1133. The abbey owes its name to a relic of the Holy Cross presented to it in the 12C by Duke Leopold V.

The community has remained under the rule of the Cistercian order since its foundation and is still active today. It runs its own college of philosophy and theology for student priests. Its economy is based on agriculture, forestry, winemaking and tourism.

TOUR ⏲

Although the foundations date from the 12C, most of the buildings with the exception of the church and the cloister are from the 17C. In the abbey courtyard stands the **Trinity Column** by the Venetian Giovanni Giuliani (1663-1744), who also created a number of other works for Heiligenkreuz.

★ **Stiftskirche** – The façade of the abbey church is Romanesque, and is typically Cistercian with its three windows and lack of a tower. The nave is Late Romanesque in style, completed in 1187, while the Gothic hall chancel was added just a century later. Its fittings date from the 19C. The neo-Gothic altar, behind which is a tabernacle containing the relic of the Cross, is surmounted by a modern

The Cistercian Order

This reforming Benedictine Order took its name from the monastery of Cîteaux in France, which was founded by Robert of Molesmes in 1098. Under Bernard of Clairvaux the order grew rapidly, and by his death in 1153 there were already more than 350 religious foundations throughout Europe. St Bernard forbade the levying of tithes, as well as the acquisition or receiving of land, and encouraged precise observance of the strict Benedictine rules.
Cistercian architecture also follows these strict principles. The churches are simple and without decoration; there is no bell-tower, only a ridge turret, and no coloured glass, only *grisaille* painting being allowed. All the greater was the care taken over the design and execution of the buildings, whose beauty is in their harmonious proportions and the purity of their lines. The initial austerity of Cistercian architecture mellowed over the centuries, with the result that pictures and statues are now to be seen in Cistercian churches.
The order still remains true to the *charta caritatis* promulgated in 1115, and has 300 monasteries and convents all over the world.

copy of a Greek Byzantine cross. The other furnishings are Baroque in style, including fine **choir stalls** by Giuliani with busts of Cistercian saints and a Descent from the Cross and Apparition of St Bernard by Johann Michael Rottmayr.

Cloister – The cloister adjoining the south side of the church dates from the 13C. The stylistic development during its construction is clearly visible from a comparison of the Romanesque arches of the north side and the Gothic arches of the south side. Two sculpture groups by Giuliani attract attention, a *Washing of the Feet* group and *The Sinner anointing the feet of Jesus*. On the south side is the nine-sided fountain room (late 13C) with fine tracery and a Renaissance basin for the ablutions. The grey-black medieval **stained-glass windows** show members of the Babenberg dynasty.

Annakapelle (St Anne's Chapel) – The now Baroque chapel was used in the Middle Ages as a library where the liturgical books were kept. Since the word was considered the best way of spreading the faith, the rooms in which the books were stored were called the "Armarium" (weaponry).

Chapter-house – The square room in which the abbots were elected and the novices clothed in the habit of the order, and the Benedictine rules were read, also houses the tombs of the Babenbergs. All the members of the family are shown in murals, and the most magnificent tomb, with a fully sculpted lid, is that of Friedrich II, damaged during the Turkish invasions.

R. Chéret/MICHELIN

Detail of a sacristy cupboard, Heiligenkreuz

Totenkapelle (Chapel of the Dead) – In the former *parlatorium*, the only room in which speaking was allowed, the monks are now laid out before burial. Giuliani was responsible for the decoration of the chapel. The Dancing Skeletons might appear somewhat macabre, but they nonetheless represent the Christian hope that death does not mean the end and is therefore robbed of its power.

Fraterie – This was the monks' workshop in the Middle Ages. Part of the original 13C painted decor is still visible.

Sacristy – The sacristy is reached by crossing a small courtyard. The attractively decorated room has an old lavabo recess, and is 18C in style, even with some Rococo touches. The four splendid **sacristy cupboards** were made by lay brothers in the early 19C, with exceptionally fine marquetry as proof of their artistry.

In the small village cemetery is to be found the grave of Mary Vetsera (*see MAYERLING*), whose gravestone bears the inscription: "Man springs up like a flower, only to be broken." Since her death certificate gave the cause of death as suicide, Mary Vetsera was buried at Heiligenblut in great secrecy at dead of night.

Schloß HERBERSTEIN★

Steiermark

Michelin map 926 folds 24 and 37

The fortress of Herberstein is perched on a rocky spur, surrounded on three sides by the course of the Feistritz, in the middle of a rugged gorge. Its origins date back to over 700 years ago. After the initial building was completed in the 13C, numerous modifications and extensions were carried out until the 17C, resulting in the final magnificent palace compound with its elaborate layout. The Gothic, Renaissance and Baroque styles have left their mark on the building in the form of architectural features typical of each period. In this way, Herberstein retraces very vividly cultural evolution from the early Middle Ages up to modern times.

The history of the Herberstein family, which has occupied the castle without a break from 1290 to the present, is intricately linked with that of the building itself.

TOUR ⊙

The walk from the car park to the castle *(15min on foot, or take the transport provided, "Tikiba-Express")* provides a good view of the church and presbytery in St. Johann-bei-Herberstein, formerly part of an Augustinian abbey.

The castle can be visited as part of a tour of "Herberstein in times past", which includes some of the oldest parts of the building. The historical exhibition on "Life in the castle" illustrates the life of the Count of Herberstein at the beginning of the 20C.

Tier- und Naturpark ⊙ – The zoo at Herberstein has a history dating back to the 17C. It is home to animals from five continents, including grey and polar wolves which inhabit special subterranean galleries where they can be watched through viewing panels. Feeding time for the wolves, cheetahs, pumas and monkeys proves popular with visitors as well as the animals themselves.

Historical gardens – These were restored in 1997 following old designs and a picture dating from 1681. In the centre of the park stands the rose pavilion with a fountain of youth. The geometrically arranged beds with various predominating colours are supposed to symbolise different times of the day and types of human temperament. The "multimedia space" in the Siegmund garden forms a bridge between old and new.

Tikiba-Kinderland – Here younger visitors to Herberstein will find a climbing frame, a mini-zoo with animals that can be stroked and various other entertainment specially developed with them in mind. The exotic-sounding name is derived from the German words for animal, child and tree (**Ti**er, **Ki**nd, **Ba**um). There is also a café-restaurant serving snacks and light refreshment.

Burg HOCHOSTERWITZ★

Kärnten

Michelin map 926 fold 35

9km/6mi east of St. Veit an der Glan – Local map see ST. VEIT AN DER GLAN

Hochosterwitz Fortress occupies a spectacular **site**★★ above the St. Veit an der Glan basin and on the border of the Zollfeld, rated as the cradle of Carinthia. The distinctive rounded form of the limestone outcrop on which the fortress stands, rising to 150m/490ft above the surrounding countryside, as well as the impressive outline of the fortress and its defence works can be seen from several miles off.

Documented for the first time in 1200, the castle remained in the hands of the lords of Osterwitz until 1478. In 1541 it was passed to the Khevenhüller family initially as a security, until Georg Khevenhüller was finally able to purchase it from Archduke Karl in 1571.

Georg Khevenhüller was Chief Equerry and Counsellor to emperors Ferdinand I, Maximilian II and Rudolf II, besides being Governor of Carinthia. As the threat of Turkish invasion was omnipresent in the 16C – he had fought against them himself in Styria and Hungary – Georg Khevenhüller invested considerable sums between 1571 and 1586 to convert the castle into a fortress. He was also the person responsible for ensuring that it should remain in the hands of his family in perpetuity. It was not always easy to comply with his orders as the counts and later princes of Khevenhüller converted to Protestantism and many of Georg's descendants were forced into exile during the Counter Reformation. Despite setbacks over the centuries, however, the fortress still remains in the hands of the Khevenhüller family.

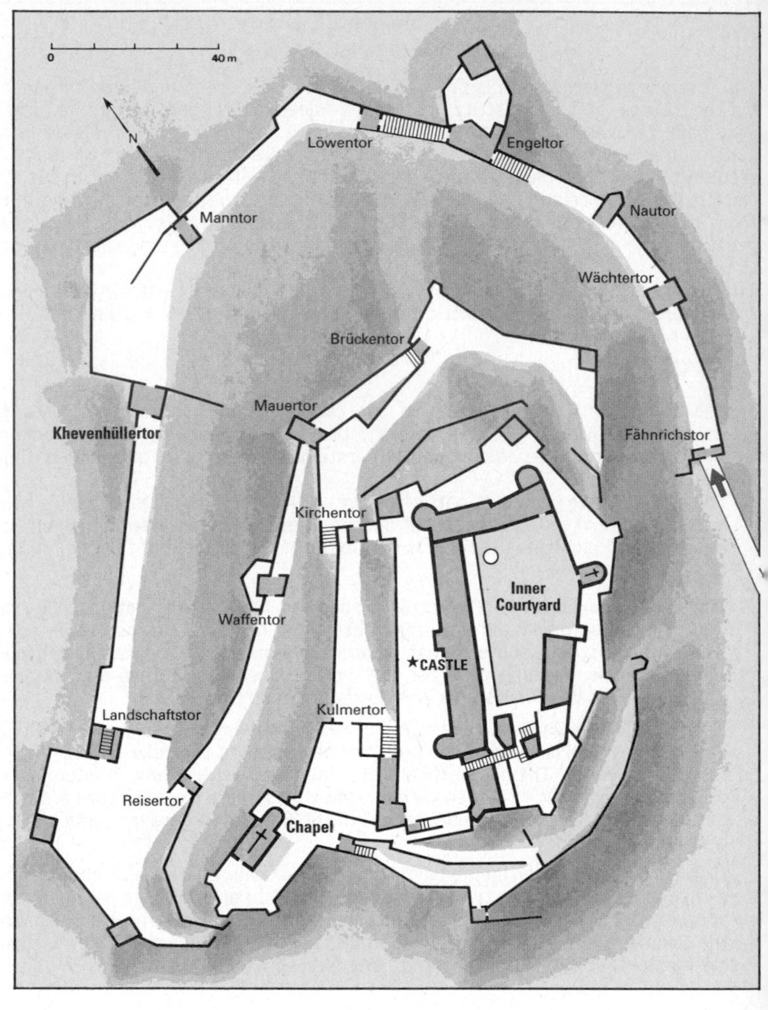

TOUR ⊙

Drive through the hamlet of Hochosterwitz at the foot of the rock and take the by-road up to the castle. Leave the car in the car park.

From here the battlemented castle is reached either on foot up a ramp *(about 30min walk)* or via the spectacular lift which takes visitors up the sheer rock face. There are 14 gateways along the way; the natural gaps in the ravine were used to form centres of resistance isolated behind drawbridges. The grandest gateway is the seventh, known as the **Khevenhüllertor** (1582), surmounted by a lion's head, the family coat of arms and a bust of Georg Khevenhüller dressed as a military leader.

At the end of the winding approach ramp, which gives many **views** of the hilly St. Veit region, in which the tallest mound is the Ulrichberg, the path passes the castle chapel (Burgkapelle) and reaches the **inner courtyard** (Innerer Burghof), where there is now an inn.

Certain rooms in the castle are open to visitors, who will find out further information about the Khevenhüllers and be able to see family portraits and a fine collection of arms and armour, recalling the fact that in its heyday Hochosterwitz boasted a remarkable armoury capable of equipping some 700 men.

Schloß-Museum HOHENBRUNN★★

Oberösterreich

Michelin map 926 fold 9 – 1.5km/1mi west of Markt St. Florian

Too large for a hunting lodge and too open to the surrounding country ever to have made any pretence at defence, Schloß Hohenbrunn, with its many windows and handsome arcades, is set like a Palladian villa in an attractive natural setting.

It was built between 1722 and 1732 for a prior at the abbey of St. Florian, on a piece of land which he had inherited from his family. The buildings, erected on a square plan round a central courtyard, were designed by one of Austria's most celebrated Baroque architects, the Tyrolean **Jakob Prandtauer**. Hohenbrunn is in fact the only castle that can be attributed with any certainty to Prandtauer, to whom the abbeys at Melk and Herzogenburg are attributed. He also put the final touches to the abbey of St. Florian and, after his death, the work was completed by Jakob Steinhueber, a foreman working at the abbey. The castle owes its name (Hoher Brunnen meaning high fountain) to a pumping appliance originally installed in a tower flanking the south façade.

Fremdenverkehrsamt Oberösterreich, Linz

Schloß Hohenbrunn

The castle was in a state of considerable disrepair in 1963 when it was bought from the abbey of St. Florian and restored under the auspices of the local provincial authority. Since 1967 it has housed an interesting hunting and fishing museum.

★★ JAGD- UND FISCHEREIMUSEUM ⓥ

The exhibition of numerous weapons, models, plaster casts of footprints and stuffed animals provides a fascinating and informative exploration of hunting in Upper Austria. Objects of historic interest include the hunting clothes of Emperor Franz Joseph I and an extraordinary rifle (3.12m/10ft 3in long) belonging to Archduke Karl Salvator. The **porcelain collection** is unparalleled in Europe.

A tour of the museum provides an opportunity to visit most of the castle. Even the non-specialist visitor will find interest in the exhibits which in no way detract from the elegant but rural character of the castle interior.

HOHENTAUERNPASSSTRASSE★

Steiermark

Michelin map 926 folds 22 and 35

Over the pass (alt 1 265m/4 150ft) through the Hohe Tauern, also known as the Triebener Tauern or **Rottenmanner Tauern**, leads a narrow road locally called the **Tauernstraße** (the Tauern Road). This was used long ago by the Romans as a link between Juvavum (Salzburg) and Virunum (near Klagenfurt).

The freshness and tranquillity of the Pölstal makes this difficult mountainous section worthwhile. Near Möderbrugg the valley is dotted with dilapidated mining or industrial buildings, survivals of a vanished industry based on silver mining and silver and metal work by artisans. Compared with the Pölstal, the crossing of the Schober pass by the main road from Trieben to Leoben is a mere formality.

FROM JUDENBURG TO LIEZEN *73km/45mi*

The steep gradients on the north slope of the pass call for great care. It is best to travel from Judenburg to Liezen in order to take this section downhill.

Judenburg – *See PACK- und STUBALPENSTRASSE.*

Branching off from the Vienna-Klagenfurt road, 6km/4mi from Judenburg, the Trieben road crosses to the north bank of the Mur. It climbs briefly on the last slopes of the Falkenberg – there are pretty views upstream of the wide valley overlooked by the Bocksruck – to enter the Pölsbach Valley over the slight shelf of the Pölshals. To the rear, the ruins of Reifenstein *(right)* dominate the industrial settlement of Pöls (cellulose industry). Ahead, far off, the jagged crests of the Hochschwung loom on the horizon.

Unterzeiring – The buildings of a formerly fortified priory attached to Admont and the crumbling castle ruins of Burg Hanfelden lend distinction to this village.

Oberzeiring – *1.5km/1mi off the Hohentauern road (take the fork signposted Unterzeiring).* This is an old mining village with a disused silver mine, **Silberbergwerk** ⓥ, open to the public.

Möderbrugg – Several man-made waterfalls, here enclosed in old wooden troughs, recall the time when the village rang with the noise of the little hammers used for iron beating (the water was used for cooling).
Huge squat barns are visible one above the other, on the slopes of the Pölstal. After the tiny resort of St. Johann am Tauern the climb becomes steeper. To the left rises the Großer Bösenstein, from the foot of which the Polster pass rises in a smooth curve. At last one reaches the upper combe of the pass, a quiet setting for the little resort of Hohentauern.
On the north slope of the mountain the road plunges into the Wolfsgraben, a dark gorge of the Triebenbach, to emerge finally on the mountainside above Trieben. The Paltental unfolds between Trieben and Selzthal. The valley is used by the main road from Graz to Salzburg.

Rottenmann – This little town was once enriched by the traffic in salt. It still has its *Straßenplatz*, its priory near the church, some traces of town walls (behind the church on the mountainside), and makes a pleasant halt.
The high perched shape of the fortress of Strechau, formerly a refuge for Protestants in Upper Styria, lends attraction to the drive from Rottenmann to Selzthal. At **Liezen** there are extensive views of the Enns gap and, from the bridge over the torrent, the Großer Grimming (alt 2 351m/7 713ft), an outcrop of the Dachstein (southwest).

INNSBRUCK★★

L Tirol

Population 130 000

Michelin map 926 fold 30

Local maps see Excursions below and SEEFELDER SATTELSTRASSEN

Alt 574m/1 883ft

Innsbruck (literally, Bridge over the Inn) is at the junction of the Inn Valley and the ill gap, on the busy road which runs, parallel with the equally busy railway line, towards Italy. Several million cars a year are driven along it towards the Brenner pass and the south. Innsbruck is the cultural and tourist capital of the Tyrol and, except for Grenoble and Bolzano, the only town of more than 100 000 inhabitants within the Alpine range.
The view along the Maria-Theresien-Straße towards the steep slopes of the Nordkette (Karwendel mountain range) combines townscape and landscape to form a **picture**★★ which is one of the most magical in Europe.
Many aspects of local behaviour show how closely man is linked with mountain life. At Innsbruck itself, though the altitude is less than 600m/2 000ft, it is not unusual, in winter, to see employees and students devoting their midday break to the ski runs starting from Seegrube, the halfway station of the Nordkette cable-car. The 1964 Winter Olympic Games marked a decisive development in the tourist amenities of Innsbruck: a ski jump was constructed at Bergisel, an ice-stadium erected (indoor ice

Inn riverfront

rink) and an airport built. The superior quality of these facilities brought to the city the 1976 Winter Olympic Games - the already existing installations were improved and new sports facilities built.
The city is almost overrun by tourists in the summer but benefits from the historic centre having been made into a pedestrianized zone. The relative lack of industry has enabled Innsbruck to keep its charming provincial character, once the main thoroughfares are left behind.

HISTORICAL NOTES

The Tyrol came into existence as a state in the 12C, at the heart of the Alps, then under the jurisdiction of the counts of Tyrol, whose seat was above Merano.
In the 14C the Tyrol came under the Habsburgs. Power weighed in favour of the territories in the Inn Valley, on the northern slopes of the mountain chain, and Innsbruck, now the capital, enjoyed a long heyday, particularly during the reign of Maximilian I.

"The Last Knight" – **Maximilian of Habsburg**, a forceful personality who was especially fond of the Tyrol, was invested with Imperial rank in 1508. He had a passion for hunting, believing that this sport was of prime importance for royalty, since it enabled them to make contact with their more humble subjects.
Maximilian took as his first wife Maria of Burgundy, the daughter of Charles the Bold, and by the increase of territorial power which their union brought him, justified the couplet so often applied to the Habsburg monarchy in later days:

"Bella gerant alii, tu, felix Austria, nube
Nam quae Mars aliis, dat tibi regna Venus."
ie "Let others war, thou, happy Austria, wed;
What some owe Mars, from Venus take instead."

The Emperor's second marriage with Bianca Maria Sforza was celebrated with great pomp and ceremony in 1494.
Soon afterwards the Emperor had the famous **Goldenes Dachl** erected. This depicted him with his two wives and became the town's emblem. In fact his attachment went further than this; he chose Innsbruck as his burial place and ordered the sumptuous Hofkirche as his mausoleum. This building, however, never received his remains, as the town gates were closed against the already dying Emperor by the burghers, exasperated at the debts left by the noblemen in his suite. He was forced to go on to Wels, where he died in January 1519, and was buried at Wiener Neustadt, his birthplace.

Good days and bad (18C) – In 1765 the town was enlivened by new celebrations, dynastic this time. The Imperial family was celebrating the marriage of Leopold, Grand Duke of Tuscany, with the Infanta of Spain, Maria Ludovica. A triumphal arch was erected at the head of Maria-Theresien-Straße. Then Emperor Franz suddenly died. That is why the triumphal arch, which dates from these events, is devoted equally to earthly glories and to funeral trappings.

TRAVELLERS' ADDRESSES

Tourist information

Innsbruck-Tourismus (tourist information), Burggraben 3/11, 6021 Innsbruck, ☏ 05 12/5 98 50, Fax 05 12/59 85 07.
Opening times: Mon-Fri 8am-6pm, Sat 8am-noon. Closed on Sun.

Innsbruck-Information (sales and bookings office for tickets, Innsbruck Cards, room reservations, city tours etc), Burggraben 3, 6021 Innsbruck, ☏ 05 12/53 56, Fax 05 12/53 56 14.
Opening times: Mon-Sat 8am-7pm, Sun and public holidays 9am-6pm. Ticket office open Mon-Fri 8am-6pm, Sat 8am-5pm. Closed on Sun.

Tirol-Werbung, Maria-Theresien-Straße 55, 6020 Innsbruck, ☏ 05 12/53 20 0.
Opening times: Mon-Fri 8am-6pm.

A monthly programme of events is available from the Innsbruck-Tourismus and Innsbruck-Information at the end of the month for the month to come. Innsbruck also has its own **Web site** *(www.tiscover.com/innsbruck).*

Innsbruck Card

These special visitors' tickets are available for a variety of durations (24, 48 or 72hr) and cover free travel on public transport, including a cable-car trip (up and down) on each of the Hungerburg-, Nordketten- and Patscherkofelbahn services, and free or reduced-price entry to numerous museums and sights (including the Swarovski Kristallwelten at Wattens). The Innsbruck Card is on sale from Innsbruck-Information for 230S (24hr), 300S (48hr) or 370S (72hr). For further details, call ☏ 05 12/53 56.

City tours

Walks (1hr) - June-Sept at 2pm, with an additional walk at 10am in July and Aug.

City tours - Long tour (2hr) all year daily at noon, June-Sept additionally at 2pm. Short tour (1hr) in summer Mon-Sat at 10.15am, noon, 2pm, 3.15pm. Details from tourist information, ☎ 05 12/53 56.

Cultural tours on particular themes are run all year on Sat. There are additional evening tours May-June at 7pm and July-Aug at 8pm, also June-Sept Fri at 7pm. Details from PerPedes, ☎ 05 12/27 37 00.

Public transport

It is advisable to buy a ticket before your journey, since you can only get single tickets from the bus driver and have to pay a surcharge.
The 24hr ticket gives you as many trips as you want within the city limits. Alternatively there are four-journey tickets, and weekly and monthly tickets to choose from.
Tickets are available from Innsbruck-Information, the Innsbruck transport authorities (Stainerstraße 2, ☎ 05 12/5 30 70) and tobacconist's shops with the appropriate sign. Further information can be found on the Internet *(www.ivb.at)*.

Inner city car parks

Congress-Garage, Herrengasse/Rennweg (daily until midnight); Europahaus, Meinhardstraße (daily 7am-10pm); Parkgarage Landhausplatz, Wilhelm-Greil-Straße (daily 7am-1am); Sparkassengarage, Erlerstraße (Mon-Fri 7am-9pm, Sat 8am-5pm); Maria-Theresien-Garage, Erlerstraße (daily 24hr), Parkgarage Altstadt, Tschamlerstraße (daily 7am-1am); City Parkgarage, Kaiserjägerstraße (daily 24hr).

Post offices

Main post office: **Hauptpostamt**, Maximilianstraße 2, Mon-Sat 7am-11pm.
Station post office: **Bahnpostamt**, Bruneckerstraße 1, Mon-Sat 6.30am-9pm. ☎ 05 12/50 00.

Shopping

The main shopping streets include Maria-Theresien-Straße, the pedestrian zone in the old town centre around Herzog-Friedrich-Straße, and Museumstraße.

M. Hertlein/MICHELIN

Herzog-Friedrich-Straße

Markets
Franziskanerplatz: farm produce every Thurs 9am-1.30pm, bric-à-brac every Sat 7am-1pm.
Sparkassenplatz: farm produce every Fri 9am-2pm.
Rathaushof: flea market every 1st and 3rd Sat in the month 7am-1pm.
Christmas markets (Christkindlmärkte) are held in the old town and on Landhausplatz from the end of Nov to just before Christmas.

Souvenirs
Craft goods and traditional costume (Trachten): Tiroler Heimatwerk, Meraner Straße 2-4.

Entertainment

Tiroler Landestheater, Rennweg 2, ☎ 05 12/5 20 74.

Kellertheater, Adolf-Pichler-Platz 8, ☎ 05 12/58 07 43.

Theater an der Sill, Kravoglstraße 19, ☎ 05 12/36 29 29.

Tiroler Volksbühne Blaas, Maria-Theresien-Straße 12, ☎ 05 12/58 60 01.

Kulturgasthaus Bierstindl, Klostergasse 6, ☎ 05 12/57 57 57. Old Innsbruck folk theatre, chivalry plays.

Treibhaus, Angerzellgasse 8, ☎ 05 12/58 68 74. Range of performances including cabaret, jazz and world music.

Utopia Kulturzentrum, Tschamlerstraße 3, ☎ 05 12/58 85 87. Concerts, events, performances, exhibitions.

Casino Innsbruck, at the Holiday Inn Hotel, Landhausplatz/Salurner Straße 15, ☎ 05 12/58 70 40 0.

Cinemas

Cineplexx, Wilhelm-Greil-Straße 23, ☎ 05 12/58 14 57.

Metropol Multiplex, Innstraße 5, ☎ 05 12/28 33 10.

Central, Maria-Theresien-Straße 17, ☎ 05 12/58 80 78.

Original-version films are shown at **Cinematograph** (Museumstraße 31, ☎ 05 12/57 85 00) and **Cine-Royal** (Innrain 16, ☎ 05 12/58 63 85).

Eating out

Ottoburg – Herzog-Friedrich-Straße 1, ☎ 05 12/58 43 38. Top-quality restaurant in one of Innsbruck's oldest buildings. Several tastefully fitted wood-panelled rooms. Reservation recommended.

Goldener Adler – Herzog-Friedrich-Straße 6, ☎ 05 12/57 11 11. Elegant Tyrolean style restaurant. Some of the more illustrious guests at the hotel of the same name (listed by the entrance) include Mozart, Heine, Camus and Sartre.

Weißes Kreuz – Herzog-Friedrich-Straße 31, ☎ 05 12/5 94 79. Traditional Tyrolean inn with various rooms decorated in rustic style.

Hirschen Stuben – Kiesbachgasse 5, ☎ 05 12/58 29 79. Charming contrast between modern decor and very old vaulting, with rotating exhibitions of works by contemporary artists.

Fischerhäusl – Herrengasse 8 (by cathedral passage), ☎ 05 12/58 35 35. Restaurant slightly difficult to find, with a peaceful inviting garden.

Cafés and bars

Café Central – Gilmstraße 11. Vienna coffee house style decor: stucco ceiling, chandeliers, palms – very classy!

Konditorei-Café Munding – Kiesbachgasse 16. This coffee house with the pleasant summer terrace is supposed to be the oldest cake shop in the Tyrol.

Krahvogel – Anichstraße 12. Cosy bar with a limited selection of food and a garden in the back courtyard.

Bellini's – Meranerstraße 5. Italian is the watchword for this modern café-bar which offers a taste of Italy in the middle of Innsbruck.

Theresienbräu – Maria-Theresien-Straße 53. Slightly off-the-wall bar aimed at a younger clientele with tasty beer brewed on the premises.

Sweet Basil – Herzog-Friedrich-Straße 31. Restaurant and two bars occupying several floors. Elegant, welcoming and very enjoyable.

Elferhaus – Herzog-Friedrich-Straße 11. Wide selection of beers from all over the world and a small range of food.

Piano – Herzog-Friedrich-Straße 5. Long café-bar with small picture gallery and several comfortable sofas in which you can take the weight off your feet after a strenuous walk around town.

Papa Joe's – Seilergasse 12. Grill, fast-food and bar. Hint of Latin America in the decor (which is fairly eclectic) with fans and a small "waterfall".

Hofgarten-Café – Very popular summer meeting place with a large terrace in the Hofgarten.

Café-Club Filou – Stiftgasse 12. Bar, restaurant and disco. Variety of seating ranging from bar stools to chairs and sofas. Drinks include beer, cocktails and even champagne.

Tip: in the **Ing.-Etzel-Straße** (level with the junction with Dreiheiligen-Straße) in the arches beneath the railway line there is something to suit every taste, from pizza outlets to music bars and trendy wine bars.

Dates for your diary

Tanzsommer: June-July. High quality dance performances by international artistes.

Innsbruck Festival of Old Music/Ambraser Schloßkonzerte: July-Aug.

GENERAL VIEW

In the town itself the belfry (Stadtturm - *see below*) gives the best view. To get a more general view go up to the **Hungerburg★ (AY)**, either by car via the Alte Innbrücke (Old Bridge over the Inn), the Höttinger Gasse, the Hötting Church and the Höhenstraße, or by **funicular** ⌚ (Hungerburgbahn). From the terrace there is a view of the whole town and the majestic peaks of the Serles and Nockspitze marking the entrance to the pretty Stubaital to the south.
Travellers descending by car from the Brenner by road no 182 should look for the view at Sonnenburgerhof on one of the last bends in the road; from this corner by the tram crossing there is a remarkable **view★★** of the whole of Innsbruck.

★ OLD INNSBRUCK

★ **Maria-Theresien-Straße (CZ)** - This lively "street-square" has an imposing **vista★★** of the Nordkette, with its rocky crown rising to an altitude of 2 334m/7 657ft. A variety of attractive old houses are to be found in this street, such as the Palais Lodron at no 7, the Palais Troyer (1681-83) at no 39, the early 18C, Baroque style Palais Trapp at no 38 and the Palais Sarnthein at no 57. It is worth taking the time to appreciate the beautiful façades on either side of the street.

Triumphpforte (CZ F) - This triumphal arch is a memorial to the joys and sorrows that the year 1765 (marriage of Archduke Leopold) held in store for the Imperial court and Tyrolean residents. The monument is crowned with a medallion of Franz I and Maria Theresa on its south side, with images of the engaged couple on the left (the right features the bridegroom's sisters, Maria Christina and Maria Antonia, better known as French Queen Marie-Antoinette).
The north side is decorated with funerary images with a medallion of the Emperor held by the angel of death and watched over by a grieving woman, in memory of Franz I's untimely end.

Altes Landhaus (DZ) - *No 43*. This palace, an excellent example of secular Baroque architecture, was built in its present form by Georg-Anton Gumpp between 1725 and 1728 and is now the seat of the Tyrolean provincial assembly and government. The Gumpp family of architects are responsible for several of Innsbruck's

Triumphpforte

most notable buildings: Wilten Abbey, the Spitalkirche, the Jesuit church, among others. The niches in the stuccoed staircase of the Landhaus contain statues and busts of gods, while the ceiling features the motif of the Tyrolean eagle with a map of the province.

Annasäule (**CZ A**) – This monumental column, set up in 1706, commemorates the liberation of the Tyrol from Bavarian invaders on St Anne's day 1703 during the War of the Spanish Succession. The Virgin Mary has the place of honour on the top of the slim column, St Anne appearing only on the base beside St George and the dragon, once the protector of the Tyrol. Here too are St Vigilius and St Cassianus, who are the patron saints of Trent and Bressanone.

A continuation of the Maria-Theresien-Straße is the **Herzog-Friedrich-Straße**, a busy street whose old arcades contain shops. In the centre of the street stands the Goldenes Dachl. On the vaulting beneath the arcade at no 35, note the remarkable fresco of the Imperial eagle dating from 1496.

Stadtturm (Belfry) ⌚ (**CZ B**) – The belfry forms part of the old town hall of 1358. The tower has a square base from which rises a slim octagonal Renaissance structure, bristling with rounded turrets and crowned with an onion dome. A staircase leads to a viewing platform from which there is a fine **panorama**★ over the city.

★ **Goldenes Dachl (Little Golden Roof)** (**CZ**) – This ornate structure, finished c 1500, was added as a spectator balcony to the façade of the main building. According to a tradition, which the most cultivated Tyrolese are sorry to see denied by irrefutable evidence, it was Friedrich the Penniless, Duke of the Tyrol (1406-39), who, wishing to put an end to the jokes about his poverty, had the little roof of the structure, in full view of passers-by, covered with golden coins. As a matter of fact, the work dates from the reign of Maximilian and symbolizes the power of the Habsburgs. The whole thing, Gothic in style with its decoration growing richer as it rises towards the roof, bears witness to the growing influence of the Renaissance.

The balustrade on the first floor is adorned with a frieze of delicately carved coats of arms, representing, from left to right, Styria (set back), Austria, Hungary, the Holy Roman Empire (a double-headed eagle), the kingdom of Germany (a single-headed eagle and a golden fleece), Philip the Fair (Maximilian's son), the Sforzas of Milan and the Tyrol (set back).

A. Niederstrasser/ÖSTERREICH WERBUNG

The second band of reliefs includes, in the centre, two pictures of Maximilian. On the left, the Emperor turns towards his second wife, Bianca Maria Sforza, who can be recognized by her long hair and her Italian headdress. The portrait of Maria, Maximilian's first wife, wearing the Burgundian headdress, completes the trio. On the right, Maximilian stands between his councillor (on the right) and his jester (on the left). The side panels each represent a couple of acrobatic dancers. The ensemble, the amusing work of a Swabian sculptor, Niklas Türing the Elder, who was for a long time unknown, was used as the royal lodge during popular festivals and when tournaments were held. All the original carvings, owing to their damaged condition, have been replaced by copies but the originals can be inspected in the Tiroler Landesmuseum Ferdinandeum *(see below)*.

Maximilianeum ⌚ – A room behind the Goldenes Dachl has been laid out as a memorial to Maximilian, with some fine exhibits intended to make him seem more real; particularly striking is the portrait of the dead Emperor. It is well worth taking the time to watch a 20min video film about his life and times.

★ **Helblinghaus** (**CZ**) – This house at the opposite corner of the Herzog-Friedrich-Straße was given a Rococo

M. Hertlein/MICHELIN

Helblinghaus

facing in the 18C, displaying lavishly decorated window frames and a highly decorated pediment. The arrangement of the windows in convex bows – a remedy for the lack of sunlight in the narrow streets of old cities – is still often seen in southern Germany. Further to the left, towards the quays on the river, is the historic inn named the Goldener Adler (Golden Eagle) (**E**). It is proud of the guests it has received since the 16C and displays their names on a marble plaque outside.

Return along Maria-Theresien-Straße, to take Pfarrgasse, which leads to the Domplatz.

Dom zu St. Jakob ⏲ (**CZ**) – There has been a church on this spot since 1180, but successive buildings were destroyed by fire or earthquake, so that the cathedral did not receive its present form with its characteristically curving, two-towered façade and the great dome over the chancel until the early 18C.

The **interior★**, in the Baroque style, is roofed with domes – three on the nave and a dome with a lantern on the chancel – decorated in 1722 by the famous Asam brothers from Munich, Cosmas Damian (painter) and Egid Quirin (stucco worker); their compositions, with clever effects of perspective, glorify the Trinity and the intercessions of St James. Above the high altar the picture of *Our Lady of Succour* (Mariahilf), painted by Lucas Cranach the Elder, is still an object of veneration. Originally intended for the Kreuzkirche in Dresden, it was presented by the Elector of Saxony to Archduke Leopold of the Tyrol, who took it with him on all his travels. The picture was not installed in the cathedral until 1650.

In the north transept is the canopied tomb of Archduke Maximilian (who should not be confused with the Emperor of Austria), a Grand Master of the Teutonic Order, who died in 1618. This tomb, which was restored to its original state in 1950, adds to the furnishings of the church a note of gravity which contrasts with the decorative exuberance of the pulpit and organ.

Daily at 12.15pm the Friedensglockenspiel (peace chimes) sounds from the north tower.

Round the cathedral of St. Jakob is the colourful old town with its ancient, balconied houses with picturesque signs, reliefs, stuccowork and frescoes.

Turn back. At the Goldenes Dachl, turn left onto the narrow Hofgasse, then, after a covered alley, left again onto Rennweg, which skirts the Hofburg.

★ **Hofburg** ⏲ (**CZ**) – On the site where the Habsburg princes of the Tyrolean branch of the family (Leopold III, Friedrich IV the Penniless and Sigismund the Rich) had little by little had a large and rather disjointed building constructed, Maximilian I had a castle of the present dimensions built, which was modified under Maria Theresa between 1766 and 1770. The long façade, flanked by two domed towers, was finished in 1770 and is a typical example of the evolution of Baroque secular architecture in Innsbruck.

Inside, the state rooms, which may be visited, are devoted to the glories of the Tyrol and of the Habsburg monarchy, especially the **Riesensaal★★** (Gigantic Hall). This state room, lined with stucco panels with a porcelain finish, is about 31.5m/100ft long. The ceiling fresco was painted by Franz-Anton Maulpertsch in 1776. The main theme is the triumph of the House of Habsburg-Lorraine, personified by two women holding their hands out to one another (note among the symbols the green shoot sprouting from a dead tree trunk).

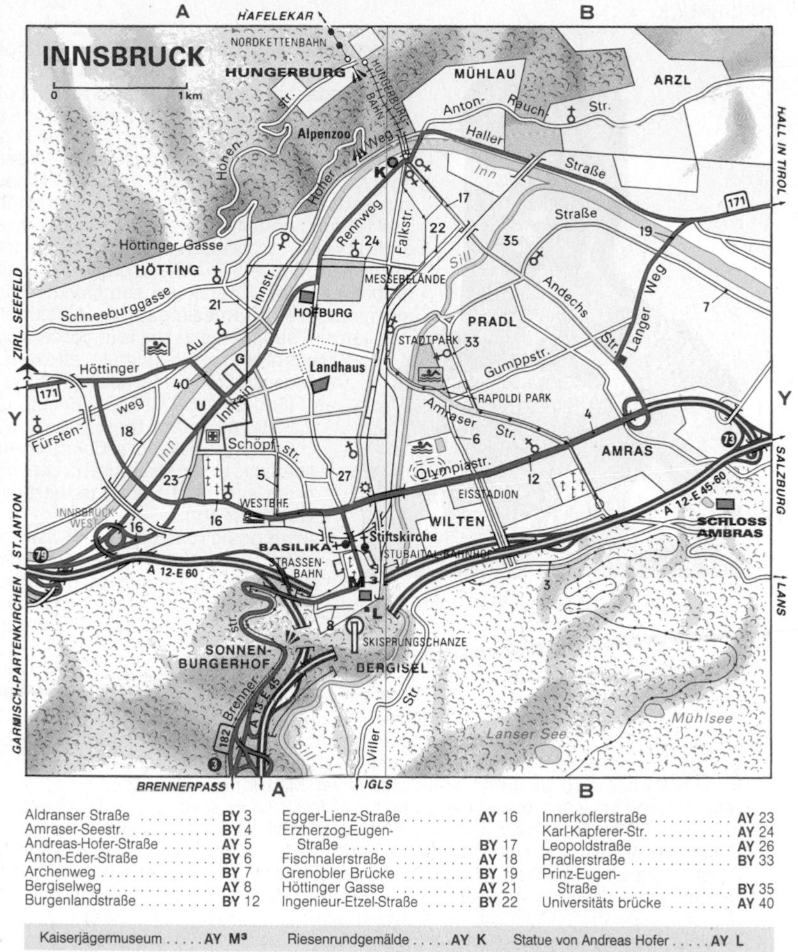

On the walls are full-length portraits of Maria Theresa's children following the Imperial couple in procession. Numerous other portraits include those of Louis XVI and Marie-Antoinette.

The private apartments house some fine paintings and tapestries.

Return to the Rennweg and enter the Hofkirche (enter through the Tiroler Volkskunstmuseum to the left of the church).

Hofkirche ⌚ **(CZ)** – This church was built by Ferdinand I (Emperor from 1556 to 1564) who finally implemented the projects of his grandfather Maximilian I. The nave with its three aisles, all equal in size, built to contain Maximilian's mausoleum, is still Gothic in style, although masked in part by Renaissance (tower, entrance porch, capitals) and Baroque (stuccowork) additions.

On the gallery are placed the 23 statuettes of the protecting saints of the Habsburg family. The comparative grace of these effigies contrasts with the sombre colossi who actually stand guard over the tomb.

★★ **Maximilian's Mausoleum** (Grabmal Kaiser Maximilians I) – This tomb is the most important specimen left to us of German Renaissance sculpture. The Emperor intended it to glorify the splendours of his reign and also to record the flawless legitimacy of the Holy Roman emperors as the heirs of the caesars.

The original plan was grandiose but not beyond the bounds of possibility, for Innsbruck at that time enjoyed international renown for its bell founders and armour makers. The plan included, in particular, 40 large statues, 100 small bronzes of saints and 34 busts of Roman emperors. In spite of a century of work this programme was not fully completed when, in 1584, the casting of the kneeling statue of Maximilian, which crowns the structure, marked the end of the work.

The 28 impressive, larger-than-life-size statues of the "black fellows", as the people of Innsbruck call them, all in bronze except two which are in copper, stand on guard over the empty tomb. A torch could be set in the right hand of each during funeral services. The choice of figures is sometimes unexpected: it takes into account the ties of blood and marriage. Here are the royal families of Habsburg, Burgundy and Austria, but also the purely sentimental lineage of heroes of chivalry or precursors

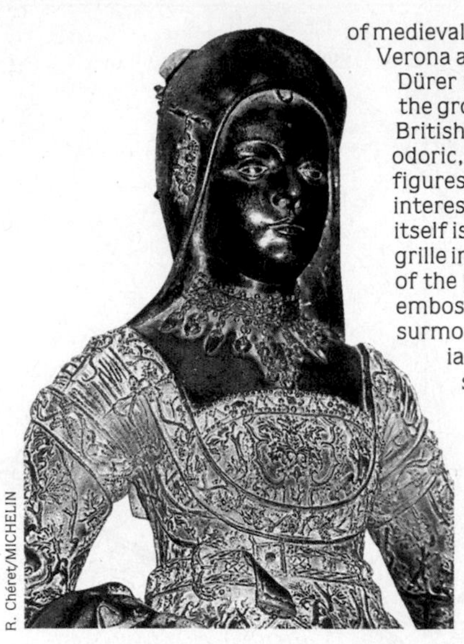

Mausoleum of Maximilian I – detail

of medieval Christianity: King Arthur, Theodoric of Verona and Clovis. The contribution of Albrecht Dürer undoubtedly raises the artistic level of the group, with the statues of King Arthur – a British-looking type in armour! – and of Theodoric, a supple and vigorous work. These figures are of inestimable value to those interested in the history of fashion. The tomb itself is surrounded by a splendid Renaissance grille in which, according to the Tyrolean taste of the period *(see STAMS)*, wrought iron and embossed sheet metal are combined. It is surmounted by the kneeling statue of Maximilian and supported at the four corners by statues of the cardinal virtues, all carved by **Alexandre Colin** of Mechelen (Malines) in Flanders (1527-1612). Reliefs in marble, all except three panels, by this same Alexandre Colin, cover the sides of the structure, depicting great events of the reign (battles, weddings etc).

After going round the tomb visitors should make sure they look at the Renaissance furnishings of the chancel and church and, on the north side, the gallery known as the Princes' Chancel and the 1567 stalls.

The Hofkirche has also acted as the national church of the Tyrol since the revolt in 1809. It contains the tomb and memorial of **Andreas Hofer** (1767-1810), hero of the Tyrolean uprising against Napoleon near the exit.

★★ **Silberne Kapelle** ⊙ – This separate chapel, built by Archduke Ferdinand II of Tyrol so that he might rest beside his wife who was a commoner, was finished in 1587. It owes its name to the large embossed silver Madonna, surrounded by designs representing the symbols of the Litanies, which is to be seen on the altarpiece of rare wood. The first bay, near the entrance on the left, contains the tomb of Philippine Welser, the beloved wife of Ferdinand, and is one of the most highly finished works of the Flemish master Alexandre Colin *(see above)* in his maturity. Nearer to the altar, the funeral statue of Ferdinand, by the same sculptor, depicts the deceased in full armour. His actual armour is displayed separately on a console, in a kneeling position, facing the altar. A small 16C cedarwood organ, of Italian origin, completes the collection of works of art housed in the chapel.

Hofgarten (**DZ**) – This public park with parrots allowed to roam free was laid out in the 16C under Archduke Ferdinand II, and was at the time one of the most ambitious gardens north of the Alps. Given a Baroque character under Maria Theresa, it was finally landscaped as a less formal park in the early 19C.

★★ **Tiroler Volkskunstmuseum** ⊙ (**CDZ**) – With the reputation of being one of Europe's finest regional museums, it covers the folk art of the whole of the Tyrol, that is including South Tyrol. The ground floor of this museum displays a collection of Tyrolean Christmas crib scenes from their origins to the present. The upper floors contain, most notably, beautiful panelled rooms with stoves which come from the houses of a variety of classes: nobility, merchants and farmers. Those on the first floor feature essentially Gothic style decoration, while those on the second floor date from the Renaissance and Baroque.

On the first floor are models of various Tyrolean farmhouses, along with skilfully decorated furniture, farming implements, tools, woodcarvings from the Grödner Tal region, musical instruments and games. There are some interesting examples of masks and costumes worn during carnival season in Imst and the area around Innsbruck. On the second floor there is a valuable collection of religious folk art, painted and carved farmhouse furniture and costumes worn by the farming community during festivals. The exhibits on display come from the old Tyrol, which included what is now the Trentino region of Italy and the Ladin valleys around the Dolomites.

Take the Angerzellgasse onto Museumsstraße to get to the "Ferdinandeum".

★ **Tiroler Landesmuseum "Ferdinandeum"** ⊙ (**DZ M²**) – *Scheduled to be closed for restoration from July 2001 to December 2002.* Although it possesses not inconsiderable prehistory and early history collections, this museum is devoted essentially to the development of the fine arts in the Tyrol from the Romanesque to the present, including masterworks from the Gothic age (Multscher, Pacher) and the Baroque (Troger). Many of the works displayed also have historic importance: the 1370 chapel altar of Schloß Tirol, the original bas-relief sculptures of the Goldenes Dachl etc. There is also a good collection of Dutch masters. In the basement is a relief model of the Tyrol at a scale of 1:20 000.

INNSBRUCK

Adolf-Pichler-Platz	CZ 2
Anichstraße	CZ
Bozner Platz	DZ 10
Burggraben	CZ 14
Domplatz	CZ 15
Herzog-Friedrich- Straße	CZ 20
Ingenieur-Etzel- Straße	DZ 22
Kiesbachgasse	CZ 25
Landhausplatz	CZ 26
Leopoldstraße	CZ 27
Maria-Theresien-Straße	CZ
Marktgraben	CZ
Meinhardstraße	DZ 28
Meraner Straße	CZ 30
Museumstraße	CDZ
Pfarrgasse	CZ 32
Stiftgasse	CZ 37
Südbahnstraße	DZ 38

Annasäule	CZ A
Goldener Adler	CZ E
Stadtturm	CZ B
Triumphpforte	CZ F
Tiroler Landesmuseum "Ferdinandeum"	DZ M²

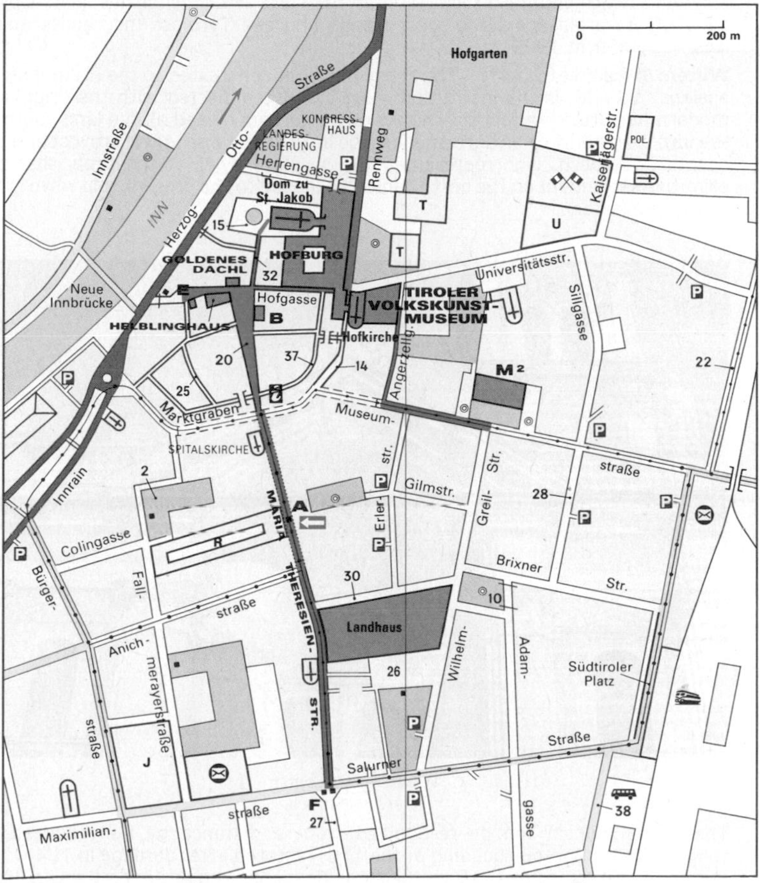

ADDITIONAL SIGHTS

Hungerburg and Hafelekar

Riesenrundgemälde (Bergisel Panorama) ⓥ **(ABY K)** – *Beside the Hungerburg funicular station.* This huge circular oil painting depicting the Battle of Bergisel on 13 August 1809 was painted in 1896 in honour of Andreas Hofer, hero of the Tyrolean uprising against Napoleon. Such panoramas were all the rage in the 19C. It is an amazing technical achievement (10m/33ft high by 100m/330ft long), completed in six months, which transports the spectator to the heart of the action by a successful use of perspective and supplementary decoration between the scene and the viewer.

Alpenzoo ⓥ **(AY)** – The pleasure of a visit to this Alpine zoo is further enhanced by the beauty of the site it occupies, the highest for a zoo in Europe, on a south-facing slope with a far-reaching view of the Inn Valley. The zoo gives visitors an overview of the fauna, both past and present, found in the Alpine region. Over 2 000 animals from 150 species, including mammals, birds, reptiles and amphibians, are on display. In the unique cold-water aquarium rare indigenous species of fish may be seen.

★★ **Hafelekar** ⓥ – Alt 2 334m/7 657ft. *About 2hr trip using the cable-car from the Hungerburg.*
A magnificent viewpoint for the Inn Valley and the Stubai Alps (south), and the rugged limestone cliffs of the Karwendel (north).

Innsbruck-Wilten, Bergisel and Amras

The district of Wilten is where the River Sill, running down from the Brenner, emerges from its final gorge to flow towards the alluvial delta. This was the site of the Roman town of Veldidena. To the south it abuts on Bergisel, a wooded eminence which became a sacred spot in the Tyrol after the battles on its slopes between Bavarian and Napoleon's troops and the Tyrolese insurgents under Andreas Hofer in 1809.

Wilten: Stiftskirche ⓥ (**ABY**) – The abbey of Wilten, entrusted to the Premonstratensians in 1128, is the institution most closely connected with the origins of modern Innsbruck. In fact the monks of St Norbert owned all the land south of the Inn. It was only by an agreement made in 1180 between their provost and the counts of Andech, who represented the secular power at the time, that the primitive settlement on the north bank was moved to the present "old town" (the Hofburg quarter).

M. Hertlein/MICHELIN

Wilten Abbey Church

The church, which can be recognized from a distance by its yellowish-red roughcast, is a Baroque building of the 17C, restored after damage in 1944. The façade, transformed in 1716 by the same architect who designed the Landhaus *(see above)*, is deeply convex on each side of the doorway, which is guarded by two stone giants wearing the warrior costumes of classical tragedy. They represent Aymon, on the left, and Thyrsus, on the right *(see below)*.

In the narthex, enclosed by a magnificent **grille**★ dating from 1707, with luxuriant adornments of foliage, is another statue, also in wood with more naive carvings (c 1500). This is the giant Aymon who came from the Rhine Valley; according to tradition he founded the abbey as an act of expiation for his murder of the local giant, Thyrsus. He also rid the nearby Sill gorge of a tiresome dragon for good measure.

The building proper has a certain distinction with its series of altarpieces in black wood, relieved with gold, but many of the paintings and the stuccowork adorning the vaulting had to be restored. Above the high altar, note the work known as Solomon's Throne (1665), a sort of gallery on a reduced scale, framed between columns and lions, which draws the eye in towards the focal point of Christ seated on a throne.

★ **Wilten: Basilica** ⓥ (**AY**) – In order to perpetuate devotion to Our Lady of the Four Columns, who had been the object of a popular pilgrimage at Innsbruck since the Middle Ages, the Premonstratensians of the nearby monastery had the parish church of Wilten completely restored between 1751 and 1756. The church was raised to the status of a basilica in 1957.

The building's sumptuous **interior** bears witness to the skill of the artists of the Rococo period, and especially of a team of decorators formed by a stucco-moulder, Franz-Xaver Feichtmayr, of the Wessobrunn School, and a painter from Augsburg, Matthäus Günther. Stuccowork in the form of flowers, scrolls and angels is arranged most successfully in the escutcheons. The fine paintings on the vaulting depict the Virgin Mary as an intercessor (chancel) and the Biblical figures, Esther and Judith (nave). The statue of the Virgin Mary, particularly venerated by pilgrims, is enthroned in glory at the high altar, under a baldaquin supported on marble columns.

Bergisel (**ABY**) – *Reached by car via the Brennerstraße, the Bergiselweg and the avenue leading into the park.* This wooded hill has been laid out as pleasant walks and many city people come to it in search of rest or pleasure. The ski jump in the background recalls the 1964 and 1976 Winter Olympic Games. Several monuments, especially the statue of Andreas Hofer (**AY L**), commemorate the fighting in 1809; the "panorama" depicting the fighting is on the far side of the town *(see above)*.

The **Kaiserjägermuseum** (Memorial to the Imperial Light Infantry) ⏲ (**AY M**[3]) contains mementoes of the 1809 uprising and of the Tyrolean crack corps (arms, uniforms and paintings), which was disbanded in 1918.

From the various rooms, and especially from the moving First World War memorial on the ground floor, there are **views**★ of the town of Innsbruck and the mountain barrier of the Nordkette.

★ **Schloß Ambras** ⏲ (**BY**) – *From the centre of Innsbruck take Olympiastraße east; by the skating rink turn right; after passing under the motorway turn left onto the Aldrans road; after 500m/550yd turn left to Schloß Ambras.*

Archduke Ferdinand II (1529-95), son of Emperor Ferdinand I and Prince of the Tyrol, had the medieval castle of Ambras rebuilt as a Renaissance palace. He lived here with the beautiful Philippine Welser, his first and morganatic wife. In order to house his considerable collections, the prince built the **Unterschloß**, his own private museum, which still exists. The present display includes his famous **Kunst- und Wunderkammer**, a cabinet of curiosities, and his **Rüstkammern**★, rooms full of armour.

The **Hochschloß** (upper castle) originally contained the residential quarters; today there is furniture from the 16C and 17C and the **portrait gallery**★ with Habsburgs from 1300 to 1800 and the most important figures in European history of the time. One prize exhibit is Emperor Maximilian's Georgsaltar (Altar of St George), shown as part of the **Collection of Medieval Sculpture**. One can also see remarkable frescoes in the inner courtyard, and Philippine Welser's bath.

To the south of the Hochschloß, Archduke Ferdinand had the magnificent **Spanischer Saal**★ (Spanish Hall) built for entertaining on a grand scale. It is here that the Schloß Ambras concerts are given every summer.

★★TOUR OF THE MITTELGEBIRGE

105km/65mi including final ascent to the Brenner pass. The route follows a narrow corniche road with hairpin bends and a gradient up to 1 in 7 in places (not suitable for caravans). Leave Innsbruck by the Hall in Tirol road (**BY** *on town plan*).

★ **Hall in Tirol** – *See HALL IN TIROL.*

The road to Tulfes crosses the Inn, goes under the motorway and, as it climbs, gives attractive views of the town of Hall, with its three church towers at the foot of the rocky cliffs of Bettelwurf range in the Karwendel massif.

About 2km/1mi after the bridge over the Inn in Hall, the road reaches the **church of St Francis Borgia** (1677), with the ground plan of a four-leaf clover, which looks like a small simplified copy of the church of St Charles Borromeo at Volders.

★ **Church of St Charles Borromeo at Volders** ⏲ – The unusual main building with a clover-leaf ground plan was constructed between 1620-54 and given its present appearance in 1710. Distinctive features of the church are its six cupolas, reminiscent of an oriental building, and the onion dome with three corner turrets at its base.

Seen through the fine Baroque screen, the church interior is clearly the work of master craftsmen. The ceiling frescoes (1765-66) by Troger's pupil **Martin Knoller** (1725-1804) illustrate the life of Milan cardinal Charles Borromeo. The painting above the high altar by the same artist (1769) depicts the saint giving Holy Communion to a plague sufferer.

Continue along the same road above Volders towards Watten. There, follow the signposts to "Swarovski" and "Kristallwelten".

★ **Swarovski Kristallwelten in Watten** ⏲ – The underground exhibition is a publicity vehicle for the Swarovski company based here and famous for its cut crystal objects. An overgrown fountain shaped like a giant head seems to guard the entrance to this magical sparkling world of crystal designed by Vienna artist André Heller. The entrance foyer with a display of the largest and smallest cut crystals in the world and works by internationally famous artists (Keith Haring, Niki de St.-Phalle, Salvador Dalí) is followed by seven "magic chambers" containing fantastic, mystical, meditative installations combining sound, light, objects and natural crystals in every shape and hue.

Retrace the route to St Francis Borgia Church, and turn left to Rinn and Tulfes.

A short, wooded and bendy stretch of road leads to a mountain plateau with meadows, where the picturesque villages of Tulfes, Rinn, Wiesenhöfe, Sistrans and Lans can be seen in succession against the backdrop of the Nordkette range (right).

✲ **Igls** – The "Innsbruck winter sports resort" has hosted the Winter Olympic Games twice (1964 and 1976) and consequently boasts a substantial tourist infrastructure. The **Patscherkofel** (2 247m/7 372ft), which can be reached by **cable-car** ⓥ, offers many possibilities for walking tours in summer and winter sport (including accompanied bob-sleigh rides on the Olympic run) with guaranteed snow well into the spring. Other attractions include the largest forest exclusively of stone pines in the eastern Alps (stone pine trail from the mountain hotel to Tulfes, about 3hr), Innsbruck University's Alpine garden and the highest-lying botanical gardens in Austria (open all hours from June to September, by the upper cable-car station at 1 964m/6 444ft).

Carry on towards Patsch/Matrei.

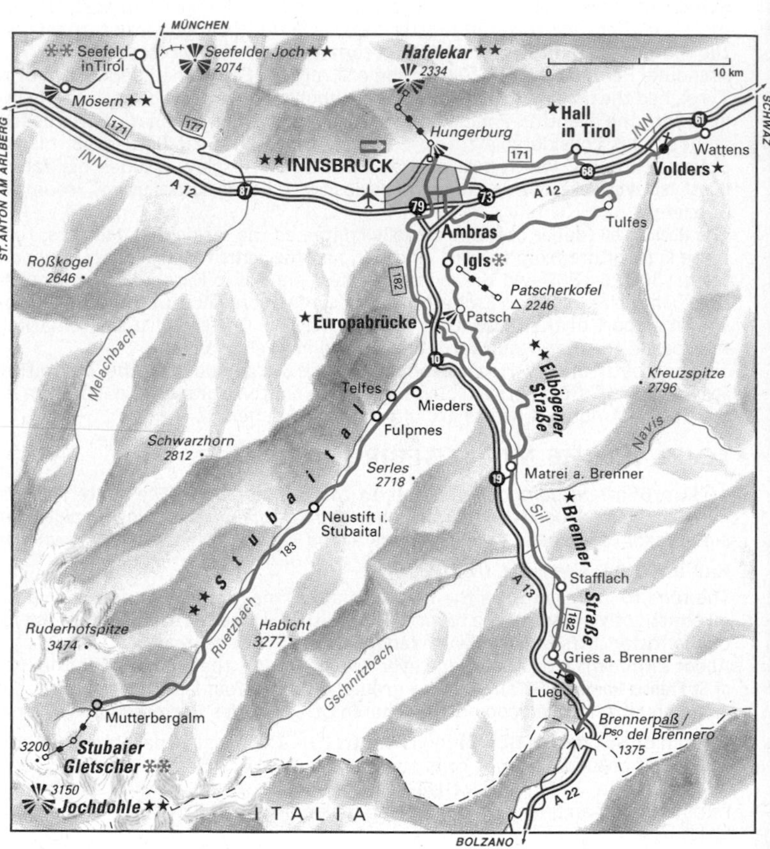

★★ **Ellbögener Straße** – This mountain road, which was once used for carting salt, leads through several tiny villages and hamlets, giving fine views of the Sill Valley. The approach to Patsch offers a splendid **view**★ along the length of the Stubaital, with the Europa bridge *(see below)* spanning the Brenner motorway in the foreground. To the left is the pyramidal Serles peak (2 718m/8 918ft) and in the background the snow-capped summit of the Habicht (3 277m/10 752ft). At the end of the valley the craggy peaks of the Zuckerhütl (3 511m/11 520ft) can be seen. After Gedeir, the road begins to drop down into the valley, ending at Mühlbach. It then crosses the Sill and joins the Brenner road (Bundesstraße 182) in Matrei am Brenner.

At this point, you can either take a detour left as far as the Brenner pass and Italian border *(32km/20mi there and back)*, or turn immediately right towards Innsbruck.

★ **Brennerstraße** – The Brenner pass (alt 1 375m/4 510ft) is the lowest route across the Alps and the only one crossed by a main railway line in the open air (since 1867). The first Brenner road was built in 1772. The Brenner toll motorway (A 13) was opened to motorists in 1969 to speed up through traffic. However, tourists who have time at their disposal would be advised to use the old pass road (Bundesstraße 182) instead, as it offers better views of the Sill Valley.

From Matrei am Brenner to the Brenner pass – After leaving Matrei and its main street lined with pretty, orieled houses, the road reveals a view of the **Navis Valley**, with the tiny white churches of St. Kathrein (left) and Tiezens (right) visible at the far end of the valley. It then runs along the lush green Sill valley, through some idyllic scenery. At the entrance to Stafflach, there is a view of the snow-capped crests of the Zillertaler Alps to the left. Shortly before climbing to the pass, on leaving Gries, the **chapel of St. Christopher and St Sigmund at Lueg** comes into sight. The interior of this superbly restored chapel, complete with shingle roof and Romanesque bell-tower, was converted to the Baroque style between 1684 and 1686. The road then continues its climb to the pass and Italian border.

Retrace your route back to Matrei.

From Matrei am Brenner to Innsbruck – On leaving Matrei the road follows a mountain route above the left bank of the Sill before dropping down towards Innsbruck in a seemingly never-ending series of hairpin bends. About 11km/7mi after Matrei it crosses the **Europa bridge**★ (785m/0.5mi long, 190m/623ft high) and shortly afterwards arrives at a parking area with a panoramic viewpoint. From here, the colossal construction appears even more impressive seen from a worm's-eye view. Shortly before Innsbruck, the Bergisel Olympic ski jump comes into view. Straight after the city information point, it is possible to stop on the right, just before a left-hand bend (opposite Sonnenburger Hof, **AY**), to enjoy a **view**★ of the whole of Innsbruck. The road then leads to the city centre via Wilten.

Oberes INNTAL★

Tirol

Michelin map 926 folds 28 and 29

Since the southern frontier of Austria was brought back, in 1919, to the crest line of the Alps, the Inn Valley has become the backbone of the Tyrol. For 185km/115mi, from the Finstermünz ravine to the Kufstein gap, the scenery is typical of the longitudinal furrows of the Alps. Here the last phases of the Ice Age made characteristic changes in the relief, as in the **Mittelgebirge** (Pre-Alpine) area round Innsbruck, and spacious plateaux are relatively well populated because of their favourable site.
Below Landeck the Inn Valley emphasizes the meeting of the pale cliffs of the limestone Alps (north) and the more solid dark rocks of the crystalline central massifs (south). In the latter, dark coloured rocks of a heavier shape predominate. The Sellraintal, a tributary valley which joins the Inn Valley opposite the promontory of the Martinswand, between Zirl and Innsbruck, marks the traditional boundary between the upper and lower valleys of the Inn (Oberinntal and Unterinntal).

FROM NAUDERS TO IMST *104km/65mi*

❄ **Nauders** – The popular winter sports resort dominated by Schloß Naudersberg, has ideal skiing conditions for downhill and cross-country skiers at an altitude where the snow is reliable. A ski pass is available for the area covering Nauders and Schöneben and Haider Alm over the Italian border, some 110km/68mi of ski slopes (Schiparadies Reschenpass). Nauders is also a departure point for mountain bike tours around the "Dreiländereck" (the point where the Swiss, Italian and Austrian borders meet), where there are 600km/370mi of tracks of varying degrees of difficulty.
Leaving the Nauders basin, where there are still grain crops ripening at over 1 300m/4 000ft, as in the nearby Alto Adige Valley in Italy (Val Venosta or Vintschgau), the road plunges into the Finstermünz gorge.

★ **Finstermünzpaß** – This grim gorge forms the natural frontier between the Tyrolean Inn Valley and the Lower Engadine and the Alto Adige.
Though the Engadine road runs along nearer the floor of the gorge, the road from Nauders plunges into it through a narrow rocky gap guarded by the massive old **Fort Nauders** (1834-40).
Downstream from the Hochfinstermünz hotel the road clings precariously to the cliffs of the right bank. After three rock-vaulted tunnel passages there is a viewing terrace to the left of the road. From here there is a view far along the Inn Valley. Directly opposite is the sickle-shaped gorge cut by the Schnalklbach, flowing down from the Grisons stretch of the Samnaun Valley in Switzerland.
After the viewpoint, the road leads through thick evergreen forest down to the valley floor, which is reached at the Kajetanbrücke (St Gaëtano) bridge.

Straight after the bridge it is possible to turn left into the Lower Engadine Valley (signposted St. Moritz).

After crossing the Inn, the road runs along the wide green valley floor, past **Pfunds** and on up the course of the Inn, giving the first views of the Kaunergrat peaks. Between **Ried** and **Prutz** stand the ruins of Laudeck on a rock to the left, flanked by the little, white church tower of **Ladis**.

***In Prutz the road forks off to the right into the* Kaunertal★★★** *(see entry).*

The stretch of road from Prutz to Landeck includes frequent sections of cliff road above the Inn, passing one imposing rockface after the other dropping right down to the road itself.

Landeck – *See ARLBERGGEBIET* 1.

From the road through Landeck, the ruins of **Schrofenstein** can be seen straight ahead half way up a mountain slope. The fortress remains in view for some time along the road to Zams.

Zams – Most of the village was destroyed, along with its church, by a fire in 1911. The church was rebuilt further west, and since the tower walls survived the fire the church boasts a free-standing bell-tower, a relatively unusual feature for the Tyrol. On leaving Zams, the wooded mountain peak crowned by the **Kronburg** Fortress can be seen. A monastery of the same name is located in a hollow on its right slope. After passing **Schönwies**, there is a view straight ahead of the solitary, pointed Tschirgant peak (2 370m/7 776ft). The road begins to climb again and there are several stopping bays to the right of it offering opportunities to make a brief halt to enjoy the views of the Inn Valley at your leisure. At last the road emerges into the wide Imst basin, cut at either end by wooded gorges, in sight of the jagged crests of the Stubaier Alps (east).

Imst – The delightful upper town (Oberstadt), with its numerous pretty fountains surmounted by old statues, nestles round the imposing 15C **parish church** (Pfarrkirche Mariae Himmelfahrt). The church interior was redecorated in the Baroque style in the 18C. The church itself was seriously damaged by a fire in 1822, although the Gothic doorways and exterior murals on the west and south façades (late 15C, early 16C, depicting among other things St Christopher and scenes from Christ's Passion) were spared. After reconstruction, the church interior was "reconverted" back to the Gothic style in the early 20C. At 84.5m/277ft the church tower is the tallest in the Tyrol.

H. Wiesenhofer/ÖSTERREICH WERBUNG

Carnival time at Imst

The well-known Imst carnival, with its procession of ghosts *(Schemenlaufen)*, takes place only every fourth year *(see Calendar of events)*, however those who are interested can see the masks and costumes used on this occasion in the **Fasnachtsmuseum**. The world's first SOS-Children's Village was founded in Imst in 1949. Since then, more than 380 such institutions have been set up in 130 countries, providing orphaned or abandoned children with a new home.

★ **Rosengartenschlucht** – *This trail leaves from Imst centre, to the left of the yellow church of St. Johannes with its onion-domed tower. The walk takes 1hr 30min there and back and strong footwear is necessary.*

At first the path leads along the peacefully flowing lower course of the Schinderbach, but soon the surrounding countryside becomes more rugged, with roaring waterfalls and steep cliffs. Along the route there are fine views of the mountain scenery all around and into the valley towards Imst.

ISCHGL★★

Tirol

Population 1 350

Michelin map 926 fold 28 – Local map see ARLBERGGEBIET

Ischgl undoubtedly ranks among the most beautiful of Austria's winter sports resorts. Its setting on the **Silvretta-Hochalpenstraße**★★, at 1 377m/4 518ft above sea-level, draws holidaymakers from all over the world. Another particular point in the resort's favour is the amount of accommodation on offer, with guest beds in hotels of every category of comfort. Possibilities for whiling away one's leisure hours include the Silvretta and Freizeit Centers which contain an indoor swimming pool, a sauna, eight tennis courts, a billiards room and a bowling alley. And if you want to have fun in the evening after your activities on the slopes, you have come to the right place, as Ischgl goes in for some intensive après-ski.

In summertime, Ischgl is transformed into a peaceful holiday resort, quite unlike its winter alterego. It is an ideal stopover for those exploring the Arlberg region.

Ischgl

✻✻ **Alpine ski slopes** – The ski slopes at Ischgl and the neighbouring Swiss resort of **Samnaun**✻ (alt 1 840m/6 037ft) belong to the Silvretta-Ski- and Funsportarena (alt 1 400-2 900m/4 600-9 500ft) which has 200km/124mi of pistes and 41 ski lifts. Almost the entire site lies over 2 000m/6 550ft above sea-level, with the result that snow cover remains excellent until early May. Connections between the mountain slopes are good, enabling skiers to get maximum benefit from the variety of pistes which cover this vast resort.

Several of the ski slopes have really made a name for themselves, in particular the magnificent descents from the Palinkopf peak to Samnaun and the Gampenalp. For less high-powered skiing, the best slopes are those towards Switzerland and the Velillscharte.

For **cross-country skiers** there is a ski track towards Galtür *(see SILVRETTA-HOCHALPENSTRASSE)*, from where there are more possibilities available.

★ **Pardatschgrat** ⌚ – Alt 2 624m/8 609ft. *In winter take the Pardatschgratbahn up; in summer and winter the Silvrettabahn gives access as far as the Idalp (2 320m/7 612ft).* There is a particularly pretty view of the Paznaun Valley if you sit facing the way the cable-car is going. The houses of Ischgl lie scattered at the foot of the Seeköpfe and Küchlspitze (alt 3 147m/10 325ft) peaks. From the station at the top there is a good view of the ski slopes surrounded by the Vesulspitze, Bürkelkopf, Flimspitze and Piz Rots summits. Directly to the south lies the Fimbatal, dwarfed by the Fluchthorn massif.

Readers should note that an almost identical view can be enjoyed from the Idalp summit (alt 2 311m/7 582ft), which is reached by the Silvretta-Seilbahn (cable-car).

★★ **Trida Sattel** – Alt 2 488m/8 163ft. *Take the cable-car up from Samnaun or follow the ski tracks from Ischgl.* From the terrace of the mountain restaurant, the **view**★★ extends southwards over the sheer Stammerspitze, Muttler and Piz Mundin peaks, and to the southeast over the Ötztaler Alps. To the north lie the ski slopes across the Swiss border, at the foot of the Bürkelkopf.

An even more far-ranging **panorama**★★ can be enjoyed from the Visnitzbahn and Mullerbahn chair-lifts.

Bad ISCHL

Oberösterreich

Population 14 000

Michelin map 926 fold 20 – Local map see SALZKAMMERGUT – Alt 469m/1 539ft

Bad Ischl is in the heart of the Salzkammergut and is the Austrian watering-place where the reign of Franz Joseph has left the greatest marks of luxury, having been for 70 years one of the most brilliant centres of fashionable life in Europe. The therapeutic properties of its saline waters were brought to public notice about 1820 by a Viennese practitioner, Dr Wirer, and were confirmed by some historic cures, such as those which justified the nickname "Princes of the Salt", given to the children of Archduchess Sophia born here, the most famous being the future Emperor, Franz Joseph.

By establishing his summer quarters at Ischl, near his favourite hunting grounds, **Franz Joseph** turned the spa into a holiday resort which attracted many crowned heads, composers such as Anton Bruckner, Johann Strauss, Emmerich Kálmán, Karl Millöcker and Franz Lehár (whose villa is now a museum), painters such as Ferdinand Waldmüller and Rudolf von Alt, the poet Nikolaus Lenau and the playwright Johann Nestroy. With the disappearance of court life, the spa has concentrated its efforts on the renewal of its facilities, in rebuilding the medical establishment (Kurmittelhaus) and in modernizing the majestic Kurhaus or casino.

SPA

The parks and Biedermeier style buildings cluster in a setting of densely wooded mountains, on the inside of a loop at the confluence of the River Traun and River Ischl. The **Auböckplatz (B)**, bordered by the drinking hall *(Trinkhalle)*, a former pump room (1831), and the parish church, reconstructed at the end of the reign of Maria Theresa, is the traditional centre of town life.

The Auböckplatz is linked to the Elisabethbrücke, a bridge spanning the Traun, by the **Pfarrgasse** (**B 16**), the main shopping street of Ischl, which retains such survivals from 19C spa life as the Zauner Café and pastry shop. The Pfarrgasse ends at the **Esplanade** (**A**), a shady walk beside the Traun, which was once the domain of the rich *Salzfertiger* (salt refiners) who were responsible for storing salt for the Treasury before it was sent downstream. One of their dwellings, the Seeauer House (no 10), with a Rococo façade and triple gables, has kept its original character. The parents of Franz Joseph stayed there between 1844 and 1877; Franz Joseph and his wife Elisabeth lived there in 1853. Later it became a hotel and now it houses the local museum.

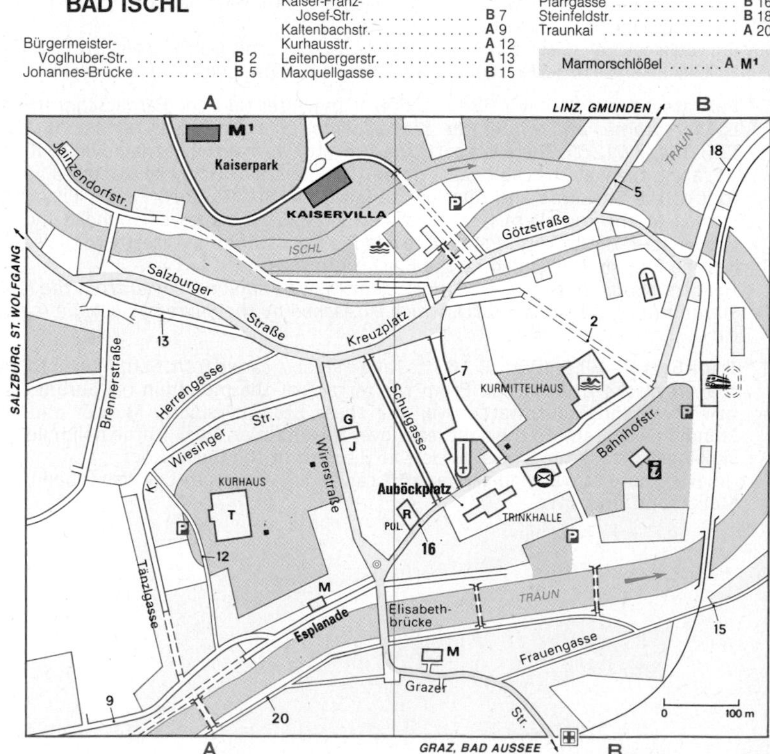

★ KAISERVILLA ⓥ (A)

The Imperial villa stands to the north of the town, on the left bank of the Ischl, in a magnificent landscape garden, the **Kaiserpark**. It was given to the Imperial couple as a wedding present by Archduchess Sophia. Though it has Classical colonnades, the house reveals the simple character of Franz Joseph by the importance given to hunting, of which he was an ardent devotee, and the sovereign disregard of modern comfort and amenities to be found in his private apartments (the study and the bedroom). One of the more moving parts of the tour is the visit to **Empress Elisabeth**'s Grey Salon, off which lie her oratory and study. This is exactly as it was on 16 July 1898, when "Sissi", as she was affectionately known, left for Geneva, where she was to be assassinated two months later by an Italian anarchist.

CAT'S COLLECTION

Sissi, with Romy Schneider and Karlheinz Böhm

It was in the Kaiservilla that Franz Joseph signed the fateful declaration of war with Serbia on 1 August 1914.

Marmorschlößl (**M**[1]) – In the park is the little "marble palace", Empress Elisabeth's tea house and a favourite retreat of hers; it now houses a photography museum, **Photomuseum** ⓥ.

KAISERGEBIRGE★★

Tirol

Michelin map 926 folds 18 and 19

The limestone massif of the Kaisergebirge is surrounded by the continuous belt of valleys in which Kufstein, Walchsee, Kössen, Griesenau, St. Johann in Tirol and Ellmau stand. It is popular with mountaineers, and is the outermost bastion of the northern Kalkalpen (Limestone Alps). This fact enables the peaks of its outer limits to be easily distinguished.

The Kaiser Valley between Kufstein and the Stripsenjoch breaks the Kaisergebirge range in two: a higher, "wilder" chain to the south (highest peak Ellmauer Halt, 2 344m/7 690ft), known as the **Wilder Kaiser** and easily distinguished by its steep, craggy cliffs lining the Kitzbühel and more especially the Ellmau horizon; and the "tamer" chain to the north (highest peak Pyramidenspitze 1 977m/6 487ft), known as the **Zahmer Kaiser** and characterised by more gentle, Alpine pasture-covered slopes. The easiest way of reaching the heart of the mountain range is from the east via the Kaiserbach Valley.

WILDER KAISER

1 From Lofer to Kufstein *68km/42mi*

★ **Lofer** – The village of Lofer, with the delicately chiselled, snow-flecked cliffs of the Loferer Steinberge in the background, makes a delightful scene. Its onion-domed church tower stands in front of a natural amphitheatre, through which the peak of the 2 487m/8 160ft Großer Reifhorn can be seen between the wooded foothills of the Großer Ochsenhorn (2 511m/8 238ft) and the Breithorn (2 413m/7 917ft).

Imposing houses adorned with deep overhanging balconies and ornate façades decorated with flowers and paintings can be found all along the narrow streets, in which traffic is restricted. Lofer is a well-known departure point for ramblers. Particular favourites include walks to the Auerwiesen, Loferer Alm or the **Maria Kirchental pilgrimage church** *(see SAALACHTAL)*.

Leave Lofer on B 312 towards St. Johann.

The valley narrows to the width of the wooded ravine known as the Paß Strub (memorial on a rock base to the right of the road commemorating the fighting by Tyrolean rebels against Napoleon), where the torrent swirls and foams.
Those with time should take a brief detour to **Strub**, by turning left about 3km/2mi after the memorial. The charming, if less well maintained than B 312 to which it runs parallel, stretch of road between Strub and Waidring contains many splendid examples of traditional Tyrolean farmhouses (living quarters, stables and granary all under one roof).

Waidring - At the centre of this little town is a square with a fountain. A number of old farmhouses with flower-bedecked balconies and ridge turrets make a charming picture. The parish church (1757-64) features beautiful stuccowork and pastels in the Rococo style.

Return to B 312 and carry on towards St. Johann.

Erpfendorf - *Turn left off the road towards the town centre.* The church, finished in 1957, is the work of Clemens Holzmeister, a master of contemporary religious architecture in Austria and designer of the new building for the Salzburg Festival. The exterior is a mixture of the traditional (tower, shingle roof) and the modern and blends in perfectly with the rest of the town. Inside the church is a monumental Crucifixion group, integrated into the roof beam construction above the nave.
The route through the Leukental from Erpfendorf to St. Johann offers fine views of the Wilder Kaiser, from both Kirchdorf and St. Johann.

✻ **St. Johann in Tirol** - *See ST. JOHANN IN TIROL.*

It is the section from St. Johann to Ellmau which offers the most distinct views of the south wall of the Wilder Kaiser, with the Treffauer (2 304m/7 559ft) as its outwork.

★ **Spitalskirche zum Hl. Nikolaus in der Weitau** - *Shortly after leaving St. Johann, turn right off the main road towards Rettenbach/Weitau. After about 1km/0.5mi the road re-enters St. Johann (signpost). Straight afterwards, to the right, is this little church, surrounded by the buildings belonging to the Weitau Agricultural College.* The church was founded in 1262 for a home for the poor, and converted into the Gothic style in c 1460 and the Baroque style (roof turrets, round-arched windows and interior decor) in the 18C. In 1744 Simon Benedikt Faistenberger from Kitzbühel painted the ceiling frescoes (St Nicholas as patron of the poor in the chancel, the Fourteen Auxiliary Saints and St John of Nepomuk in the nave). In 1745 Josef Adam Mölk from Vienna created the murals. The church window behind the altar is the oldest preserved stained-glass window in the Tyrol (c 1480). The church also houses the oldest bell in the Tyrol (1262) *(not on show to the public)*.

Ellmau - This little village, a relatively sleepy farming community until the Second World War, has transformed itself into a smart tourist resort. A footpath leads off from near the Baroque parish church of St Michael to the **Maria-Heimsuchungs-Kapelle** (1719), Ellmau's trademark feature, located on a hill above the town. From the chapel there is a fine view of the town against the backdrop of the Kaisergebirge mountains.

Hintersteinersee - *About 4km/2.5mi after Ellmau, turn right towards Scheffau/Hintersteinersee. The road goes through* **Scheffau** *and*

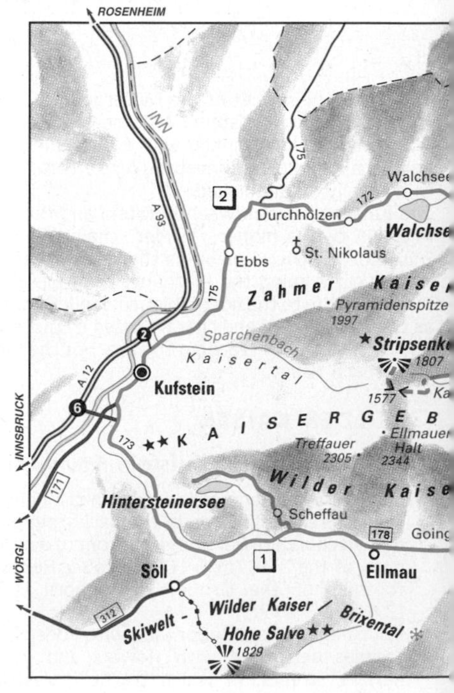

reaches the bank of the lake after a steep, winding stretch of about 5km/3mi. Car park. The crystal clear waters of this mountain lake reflect the rocky crags of the Wilder Kaiser. The lake offers the opportunity of bathing or a lakeside walk.

Return to B 312 and carry on towards Wörgl.

Söll - This charming little town, lying in a hollow, is grouped round the church of St Peter and St Paul, built between 1764 and 1768 and boasting fine Baroque interior decor richly decorated with stuccoes and frescoes. To the south lies the Hohe Salve with its unmistakable rounded summit.

★★ **Hohe Salve** - Alt 1 829m/6 000ft. **Cable-car and chair-lift** ⌚ *to the summit. Lower station is about 1km/0.5mi southwest of Söll, signposted "Bergbahnen".* From the summit with its tiny church and a restaurant there is a marvellous **panorama**★★ to the south, taking in the Brixen Valley, the Kitzbüheler Alps (Großer Rettenstein) and, further off in the distance, the Hohe Tauern (Großvenediger) and the Zillertaler Alps. To the north, the horizon is dominated by the jagged rocky peaks of the Wilder Kaiser.

A path, best negotiated on foot, to the left of the lower station leads after 500m/550yd to the **Stampfanger pilgrimage chapel** (1670, modern building 1757), idyllically situated on a rocky pedestal above the Stampfangerbach. The chapel itself can only be reached across a covered bridge.

✲ **Skiwelt Wilder Kaiser-Brixental** - This ski area encompasses eight winter sports resorts from the Wilder Kaiser (Going, Ellmau, Scheffau, Söll, Itter) and the Brixen Valley (Brixen, Westendorf, Hopfgarten). It is virtually possible to ski across the entire area with its 250km/155mi of ski runs and 90 ski lifts without needing to take off your skis, although some of the connections between individual mountains can be a little arduous. This large ski area set amid medium-altitude mountains is ideal for skiers who prefer a more gentle and relaxed style of skiing. There are numerous untaxing ski runs through the forest. More experienced skiers will be drawn to the black run on the Hohe Salve.

For easiest access to the ski area, the resorts of Scheffau, Söll and the pretty town of Brixen are to be recommended.

For those interested in cross-country skiing, there are 110km/68mi of ski tracks divided between the various resorts, of which 30km/19mi each are concentrated around Söll and Hopfgarten.

Take B 312 back northeast and after 2km/1mi turn right towards Kufstein.

Road 173, known as the Eibergstraße, leads into the Weißbach gorge, at the far end of which the fortress of Kufstein comes into view to the right.

Kufstein - *See KUFSTEIN.*

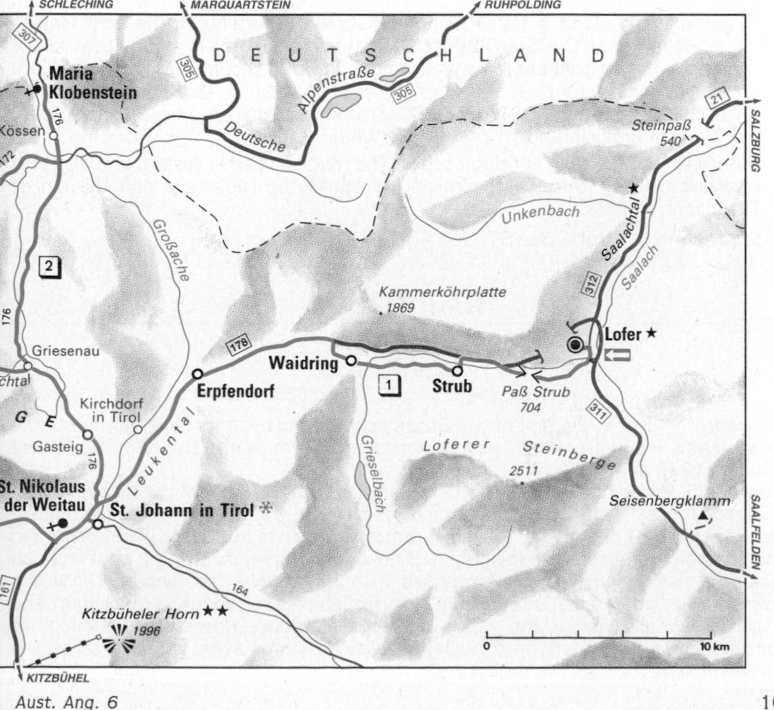

ZAHMER KAISER

2 From Kufstein to St. Johann in Tirol *61km/38mi*

Skirting the Kaisergebirge to the north, the road continues first at the foot of the slopes of the Zahmer Kaiser and then through a harsher landscape towards the imposing Wilder Kaiser rockface. It passes through villages like Ebbs or Walchsee where the comfortable houses are reminders of the proximity of Bavaria.

Kufstein - *See KUFSTEIN.*

North of Kufstein the Kaisergebirge massif ends above the alluvial plain of the Inn in great precipices, cut through by the terminal gorge of the Sparchenbach, a torrent whose valley - the Kaisertal - runs into the heart of the massif. Leaving the foot of these cliffs, the road provides an extensive view of the Ebbs plain, dominated by the pilgrim church of St. Nikolaus (1490), which is perched on a wooded foothill.
Take road 172 east towards Kössen. Between Durchholzen and the Walchsee the corridor opens out into an attractive valley, partly drowned by the lake and overlooked by a few peaks of the Zahmer Kaiser.

Walchsee - The road leads along the north shore of the lake (of the same name as the village), which is used for water sports and has attracted a healthy level of tourism to the village.

Maria Klobenstein - *A side road leads for about 8km/5mi up the Klobenstein pass. In Kössen, turn onto road 176 towards Schleching. 3km/2mi from town there is a signpost to "Wallfahrtskirche Maria Klobenstein". Follow the road for 500m/550yd until you reach a parking area to the left of it, before the tunnel. A short footpath leads to the chapel.*
The Ache, which rises as a surging torrent in the Kitzbüheler Alps and flows towards the Chiemsee under a series of different names (Kitzbüheler Ache, Tiroler Ache, Kössener Ache), forces itself through a narrow gap just behind **Kössen** forming the natural border between the Tyrol and Bavaria.
Below the road, which runs through this picturesque gorge linking Kössen with Schleching in Bavaria, stands the pilgrimage chapel of Maria Klobenstein which unusually features two church interiors one inside the other (1707 and 1733). Beneath the chapel a rock split into two and several metres high can be seen - this is the "Klobenstein" (cleft rock) to which the locality owes its name.

Take road 176 back, heading south, until it reaches Griesenau and the entry to the Kaiserbach Valley. From the junction, a **toll** *is levied on the road. After 5km/3mi, park the car at the car park by the Griesener Alm.*

Ascent of the Stripsenkopf - *4hr on foot there and back. Nearly 800m/2 623ft difference in altitude. The path gets more demanding between the Stripsenjoch pass and the summit, so should only be attempted by experienced ramblers with suitable footwear.* The climb begins from Griesener Alm (1 024m/3 360ft) on the other bank of the Kaiserbach. Initially, the path is well maintained and waymarked "Stripsenjoch". About a 1hr 30min walk should bring you to the Stripsenjoch mountain refuge at 1 605m/5 266ft. Skirt the refuge to the right and then follow the red-white "Stripsenkopf" waymarkings. The path becomes steeper and there are one or two tricky rock passages. After about 30min, you should reach the Stripsenkopf summit (1 807m/5 928ft) from where there is an excellent close-up **view**★ of the imposing north face of the Wilder Kaiser.

Return to road 176 and continue south. The road ends after **Gasteig**, with a pretty **panoramic descent**★ through the meadows above the Leukental and the dip of St. Johann in Tirol.

✻ **St. Johann in Tirol** - *See ST. JOHANN IN TIROL.*

KAPRUN✻

Salzburg

Population 2 800

Michelin map 926 fold 32 - Alt 786m/2 579ft

This peaceful town at the foot of the Großglockner road owes its development to the construction of a hydroelectric power station upstream of it in the Kapruner Valley between 1938 and 1951.
From 1965, the linking of the Schmieding glacier with the flank of the Kitzsteinhorn has made it possible to ski all year round. As a result, Kaprun has gradually made a name for itself as one of the leading summer ski resorts in Europe. The resort can also boast numerous leisure facilities (18-hole golf course, swimming pool etc) and took on a new dimension by linking itself with **Zell am See**✻ *(see entry)*. These two towns, separated by a distance of only 7km/4mi, have evolved into a huge sport and relaxation complex under the name of **Europa-Sportregion**. However, the village of Kaprun itself, at the mouth of the valley, is quite a distance away from the ski slopes *(some form of transport is necessary)*.

During the summer the Kapruner Valley, famed for its magnificent mountain setting, has numerous interesting footpaths to offer the visitor. The **Alexander-Einziger-Weg** from the Alpincenter (upper section of the Kitzsteinhorn) to the summit of the Maiskogel is well worth a detour *(beforehand, enquire at the tourist office about bus times to the Kitzsteinhorn car park)*.

★★ KAPRUNERTAL

Allow a day (at least 2hr 30min for the Kitzsteinhorn and at least 4hr for the reservoirs, which are only accessible between late May and mid-October).

The Kapruner Valley lies between the ice-capped summits of the Hohe Tauern and the green, shimmering waters of the **reservoirs**★★, lying one above the other, attached to the hydroelectric power scheme. The Glockner-Kaprun power station is one of the most pioneering and successful achievements of Austrian technology.

Located 2km/1mi upstream of the town, the **Kraftwerksgruppe Glockner-Kaprun** ⓥ (output: 220 000kW) is the lower station of the power complex. The road becomes noticeably steeper at this point, while the valley tucked between sheer cliffs appears ever more barren. Further up ahead looms the wall of the Limberg dam. *Park the car at the foot of the Kitzsteinhorn ski lift.*

Markowitsch/ÖSTERREICH WERBUNG

Kapruner Valley

★★★ **Kitzsteinhorn** ⓥ – *Take the cable car, which gives a view of the surrounding landscape. The underground funicular closed in November 2000 after a tragic fire, and it is uncertain when it will reopen.*

The **trip**★★ between two particularly sheer rock faces is most impressive. Finally, the cable-car reaches Langwied station (alt 2 000m/6 562ft), which is the departure point for the ski slopes during winter.

Take the Langwiedbahn up as far as the upper section and the **Alpincenter** station (alt 2 452m/8 045ft, restaurant). There is a beautiful view of the Kitzsteinhorn massif and the summer ski slopes.

The connecting cable-car climbs to 3 029m/9 938ft above sea-level, reaching a snow-covered mountain ridge just below the summit (alt 3 203m/10 503ft, accessible only to mountaineers). From the upper station climb to the second level of the viewing terrace. Straight ahead stands the Großvenediger, dominating the whole **panorama**★★★. To the left are the Granatspitze and the Stubacher Sonnblick, and to the right tower the peaks of the Zillertal, Kitzbüheler Alps, Zell am See with its lake and numerous limestone ridges from the Wilder Kaiser as far as the Hochkönig. On a clear day the view stretches as far as the Zugspitze on the other side of the Karwendel range.

Go down three floors and follow the tunnel for 360m/390yd to the "Glocknerkranzl" terrace. From this terrace there is an impressive **view**★★ of the Großglockner, flanked by the Bärenkopf and Hoher Riffel peaks.

Kitzsteinhorn ski slopes These are open all year round. Admittedly, the total area covered is relatively modest (15 ski lifts and 35km/22mi of ski runs), but it offers fantastic snow conditions in a spectacular setting between 2 000m/6 500ft and 3 000m/10 000ft above sea level. The facilities are among the most modern and comfortable anywhere in Austria. The ski runs are suitable for all levels of ability, with a slight preponderance of easier runs.

Return to the lift and travel down to the Kesselfall-Alpenhaus car park.

★★ **Hydroelectric dams** – A bus runs to the lower station of the Lärchwand funicular. During the ascent there is a good view of the valley through which you have just travelled, and also of Kaprun. At the upper station, the wall of the Limberg dam comes into view, with the Wiesbachhorn, the Bärenkopf and the Klockerin peaks in the background.

Limbergsperre – The Limberg dam (alt 1 672m/5 486ft) is an arch gravity dam measuring 120m/394ft high by 357m/1 171ft along the top of the dam wall. The power station at the foot of the dam wall receives water from the Mooserbodenspeicher reservoir opposite and expels it into the Wasserfallboden reservoir behind the dam.

From the upper station, take a bus which travels along the Mooserbodenstraße, 1 700m/1mi of which cuts through tunnels, to the Mooser dam. During the drive, there is a good view, initially close at hand and then from above, of the **Wasserfallboden reservoir**★ in its marvellous isolated mountain setting.

★ **Mooser- und Drossensperre** – Alt 2 036m/6 680ft. Both valley exits of the Mooserboden are blocked by arch gravity dams lying to the east and west of the so-called Höhenburg. The **Mooserboden reservoir**★★, lying amid spectacular Alpine scenery at the foot of the ice-clad Hohe Tauern, makes an indelible impression on visitors. Crossing the first dam, there is a wonderful **view**★★ down onto the green waters of the Wasserfallboden, against a mountain backdrop formed by the Leoganger Steinberge and the Steinernes Meer.

A 12km/7.5mi long gallery carries melt water from the Pasterzen glacier and water from the Leiterbach, collected daily in the Margaritze overflow reservoir at the foot of the Großglockner, to the Mooserboden.

KARWENDELGEBIRGE★

Tirol und Bayern (Germany)

Michelin map 926 fold 17 – North of Innsbruck

The limestone massif of the Karwendel (highest point: the Birkkarspitze, 2 749m/9 019ft), whose first section, the Nordkette, lies north of Innsbruck, can also be seen as an impressive feature from the Mittenwald (in Germany) or from the road to the Achensee. Only an excursion into the Rißbach Valley, with a possible detour through Bavaria, will enable the motorist to get near the greyish, pitted cliffs, the *Kar* which give these mountains their character. If time is scarce, it is worth driving as far as the Achensee, the largest lake in the Tyrol.

1 FROM THE INN VALLEY TO THE SYLVENSTEIN DAM (GERMANY) *39km/24mi*

Beginning at the Inn Valley *(exit on motorway "Wiesing-Achensee")*, the panoramic road climbs up to Eben.

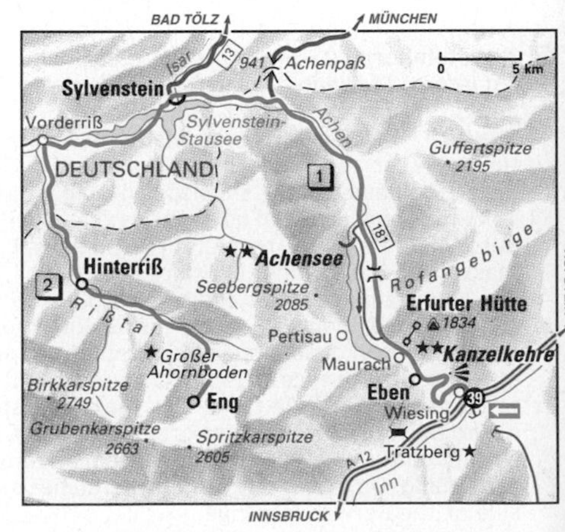

★★ **Kanzelkehre** – This terraced viewpoint is laid out on a curve. The **view**★★ looks down on the Inn Valley and the lower Ziller Valley, which is dotted with very sharp steeples (Wiesing in the foreground). The scale of these valleys, with their attractive landscapes fashioned by human activity over many centuries, makes a fascinating contrast to the surrounding mountains. The Rofangebirge mountain peaks tower up to the north.

Eben – The church of this village contains the chalice of St Notburga, who is much venerated in Bavaria and the Tyrol as the patroness of workers.

Erfurter Hütte ⏲ - Alt 1 834m/6 033ft. *Ascent by cable-car.* This hut, the departure point for climbing expeditions to scale the Rofangebirge massif, is set in a magnificent panorama above the Achensee and the Karwendel.

★★ **Achensee** - Visitors will be interested in the local anomaly of the parting of the waters between the Isar (to the north) and Inn (to the south) basins. The lake empties through the Achenbach, a tributary of the Isar, though the sheet of water lies in a hanging valley over the trench formed by the Inn. A morainic barrier, created by the former Inn glacier, explains this phenomenon. Engineers have taken advantage of the site by tapping the waters of the Achensee for the benefit of the electrical power station about 350m/1 150ft lower down, near Jenbach, in the Inn Valley.

The road climbs steeply again, offering the finest **view**★★ of the Karwendel summits, which rise massively round Pertisau on the opposite shore.

To drive along the edge of the lake, turn round at the village of Achensee and use the old road (one way: north-south).

Austro-German border just after Achenwald. There is the option of turning right and driving across the Achen pass to the Tegernsee in Bavaria (about 18km/11mi from the border). Turn left onto road 307 to the Sylvenstein dam.

Sylvenstein-Staudamm - This dam regulates the dreaded floodwaters of the Isar. Water is conducted from the vast reservoir into an underground power station to generate electricity.

2 FROM THE SYLVENSTEIN DAM (GERMANY) TO ENG *37km/23mi*

The road, for part of which a **toll** *is charged, is narrow and winding and cannot be used from November to May.*

Sylvenstein-Staudamm - *See above.*

On leaving the banks of the artificial lake, and reaching Vorderriß, turn left into the deep Riß Valley and crosses the Austro-German border.

Hinterriß - The hunting lodge built in the 19C for the Duke of Coburg-Gotha is a favourite holiday resort of the Belgian royal family.

Use binoculars to scan the slopes and steep cliffs overlooking the road, to see some of the 5 000 chamois which still live on the massif.

Eng - The road ends here, in the **Großer Ahornboden**★, a grassland where the maples glow with magnificent colours in the autumn in an otherwise severe landscape. The walls of the Spritzkarspitze (alt 2 605m/8 547ft) and the Grubenkarspitze (alt 2 661m/8 727ft) form a natural amphitheatre marking the end to the valley.

KAUNERTAL★★★

Tirol

Michelin map 926 fold 29

This long valley, through which leads one of Europe's highest roads, the Kaunertaler Gletscher-Panoramastraße (Kaunertal Glacier Panoramic Road; highest point: 2 750m/9 022ft), is the ideal place for a day trip, with its magnificent mountain scenery and large reservoir. Skiing is possible all year round on the Weißseeferner glacier.

Ideally you should set off early in the morning. Exploring the valley in its entirety involves first a drive to the Weißseeferner glacier, then going to the Karlesspitze summit, then a hike to the Gepatschferner glacier and along the road to Piller. From here, it is possible to follow the **Pitz Valley**★★★ *(see PITZTAL) which runs parallel to the Kauner Valley. Allow at least 6hrs not including rests.*

★★ FROM PRUTZ TO THE WEISSSEEFERNER GLACIER *40km/25mi*

In Prutz, turn left off the Bundestraße 315 towards Switzerland and Italy. The road runs alongside the River Faggenbach in a deeply incised, green valley at the foot of the Köpfle (alt 2 834m/9 298ft) and Peischlkopf (alt 2 913m/9 557ft) peaks.

After 12km/7.5mi, the road passes through the village of Feichten. From here on a toll is payable. The valley becomes considerably wider, and there are fleeting glimpses of the Gletscherkessel lying in the distance. After 10km/6mi of steep climb through a beautiful forest, the road brings you to the Gepatsch reservoir *(car park)*, the largest in west Austria. There is a very pretty **view**★ of the lake and the Weißseespitze (alt 3 526m/11 568ft). The road runs along the left bank of the lake for 6km/4mi, sprayed by numerous **waterfalls**★ as it goes. The best view of the long lake with its border of pine trees is to be had after the Faggenbach bridge.

From bend 12, there are impressive **views**★ of the splendid tongue of the Gepatsch glacier. The look-out point in bend 7 gives a magnificent **view**★★ as far as the Weißseespitze, the Fluchtkogel (alt 3 497m/11 473ft) and the Hochvernagtspitze (alt 3 535m/11 598ft).

The surrounding landscape becomes ever more rocky, as vegetation thins out. There is a **view**★ to the right of the picturesque Krummgampen Valley with its reddish cliffs. Shortly after this, the Weißsee comes into sight on the left. The final, steep stretch of road leads to the edge of the Weißseeferner glacier, where the road comes to an end (alt 2 750m/9 022ft). You are now in an all-year ski area served by three chair-lifts, five T-bar lifts and a practice lift (highest altitude: 3 160m/10 367ft).

★★★ASCENT TO THE KARLESSPITZE

★★★ **Wiesenjaggl-Sessellift (Chair-lift)**⌚ - Alt 3 010m/9 875ft. *45min there and back.* During the ascent in the chair-lift and on the summit itself, visitors find themselves surrounded by magnificent **mountain scenery**★★★. Besides those peaks already mentioned, the view encompasses those of Ölgruben and Bligg.

★★ **Walk to Klettersteig Panoramablick** - Alt 3 160m/10 367ft. *1hr there and back from the upper station of the chair-lift. The path leads through snow (mountain boots, sunglasses and warm clothing are essential). The walk is not particularly difficult, but it is quite taxing, as the path is very steep.*
This excursion offers even inexperienced hikers the rare opportunity of seeing a glacier at close hand without running any risks. The walk leads to a pass at the foot of the **Karlesspitze**, from where there is a **view**★ to the south over the Dolomites and to the southwest over the Swiss Alps.

Return to the car and drive back down to the Faggenbach bridge (car park).

★★HIKE TO THE GEPATSCHFERNER GLACIER

1hr 15min there and back from the bridge

The path runs along the right bank of the river. After about 100m/110yd, it brings you to a huge waterfall. There follows a very steep climb through pretty countryside, in which the reddish colour of the cliffs dominates. Numerous Alpine flowers bloom along the way. Finally the path reaches a point near the Gepatschferner glacier, which is the largest in Austria. There is a fine **view**★★ of the S-shaped tongue of the glacier. The rocky cirque is closed off by the Rauher Kopf and Schwarze Wand peaks.

★PILLERPASS-STRASSE

20km/12mi as far as Wenns

A drive along this road leading through a pretty medium-altitude mountain landscape is an ideal way to round off a sightseeing trip to the Kauner Valley. At 9km/6mi after the toll booths, turn right and drive up to the holiday resorts of Kauns and then Kaunerberg. Nearby, there are good **views**★ of the lower stretch of the Kauner Valley.
Carry on towards Piller *(take a left turn 450m/500yd or so after entering Kaunerberg)*. Having gone through the hamlet of Puschlin, the road brings you to the pass, at an altitude of 1 559m/5 115ft. The road then winds its way tortuously through extensive forest, across the Venet massif, before passing through the village of Piller and finally running into the **Pitz Valley**★★★ *(see PITZTAL)* at the level of Wenns.

KITZBÜHEL❄❄

Tirol

Population 7 872

Michelin map 926 folds 18 and 19 - Alt 762m/2 500ft

Kitzbühel is one of the oldest and most exclusive holiday resorts in the Austrian Alps. The valley in which it lies would appear to have been inhabited long before recorded time. The village itself developed thanks to its favourable geographical location on the main route from Venice to Munich. Its economic growth was further assured by rich local mining deposits. In 1255 it was granted the charter of market town, and in 1271 elevated to that of town.
Until the end of the 19C, Kitzbühel developed peacefully, untouched by the destruction of war. At that time, the town's inhabitants sent for a delivery of skis from Norway, so that they could try the sport out on the slopes of the Kitzbüheler Horn. However, it was not until 1931 that the **Hahnenkamm** opposite was opened to skiers in its turn.
The village rapidly developed its tourist industry, drawing holidaymakers from all over Europe, especially from Great Britain and Germany. The seal was put on its reputation with the construction of one of the most famous and testing World Cup downhill ski runs - the **Streif**.

In spite of this evolution, Kitzbühel retains some of the atmosphere of the fortified medieval village it once was. Its original site, on a terrace enclosed by two torrents gushing down from the Hahnenkamm, can still be discerned, despite the ever expanding suburbs. The nucleus of the town is formed by two pedestrian streets, the "Vorderstadt" and the "Hinterstadt", which are lined by elegant gabled Tyrolean houses. Numerous smart boutiques make this a tempting place to while away time window-shopping.
Kitzbühel can accommodate up to 7 200 visitors, mainly in hotels and guesthouses. Besides skiing, there are plenty of other sport and leisure activities on offer: ice-skating, curling, swimming (indoor pool with a health centre), casino.
The resort is popular with those on summer holiday as well. It has made quite a name for itself as the hub of Austria's tennis circuit (international tournaments are hosted here) and as one of the country's leading golf venues (two nine-hole and one 18-hole courses). Furthermore, it can boast a hang- and paragliding school and several riding centres. However, the main leisure activity during summer months is hiking, along some of the 200km/124mi of waymarked footpaths, which principally run along the ski slopes. These paths are suitable for those in search of an untaxing ramble, picturesque scenery and spectacular views *(lifts have been installed, as an alternative to walking, to give access to some of the best viewpoints).*

Kitzbühel Alps – Between the Wörgl-Saalfelden gap and the upper valley of the Salzach, the smoothly rounded Kitzbühel Alps reach an altitude of 2 362m/ 7 749ft at the Großer Rettenstein. Known locally as Grasberge (grass mountains), they form a charming and tranquil pastoral landscape.

The contrasting shapes and colours of the surrounding massifs – the jagged walls of the Wilder Kaiser in the north and the enormous ridge of the Hohe Tauern in the south – make the Kitzbühel Alps much sought after for the quality of their views.

Ascher/PIX

Kitzbühel in the snow

** **Ski slopes** – These are spread over four separate areas: **Hahnenkamm-Steinbergkogel-Pengelstein** (alt 750-1 970m/2 450-6 450ft), **Kitzbüheler Horn** (alt 750-2 000m/2 450-6 550ft), **Stuckkogel** (alt 900-1 580m/2 950-5 180ft) and **Paß Thorn** (alt 930-1 980m/3 050-6 500ft). Buses transport skiers to each mountain. There are 64 ski lifts leading to 55 ski runs covering a total distance of 158km/98mi. In contrast to the sporty image that the resort has acquired through the international competitions held here, the ski slopes are principally suited to more gentle skiing, with long, pleasant runs through pine forests ranging from relatively easy (Pengelstein, Kaser) to middlingly difficult (Fleck, Oxalm-Nord). Only about 12km/7.5mi of ski runs cover steeper terrain, mainly in the area of the Steinbergkogel peak. Because of the resort's relatively low altitude, snow does tend to disappear from some of the slopes as early as March, however.
To avoid the long queues at the Hahnenkamm massif, day trippers would be better off travelling to the neighbouring Kirchberg peak, where the Fleckalm cable-car gives access to the heart of the mountain range in 15min. The flank of the Kitzbüheler Horn opposite, which is equipped with modern ski lifts, is not to be missed, especially when snow conditions are good, as it is then possible to ski right down into the valley.

SIGHTS

Pfarrkirche (A) – Like the neighbouring Liebfrauenkirche the church is set off by its raised site. The slender tower flanks a 15C Gothic triple nave, whose large overhanging roof, covered with shingles, gives it a distinctive mountain style. The nave is not without grace. The talent of a local family, the **Faistenbergers**, who were all well-known artists in the 17C and 18C, is represented by the high altar, by Benedikt Faistenberger (1621-93) and the painted ceiling of the Chapel of St Rosa of Lima by his grandson, Simon-Benedikt (1695-1759).

Liebfrauenkirche (B) – This two-storeyed church is distinguished by a massive square tower, compared with which the nave seems very small. The Baroque interior of the upper church includes a ceiling fresco of the Coronation of the Virgin by Simon-Benedikt Faistenberger (1739) and a Rococo grille (1778).
A 17C painting of Our Lady of Succour (Maria-Hilf) after Cranach the Elder reminds us of the important role this church played as a place of pilgrimage until the 19C.

Museum Kitzbühel (**M**) – This local museum is housed in the oldest building in the town, a former grain store; its collection will be instructive to visitors interested in the origins of the town, which belonged to Bavaria for nearly 1 000 years.

KITZBÜHEL

Bichlstraße	2
Franz-Reich-Str.	4
Graggaugasse	5
Hammerschmiedstr.	7
Hinterstadt	8
J.-Pirchl-Straße	10
Klostergasse	12
Malinggasse	13
Vorderstadt	15

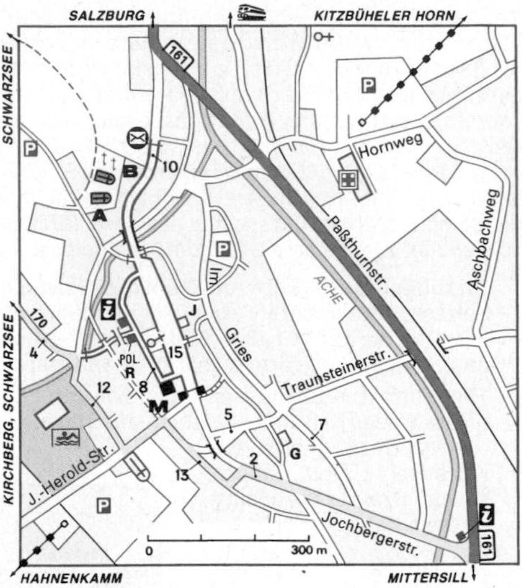

Heimatmuseum ... M Liebfrauenkirche ... B Pfarrkirche ... A

EXCURSIONS

★★ **Kitzbüheler Horn** – Alt 1 996m/6 549ft. *Allow 1hr 30min there and back. Take the cable-car up (in two stages).*
There is a fabulous **panorama**★★ of the jagged peaks of the Kaisergebirge to the northwest, the Kitzbühel ski slopes at the foot of the Rettenstein to the southwest and the Hohe Tauern with the Großvenediger and Großglockner summits to the south.
Return to the upper cable-car station, from where the limestone massif of the Loferer Steinberge can be seen lying to the east.
In the summer, the Kitzbüheler Horn is a departure point for an interesting **ramble to the Bichlalm** (alt 1 670m/5 479ft – *allow 3hr and wear stout footwear*). From here, take the chair-lift back down into the valley, and then the bus back to town *(enquire in advance about timetables at the tourist office).*

★ **Ehrenbachhütte (Hahnenkamm-Massiv)** – Alt 1 802m/5 912ft. *Take the cable-car up from Klausen (near Kirchberg), 45min there and back.*
There is a good **view**★ of the Wilder Kaiser, the Hohe Salve, the Kitzbüheler Horn and the Großer Rettenstein peaks.
In the winter, it is possible to ski up to the **Steinbergkogel** summit (alt 1 975m/6 480ft), from where there is a wide-ranging **panorama**★★ (Hohe Tauern, Leoganger Steinberge).
In the summer, ramblers can walk from the upper cable-car station to the Jufenkamm ridge, and then follow the path along the ridge south to the Pengelstein mountain refuge and on to the **Schwarzkogel**★ summit (alt 2 030m/6 660ft).

Schwarzsee – *5km/3mi on the Kirchberg road and the lake road to the right (level crossing). It is, however, more agreeable to walk all the way via the Liebfrauenkirche and the Lebenberg road (northwest of the town plan).*
This lake offers the opportunity of bathing within view of the Kaisergebirge.

Paß Thurn – Alt 1 273m/4 176ft. *20km/12mi south. Leave Kitzbühel on the road to Mittersill.* The best-arranged **viewing point**★ for cars to stop at is about 1 800m/5 900ft beyond the crest, on the Oberpinzgau slope, close to the "Tauernblick" snack bar. From this point there is an end view of the Hollersbachtal, which runs south towards the main crest of the Hohe Tauern range.
The slopes overlooking the pass are the ski fields of the resort of Mittersill.

KLAGENFURT

🄻 Kärnten

Population 90 000

Michelin map 926 fold 35 – Local map see WÖRTHER SEE – Alt 446m/1 463ft

Klagenfurt was founded in the 12C by Hermann von Spanheim, Duke of Carinthia. Although it was an important centre for trade, it was not Klagenfurt that was capital of the province but St. Veit an der Glan until the 16C. In 1518 Emperor Maximilian had the town elevated to capital of Carinthia.

A site on the banks of the warmest Alpine lake in Europe and a mild southern climate have ensured that Klagenfurt enjoys huge popularity as a holiday destination. For over 400 years the town and nearby lake, Wörther See, have been linked by a canal: the **Lendkanal** flows directly into the lake, past green banks dense with plant life and beautiful villas dating from the turn of the century.

TRAVELLERS' ADDRESSES

Tourist information

Klagenfurt-Tourismus, Rathaus, Neuer Platz, 9010 Klagenfurt.

Opening times: May-mid Oct Mon-Fri 8am-8pm, Sat, Sun and public holidays 10am-5pm; mid Oct-Apr Mon-Fri 8am-6pm, Sat, Sun and public holidays 10am-1pm. ☎ 04 63/53 72 23, Fax 04 63/53 72 95.

From May-Sept a monthly calendar of events is issued by the tourist office, otherwise refer to the annual calendar of events.

For more detailed information about the town, consult the **Web site** at *www.info.klagenfurt.at*

"Kärnten Card"

This "Carinthia Card" is useful further afield than just in Klagenfurt. It is available May-Oct and is valid for up to three weeks. Almost 90 sites/activities of interest (museums, cable-cars, boat trips, leisure parks and swimming pools) in Carinthia can be visited free of charge and in some cases as often as you like with this card (however, the card is not transferable). It also entitles you to free travel by local rail and bus. It is on sale at local Carinthian tourist offices for 385S. For further details about the card, call the hotline ☎ 04 63/30 00.

City tours

From July-Aug, free guided tours of the town on foot are available daily (except on Sun and public holidays) at 10am; during the rest of year for groups only (apply at the Klagenfurt-Tourismus office).

Public transport

It is advisable to buy your ticket before starting on your journey, since a supplement is payable when buying it from the bus driver.

With the **Stadtkarte** (town ticket) you can make as many journeys as you like in the space of 1hr on the Klagenfurt transport system; the same applies for different periods to the **24-Stunden-Karte** (24hr ticket) and the **7-Tage-Karte** (weekly ticket), which are each transferable.

Information about public transport as well as all tickets is available from the ticket sales office on the Heiligengeistplatz (Quelle-Passage, open Mon-Fri 6.30am-2.30pm, ☎ 04 63/52 15 42) or from tobacconists' shops (Trafiken). For telephone information about timetables, call ☎ 04 63/52 15 34 (5am-midnight).

Inner city car parks

No charge: St. Ruprechter Straße; Rosentaler Straße (Messegelände exhibition centre); Krassnigstraße.

Short-stay parking zones in the town centre are indicated by blue lines.

Long-stay, fee-paying car parks: Parkplatz Waaggasse; Parkgarage Geyerschütt (multi-storey); and the following underground car parks (Tiefgaragen): Apcoa on the Neuer Platz; Apcoa on the Heiligengeistplatz (Woolworths' store); Apcoa Dobernigstraße; and the Tiefgarage on the Domplatz.

Post offices

Hauptpostamt (main post office): Benediktinerplatz; open Mon-Fri 7.30am-8pm, Sat 7.30am-1pm.

Post am Bahnhof (station post office): open round the clock.

Shopping

Most of the department stores and shops, as well as the exclusive boutiques, are situated on the Alter Platz and Neuer Platz, and in the Bahnhofstraße, Kramergasse, Wienergasse, Burggasse and Paradeisergasse.
Pedestrianized area: Kramergasse, Wienergasse, Tabakgasse, Renngasse, Alter Platz and Dr.-Arthur-Lemisch-Platz.

Markets
Benediktinerplatz: weekday market daily except Wed 8am-5pm, Grand Market Thur and Sat 7am-noon.
Pfarrplatz: organic farm produce market every Fri 6am-noon.

Souvenirs
Craft goods and traditional costume (Trachten): Kärntner Heimatwerk, Herrengasse 2.

Entertainment

Stadttheater, Theaterplatz 4, ☎ 04 63/5 52 66. Theatre, music and dance.
klagenfurter ensemble, Südbahngürtel 24, ☎ 04 63/30 01 00. A professional troupe with its own home theatre has evolved from an amateur one founded in 1979, and now puts on theatre, music and children's productions.

Cinema

Kammerlichtspiele, Adlergasse 1, ☎ 04 63/5 40 51.
Wulfenia Kinozentrum, Luegerstraße 5, ☎ 04 63/2 22 88.
Volkskino, Kinoplatz 3, ☎ 04 63/31 98 80.
Carinthia Lichtspiele, Ehrentaler Straße 28, ☎ 04 63/4 22 56.

Eating out

Gasthaus Pumpe, Lidmanskygasse 2; **Gasthof Pirker**, Adlergasse 16; **Hirter Botschaft**, Bahnhofstraße 44; **Restaurant Wienerroither**, Neuer Platz 10; **Restaurant 5er**, Kaufmanngasse 5; **Restaurant Landhauskeller**, Landhaushof 1.

Cafés and bars

Cafés Café Domgassner, Domgasse 12; **Café Janach**, Bahnhofstraße 5; **Café Musil**, 10.-Oktober-Straße 14; **Café Segafredo**, Alter Platz 30; **Café am Neuen Platz**, Neuer Platz; **Café 7. Himmel**, Osterwitzgasse 12.

Popular bars Bierhof zum Augustin, Pfarrhofgasse 2; **Biergarten Marhof**, Stift-Viktring-Straße 18; **Künstlerhauscafé**, Goethepark 1; **Napoleonstadel "Haus der Architektur"**, St. Veiter Ring 10. Live music is played in the blues and jazz cellar **Kamot**, Bahnhofstraße 9. There is dancing at **Scotch Dancing**, Pfarrplatz 20; **Fun Factory &oy Dancing**, Gerberweg/Südring. Genuine cocktails are prepared in these bars: **Meyer Lansky**, Herrengasse 6; **Camino**, Rennplatz 2; **Lemon Bar**, Pfarrplatz 20; **Gates Internet Café**, Waagplatz; **Rockefeller Bar**, Osterwitzgasse 5; **Joe's Bar**, Arcotel Hotel Moser-Verdino, Domgasse 2.

Dates for your diary

Singing, dancing and music under the maypole: in May, traditional shows in the Landhaus courtyard.

Musikforum Viktring: in July and Aug. Master classes and series of concerts on modern music and jazz. Details from ☎ 04 63/28 22 41.

Altstadtzauber ("Old town magic"): last weekend in Aug. Brings together internationally known artists and music groups performing on several stages, with a big flea market.

Christkindlmarkt (Christmas market): in Dec on the Neuer Platz.

★★ OLD TOWN

The idyllic old town, which really comes to life in the summer, reflects almost 800 years of local history. Master architects from Italy are behind the town's present appearance with a regular grid pattern of streets, dating from the 16C and 17C. They are also responsible for over 50 picturesque arcaded courtyards, many of which are open to the public. The town boasts numerous fine squares, forming architectural highlights around the old town, which has been awarded the Europa-nostra prize three times.

Neuer Platz (**Y**) – This large regular square is at the heart of the old town. Its main attraction is the **Lindwurmbrunnen**★ or Dragon Fountain, which has become the emblem of Klagenfurt. The great monster was created by brothers Ulrich and Andreas Vogelsand between 1582 and 1593 from a block of chloride slate. The basin was added in 1624, and the Hercules figure in 1636. The monument to Maria Theresa, Austria's earliest to this monarch, was built in 1765; the bronze statue dates from 1873.

Each of the houses around the Neuer Platz has its own history and most are of historical value architecturally. The original Palais Porcia (now a hotel) dated from the late 18C, although the present building is a successful reconstruction. The **town hall** (Rathaus) on the west side of the square is original, despite having undergone substantial modification over the centuries; the core of the building dates from 1580. On the east side stands the 16C Adler-Apotheke with charming Rococo stucco decoration inside.

★ **Alter Platz (Y)** – Beautiful mansions dating from the 16C with Baroque façades and Renaissance arcaded courtyards lend a certain grandeur to this street-square at the heart of the old town. The **old town hall** (Altes Rathaus), built in 1600 and now called the Palais Orsini-Rosenberg, features a charming Renaissance doorway and a three-storey arcaded courtyard. To the west the Haus zur Goldenen Gans (Golden Goose), a gift from Emperor Friedrich III and one of the town's oldest houses, closes off the square. On the southwest corner stands the **Palais Goess** with a Late Baroque pilastered façade.

The Trinity Column (Dreifaltigkeitssäule), customarily found in Austrian towns, is also in evidence on the Alter Platz. It was built in 1689, in gratitude for the town's deliverance from the plague, and features motifs symbolising the world religions: a sphere, a crescent moon and a double cross.

Turn out of the Alter Platz into Wiener Gasse, at the end of which is the **Ossiacher Hof**, built in 1627, acquired by the foundation of this name in c 1750. Towards the end of the 18C the façade was transformed into the neo-Classical style. The magnificent building also boasts two fine inner courtyards.

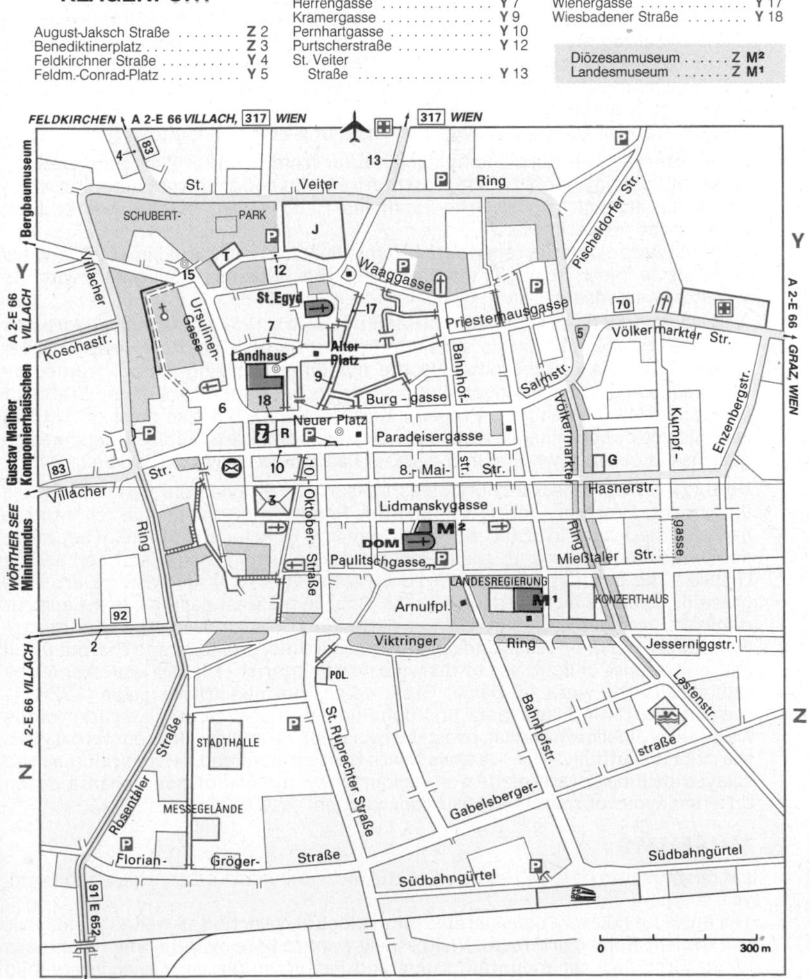

Großer Wappensaal, Landhaus, Klagenfurt

Stadthauptpfarrkirche St. Egyd – This church was built in 1692 and had a neo-Baroque façade added to it in 1893. The onion domes date from the 18C. The wide interior is richly decorated with galleries and sumptuous fittings. The ceiling paintings on the barrel vaulting are the work of Joseph Mölck, and those on the chancel vaulting are by Joseph Fromiller. Tombstones spanning four centuries testify to the importance of this church. The most recent was erected in 1998 to the French-American author Julien Green, who requested that he be buried in Klagenfurt "City of Joy and Peace".
From in front of the porch tower there is a fine **view★** of the town.

Landhaus (**Y**) – This imposing building not far from the Alter Platz embodies the power of the body of political representatives who had their seat here. It used to house the arsenal as well. The Landhaus is now used as the seat of local government for Carinthia.
Architect Antonio Verda contributed to this building, completed in 1590, and his influence is most strongly discernible in the **Renaissance courtyard★** with its two-storey arcaded gallery.

★ **Großer Wappensaal** ⏲ – This unique state hall on the first floor of the central block was decorated by one of Carinthia's most important Baroque painters, **Joseph Fromiller** (1693-1760). He painted not only the magnificent ceiling fresco, framed by *trompe-l'œil* galleries and depicting a scene showing members of the States of Carinthia paying homage to Emperor Karl VI (1728), but also most of the 665 heraldic shields adorning the walls and window embrasures, representing the coats of arms of noblemen who sat in the States Parliament between 1590 and 1848.

★ **Dom** (**Z**) – The cathedral church was built in 1578 under the Lutheran States Parliament. However, during the Counter Reformation the church fell into the hands of the Jesuits in 1604, who dedicated it to St Peter and St Paul. They made numerous alterations to it, most importantly enlarging the chancel and adding chapels. The building was destroyed by a fire in 1723, and visitors are thus greeted nowadays by a Baroque interior. Only on the west gallery has the opulent original stucco decoration by Gabriel Wittini in 1668 survived. The later stucco-work (after 1730) by Kilian and Josef Pittner are more delicate and charming still and lend a sense of lightness to the wide well-lit interior. The **high altar**, framed by columns, is the work of Daniel Gran, while the magnificent **pulpit** (1726) is attributed to Carinthian artist Christoph Rudolph, along with the execution of the **Apotheosis of St John of Nepomuk**, designed by Joseph Fromiller. This counterbalances the pulpit beautifully. The **side altars★** with their straight and twisted columns and splayed pediments are made very colourful by the use of more than a dozen different types of marble in their construction.

MUSEUMS

★ **Landesmuseum** ⏲ (**Z M**[1]) – A visit to the museum unlocks Carinthia's thousand-year history.
The museum houses a considerable mineralogical collection as well as prehistoric and Ancient Roman artefacts. Visitors will want to pore over the fine relief maps of the Großglockner mountain range and Pasterzen glacier. Other interesting

exhibits include models of mines and the "dragon skull", a fossilised woolly rhinoceros skull found in the Zollfeld in 1335 and said to have inspired the designer of the Lindwurmbrunnen. Also impressive is a large **mosaic floor★** from the Roman city of Virunum which depicts Dionysius in a ring of bacchantes.

The 15C and 16C are represented by numerous works of religious art, including the imposing St. Veit altarpiece (c 1470). Note also Paola Gonzaga's **bridal chests★** (c 1477) decorated with colourful reliefs based on designs by Andrea Mantegna.

Opposite the museum, a lapidary display has been set up, exhibiting a large collection of Ancient Roman stone memorials. These come from the Zollfeld, located halfway between Klagenfurt and St. Veit, once the site of the Ancient Roman provincial capital Virunum, near the modern site of Maria Saal Church *(see entry)*. Note especially the reconstruction of a Celtic fountain.

★ **Diözesanmuseum** ⓥ (**Z M²**) – The museum aims to give a good general picture of religious art in Carinthia from the 12C to the 18C; it displays examples of all the arts: gold- and silverwork, tapestry and embroidery, sculpture and painting. Next to immensely appealing specimens of folk art, there are outstanding **works of art★** such as the rare 12C **processional cross** (ironwork with traces of gilding) or the fine **Magdalen window★** dating from 1170, the oldest of its kind in Austria but of strikingly modern design.

★ **Bergbaumuseum** ⓥ (**Y**) – *Access via the botanical gardens. Take warm clothing with you, as the temperature is 9°C/48°F.*

The old air-raid galleries in the Klagenfurt Kreuzbergl are now home to the oldest museum on mining in Carinthia. A variety of rare and valuable exhibits illustrate local mining history.

The best and largest mineral samples from Carinthia are on display as if in a treasure chest, such as an enormous chunk of cairngorm weighing about 200kg/440lb and measuring 1m/3ft in height. A display of fossils charts geological eras spanning a period of over 500 million years. Since the various display areas have been impeccably academically researched, visitors are sure to learn a lot from the exhibition.

If you leave the museum while it is still daylight and emerge into the delightful botanical gardens, the contrast between the two worlds could not be greater.

EXCURSIONS

Minimundus – *3km/2mi west of Klagenfurt. Leave via the Villacher Straße* (**YZ**).

More than 170 scale models (1:25) of world monuments made of authentic materials, from Big Ben to the Statue of Liberty, and the Eiffel Tower to St Mark's in Venice, are displayed in a park-like setting.

Since great care is taken to create exact replicas, construction of a model can take up to five years. In spite of the reduction in size, some of the models nonetheless occupy the area of a detached house (the Vatican, the Dresden Zwinger). Every building in Minimundus is dwarfed by the 22m/72ft CN tower, the original of which is in Tokyo.

R. Chéret/MICHELIN

Minimundus – tour the world on foot

Gustav-Mahler-Komponierhäuschen ⓥ - *Follow the road along the south bank of the Wörthersee from Minimundus. Leave the car at the car park opposite Maiernigg beach. 30min on foot there and back.*
The log cabin hidden in the forest is pretty unprepossessing, but lovers of **Gustav Mahler**'s music are sure to be moved by it nonetheless. The composer created some of his masterpieces here between 1900 and 1907, including Symphonies Four to Eight and the Rückert Lieder. Employed as director of the Hofoper in Vienna during the year, Mahler only got the chance to compose during his summer holidays.

★ **Pörtschach** - *10km/33mi west of Klagenfurt along road 83.* Its unusual site on a peninsula jutting into the north side of the Wörthersee determined Pörtschach's development into a popular tourist resort, with elegant villas and hotels half-hidden by abundant foliage. A promenade path with colourful flowers in season runs all round the tiny tongue of land, while the town itself is characterised by grand villas.
Besides Schloß Leonstein perched on a rock southwest of town, the classic walk from Pörtschach is to the "Gloriette", a belvedere giving a view of the lake and the Karawanken mountains *(30min on foot; a lot of steps).*

St. Kanzian Lakes - *20km/12mi east of Klagenfurt. Leave by road no 70, the Völkermarkter Straße* (Y). This well-wooded lake district offers swimming and windsurfing as well as tennis and riding and an extensive network of signposted footpaths.
The Klopeinersee has a built-up lakeside with all kinds of water-based activities reached by private as well as public roads. The Turnersee and Kleinsee are quiet by comparison.
The road from Klagenfurt to St. Kanzian runs on a bridge over the Völkermarkter Stausee, an artificial lake formed by damming the Drava *(bathing forbidden).*

KLEINWALSERTAL★

Vorarlberg

Population 5 300

Michelin map 926 fold 15 - Local map see BREGENZERWALD

Alt of resorts: 1 086m/3 563ft to 1 244m/4 081ft

The Kleinwalsertal, which forms a tiny mountain area of about 100km²/38sq mi, is a region isolated from the rest of Austria by the peaks of the Allgäu Alps and is thus exclusively oriented towards Germany - whether it be economically or through tourism.

Walser Colonization - The upper Breitach Valley was settled and cleared in the late 13C by emigrants of Germanic origin from the Upper Valais - the Walser. Until 1930, when the modern road was built, the valley retained a strongly individual character, reflected in the widely scattered houses.

A unique administration - The Walser settlers passed under the sovereignty of the Habsburgs in 1453, so that they found themselves Austrian subjects when the national frontiers were fixed. The customs agreement of 1 May 1891 made the area part of the German economic area (currency, customs), although it remained Austrian sovereign territory.
The originally, uniquely agricultural valley has undergone a complete transformation and now earns its living almost exclusively from tourism. Despite the extremely well-developed tourist infrastructure, visitors will still find numerous secluded spots in side valleys, off the beaten track, which are the true highlights of this valley region.

Holiday region - The joint Kleinwalsertal and Oberstdorf ski pass puts a total 55 cable-cars and ski lifts at your disposal. There are also more than 50km/30mi of footpaths covering the valley that are kept clear for ramblers even in winter. In summer, there are walks of various levels of difficulty between altitudes of 1 100m/3 609ft and 2 500m/8 203ft.

FROM OBERSTDORF (GERMANY) TO BAAD

14km/8.6mi from the border

★★ **Oberstdorf** - Charming mountain air health resort and winter sports centre at the foot of the majestic Nebelhorn. *Traffic is barred from the town centre.*

Leave Oberstdorf on B 19 heading south. After about 5km/3mi you reach the Austrian border.

The road through the Kleinwalsertal (B 201) passes one after the other **Riezlern**, **Hirschegg**, **Mittelberg** and its offshoot **Baad**, closing off the valley. The highest mountain at the end of the valley is the imposing Großer Widderstein summit (2 533m/8 311ft).

Walsermuseum ⊙ – *In Riezlern tourist office*. Exhibition on the history and way of life (including traditional costume) of the valley and its inhabitants. On the second floor is a reconstruction of a typical Valaisian chalet and an Alpine dairy hut.

Wintersportmuseum ⊙ – *In the Walserhaus in Hirschegg*. The evolution of various winter sports from the late 19C to around the Second World War is retraced with the help of numerous exhibits on the first and second floors of the Walserhaus. The emphasis is naturally on the Kleinwalsertal itself, but there is also material about other Austrian regions, Switzerland, Canada etc. The display includes old-fashioned skis and skates, toboggans and sleighs, as well as more unusual items such as barrel staves used as a short kind of ski, or the "basin" ski in which small children were tucked up in order to be able to enjoy the joys of winter with everyone else.
Visitors to the Kleinwalsertal should be sure to look at an authentic surviving example of a traditional Valaisian chalet.

Walserhaus – *Turn left towards Baad from Mittelberg*. After about 1.7km/1mi, to the right of the road, is a distinctive stone-roofed building originally built as a one-room house in 1552 *(Bödmerstraße 82 – not open to the public)*.

KLOSTERNEUBURG★

Niederösterreich

Population 30 500

Michelin map 926 fold 12 – Local map see DONAUTAL – Alt 192m/630ft

In 1113, on marrying Agnes, the daughter of the Salian emperor, Babenberg Margrave Leopold III moved his court from Melk to Klosterneuburg. He had his stronghold built on a hill that had probably been settled by the Romans. In 1114, he founded an abbey there run – as it still is – by Augustinian canons.
In 1298 Klosterneuburg was granted its town charter. Blessed over the centuries by periods of prosperity, it developed into the lively town it is today.

ABBEY (STIFT) ⊙

Guided tour about 1hr in the following order: Stiftsplatz, church, cloisters, Imperial apartments. The abbey museum may be visited separately, without a guide.

Stiftsplatz – You cross this square to get to the church and the Imperial apartments. In its centre is a Gothic column of 1381 bearing reliefs of Christ's Passion. Opposite the side entrance to the abbey is the Sebastianikapelle *(not open to the public)*.

Stiftskirche (Abbey church) – This Romanesque basilica with three aisles dates from 1114-36, but has been modified a number of times over the centuries, most particularly in 1634 when it was converted into a Baroque style building by Giovanni Battista Carlone and Andrea de Retti. The **church interior**★ is Baroque throughout, the final work on the project having been completed in 1730. On entering the church it is immediately obvious that great artists have been at work here, and that they have successfully worked as a team to produce a remarkable and harmoni-

M. Hertlein/MICHELIN

Abbey church

ous result. The **ceiling frescoes** in the nave were executed by Georg Greiner c 1689. Shortly after this, the six side altars decorated with sculptures by the Späz brothers made their appearance. The high altar itself is the creation of **Matthias Steinl**, as is the sounding board above the marble pulpit, and more especially the beautiful **choir stalls** decorated with 24 Habsburg coats of arms. The altar painting is by Johann Georg Schmidt, while the ceiling frescoes above the chancel, depicting the *Assumption of the Blessed Virgin Mary*, are by Johann Michael Rottmayr. The Baroque organ of 1636 is famous for its fine sound and was greatly admired by Anton Bruckner.

Kreuzgang (Cloisters) – These date from the 13C and 14C and are a fine example of Early Gothic architecture with Burgundian influence. The old pump house contains a remarkable seven-armed **bronze candelabra**, a Veronese work dating from the 12C, symbolizing the Tree of Jesse.
The Leopoldskapelle contains some wonderfully luminous **stained glass**★ dating from the 14C. The chapel also houses the tomb of Leopold III, who was canonized in 1485. His bones are kept in a reliquary above the famous Verdun altarpiece *(see below)*. The Freisingkapelle contains the reclining figure of Berthold von Wehingen, the Bishop of Freising who died in 1410.

★★ **Verdun altarpiece** – At the end of the 12C Prior Werner commissioned from Nicolas of Verdun a "great enamel picture" as a cover for the ambo of the abbey church. The artist made 46 gilded and *champlevé* enamelled panels. After a fire in 1331 they were refashioned as an altarpiece, and six enamel panels and four panel paintings were added. The altar has three rows of famous scenes from the Old (upper and lower panels) and New (central panel) Testaments. The execution of the gilded figures on the multicoloured, but predominantly blue background is more typical of the Rhineland than Nicolas of Verdun's Meuse Valley.

Nicolas of Verdun

We know little more of Nicolas of Verdun (late 12C/early 13C) than that he was a goldsmith and enameller from Lorraine. The panels on the sides of the Dreikönigsschrein (Shrine of the Three Kings) in Cologne Cathedral are attributed to him, but his name is only known to us from inscriptions on two works, the Mary Shrine in Tournai Cathedral and the enamelled panels in Klosterneuburg, which are among the masterpieces of medieval art.

★ **Stiftsbau (Abbey building)** – Under Emperor Charles VI, father of Maria Theresa, the impressive abbey building complete with domes took on its present appearance. The aim of the original plans was to emulate Philip II's Escorial monastery near Madrid. As a counterbalance to the abbey church, intended to embody spiritual strength, the abbey was supposed to emanate worldly power. However, these ambitious projects were only ever realized in part, with the initial completion of one eighth being augmented by further construction in the 19C, taking the total to a quarter of the original design. The architect was Donato Felice d'Allio, who firmly left his own mark on the building, despite the fact that the influence of Fischer von Erlach makes itself felt.
The Imperial staircase, generous in dimension but somewhat impoverished in ornamental detail, leads up to the **Imperial apartments**, some of which contain valuable furnishings. Note in particular the Gobelins Room, adorned with priceless tapestries which were woven in Brussels at the beginning of the 18C and which depict scenes from the life of Telemachus, son of Odysseus. The cupola of the oval marble room is decorated with a fresco by Daniel Gran, portraying the *Apotheosis of the House of Habsburg*.

Library – With its 200 000 volumes, 1 250 manuscripts and 850 incunabula this is the largest private library in Austria.

★ **Stiftsmuseum** ⓥ – Above the Imperial apartments is the abbey museum, which contains many interesting items including the **four panel paintings**★ from the wings and the back of the Verdun altarpiece, the Archduke's hat (Augsburg 1616), and a collection of Gothic panel paintings.

ADDITIONAL SIGHT

Martinstraße – This narrow, slightly sloping street is a picture of idyllic calm. It is lined by pretty town houses, including the Kremsmünsterer Hof (no 12) and the Martinschloß (no 34). The street leads up to the **Martinskirche**, the oldest church in Klosterneuburg (first documented in c 800), which boasts some sumptuous Baroque fittings.

★ **Sammlung Essl** ⏱ - An der Donau-Au 1. This exhibition space for the collections of art-collecting couple the Essls opened in 1999. The building, which was designed by Tyrolean architect Heinz Tesar specifically to house the more than 4 000 works of art (storage and exhibition galleries, sculpture park), is striking because of its multiform architecture. It houses temporary exhibitions displaying post-1945 art, with a particular emphasis on Austrian painting. The private museum, set up without any public subsidy, gives an almost complete, and certainly unique, overview of Austrian post-war and contemporary art, setting it in its international context.

EXCURSION

Kierling - Heading west from the Stadtplatz along the Kierlinger Straße, one comes to this village where **Franz Kafka** died of tuberculosis in the former sanatorium. There is a small museum with memorabilia of the great writer.

KREMS und STEIN★★

Niederösterreich

Population 23 120

Michelin map 926 fold 11 - Local map see DONAUTAL - Alt 221m/725ft

At the eastern end of the Wachau, **Krems** stands on the left bank of the Danube at the foot of terraced loess hills covered with vineyards famed for their wine. This large settlement in fact consists of three towns in one, along with **Stein** and **Und**, giving rise to the Austrian joke: "Krems Und (and) Stein are three towns".
Krems was for a long time the home of the painter Martin Johann Schmidt (1718 1801), known as **Kremser Schmidt**, who was responsible for much work in the churches and abbeys of Austria.

KREMS

★ **Piaristenkirche** (**BZ**) - Dominating the old town, this is an unusual church with an elevated chancel and a triple hall nave. Both chancel and nave have fine network vaulting. The seven huge windows making up almost the whole of the south wall flood the interior with light as in no other church in Austria.
The chancel was completed in 1457 and the nave between 1511 and 1515, manifestly inspired by the Stephansdom in Vienna.
The Jesuits were given the church in 1616 and it is they who were responsible for the chapel dedicated to St Francis Xavier of 1640. In 1776 Maria Theresa put the church and the adjoining college in the charge of a congregation of Piarists, an educational order who still officiate today. The fresco at the entrance showing the death of St Francis Xavier at the gates of China is the work of Kremser Schmidt, as is the majestic Assumption forming the centrepiece of the **high altar** of 1756. A further six paintings by this artist adorn the body of the church. Notable too are the **choir stalls**, still with stylistic features of the Early Renaissance although dating from well into the 17C.

Pfarrkirche (**BZ**) - This Early Baroque church, completed in 1630 under the Italian architect Cyprian Biasino, has a sumptuously decorated interior. The nave and chancel vault are adorned with frescoes painted at the end of the 18C by Martin Johann Schmidt.

★ **Weinstadtmuseum** ⏱ (**BZ M**) - The former Dominican monastery has regained its structural integrity in its last restoration, and provides a delightful setting for this "town of wine" historical museum, which has been put together with much skill and taste. The various rooms are devoted to subjects such as "Pleasures of the table", "Trade and craft work" and "Civic pride". Winemaking is naturally given special emphasis. An inconspicuous little statuette in Room 1 is of particular interest; known as **Fanny vom Galgenberg**★, it is Austria's oldest work of art, possibly 32 000 years old, and is the only representation of a woman from the Aurignacian period in the world.
The 13C and 14C Gothic church is plain to the point of austerity, as was required by the Mendicant Order, but still has some fine 13C frescoes.
The cloister is surrounded by the monastery buildings. Its eastern gallery, whose pointed Gothic vaulting and decorated gables had been hidden by later building work, has been restored to its original form.

Obere und Untere Landstraße (**BZ 18, 26**) - This is the main artery of old Krems, approached from the west through the Steiner Tor, a monumental gateway dating from 1480 surmounted by a Baroque octagonal lantern and flanked by a pair of towers with pepper-pot roofs. The main street itself has many old houses with Renaissance or Baroque façades.

Bürgerspitalkirche (BZ) – This elegant Gothic chapel is all that remains of the old town hospice built here in the 15C. The peaceful atmosphere of the interior with its single rib-vaulted nave is conducive to contemplation. The high altar is flanked by two superb gilded wooden statues, the work of Matthias Schwanthaler.

STEIN

Stein extends along a narrow strip of river bank parallel to the Danube and is bordered by terraced vineyards to the north. This site, together with some extraordinarily old buildings, contributes greatly to the town's charm. Some of the original town wall and a number of houses have survived from the Middle Ages and Renaissance period. It is thus a rare treat to stroll along the main street, the Steiner Landstraße, and through some of the narrower alleys climbing the hillside.

★ **Old houses** – Along the **Steiner Landstraße**, which is delimited by Krems to the east and the Linzer Tor gateway to the west, and which opens out here and there into small squares, stand several very well preserved elegant town houses and courtyards. Most of these are two or three storeys high and reflect the wealth of this rich commercial town. The houses to the west of the street, between the Pfarrkirche and the Reisperbach, boast some particularly sumptuous façades.

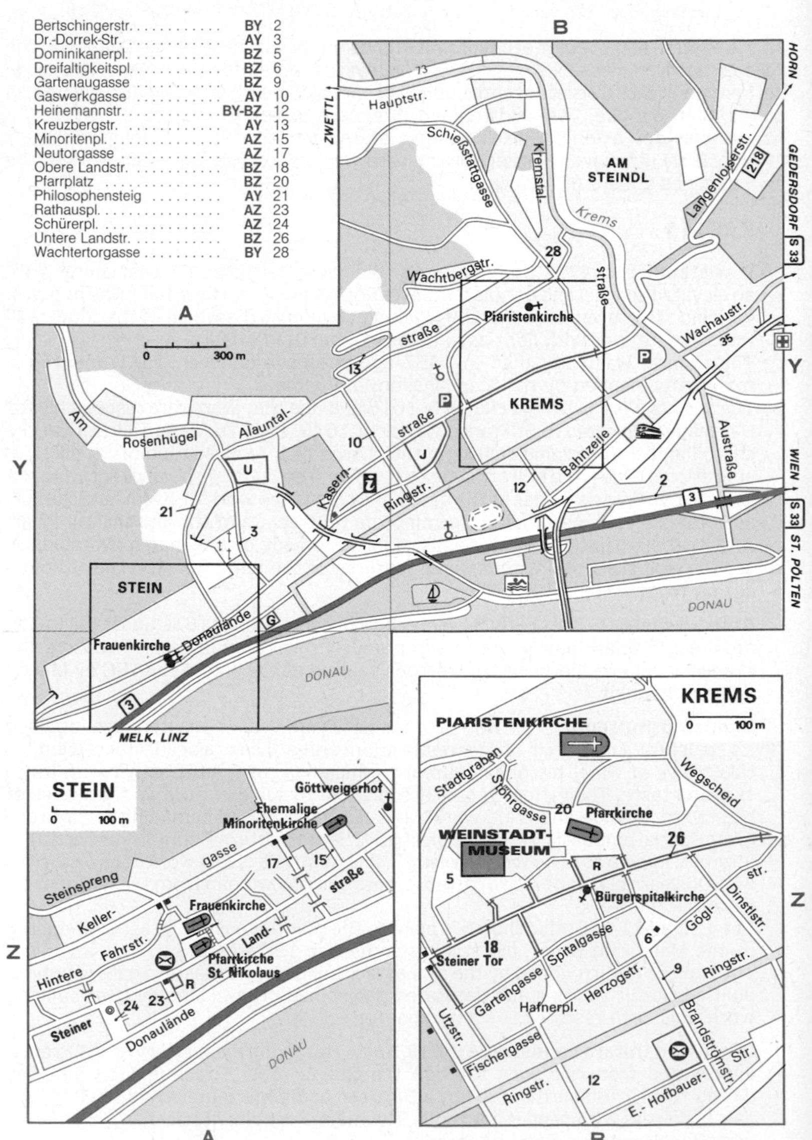

Pfarrkirche St. Nikolaus – The parish church stands in the centre of town and, along with the **Frauenkirche** behind it, dominates the town's skyline. The mighty west tower with its delicate, curved Baroque dome is particularly eye-catching. Inside the church are a ceiling fresco and altar paintings by Kremser Schmidt.

Former Minoritenkirche – This triple-aisled basilica with pillars was consecrated in 1264. Its tower dates from 1444. The 14C **frescoes** are particularly interesting. Those in the chancel depict the Virgin Mary enthroned with donors. It is now an art gallery.

Göttweigerhof – *Göttweigerhofgasse 7.* This complex, already described as a court in 1286, ceased to belong to Göttweig Abbey in 1839. The **chapel** is decorated with Early Gothic **frescoes**, which were painted between 1305 and 1310 and which rank among the most interesting of their kind in Austria.

EXCURSIONS

★ **Kremstal** – *16km/10mi. Leave Krems on the Kremstalstraße and the road to Zwettl* (**AY**).
As soon as it leaves the town, the road joins the River Krems and runs along its left then right bank through a pleasant landscape of loess hills where vines and fruit trees – peaches, plums and apricots – are grown on terraces.
Soon the church and ruined castle of **Rehberg**, perched on a rocky spike, come into view and then the Gothic tower of **Imbach** Church.
Soon after Imbach appears the proud shape of the ruined fortress of **Senftenberg**, crowning a bluff. Beyond the attractive village of Senftenberg, the valley narrows between rock outcrops and becomes wild and solitary.

Turn back to Krems at Untermeisling.

★ **Stift Göttweig** ⌚ – *6km/4mi south of Krems on the road to St. Pölten* (**BY**). The massive, pale-coloured abbey buildings with their corner turrets and onion domes rise four-square from the surrounding countryside on the side of a hill, making an unforgettable sight. The striking architecture of this Benedictine foundation has earned it the local nickname "Austria's Monte Cassino" (after the Italian abbey where the Benedictine Order originated).
In 1094, the first Benedictine monks arrived at the Augustinian canonry founded by St Altmann in 1083. After the great fire of 1718, work was begun on reconstructing the Baroque abbey following plans by Johann Lukas von Hildebrandt; however, the project was to remain unfinished.
The abbey church's **façade**★, with its two squat corner towers, the narthex, the four Tuscan columns and a balustrade running above, could perhaps be less heavy, but its expansive theatricality is nonetheless satisfying. The church interior is richly decorated with elaborate stuccowork. The mighty high altar (1639) and pulpit are the work of Dutch master Hermann Schmidt. Note the organ case which dates from 1703.
The western wing of the abbey houses the monumental **Imperial staircase**★ with a ceiling fresco by **Paul Troger** (1739) depicting the *Apotheosis of Charles VI*. The stairwell, completed by **Franz Anton Pilgram** in 1739 and a masterpiece of elegance and spaciousness, rises up three storeys.

Stiftsarchiv Göttweig

Imperial staircase, Göttweig Abbey

KREMSMÜNSTER★

Oberösterreich

Michelin map 926 fold 21 – 8km/5mi west of Bad Hall

The impressive Benedictine abbey of Kremsmünster stands among the hills rising between the foothills of the Alps and the Danube, on a bluff which overlooks the Krems Valley. The tourist coming from the east suddenly sees the tall façade of the monastery buildings, from which emerge the two domed towers of the abbey church and, on its right, the "mathematical tower".

The abbey was founded in the second half of the 8C and was the work of Tassilo III, Duke of Bavaria. According to legend, Gunther, the son of Tassilo, was mortally wounded by a wild boar when hunting in the forests which then covered the domain. Tassilo decided to create a religious community on this spot in memory of his son. The present appearance of the abbey church and its monastery buildings dates from the 17C and 18C. Great architects – Carlo Antonio Carlone, Jakob Prandtauer – and talented painters – Altomonte, Kremser Schmidt – participated in the transformation of the abbey into the Baroque style.

ABBEY (STIFT) ⏲ *2hr 30min for a complete tour*

Park the car in the outer court of the abbey. Tickets on sale in the abbey shop in the first courtyard, near the fish pond.

★ **Fischbehälter** – *Accessible independently of the guided tour.* The **fish pond** was built by Carlone and enlarged by Prandtauer between 1690 and 1717. It brings an unexpected note to the abbey buildings with its five basins, surrounded by arcades and adorned with statues (Samson, David, Neptune, Triton) spouting water, which suggest the elegance of the Italian Renaissance. It was restored in 1971, with the exception of the ceiling frescoes which had been too affected by damp to be treated.

Stiftskirche (Abbey Church) – Only the twin towers suggest that this is in fact a church. The basilica, essentially transitional Romanesque-Gothic, was transformed into the Baroque style by **Carlo Antonio Carlone** after 1680. The ceiling frescoes by the three Grabenberger brothers are set amid richly sculpted stuccowork. Sumptuously framed pictures stand on 12 altars. The really unusual feature of the church is however the 24 **marble angels** on either side of these, including 16 that are particularly finely sculpted, the work of Michael Zürn the Younger between 1682 and 1686.

Stiftsgebäude (Abbey Buildings) – The **Kaisersaal** (Emperors' Hall) owes its name to portraits of the Holy Roman Emperors (from Rudolf of Habsburg to Charles VI). The pictures were painted at the end of the 17C by Altomonte. Ceiling frescoes and stucco mouldings of great delicacy adorn this state hall.

Kept in the Schatzkammer (treasure chamber) is the famous **Tassilo chalice**★★★, presented to the monks by the duke at the end of the 8C. It was used in 765 as the wedding chalice at the marriage of the duke to Luitburg, the daughter of the Langobard king. This is the oldest piece of goldsmith's work in the Austro-Bavarian area, made of copper gilt, inlaid with niellated silver plaques; the decorative designs and characters – Christ and saints – show the influence of the earliest Christian art, the Anglo-Irish.

The collections of paintings are exhibited in several galleries on the second floor. The unusually extensive **library**★ (65m/213ft long) contains a total of 165 000 volumes; it recalls the old Benedictine adage that a bookless abbey is like a fortress without an armoury.

Trumler/ÖSTERREICH WERBUNG

Tassilo chalice

★ **Mathematischer Turm** – The "mathematical tower", or observatory, is about 50m/164ft high. It contains extensive collections relating to paleontology, physics, mineralogy, zoology, anthropology and astronomy. Though built between 1749 and 1758 it has a decidedly modern appearance. From the top the view stretches as far as the Alps.

KUFSTEIN

Tirol

Population 14 500

Michelin map 926 fold 18 – Local map see KAISERGEBIRGE – Alt 499m/1 637ft

Kufstein, the last Austrian town in the Inn Valley, lies at the foot of a rocky outcrop crowned with a mighty fortress. Not far away is the Kaisergebirge range *(see entry)*, easily reached by the Wilder Kaiser chair-lift (**Y**), which explains in part why the little town has become a lively and popular tourist resort.

General view (**Z**) – To appreciate the **site**★ of the castle at its best, climb the Heldenhügel, a wooded rise topped by a memorial statue to Tyrolean freedom fighter Andreas Hofer.

FORTRESS (FESTUNG) ⌚ (Z)

Like its prestigious neighbour Salzburg, Kufstein owes much of its character to the citadel which dominates the town.

Starting from the Unterer Stadtplatz, leave the church, and make for the Festungshof *(left)* which contains the auditorium for the Heldenorgel *(see below)*. Pass through the walls by a covered stairway beneath the Bürgerturm (Burghers' Tower) – the pipes of the Heldenorgel can be seen from here.

Other possible access: take the lift at the foot of the rock along the Inn-Promenade.

A gateway leads to the Tiefer Brunnen to the right, a well with a shaft c 60m/197ft deep reaching right down to the water level of the Inn. From here, a 170m/186yd underground passage through the rock leads to the "Peacock tail" (Pfauenschweif) gateway, and then left through it to the Wallachen and then the Caroli bastions, which forms a **viewpoint**★ overlooking the River Inn and the wooded Pendling, a small mountain range.

KUFSTEIN

Street	Square
Hans-Reisch-Str.	Z 2
Innbrücke	Z 4
Innpromenade	Z 5
Kaiserbergstr.	Y 7
Langkampfener Str.	Y 10
Madersperger Str.	Z 12
Marktgasse	Z 14
Maximilianstr.	Z 15
Neuhof	Z 18
Oberer Stadtplatz	Z 19
Otto-Lasne-Str.	Y 22
Praxmarerstr.	Z 23
Römerhofgasse	Z 24
Schillerstr.	Z 25
Stuttgarter Str.	Y 26
Südtiroler Platz	Z 27
Thierseestr.	Y 28
Unterer Stadtplatz	Z 29
Willy-Graf-Str.	Y 30

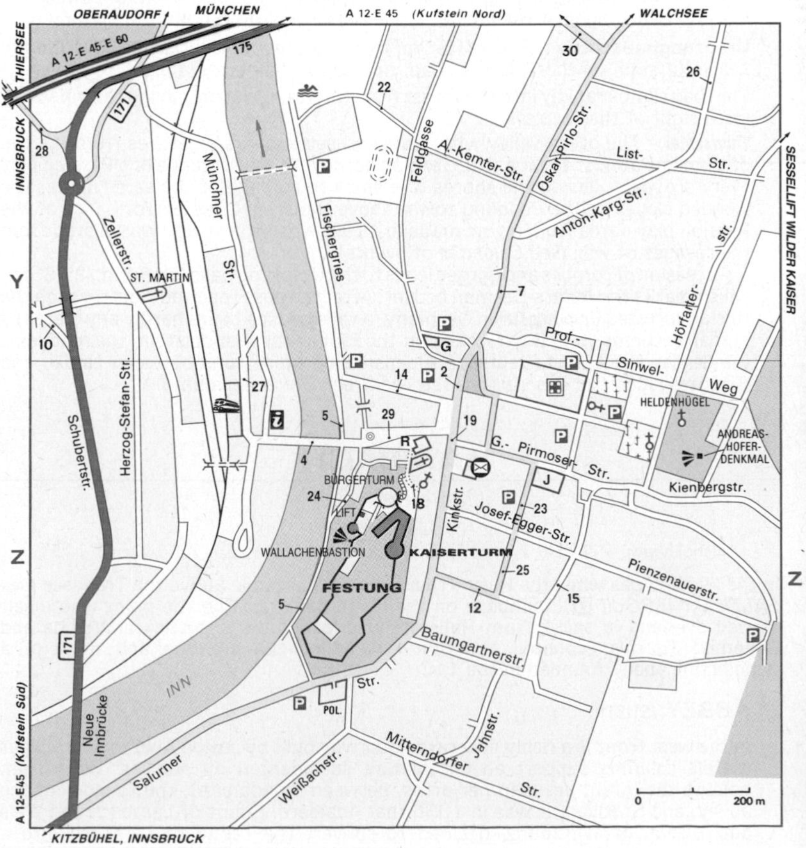

There is a view across the Inn of the Kitzbühel Alps, to the left, and in clear weather as far as the snows of the Stubai Alps, southwest of Innsbruck.

Festungs- und Heimatmuseum – The local museum houses an array of objects collected by the Kufstein local history society. Of particular interest are the rooms devoted to illustrations of the fortress through the ages.

★ **Kaiserturm** – This colossal tower, completed in 1522, rears up, with walls up to 4.5m/15ft thick, on the highest point of the rock.
The interior is arranged round a huge central pillar, encircled by a vaulted gallery. The design can be clearly seen from the second floor, at the beginning the tour. On the third floor 13 cells are reminders of the captives imprisoned at Kufstein in the 19C, when the castle was a State prison.

Heldenorgel ⊙ – This instrument, known as the "Heroes' organ", was first played in public in 1931. It was built in the top storey of the Bürgerturm to commemorate the German and Austrian dead from the First World War. The recitals can be heard for several miles round the town in still weather *(daily at noon, from early June-mid Sept additionally at 6pm)*. Indisputably the largest instrument of its kind in the world, since 1971 the organ has been able to boast 4 307 pipes and 46 registers. The organist's keyboard and the gallery for the audience are at the foot of the rock.

EXCURSION

Schloß Mariastein – *12km/7.5mi southwest of Kufstein. Leave the car in the valley and climb the last section of route up to the castle on foot.*
In the 14C in a small peaceful valley running parallel to the Inn a fortified tower was built on a huge rocky outcrop. It was called "Stein" (rock) and became a site of Marian pilgrimage after a Lady Chapel was built here.
Cross the courtyard and climb the tower staircase. The Knights' Hall (Rittersaal) on the second floor houses the **Schloßmuseum** ⊙(Tyrolean royal crown and sceptre, numerous ex-votos etc) Two chapels have been built one above the other on the upper storeys. The lower is the **Kreuzkapelle** (Chapel of the Cross), which is still Late Gothic (1550). The upper **Gnadenkapelle** (Chapel of Miracles), decorated in the Baroque style, has been restored to its original harmonious appearance since the windows were rebuilt and the tracery added to them in the 19C removed. The venerated statue of the Virgin Mary and Child dates from 1450.
Before leaving the valley, climb the slope opposite the Mariastein to admire the tower outlined against the crests of the Kaisergebirge range.

★ **Ursprungpaßstraße** – *25km/15.5mi from Kufstein to Bayrischzell (Germany). Leave Kufstein on the Thiersee road, northwest of the town plan.*

The road climbs rapidly into the forest from Kufstein, and on leaving the Inn Valley loses sight of the fortress.

Thierseetal – The green valley with scattered settlements stretches from the top of the climb almost as far as the German border. Thiersee, venue of a Passion play every six years, lies on the shores of a small round lake of the same name. The wooded slopes of the Pendling tower above the scene. The performance of the Passion play dates from a vow made in 1799, when the village was spared from the ravages of war *(see Calendar of events)*.
A succession of combes and gorges leads to the Ursprung pass (alt 849m/2 785ft), which marks the Austro-German border. After the pass the road runs through the thickly forested **Ursprungstal** in Germany, a valley which bears hardly any traces of human settlement. In Bayrischzell, at the foot of the Wendelstein, the road joins the **German Alpine Road** (Deutsche Alpenstraße) which runs between Lindau and Berchtesgaden *(for description, see The Green Guide Germany)*.

LAMBACH

Oberösterreich

Population 3 170

Michelin map 926 fold 21 – 15km/9mi southwest of Wels – Alt 349m/1 145ft

In the Middle Ages when the River Traun was not navigable above the Traunsee *(see SALZKAMMERGUT* 2*)*, Lambach on the north bank became the point where salt carried overland in sacks from Hallstatt was loaded on to boats for Vienna and Bohemia. To this economic function was added the prestige and fame of a Benedictine abbey founded in the 11C.

★ ABBEY (STIFT)

In the west front is a richly decorated doorway built by Jakob Auer in 1693. Four marble columns support an entablature surmounted by statues: the Virgin, holding the Infant Jesus in her arms, between St Adalbero, the founder of the abbey, and St Kilian. It was in 1056 that Adalbero, Count of Lambach and Wels and Bishop of Würzburg, decided to convert the castle at Lambach into a

Benedictine abbey. Evicted from his see on several occasions by the German emperor, Henry IV, in the course of his Investiture struggle with Pope Gregory VII, Adalbero undertook a number of journeys in the Papal States. It was no doubt during these travels that he acquired his taste for the kind of Byzantine frescoes then to be seen in Lombardy and the Veneto.

Stiftskirche (Abbey Church) ⓥ – In the 17C the abbey was rebuilt according to Baroque precepts. The Romanesque chancel and transept, at the west end of the church were abandoned in order to reorientate the church to face the east. The chancel was demolished but the transept was retained, outside the new edifice, in order to support the extra load of the towers (estimated at 900t). The walls were doubled in thickness too, thereby covering up the frescoes for more than two centuries and guaranteeing their preservation.

★★ **Romanesque frescoes (11C)** – Uncovered and restored in 1967, they are the only ones of their kind in the whole of Austria. It is likely that they were completed for the consecration of the abbey in the year of Adalbero's death (1090).
Both in terms of style and subject matter, the frescoes owe more to Byzantium than to Western Europe. Among the great variety of figures, one particular scene in the central dome stands out, the **Virgin Mary and Infant Jesus accompanied by two Midwives**. This unusual subject is perhaps intended as an affirmation of Christ's truly human birth. To the left, the Three Wise Men bring their gifts. More difficult to distinguish is the subject matter in the south dome; this represents the city of Jerusalem and Herod interrogating the Wise Men. The fact that a number of scenes are based on the life of Herod is not without relevance to the contemporary quarrel between secular power (the emperor) and spiritual power (the Pope). In terms of technique, most of the work is "a fresco" with occasional touches of "secco".

Klostergebäude (Abbey Buildings) – The abbey is composed of three complexes: the first to the north of the church around the cloisters, the second – horseshoe-shaped – around the abbey courtyard, and the third around the rectangular abbey garden. In the west wing of this section, called the "New Convent", there is the Baroque **abbey library** with frescoes by Melchior Seidl.
The north wing houses the **refectory** on the ground floor, a well proportioned room with outstanding stucco decoration by Diego Francesco Carlone and frescoes by Wolfgang Andreas Heindl.
The **dispensary** on the floor above also contains some beautiful stuccowork.

★ **Kleines Theater** – The abbey has its own theatre, the only one of its kind to have survived in Austria. The stage dates from 1769. On 23 April 1770, while on her way to marry the future Louis XVI, **Marie-Antoinette** of Austria stayed at the abbey with her mother and their retinue. An improvised play, *The Marriage Contract*, was staged for their entertainment; it made the 15-year-old Marie-Antoinette laugh so much that she had to be reminded that such behaviour was not appropriate for a future queen of France.
Another famous name associated with the abbey is that of **Mozart**, who is supposed to have written the **Lambach Symphony** while staying here.

H. Wiesenhofer/ÖSTERREICH WERBUNG

Dreifaltigkeitskirche, Stadl-Paura

★ PFARR- UND WALLFAHRTSKIRCHE STADL-PAURA

2km/1mi. Leave Lambach to the south. Cross the River Traun and turn right after 500m/550yd towards the mound on which the church is built.
The **Dreifaltigkeitskirche** was built as the result of a vow. In 1713, when the whole land was being ravaged by plague, Abbot Maximilian Pagl swore to build a

church dedicated to the Holy Trinity as soon as the country had been delivered from its torments. Between 1714 and 1725 he constructed one of Austria's most unusual Baroque monuments.

Everything in the building, designed by the Linz architect Johann Michael Prunner, is a symbol; faith in the Trinity is expressed in the plan itself, the circular nave being inscribed within an equilateral triangle formed by the three chancels. This architectural conceit, mixing logic with theatre, is continued throughout, regardless of liturgical convenience, and hence there are three façades, three portals, three altars, three miniature organs and three sacristies. The frescoes in the dome and the altar paintings are by Carlo Antonio Carlone, Martin Altomonte and Domenico Parodi.

LECH***

Vorarlberg

Population 1 270

Michelin map 926 fold 28 – Local map see ARLBERGGEBIET – Alt 1 447m/4 747ft

Lech is indisputably the prettiest holiday destination in the Austrian Alps and one of the few resorts in the northern Alps to have made a name for itself as an international winter sports venue.

Lech has won its reputation thanks in part to its merging with the neighbouring resorts of **Zürs**** and **St. Anton**** *(see separate listing)*, to create a ski area capable of meeting the most demanding standards, but most of all because of its insistence on quality above quantity. Here, biggest is not allowed to be best, and tourist facilities have been built very much with the welfare of the natural environment in mind.

For this reason, guest capacity is only about 7 000, or three to six times smaller than the demand in the other major European winter sports resorts listed above. Accommodation is furthermore quite dispersed, consisting mainly of hotels and family guesthouses in the luxury category. Après-ski catering in Lech emphasises the art of living, with exclusive boutiques, elegant cafés, gourmet restaurants and cultural activities.

Lech also has plenty to offer in the summer months, when life takes on a much calmer pace. Although there are no particularly breathtaking panoramas, the soft green meadows of the surrounding countryside are most restorative. The area lends itself especially to rambling *(see Excursions below)* and mountain bike tours, most popularly in the Formarin, Ferwall and Moos valleys. One of Lech's major attractions is the 1 200m²/12 917sq ft open-air swimming pool in a pretty woodland setting. Anglers can choose between lakes such as the Formarinsee, Spullsee, Zürssee or Zugweiher *(details of fishing permits available from the Lech tourist office)*.

Gritscher/ÖSTERREICH WERBUNG

Lech centre

★ SITE

The town of Lech, covering an area of 90km²/35sq mi, lies on a mountain plateau (alt 1 444-1 717m/4 738-5 633ft). Limestone peaks (the Mohnenfluh and Braunarlspitze to the north, Rote Wand to the west, Schafberg and Omeshorn to the south and Rüfispitze to the east) tower above the lush Alpine pastures and woodland which grows at up to 1 800m/5 900ft above sea-level. Although difficult access roads and the sheer cliff faces of Omeshorn and Rüfikopf lend the area an undeniably mountainous aspect, the mountains around Lech are not in fact that high. None of the surrounding peaks are taller than 2 700m/8 850ft, and there is not a single glacier in sight.

The town of Lech is spread along the banks of the river of that name. Lech town centre lies on the intersection of the river valley with the valley in which Zürs is situated. With the exception of the Gothic **church** (14C), and one or two farmhouses from the days of the Valais (Haus Anger no 19) and of the court in the Weißes Haus (16C) opposite the Hotel Krone, Lech retains little physical evidence of its past.

Further uphill the resort of **Oberlech** (alt 1 700m/5 577ft) stands on a slope of the Kriegerhorn. This part of town is blessed with plenty of sunshine and offers excellent snow conditions and a sweeping view. In winter Oberlech is car free and only accessible by cable-car.

For holidaymakers seeking respite from the hubbub of the ski slopes and other holidaymakers, the hamlets of Zug to the west and Stubenbach to the east offer a calmer alternative.

SKI SLOPES

The **Arlberg ski slopes**✲✲✲, which encompass from north to south the resorts of Lech, Zürs, Stuben and St. Anton am Arlberg, are the largest and most varied in Austria. They include over 200km/124mi of maintained and 220km/137mi of unmaintained ski runs, to which 86 ski lifts give access. It is possible to ski from Lech to Zürs and back, and likewise from Stuben and St. Anton. To get from Zürs to Stuben or St. Anton, however, it is necessary to take the bus.

The **ski area**✲ attached to Lech extends over two mountains. Most of the ski runs are to be found on the Kriegerhorn and the Zuger Hochlicht (alt 1 450-2 377m/4 757-7 799ft). The guaranteed snow cover and the gentle slopes make skiing here an enjoyable and relaxing experience. The Mohnenmähderpiste (very easy) and the Steinmähderpiste (for those of average ability) are definitely worth a try. Experienced skiers will prefer the Rüfikopf opposite (alt 1 450-2 362m/4 757-7 749ft). This is the departure point for two off-piste runs (the Langerzug and the Tannegg), which can be tackled with an accompanying ski instructor.

Holidaymakers should also enquire about the ski slopes at Zürs and St. Anton, which also have plenty to offer by way of enjoyment.

VIEWS FROM THE PEAKS VIA SKI LIFT AND CABLE-CAR

★★ **Zuger Hochlicht** – Alt 2 377m/7 799ft. *In winter accessible to skiers only, allowing 1hr 30min there and back. Take the Schlegelkopf and then the Kriegerhorn chair-lifts, followed by the Mohnenfluh cable-car. In the summer, it is possible to take the* **Petersboden chair-lift** ⓥ *from Oberlech, and then do the tour of the Zuger Hochlicht round via the Mohnenfluhsattel gap and on to Butzensee Lake (2hr 15min there and back on foot).*

From the Kriegerhorn (alt 2 173m/7 129ft) there is a broad view of the Zuger Valley against a backdrop of the Rote Wand cliffs, to the west, and of the Zuger Hochlicht ski slopes, framed between the peaks of Braunarlspitze and Mohnenfluh, to the north. To the south lies Zürs in its valley, at the foot of the majestic Rüfispitze and the precipitous Roggspitze.

The Zuger Hochlicht reveals a beautiful **panorama**★★ of the Arlberg region, the Lechtal Alps and the Rätikon (especially the eye-catching peak known as the Drei Türme, or "three towers"). There is an all-round panorama from the peak itself, reached in a few minutes from the far left end of the cable-car station. The Hochtannberg pass road can be seen further below.

★ **Rüfikopf** ⓥ – Alt 2 362m/7 749ft. *Take the cable-car.* There is a beautiful overall view from this summit of the holiday resort and Lech ski slopes, at the foot of the rocky Mohnenfluh and Braunarlspitze peaks. The Rüfikopf is a good departure point for a ski trip to Zürs.

EXCURSIONS

The Lechtal Alps offer numerous possibilities for walking and hiking tours, with 200km/124mi of waymarked paths.

★ **Spullersee** – *Take the bus to the lake (from the stop in front of the post office; enquire at the tourist office for the timetable). Allow 30min. Cars can be parked in Anger underground car park (free during summer) opposite the post office. Before 9am and after 3pm, motorists can drive to the lake in their own car; there is a toll levied on this stretch of road.*

This beautiful **drive★** leads through charming, green countryside. Level with the toll booth, there is a municipal swimming pool set in the woods. Then the road passes through the pretty village of Zug, with Alpine pastures, through which the Spullerbach winds a course, stretching on either side in between clumps of fir and larch.

Finally after a very steep climb the road reaches the **Spullersee★**, which lies in a spectacular setting in a natural amphitheatre 1 827m/5 994ft above sea-level. The major summits are the Plattnitzer Spitze and Rohnspitze to the south, the Wildgrubenspitze to the east and the Spuller Schafberg (alt 2 679m/8 789ft) and Pfaffeneck to the north.

★ **Formarinsee** – *Take the bus to the lake. The first half of the trip is identical to that described above. Allow 30min for the bus ride and then 10min walk downhill on a good footpath.*

The Formarinsee (alt 1 789m/5 869ft) lies at the foot of the Rote Wand (alt 2 704m/8 871ft).

★★ **Walk from the Formarinsee to the Spullersee** – *Allow 4hr for this quite taxing walk, parts of which should be tackled with care. Difference in altitude is about 600m/2 000ft. Climbing boots are essential. This excursion is dangerous in mist or fog, or if the ground is damp.*

Take the bus which goes to the Formarinsee. On arrival at 1 871m/6 138ft, instead of walking down to the lake, take the footpath climbing gently up to the left *(waymarked in yellow)*. The path, dotted with Alpine roses, leads right along the edge of the cliff, offering lovely views of the Formarinsee below before reaching the **Freiburger Hütte** (mountain refuge).

From here take path no 601 towards the Ravensburger Hütte *(waymarked in red)*. After 30min of easy climb towards the Formaletsch range the path crosses a picturesque limestone plateau, a real sea of rocks, known aptly enough as **Steinernes Meer** *(Take care! Do not leave the waymarked path.)*

The path becomes clearer again and climbs steeply and tortuously up to the **Gehrengrat**, where chamois and ibex are frequently to be seen. There is a good view of the Verwall range, the Kloster Valley and the Rätikon. A very steep path leads from the summit down to the Spullersee *(allow 1hr 30min; follow signs to Ravensburger Hütte, or "RH")*. On reaching the lake, turn left. After about 5min, the path comes to the bus stop for the return trip to Lech.

Oberes LECHTAL

Vorarlberg und Tirol

Michelin map 926 folds 15, 16 and 28

Upstream from Reutte the Lech Valley hollows out a deep furrow for 60km/37mi between the Allgäu and Lechtal Alps, parallel to the Inn Valley. The unusually uniform valley has few terraces and is therefore relatively sparsely inhabited. The poor yields from local agricultural terrain caused many valley inhabitants to seek work elsewhere and not return to their home villages until their old age, in some cases quite well-off. There they built themselves grand houses, many of which have beautifully painted façades.

FROM WARTH TO REUTTE *61km/38mi*

The road between Warth and Steeg can be closed (not more than 3 days) owing to avalanches. On the whole, it is not usually possible to drive between Lech and Warth in winter.

Between Warth and **Steeg** the road goes through a series of gorges, before entering a harsh landscape of forest and rocks where it runs along mountain slopes with the Lech gushing along at the foot of them. In the hamlets of Hägerau and Holzgau, beyond Steeg, there are several houses with especially fine painted façades, the work of the Zeiller family of painters from Reutte *(see below)*.

Elbigenalp – The Tyrolean tradition of woodcarving is still very much alive in this village (woodcarving colleges). In 1768 the painter **Joseph Anton Koch**, well known for his "heroic" landscapes and one of the most talented figures among the German Romantics, was born in the suburb of Untergiblen. Elbigenalp is also the birthplace of artist **Anna Stainer-Knittel** (1841-1915) who became a famous local figure better known as "**Geierwally**" and immortalised in novel, and on stage and screen.

Pfarrkirche St. Nikolaus – The church stands on the edge of the village and is enclosed by the graveyard walls. Its sharp pointed spire has made it one of the most distinctive images of the upper Lech Valley. The exuberant Baroque interior with a riot of almost luminous fresco decoration is the work of Johann Jakob Zeiller *(see Reutte below)*. Alongside the main church is the small 15C Martinskapelle,

M. Hertlein/MICHELIN

Ceiling fresco in St. Nikolaus church, Elbigenalp

in which the crypt once served as a charnel house. The chapel interior is decorated with 15C frescoes and a painted panel representing *The Dance of Death*, a traditional 19C work. Various scenes have been reproduced on a larger scale in niches in the graveyard wall.

After Elbigenalp, delightful side valleys open up to the right of the road, cutting into the Lechtaler Alps: Gramaiser Tal near **Häselgehr**, Bschlaber Tal near **Elmen** and Namloser Tal (literally "valley without a name") near **Stanzach**. For the final stretch of this trip, beyond Stanzach, the Lech flows along a relatively broad bed with sprawling gravel banks interspersed along it.

Reutte – The market town of Reutte is the administrative and economic capital of the Außerfern district. In summer, Reutte's altitude of 854m/2 802ft and proximity to the mountains make it a good starting point for numerous walks. It also has a good infrastructure for sport, much appreciated by skiers, who patronise the little resort in winter. Furthermore, Reutte is the home town of the Zeiller family of painters, whose Baroque frescoes adorn many a church interior in the Tyrol and south Germany. The most notable member of the family is **Johann Jakob Zeiller** (1708-83), whose masterworks include the frescoes in the Bavarian Benedictine foundations at Ettal and Ottobeuren (together with his cousin Franz Anton Zeiller). In Reutte itself, the painted façades of the "Grünes Haus" (Green House) at Untermarkt 25, and "Schönes House" (Beautiful House) or "Zeiller-Haus" at Untergsteig 1 are attributed to him.

Heimatmuseum ⏲ – *In the Grünes Haus*. The local museum collections focus mainly on works by the Zeiller family and their pupils, as well as the history and customs of the local district.

LEOBEN

Steiermark

Population 32 010

Michelin map 926 fold 23 – Alt 541m/1 775ft

Leoben, whose name is derived from the Slavonic root *"liub"* meaning "pretty", is the seat of the Montanuniversität, a famous metallurgy and mining university, and the centre of the Styrian metalworking industry since the Middle Ages. The proximity of the Erzberg with its iron deposits *(see EISENERZ)* has encouraged the development of the metallurgical industry in Donawitz to the northwest. Leoben's industrial suburbs form a striking contrast to their Alpine surroundings.

It was in Leoben that Napoleon, having fought his way as far as the Mur Valley, signed a peace treaty with Austria on 18 April 1797 as a preliminary to the Treaty of Campo-Formio. But Leoben did not escape unscathed from the later wars with the French, which culminated in 1809 in the Battle of St. Michael.

SIGHTS

Old town – Gracious houses around the **Hauptplatz**, such as the house on the corner with the Homanngasse or the red **Hacklhaus** dating from 1680, with its sculpted decoration, testify still to the wealth of the iron merchants of former times. The column in memory of the plague *(Pestsäule)*, which features a sculpture group of the Trinity and saints, was put up in 1717. More beautiful old houses can be seen in the Dominikanergasse and the Homanngasse. The old town wall, in many places hidden or incorporated into other buildings, is best preserved where it runs alongside the River Mur. Here stands the **Schwammerlturm** (Mushroom Tower) of 1616, which gets its name from the mushroom-like shape of its roof. Another tower, the Freimannsturm in the Glacisgasse, dates from 1480.

★ **Stadtpfarrkirche St. Xaver** ⊙ – Built as part of the once powerful Jesuit College founded in 1613, this Early Baroque structure from 1660-65 is attributed to the architect Pietro Francesco Carlone. Its façade of pilasters and mouldings is flanked by two towers, and has above the doorway a sculpture of the missionary St Francis Xavier surrounded by Indians complete with feather headdress.

The interior with its pilastered walls impresses by virtue of the simplicity of its architecture, which allows the original **furnishings**★ of 1670, preserved in their entirety, to stand out all the more with their profusion of gold and black, a style typical of Jesuit Baroque churches in Austria. The richly gilded main altar with its twisted columns fills the whole end wall of the choir, framing a painting of St Francis Xavier in glory by the German artist Heinrich Schönfeld, whose work is also to be seen in Salzburg Cathedral. The pulpit has representations of the four Evangelists and a Salvator Mundi (Saviour of the World) statue above the sounding board. The decoration of the pulpit and of the six side altars is probably from the studio of Ägidius Meixner.

Kirche Maria am Waasen – West of the town, near the bridge over the Mur, the Gothic church of Maria am Waasen has 15C stained-glass windows in the chancel; they depict the Apostles, the Coronation of the Virgin and scenes from the Life and Passion of Christ.

Stift Göss ⊙ – The buildings of the former Benedictine convent, secularized more than 200 years ago, are now home to the famous Gösser brewery. The **church** with its early-14C chancel and 16C nave can be viewed, noting in particular the first two of the massive pillars, twisted like coils and resting on star-shaped bases. The furnishings date from the late 18C. The Early Romanesque **crypt** may only be viewed on a guided tour. The **south porch**★ of 1520 has fine stone carvings.

LIENZ

Tirol

Population 11 700

Michelin map 926 fold 32 – Alt 678m/2 224ft

Lienz lies in the shadow of the Dolomites, whose deeply wrinkled rocky slopes justify their popular nickname of *Unholde* – "fiends". The town is the southern terminus of the road to the Großglockner and the Felbertauern. It is also the chief town in the Osttirol district of Austria, which has been cut off from the central part of the province of Tirol and from Innsbruck, the provincial capital, since the transfer of the Pustertal (Val Pusteria) to Italy in 1919. Only in 1967 with the opening of the Felbertauern tunnel was the situation changed. The small ravine of the Drava known as the Tiroler Tor (Gate of the Tyrol) about 15km/9mi downstream, between Nikolsdorf and Oberdrauburg, has marked the natural frontier with Carinthia since the 16C.

SIGHTS

Schloß Bruck and the Regionalmuseum Osttirol ⊙ – This castle is a former fortress of the counts of Görz (now Gorizia). Their estates, extending from the Tauern to Istria, enabled the Habsburgs, who inherited them in 1500, to practice their policy of expansion to the south.

The castle now houses the museum of the East Tyrol, which is devoted among other things to local antiquities, folklore and handicrafts. The Knights' Hall (Rittersaal) still has its original painted Romanesque timbered ceiling. The

LIENZ

Albin-Egger-Straße	2	Grafendorferstraße	6	Muchargasse	15
Andrä-Kranzgasse	3	Haugerplatz	7	Patriasdorferstraße	16
Emanuel-von-Hibler-Str.	4	Hauptplatz	8	Rosengasse	17
		Johannesplatz	10	St. Michaelsgasse	18
		Kärntner Str.	12	Schweizergasse	20
		Messinggasse	13	Südtirolerplatz	21

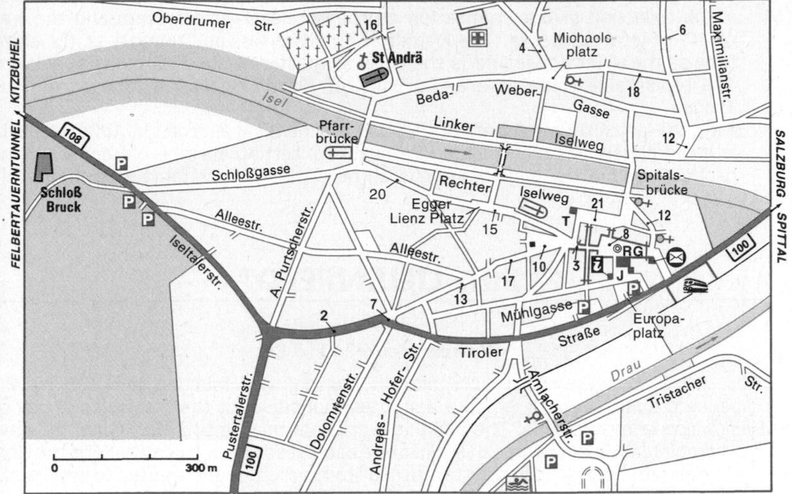

two-storey chapel houses, under its 15C Gothic vaulting, some frescoes dating from 1495 and, on the lower storey, the "Görzer" altarpiece from Michael Pacher's School.

The large **Albin-Egger-Lienz gallery** gives a comprehensive review of the work of this painter (1868-1926), who was often inspired by the Tyrol and its inhabitants. His powerful and unadorned expressionism recalls the work of Swiss painter Ferdinand Hodler. The museum also exhibits the work of contemporary artists.

The fragments of stonework collected in the section on Roman archeology come mostly from the excavations at Aguntum and Lavant-Kirchbichl, which those interested in archeology may see east of the town, on either side of the Drava.

Pfarrkirche St. Andrä - This church has a Late Gothic nave and an 18C chancel. During its restoration in 1968 mural paintings of the 14C, 15C and 17C were discovered.

The **organ**, created in 1618 by Passau master Andreas Putz, is one of the oldest in Austria. The Renaissance backdrop is the creation of a workshop from Brixen (Italian: Bressanone) and has survived almost entirely in its original form.

Under the gallery are the magnificent **tombstones**★, in Salzburg marble, of Count Leonhard (1506-07), the last of the Görz-Tirol line, and his successor, Michael von Wolkenstein (with his wife, Barbara von Thun, 1510).

Within the once fortified graveyard stands the **local war memorial**, a chapel enclosed by arcades to the war dead and built by Clemens Holzmeister in 1924-25. It contains the tomb of Albin Egger-Lienz, who painted the four-part cycle of paintings which provoked enormous controversy because of the accusation it expresses, and has even led to the temporary closure of the chapel. Seldom have the horrors of war been depicted so vividly. *Key to the chapel can be obtained from Pfarrgasse no 13.*

EXCURSION

★ **Pustertaler Höhenstraße** - *About 30km/18mi. Leave Lienz on road no 100. At the exit to Leisach turn right towards Bannberg and follow the "Pustertaler Höhenstraße" signs.*

This mountain road hardly carries any traffic and we recommend it to all those interested in exploring this region. The road runs high above the valley floor and offers ever finer views of the Lienz Dolomites stretching along to its left. The soft green countryside is dotted with charming hamlets with slate-roofed farmhouses and churches. Beyond **Kosten** the road heads northwest and the peaks of the Defereggen Alps come briefly into view.

★ **Anras** - Excavations show that this town on a sun-exposed terrace has been inhabited for over 2000 years. It was the economic and religious centre of the Puster Valley for centuries. After the 13C, Anras came under the jurisdiction of the Brixen bishopric (South Tyrol, Italian: Bressanone), as testified by the

Pfleggerichtshaus ⏲, restored in exemplary fashion by the Munich Messerschmidt foundation. This court house was built between 1754 and 1757 and was used as the temporary summer residence of the bishops of Brixen. It houses a rich collection of documentation on the Tyrolean penal system and the way of life of local residents. The **Pfarrkirche St. Stefan** was built almost at the same time as the court house and is the work of master mason Franz de Paula Penz. The remarkable frescoes are the work of Martin Knoller, a student of Paul Troger.

Asch, the last settlement before the road rejoins the main road in Abfaltersbach, is a completely unspoilt village in a beautiful setting, its fine old houses being grouped around the pilgrimage church of Mariae Himmelfahrt, consecrated in 1765.

Stift LILIENFELD★

Niederösterreich

Michelin map 926 fold 24

This, the largest monastery complex in Austria, was founded in 1202 by the Babenberg duke, Leopold IV, as a daughter foundation of the Cistercian abbey of Heiligenkreuz near Vienna. The building work continued until 1263, when the nave was completed. However, in 1219 Lilienfeld had already been given a relic of the Holy Cross by its founder, who had just returned from a crusade and wanted to emphasize the importance of the new foundation.

The abbey experienced many vicissitudes, suffering great poverty in the 15C, but rising to such a position of power by the 17C that the abbot was able to oppose the appointment of Richelieu as Abbot General of the order. Lilienfeld was successfully defended against the Turks in 1693, but a century later danger threatened from another quarter when Joseph II secularized the abbey in 1789, thus paving the way for looting and destruction of its art treasures. His successor Leopold II rescinded the order a year later.

TOUR ⏲

Basically, the buildings are in a transitional style between Romanesque and Gothic, but in the Baroque period some major parts were renewed or added, such as the convent buildings with their corner towers; the west tower of the abbey church also dates from this time (1703).

Stiftskirche – This is the largest church in Lower Austria, 82m/269ft long by 21m/69ft wide. The pillared basilica is essentially Romanesque in concept with its cruciform ground plan and the round-arched windows, but Gothic features include the addition of flying buttresses. The Early Gothic **west doorway**★ is most impressive with its deeply splayed sides and numerous small columns with crocket capitals. The interior is dominated by the Gothic vaulting and massive crossing pillars, and is unusual in having a straight end to the choir with a double ambulatory. The **Baroque furnishings**★ fit in remarkably well with the medieval architecture. The predominant tone is the black of the Türnitz marble from which the altars, the pulpit, the choir organ case and the memorial to the founder of the abbey are made, lit up by the lavish gleaming gold leaf. The painting on the high altar is of the Assumption of the Virgin Mary by **Daniel Gran** (1746).

★ **Cloister** – Like the church, this could well be the work of Burgundian craftsmen, and was built in the mid 13C. The ribbed vaulting is supported on finely proportioned consoles by clustered pillars of attractively coloured stone. On the north side are remarkable stained-glass windows from the first half of the 14C. The **chapter-house** is one of the oldest parts of the whole complex, with stone benches running round the square room and four circular pillars. Over the

The bridge saint

St John of Nepomuk was born in Bohemia in 1340 and went to Prague in 1370, initially as a priest and subsequently as vicar-general to the archbishop. In a dispute between the archbishop and King Wenceslas I, he stood up for the rights of the church and in particular the confidentiality of the confessional – he is said to have been the queen's confessor. For this reason, in 1393 the King had him tortured and then thrown from the bridge into the Vltava. So statues of this martyr were placed on many bridges in South Germany, Bohemia and Austria.

cellarium, a well-preserved storage cellar from the 13C, is the impressive two-aisled, lay brothers' **dormitory**, the only one of its kind to have survived from the Middle Ages in Austria.

★ **Library** - As is always the case in a monastery, this is one of the finest rooms. Dating from 1700, it has magnificent stucco decoration and ceiling frescoes, the work of lay brothers, as are the richly inlaid bookcases and doors.
There is an adjoining picture gallery with a collection of paintings that is worth seeing.

TOWN

On the other side of the Bundesstraße 20 and the River Traisen is the **town of Lilienfeld**, which achieved fame by virtue of the Alpine skiing technique of the same name developed by Mathias Zdarsky in 1897. The little **Bezirksheimatmuseum** (local museum), housed in a 14C Gothic gatehouse, is devoted to this local hero.

Nepomuk group, Lilienfeld

The Nepomuk group★ is of special interest, as one of the few not on a bridge but on the river bank of the Traisen *(Dörflstraße)*, since the bridge was moved 50m/164ft upstream at the end of the 18C. It is a particularly striking example, with hardly an equal in the rest of Austria, carved in pale sandstone in 1712 by the sculptor Christoph Brandl from Wilhelmsburg. Its date can incidentally be established by adding up the capital letters on the base which correspond to Roman numerals (this is known as a chronogram).

LINZ★

L Oberösterreich
Population 197 960
Michelin map 926 fold 9 - Local map see DONAUTAL - Alt 266m/873ft

Linz, the capital of Upper Austria, is built on both banks of the Danube, at a point where the valley opens out after a narrow section. Three bridges link the city with its suburb of Urfahr, on the left bank.
As a bridgehead, Linz owes a good deal of its prosperity to the Danube. Today it is an important industrial city, whose dynamism is symbolized by the **Neues Rathaus** (**Z R**). Opened in 1985, this ultra-modern city hall stands on the north bank of the river near the Nibelungen bridge.

A daughter of the Danube - The Romans had already recognized the importance of this crossroads site, commanding both the Danube Valley and the former salt road, which extended from Hallstatt in the Traun Valley to Bohemia. From the Middle Ages onwards, shipping on the Danube contributed to the growth of the town, which was well fitted to take a leading role in river traffic, owing to its wood and iron industries. Today, large scale engineering works have made the port of Linz the biggest on the middle Danube.

Talent welcomed - The German astronomer **Johannes Kepler** (1571-1630) lived in Linz and it was here that he wrote his best-known work *Harmonice mundi*. Closer to our time, the Austrian writer **Adalbert Stifter** (1805-68), considered by Nietzsche to be one of the great masters of 19C German prose, was Director of the city's schools. Linz was a staging-post for **Mozart** in the course of his many tours; in 1782 he wrote his 36th symphony, the "Linz Symphony", here in just four days for a concert he was due to give at the city theatre. **Beethoven** too composed a symphony in Linz, his Eighth, but more than any other composer, the city cherishes the memory of **Anton Bruckner** who was cathedral organist here for 12 years. Every year Linz keeps his memory alive through its international festival of classical music, the Brucknerfest.

Capital of industry – The first train in Austria ran between Linz and Budweis (now Ceské Budejovice in the Czech Republic) in 1832, and the rapid development of railways encouraged the building of engineering and textile factories between the old town and the confluence of the Danube and the Traun. This enabled Linz to expand and absorb Scharlinz, Bergern and Kleinmünchen, which are now part of its southern suburbs.

Since the end of the Second World War industrial development has accelerated with emphasis on chemicals and other heavy industries.

Nowadays, the VÖEST-ALPINE concern in its steel, assembly and industrial machinery sectors, and the companies on the ÖMV industrial chemistry site (Chemie Linz and Agrolinz Melamin) between them employ almost 20 000 people. Their equipment and production processes are among the most modern in Austria and this, plus the fact that both industrial groups concentrate their efforts on production for export, means that they are of great economic importance to Linz and the region.

GENERAL VIEW

We recommend that you approach Linz along the Danube, preferably from the west. However, it is from the Pöstlingberg hill (alt 537m/1 762ft) that the most interesting general view of the town can be enjoyed.

★ **Pöstlingberg** ⏲ (**X**) – *4.5km/3mi north-west. On the left bank of the Danube beyond the north end of the Nibelungenbrücke turn left into Rudolfstraße, then right into Hagenstraße. After a level crossing the road climbs quickly. Turn right by the oratory. Leave the car in the car park below the church.*

From a flower-decked terrace below the pilgrimage church there is an extensive **view**★ from nearly 300m/1 000ft down into the Danube Valley, where Linz is spread out along the south bank in a basin encircled by hills; on the north bank lies the built-up area of Urfahr. It is easy to make out the city centre with its shopping avenues and the extensive industrial suburbs with their factory chimneys. Southwards, serving as a backcloth to this fine urban panorama, rise the foothills of the Alps.

★ OLD LINZ (Z)

Leave from the Hauptplatz. Follow the route marked on the town plan.

Hauptplatz – This large square laid out in the 13C is strikingly large (219x60m/719x197ft). In the centre stands the Trinity Column *(Dreifaltigkeitssäule)*, erected in 1723 by order of the States of Upper Austria (provincial assembly) and the local council and population to commemorate the escape of the town from plague, fire and Turkish invasion. With its statues and che rubs in white marble, and the group representing the

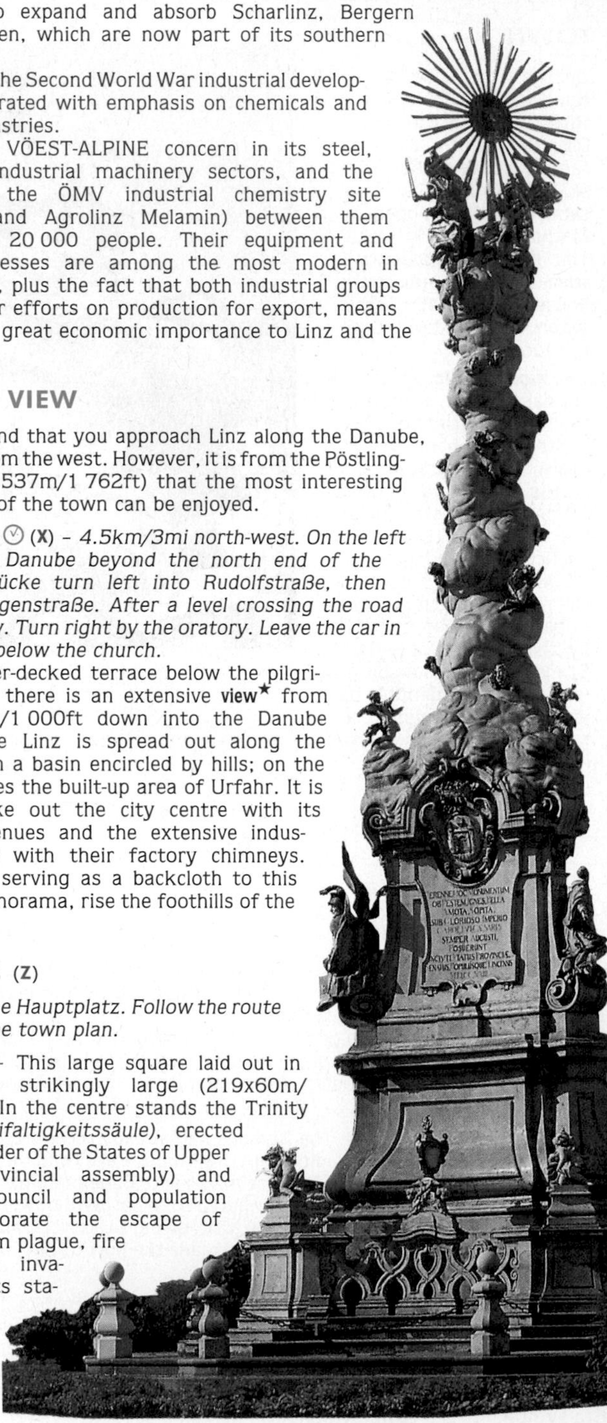

Trinity Column on the Hauptplatz, Linz

Bali/BILDAGENTUR BUENOS DIAS

TRAVELLERS' ADDRESSES

Tourist information

Tourist-Information, Hauptplatz 1 (Altes Rathaus), 4020 Linz.
Opening times: Mon-Fri 8am-7pm, Sat 9am-7pm, Sun and public holidays 10am-7pm (Nov-Apr until 6pm in each case). ☎ 07 32/70 70 17 77, Fax 07 32/77 28 73.
Tourist-Information, Urfahrmarkt 1, 4040 Linz.
Opening times: July-Sept daily 10am-6pm; Oct-June Mon and Thur 8am-4pm, Tue and Fri 8am-1pm. ☎ 07 32/70 70 29 39.

Further information can be found about Linz at the following **Web site**: *www.tiscover.com/linz*

Linz City Ticket

This entitles you to a city tour, a 10% reduction on a river trip on the Danube, free entry to the Botanischer Garten (Botanical Gardens) and to the Ars Electronica Center as well as one of the Linz museums, an "Erlebniskarte" (a combined ticket for the Pöstlingbergbahn (Pöstlingberg mountain railway) and the no 3 tram) and a voucher for food and drink. The Linz City Ticket can be obtained from the tourist Information offices on the Hauptplatz and Urfahrmarkt and costs 299S.

Trips on the Danube

Boat trip between Passau-Linz-Passau
Donauschiffahrt Wurm & Köck, Untere Donaulände 1, 4020 Linz, ☎ 07 32/78 36 07, or Höllgasse 26, 94032 Passau, Germany, ☎ +49 8 51 92 92 92.

Boat trip between Krems-Linz-Krems
Donauschiffahrt Ardagger, 3321 Ardagger 155, ☎ 0 74 79/6 46 40.

City tour

Linz-City-Express: tour in a miniature train with commentary (25min) – in season 10am 6pm, hourly (if demand is heavy, every 30min). Leaves from the Hauptplatz. Details from the tourist information offices.

Public transport

Individual tickets (Tageskarten for one day's travel, Strecken- or Kurzstreckenkarten for a certain distance) can be obtained from the ticket machines, while **multiple tickets** (Mehrfahrtenkarten) for six journeys and transferable **runabout tickets** (Netzkarten), valid for several days and giving unlimited travel on buses and trams, are available from ticket offices in Trafiken (tobacconists' shops). Information on public transport services is provided by ESG-Kundenzentrum, Landstraße 85/1 ☎ 07 32/78 01 70 02.

Inner city car parks

No charge: Urfahr market site; Station car park
Fee-paying: City-Parkhaus (multi-storey) Bethlehemstraße 12; Mozart-City-Center, Mozartstraße 12-14; Tiefgarage Hauptplatz, Tiefgarage Hessenplatz (underground car parks); Bahnhofgarage, Kärntnerstraße 18-20.

Post offices

Main post office: Hauptpostamt, Bahnhofplatz 11, open daily 6am-midnight
Sub-post offices Domgasse 1, Bismarckstraße 2, Volksfeststraße 2, Schmiedegasse 14 (usually open 8am-noon and 2-6pm).

Shopping

Shops and department stores are to be found in the Landstraße, which is pedestrianized from the Hauptplatz to the Bürgerstraße (for about 2km/ 1.25mi), and its side streets; there are exclusive boutiques in the arcade on the Landstraße. The Herrenstraße has another pedestrian shopping precinct.

Markets
Südbahnhof: daily market in the mornings, with a large market on Tues and Fri.
Hauptplatz: farmers' market every Fri 10am-2pm, flea market every Sat 6am-2pm.

Souvenirs
Craft goods: Heimatwerk, Landstraße 31; Linzer Torte (local speciality, kind of jam tart): Café Jindrak (several branches, including Herrenstraße 22).

Entertainment

Landestheater (Provincial Theatre), Promenade 39, ☎ 07 32/7 61 11 00.
Theater Phönix, Wiener Straße 25, ☎ 07 32/66 65 00.
Konzerthaus Brucknerhaus, Untere Donaulände 7, ☎ 07 32/7 61 20.
Posthof, Posthofstraße 43, ☎ 07 32/7 70 54 80. Cabaret, stand-up, theatre, dance, broad range of musical events.
Casino Linz, Rainerstraße 2-4, ☎ 07 32/65 44 87.

Cinemas

Central Kinocenter, Landstraße 36, ☎ 07 32/77 16 60.
City Cinema, Am Grabem 30, ☎ 07 32/77 60 81.
Kolosseum, Schillerplatz 1, ☎ 07 32/66 30 86.
Hollywood Megaplex, Pluskaufstraße 12, in Pasching, ☎ 0 72 29/6 93 00 15.

Arts cinemas:
Café Kino Cinematograph, Obere Donaulände 51, ☎ 07 32/78 56 03.
Moviemento, Dametzstraße 30, ☎ 07 32/78 40 90 50.

Eating out

Kremsmünsterer Stuben, Altstadt 10, ☎ 07 32/78 21 11.
Josef - Das Stadtbräu, Landstraße 49, ☎ 07 32/77 31 65.
Stieglbräu zum Klosterhof, Landstraße 30, ☎ 07 32/77 33 73.
Sturm's Wirtshaus, Am Pöstlingberg 12 (with a panoramic view of the town), ☎ 07 32/73 14 83.
Ursulinenhof, Landstraße 31, ☎ 07 32/77 46 86.

Cafés and bars

Cafés
Café Glockenspiel, Hauptplatz 18; **Café Jindrak**, Herrenstraße 22.

Many of the most popular bars are in the old town, such as **Grand Café-Daniel Sassi** (in the arcade, Spittelwiese 8). Other good places to go include the **Irish Pub** (Hessenplatz 19), **S'Kistl** (Altstadt 17), and **S'Linzerl** (Hofberg 5). To listen to music, head for **17er Keller** (Hauptplatz) or the **Kasper-Keller** (Landstraße 24, food available, jazz jam session every Tues, admission free), **Stieglitz im Klosterhof** (Landstraße 30) or **Joe's bar** in the Arcotel (Untere Donaulände 9).

Dates for your diary

Linz Fest: May. Wide range of musical entertainment including pop, hip-hop, jazz, soul, folk and popular Viennese music.

Klangplatz Hauptplatz: June-Aug, every Fri. Jazz, pop or rock music concert on the Hauptplatz.

Linzer Pflasterspektakel: one weekend in July. Cabaret artists, musicians and travelling entertainers from all over the world transform the centre of Linz into a big stage.

Festival Ars Electronica: Sept. Performances using and discussions on the use of electronic media (symposia, happenings etc).

Internationales Brucknerfest: Sept-Oct. Concerts of classical music.

Holy Trinity at the top, it is a fine example of the Baroque *Pestsäulen* (plague columns) which were set up in many towns of the Empire at that period.

Leave the square along the Domgasse (**5**) *to the southeast.*

Alter Dom St. Ignatius ⌚ – This church was built for the Jesuits in the second half of the 17C. Designed by Pietro Francesco Carleone, it is the city's most important Baroque church, and served as diocesan cathedral from 1785 to 1909. The simple façade is in striking contrast to the interior, where stucco, pink marble columns, an elaborately carved pulpit and choir stalls and a high altar adorned with marble statues make up a highly elaborate decor.
A medallion to the left of the entrance recalls Bruckner's 12-year service as organist here, during which time he had the organ – originally from Engelszell Abbey – rebuilt according to his specifications.

Turn right into the Graben (Moat); continue into the Promenade (**30**)*; turn right to the Landhaus.*

Landhaus (**L**) – This building, which is the headquarters of the provincial government, was erected in the second half of the 16C. The inner court is lined on two sides with arcades and has an octagonal fountain in its centre. On the base of the fountain, seven figures representing the planets recall that the great astronomer and mathematician Johannes Kepler taught between 1612 and 1626 at the regional secondary school, which was then in the Landhaus.

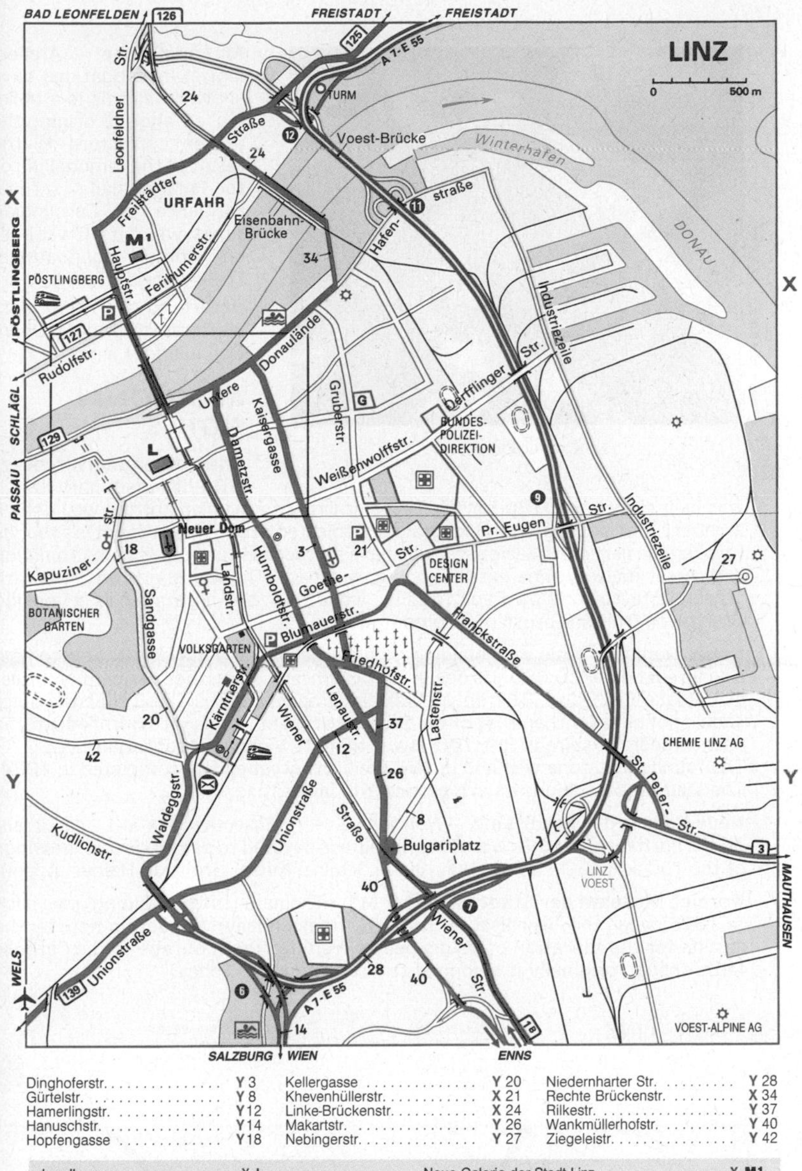

Landhaus .... X L

Neue Galerie der Stadt Linz .... X M¹

The north door, opening onto the Klosterstraße (**22**), is a fine work in the Renaissance style. The windows of the room over the passage are in harmony with the architecture of the doorway.

Minoritenkirche ⓥ (**D**) - The Gothic church, founded in the 13C by the Minorite Brothers or Franciscans, was remodelled in the Rococo style in the 18C.
Interest lies in its decoration. The altarpiece on the high altar by Bartolomäus Altomonte represents the Annunciation; the altarpieces on the six side altars were executed by Kremser Schmidt.

Take the Altstadt north.

Schloß - The oldest part of the palace, which was the residence of Emperor Friedrich III, dates from the end of the 15C.
It houses the art and historical collections of the provincial museum.

★ **Schloßmuseum** ⓥ (Part of the Oberösterreichisches Landesmuseum) - On the first floor, the history of art in Upper Austria is traced from the Middle Ages to the Rococo period. There is a large collection of weapons. On the second floor are to be found collections of popular art and folklore. Reconstructions of Gothic and Renaissance interiors are also on view as well as a 19C painting gallery.
Cross the many courtyards in the palace to descend to a terrace from which there is a pleasant view of the Danube, the Pöstlingberg hill and the first hills of the Mühlviertel.

Griedes/ÖSTERREICH WERBUNG

Linz headdress

Martinskirche – Archeological investigations have shown that this is a building of ancient origin; the present structure is the result of the remodelling of the Palatine hall of a royal residence of Carolingian times, which itself was built on Roman foundations. The chancel is Gothic.

Return to the Hauptplatz via the embankment (Obere Donaulände).

ADDITIONAL SIGHTS

★ **Priesterseminarkirche** (Z) – The little seminary church was built early in the 18C for the Teutonic Order to the plans of the well-known architect Johann-Lukas von Hildebrandt. Dedicated to the Holy Cross, it is a tour de force on the part of its designers, who have succeeded in investing a small building with great majesty. The exterior is highly ornate. The vaulting is adorned with graceful stuccowork by Paolo d'Allio, while over the high altar is a moving Crucifixion from the brush of Altomonte.

Neuer Dom (Y) – This vast building is the largest church in Austria, able to hold a congregation of 20 000. Its designer was Vincent Statz, then resident architect at Cologne Cathedral. The only constraint imposed on him was that the spire should not be taller than that of the Stephansdom in Vienna; at 134m/440ft, the new cathedral's spire is 3m/10ft lower than its Viennese counterpart.
The foundation stone was laid in 1862 and the great edifice completed in 1924. The stained-glass windows are particularly interesting.

Neue Galerie der Stadt Linz – Wolfgang-Gurlitt-Museum ⏱ (X M[1]) – *In Urfahr on the north bank of the river.* The museum is devoted to paintings and drawings of the 19C and 20C (Kokoschka, Klimt, Schiele, Kubin, Hrdlicka, Rainer, Appel).

Nordico Museum der Stadt Linz ⏱ (Z M[2]) – The name of the building goes back to 1675, when the "Nordisches Stift" (Northern Abbey) was set up here by the Jesuits for the education of young people from Northern Europe of the Catholic faith, though originally it belonged to Kremsmünster Abbey.

LINZ

Altstadt	Z 2	Klosterstr.	Z 22
Domgasse	Z 5	Promenade	Z 30
Elisabethstr.	Z 6	Rathausgasse	Z 32
Hagenstr.	Z 10	Rechte Donaustr.	Z 35
Hofgasse	Z 15	Schmidttorstr.	Z 38
Honauerstr.	Z 17	Theatergasse	Z 39

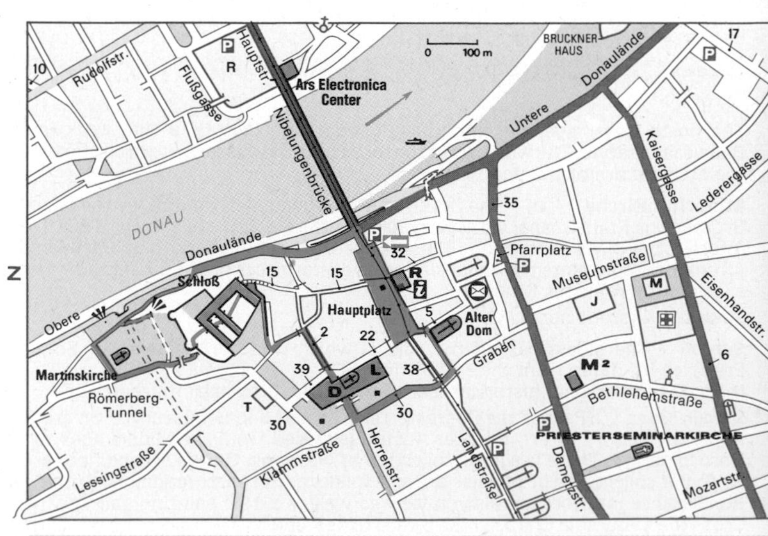

Landhaus	Z L	Neue Rathaus	Z R
Minoritenkirche	Z D	Nordico-Museum der Stadt Linz	Z M2

The museum's displays, presented on all three floors, are devoted to the history of the city and also to the history of art and culture.

Ars Electronica Center ⓥ – This "museum of the future" is entirely devoted to digital media, with the latest in technology from a 3-D installation to computer simulation and a Cyber City presented in an interactive centre.

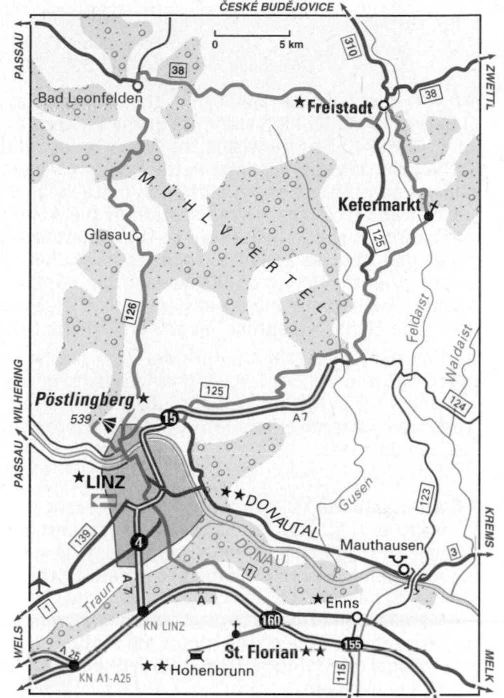

EXCURSIONS

★★ **Stift St. Florian** – *18km/11mi – see local map. Leave Linz on ③, road no 1, going southeast towards Enns (Y). In Asten turn right under the motorway to St. Florian. The village is overlooked by its great abbey (see Stift ST. FLORIAN).*

MÜHLVIERTEL *Round tour of 90km/56mi*

The Mühlviertel, the district of the Mühl, a small river which flows into the Danube above Linz, is a hilly upland stretching between the Danube and the Czech frontier and varying in height between 600m/2 000ft and 1 000m/3 000ft. The underlying rock is granite, which has been quarried extensively along the steep bank of the river, as at Mauthausen. The region beyond has wide valleys covered with a dark green carpet of forests contrasting, in its melancholy, with the Danube Valley, where the towns are more frequent.

Leave Linz on the road (no 126) north to Bad Leonfelden.

As soon as it leaves Linz the road enters a little verdant gorge and begins to climb gently, sometimes among rocks, sometimes among orchards. Firs take the place of fruit trees and become denser after Glasau. The wild nature of the hills, where meadows alternate with fir forests, grows more marked near Bad Leonfelden. About 500m north of the town bear right towards Freistadt. The well-engineered road runs through quiet countryside.

★ **Freistadt** – *See FREISTADT.*

Directly after leaving Freistadt, leave the Linz road and cross to the east bank of the Feldaist.

Kefermarkt – Kefermarkt stands on the left bank of the Feldaist, in a restful, hilly landscape marking the transition between the Mühlviertel and the granite plateaux of the Waldviertel north of the Danube.

St. Wolfgangskirche ⓥ – This Gothic church contains a remarkable **altarpiece**★★ of carved wood, which ranks among the finest of its kind. Author **Adalbert Stifter**, under whose direction the altarpiece was restored between 1852 and 1855, mentioned it in his great novel *Nachsommer* (Indian Summer, 1857).

The altarpiece is in the chancel, behind the high altar. It is outstanding for its monumental size – it is more than 13m/40ft high – the beauty of its proportions and the carved decoration, which show the exceptional skill of the artist.

The altarpiece was made at the end of the 15C by an unknown sculptor and was probably painted. Today all its carving, in high or low relief, is in natural limewood. Under richly carved canopies three figures – St Wolfgang, flanked by St Peter and St Christopher – occupy the central panel. The skill of the drapery and the expression of the faces recall the admirable composition of the altarpiece in the Pfarrkirche in St. Wolfgang in the Salzkammergut, a masterpiece by Michael Pacher.

On the shutters flanking the central panel are depicted the Annunciation and the Birth of Christ *(above)* and the Adoration of the Magi and the Dormition of the Virgin Mary *(below)*.

At the main crossroads in Kefermarkt turn right towards the railway station; cross the track and the Feldaist. After 7km/4mi turn left onto the main road, no 125, connecting Freistadt and Linz.

MALLNITZ*

Kärnten

Population 1 014

Michelin map 926 fold 33 – Alt 1 190m/3 904ft

At the foot of the Goldberg, the Ankogel and the Hochalmspitze, the last 3 000m/10 000ft high summits in the Eastern Alps, Mallnitz extends over an area of 110km²/42.5sq mi within the Hohe Tauern National Park.

During the summer Mallnitz is the point of departure for first class **hikes and Alpine tours**. A magnificent route, although quite long *(8hr on foot)* is the Göttinger Weg, which leads from the second section of the Ankogel railway up to the **Hagener Hütte** mountain lodge and then down to the mountain inn of Jamnig, from where the bus takes you back to Mallnitz. Another lovely hike leads to the Arthur-von-Schmidt-Hütte mountain lodge on **Dösner See** *(4hr 30min there and back)*. For less serious walkers, we recommend the easier route to the Stappitzer See *(20min there and back from the Hotel "Alpenrose" at the end of the road)*.

During the winter, the chair-lift serves a **ski area** which is restricted to a 15km/9mi piste, but which does however provide plenty of opportunities for off-piste skiing and ski tours. The 1 400m/4 600ft difference in altitude is enticing. Excellent snow conditions attract skiers late into the winter season, above all from the second section upwards.

Mallnitz has 4 cross-country skiing courses totalling 25km/15.5mi.

★★ **Ankogelbahn** ⌚ – In two sections. From the last mountain station, a 10min walk brings you to **Hannoverhaus** mountain lodge (alt 2 722m/8 930ft). A beautiful **panorama★★** opens up from here to the east, looking out over the Ankogel and the Hochalmspitze peak, to the west over the Hohe Sonnblick and the Schareck, to the south over the Seebach Valley at the foot of the Maresenspitze peak.

From the terrace of the mountain station, mountaineers set out to conquer the Ankogel (alt 3 246m/10 649ft), although it is only recommended to experienced Alpine climbers.

EXCURSION

Obervellach – *9km/6mi south of Mallnitz.* The **church★** is a massive building of the Late Gothic period (beginning of the 16C). It contains valuable works of art, including the 1520 **altarpiece★** of the Dutch Master Jan van Scorel, on the north side altar, depicting the Holy Family between St Christopher and St Apollonia. Also notable is the 1509 fresco of the 14 "auxiliary saints" in the chancel (from whom the people used to expect cures for the most diverse ills). Also in the chancel is a low relief of the Garden of Olives, and various statues forming an excellent Gothic ensemble of the 16C.

MALTATAL★★

Kärnten

Michelin map 926 fold 33

A 30km/18.5mi stretch of road leads through this magnificent valley, one of the most beautiful destinations in Carinthia, extending from Gmünd *(see GMÜND Kärnten)* to the foothills of the Hohe Tauern National Park.

It became especially famous after the Kölnbrein dam and the reservoir were built, but it owes its attraction above all to its highly diverse landscape. Until just beyond Malta the valley is wide and the countryside alternates between green meadows and wooded outcrops. Then the valley becomes narrower, before opening onto the magnificent glacier panorama of the Ankogel massif and the Hochalmspitze peak in the final stretch.

This is a conservation area and is particularly suitable as a point of departure for both **medium and high altitude Alpine hikes**.

The village of **Malta** at 840m/2 755ft above sea-level is an entrancing holiday spot. The church of Maria Hilf, which dates from the 15C, houses some fine 14C and 15C frescoes, including a rare image of Mary in Labour on the south wall. The Baroque decor is beautifully uniform. The high altar and pulpit were made in 1730.

SIGHTS

★★ **Malta-Hochalmstraße** – Above Malta, a toll is payable to drive the last 18km/11mi to the dam. The regular gradient of this excellently laid out road is a maximum of 13%, leading over nine bridges and through seven tunnels, including one especially impressive one, which is designed as a hairpin bend. Single line traffic alternates at two narrow points. A particular attraction of the road is

Y. Bontoux

Kölnbrein dam

its luxuriant vegetation (spruce, larch, alder and birch) and the waterfalls, 30 in all, which roar down into the valley. The Fallbach (level with the road branching off to the Gießener Hütte), the Melnikfall and the Hinterer Maralmfall are particularly impressive examples *(the brochure handed out at the toll point gives details about the waterfalls and tunnels).*

★ **Kölnbreinsperre** – The road ends here at 1 900m/6 233ft above sea-level. The dam is 200m/656ft high, 41m/134ft thick at the base and a total of 626m/2 054ft wide, making it the largest dam in Austria. The reservoir covers an area of 225ha/556 acres, and its volume is 200 million m^3/7 063 million cu ft, the same size as the Ossiacher See. Apart from its phenomenal technical capacity, the aesthetic design of this concrete colossus with its flowing, parabolic shape, is well worth seeing. *During high season, there are guided tours of the dam on the hour.*

In the panoramic look-out tower standing on the right of the dam there is an **information centre** ⌚, with films about the Hohe Tauern National Park, and a multimedia display on the construction of the Kölnbrein dam. The **Tauernschatzkammer**★ is indeed a treasure trove of beautiful rock crystals and other minerals from the local area.

The dam is the point of departure for some wonderful walks. The hike along the lake (also suitable for inexperienced hikers), which provides a wonderful view over the **surrounding Alpine landscape**★★, should not be missed. Visitors with more stamina should climb the Arlscharte.

★★ **Hike to the Arlscharte and the Arlhöhe** – *3hr 45min return trip on foot from the dam. Go towards the "Osnabrücker Hütte" mountain lodge.* The trail leads along the northern bank of the lake and soon proffers a magnificent view over the Ankogel glaciers. After walking for 45min, you will reach a memorial to a tragic accident which occurred during the building of the dam.

Turn to the right and walk on up the relatively steep Alpine flower trail. After 10min, the trail divides; turn left (the right hand trail leads to the Jägersteighütte mountain lodge). The trail, which is marked in red and white, climbs fairly steeply to the peak, which takes 45min to reach.

From the peak, the view extends over Pfringersee Lake below and over the Schödertal Valley. Opposite there is a **view**★★ over the two artificial lakes, over which tower the Kölnbreinspitze peak and its small glacier on the left and the impressive massif of the Hochalmspitze peak on the right.

Walk a few metres towards Pfringersee, then turn left and follow a waymarked trail *(red cross on a white background)*, which leads to an elevated point and then follows a kind of ridge trail. After 20min you will reach the **Arlhöhe** (alt

2 326m/7 631ft), where you will find an orientation map. There is a magnificent **panorama★★** over the artificial lake, over the furthest end of which tower the gleaming glacier of the Hochalmspitze and the rocky mass of the Schwarzhorn. Further to the right rise the Tischlerspitze peak and the Tischlerkarkopf (glaciers in the Ankogel range). In the north the Zwölferkogel dominates the deep Schödertal Valley. Return to the dam along the same trail.

★ **Excursion to the Gößkarspeicher** – *Return trip involving a 1hr drive and 45min on foot.* Halfway between Malta and the toll point, turn to the left towards the Gießener Hütte mountain lodge. The narrow 12km/7.5mi mountain road is quite steep (800m/2 625ft difference in altitude) and follows the course of the Gößbach, even fording the river bed at one point (danger, especially during bad weather; watch out for flood warnings). The rugged countryside is refreshingly unspoiled.

Since no cars are allowed along the last section, continue on foot to the Gößkar reservoir *(15min climb)*. This is a beautiful **wooded area★**, over which tower the Großer Gößspitze and the Dösnerspitze peaks.

Walk right along the left bank of the lake. Fantastic **view★** over the Hochalmspitze peak and its glacier, from which waterfalls simply thunder down.

Return to the reservoir, continue to its end and then to the right along the meadow (through a fence) until you reach a wide, moderately steep trail. **View★** over the rocky peaks of the Riekenkopf and the Pfaffenberger Nocken. Walkers return from here to the car park; hikers can climb up to the Gießener Hütte mountain lodge, from where the climb to the legendary Hochalm peak commences.

MARIA SAAL★

Kärnten

Population 3 220

Michelin map 926 fold 35 – 7km/4mi north of Klagenfurt – Alt 504m/1 654ft

Maria Saal is located near the site of the former Roman city of Virunum, capital of Norica. The city's ruins are scattered over the Zollfeld plain, between Klagenfurt and St. Veit.

In the 8C to 9C, following the Barbarian invasions, Carantania (as Carinthia was then known) was the centre from which the reconversion of the province to Christianity began. This was the sphere of activity of the Apostle of Carinthia, Bishop Modestus from Salzburg, in the second half of the 8C. He also founded the original church of Maria Saal, of which no trace now remains.

The name Maria Saal is probably derived from the Celtic "Sol", meaning "densely wooded", a name which is found elsewhere in the Zollfeld area.

★★ CHURCH (KIRCHE)

The present Gothic building was built between 1430 and 1460. It is protected by a fortified enclosure, which once also included the churchyard, recalling how exposed the Zollfeld was as a bastion of Christianity against the threat of Turkish invasion right up to the 17C. The fortified walls proved their worth in 1482, when Hungarian mercenaries unsuccessfully laid siege to the church.

Among the buildings around the church note especially the **charnel house** or **ossuary.** This is essentially a circular Romanesque baptistery chapel, which was extended upwards in the 15C and encircled by a two-storey arcaded gallery. Although the building has nine corners, it is referred to as an octagon. In 1751 the lower chapel had a Holy Sepulchre added to it. In front of the ossuary stands a Gothic graveyard lantern dating from 1497.

Exterior – With its twin towers of volcanic stone, decorated with delicate blind arcades, and its vast stone roof, made of 180 000 greyish stone slabs, the church makes a striking impression. Many stone reliefs and tombstones are sealed into the south and west walls. Roman stone work includes the bas-relief sculptures of Achilles dragging the corpse of Hector and the **Roman mail wagon★**, which in fact shows the journey of a dead soul into the afterlife. The magnificent **Keutschacher Epitaph★**, a red marble tombstone, depicts the Coronation of the Virgin. It was made in c 1510 in Salzburg, commissioned by Archbishop Leonard von Keutschach, whose main memorial is in Hohensalzburg Fortress *(see SALZBURG)*.

Among the tombstone reliefs in the porch is another interesting Roman example depicting the mother wolf with the twins Romulus and Remus.

R. Chéret/MICHELIN

Keutschacher Epitaph, Maria Saal

Interior – The triple-naved church is a typical Late Gothic building. The bays of the ribbed vaulting above the nave are decorated with frescoes growing out of calyxes, depicting the genealogy of Christ. They date from 1490 but were not uncovered until the early 20C. The sumptuous furnishings indicate the great importance that this pilgrimage church had.

The **high altar** dating from 1714 sets off the statue of the Madonna venerated by pilgrims, a 1425 stone figure in the "soft" style. On the north wall of the well-lit chancel is a remarkable medieval fresco of the Three Magi (1435). The north chancel contains the splendid **Arndorfer altarpiece★**, depicting the Coronation of the Virgin Mary carved by craftsmen from the Villach workshops in c 1520. The south chancel contains the St George altarpiece dating from 1526, a rather severe work which depicts the saint as the Dragon-Slayer symbolising the victory of Christianity over heathenism. The fresco on the south wall illustrating the salvation of the Apostle Peter on the Sea of Galilee was painted by Herbert Boeckl in 1928. The artist has depicted Peter with the features of Lenin, thereby symbolising the fall of Bolshevism and Communism in advance of events themselves.

Of considerable interest from the point of view of the church's history is the **tomb of St Modestus★** contained in the left side aisle in the Saxon chapel donated in 1451. Beneath a stone Romanesque altar-table supported on six small pillars is a Romanesque children's sarcophagus containing the saint's bones. A gravestone from Virunum serves as a lid.

Log cabin construction

This method of construction has been typical in Carinthia for centuries. It is used for living quarters and outbuildings (barns, drying sheds, bee hives). Beams of straight-grained timber from evergreen trees (pine, larch) are laid horizontally one above the other, alternating crown and root end of the timber. To build corners the beams are dovetailed into each other to strengthen the join. This corner join has taken on a variety of forms since the 16C – swallow's tails, bells, faces – and it is now therefore often possible to tell the age of a building by it. The gaps between the beams were padded with moss or straw matting; a special kind of moss was used for this. Gaps in the walls were also sometimes filled in on the outside with a clay wash.

The richly decorated pulpit with the fathers of the Ancient Roman church is counter-balanced by a depiction of the Glorification of St John of Nepomuk opposite it. Both works were created in 1747 and are attributed to Johann Pacher. The Baroque **organ** (1735) by Johann Martin Jäger from Klagenfurt has a beautiful tone.

★KÄRNTNER FREILICHTMUSEUM ⏲

300m/330yd north of the village centre. 45min.

Some 40 old buildings have been dismantled and then reassembled here in a hilly wooded setting of 4ha/10 acres. They include farmhouses, stables, barns and a variety of outbuildings. By preserving exhibits representative of rural activities, the museum goes to the heart of country life in Carinthia in past centuries, particularly in the interiors and furnishings.

Most of the buildings are **built of logs**, and some are thatched with straw while others are roofed with wooden shingles. The living quarters have a smoking room with an oven and an open hearth.

Particularly interesting examples include the Hanebauerhaus from St. Jakob ob Gurk, the early-17C Bodnerhaus, the Salzerhaus (1767) from the Katschtal, the Urchhaus from the Rosental and the Kramerhaus, a house with a cross passage giving access through the inside. The Lavanttaler Haus is one of the oldest houses in the museum; parts of it date from 1631.

A reconstructed covered wooden bridge leads to the mill area. There is a mill wheel with the miller's room beneath it, a turbine-like mill from Upper Carinthia and a saw-mill, all of which clearly illustrate the difficult working conditions, but also well thought-out systems of early mechanisation which saved the workers from some considerable effort.

MARIAZELL★

Steiermark

Population 1 930

Michelin map 926 fold 23 – Alt 868m/2 848ft

Mariazell is the most frequented place of pilgrimage in Austria. It is also a popular summer and winter resort, occupying a charming **site**★ on the gentle slopes of an escarpment, out of reach of morning mists (fine cloud effects in still weather) and dipping towards a verdant Alpine basin. This extreme eastern end of the Alps, very jagged in outline, includes wild areas (massifs of the Hochschwab and the Ötscher, the Salza Valley, etc) in spite of its modest altitude. A good impression of the region can be obtained by climbing to the **Bürgeralpe**, served by frequent **cable-cars** ⏲ from the centre of the town.

Pilgrimage – It was in 1157 that Benedictines from St. Lambrecht Abbey founded a priory here. As early as the beginning of the 14C the first rescripts of indulgences appeared here, testifying to the attraction of the church for crowds of Christians. In 1370 Ludwig the Great of Hungary, won a victory over the Turks which he attributed to the Virgin of Mariazell and had a chapel built here in thanksgiving, which is still standing. From that time on, the worship of the Virgin of Mariazell, also venerated in Hungary and the Balkans, symbolized more and more the spiritual forces which guaranteed the cohesion of the Austrian Empire. Even today pilgrims from all over the former Habsburg Empire make the pilgrimage in large numbers to Mariazell, which is regarded as their spiritual centre by the Catholic peoples of the Danube countries. The most important ceremonies are on 15 August and 8 September. For the rest of the summer the largest crowds assemble on Saturday evenings, when a great torchlight procession takes place.

★BASILICA

In the 17C the growing number of pilgrims made it necessary to enlarge the original Gothic building which dated back to the 14C. The architect, **Domenico Sciassia** was given the task (1644-1704). He kept the nave but demolished the chancel to replace it by two vast bays, one of which was roofed by a dome. When he remade the façade, he left the Gothic porch intact between the two new and much squatter onion-capped towers. This unusual combination has become the emblem of this pilgrim city. The main doorway still has its carved Gothic tympanum, whose lower register is devoted to the history of the pilgrimage.

Enter the church. The brilliant structure of the Gnadenkapelle marks the transition from the Baroquized Gothic main building to the after-nave, which is 17C.

West Nave – This is nothing other than the former Gothic building, whose slim design can still be distinguished in spite of the Baroque shell and the width gained by including the former buttresses inside the building. By means of this last

device, Sciassia made room along the aisles for a series of side chapels, and on the first storey for a gallery whose large windows give an exceptional degree of light. To appreciate fully the details of the Baroque decoration - stucco and paintings - one should walk along these galleries.
The chapel in the north aisle dedicated to St Ladislas, King of Hungary, until recently housed the mortal remains of Cardinal Mindszenty, Primate of Hungary, now transferred to Esztergom in that country.

Gnadenkapelle (Chapel of Miracles) - The chapel, built on a trapezoidal plan in the centre of the church, shelters a Romanesque statue, always in full regalia, of the Virgin of Mariazell. She stands beneath a valuable silver baldaquin resting on 12 columns designed by Joseph Emmanuel Fischer von Erlach the Younger (1727). The enclosing grille, also of silver, was ordered by Maria Theresa from Viennese silversmiths in 1756.

East Nave - This truly monumental piece of Baroque architecture is superbly proportioned. It forms a second, inner nave, beyond a false transept. The first bay is lit by an oval lantern-dome which harmonizes with the extended shape of the whole church. The second square bay, which closes the perspective, contains the majestic high altar by Johann Bernhard Fischer von Erlach, which was completed in 1704 and inspired by the commemorative arches of antiquity. The statues of the Crucifixion group, like those of the great angels guarding the Gnadenkapelle are copies of the solid silver statues which were melted down to meet the needs of the Austrian treasury during the Napoleonic Wars.

Schatzkammer (Treasury) ⓥ - The display includes a remarkable brocade chasuble, (c 1500) with high relief embroidery of saints under canopies, and various robes for attiring the Virgin of Mariazell. Ex-votos from the 15C to 20C can also be seen.

EXCURSION

★ **Erlaufsee and Gemeindealpe** - *Round tour of 20km/12mi. Leave Mariazell on the road to Bruck an der Mur. On reaching the valley floor turn right onto the Lunz road.*

Marienwasserfall - *Access to the waterfall is by the hotel of that name.* This small cascade flows like a shimmering veil over a rocky niche containing a copy of the Mariazell Madonna.

Go back to the car. At a junction of three roads, bear right.

Erlaufsee - The road emerges from the woods and runs along the south shore of the lake, celebrated in song by Schubert. The scene is dominated to the northwest by the summit of the Gemeindealpe.

At the end of the lake, turn left towards Mitterbach and stop at the chair-lift station (Alpensesselbahn) for the Gemeindealpe.

★ **Gemeindealpe** - Alt 1 626m/5 335ft - *About 1hr 30min there and back, including 1hr by chair-lift.* From this height one can enjoy a general **view** of the Ötscher massif, overlooking a mountainous area cut across by the furrows of the Ötschergraben and the Tormäuer. In the opposite direction the water of the Erlaufsee lies in the foreground of the Mariazell basin. In clear weather the bastions of the Dachstein (southwest) are visible.

Return to the lower station and make for Mitterbach and from there to Mariazell by the direct road.

MATREI IN OSTTIROL*

Tirol

Population 4 900
Michelin map 926 fold 32 - Alt 1 000m/3 300ft

The popular holiday resort of Matrei in East Tyrol lies in beautiful and diverse surroundings at the junction of the Tauerntal, Virgental and Iseltal, and boasts the third largest municipal area in Austria. Thanks to the natural barriers provided by the Hohe Tauern in the north, the region boasts an especially pleasant climate. The market town lies in a restful low mountainous area and is framed by the highest and most beautiful peaks in Austria (Großglockner in the east and Großvenediger in the west). Thanks to its extraordinary position it has become a well-known point of departure for **hikes**★★★ into the Eastern Alps.

During the winter the **ski area**★ offers satisfactory conditions for skiers. Three chair-lifts and three T-bar lifts lead to 30km/18.5mi of pistes of between 1 000m/3 300ft and 2 400m/7 900ft in length, some with artificial snow. It is a particularly attractive resort for lovers of long distance skiing and ski tours, with 24km/15mi of long pistes and vast off-piste areas.

Y. Bontoux

A fresco in St. Nikolauskirche

SIGHTS

Pfarrkirche St. Alban – Only the church tower bears witness to the original Gothic style of the building. It was converted to the Baroque style at the end of the 18C (ceiling frescoes by Franz Anton Zeiller, 1783).

St. Nikolauskirche – *Approach by car. From the main square in Matrei, drive over the bridge to Lienzer Straße, then turn onto the second small street on the left (Bichler Straße). Drive to the end of the street and leave the village. The road leads over a bridge and then right past a wooden well. Turn right at both the next sets of crossroads. The road is no longer tarmacked, but is quite drivable. Turn right onto the next small road, which leads to the church situated in a beautiful location above Matrei.*

St. Nikolaus is a Romanesque building dating from the second half of the 12C, and is unquestionably one of the most interesting churches in the Tyrol. Inside, the narthex and the dome are worth seeing. These were converted to the Gothic style in around 1470. The choir, a special feature, is situated in a tower and is two storeys high, decorated with important 13C **frescoes**★. The lower storey represents scenes from the Creation (Adam and Eve are noteworthy). The upper storey is reached via a double staircase and is even more interesting. The frescoes show the four elements, which carry the 12 Apostles and the Evangelists. Note the three beautiful sculptures from the 15C, of St Nicholas, St Alban and the Virgin and Child.

EXCURSIONS

★★ **Europa-Panoramaweg** – In the summer it is worth buying a ticket which includes the valley trip with the Glocknerblick chair-lift and the return trip to Matrei in the bus *(ask for times at the tourist information office)*. You should plan an entire day for the interesting trip to Kals-Matrei pass and to Großdorf *(1hr 45min of which is an easy walk)*. Hikers will want to climb up to the Blauspitze peak.

★★ **Goldriedbahn** – Alt 2 150m/7 054ft. *40min trip in two sections.* Magnificent **view**★★ over the steep rocky mass of the Kendlspitze peak, the Virgental (Virgen Valley), the Kristallkopf and the Großglockner.

★★ **Walk to the Kals-Matrei-Törlhaus** – Take the so-called Europa Panoramaweg trail at the mountain station of the chair-lift. About 60 "ten-thousand-footers" can be seen from this easy trail. After 25min you reach the highest point on the trail (alt 2 259m/7 411ft), which boasts a magnificent **view**★★ over the Großvenediger in the northwest. The trail to the Törlhaus which is bordered with willowherb runs along opposite the glaciers of the Großglockner through a larch forest. The Kalsertal Valley, and on the right the Schober group, can be seen from the pass.

★★ **Hike to the Blauspitze** – *2hr 45min return trip from the Kals-Matrei pass. Recommended excursion for experienced hikers. Climbing boots are essential for climbing up to the peak.*

Take the ridge trail towards Sudetenhütte mountain lodge. Turn right after almost 1hr *(trail waymarked with red crosses)*. Care is needed at the end of the well secured (roped) section. A magnificent **panorama**★★, especially over the glaciers of the Großglockner, can be enjoyed from the first peak. The impressive ridge trail to the cross is only recommended to experienced mountaineers who have a good head for heights.

★★ **Kalsertal** – Climb down from the Kals-Matrei pass on the other side. In 1hr you will reach the mountain station of the Glocknerblickbahn railway. Take the train down into the valley. The trip to Großdorf offers a magnificent **view**★ over the valley. Then walk to Kapellenplatz and take the bus back into Matrei. It is best to sit on the left in the bus so that you can see the impressive valley sides. On the final bends into the Iseltal, you will capture a brief **view**★ over the Dolomites to the south.

★ **Virgental** – *18km/11mi drive from Matrei to Ströden.* This beautiful valley to the south of the glacier of the Großvenediger is an interesting excursion destination for all summer visitors in the Matrei area. The dense forests in the lower part and the Alpine mountain scenery in the upper part are impressive. Prägraten (alt 1 310m/4 298ft) is the most beautiful holiday resort in the valley.

The Umbal falls at the end of the road are well worth a visit.

Burg MAUTERNDORF★

Salzburg

Michelin map 926 fold 34

The castle overlooks an ancient route, once used by the Romans, which now links the Hohe Tauern mountains and Salzburg. There is evidence that there was a customs post *(Mautstelle)* here as early as 1002. The village of **Mauterndorf** owes much of its dignity to a number of substantial buildings, many of them embellished with bay windows and stepped gables.

The first castle was built by the archbishops of Salzburg in the middle of the 13C to enable them to keep a close eye on their possessions in the Laugau; it was not until 1339 that the castle chapel was built and the frescoes painted.

Prince-Archbishop Leonhard von Keutschach was particularly fond of the castle. In 1494 he added a room above the chapel; visitors may see the mural decorations and the bed recess.

"The Archbishop's Turnip"

The story goes that **Leonhard von Keutschach** led a lively student life as a young man, rarely heeding his family's advice. One day, on a visit to Pinzgau, he was walking in a turnip field with his uncle Wolf zu Alm, who soundly berated him on the subject of his studies. Piqued by the young man's impertinent reply, the uncle flew into a rage and threw a turnip at him saying, "If you don't mend your ways, I will never receive you again!" The turnip changed Leonhard's life; he applied himself to his studies and later became Prince-Archbishop of Salzburg. In gratitude, he had a turnip included in his coat of arms, which appears in various places at Mauterndorf.

TOUR

The exterior of the **keep** in the main courtyard is well worth examining. A security device, typical of medieval keeps, controlled the entrance. The only access was through a door which was always in view, about 8m/26ft above ground level (left of the fresco of St Christopher). This door was approached by means of a wooden gallery against the wall linking the keep to a separate building. In the event of an attack, this vulnerable link could be quickly removed and the keep isolated. The existence of a late-15C **fresco of St Christopher**, patron saint of travellers, strongly suggests that in the Middle Ages the main road passed through the castle courtyard, thus facilitating the collection of toll charges. Most of the present buildings date from the spate of construction from 1546 to 1559, although there was also some major, albeit respectful, restoration work carried out in 1896. Since 1968 the castle has been owned by the Land (Province) of Salzburg; it houses an interesting museum of local arts and traditions, the **Lungauer Landschaftsmuseum** ⌚.

MAUTHAUSEN

Oberösterreich

Population 4 350

Michelin map 926 fold 9 – 25km/16mi east of Linz

Local map see DONAUTAL – Alt 250m/820ft

Mauthausen's provincial-style houses run down almost to the banks of the Danube. The sleepy little town has a traditional market place with a stone fountain playing under the shade of two great plane trees. The Late Gothic **Pfarrkirche St. Nikolaus** has altarpieces by Kremser Schmidt, and to the south of the church a remarkable Romanesque charnel house from the beginning of the 13C with fragments of frescoes from the same period. On the eastern edge of the town stands all that remains of the 11C **Heinrichskirche**, the Gothic chancel of which was added around 1400. With its walls rising from the waters of the Danube, the old fortress of **Schloß Pragstein** now plays a peaceful role as the local museum.

Until 1938, when Austria was annexed to Hitler's German Reich, Mauthausen was known only for its granite quarries, which supplied most of the paving stones for Vienna. One of the quarries was used as a Nazi concentration camp, which made the name of Mauthausen one of the most sinister under their rule. In 1949 the Austrian Government declared the camp to be a historic monument. By that time many of the buildings had been destroyed.

Konzentrationslager (Concentration Camp) ⏲ – From 1938 until 5 May 1945 about 200 000 people were imprisoned at Mauthausen and its 49 subsidiary camps, over 100 000 of whom died. Some of the huts and rooms in which the prisoners suffered and died still stand. One of the buildings has been turned into a museum with photographs and other documentary material on the horrors perpetrated in this sinister place. Outside the camp limits are the memorials set up by countries whose people perished here. Below the plateau is the "Todesstiege" (Staircase of Death), leading to the quarry.

MAYERLING

Niederösterreich

Michelin map 926 fold 25 – 36km/22mi southwest of Vienna

Local map see WIEN: Excursions

At the end of the 19C Mayerling was the setting for a tragedy that shook the world of the day.

A tragic love story – The secrecy with which the Imperial family surrounded the events of January 1889 gave rise to the most fanciful theories. Nonetheless, with the help of recently discovered documents, most of the drama can be recreated. In 1888 the **Archduke Rudolf**, only son of Emperor Franz Joseph and Empress Elisabeth and heir to the throne of Austria-Hungary, was 30 years old. His support for the parliamentary opposition in Hungary together with his liberal ideas frightened the aristocracy. His lack of faith angered the Church; and his dissolute life, worsened by his unhappy marriage with Stephanie of Belgium, created estranged relations with his family. His last conquest was made at a ball at the German Embassy, where he made the acquaintance of a girl of 17, Maria Vetsera. He fell in love with her and his love was returned. Hearing of this liaison, the Emperor decided to put an end to the scandal. On 28 January 1889 he had a stormy interview with his son during which he told him of the refusal of Pope Leo XIII to annul Rudolf's marriage and of his own opposition to a divorce; he also demanded that he reveal the names of the Hungarian conspirators. Refusing to betray his friends and weary of a situation full of insuperable problems, Rudolf, already depressed, resolved

ROGER VIOLLET

Archduke Rudolf

to commit suicide with his loved one. The following day, he did not appear at dinner but shut himself away with Maria in the hunting lodge at Mayerling that he had acquired in 1887. On 30 January they were found dead. Maria was the first to die. Rudolf then wrote to his mother, his wife, and his very old friend Maria Caspar (Mizzie), before shooting himself at dawn.

CHAPEL AND MEMORIAL ⊙

In the village, follow the signs to "Ehemaliges Jagdschloß - KARMEL St. Josef".

After the death of Rudolf and Mary Vetsera, Emperor Franz Joseph had part of the hunting lodge sectioned off and new rooms added to it to accommodate a Carmelite convent. On the site of the bedchamber in which the tragedy took place, a neo-Gothic memorial chapel was built. The high altar stands on the spot once occupied by the bed in which the dead couple were found. In this part of the building added after the death of the Crown Prince, leading off from the chapel, are rooms set up in memory of the dead prince, containing furniture from the hunting lodge, photographs and drawings.

Almost a century later, this tragic story continued to arouse a certain fascination. Sir Kenneth Macmillan choreographed the ballet *Mayerling* to music by Liszt for the Royal Ballet of London, which first performed it in 1978.

Stift MELK★★★

Niederösterreich

Michelin map 926 fold 10 - Local map under DONAUTAL - Alt 213m/699ft

The abbey of Melk, which crowns a rocky bluff overlooking the Danube more than 50m/150ft above the river, is the apogee of Baroque architecture in Austria.

The cradle of Lower Austria - The princely family of Babenberg, who were natives of Bavaria, established their rule on the site of a Roman stronghold at Melk, fixing their seat there at the end of the 10C. Recalling the fate of the Nibelungen - Melk is said to be the Medelike of the famous story - the Babenbergs continued down the Danube Valley and established their court first at Tulln, then at Vienna.
At the end of the 11C, Leopold III von Babenberg handed over his castle to the Benedictines, who converted it into a fortified abbey. The spiritual and intellectual renown of Melk spread through the whole of Lower Austria.

Days of storm and days of glory - The spread of the Reformation hindered the development of monastic life. The Turkish invasion in 1683 sowed ruin and chaos beyond Vienna, and many of the monastery estates were ravaged. The abbey itself was gutted by fire but was entirely rebuilt from 1702 onwards in its present form. Several rulers of the House of Habsburg, including Maria Theresa in 1743, and other famous people such as Napoleon, stayed at the abbey, which succeeded in conserving its art treasures throughout all the years of its history.

MELK

Abbe-Stadler-Gasse 2
Abt-B.-Dietmayr-Straße 3
Bahngasse 5
Fischergasse 6
Fisolengasse 7
Hauptplatz 9
Hubbrücke 10
Josef-Büchl-Straße 12
Kaiblingerstraße 13
Kirchenplatz 14
Kremser Straße 16
Nibelungenlände 17
Pischingerstraße 19
Prinzlstraße 20
Rathausplatz 21
Roseggerstraße 23
Stadtgraben 24
Stiftsweg 26

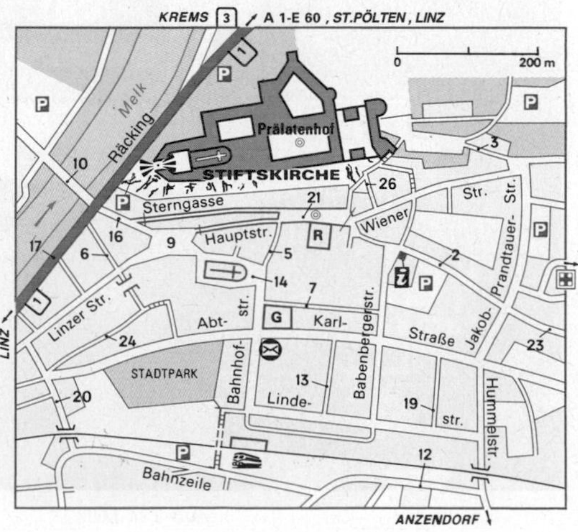

TOUR ⏲

High above Melk's main street (Hauptstraße) lined with fine town houses, stands the south façade of the abbey, extending for some 240m/785ft.

The abbey can be reached directly on foot from the Stiftsweg (**26**). *The road approach is from the east end of the town; follow signs marked "🅿 Stift Melk".*

In 1702 Abbot Dietmayr laid the first stone in the rebuilding of the monastery. The architect, **Jakob Prandtauer**, managed to make the best of the difficult trapezoid site and to create a structure perfectly in harmony with the situation. After his death in 1726 the work was completed with the help of his plans by his pupil, **Josef Munggenast**.

The outer gateway, giving access to the first courtyard, is framed by the statues of St Leopold and St Coloman, the abbey's patrons, and flanked by two bastions built in the 17C and 18C. On the inner gate is the abbey coat of arms. Directly beyond a vestibule with a painted ceiling depicting St Benedict, the founder of the Order, is the **Prälatenhof** (Prelates' Courtyard), a fine group of buildings, its walls adorned with statues representing the Prophets. The dome of the abbey church may be seen beyond the fountain.

Kaisergang – *Access via the Imperial staircase.* The Emperors' gallery, which is 196m/644ft long, provided access to the chambers reserved for important visitors. It is hung with paintings of the kings and regents of Austria. Several of the former Imperial rooms have been converted into a museum containing the Melk Cross of 1363, a Gothic altarpiece by Jörg Breu, and various objects illustrating the abbey's history and current objectives.

Marmorsaal – Preceded by a vestibule with portraits of the builder of the Baroque abbey (Dietmayr) and its architect (Prandtauer), the Marble Hall impresses the visitor less by the lavishness of its decoration than by the strength of its design, which is dominated by a series of pilasters covered in a reddish-brown stucco in imitation of marble *(Marmor)*.

The allegorical ceiling fresco, "The goddess of Reason guiding Humanity from the darkness of uncivilized existence towards the light of civilization and culture", was painted in 1732 by **Paul Troger**, whose blue tones are famous.

Terrace – This is situated at the very tip of the rocky spur, over the elegant portico linking the symmetrically designed Marble Hall and Library. It affords a fine view of the Danube and the façade of the abbey church.

Bibliothek (Library) – Like the Marble Hall, the Library is two storeys high and has a fine ceiling painted by Paul Troger symbolizing Faith. It contains 100 000 books and 1 800 manuscripts. The gilded wood statues at the entrances represent the four faculties; the woodwork and gilding of the interior add to the splendour.

Abbey of Melk

★★★ **Stiftskirche** – The abbey church is surrounded by the abbey buildings but dominates the group with the symmetrical towers of its west front and its great octagonal dome *(see Introduction: ABC of architecture).*

The interior gives a great impression of lightness, which is due to the many windows, the sweep of great fluted pilasters and to a judicious use of colours, in which brownish-red, grey, orange and golden tones are mingled.

The lavish decoration includes frescoes, gold ornaments and marble.

The vaulting of the nave, the dome and the altars are crowded with figures. In the dome, which is 65m/213ft high, are enthroned God the Father, Christ, the Evangelists and the Doctors of the Church. On the nave vaulting St Benedict is triumphantly received into Heaven. All these paintings are by **Johann Michael Rottmayr**, as well as those on the side altars depicting the Adoration of the Magi, St Michael and the Baptism of Christ. Paul Troger did the paintings on the other side altars, among them St Nicholas and St Sebastian, while the Italian painter Hippolyto Sconzani was responsible for the wall paintings.

In the midst of these riches the eye is caught by the high altar. In the centre of the group of statues, the two Princes of the Apostles, St Peter and St Paul, to whom the church is consecrated, take leave of one another before their martyrdom.

EXCURSION

★ **Schloß Schallaburg** ⌚ – *6km/4mi south of Melk towards Anzendorf.*

The castle has substantial Romanesque remains and a Gothic chapel, but it is the great 16C **Renaissance arcaded courtyard**★ which makes the most striking impression, as if it had been moved by magic from faraway Rome to its present Alpine surroundings.

The Austrian predilection for arcaded courtyards is repeated here with an extraordinary profusion of terracotta ornamentation. Statues, atlantes, caryatids, floral motifs, cartouches and ornamental keystones are boldly and harmoniously combined to form a masterly composition in the Antique taste of the period.

Today, Schallaburg is an exhibition and cultural centre for the province of Lower Austria, used every summer for prestigious exhibitions.

MILLSTATT★

Kärnten

Population 3 200

Michelin map 926 folds 33 and 34 – Alt 604m/1 982ft

Millstatt lies on the north shore of the **Millstätter See**, a lake which boasts summer water temperatures of up to 26°C/82°F. Owing to its lakeside beach and its favourable climate, Millstatt has become a very popular summer resort.

The lake (12km/7.5mi long and more than 1km/0.5mi wide) reflects the distant peaks of the Kreuzeck and Reißeck (northwest), outcrops of the Tauern range. The mountain setting and the peaceful, wooded shore on the south side of the lake provide a tranquil backdrop for this long narrow stretch of water.

As cultural centre of Upper Carinthia, Millstatt hosts a series of concerts, the Internationale Musikwochen, between May and October.

★ ABBEY (STIFT)

The abbey's history has been a turbulent one, and can be divided into three main periods. It began life as a Benedictine monastery under the abbey of Hirsau (before 1077-1469), then it became the seat of the Knights of St George (1469-1598), and finally it fell into the hands of the Jesuit Order (1598). In 1773, when the Jesuit Order was annulled by the Pope, the monastery became State property. Each of these periods has contributed significantly to the overall architecture and its contents, however, first prize has to go to the Romanesque period which bequeathed the outstanding cloisters and west door. The **abbey museum** ⌚ gives a good insight into history of the abbey and the works of art, both religious and secular, that it contains.

The site of the 15C castle of the Grand Master of the Knights of St George is now occupied by a hotel.

★ **Stiftshof (Abbey courtyard)** – The 1 000 year old "Judgement" lime tree, and two tiers of galleries with Italian arches, form a colourful scene. The elegance of this 16C architecture reveals the riches of the Order of St George, which was founded by the Emperor Friedrich III, to assist in the defence of Christianity against the Turks. In spite of its Imperial foundation, the Order never won any political power. Furthermore, its few members were incapable of repelling the Turks, with the result that the Turks stormed unimpeded through to Carinthia a total of five times between 1473 and 1483, and in 1478 even set fire to the abbey itself.

Ph. Roy/EXPLORER

Abbey cloisters at Millstatt

★ **Kreuzgang** (**Cloisters**) ⊙ – *Enter from the east side of the courtyard. In summer, the cloisters can only be visited as part of a visit to the abbey museum. It is open without this restriction for the rest of the year.* The cloisters were endowed with Gothic vaulting by the Knights of St George at the beginning of the 12C. They still possess the Romanesque blind arcades with slim marble columns and the **cushion capitals**★ lavishly decorated with animals or symbolic plants. In the east gallery, which is the most open, may be seen the design, often reproduced in tourist literature, of a gnome and a lion each supporting a slim column. In front of a former communicating door into the church are two detached columns, each resting on a sculptural group representing a woman (the Church) taming a monstrous male figure (the pagan world).

Return to the abbey courtyard to go up to the church.

Stiftskirche – The porch contains a magnificent marble **Romanesque west door**★★, whose decorative designs in the covings – rolls, braids – are preserved in all their extraordinary delicacy. Masks and animals along the ends of the small columns represent the struggle between good and evil. The tympanum shows Abbot Heinrich II (1166-77) paying homage to Christ in his abbey church.

Interior – The interior owes its network vaulting, with historiated keystones, to the Knights of St George and its magnificent Baroque furnishings to the Jesuits. The richly crocketed **high altar**★ was made in 1648 and features two pairs of gilded columns entwined with vines, in between which there are larger than life-size statues of St Domitian (left) and Margrave Leopold III (right). The altar is flanked by angels carrying horns of plenty which were added in 1716. The gilded Rococo pulpit was made in the year that the Jesuit Order was annulled. Black and gold are the predominant colours on the altar of St Ignatius in the left aisle and that of St Francis Xavier in the right.

There are one or two noteworthy **frescoes** adorning the church, such as the Last Judgement (1515) on the south wall (to the right of the altar to St George at the far end of the south aisle). The second column along in the nave, on the south side, still features paintings dating from 1430. Two side chapels, facing one another, contain (on the left) the Tombstone of Grand Master Siebenhirter (d 1508), and (on the right) that of Grand Master Geumann (d 1533), both carved from red marble.

Oberes MÖLLTAL★

Kärnten

Michelin map 926 fold 32

The winding Möll Valley, a tributary of the Drava, forms an important communication route. In its upper part from Heiligenblut to Winklern it provides a kind of continuation for the Großglockner road; in its lower section, between Winklern and Möllbrücke, the road has developed into an important transit route between the Dolomites, Lienz and the Carinthian lakes.

FROM HEILIGENBLUT TO LIENZ *38km/24mi*

✲ **Heiligenblut** – *See HEILIGENBLUT.*

South of Heiligenblut, after the Zlapp outcrop over which the River Möll thunders as a torrent, the road drops steeply to a lower level in the valley. The peak of the Großglockner is now out of sight.

The Möll Valley, quiet and green, is dotted with houses of dark wood lending a touch of mountain scenery to this section. In the meadows are crop drying racks.

Döllach - The history of this elegant village, once of primary importance for the Möll Valley as a gold and silver mining centre, is well presented in a small museum, located in **Schloß Großkirchheim**. This formidable building was built in 1561 by the Melchior Putz (mine-owner) works.

Shortly after Döllach a few harp-shaped hay and grain drying racks can be seen to the right of the road - these were once a common sight throughout the region. Downriver of Mörtschach there is a fine first view, to the south, of the cliffs and pinnacles of the Dolomites at Lienz.

At Winklern the road forks. The Möll Valley turns abruptly east between wooded slopes, while the road to the **Iselsberg pass** (alt 1 204m/3 950ft) branches off to the southwest. Stopping at the first parking spot beyond Winklern is an absolute must, to admire the view of the valley below and the countryside in the distance: the **panorama**★★ of the Möll Valley is simply unforgettable.

The **descent**★ from Iselsberg to Lienz is a magnificently designed stretch of road which is a real experience to drive along. The first two bends are good places to stop (Gasthaus Dolomitenblick). The grey crags of the Lienz Dolomites seem almost close enough to touch. The upper Drava Valley can be seen stretching away towards the southwest.

Lienz - *See LIENZ.*

MÖLLTALER GLETSCHER★★

Kärnten

Michelin map 926 fold 33

This particularly picturesque mountain region is home to long Alpine lakes, which are used to generate hydroelectricity, along with a ski area where it is possible to ski almost all year round.

★★ **Mölltaler Gletscherbahnen** - Alt 1 250-3 120m/4 101-10 237ft. *9km/5.5mi from Flattach to Innerfragrant and the lower cable-car station for the new Stollenbahn (alt 1 250m/4 101ft). From here take the underground funicular and a cable-car on up to the Eissee mountain restaurant at 2 798m/9 180ft (allow about 40min there and back).* The ski area on the glacier, where snow is guaranteed virtually all year round, is served by two chair-lifts and two ski tows and offers a total of 47.5km/29.5mi of downhill pistes. Ski enthusiasts can cavort about to their heart's content here from June to April. From the upper cable-car station - view of the numerous mountain lakes and reservoirs of the Wurten region - there are plenty of options for ramblers to hike to the Schareck peak (3 122m/10 243ft) and the Baumbach peak (3 108m/10 197ft). The Schareck peak can also be reached by chair-lift, which leaves from the upper cable-car station. From this peak there is a broad panorama of the surrounding Hohe Tauern, in which it is possible to pick out some 30 summits over 3 000m/10 000ft high, including the Großglockner.

MONDSEE

Oberösterreich

Population 3 015

Michelin map 926 fold 20 - Local map see SALZKAMMERGUT

Alt 481m/1 578ft

Up to 1791 the history of Mondsee is intermingled with that of its Benedictine abbey. Nowadays many tourists are attracted to this township, which bears the same name as the nearby lake whose shady banks are approached from the town along an avenue of lime trees.

The **Mondsee**★, a lake shaped like a crescent at the foot of the cliffs of the Drachenwand and the Schafberg, is the most temperate in the Salzkammergut. The lake has become even better known since the section of the Salzburg-Vienna **motorway**★ along its north shore was opened.

The neighbouring region still produces one of the rare strongly flavoured Austrian cheeses, known as Mondseer.

Weinhaeupl/ÖSTERREICH WERBUNG

Mondsee seen from the Schafberg

SIGHTS

★ **Pfarrkirche** – This late-15C church once belonged to an abbey, whose former buildings stand on the left of the square. The present façade, with its Baroque helmeted towers, was remodelled in 1740.
The interior escaped the Baroque influences of the 17C – as the monastery was in financial difficulties – and has preserved its Gothic network vaulting. **Meinrad Guggenbichler** (1649-1723) who is known in Austria's art history as the Sculptor of Mondsee, endowed the different halls with furnishings (seven of the 13 altars) which give a great unity of style. The altar of the Holy Sacrament, on the lower left-hand side, with its twisted columns supported by cherubs, is one of his most characteristic works. The altar to St Sebastian (facing the other altar) is well known with its statue of St Roch and is Meinrad Guggenbichler's last known work. In the choir is a remarkable colourful gate to the sacristy. The seven charming little statues surmounting the arch, like this masterpiece of Gothic ironwork, date from the 15C.

Heimat- und Pfahlbaumuseum ⏲ – Installed in various parts of the former abbey, the museum presents local antiquities (one phase of the Neolithic Era being known as the "Mondsee Culture") and traditions.
A photographic sequence illustrates the making of *Einbaum* boats, cut from a single tree, of which some were in use until recently. In the upstairs part of the church, under the Gothic arches of the monks' library, the history of the abbey and the display of manuscripts (reproductions) is featured. Also exhibited are works of Meinrad Guggenbichler and religious works of art from the abbey.

Freilichtmuseum Mondseer Rauchhaus ⏲ – The smoke house is a primitive wooden chalet (mentioned in records going back to the 15C), built in the local style and surrounded by outbuildings, moved here from its original site. The most noticeable feature is the old-fashioned but logical placing of the vaulted hearth, which lacks a chimney. The escaping smoke formed a rising cloud which spread out to dry the farm crops in the attics without inconveniencing the inhabitants. One or two annexes bear witness to the work of local farmers: home, silo, mill, drying sheds for linen and fruit.

Maria-Hilf-Kapelle – This 15C chapel, which has been remodelled in the Baroque style, is charmingly situated on a bluff overlooking the lake.

MONTAFON★

Vorarlberg

Michelin map 926 folds 27 and 28 – Local map see ARLBERGGEBIET

Montafon is a charming, densely populated valley. Thanks to the protection of the surrounding mountains and the positive effects of the Föhn, a warm, dry southerly wind, it is possible to grow fruit in the valley basin up to quite a high altitude, while the local breed of reddish-brown cows thrives on the Alpine meadows higher up still. Although the language spoken here is German, the harsh sounds of the local names and the building style (timber-clad stone houses with arched doors) point to the influence of the old Rhaeto-Romanic culture, which is still alive in Engadin, on the south side of the Silvretta range.

The Montafon region has fundamentally altered as a result of modern civilization and above all through the development of winter sports and electricity production (Rodund power station at Vandans). It has been popular for some time as a relaxing holiday area offering a broad range of activities (downhill and cross-country skiing, hiking). The famous **Silvretta-Hochalpenstraße**★★ mountain road also runs through the Montafon.

FROM BLUDENZ TO PARTENEN

40km/25mi - allow at least one day

Bludenz - *See ARLBERGGEBIET* 1.

Turn left in St. Anton in Montafon towards Bartholomäberg. The small mountain road takes you along a spectacular route high above the valley floor.

Bartholomäberg - Beautifully situated, this scattered settlement is strung out along a sunny terrace. From the churchyard around the **Pfarrkirche** there is an impressive **panorama**★ of the village of Vandans at the foot of the sharp Zimba peak (alt 2 643m/8 671ft) and of the villages of Schruns and Tschagguns, over which tower the lofty summits of Schesaplana (alt 2 965m/8 842ft) and Drusenfluh, the **Drei Türme** (a rocky massif in the form of three towers standing one behind the other) and the Sulzfluh.

The **Baroque interior furnishings**★ of the church form one of the most beautiful art treasures of Vorarlberg. The high altar and the pulpit are the work of Georg Senn (1737). The organ, which dates from 1792, is one of the finest instruments in Austria. The triptych dedicated to St Anne (1525) on the right-hand side of the nave is especially interesting.

Continue towards Innerberg. After about 1km/0.5mi, there is a magnificent **view**★ to the right over St. Gallenkirch at the foot of the Valiseraspitze peak, and opposite over the Kreuzjoch massif, as well as the Silbertal Valley and the Verwall range.

In Innerberg (alt 1 161m/3 809ft), turn right towards Silbertal. Turn left on the main road at the bottom of the valley and park at the foot of the Kristbergbahn railway.

★ **Kristbergbahn** ⓥ - The Kristberg inn (alt 1 430m/4 691ft), with a chapel nearby, can be reached in 5min from the mountain station. It affords an especially beautiful **all-round view**★ over the Montafon.

Hikers can climb up to the Kristbergsattel and then follow the ridge path to the left as far as the **Ganzaleita** viewpoint (alt 1 610m/5 282ft), from where the view encompasses the Lechtaler Alps and the Rote Wand.

At the Litz, a mountain torrent, continue towards Schruns. The route takes you through an unspoiled **natural landscape**★ which boasts luxuriant vegetation.

Y. Bontoux

Drei Türme mountains

✻ **Schruns** - Alt 690m/2 264ft. This holiday resort and local capital of the Montafon is located in a broad section of the valley and has good accommodation and leisure facilities (swimming pool, 15 tennis courts). In the summer it is an ideal point of departure for hikes in the medium-altitude mountains. In the winter, the **ski area**✻ (40km/25mi of piste) is especially suitable for beginners and for relaxed skiing. Plenty of easy ski runs in the foothills of Kreuzjoch and Fredakopf offer excellent skiing conditions. Good skiers can try their hand at the off-piste section at Sennihang. The attraction of the area lies in its considerable differences in height (700-2 400m/2 300-7 100ft), which result in landscapes ranging from Alpine scenery devoid of vegetation to wooded areas beneath the Kapell. Snow machines mean that it is possible to ski all the way down to the lower station of the Hochjochbahn.

Ski passes are available to tourists (three days or more), which are valid for the entire Montafon Valley with its 73 ski lifts and 210km/130mi of piste. Buses run regularly between the individual locations (Tschagguns-Vandans, Schruns, Kristberg, Gargellen, St. Gallenkirch and Gaschurn). **Cross-country skiers** are restricted around Schruns to 13km/8mi of easy tracks. The surrounding locations provide more opportunities: 11km/7mi of more demanding cross-country tracks on the Kristberg at between 1 450m/4 757ft and 1 550m/5 085ft in altitude, 6km/4mi in Tschagguns and 8km/5mi in Vandans, as well as the extensive cross-country ski area in the Hochmontafon.

★ **Sennigrat** ⓥ - *1hr there and back.* First take the Hochjochbahn cable-car *(charge for parking)* or the Zamangbahn cable-car *(only operates in winter, free parking)* to the **Kapell** (alt 1 850m/6 069ft). Enjoy the view down into the valley and the many scattered chalets of Schruns. Then take the chair-lift up to the Sennigrat (alt 2 210m/7 250ft). Here the **panorama**★ takes in the Kreuzjoch area, the Madrisa massif above the Gargellental Valley, and the Rätikon (Sulzfluh, Drei Türme, Schesaplana) with Silbertal and Arlberg in the background.

★★ **Hike to the Kreuzjoch and the Zamangspitze** - *4hr on foot there and back. Plenty of opportunity to shorten the route: for walkers, just go as far as the mountain lodge and the lake path (just under 2hr). Climbing boots are recommended.*

The Wormser Hütte mountain lodge (alt 2 305m/7 562ft) can be reached in 20min. From the lodge, follow a ridge path to the Kreuzjoch (the Kreuz or cross itself is at an altitude of 2 395m/7 857ft) and then on to the Zamangspitze peak (alt 2 386m/7 828ft), from where a **panorama**★★ opens up over the Silvretta massif and the Hochmontafon. Return to the lodge along the same route and continue along the lake path past **Herzsee** and **Schwarzsee** lakes back to the Kapell, returning to Schruns in the cable-car.

Behind Schruns the road winds up the Hochmontafon. It leads through **St. Gallenkirch**✻ **(alt 900m/2 950ft) and Gaschurn**✻ **(alt 1 000m/3 300ft) and finally, after Partenen, to the Silvretta-Hochalpenstraße**★★ *(see entry)*.

✻ **Silvretta Nova ski area** - The villages of St. Gallenkirch and Gaschurn have joined together to create an extensive, varied ski area with 33 ski lifts and 100km/62mi of piste between 900m/2 950ft and 2 300m/7 550ft in altitude. Good skiers use the black Buckelpiste and the ski run into the valley from the Schwarzköpfle, and, on powdered snow, the **Ziglamstrecke** run at the foot of the mountain peak, which provides a remarkable **view**★★ over the Silvretta group. The pistes from the Gampabing lift are suitable for skiers of average ability.

Gargellen, the highest village in the Montafon (alt 1 423m/4 668ft), 8km/5mi up the valley from St. Gallenkirch, offers interesting Alpine ski pistes.

For cross-country skiers there are connected ski runs in the floor of the valley between St. Gallenkirch and Partenen. In addition, a 15km/9mi cross-country track, which runs around the Silvretta reservoir at an altitude of 2 030m/6 660ft, can be reached with the funicular railway and the bus.

★★ **Valisera cable-car** ⓥ - Alt 2 100m/6 890ft. *Around 45min there and back from St. Gallenkirch.* There are some beautiful views over St. Gallenkirch and Schruns during the first extremely steep and wooded section. From the mountain station the view extends over the rocky peak of the Reutehorn, which dominates the Gargellental Valley. During the second section there is a good view over the ski area. Opposite the top station lie the Heimspitze and Valiseraspitze peaks. To the southeast, the Silvretta group is visible, and to the north the Zamangspitze peak and the Verwall range can be seen. The Bella Nova restaurant is just a few steps away, and provides a view over the magnificent Gargellental Valley.

★ **Versettla cable-car** - Alt 2 010m/6 594ft. *45min there and back from Gaschurn.* Descend to the Höhenrestaurant from the mountain station. **View**★ over the Silvretta range (Piz Buin, Großer Litzner, Großes Seehorn) and the whole of the Silvretta Nova ski area. A broader panorama can be enjoyed from Burg and Versettla *(take the Burg ski lift in the winter, and the Versettlaweg path in the summer)*.

MURAU

Steiermark

Population 2 630

Michelin map 926 fold 34 – Alt 829m/2 720ft

Charmingly situated in the upper Mur Valley, the small town of Murau was already celebrated at the end of the 19C for its clean air and pleasant climate. Owing to the protection of the Niedere Tauern hills, rainfall is very moderate.

SIGHTS

Old Town – The castle at Murau was built by Ulrich von Liechtenstein; outside the castle walls he established a market which was to play an important local role during the Middle Ages.

The historic town centre, on the north bank of the River Mur, with its narrow streets and innumerable shops, is endowed with undeniable southern charm. The Raffaltplatz, for instance, shaded by chestnut trees and ringed by houses with smart, multicoloured façades, suggests a certain Italian influence.

The parish church of St. Matthäus can be reached from Anna-Neumannstraße or Schillerplatz by narrow pedestrian alleys and a covered flight of steps.

★ **Stadtpfarrkirche St. Matthäus** – The church, which stands on a hillside below the castle, was dedicated to St Matthew on completion of the chancel in 1296. The Gothic character of the building, with its majestic nave and splendid decorations, was not destroyed by alterations carried out in the first half of the 17C. There are several beautiful **frescoes** dating from the 14C to the 16C, including a 14C St Anthony and his pig in the south transept, an Entombment of Christ (1377) and an Annunciation on the south wall of the nave. The north transept was decorated in the late 16C to early 17C with a large number of small paintings (executed on dry plaster) in the form of epitaphs for deceased members of the House of Liechtenstein. The magnificent **Baroque high altar**★ (1655) was created by local artists who placed at its centre a Gothic Crucifixion (1500); the sky-blue tabernacle is complemented by wood and gilt work. The heavy pulpit was sculpted in the Late Baroque style in 1777 by an artist from Freisach.

Schloß – *Access on foot by the long wooden staircase to the north of the church. Only the interior courtyard is open to visitors.* The first castle was built by Ulrich von Liechtenstein in 1232; all that remains of it are the cellars and a well 48m/157ft deep. It occupied a commanding position in the Mur Valley, at a point where the river becomes wider, and guaranteed the autonomy of a region in which prosperity was derived from iron ore and salt as well as commerce.

The present castle was built between 1628 and 1643 by Count Georg-Ludwig von Schwarzenberg; the tall façades of the courtyard rest on cloister galleries, the arcades of which are supported by stout twin pillars. The austerity of the façades of the inner court is tempered by the elegant chapel door and by round-headed windows and oculi.

★ **Leonardikapelle** – *1km/0.5mi south of the old town. Take the road to the Frauenalpe; after 300m/330yd turn right onto Leonhardweg, a footpath which leads to the chapel.*

This Gothic building was already a place of pilgrimage in 1439. During the walk up to the chapel there is the opportunity to pause by the side of the **pond**★, a wild and peaceful spot. The pleasant walk round the pond *(20min)* provides romantic views of the chapel surrounded by greenery.

S. Bohviac/BILDAGENTUR BUENOS DIAS

Murau

EXCURSIONS

Mur Valley by train (Murtalbahn) ⌚ – *74km/46mi there and back – about 5hr.* This picturesque excursion is made by **steam train** along the Murau-Tamsweg line. Bicycles can be taken on the train, and can be hired from the stations at Murau and Tamsweg, so it is possible to make a voyage of discovery of the valley combining both these modes of transport.

Oberwölz – *27km/17mi northeast of Murau. Leave town on Bundesstraße 96 going east; in Niederwölz take the road to Oberwölz.*
This small medieval town at the foot of its 12C castle, Schloß Rothenfels, was settled as early as the Hallstatt period, after which it developed over the course of its eventful history from village to market town, before finally obtaining its civic charter in around 1300. At this time, Oberwölz was a well-off community which owed its wealth to the salt trade and silver-working. Of the fortified town wall built during this period, there remain large sections complete with fortified towers and three gateways. The remains of the wall encircle the pretty historic town centre, which is bright with flowers in season.

★ **Sigismundkirche** – This chapel, which is very close to the Gothic parish church and first recorded in 1360, was founded to serve the town's former hospital. The back of the chapel, which housed the patients, consists of an enormous gallery supported by intersecting ribs; this part of the church is roofed by a complex arrangement of rib vaulting rising from three pillars.

MURTAL

Steiermark

Michelin map 926 folds 23, 37 and 38

The route described below runs up the deeply wooded Mur Valley for some 70km/43mi. This is only about one-seventh of the course of the river, which rises in the Radstädter Tauern, in the Salzburg district, and ends in Hungary, 483km/300mi away, where it joins the Drava, a tributary of the Danube.

FROM GRAZ TO LEOBEN *70km/43mi*

★★ **Graz** – *See GRAZ.*

*Leave Graz on the road to Bruck an der Mur (**AX**).*

Once the road has crossed to the east bank, wooded hills appear and then rock outcrops.

★★ **Österreichisches Freilichtmuseum (Austrian Open-air Museum)** ⌚ – *In* **Stübing**. This museum of Austrian traditional rural architecture occupies an area of 60ha/148 acres in a tributary valley of the Mur. About 90 original farmhouses with their annexes have been reconstructed on this site and aligned east to west to correspond with the geography of the country, so that visitors start with Burgenland in the east and head west past examples of buildings from the other Austrian provinces before ending up in the westernmost Austrian province, the Vorarlberg. All the buildings have been fitted out with appropriate furnishings or tools and equipment depending on their purpose, thus giving the visitor a nostalgic glimpse of ways of life and working methods of the past. The museum also puts on temporary exhibitions on rural life and traditional culture, installed in two exhibition buildings.
For illustrations of traditional Austrian architecture, see the section on Traditional Austria in the Introduction.

North of **Peggau**, a large industrial town covered in dust from its cement factories, beside the road (right) rises an impressive limestone cliff. In the mountain behind lies the Lurgrotte, an underground network of galleries.

★ **Lurgrotte (Peggau entrance)** ⌚ – *The temperature in the cave is only 10°C/50°F all year round, so visitors in summer should remember to bring warm clothing with them.* The walk beside the underground river formed from melt-water goes back some 2km/1mi into the cave interior, past several amazing concretions such as the stalactite of the "Prince", perhaps the most impressive, which weighs 3t and is almost 4m/13ft long.
The valley, often bordered by rocky slopes, becomes greener and more picturesque. There is an attractive view from the bridge on the by-pass of the town of Frohnleiten *(see entry)*, whose houses cluster at the foot of the church on the steep bank of the River Mur. The long leats, which supply the Laufnitzdorf and Pernegg power stations, have created new stretches of water parallel to the river.

★ **Bruck an der Mur** – *See BRUCK AN DER MUR.*

West of Bruck the road follows the south bank of the Mur, which runs in a west-to-east direction. To the left you see the Brucker Hochalpe, a limestone massif whose highest summit the Roßeck is 1 664m/5 460ft. The valley now widens and becomes more and more industrial until it reaches Leoben.

Leoben – *See LEOBEN.*

NEUSIEDLER SEE★★

Burgenland

Michelin map 926 fold 26

The Neusiedler See (only 113m/370ft above sea-level) is the most westerly example of a steppe-type lake, and is one of the great attractions of the Burgenland. The term "steppe" may seem surprising given the proximity to Vienna, but in fact the Hungarian Puszta starts right here, where the last foothills of the Leithagebirge come to an end.
The lake has an area of 320km²/124sq mi, of which the major part belongs to Austria, only the southern tip being in Hungary (one fifth of the total surface).

A capricious lake – Among the peculiar features of the Neusiedler See is the huge expanse of reeds which surrounds it, in places up to 5km/3mi wide, and its shallow, relatively warm and slightly salty water. Its depth varies between 1m/3ft and 1.5m/5ft, and is nowhere more than 2m/7ft.
There is no permanent natural outflow and only one tributary of any size, the Wulka, which is an almost negligible factor as the volume of normal evaporation is four times the quantity of water that flows in. The bulk of the water must then come from precipitation, melting snow (there are heavy snowfalls in winter) and ground water. When a strong wind blows for some time in the same direction, the waters are driven towards one shore, while the level on the near shore drops perceptibly. When the wind drops, the lake returns to its normal level and appearance.
It even sometimes happens that the lake dries up altogether (the last time was between 1868 and 1872), only to reappear one day as mysteriously as it vanished.

Geography and landscape – To the east of the lake is the flat Parndorfer Platte and the Seewinkel, an area of grassland divided up by salty pools and ponds which has increasingly been reclaimed as land for crops and orchards. The western shore is quite different, its horizon being formed by two lines of hills, the Leithagebirge and the Ruster Höhenzug, at whose foot vegetables, maize, vines and fruit trees (even almonds) flourish in the rich ochre soil and gentle climate.

National park – In 1992, the Nationalpark Neusiedlersee-Seewinkel was formed, extending either side of the national frontier and jointly administered by Austria and Hungary. The aim of the park is to safeguard the flora and fauna of this transitional zone between the Alpine and Eurasian regions.

A Garden of Eden – Many thousands of plants flourish in this apparently rather dry tract of country, including spring adonis, dwarf iris, Austrian sage, Austrian flax and sea asters to name but a few. The impenetrable thickets of reeds surrounding the lake and the Seewinkel salt pools provide habitats for an unusually large variety of animals, which include some rarely seen in Europe such as the shy Aesculapius snake and the South Russian tarantula.

A paradise for birds – The whole area forms a unique nature reserve, in which numerous migratory birds settle and make their nests. The birdwatchers' hides are the only objects sticking up from the flat and featureless landscape, where more than 250 varieties of bird can be observed.

Vienna's "seaside" – Apart from Podersdorf which is right by the water, every village near the lake has its little bathing-beach, normally reached by a roadway between two hedges of reeds. Owing to its proximity to the capital (50km/31mi), it is popular with the Viennese for aquatic sports in summer and ice sports (especially ice-yachting) in winter.

A great wine area – The vineyards of the Burgenland, terraced on the slopes or lying in the plain, enjoy plenty of sunshine and produce excellent vintages, the wines of Rust, Mörbisch, Gols and Ilmitz being particularly prized for their fruity bouquet. All the places on the Austrian shores of the lake have their **Buschenschenken**, wine-parlours with gardens where a fruity white wine is served, guaranteed to put anyone into a good humour.

FROM NEUSIEDL TO EISENSTADT *69km/43mi*

Neusiedl am See – The place which gives the lake its name has a few sights of its own: a ruined castle from the 13C, a church from the 15C, and the **Pannonisches Heimatmuseum** ⏲ *(Kalvarienbergstraße 40)*, the local museum which is devoted to folk art and customs.

Leave Neusiedl going northwest and join the road to Eisenstadt, then 2.4km/1.5mi after Donnerskirchen turn left for Rust.

★ **Rust** – Rust is not only famous for its storks' nests, to which the birds return faithfully every year, but also for its wine. It is a prosperous wine-growing centre, which, back in 1681, bought its charter as a "free royal borough" from Leopold I with 30 000l/6 600gal(UK) of wine and 60 000 gold coins. In 1989 the world's first German-speaking wine academy was founded in the 16C lakeside courtyard, offering seminars and other wine-related events.

Nightingale
European Bee-eater
Whinchat
Little Ringed Plover
Lakeside Birdlife
Partridge
Coot
Bar-tailed Godwit
Great Egret
M. Guillou/MICHELIN

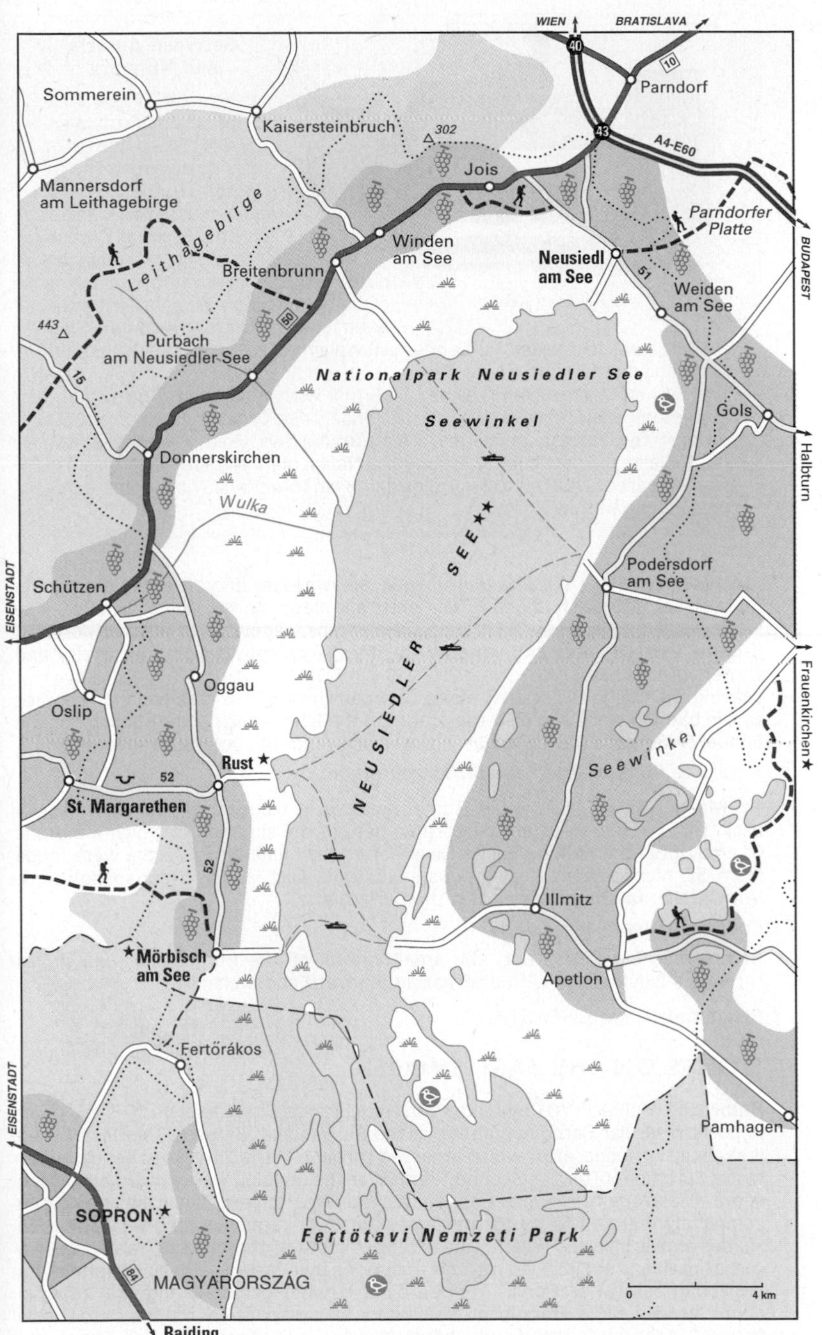

This pretty place has many a picturesque view to offer the visitor: charming Renaissance and Baroque façades with oriels and huge carved doorways, attractive inner courtyards with arcades, and the partially preserved fortified town wall. Its considerable architectural heritage has led to the whole of the old town's being made a conservation area.

Fischerkirche – *On the west side of the Rathausplatz*. The fortified Fisherman's Church, surrounded by a wall, has an irregular ground plan, and impressive **frescoes★** inside dating from the 14C and 15C. Note in particular the three statues on the altar to the Three Magi, in the Late Gothic style, in the side aisle, and the fine organ from 1705.

From the village a causeway through the rushes leads to the **Seebad Rust** ⏲, the bathing resort with its buildings on piles connected by pontoons.

M. Guillou/MICHELIN

House in Apetion

Between Austria and Hungary

As a result of the Treaty of Saint-Germain-en-Laye (1919), parts of the three western *comitats* (provinces) of Hungary passed to Austria, and it is from these that the present province of Burgenland is formed, which consequently shows a certain undeniable Magyar influence. Even today there are still bands in Siegendorf, Trausdorf an der Wulka and **Apetion** playing the *tanburica*, a mandolin-like instrument.

The Burgenland has retained its racial mix with Hungarian, Romany and Sinti ethnic minorities, as well as descendants of Croat refugees from the time of the Turkish invasions. These minorities liked to settle in the Burgenland and particularly around the Neusiedler See, since this area had formed part of a buffer zone which had been intentionally depopulated by the Hungarian rulers.

★ **Mörbisch am See** – With its picturesque alleyways leading off either side of the main street, Mörbisch is one of the prettiest places on the Neusiedler See. The whitewashed houses nearly all have stone steps leading up to pillared porches, brightly painted doors and window shutters, corn cobs hanging up to dry and flowers everywhere.

Leaving the village to the east along the road through the reed-beds, one comes to the bathing place and also the stage on the lake, which is the setting for the annual **Seefestspiele** (Lake Festival) presenting magical operetta productions.

Return to Rust; bear left for St. Margarethen.

St. Margarethen – In the old Roman quarry, in front of an impressive rocky backdrop, Passion plays are performed here in the summer, in which hundreds of amateurs take walk-on parts. Several famous buildings in Vienna were made from St. Margarethen's calcareous sandstone, such as the Stephansdom, the Votivkirche, the Burgtheater and the Parlament.

Continue towards Eisenstadt.

Before reaching Eisenstadt, the small capital of the Burgenland, one drives through a hilly district with alternating vineyard and orchards.

★ **Eisenstadt** – *See EISENSTADT.*

SIGHTS ON THE EAST SHORE

Halbturn – Built in 1701 by Lukas von Hildebrandt, **Schloß Halbturn** ⌚ is the most important secular Baroque building in the Burgenland. Emperor Charles VI used it as a hunting lodge, after which it passed through Maria Theresa to her daughter Maria Christina. After the Second World War the building was ravaged by looting and a disastrous fire, which only spared the central part. But it has now been completely restored to its former glory, with its façade looking very smart in shades of pale blue and cream. The extended front of the house is framed by two corner pavilions and divided into nine sections by pilasters with fine capitals. Its projecting central section is topped by a curving gable bearing the Imperial double-headed eagle. **Franz Anton Maulbertsch** was responsible for the remarkable **frescoes**★ in the garden room, which fortunately survived the 1949 fire. The ceiling fresco portrays the Allegory of Time and Light, a masterly composition in vibrant colours.

★ **Frauenkirchen** – The famous **pilgrimage church** ⌚ radiates Italian elegance, but then its architect was Francesco Martinelli, the stuccowork was by Pietro Conti and the frescoes by Luca Columba. Prince Paul Esterházy had commissioned them with the task of building and decorating the church, completed in 1702. The sumptuous altar frames the devotional image, an Early Gothic statue of the Virgin Mary (c 1340), which is clothed, as was the custom in the Baroque period. Of particular interest are the first side altar on the north side, with a rare painting of the Madonna Lactans (breast-feeding), and the painted choir stalls in the organ gallery.

On the south side of the church there is an unusual **Calvary**, with the stations spirally arranged and figures more than life size, as well as a Crucifixion group.

OBERNBERG AM INN

Oberösterreich

Population 1 680

Michelin map 926 fold 7 – 37km/23mi south of Passau – Alt 352m/1 155ft

The market town of Obernberg, founded in c 950, was ruled from Passau for many years. In 1779, together with the Inn region, it passed under the aegis of Austria. The town stands on the south bank of the Inn, which marks the frontier between Austria and Germany.

Marktplatz – This large well-preserved market square has at its centre a carved stone fountain. It is framed by elegant houses with brightly coloured façades, some of which are decorated with stucco. Note in particular the stucco façades of the Wörndlehaus, the Apothekerhaus and the Schiffmeisterhaus, which are the work of Bavarian master Johann Baptist Modler (c 1740). From the middle of the square the fretted gables, and the silhouette of the onion-domed tower of the church, make a pleasant picture.

OBERTAUERN**

Salzburg

Population 400

Michelin map 926 fold 33 – Alt 1 739m/5 705ft

The holiday resort of Obertauern lies on a broad terrace on the Radstädter Tauernpaß *(see RADSTÄDTER TAUERNPASS)*. In contrast to most of the other Austrian mountain locations, it did not develop from an existing village, but was set up purely as a winter sports location. It is surrounded by one of the most beautiful ski areas in the northern Alps.

During the summer, Obertauern provides some interesting hiking destinations, in particular the **Seekarspitze peak★★** (alt 2 350m/7 710ft; *3hr 30min round trip*) and the **Gamsleitenspitze-Zehnerkarspitze-Glöcknerin-Wildsee circuit★★** *(allow 6hr 30min for the whole circuit; for experienced hikers only).*

Day trippers can park at car park P1 at the outskirts of the village.

** **Ski area** The Obertauern (alt 1 650-2 350m/5 410-7 710ft) area's main attraction is its guaranteed snow, but it can also boast 26 ski lifts leading to 120km/75mi of piste. Its somewhat modest size is more than made up for by the quality of the facilities. Only a few other Austrian winter sports locations offer such modern, comfortable equipment and pistes and ski runs of such differing degrees of difficulty.

Experienced skiers can hone their skills on the impressive Buckelpiste, or humpbacked piste, along the Gamsleitenbahn 2, which includes a difference in altitude of 360m/1 181ft, and on the ski run on the Hundskogel. For fairly good skiers there are some magnificent pistes in the area of the Seekarspitze summit, while for beginners the more or less flat slopes immediately surrounding the village, at Sonnenlift and Kurnenlift, are suitable.

VIEWPOINTS

★ **Zehnerkarseilbahn cable-car** – Alt 2 192m/7 191ft. *45min there and back.* The cable-car runs to the foot of the Zehnerkarspitze peak (alt 2 381m/7 811ft). Beautiful **all-round view★** over the massif around Obertauern from the Seekarspitze to the Gamskarspitze. After dropping 200m/650ft, the ski run offers a view of the far-distant limestone massif from the Tennengebirge to the Dachstein.

★★ **Gamsleitenbahn 1 and 2** – *Accessible to skiers.* Turn left at the mountain station of the second chair-lift (alt 2 313m/7 588ft) and approach the furthest end of the piste. Magnificent **view★★** over Mosermandl and the rocky ridges of the Kesselspitze. The Gamskarspitze and the Plattenspitze peaks tower opposite.

★★ **Seekareck** – *Accessible to skiers using the Grünwaldkopf and Seekareck chair-lifts.* Turn left at the mountain station (alt 2 160m/7 086ft). In a few minutes you will reach a raised bit of ground, from which you can see the Großglockner.

When there is no risk of avalanche and the trail has been cleared, it is well worth climbing up to the peak (alt 2 217m/7 273ft; *10min on foot*). Wonderful **panorama★★** over the Radstädter Tauern, the Dachstein and the Hohe Tauern.

★ **Panoramabahn** – Alt 2 208m/7 244ft. *Accessible to skiers.* The view stretches over the Schladminger Tauern. A wonderful **view★★** over the Hohe Dachstein and the Radstädter Tauern can be seen from the red piste, which leads along the left side of the Seekarspitzbahn down to the valley.

★ **Hundskogelbahn** – Alt 2 136m/7 008ft. *Accessible to skiers.* **View★** over the Bischofsmütze, the Tennengebirge and the Großglockner.

ÖTSCHERMASSIV★

Niederösterreich und Steiermark

Michelin map 926 folds 23 and 24

The mountainous area south of St. Pölten, between the Wienerwald and the Eisenerz Alps, is part of the limestone Pre-Alps. The first foothills, which are wooded and 600m/2 000ft to 800m/2 600ft high, give way to a succession of minor ranges, reaching an altitude of 1 893m/6 211ft, at the massive peak of the Ötscher (from an old Slavonic word Otan meaning godfather), which can be seen at a great distance, especially when approached from the north.

ROUND TRIP STARTING FROM MARIAZELL *112km/70mi*

★ **Mariazell** - *See MARIAZELL.*

Leave Mariazell by road no 21 (east) which runs steeply downhill, enters the Salza Valley and follows the stream closely. In Terz the picturesque road turns north and plunges into a gorge with rocky sides to which conifers cling.

St. Aegyd lies in the Unrecht Traisen Valley, which is lined with factories and sawmills. Beyond Hohenberg the limestone cliffs are broken, here and there, by well developed natural amphitheatres.

In Freiland turn right onto road no 20 to Lilienfeld.

★ **Stift Lilienfeld** - *See Stift LILIENFELD.*

From Lilienfeld return south; in Freiland continue southwest (road no 20).

The road, which is pleasant and picturesque, becomes more and more enclosed, first between wooded slopes, then in a rocky gorge where there are outcrops of schist. Reservoirs supply small factories, including paper mills at Dickenau.

Beyond Türnitz, the well-laid road climbs steadily, offering wider and wider views of limestone ridges of 1 200m/4 000ft to 1 400m/4 600ft. A series of hairpin bends leads to the village of Annaberg.

Annaberg - The village stands on a col, facing the Großer Ötscher. The beautifully situated pilgrimage church is well known to the faithful on their way to Mariazell. The first building, a timber chapel, was erected here in 1217, though the present church is 14C-15C. It is dedicated to St Anne, as the Madonna and Child with St Anne (15C) on the high altar shows, and still has fine ogive vaulting but was decorated in the Baroque style in the 17C and 18C.

The ceiling of the small south chápel is adorned with frescoes and stucco; cherubs and statues overload the high altar and side altars, and there is a mass of gilding and carving on the pulpit and the organ-loft.

During the hairpin bend descent, the Ötscher, towering 1 000m/3 280ft above, stands out clearly to the west. Josefsberg is the start of a pleasant run downhill among fir woods, with fine vistas towards the Gemeindealpe (alt 1 626m/5 335ft) on the right. People throughout this region live on cattle raising and forestry. In the valleys there were once many little forges, working the Styrian iron ore from the nearby Eisenerz. Today they have disappeared.

To the right of the road lies the artificial Erlaufstausee Lake, barring the upper course of the Erlauf. On leaving Mitterbach turn right and drive beside a second lake, the natural Erlaufsee.

Return to Mariazell.

ÖTZTAL★★

Tirol

Michelin map 926 fold 29 or 218 folds 8 and 9

The Ötztal, which is remembered by mountaineers as a series of shining glaciers - total surface area: 173km²/67sq mi - is a deep valley running into the Inn and consisting for 50km/31mi of ravines separated by isolated basins, where the patriarchal traditions of Old Tyrol have long been observed.

When mountains unite more than they divide - The **Ötztal Alps** include the highest point in the northern Tyrol, the Wildspitze (alt 3 774m/12 382ft). Students also learn that the highest parish in Austria, Obergurgl (alt 1 927m/6 321ft) and the highest permanent human habitation in the country, **Rofen** near Vent (alt 2 014m/6 608ft), are in the upper basin of the Ötztal.

Until the First World War these places were more closely connected with the Alto Adige to the south, from which their people originally came, than with the Inn Valley. For a long time the inhabitants preferred to trudge through snowfields on wide passes like the Hochjoch or Niederjoch, at an altitude of nearly 3 000m/10 000ft, rather than make their way along the floors of the gorges of the Ötztaler Ache, on unsafe roads exposed to floods, falling stones and avalanches.

When the **Timmelsjoch road** was completed, in 1969, the isolation of the Ötztal came to an end, at least in summer.

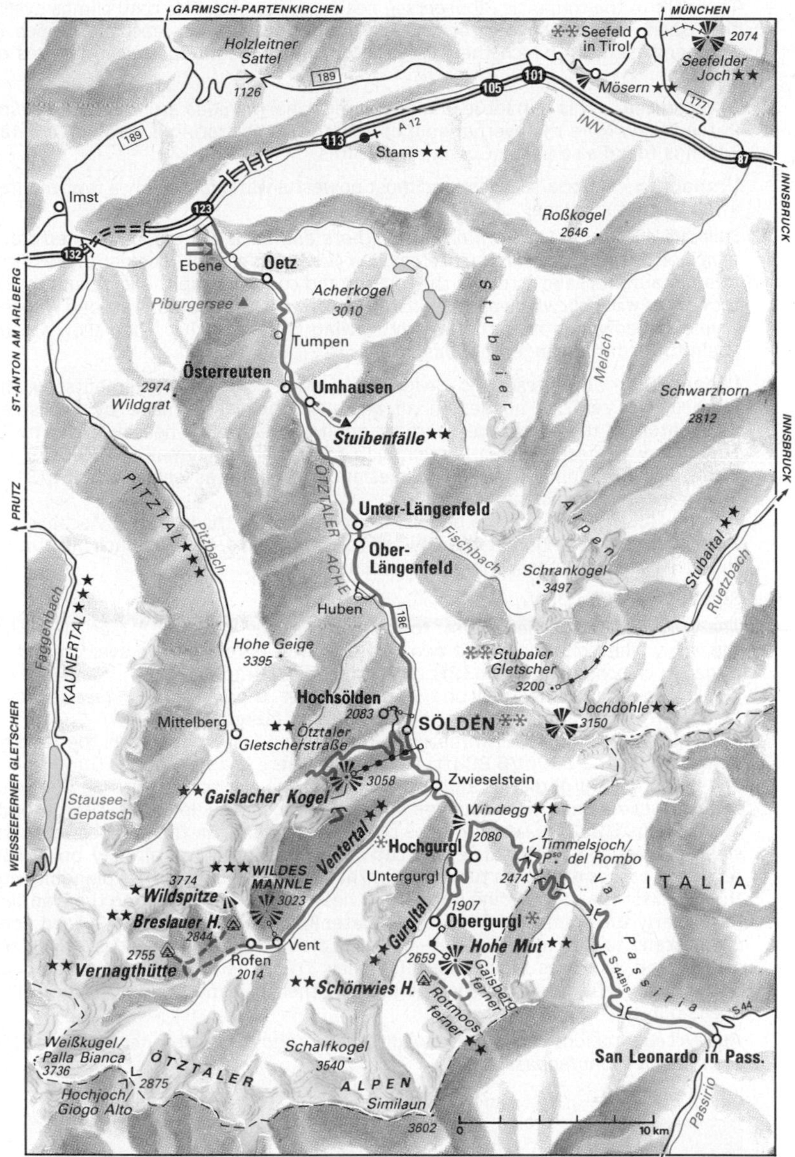

FROM THE INN VALLEY TO SAN LEONARDO IN PASSIRIA

(ST. LEONHARD IN PASSEIER) *88km/55mi*

On the Italian side the road is generally snow free from mid-June to mid-October. The route demands care (no crash-barriers) and has an irregular surface, especially in the tunnels. Trailers, caravans, buses and trucks are forbidden.
On the Austrian side, however, the road is generally open all year round, at least to Hochgurgl.

The Bundesstraße 186, turning off the busy Inntal road, runs through pleasant pine woods among piles of debris brought down from the Ötztaler Ache which has been deeply furrowed by the torrent. This flows beneath the picturesque covered bridge at Ebene to enter the Ötz basin, which is dominated by the rocky tooth of the Acherkogel. Chestnuts, fields of maize and peach and apricot orchards show that the Ötztal corridor, running due south, attracts the warm air of the Föhn.

Oetz – The village is well sited on the last levels of the sunny slope on which the large church is built. Several buildings have a traditional air, for example, the Gasthof Stern with its flower-decked oriel and painted façade.

The walk to the romantic Piburgersee nearby is popular. The road climbs over a first shelf, crossed by the torrent in a muddy stream. It reaches Tumpen in another basin into which the Tumpenbach, on the right, pours in a series of cascades.

Österreuten – This hamlet is one of the most harmonious architectural groups in the valley. Note the overhanging upper storeys sheltering a veranda, a detail which is found also in the Cortina Dolomites.

Umhausen – Austria's largest and most powerful waterfall is only a few minutes away from this village.

★★ **Stuibenfälle** – *About 1hr 30min on foot there and back along a signposted track which begins at the tourist office pavilion (Verkehrsverein).* The path leads first to a restaurant-chalet, crosses the torrent and continues up the left bank to the foot of the **waterfall**, which plunges 150m/492ft into the depths. A second wooded ravine lies downhill, near the swiftly flowing Ötztaler Ache. The valley widens again to form the Längenfeld basin.

Längenfeld – This resort is divided into two separate settlements by the Fischbach torrent. It nestles in an angle of the valley made by the steep promontory of the Burgstein. There are good walks through nearby larch woods. Together with nearby **Huben** Längenfeld offers the holidaymaker 150km/93mi walks, several climbing training courses and two climbs as well as a 50km/31mi network of cycle tracks.
Beyond Huben, a long ravine begins, narrowing after the bridge at Aschbach to a **gorge**★ covered with larches. Below the mountain road, the Wildbach hurls itself thunderously over massive blocks of rock.

❄❄ **Sölden** – *See SÖLDEN.*

The valley forks in Zwieselstein: to the right lies the **Ventertal**★★ *(see SÖLDEN)*, the valley which gave access to two of the earliest border passes over the Alpine ridge (Hochjoch 2 875m/9 432ft, Niederjoch 3 019m/9 905ft).
This itinerary takes the valley on the left, however, the **Gurgler Tal**★★ *(see separate listing)* with the famous winter sports resort of **Obergurgl**❄.
After a steep climb the Timmelsjoch road drops briefly to reach the **Windegg viewpoint**★★ (alt 2 080m/6 824ft) from which there is a view of the Gurgl Valley and the Great Gurgl glacier and, to the north, the cleft of the Ötztal. The road begins to climb once more through an austere landscape up to the Timmelsjoch (alt 2 509m/8 232ft), which marks the Italian border. On the steeper southern slope of the pass the road, often cut out of the rock and already on Italian territory, passes through a tunnel 700m/nearly 0.5mi long, before plunging into the Val Passiria and providing impressive views of the crest marking the frontier, particularly the Monte dei Granati (Granatenkogel) to the south. The road does not descend to the river level but continues along the mountainsides, which are often steep, as far as Moso (there is a view from the terrace of the Gasthaus Saltnuß, alt 1 630m/5 346ft). The journey then becomes easier as the valley opens out.

At San Leonardo one can join the road from Merano to the Brenner by way of the Monte Giovo (Jaufenpass).

"Ötzi"

In 1991 a pair of climbers discovered a mummified body in the snow while climbing in the Similaun range in the Ötztaler Alps. This rather gruesome discovery soon turned out to be an archeological sensation, as the body proved to be that of a person from the fourth millennium BC! The mummy, fondly nicknamed "Ötzi", had been particularly well preserved due to the environmental conditions in the glacier. Even his organs were still intact, so that it was possible to draw conclusions about his diet and the circumstances of his death. He was caught while in the mountains by a sudden drop in temperature accompanied by snowfall which proved too much for him in spite of his good thick clothing of furs and a grass cloak.
As the mummy was found on Italian territory, it is now on display in the South Tyrol Archeological Museum in Bolzano (Bozen).

OSSIACHER SEE★

Kärnten

Michelin map 926 fold 34 – Local map see WÖRTHER SEE

Ossiach Lake, not yet over-frequented by tourists, lies a little set back from the Villach basin, tucked amid the wooded slopes of the Gerlitzen, the Hexenberg and the Ossiacher Tauern. It is Carinthia's third largest lake, measuring 11km/7mi long by 1.5km/1mi wide, and reaching a depth of 46m/150ft. Its inviting shores are perfect for bathing and generally chilling out. From spring to autumn, three boats operate on the lake, providing a regular service to all the resorts. Those with enough time may like to choose a cruise which takes 2hr 30min.

★TOUR OF THE LAKE

Starting from Villach *66km/41mi*

★ **Villach** – *See VILLACH.*

From Villach Bundesstraße no 94 leads into the alluvial plain partly occupied by the lake. Ahead and to the right the ruins of Landskron stand on a spur. The road skirts the north shore of the lake, at the foot of the steep slopes of the Gerlitzen.

H.A. Jahn/VIENNASLIDE

Ossiacher See

★★ **Gerlitzen** – The Gerlitzen summit (alt 1 909m/6 263ft) dominates central Carinthia, its foothills running down to the water's edge of Ossiach Lake. The mountain is one of the outposts of the largely rock massifs of the central Alps. In winter its numerous mountain hotels, cable-car from Annenheim up to the Kanzel, many ski lifts and sunny slopes attract skiers from Austria and much further afield.

Ascent of the Gerlitzen – *From Bodensdorf on the north shore of the Ossiacher See make for Tschöran, where the little mountain road to Gerlitzen starts (12km/7.5mi, toll levied).*

After winding through woods and pastures, the road ends at an altitude of 1 764m/5 787ft. A large complex called "Dorf und Hotel Gerlitzer Alpen" has developed here. Finish the climb on foot or, if necessary, by **chair-lift** ⌚.

The **panorama**★★ embraces, southwards, the three lakes at Ossiach, Wörth and Faak and, beyond the Drava Valley, the long barrier of the Karawanken. To the north, the view encompasses the mountainous district known as the Nockgebiet. The permanently snow-covered slopes of the glaciers of Hochalm and the Ankogel (in the Hohe Tauern range) glitter in the northwest.

Return to the lake. The road carries on east to Steindorf. Turn right off the main road here onto the road which follows the south shore of the lake.

Ossiach – The former Benedictine **abbey** of Ossiach (now transformed into a hotel) was founded in the 11C. In the 16C and 17C it had periods of splendour, as in the summer of 1552, during which the abbot, when receiving Emperor

Charles V, sailed a fleet of galleys on the lake for his Imperial visitor. In 1783 the abbey was dissolved on the orders of Emperor Joseph II. It subsequently took on a number of different roles: stud farm, military base, convalescence home. These varied functions all took their toll on the building, as nobody thought to take care of its upkeep. The cloisters were even demolished in 1816. Since 1946 the abbey buildings have belonged to the Austrian Forestry Commission and it has at last been possible to restore them. They now house a hotel. Ossiach is well known far beyond national borders as a venue of the Carinthian Summer festival.

★ **Church** ⏲ – The church's exterior is dominated by the massive tower above the transept crossing. Inside, the originally Romanesque triple-naved pillared basilica was completely transformed into the Baroque style between 1741 and 1745. This is particularly successful in the delicately coloured **stuccowork** by masters from the Wessobrunn School in Bavaria, the lace-like patterning lavishly adoring the interior. The ceiling painting is the work of the local artist, **Joseph Ferdinand Fromiller**, the famous Carinthian Baroque painter, who also worked in the Landhaus at Klagenfurt; his work contributes to the harmonious general impression.

In the Gothic baptistery chapel, to the left of the entrance, is one of the most valuable of the 60 Late Gothic altarpieces to be found in Carinthia. This **carved altarpiece**★ is thought to have been created in one of the St. Veit workshops in the early 16C. The central panel depicts the Virgin Mary between St Margaret and St Catherine; on the side panels are the Apostles, in groups of three. This work by an anonymous master is characterised by the faces' heavily emphasised chins and the short chests of the women figures.

As the tour of Ossiacher See ends, the ruins of Landskron appear once more against the distant crests of the Villacher Alps.

Burgruine Landskron – *See VILLACH.*

Take the road back to Villach, which runs parallel to a drainage channel of the lake.

PACK- und STUBALPENSTRASSE★

Steiermark und Kärnten

Michelin map 926 folds 35 and 36

Between the valleys of the River Mur and River Lavant and the Graz basin rise the gentle, wooded heights of the Pannonian Pre-Alps. These mountains, known as the Koralpe, the Packalpe, the Stubalpe and the Gleinalpe, form a barrier less by their height, which hardly exceeds 2 000m/6 500ft, than by their solitude. The inter-regional road from Graz to Klagenfurt passes over the Packsattel, whereas the old road from Graz to Judenburg via Köflach crosses the Stubalpe, cutting off the wide bend of the River Mur.

★ STUBALPE

From Judenburg to Köflach *44km/27mi*

Beware of the steep gradient on the east slope of the Gaberl pass (maximum 1 in 5) between Puffing and the Salla Valley.

Judenburg – The town is densely built up on its spur, around the foot of a tall tower which has become the emblem of the town. Judenburg, located at the point where five trade routes converged, is the oldest commercial centre in Styria. From 1103, records show that there was a Jewish community here, which held the reins of the trade and usury activities. In 1496, as elsewhere in Styria, Emperor Maximilian I had the Jews driven out. Numerous old buildings and courtyards from the historic town centre survive, clustered around the **Neue Burg**.

The mountainous stretch of the "Gaberlstraße" begins at the village of Weißkirchen. The tortuous road rises in stages through the fir trees to the crest, which it follows nearly to the Gaberl-Sattel. There are many attractive vistas north and south through woodland into the nearby valleys. Behind, the Aichfeld plain (in the Judenberg-Knittelfeld region) lies at the foot of the bare crests of the Niedere Tauern, which stretch northwest. The main ridge of the Stubalpe is crossed at the **Gaberl** pass (alt 1 547m/5 075ft – *inn*).

On the east slope of the pass, the road drops suddenly into the wild and narrow wooded **Salla Valley**, reaching its floor at a tiny village of the same name. Here and there a large farmhouse or an old mill stands by the torrent. The sawmills and

scythe factories *(Sensenwerke)* which introduced industry to the valley, may still be seen, though some are now in ruins. (Styrian scythes have a worldwide reputation).
The valley opens out again.

Köflach - The industry of this town is based on the opencast lignite extraction nearby (the Köflach mine is the most productive in Austria). At the beginning of September the annual "Lipizzaner Almabtrieb" takes place, when the famous white stallions are driven down from the Alpine pastures to their winter quarters at Piber stud farm.

★ **Gestüt Piber** ⓥ - *3km/2mi northeast of Köflach.* Piber's claim to fame rests on the beautiful **Lipizzaner stallions**, a race prized during the Baroque period, which are bred here. The stallions are sent to the Spanische Reitschule in Vienna *(see WIEN)*, where it is possible to watch them in displays of classical horsemanship. A visit to the stables and a walk in the fields nearby will give a close view of the famous Lipizzaners. Born bay or black, the horses acquire their white coats between the ages of four and 10. In exceptional cases a Lipizzaner may retain its dark coat, which makes it a highly prized example called a "Hofburg bay".

Wiesenhofer/ÖSTERREICH WERBUNG

Lipizzaner stallions at Piber stud farm

★ PACKSATTEL

From Köflach to Wolfsberg *52km/32mi*

Köflach - *See above.*

After leaving Köflach, the route passes the opencast lignite pits and then climbs up the side of an outlying hill a little distance from the main Packalpe ridge. There are good views down into the industrial valley, particularly after Edelschrott; the bright white outline of the pilgrimage church at Maria Lankowitz stands out, as do the chimneys and cooling towers of the thermal power station at Vottsberg. The road runs along the enclosed Teigitschbach Valley but the views open out as it begins the final climb up towards the village of Pack.

Pack - Favoured by the proximity of the **Packer Stausee** (an artificial lake with boating and bathing facilities), this little place also enjoys a peaceful **panorama**★ of the wooded foothills of the Pannonian Pre-Alps and the Graz plain. The construction of the Graz-Wolfsburg motorway has freed the village from through traffic and allowed it to reclaim its past atmosphere.
In gentle pastoral surroundings the road reaches the Packsattel, which is also known as the Packhöhe or the Vier Tore (Four Gates - alt 1 166m/3 825ft), and then drops into an even quieter and more thickly wooded zone. The motorway also passes over the Packsattel, at an altitude of 1 061m/3 480ft, without exceeding an average gradient of 1 in 25 from Graz.
A series of hairpin bends below the Preitenegg ridge lends a little variety to this descent of the Carinthian slope, during which one can see, in the distance, the crests of the Saualpe, rising in series to the west. If the weather is clear, the rocky barrier of the Karawanken can be seen, to the south, through the Lavanttal gap. This section of the route ends at the foot of the sombre Schloß Waldenstein. It then winds along the ravine of the Waldensteiner Bach to join the equally deep Lavant Valley at Twimberg.

★ **Lavant Valley Motorway Bridge (Autobahnbrücke)** – 1 079m/3 500ft long and 165m/541ft high, this bridge is taller than the Stephansdom in Vienna. It is among the 10 longest bridges in Austria and it is Europe's second highest bridge built on piers.

Wolfsberg – The town lies at the foot of the château of the counts Henckel von Donnersmarck *(not open to the public)*, which was reconstructed in the 19C in the Tudor style. The town centre is the Hoher Platz, a square adorned with a column to the Virgin Mary and surrounded by fine houses in the Biedermeier style.

PETRONELL-CARNUNTUM★

Niederösterreich

Population 1 200

Michelin map 926 fold 13 – Alt 330m/1 082ft

On the site of Petronell and in the neighbouring community of Bad Deutsch-Altenburg, numerous remains have been uncovered of a long-vanished Roman town, which was built on the Danube in 1C AD. The Illyrian and Celtic town of Carnuntum was on the famous Amber Road then linking Italy with the Baltic. A garrison was set up here in AD 15 when Emperor Tiberius decided to send to the Danube his formidable 15th Legion, the so-called Appollinaris, to resist the onslaught of the Marcomanni.

The Capital of Upper Pannonia – Pannonia, which largely corresponded to modern Hungary, was conquered under Augustus after the rebellion of AD 16. In the early decades of the 2C Carnuntum became the capital of the province of Upper Pannonia, and under Emperor Hadrian was given the status of a municipium, which meant that its inhabitants were Roman citizens.

In 171 Emperor Marcus Aurelius came to Carnuntum in person – he is said to have written part of his *Meditations* here – in order to drive back the Marcomanni and the Quadi (Goths); he finally subdued them in 174. He subsequently returned to the camp of Vindobona (Vienna); it is thought that he died there of an epidemic in 180.

In 308 the Imperial Conference for the rescue of the Empire was convened in Carnuntum. But for the town the end was near. First the Goths and then the Huns destroyed it completely in 407.

SIGHTS

★ **Freilichtmuseum Petronell** ⏲ – *Information Centre, Hauptstraße 296.* The sites of the Roman excavations cover an area of 8km²/3sq mi and form in effect an open-air museum. Begun in 1885, the excavations have revealed the camp of the 15th Legion, including the field hospital. In particular two **amphitheatres** were discovered: Amphitheatre I, with an arena in the form of an ellipse 72m/236ft long and 44m/144ft wide and rows of seats rising in steps, can hold 6 000 to 8 000 people. In its centre is a rectangular basin supplied with water by a channel for cleaning the arena. Amphitheatre II, which can accommodate 13 000 spectators, also has an ellipsoid arena, with two gateways. The south gateway has a basin which is thought to be an Early Christian baptistery.

In the civilian part of the town, which had up to 50 000 inhabitants, were situated the **Great Baths** as a temple to pleasure. The structure is also sometimes called a "ruined palace", and is one of the largest remains of a building from Antiquity found north of the Alps, since the Baths were converted in 308 to accommodate the Imperial Conference. Close by is a reconstruction of the Temple of Artemis, and much further away to the south the 20m/66ft high **Heidentor** (Heathens' Gate), one of the four town gates of Carnuntum.

Round Chapel – *Level with Hauptstraße 173. Access through the car park of the Hotel Mark Aurel.* On the right side of the street is this very original round chapel dating from 1200, with its pointed roof and semicircular choir. The individual character of the building is further emphasized by the simplicity of the façade with its three-quarter columns and arcades carried on consoles. There is a relief on the **Tympanum**★ over the entrance showing the baptism of Christ, an indication that the chapel must originally have been used as a baptistery.

Pfarrkirche der hl. Petronilla – The parish church dedicated to St Petronilla, founded in about 1078 by Bishop Altmann of Passau, stands in the centre of the village, surrounded by graveyard walls. Although badly damaged by the Turks in 1529, it retains its beautiful Romanesque apse to the choir.

★ **Archäologisches Museum Carnuntinum** ⏲ – *Badgasse 40-46.* The archeological museum opened by Emperor Franz Joseph in 1904 has been splendidly restored and reorganized.

The huge quantity of finds made in this area becomes clear when one considers that only 5% of the relics excavated are exhibited. In this remarkable collection it is the sculptures that stand out in particular. Among the most striking is the marble statuette of the **Dancing Maenads of Carnuntum**★ (2C, *upper floor*).

The exhibits on the ground floor mainly relate to the **Mithras cult** and come from the Mithraeum, an underground place of worship revealed by the excavations. Mithras was a Persian god, particularly venerated by Roman soldiers in the 2C, associated with fire and the sun. In the early centuries AD this mystery religion, into which members were admitted in seven stages of initiation, won the status of a world religion through its protection by various Roman emperors and became serious competition for Christianity. As the latter gained ground, however, the cult of Mithras declined, finally disappearing almost as quickly as it had initially won popularity.

Harrach'sche Gemäldegalerie - *The Concert* (c 1500)

Graf Harrach'sche Familiensammlung/SCHLOSS ROHRAU

EXCURSION

Rohrau - *4km/2.5mi south of Petronell-Carnuntum.* Here in the 16C castle is the **Harrach'sche Gemäldegalerie**★★ ⓥ, the largest and most important private art collection in Austria with works by 17C and 18C masters from Spain, Naples and Rome, and 16C and 17C masters from Holland and Flanders. One of the most famous exhibits is *The Concert* (16C), a particularly graceful painting of half-length female figures, presumably by a Dutch artist.

Rohrau was where the composer **Joseph Haydn** was born, on 31 March 1732, in the thatched **Geburtshaus Joseph Haydns** ⓥ on the main road leading through the village.

PITZTAL★★★

Tirol

Michelin map 926 fold 30

The long Pitztal Valley, which runs from north to south, is bordered in the west by the Kaunertal Valley and in the east by the Ötztal Valley. It is famous for the extraordinary Alpine scenery in its upper reaches. It is enclosed by a massive glacier basin, over which towers the 3 774m/12 382ft high **Wildspitze** peak, the highest point in the Tyrol.

SIGHTS

★ **Road from Arzl to Mittelberg** - *39km/24mi - allow 45min.* The road leads through numerous villages and hamlets. After 18km/11mi, the glaciers of the Pitztal Valley come into view at Hairlach. 4km/2.5mi later, the road passes through St. Leonhard. The mountain slopes draw further away from the road. The scenery is characterized by forest, little waterfalls and the Pitzbach, which the road follows to Mittelberg, where it ends. From here, lifts take you up to the glaciers.

★★★ **Hinterer Brunnenkogel** ⓥ - Alt 3 440m/11 286ft. *Around 2hr there and back. Anyone wishing to take a trip to Riffelsee Lake (on the same day or on the following day) should buy a combined tourist excursion ticket.*
You should take sunglasses, sturdy shoes which are also suitable for snow, warm clothing (even in summer) and, if possible, binoculars.
First take the Pitzexpress funicular railway. After travelling underground for 3.7km/2.3mi, you will reach the foot of the Pitztal glacier at an altitude of 2 860m/9 383ft. Continue on the Pitz-Panoramabahn, the highest cable-car in Austria.

From the mountain station you will reach the peak in a few minutes, and will be able to enjoy the fantastic **Alpine panoramas★★★**. The Hinterer Brunnenkogel is located in a magnificent situation right in the centre of a massive glacier basin. The Wildspitze peak towers majestically over this grandiose landscape. On the right you can see the Taschachferner glacier, which rolls down the slope at the foot of the impressive Hochvernagtspitze peak. In the background you can also see the peaks of the Kaunertal and Ötztal valleys.
In the west a long, rugged rocky face with the Ögrubenspitze and Bliggspitze peaks rises up opposite the Wildspitze. In the north you can see right up to the last hamlets in the Pitztal, flanked by the Watzespitze peak and the Hohe Geige.

✻ **Pitztal glacier ski area** – A cable-car, four T-bar lifts and a chair-lift lead up to the 25km/15.5mi long piste which is well covered in snow. The ski area, which is normally open from the autumn right up to June, is suitable for skiers of all levels, although easy runs predominate.
Other ski slopes in the Pitztal include the Hochzeiger (Jerzens) and Riffelsee ski areas.

★ **Excursion to the Riffelsee** ⏲ – Park the car in Mandarfen, a hamlet 1km/0.5mi below Mittelberg. Ride up in the cable-car. This excursion is especially recommended as part of a hike.
During the trip you will enjoy interesting **views** over the valley, and of the Kerlesferner glacier to the south. From the cable-car mountain station (alt 2 300m/7 546ft), there is a wonderful view over Riffelsee Lake, which is surprisingly light in colour and large in size in view of its altitude. The **landscape★** is dominated by the Seekogel. A walk around the lake is recommended.
Hikers with plenty of stamina can take the Fuldaer Höhenweg ridge trail, which leads southwards directly along the mountainside to the **Taschachhütte** mountain lodge at an altitude of 2 432m/7 979ft. It is located at the foot of the Hochvernagtspitze peak and the Taschachferner and Sexegertenferner glaciers *(day trips)*.

PÖLLAU★

Steiermark

Population 1 860

Michelin map 926 south of fold 24 – Alt 427m/1 401ft

The market town of Pöllau lies in the heart of a small, undulating region well away from the major tourist routes; it is the main town of the Pöllauer Tal (Pöllau Valley). Much of the surrounding countryside, which encompasses six townships, has been turned into a game park (124km²/48sq mi); it is crisscrossed by 100km/62mi of waymarked paths and boasts large wooded areas that are well stocked with animals. The park is dominated to the east by the summit of Rabenwaldkogel (1 280m/4 198ft) and to the west by the Masenberg (1 261m/4 135ft), both highly popular areas with walkers.
In an area of limited agricultural activity, vines occupy a significant niche in the local economy. In the season, there are a large number of traditional bars *(Buschenschenken)* to be found in the countryside, serving good quality wines, sometimes to the accompaniment of accordion music.
The charm of Pöllau is due in part to its beautiful old tiled roofs.

SIGHTS

Marktplatz – This traditional market place, with its column to the Virgin Mary, is characterized by the southern air of many of its old façades. The narrow streets leading into the square have preserved the provincial flavour of their simple, unsophisticated architecture.
To the north of the square, a door set in a pedimented building adds a note of discreet solemnity to the surrounding rural gaiety. The door opens into the old abbey, a vast, almost circular area, round which the market town has grown.

Stift – This abbey of canons regular under the Rule of St Augustine was founded in 1504 by a nobleman of Pöllau, Hans von Neuberg. The new foundation had a troubled time during the 16C, when Styria was racked by religious disputes and particularly by Turkish raids.
By the end of the 17C the abbey had become prosperous and it was then rebuilt in the Baroque style. Less than a century later, at the time of Austria's secularization in 1785, it was closed down by Emperor Joseph II and turned into a private residence. The old abbey buildings now belong to the town.

★ **Abbey church** – The plans for this huge building were drawn up by **Joachim Carlone**, a member of the celebrated family of Graz architects. The prior wished the new church to bear as strong a resemblance as possible to St Peter's in Rome. Rebuilding took place between 1701 and 1709 in the form of a Latin cross with a cupola over the transept crossing.

The dimensions are impressive: nave and chancel 62m/203ft long, transept 37m/121ft wide, cupola 42m/138ft high, creating an unusually large space for a community numbering only about 10 priests.

The remarkable **decor** is a delightful blend of paintings, gold, stuccowork and opulent sculptures. The frescoes in the nave and cupola are by **Matthias von Görz**, a Styrian painter heavily influenced by the Italian artists with whom he worked when he was studying in Italy. The hallmarks of this regional painter are the use of bright colours, a somewhat simple serenity, a passion for light and considerable skill at *trompe-l'œil*. It took him 12 years to finish decorating the church. In the vault of the **cupola**, the nine choirs of angels celebrate the Trinity; from between the eight windows, allegorical figures of the virtues look up towards heaven. The vault of the nave is decorated with the fall of the wicked angels, the veneration of the cross, the adoration of the Lamb of God by all the saints, and the Blessed Virgin Mary enthroned and surrounded by her court.

The **high altar** is decorated with an enormous painting, representing the martyrdom of St Vitus, executed by the artist Joseph Adam von Mölk in 1779. The 24-stop **organ**, built in 1739, stands on an arcaded gallery, beneath a ceiling fresco of David playing the harp.

EXCURSIONS

★ **Pöllauberg** – *6km/4mi northeast of Pöllau.* Pöllauberg Church, which seems to float in mid-air, in fact crowns the top of a steep hill and is visible for miles around. This tiny village grew up at the foot of the celebrated pilgrimage church which dominates the Pöllau Valley. From this natural balcony, it is possible on a clear day to see as far as the Hungarian plain.

★ **Church** – On reaching the top of a flight of seven steps, it is initially surprising to see an elegantly ribbed axial pillar concealing much of the chancel from view. This pilgrimage church was built between 1375 and 1379 according to an unusual design; two naves of equal size and with intersecting ribs in the vaults are separated by three columns, which stand in the central aisle and are so carefully sited in relation to the chancel that there is a clear view of the celebrant from every seat.

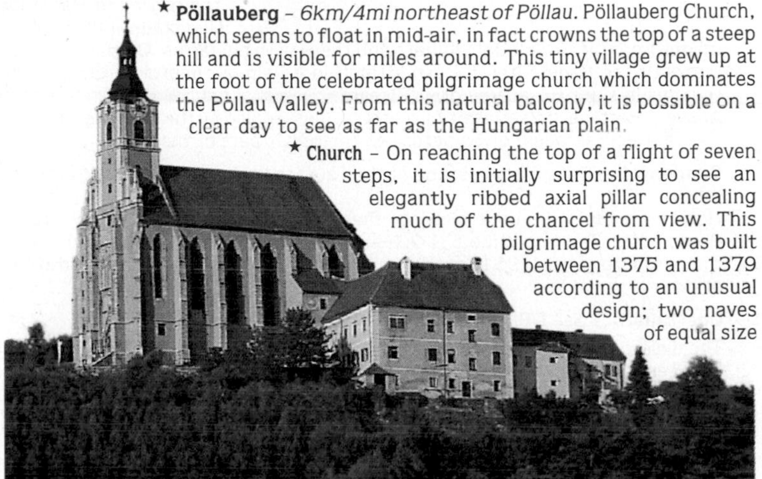

GEORG MIKES

Pilgrimage church at Pöllauberg

The large and sumptuously decorated high altar was built in 1714 around a statue of the Virgin Mary. The pulpit, which is lavishly decorated with gold, dates from 1730.

★ **Schloß Herberstein** – *23km/14mi south of Pöllau. From Kaindorf take the Graz road; in Kaibing turn off towards St. Johann bei Herberstein.* *See Schloß HERBERSTEIN.*

RADSTÄDTER TAUERNSTRASSE★

Salzburg

Michelin map 926 folds 20, 33 and 34

This road was much used in the Roman era and is still marked by military milestones which have been recently re-erected. The road, which crosses the summit of the Niedere Tauern at 1 700m/5 577ft, connects the upper valleys of the Enns and the Mur. In the Middle Ages it was one of the lines of expansion towards the south pursued by the archbishops of Salzburg.

The **Lungau**, in the upper Mur Valley, is the only remaining relic of these ambitions. Until the opening of the Tauern motorway, it was one of the most remote and tradition-bound areas of the Alps and is still linked politically with the Salzach region.

FROM RADSTADT TO ST. MICHAEL IM LUNGAU *67km/42mi*

Radstadt - Radstadt, built on a regular, square layout by the Salzburg bishops at the end of the 13C, is still enclosed by the original fortified walls with their towers. On the west side, part of the moat has also survived. This pretty town occupies a fine **site★** at the junction of two spectacular scenic roads, the Dachsteinstraße and Radstädter Tauernstraße. To the north towers the Roßbrandgipfel summit *(see DACHSTEIN)*, from where there is a breathtaking view of the surrounding mountain ranges, and to the south the Kemathöhe (alt 1 577m/5 174ft), which is excellent for downhill skiing in the winter. Together with neighbouring resort Altenmarkt, 20km/12mi of ski runs have been laid out.

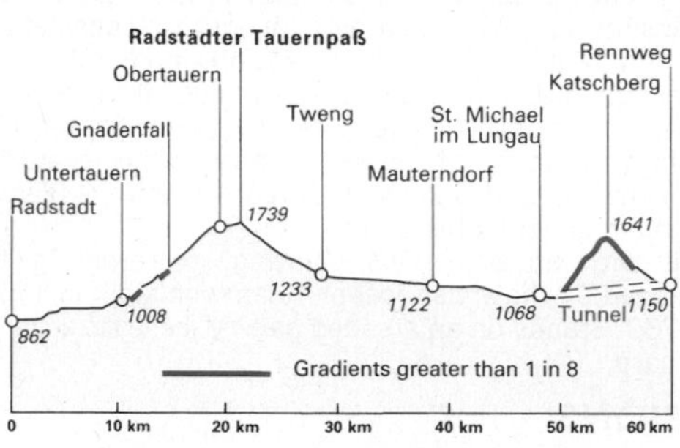

The charming countryside around Radstadt boasts a number of interesting manor houses, such as those of Tandalier and Mauer, in the traditional Salzburg style (wide, overhanging roofs, corner turrets and watchtowers).

The run from Radstadt to Untertauern unfolds above magnificent meadows, dotted here and there with big farms. On the horizon, the crests of the Radstädter Tauern stretch in an almost unbroken line. Radstadt remains in sight for a time downstream.

Above Untertauern a series of hills and ravines, cooled by the shade of maples and the Taurach cascades, gives access to the upper part of the valley.

Gnadenfall - This pretty cascade of the Taurach leaps a wooded shelf in two light falls.

Hotels are dotted about among the larches and spruces below the pass (Radstädter Tauernpaß: alt 1 739m/5 705ft). About 800m/0.5mi short of the pass a modern (1951) statue of a Roman legionary stands guard over the bridge.

❄❄ **Obertauern** - *See OBERTAUERN.*

The descent of the south approach to the pass involves a forbidding section but between Tweng and Mauterndorf pleasant clearings appear on the banks of the calmer Taurach. Soon the roofs of the castle of Mauterndorf emerge from the trees.

★ **Burg Mauterndorf** - *See Burg MAUTERNDORF.*

★ **Tamsweg** - *See TAMSWEG.*

★ **Schloß Moosham** ⌚ - This former fortress of the archbishops of Salzburg was restored and refurnished last century. In the arolla (pine) panelled rooms on the second floor and in the vaulted chancellery there are considerable collections of furniture and art objects. Ask for the explanation of the comical picture of people classified by their characteristic features in the bedroom on the second floor.

The castle's **lower courtyard★** provides a lasting and picturesque memory: the stillness, the grass and the surrounding wooden galleries. The old well is 64m/210ft deep.

St. Michael im Lungau - Benefiting from the exceptional sunshine enjoyed by the upper Mur Valley, this resort is a busy place with a huge modern youth hostel. Next to the Gothic parish church is the "Wolfgangkapelle", an elegant little building on an octagonal plan.

With its numerous ski lifts giving access to the fine ski slopes all around, St. Michael, together with St. Margarethen and Mauterndorf, is a particularly attractive centre for winter sports.

From St. Michael, to get to the Carinthian lakes, drive south along the old* Katschbergstraße*, reaching Spittal an der Drau via Gmünd (see respective entries).

Alternatively, a quicker route to that over the pass (1 641m/5 384ft) is along the A99 and through the toll-paying* Katschbergtunnel*.

RATTENBERG*

Tirol

Population 540

Michelin map 926 fold 18 – Alt 514m/1 686ft

This tiny frontier town was a subject of dispute between the Tyrol and Bavaria until 1505, when Maximilian of Austria annexed the lower Inn Valley as far as Kufstein. Rattenberg took advantage of a bottleneck in the alluvial plain of the Inn, which enabled it to control traffic on the road and on the river.

Renaissance townscape – By the 17C the silver mines on which Rattenberg's prosperity had been based were exhausted. In its impoverished state, the town was unable to improve or replace its building stock, which accounts for its appearance today, an almost perfectly preserved example of Renaissance urban design. The old town, squeezed between the Inn and the Schloßberg, forms a triangle whose longest side, parallel to the river, is barely 300m long. This densely populated area has only two streets, intersected here and there by narrow alleyways. The building of the motorway has happily freed the main street from choking traffic.

Glass-making – Among other Tyrolean specialities, Rattenberg manufactures engraved and finely modelled glassware, both in the town itself and in Kramsach on the north bank of the Inn.
Rattenberg styles itself "the town of glass" (Glasstadt), though the well-known technical college specializing in glass technology is actually in Kramsach.

Bohnacker/ÖSTERREICH WERBUNG

Rattenberg

SIGHTS

* **Hauptstraße** – The most characteristic houses have plain façades under dull-coloured roughcast, adorned with some stucco, with window and door frames in pink marble and crowned with a horizontal pediment. As one can see from the castle *(for access see below)*, the pediment does not conceal a flat roof, which would be unsuitable in an Alpine climate, but a furrowed roof *(Grabendach)* anticipating the trussed roofing of 19C workshops. This division of the roof into several ridges at right angles to the street provided better protection against fire than a single, gabled roof, and did away with the intermediate gutter, which caused trouble between neighbours.

* **Augustinermuseum** ◷ – *Pfarrgasse 8*. The Augustinian monastery was founded in 1384. In 1993 a museum was installed on the premises, with the aim of displaying Tyrolean art treasures in an appropriate setting. A large area is given over to Late Gothic sculpture, exhibited in the cloisters. Some excellent examples of local goldsmithing, the master exponent of which was Dominikus Lang, illustrate the very high standard to which this art had been refined.
Items carried in procession are exhibited up in the church gallery, among which the seated Madonna and the Mocking Group are outstanding.

★★ **Pfarrkirche St. Virgil** – Abutting the castle bluff, this Gothic church of 1473 is remarkable for its fine external stonework of pink marble.

Its twin naves, separated by four graceful columns with capitals of Antique design, are a harmonious and iridescent confection in pinks and whites. Formerly the main nave was reserved for the townsfolk, and the smaller nave for the miners. Abundant statuary, delicate stuccowork adorning the vaulting, and elegant frescoes make up the scintillating Baroque decorative scheme of about 1730, to which the finest artists of the region made their contribution. The masterly **Last Supper** in the main nave is the work of the Bavarian artist Matthäus Günther; the Transfiguration in the chancel is by Simon Benedikt Faistenberger. The statues around the **altar** in the miners' chancel were sculpted by Meinrad Guggenbichler, the famous sculptor from Mondsee.

At the far end of the church, a flight of steps leads to the chapel dedicated to Saint Notburga, born in Rattenberg in 1265.

Schloßberg – *30min on foot there and back. Go beneath the railway bridge behind the church and, on emerging from the covered way, bear right onto the path up to the castle. At the open-air theatre turn right to reach the edge of the terrace at the foot of the castle ruin.*

From this vantage point there is a good **general view** of the town, hemmed in between the Inn and the mountain, with the belfry of the Servitenkirche (13C-18C) rising above the roof ridges. Downstream, the Kaisergebirge can be seen.

EXCURSION

★ **Freilichtmuseum Tiroler Bauernhöfe** ⌚ – *7km/4mi away in* **Kramsach**. *Leave Rattenberg in the Kramsach direction and cross the Brandenberger Ache (a tributary of the Inn) towards Breitenbach am Inn. The museum car park is on the right shortly after the hamlet of Mosen.*

A good number of farm buildings from North, East and South Tyrol have been rebuilt here in a quiet Alpine setting, in the manner of a scattered settlement, enabling the visitor to appreciate the phenomenon of the Tyrolean farmhouse in all its pleasing variety. It is worth allowing plenty of time for your visit, as it can easily take 2hrs to look over all the houses.

★ **Alpbach** – *12km/7.5mi southeast of Rattenberg.* Alpbach, situated in a southern side-arm of the Lower Inn Valley, was probably first settled in about the year 1000 by Rhaetians and Bavarians. The fine houses with their flower-bedecked wooden balconies and the parish church of St. Oswald with its pointed spire stand out against the backdrop of the mountains. Its almost too perfect idyllic beauty has earned it several awards; for instance, Austrian TV viewers voted Alpbach Austria's most beautiful village in 1983, and in 1993 an international jury named it Europe's prettiest "village of flowers".

Since 1945, the Alpbach European Forum has met here every year, bringing together academics, politicians, economists and artists of all nationalities, who can discuss contemporary problems in this relaxed atmosphere. Statesmen and Nobel prize winners frequently take part in round-table symposia here.

Pfarrkirche St. Oswald – The plain exterior of this church dating from 1720, which only retains the tower of its predecessor from 1420, does not prepare us for the richly decorated interior with its fine frescoes. Baroque splendour is particularly in evidence in the fashioning of the altars. The High Altar bears the figures of St Oswald, St Martin and St Catherine, while the two side altars are framed in Rococo carvings from 1764. The left-hand one with its miraculous picture of Our Lady of the Victory has attracted thousands of pilgrims over the centuries. The Crucifixion group on the right-hand altar is by Andreas Pietzacher, a local artist from the early 19C.

REISSECK-MASSIV★★

Kärnten

Michelin map 926 fold 33

The Reißeck massif, which towers 2 400m/7 900ft over the Möll Valley at an altitude of 2 965m/9 727ft, is one of the most unspoilt places in Carinthia. Since the building of a funicular and the laying of a railway line as part of construction of the power station at Kolbnitz, the massif has been opened up to the outside world to a far greater degree. Due to its beautiful situation and the good snow conditions, holidaymakers soon began to practice skiing here. During the winter, skiers are able to reach two high altitude ski lifts, which in the summer make the ideal point of departure for hikes to the many lakes and viewpoints of the massif.

Kolbnitz – The power station is fed, from both sides of the Möll Valley, by pressure conduits collecting water from the Reißeck and Kreuzeck. Seven turbines generate about 307 million kWh/year. This installation, which was completed in 1959, required the tapping of four mountain lakes (Kleiner and Großer Mühldorfer See, Radlsee and Höchalmsee) on the Reißeck slope. The maximum drop for the winter storage power station is 1 772m/5 812ft.

★ **Reißeck funicular and railway** – *From Kolbnitz. 1hr there and back with the funicular and 15min on the train.* The funicular, made up of three sections, is quite spectacular, because of its very steep gradient (up to 1 in 1.4). A 3.5km/2.2mi journey leads up to the Schoberboden station (alt 2 237m/7 339ft), from where there is a beautiful **view**★ of the valley and the first rocky foothills of the Reißeck massif.

After travelling underground for 3.2km/2mi, the train arrives at the Reißeck mountain hotel, which is a pleasant place to stay in both summer and winter.

★ **Walk to the Mühldorfer Seen** – An easy 20min climb leads to the Großer Mühldorfer See, from where there is a **view**★ to the east over the Hohe Leier. After this the trail is quite stony, so sturdy shoes are essential *(follow the red and white markings)*. After 10min the path emerges above the Kleiner See dam. There is a beautiful **open view**★ over both lakes, which lie in an unspoiled rocky landscape. The **Riekentörl pass** (alt 2 525m/8 284ft), with the Riedbock on its left and the Redlkopf on its right, lies to the northwest.

Hikers should unquestionably climb this pass *(it takes 1hr over a quite rocky trail, but presents no technical difficulties)*, which offers a magnificent **panorama**★★ over the entire Reißeck massif.

RETZ

Niederösterreich

Population 4 370

Michelin map 926 fold 11 – Alt 252m/827ft

Retz, near the Thaya Valley, is an important wine-growing and farming centre (a visit of the **Retzer Erlebniskeller** ⏱ is possible, Austria's largest historic wine-cellar, some 12km/7.5mi long), in a hilly region which forms part of the Bohemian Forest. The **old town** still has its grid plan, ramparts and defensive towers. The town's emblem is a windmill, built in 1772 and still operational.

★ HAUPTPLATZ

This fine square is the heart of the old town. At the centre of the very large, rectangular space is a column to the Holy Trinity.

The Hauptplatz is surrounded by a few houses which are remarkable for their architecture and decoration: the **Verderberhaus** (north side) is crowned with crenellations and pierced by an arched passage; opposite (no 15) is the **Sgraffitohaus**, a handsome building with a carved doorway and a façade covered with inscribed maxims.

The **Rathaus** was created in the 16C by converting a Gothic church; the Lady Chapel has survived on the ground floor.

Schloß RIEGERSBURG★

Niederösterreich

Michelin map 426 fold 11 – 8km/5mi west of Hardegg

The unspoilt, peaceful landscape of the northeastern Waldviertel provides a backdrop for the most important Baroque mansion in Lower Austria.

Visitors are surprised when they come upon this elegant building, a precious jewel which lies hidden in its park in the midst of otherwise rural surroundings. The former moated castle was bought by Sigmund Friedrich Count Khevenhüller, Governor of Lower Austria. He entrusted master builder **Franz Anton Pilgram** with its conversion to a four-winged Baroque palace, grouped around a square inner courtyard. Pilgram was a student of Hildebrandt and was the master builder of the abbey in Göttweig. In this building, he showed what he could do. The decoration is rich, but not ostentatious, so that the building heralds the Classical style. The high quality **furnishings**★ in the house, which is still owned by the family, make it a fine example of an 18C country seat.

Schloß Riegersburg

Atlas carrying the world

TOUR ⊙

The main façade is divided by a central section with five bays and round-arched windows, and flanked by jutting corner pavilions. The tympanum shows the coat of arms of the Khevenhüller family, above which stands the figure of Atlas carrying the globe. The gable itself bears the statues of Wisdom, Unity, Justice and Honesty. The beautiful sculpted decoration, which dates from 1733, is the work of Josef Kracker.

State rooms – The **banqueting hall** (Festsaal) is reached via the three flights of the main staircase. It is remarkable that stuccowork as a means of decoration has only been used sparingly, and no gilding detracts from the beautiful proportions of the room. A *sopraporte* shows Count Johann Joseph Khevenhüller-Metsch, Maria Theresa's Chief Lord Chamberlain, whose diaries are said to have inspired the libretto for Richard Strauss' opera *Der Rosenkavalier*. The portraits of Maria Theresa and her mother Elisabeth Christine are by court painter Martin van Meytens. The **Baroque room** houses a view of Naples composed of 35 copper engravings dating from 1730 to 1775, which is a most unusual work since it shows a view from the air. The furniture in the Salon includes Queen Anne and Chippendale pieces, as well as furnishings in the Austrian Baroque style and a handsome tabernacle cupboard.
The **tower room**, hung with *toiles de Jouy* (plate-printed cotton), contains furniture from the 18C. Note the pretty travelling writing desk from England.
The **dining room** contains French furniture and houses one of the most famous portraits by Austrian painter Auerbach of Prince Eugene of Savoy. Note also the statue of a graceful blackamoor, a Venetian work.
The **stucco ceiling★** of the **Yellow Salon** depicts an allegory of princely virtue. The room is furnished with Marie-Antoinette chairs and two beautiful Florentine commodes with delicate inlaid work. The **Chinese Salon** also features a magnificent stucco ceiling. The carpet with its Chinese decorations comes from the manufacturer Zuber in Mulhouse, France. The two commodes with their precious chequered inlaid work were a gift from Maria Theresa.
In the north wing is the elegant **Schloßkapelle** (chapel), consecrated in 1755. The altar is integrated into the architectural structure and is surmounted by rich stuccowork. The altarpiece depicts St Sigismund.
The **Schloßküche** (kitchen) on the ground floor, which was in use up to 1955, and which still has its original appointments, working equipment and the large brick oven, is the only remaining manorial kitchen in Austria.
From the café in the right wing, it is possible to gain access to the park with its pond.

EXCURSION

Burg Hardegg ⊙ – *8km/5mi to the east.* Hardegg, Austria's smallest town, lying on the Thaya at the frontier with the Czech Republic, is dominated by the fortress of the same name, which is enthroned on a rocky mountain top. Its formidable keep and handsome walls create a great impression of impregnability. The origins of this strategically important fortress – highly prized because of its location in the north of the Ostmark, or East March – date back to the year 1000, but records show that extensions were added right up to the 14C.
After a chequered history, the fortress passed into the hands of the Khevenhüller in 1730 and at the end of the 19C it was converted into a mausoleum for the Lower Austrian line of this dynasty. Some of the rooms are dedicated to the memory of the unlucky Emperor Maximilian of Mexico, whose comrade-in-arms and close confidant was Count Johann Franz Carl Khevenhüller.

Schloß ROSENBURG★

Niederösterreich

Michelin map 926 fold 11

More than 1 000 years ago, the Babenbergs freed central Austria from the Magyars, so that this region could at last be settled. But in order to counter effectively the constant threat from Bohemia, the nobles built a series of castles in the strategically important Kamptal, the valley forming a north-south link to the Danube. Of these, the Rosenburg, built in the first half of the 12C, is one of the most attractive and important.

Placed at a point where the River Kamp, which has been flowing from west to east, makes a sudden turn to the south towards the Danube, it has an ideal site on a rocky spur dominating the valley. In the hands of the Grabner family in the 16C, the Rosenburg became a centre of Protestantism. It was Sebastian Grabner who had the castle transformed into a splendid Renaissance residence. The well-known song that speaks of a "castle in Austria, finely built of silver and red gold, and walled with marble stone" must date from this time. Since 1681 the Rosenburg has been owned by the counts Hoyos-Sprinzenstein.

TOUR ⊘

Entering through the gateway, one comes to the Turnierhof (jousting court or tilt-yard) of 1614 surrounded on three sides by double galleries. The name is a misnomer, since by the time it was built there were no longer any real tournaments (they went out in the 14C), and the courtyard was only used for various equestrian games. Next one comes to the second gateway, with a large **coat of arms★** over the main entrance; carved in pink limestone and sandstone, it displays the arms of the former owners, the Grabner and Polheim families.

From the forecourt overlooking the ornamental lake down below a stone bridge leads over the moat to the third gateway and the main building. This is arranged around an irregularly shaped inner courtyard, whose main feature is a fine wrought-iron well cover of 1556. The square **keep** is part of the original castle, but was altered in the Renaissance period by the addition of a balcony.

After standing nearly empty in the 18C, the living rooms and grand public rooms were furnished mainly in the style of the German Renaissance, which gives them a lived-in feeling. The **library** is of particular interest, its remarkable wooden **coffered ceiling★** being painted in the German Mannerist style of the late 16C.

R. Chéret/MICHELIN

Free flight demonstration, Schloß Rosenburg

Schloß Rosenburg is a centre for falconry, and visitors with time to spare are recommended to watch the **free flight demonstrations★** in which hunting falcons, eagles and vultures perform their routines.

SAALACHTAL★

Salzburg und Bayern (Germany)

Michelin map 926 fold 19

The valley of the River Saalach, which breaches the Northern Limestone Alps, is served by the main roads 312 and 311, forming the quickest link between Salzburg, Zell am See and the Großglockner.

Owing to the clearance made by enormous masses of glacier ice coming down northwards from the Tauern, the broadest part of the valley is to be found near Zell am See and Saalfelden, near the source of the Saalach. Below Saalfelden, on the other hand, the river rushes through a rock cleft which is considered to be one of the most impressive transverse defiles in the Alps. After Lofer the cleft is replaced by a less striking series of basins and small wooded gorges. The upper course of the River Saalach flows through the Berchtesgaden region in Germany, before joining the Salzach northwest of Salzburg.

FROM SALZBURG TO ZELL AM SEE *95km/59mi*

★★★ **Salzburg** – *See SALZBURG.*

Leave Salzburg by ③ on the plan and road no 1.

The road goes past Salzburg's WA Mozart Airport, and about 7km/4mi after leaving the city it is possible to take a left turn to **Großgmain** and the Salzburg open-air museum *(detour of 6km/3.7mi).*

Salzburger Freilichtmuseum ⓥ – More than 60 original buildings from Salzburg province representing five centuries' traditional architecture have been reconstructed on this site. The houses in the museum village have been grouped by region: Flachgau, Tennengau, Pongau, Lungau and Pinzgau. In addition, there are various exhibitions, including a collection of old tractors. The open-air museum puts on a lively programme of events on local crafts and customs. Further details on this can be obtained from the museum.

Carry on to Bad Reichenhall, administrative seat of the Berchtesgaden region in Bavaria (Germany).

★ **Bad Reichenhall** – This salt mining city is located on some of the richest and most productive salt springs in Europe (maximum salt content 24%), from which it produces table salt. The saltwater spa is used primarily for curing respiratory diseases.

Branching off at Schneizlreuth from the Deutsche Alpenstraße, the Lofer road runs within view of the distinctive peaks of the Drei Brüder (Three Brothers) in the middle distance to the south. The road then turns away temporarily from the Saalach, as its course is too deeply sunken, and climbs up to Melleck. Soon afterwards the Steinbach ravine marks the return to the Austrian frontier. This is the Steinpaß.

Between Unken and Lofer there are several bottlenecks, such as the Kniepaß with its defensive fortress, where the Saalach foams close beside the road, which give the run a touch of excitement. The northern approach to Lofer provides glimpses, directly after Hallenstein, of the central group of the Loferer Steinberge (left to right: Ochsenhorn, Großes Reifhorn, Breithorn); further south rise the Leoganger Steinberge.

★ **Lofer** – *See KAISERGEBIRGE* 1.

Making a contrast with these scenes, the **enclosed section**★ from Lofer to Saalfelden, in a former glacial gorge, is strikingly uniform.

Wallfahrtskirche Maria Kirchental ⓥ – *4km/2.5mi south of Lofer. At St. Martin bei Lofer turn right off B 311 onto a narrow toll road.*

A destination for pilgrims from all over the province, the church was built between 1694 and 1701 to the plans by the famous architect Johann Bernhard Fischer von Erlach. Its rustic yet graceful architecture recalls the cathedral at Salzburg or, even more, the sanctuary of Maria Plain *(see SALZBURG: Excursions).*

Consecrated in 1701 by the bishop of Seckau, the church was steadily decorated and furnished over the 18C and 19C as the offerings of the pilgrims mounted up. It is nicknamed, not without a touch of humour, the "Pinzgau Cathedral".

About 6km/4mi beyond Lofer the road reaches the Vorderkaser gorge, the first of the Saalach Valley's three **legacies of the forces of nature**★.

Vorderkaserklamm ⓥ – Car parking possible right by the road or a few yards off in the forest. If necessary the stretch as far as the ticket booth can be travelled by car. From the road a 2.5km/1.5mi long footpath leads through the Schüttachgraben natural recreation area, complete with pools for bathing and barbecue areas, to the ticket booth. From here *(about 45min there and back on a well laid out footpath)* an initially quite steep path leads up through the forest to the entrance to the gorge. Sections of this are quite narrow – in some places the cliffs are only 80cm/2.6ft apart. Footbridges lead past waterfalls large and small, right above the thundering torrents in some places. Passages beneath wedged rocks are some of the highlights of the walk. To return to the ticket booth from the end of the gorge, either take a slightly less spectacular path back through the forest or retrace your steps along this one.

Lamprechtshöhle ⓥ – *8km/5mi beyond Lofer. Car park and entrance right by the road. The temperature in the cave is only about 5-7°C/41-45°F, so dress accordingly! It is advisable to wear closed-in shoes as the ground is wet. 45min there and back.* The Lamprechthöhle is one of Europe's most extensive underground networks, covering a total of 44km/27mi. The section of the caves open to the public covers 700m/765yd, a tiny fraction of the whole complex, and ends after a climb up to a rocky crevice through which a waterfall tumbles. A footbridge serves as a viewing platform, from which visitors can look down into the pitch black depths and be very glad that the way back out is illuminated.

1km/0.6mi after the Lamprechtshöhle there is a signpost left to the Seisenbergklamm (gorge). Park the car at the inn or, slightly further along B 311, in the town of **Weißbach**.

Seisenbergklamm ⏱ – *Allow about 1hr for the gorge.* Flights of steps, footbridges and paths give access to the right and left sides of the Weißbach as it roars through a narrow ravine, about 600m/650yd long and up to 50m/164ft deep, divided into two sections. The spectacular appearance of the first section is surpassed nonetheless by the tortured rock formations, gouged out by the action of the water, of the dark **Dunkelklamm**, which forms the end section of the Seisenberg gorge. From the end of this, a footpath climbs steadily up through the forest, following the rock-strewn bed of the Weißbach until it reaches the Gasthof Lohfeyer, idyllically situated in an Alpine pasture against a backdrop of wooded slopes *(about 30min from the gorge to the inn)*.
South of Weißbach the road runs along the floor of a long canyon, whose ever steeper sides form part of the Leoganger Steinberge (right) and Steinernes Meer (left) ranges. From the bend by the Hotel Gut Brandlhof, one can see, in the distance, the snows of the Wiesbachhorn and the Kitzsteinhorn (Hohe Tauern) and, in clear weather, as far as the Großglockner.
The road reaches the Saalfelden basin. This section of the road offers open views. Ahead, the Tauern range can be seen clearly through the Zell am See corridor.

Saalfelden – This market town with 12 centuries of history behind it has plenty to offer visitors: a beautiful site, a historical town centre and rich and varied leisure facilities. In winter Saalfelden is particularly favoured by cross-country skiers, to whom it offers a network of 80km/50mi of ski tracks (up to 160km/99mi jointly with neighbouring Saalach Valley communities).
Towering over the resort are the imposing rock faces of the Steinernes Meer, shot through with streaks of red from the iron ore they contain, which glow in the rays of the sun. The snow-capped peaks of the Hohe Tauern are visible through the dip made by the Zellersee, completing the impressive mountain scene.

Maria Alm – *Southeast of Saalfelden. Detour of 10km/6mi.* In the middle of this town which offers plenty of sports options in both winter and summer stands a pilgrimage church of the same name, whose sharp spire rises to a height of 84m/276ft. The church exterior is Gothic and dates from the early 16C, whereas the interior is Baroque and dates from the 17C and 18C.

Return to Saalfelden and carry on to Zell. At the end of the run the road first skirts the shore of the Zeller See before finally arriving at Zell am See.

* **Zell am See** – *See ZELL AM SEE.*

SAALBACH-HINTERGLEMM**

Salzburg

Population 2 700

Michelin map 926 fold 19 – Alt 1 003m/3 291ft

With accommodation for more than 17 000 visitors, Saalbach is without doubt one of the largest winter sports resorts in Austria. It lies at the heart of the **Glemmtal** Valley, the upper part of which forms the border between the Austrian provinces of Tyrol and Salzburg. This valley runs along the Pinzgauer Grasberge on the eastern edge of the Kitzbüheler Alps close to the Zeller See. Its attraction lies in its wooded rural setting (3 800ha/9 390 acres of forest) and the harmonious contours of its broad, gently falling slopes.
Despite its development as a tourist location, the town has retained its attraction, since buildings are in the traditional style. Saalbach extends from the foot of the Schattberg in the south to that of the Spielberghorn in the north.
The onion tower of the church rises up above the heart of the town, which comprises a steep pedestrianized street with boutiques, restaurants and elegant hotels.
Further up the valley, the town of **Hinterglemm** spreads out at the foot of the Zwölferkogel. It too has developed into an important holiday resort.
Saalbach owes its reputation both to the quality of its accommodation and to its extensive ski area, in which downhill races are frequently held during the world skiing championships. The winter sports resort obviously also boasts a broad range of leisure facilities (swimming pool, ice rink, indoor tennis courts etc).
In the summer, Saalbach is a restful summer holiday destination, from where some beautiful excursions can be made, in particular the **Pinzgau path**★★ *(see ZELL AM SEE)* and the hike to the Tristkogel and to the Torsee Lake.

** **Ski slopes** – The ski slopes extend between 900m/2 950ft and 2 100m/6 890ft in altitude, forming one of the largest ski areas in Austria. A total of 60 ski lifts (including one cable railway, nine cable-cars and 18 chair-lifts) open up 200km/124mi of piste for skiers of all levels.

Sochor/ÖSTERREICH WERBUNG

Ski slope down into the town centre

The snow conditions are generally good from Christmas to April. The lack of altitude is offset by a microclimate, which ensures lower temperatures and considerably more snow than in the surrounding valleys.
This ski area is of particular interest because it encompasses around 12 peaks between which it is possible to ski, all of which have a difference in altitude of almost 1 000m/3 300ft. Lovers of wide open spaces will, however, not find any really high peaks here.
The slopes of the Zwölferkogel and the northern downhill section of the Schattberg-Ost will suit good skiers. Almost the entire ski area will please skiers who are seeking relaxation, in particular the 8km/5mi long run, which links the Schattberg-Ost with Vorderglemm (Mulden and Jausern pistes). They should also try the pistes on the Zwölferkogel (Seekar and family run), the Hasenauer Köpfl (Hochalm piste), the Reiterkogel (pistes 35 and 37), the Kohlmaiskopf (piste 51) and the Bründlkopf. The second run on the Bernkogel is particularly recommended to beginners. Take note, however, that certain unmarked pistes are reserved for snowboarders.
There are far fewer opportunities for cross-country skiing, since only a total of 18km/11mi of cross-country track are available between Vorderglemm and Saalbach and above Hinterglemm.

VIEWPOINTS

★★ **Schattberg-Ost** ⏲ – Alt 2 020m/6 627ft. *45min there and back on the cable railway.* This provides an **overall view** of the Glemmtal Valley and its ski area. In the distance are the limestone massifs of the Loferer and Leoganger Steinberge in the north and of the Hohe Tauern in the south (Wiesbachhorn, Kitzsteinhorn, Großglockner and Johannisberg).

★ **Zwölferkogel** ⏲ – Alt 1 984m/6 509ft. *30min there and back. Ride up in the cable-car from Hinterglemm or continue uphill from Kolling.* The landscape is dominated by the Hohe Penhab and by the Schattberg-West. The view stretches over the entire area around Hinterglemm.

★ **Wildenkarkogel** – Alt 1 910m/6 266ft. *45min there and back. Ride up from Vorderglemm on the Schönleiten cable-car.* From the summit, the end of the Karlift ski lift can be reached in a few moments. There is a good view from here of the Leoganger Steinberge. Walkers may like to follow piste 65 for a while, as it forms a pleasant ridge path.

SALZACHTAL★

Salzburg

Michelin map 926 fold 20

The Alpine valley of Salzach is an artery of the province of Salzburg, whose hooked shape conforms with the bent course of the torrent. Strung out between the Krimml waterfalls and Salzburg is a series of basins, separated by ravines. Until the coming of the railway, each of these isolated sections of the valley tended to lead its own life, quite separate from that of its neighbours.

LOCAL LANDSCAPES

The Pinzgau – The roads to the Gerlos *(see GERLOS-ALPENSTRASSE)* and Thurn *(see KITZBÜHEL: Excursions)* passes give views of the upper Pinzgau Valley (Oberpinzgau), which has been brought out of isolation by the growth of tourism and the construction of hydroelectric works *(see KAPRUN)*. The region of Zell am See and Saalfelden – the Mittelpinzgau – is more lively. It lies at the foot of the Steinernes Meer cliffs, which here mark the Bavarian frontier.

The Pongau – The bottlenecks of the valley between Taxenbach and Lend, upstream, and between Werfen and Golling, downstream, clearly define the Pongau basin. To the east, the Fritztal and Wagrainer Höhe roads provide easy communications with the upper Enns Valley, which explains the attachment of the Radstadt district to the province of Salzburg. Tourist traffic in the Pongau is most intense in the tributary valley of Gastein *(see GASTEINER TAL)*.

The Tennengau – Downstream from the Lueg pass, as far as Hallein, a less mountainous area unfolds. Forest cover and water courses (Golling waterfalls) nonetheless abound. Here the Salzach receives a contribution from the waters of the Lammer, flowing west from the pastoral district of Abtenau and the Salzburg Dolomites. The fine villages of the Tennengau (Abtenau, Golling, Kuchl etc), with their pretty painted and flower-bedecked gables beneath wide, overhanging roofs, have many features in common with Bavaria.

The Flachgau – Below Hallein the Salzach enters the flat land of Salzburg and adds a lively note as it flows through the dignified city of the prince-archbishops. After its confluence with the Saalach, the river forms a natural frontier between Styria and Bavaria, passing the Bavarian cities of Tittmoning and Burghausen before joining the Inn.

★1 FROM LEND TO RADSTADT *70km/44mi*

Via the Hochkönig road and the Wagrainer Höhe

The mountain section of the route between Dienten and Mühlbach has many bends and is usually blocked by snow in winter.

Lend has an industrial character (aluminium plant) and is also the place where the Gasteiner Ache ends its course in a series of falls. Leave the town on the minor road to Dienten and cross the Salzach.

W. Geiersperger/BILDAGENTUR BUENOS DIAS

Hochkönig mountains

The church at **Dienten** soon comes into sight, standing out against the Hochkönig crests whose vertical white cliffs are particularly impressive when lit by the evening sun. Dienten's flower-bedecked farmsteads are spread out along the road, giving way eventually to alpine pastures.

Between Dienten and the Dientener Sattel there is evidence of winter sports activity, with several ski tows. The highest point of the route is reached at the Dientener Sattel (1 370m/4 493ft) at the foot of the rocky barrier formed by the **Hochkönig**.

From this point the road still has several steep sections. The sharp descent into the resort of **Mühlbach** gives further views of the Hochkönig as well as glimpses of the last ridge of the Mandelwand to the east. Mühlbach is a good centre for mountain walking, with a number of huts and mountain hotels (for instance, the Arthurhaus) in the area. Copper has been mined in the district since the Bronze Age.

Take road no 311 southwards as far as St. Johann im Pongau.

The countryside to either side of the direct route from **St. Johann im Pongau** (recognisable by its trademark twin-towered church façade; the neo-Gothic Pongauer Dom was built between 1857 and 1876) to the Enns Valley is most attractive, particularly around **Wagrain**✲. After the low pass at **Wagrainer Höhe** there are views of the snow-capped Dachstein (2 995m/9 856ft) to the northeast; to the south there are glimpses up side valleys of some of the fine peaks of the Radstädter Tauern.

Radstadt - *See RADSTÄDTER TAUERNSTRASSE.*

2 FROM LEND TO SALZBURG *89km/55mi*

The Salzach Valley, closely hemmed in as far as Lend (1 *above*), opens out north of Schwarzach to form the Pongau basin.

Turn right off road 311 to St. Johann im Pongau, and follow the signposts to "Liechtensteinklamm". There is a car park by the gorge.

★ **Liechtensteinklamm** ⌚ - *Allow 1hr there and back on foot. A torch is not absolutely necessary but can be useful as there is a tunnel to go through.* Walkways with handrails alongside the cliffs enable visitors to walk through the gorge itself. Sheer - at times overhanging - rock walls and the varied and unusual formations wrought by water action on the shiny, white-streaked schist rock contribute to the charm of the gorge. At the end of the path, walkers are rewarded by the sight of a majestic **waterfall**★.

Y. Bontoux

Liechtenstein gorge

Return to the main road no 311 and go north towards Salzburg.

Bischofshofen - The largest town in the Pongau occupies a fine **position**★ in the wide Salzach Valley, with the peaks of the Tennengebirge (alt 2 400m/ 7 870ft) to the north and the Hochkönig (alt 2 941m/9 646ft) to the west. Bischofshofen is well-known to ski jumping fans as one of the venues of the Four Hills Tournament.

Pfarrkirche - *To the right of the through road when coming from the south.* This church is the lowest of three churches (the Frauenkirche and Georgskirche are the others) built on a slope and linked by a narrow road, thus forming a typical example of a "family group" of churches. The present church was built in 1450. The massive tower above the transept crossing, in the middle of the

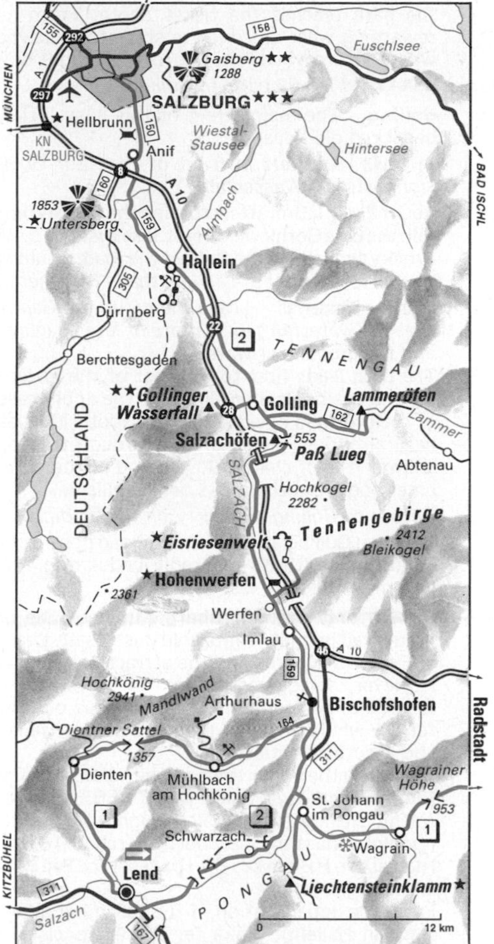

church roof, is the only example of its kind in the province of Salzburg. This is also true of the marble tomb of the Bishop of Chiemsee, who had the church built, Sylvester Pflieger, in the north transept. A copy of the Bischofshofen **Rupertuskreuz**, a processional cross that is Austria's oldest religious work of art (c 700), is on display in the church. The original is in the cathedral museum at Salzburg.

Carry on towards Salzburg. After going through Imlau, the road reveals the imposing fortress of Hohenwerfen to view. Before reaching the fortress, however, turn right in Werfen to visit the Eisriesenwelt caves.

★ **Eisriesenwelt** – *See Höhlen EISRIESENWELT.*

★ **Erlebnisburg Hohenwerfen** ⏲ – *Car parks at the foot of the outcrop on which the fortress stands. From there, 15min on foot up a shaded forest path to the fortress gateway.*

The origins of the fortress date back to the 11C. It took on its present form chiefly in the 16C and 17C, when it was extended and modernised by the archbishops of Salzburg, who used it as a military base, residence, hunting lodge and also as a prison. The guided tour of the fortress (about 1hr) includes a visit to the fortress chapel, the torture chamber and the weaponry. There is also a museum of falconry and a birds-of-prey trail in the front castle. The birds kept here – long-legged buzzards, white-tailed eagles and red kites – give twice daily **flight displays**★ *(about 30min)* demonstrating their skills as hunting birds against the impressive mountain backdrop.

Continue along the road as it runs through the impressive Werfen-Golling section of the valley. This is one of the deepest and most striking of the valleys cutting across the main east-west grain of the Alps and leading to the **Lueg pass**.

The valley makes a sharp bend and narrows even more. The cleverly engineered road leaves the river bank to cross a rise which marks the end of this section of the valley. Before reaching the geographical level of the pass at the entrance to the tunnel, turn right to the Salzach gorge.

Salzachklamm (Salzachöfen) – This gorge is one of three impressive natural features close to the pass, along with the Lammeröfen gorge and Gollinger waterfall. To the right of the approach road stands the pilgrimage church of Maria Brunneck, a Rococo building dating from 1766. From the Gasthaus Paß-Lueg-Hütte, a steep path *(45min there and back)*, slippery in rainy weather, leads to a jumble of rocks forming a natural bridge over the Salzach. It is possible, but difficult, to get right underneath the arch of the bridge by following signs marked "Dom".

About 2km/1.3mi beyond the tunnel at Lueg pass the road reaches the junction of B 159 and B 162. *Turn right towards Abtenau/Lammertal for the Lammeröfen gorge. Detour of 14km/8.7mi.*

Lammeröfen ⏲ – *Straight after the entrance to Oberscheffau, 7km/4mi beyond the junction, park the car to the left of the road next to Lammerklause guesthouse. The walk begins from the next turning left, after the bus stop. 1hr 15min there and back.* After about 25min walk through the relatively wide gorge, the path reaches the ticket booth. From here there is a shorter but more rewarding walk up concrete steps to a viewpoint beneath a natural rock vault, where a narrow cleft in the rock lets light down into the gorge below.

Take road B 162 back to Golling.

Golling – The main street of this busy little place is lined with pretty, flower-bedecked old houses.

In town, turn left in front of the "Zur Goldenen Traube" inn and follow the signposts to "Wasserfall".

About 2km/1.3mi after crossing the railway line, shortly before reaching the waterfall, the Late Gothic **church of St. Nikolaus** (1515, with Baroque interior) can be seen on a rocky pedestal to the right of the road, an unusually exposed **site★** *(footpath to the church to the right of Landgasthaus Torrenerhof in Weissenbachstraße).*

★★ **Gollinger Wasserfall** – *Leave the car in the Gasthof Hubertus car park. Remember that the waterfall can be more or less spectacular depending on the time of year and the amount of water.*

The path leads first to the foot of the lower falls which pours into a series of natural basins. It then climbs to the upper cascade which plunges under a bridge of rock formed by a landslide. A footbridge leads across the waterfall below the natural bridge, giving a view through the spray, accompanied by a refreshing shower free of charge! At the end of the path there is a viewpoint of the water emerging from the rocks on the hillside.

Return to Golling and carry on to Salzburg.

Between Golling and Hallein the road goes through the most attractive part of the Tennengau with its markedly undulating wooded valley sides. The mountains become noticeably less craggy.

Hallein and the Dürrnberg Mines – The history of Hallein has been much influenced by that "white gold dust", salt. Everyday life is concentrated nowadays in Hallein's squares and the attractive pedestrian zone at the heart of the town. However, lovingly restored old houses, sleepy alleyways and other romantic spots are still to be found in the picturesque old town. Hallein is the economic centre for the whole of the region, and a major focal point for local cultural, economic and leisure activities.

Located in the upper town on the north side of the parish church are the home and tomb of **Franz-Xaver Gruber** (1787-1863), the composer of the famous carol *Stille Nacht, Heilige Nacht (Silent night, Holy night)*, which he originally wrote for midnight mass in Oberndorf Church in 1818.

High above Hallein lies the spa resort of **Bad Dürrnberg**, site of important prehistoric archeological finds.

From the upper station of the salt mine cable-car (lower station to the south of town in Hallein), make for the entrance of the mines, heading towards Bad Dürrnberg. On the way, you will pass the pilgrimage church of Mariä Himmelfahrt, built from local pink marble, and **Keltendorf am Dürrnberg**, a reconstruction of a Celtic village and royal tomb.

Salzbergwerk Dürrnberg ⓥ – The tour of the oldest mine in the world open to the public entails a trip in the mine train, and a walk along a footpath through several galleries. A double toboggan (Doppelrutschen) takes you down into the depths of the mountain. The visit ends with a raft trip across the floodlit underground salt lake.

On the drive down to Salzburg there is the option at the crossroads in Anif, instead of turning right onto road B 150 to Salzburg, of heading straight on through the centre of town. Just where this road enters Salzburg are the zoo (Tiergarten) and **Schloß Hellbrunn★** *(see SALZBURG: Excursions).*

★★★ **Salzburg** – *See SALZBURG.*

SALZATAL★★

Steiermark

Michelin map 926 folds 22 and 23

The Salza is a tributary of the upper Enns. Among the last eastern massifs of the limestone High Alps and at the northern foot of the jagged cliffs of the Hochschwab (highest point 2 277m/7 470ft) it traces a furrow which for 70km/45mi is almost uninhabited, except for the villages of Wildalpen and Greith. It offers nature lovers opportunities for delightful expeditions through the woods and along the rapids and pools of the torrent.

FROM HIEFLAU TO MARIAZELL *80km/50mi*

Between Hieflau and Großreifling the route follows the Enns, which is dammed in several places. The setting created by the road bridge and the Wandau weir running parallel, which can be seen shortly after setting off, is most impressive.

On the section between Großreifling and Palfau the road is steep and follows a winding, uphill course under fir trees or the light shade of beeches. There are several glimpses of the smooth sheet of water below and, later, of the once more swirling torrent.
Before Wildalpen the Salza ravines are clothed in darker forest.

Wildalpen – This delightfully situated tourist centre is able to profit from the attractions of its surrounding countryside both in summer and in winter. It is primarily known as a starting point for white-water sports on the Salza (with rafts, kayaks and canoes).
The interesting **Heimat-, Pfarr- und Wasserleitungsmuseum**★ ⏲ gives a visual account of the building of the pipeline which supplies Vienna with water, a remarkable technical feat given its considerable length and only slight drop.

The second water pipeline to Vienna

Two pipelines supply Austria's capital with water. The first, laid in 1873 in the Rax-Schneeberg area of Lower Austria, had a particularly beneficial effect, as it saw an end to the outbreaks of cholera. But it soon proved to be inadequate in the face of the increasing demand for water from Vienna's more than one million inhabitants. Accordingly the possibilities for a second pipeline were investigated, and the Salza Valley, with its considerable water reserves, seemed to offer the best solution. Begun in 1900 after seven years of preparatory work and the examination of 50 springs, this second pipeline was completed in 1910. It is 191.8km/119mi long and passes over 100 aqueducts and through 19 siphon installations. It currently delivers an average of 210 000m^3/7 415 940cu ft per day, satisfying just about 59% of the capital's requirements.

The **Pfarrkirche St. Barbara** with its scalloped tower roof has fine frescoes covering the whole of the interior and remarkable furnishings, the sculpted decoration being, at least in part, the work of Josef Thaddäus Stammel *(see Stift ADMONT)* or his studio.
Above Wildalpen the river flows near the Hochschwab cliffs. The sides of the Riegerin, eroded into needles, are an impressive sight.

Brunn – *Immediately after the Postbus stop at kilometre stone 31.6, turn right.* From the Brunnen wayside shrine, only a few yards from the road, there is a **view**★ down into the bottom of the Brunntal, in the heart of the Hochschwab.
There is also a splendid **view**★★ all along the north slope of the massif, where the rocks are still fantastically shaped by erosion. The cliffs of the Türnach, opposite, are no less impressive.
Near the Kläfferbrücke *(kilometre 23.0)* on the right stands a small hut for the employees looking after the machinery for Vienna's second water pipeline.

Prescenyklause – The rock gateway *(traffic will pass through a tunnel from 2000)* leads through to a dam constructed here to make it possible to release sufficient water to float logs downstream, but it has been out of use since the Salza raftsmen ceased to carry on their dangerous trade in the mid 20C.

Weichselboden – This tiny, scattered community is dominated by the parish church, which was built between 1773 and 1777. To the southeast lies the rocky, steep-sided valley known as "In der Höll" (In Hell).
Between Weichselboden and Mariazell the road, passing for a moment out of sight of the Hochschwab, climbs steadily as far as Greith and continues above the valley, which is now wider but entirely given over to the forest. The landscape becomes gradually less mountainous and the road begins its descent to Gußwerk.

Gußwerk – There is nothing left, apart from two monumental cannons and the town's name, to indicate that it was here that the so-called Mariazeller Guß (Mariazell cast iron), which was of great importance for the arms industry of the Austrian Empire, was produced from 1740 until well into the 19C.
The road does not stay long on the floor of the Mariazell basin, but climbs in wide bends to the centre of pilgrimage.

★ **Mariazell** – *See MARIAZELL.*

SALZBURG***

L Salzburg - Population 147 000

Michelin map 926 folds 5, 19 and 20

Local maps under SALZACHTAL and SALZKAMMERGUT - Alt 424m/1 391ft

Hotels and Restaurants: see The Red Guides Deutschland or Europe

Salzburg, Mozart's birthplace, is a delight from the first sight of the outline of the Hohensalzburg, the symbol of the power of the prince-archbishops. The fortress rises over the roofs and belfries of the town, through which flow the waters of the Salzach as the river bends in its course.

A soft light bathes the shapes of its towers and churches in a wonderful setting. It enjoys the attraction of the nearby Salzkammergut, and it has the prestige of the festival drawing lovers of classical music in July and August each year.

Its picturesque streets with their wrought-iron signs, its spacious squares with sculptured fountains, and the noble architecture of its buildings inspired by bishops with a passion for construction, leave memories which linger for years.

HISTORICAL NOTES

The heritage of the prince-archbishops - The See of Salzburg was founded shortly before 700 by St Rupert and was raised in the following century to an archbishopric. In the 13C the bishops were given the title of Princes of the Holy Roman Empire. Their temporal power extended to Italy, while much of their large revenue came from the mining of salt in the Salzkammergut. Three of these overlords, while governing their estates with skill, showed a taste for building. In a little more than half a century they converted the little town, with its maze of streets, into something resembling an Italian town, with palaces and open spaces.

Wolf Dietrich von Raitenau was elected archbishop in 1587. He was a typical representative of the Renaissance: brought up in Rome and closely connected with the Medicis, he longed to make his capital the Rome of the North. When the former cathedral and the quarter round it were conveniently destroyed by fire, he turned to the Italian architect Scamozzi and asked him to build a cathedral larger than St Peter's in Rome. Raitenau's private life was more than averagely active: he had 15 children by Salome Art, a great beauty for whom he built the château of Mirabell, on the right bank of the Salzach. He was drawn into an unfortunate conflict with the dukes of Bavaria over the salt trade and lost. He was condemned by the Court of Rome and imprisoned in 1612 in Hohensalzburg Castle where he died after five years of captivity. His only project to be completed was his last, his mausoleum in the St. Sebastian cemetery.

His successor, **Markus Sittikus** of Hohenem, undertook to build the cathedral on a more modest scale and entrusted the work to another Italian architect, Santino Solari. To the south of Salzburg he had the mansion of Hellbrunn built as a country house, and the park laid out with fountains.

Paris Lodron took advantage of his long episcopate (1619-53) to complete the work begun by his predecessors. He finished the cathedral, and it was solemnly consecrated in 1628. On this occasion a mass written by the Italian choirmaster, Horatio Benevoli, was sung. It had 53 parts; eight two-part choruses, two string orchestras and two ensembles for brass, woodwind, drums and the cathedral organ. This remarkable achievement began a musical tradition which was to blossom in the following century. Paris Lodron also completed the Residence, near the cathedral, a less austere building than Hohensalzburg Castle. He opened new streets in the town, creating the face of Salzburg for generations to come.

WOLFGANG AMADEUS MOZART (1756-91)

It was in this bishops' city, which owed as much to German as to Italian influences, that Mozart was born on 27 January 1756.

A child prodigy - Leopold Mozart, a talented composer and violinist in the service of the archbishop of Salzburg, recognized early on the potential of the exceptional gifts displayed by his son Wolfgang and his daughter Nannerl, who was four years older. Leopold encouraged the development of their natural talent - the young Wolfgang had a remarkable musical memory and sophisticated ear and was composing by the age of five and a keyboard virtuoso by the age of six, having started learning to play the harpsichord two years previously. The father began to give his son a serious musical education and they undertook what was to be a memorable tour of Europe. Between 1762 and 1766, Leopold and his children were enthusiastically received in Munich, Vienna, Augsburg, Frankfurt, Paris, London and The Hague. At Schönbrunn, Empress Maria Theresa herself embraced the young Wolfgang. Paris published four sonatas for piano and violin by the eight-year-old composer, whose talent continued to blossom, strongly influenced while in London by Johann Christian Bach, the youngest son of Johann Sebastian Bach.

Mozart remained in Salzburg for three years after his return, leaving at the command of Emperor Joseph II, to go to Vienna. The nature of his genius is such that it defies explanation, but Mozart himself was aware that exceptional gifts alone were not

TRAVELLERS' ADDRESSES

Tourist information

Tourist information on Salzburg is available from: **Salzburg Information** (management, marketing, administration, hotel reservations: Auerspergstraße 7, 5020 Salzburg, ☎ 06 62/88 98 70, Fax 06 62/8 89 87 32, Web site: *www.salzburginfo.at*) and **Salzburg Congress** (Auerspergstraße 7, 5020 Salzburg, ☎ 06 62/88 98 70, Fax 06 62/8 89 87 66, Web site: *www.salzburg-congress.at*).

There are also tourist information outlets on the city perimeter and in the centre (from which annual and monthly calendars of events are available):

Open all year:
Mozartplatz, Mozartplatz 5, ☎ 06 62/88 98 73 30;
Hauptbahnhof (Main station), Platform 2a, ☎ 06 62/88 98 73 40;
Salzburg Centre, Münchner Bundesstraße 1, ☎ 06 62/88 98 73 50;
Salzburg South, Park & Ride Car Park, Alpensiedlung-Süd, Alpenstraße, ☎ 06 62/88 98 73 60;
Airport Arrivals Hall, ☎ 06 62/85 12 11 or 85 20 91 or 8 58 09 99.
Open June-Sept:
Salzburg North, Kasern motorway service station, ☎ 06 62/88 98 73 70.

Salzburg Card

This ticket, valid for 24, 48 or 72hr, gives free travel on all public transport in the city (except line 80), as well as free entrance to all sights and other price reductions (including discounts to sights elsewhere in Salzburg province etc; the brochure gives a detailed list). It is available at 200S (24hr), 290S (48hr) or 380S (72hr) from Salzburg tourist information offices, travel agencies, hotel receptions and in branches of the Salzburger Sparkasse.

"Salzburger Sommerjoker"

Those spending only one day visiting the city, with the intention of exploring further afield in the province, may find the "Salzburg Summer Joker" ticket a better alternative to the Salzburg Card. This entitles the bearer to certain reductions in the city itself for 24hr and additionally free admission to over 190 sights throughout the province of Salzburg as well as other discounts. It is available from May-Oct and is valid for 16 days maximum. It costs 495S for adults and 250S for children aged 6-14 (no charge for children younger than 6, or for the third child aged 6-14 in a family party). It is on sale at tourist offices in some branches of the Raiffeisenbank; hotels and guesthouses. For further details call ☎ 06 62/88 98 74, Fax 06 62/66 88 66 (Web site: *www.salzburg.com/sommerjoker*).

City tours and guided tours

Auf den Spuren Mozarts (In Mozart's Footsteps; 1hr 30min coach tour and 1hr in Mozart's house) – Departures daily at 9.30am, 11am, noon, 2pm and 4pm, or by request.
Panorama City Tour (1hr) – Departures daily at 10am, 11am, noon, 1pm, 3pm, 4pm and 5pm, or by request.
Information and reservations from Salzburg Panorama Tours, Schrannengasse 2, ☎ 06 62/88 32 11 0 (Web site: *www.panoramatours.at*).
Mozart City Tour (2hr) – Departures daily at 9.30am, 11am and 2pm.
Salzburg-Informativ (1hr) – Departures daily at 10am, noon, 3pm, 4pm and 5pm.
Salzburg-Exklusiv with bus trip, walk and wine-tasting (4hr) – 15 May-15 Sept daily at 2pm.
Information and reservations from Salzburg Sightseeing Tours, Mirabellplatz 2, ☎ 06 62/88 16 16.

Public transport

Information and tickets for the city bus network can be obtained from the ticket offices of the Salzburg public transport authorities (Griesgasse 21, ☎ 06 62/44 80 62 62; Lokalbahnhof (at the Hauptbahnhof), ☎ 06 62/44 80 61 66; Alpenstraße 91, ☎ 06 62/44 80 62 63). Tickets can also be bought from bus drivers, in tobacconists (Tabaktrafiken) and from ticket machines at the bus stop (tickets for a single trip should be bought in advance in blocks of five, before starting on a journey, as a supplement is charged when they are bought separately from the bus driver or a ticket machine). Tickets must be date-stamped as soon as you get on the bus.

The Salzburg transport authorities also offer transferable daily, weekly, monthly (valid from time of first use) and family-day-trip travel cards for the city area, and a 24hr ticket (valid for the whole transport network, only available in blocks of five), with which you can make as many journeys as you like. These are available from tobacconists and ticket offices (daily, weekly and monthly tickets also from ticket machines).

Inner-city car parks

Park-and-Ride: P+R-Süd, Alpenstraße (all year round, 300 spaces)
P+R-Salzburger Ausstellungszentrum (July and Aug, 4 200 spaces)
Multi-storey (fee-paying): Altstadt-Garage (1 470 spaces), in the Mönchsberg; Bahnhof-garage (150), Südtiroler Platz; Mirabell-Garage (660), Mirabellplatz; Parkgarage Airportcenter (1 445), Innsbrucker Bundesstraße; Parkgarage Auersperg (60), Auerspergstraße 4; Parkgarage Linzer Gasse (400), Glockengasse 4 (Mon-Sat); Raiffeisen-Garage (179), Schwarzstraße 13-15; Parkhaus Salzburg Airport (1 000), at the airport.
Car parks (fee-paying): Akademiestraße; Gebirgsjägerplatz; hellbrunn, Mülln; Petersbrunnstraße; Salzburg Airport.

Post offices

Hauptpostamt (Main post office): Residenzplatz 9, open Mon-Fri 7am-7pm, Sat 8am-10am.
Postschalter im Hauptbahnhof (counter at the main station): Südtirolerplatz 1, open daily 6am-11pm.

Shopping

The main shopping areas include the Altstadt (Old Town), left and right of the Salzach, the areas around the Getreidegasse, the area around the Festspielhäuser, the Mozartplatz, the Kaigasse, the Alter Markt, the Linzer Gasse, the Makartplatz and the Mirabellplatz.

Markets

Around the Andräkirche: Schrannenmarkt (fresh food, vegetables, flowers) Thur (or Wed if Thur is a public holiday) 6am-1pm.
Universitätsplatz and Wiener-Philharmoniker-Gasse: Vegetable market Mon-Fri 6am-7pm, Sat 6am-1pm.

Souvenirs

Craft goods and traditional costume (Trachten): Salzburger Heimatwerk, Residenzplatz 9; Wood carvings, busts of Mozart: Kopfberger, Judengasse 14; hand-crafted wax goods, Lebkuchen specialities: Nagy Johann & Söhne, Linzergasse 32; Mozart souvenirs: Mozartland, Getreidegasse 10; souvenir shop in Mozarts Geburtshaus, Getreidegasse 9; **Mozartkugeln** (round chocolates with marzipan and truffle filling): Café-Konditorei Fürst (inventors of the original recipe), Brodgasse 13, Sigmund-Haffner-Gasse and Mirabellplatz 5; Schatz-Konditorei, Getreidegasse 3.

Pratt-Pries/DIAF

Salzburger Marionettentheater

Entertainment

Großes and **Kleines Festspielhaus**, Hofstallgasse 1, ☎ 06 62/8 04 50. Theatre and musicals, concerts.

Landestheater, Schwarzstraße 22, ☎ 06 62/8 71 51 20. Theatre, musicals and dance.

Kleines Theater, Schallmoser Hauptstraße 50, ☎ 06 62/87 21 54. Theatre and cabaret.

Salzburger Marionettentheater, Schwarzstraße 24, ☎ 06 62/87 24 06. Mozart operas feature predictably quite highly on the programme of this world-famous marionette theatre, which also includes master works by Rossini, Offenbach, Strauss and Tchaikovsky, on recordings by prestigious orchestras. The audience in the old Hotel Mirabell with its Rococo decor is transported into another world of magic and fantasy.

Kammerspiele, Schwarzstraße 24, ☏ 06 62/87 15 12. Youth theatre, cabaret.

SZENE-Salzburg, Anton-Neumayr-Platz 2, ☏ 06 62/84 34 48. Theatre, music and dance.

Rockhouse Salzburg, Schallmoser Hauptstraße 46, ☏ 06 62/88 49 14. Jazz, folk, blues, reggae, heavy metal and rock music concerts.

Kulturzentrum Nonntal, Mühlbacherhofweg 5, ☏ 06 62/84 87 84 0. Live concerts and other events.

Casino Salzburg, Schloß Klessheim in Wals-Siezenheim, ☏ 06 62/85 44 55.

Cinemas

Central Kino, Linzer Gasse 17-19, ☏ 06 62/87 22 82.
Elmo-Kino-Center, St.-Julien-Straße 3-5, ☏ 06 62/87 23 73.
Mozartkino, Kaigasse 33, ☏ 06 62/84 22 22.
Salzburger Filmkulturzentrum, Das Kino, Giselakai 11, ☏ 06 62/87 31 00.

Eating out

Brandstätter – Salzburg-Liefering, Münchner Bundesstraße 69, ☏ 06 62/43 45 35. Restaurant in the hotel of this name; rooms range from the rustic Schankstube to the elegant Zirbelstube. Some of the best cooking in town.

K+K Restaurant am Waagplatz – Waagplatz 2, ☏ 06 62/84 21 56. This restaurant's unique selling point is as "Salzburg's first eatery": guests are fed and entertained in medieval style in a 900 year old vaulted cellar (starts at 8pm; costs 570S for a seven-course meal, welcome drink and programme of entertainment with musicians; enquire about dates; booking recommended). There is also a more "traditional" restaurant in a number of rooms spread over four floors.

Alt Salzburg – Bürgerspitalgasse 2, ☏ 06 62/84 14 76. Cosy, tastefully decorated rooms, in which local products cooked in a truly authentic Austrian fashion are served.

Bei Bruno – Makartplatz 4, ☏ 06 62/87 84 17. Separately run, elegant restaurant belonging to a luxury hotel with excellent food.

Stadtkrug – Linzer Gasse 20, ☏ 06 62/87 35 45. Small, intimate and stylish local restaurant with an extensive wine list. The ideal venue for a candle-lit dinner!

Eulenspiegel – Hagenauerplatz 2, ☏ 06 62/84 31 80. Self-declared as "Austria's most original restaurant" with the Eule bar on the ground floor and its small dining rooms full of nooks and crannies divided over several floors.

For a very special experience, you might try the **Mozart Dinner Concert**, on offer all year round in the Baroque room of the Stiftskeller St. Peter (St. Peter Bezirk I/4): 3 course menu (drinks not included) by candlelight, to the accompaniment of works by WA Mozart (performed by musicians in historical costumes). 560S. Details of dates: ☏ 06 62/82 86 95 0 or 84 84 81. Booking recommended.

The **Stiftskeller St. Peter**, ☏ 06 62/84 12 68 0, with its tradition dating back to 803, in any case offers a pleasant setting (several banqueting rooms and dining rooms) for eating out in style.

Blaue Gans – Getreidegasse 41-43, ☏ 06 62/84 24 91 0. Old vaulted premises and correspondingly traditional Austrian cooking using authentic old recipes.

Sternbräu – Griesgasse 23/Getreidegasse 34, ☏ 06 62/84 21 40. A staggering 14 different dining rooms to cater to every taste, fine arcaded courtyard. Programme of evening entertainment from May to October.

Pitter Keller – Auerspergstraße 23, ☏ 06 62/88 05 52. Earthy beer cellar with local food.

Alter Fuchs – Linzer Gasse 47-49, ☏ 06 62/88 22 00. Informal atmosphere. Daily menus are good value for money.

Krimpelstätter – Müllner Hauptstraße 1, ☏ 06 62/43 22 74. Traditional inn with a large beer garden.

Cafés and bars

Tomaselli – Alter Markt 9. Classic coffee house, where visitors never outstay their welcome.

Fürst – Brodgasse 13. Parent branch of the Konditorei-Confiserie, where the original Salzburger Mozartkugeln are made.

Bazar – Schwarzstraße 3. Stylish café with terrace overlooking the Salzach.

Café-Restaurant Winkler – Mönchsberg 32. Marvellous view of the city.

Augustiner-Bräu – Augustinergasse 4. Abbey brewery since 1621. Beer served in stone tankards. Enormous halls with something of a beer-tent atmosphere and a large, shady beer garden.

Die Weisse – Rupertgasse 10. Rustic inn with its own brewery, serving Weißbier made on the premises (since 1901).

Zum fidelen Affen – Priesterhausgasse 8. Beer and wine cellar with warm wooden panelling.

Zebra – Imbergstraße 11. Ultra-modern cocktail bar. Italian antipasti for anyone feeling a bit peckish.

Daimler's – Giselakai 17. Small restaurant and friendly bar on two floors.

Fridrich – Steingasse 15. Smart bar specialising in wine.

Saitensprung – Steingasse 11. Cocktails and wines in a homely brick-vaulted room, which stays open into the early hours.

Zwettler's – Kaigasse 3. Rustic, relaxed atmosphere for a light meal or simply to enjoy a little drink.

Shamrock Irish Pub – Rudolfskai 12. Typical exported pub, rough-stone walls, live music: rustic, but agreeable.

Vis-à-vis – Rudolfskai 24. Café, bar with brick-vaulted ceiling, bathed in blue neon light.

Salzburger Altstadtkeller – Rudolfkai 26. Live music every day at the "musical landlord's".

Dates for your diary

Mozartwoche: 3rd and 4th weeks in Jan. Solo recitals, chamber, choral and orchestral concerts.

Osterfestspiele: Sat before Palm Sun until Easter Mon. Easter music festival with opera and concerts.

Salzburger Pfingstfestspiele (specialising in Baroque music): Sat before Whit weekend until Whit Mon. Whitsun music festival with opera and concerts.

Salzburger Festspiele: end of July to end of Aug. Salzburg Festival with opera, concerts, theatre, literature and poetry readings, Lieder evenings *(see also below)*.

Ch. Strasser/BILDAGENTUR BUENOS DIAS

Salzburg Festival – "Everyman"

SommerSzene: July. Festival of alternative art: theatre, dance, performances, exhibitions (various venues around the city and immediately surrounding area).

Kulturtage: mid to end Oct. Cultural festival with opera and concerts.

Internationaler Salzburger Jazz-Herbst: early Nov. Autumn jazz festival with jazz, spirituals and Gospel music.

Krampusläufe: Exhibition of traditional customs on 2, 3 and 4 Dec in Getreidegasse; 1st Sat in Dec in Linzer Gasse.

Weihnachtsmärkte (Christmas markets): Mirabellplatz and Domplatz (late Nov to 24 Dec) and in the castle courtyard of Hohensalzburg (every weekend in Advent).

enough to produce lasting results, as indicated by his later claim that no-one had taken greater pains than he to study musical composition, there being few masters whose work he had not studied in depth.

Wolfgang Amadeus Mozart

Early career in Salzburg – In 1769, the teenage Mozart was made Concertmaster of the archbishop of Salzburg's orchestra.

Dedication – Mozart's father believed that a musician's education was not complete until he had visited Italy. This was where Wolfgang would learn to compose an opera. The young composer took the peninsula by storm. In Rome, he wrote out the famous nine-part *Miserere* by Gregorio Allegri, having heard it only once in the Sistine Chapel. On his return to Salzburg, Mozart's output was prolific.

First disappointment – Until 1777, Mozart lived for most of the time in Salzburg. Archbishop Hieronymus Colloredo, who succeeded Archbishop Sigismund in 1772, took a poor view of constant journeys abroad and his relations with his young concert master were on the whole strained. By 1777 Mozart had had a major quarrel with the archbishop, resigned his post and left for Paris, accompanied this time by his mother, who to Mozart's great distress died on the journey. In Paris, he came under the influence of Gluck, who had chosen Paris to begin his reform of opera.

During the following years the quiet life he led at Salzburg encouraged the production of many works including religious music, of which the *Coronation Mass* is a supreme example, and symphonic and lyrical pieces such as *Idomeneo*, an opera which reflects the influence of the French School. In 1781, after a further heated altercation between Wolfgang and Count Arco, representing Archbishop Colloredo, the breach was complete. Mozart left Salzburg for Vienna.

Independence in Vienna – On his arrival in Vienna, the 26-year-old Mozart had only limited means of support. He married Constanze Weber in the year he arrived, and it was in Vienna that he was initiated into the ideals of Freemasonry. Discovery of Handel's oratorios and of further works by Bach, together with the influence of his friend and mentor, Haydn, contributed to the development of his mature style. The public adulation occasioned by works such as *Die Entführung aus dem Serail* (The Abduction from the Seraglio) of 1781 and the Mass in C Minor of 1783 was not repeated, at least in Vienna, where the public failed to appreciate *The Marriage of Figaro* (1786) and *Don Giovanni* (1787). A sombre period began, lightened only by his warm reception in Prague.

The final years (1788-91) – Mozart's career was to end in poverty and destitution. Though nominated "Composer to the Imperial Chamber" by Joseph II, he never received a commission. His final operas, *Così fan Tutte* (1790) and *La Clemenza di Tito* (1791) met with a cool reception, barely mitigated by the success of *The Magic Flute* (late 1791). The great composer was to die before his time, alone and haunted by the spectre of his own death.

On 6 December 1791 the paupers' hearse carried Mozart's corpse to a communal grave in St Mark's Cemetery in Vienna. His remains have never been identified.

Mozart's music – The astonishing rate of production shown by "the divine Mozart" during his short life was equalled only by the ease with which he mastered every form of musical expression: the Köchel catalogue, which lists 626 entries, is evidence of this. As for Mozart's style, it has a charm which makes him a favourite with a wide public and is appreciated even by the unpracticed ear. Pleasant and sparkling motifs ripple beneath a rhythmic counterpoint of charming liveliness.

But spontaneity and brio need not mean lack of depth and Mozart is no buffoon or mere comic-opera musician. Though he may attract, at first, simply by easy writing, the listener finds an exquisitely pure melodic line, sometimes tinged with melancholy. Towards the end of his life this vague sadness turned into despair, forcefully expressed in the 40th Symphony in G minor, *Don Giovanni*, the late string quartets, the "tragic" quintet in G major (K 516) and the *Requiem* (K 626), composed

shortly before Mozart's own death (and not completed). Chopin was so affected by this great choral work that he requested it to be played at his own funeral. These late works reflect the emotional frustration of Mozart's life and his struggle against poverty and illness, and herald the Romantic Movement.

The Salzburg Festival ◷ – Many years were to pass before his native city was to acknowledge Mozart's outstanding place in musical history. The composer's biography was written in 1828 by Georges Nicolas de Nissen, who had married the widowed Constanze in 1809. In 1842 Salzburg put up a statue to Mozart; later the city founded a musical academy named the **Mozarteum**. In 1917 the poet Hugo von Hoffmansthal, the composer Richard Strauss and the producer Max Reinhardt conceived the idea of a Mozart Festival.

The festival was inaugurated in 1920. Those contributing have included many of the great names in 20C music – Lotte Lehmann, Bruno Walter, Toscanini, Furtwängler, Böhm... – while Salzburg itself has been affected indelibly by the personality of **Herbert von Karajan**, who was associated with the festival for over 30 years and instituted the Easter Festival (in 1967) and the Whitsun Festival (in 1973).

The festival is held every year between the end of July and the end of August. The numerous concerts and performances take place at the following locations: the great **Festival Hall** (Großes Festspielhaus – **Z**), built in 1960 by the architect **Clemens Holzmeister**, in the small festival hall (Kleines Festspielhaus) and old Summer Riding School (Felsenreitschule), the **Mozarteum**, the **Landestheater** (**Y**), the Residenzhof and the disused salt mines on Perner Island in Hallein. Mozart may be the centre of attraction but other works of the (mostly classical) repertoire are performed by the cream of the world's musical talent; every year there is a performance of Hofmannsthal's *Jedermann (Everyman)* on the cathedral forecourt. Since reforms to the festival programme introduced in 1992, the festival is placing increasing emphasis on 20C music and theatre. Since 1998, the spring festival has concentrated on Baroque music.

** VIEWPOINTS

Fine views of the city in its setting can be had both from the Mönchsberg hill whose rocky mass hems in the old town and from the Kapuzinerberg (Hettwer Bastei) on the far bank of the Salzach.

★★ **Mönchsberg** ⓥ (**Z**) – *Parking: see below.*

From the Gstättengasse (**X 12**) a **lift** goes up to a terrace just below the Café Winkler, from which there is a fine general **view** of the city. Modern Salzburg spreads out along the right bank of the Salzach, while the old town, bristling with domes and church towers, lies crowded between the river and the Hohensalzburg Fortress. To the south on the horizon are the Tennen- and Hagengebirge, the Untersberg and the Salzburg Alps; eastwards the Kapuzinerberg and, in the background, the Gaisberg, mark the city boundaries.

★★ **Hettwer Bastei** (**Y**) – *Climb up to the Kapuzinerkirche via the steep ramp reached from the Linzergasse through a covered passageway. From the church, go downhill again for about 50m/55yd, turn left and follow the sign "Stadtaussicht-Hettwer Bastei" to the viewpoint.*

The Hettwer Bastei (bastion) on the south side of the Kapuzinerberg gives fine **views** over Salzburg, particularly early in the day, when the morning light enhances the green of the many copper-clad roofs, brings out the textural qualities of the old part of the city, and emphasizes the dramatically sculpted forms of the collegiate church and the cathedral.

Return via the series of steps leading to the Steingasse.

The Steingasse, leading to the 17C Steintor (city gate), is so narrow that the marks made by carts are visible on the walls of the houses.

★★ OLD TOWN

Park outside the old town (pedestrians only) and outside the "blue zones" (east bank); underground car parking (Altstadtgaragen) is available under the Mönchsberg. Walk to the Domplatz.

Since 1997, Salzburg Old Town has been classified as a World Heritage site by UNESCO.

Domplatz (**Z**) – Three porticoes link the buildings surrounding this square, the cathedral and the former ecclesiastical palaces. In the centre is a column dedicated to the Virgin Mary (1771).

Ball/BILDAGENTUR BUENOS DIAS

SALZBURG

Auerspergstraße .... V 3
Bürglsteinstraße .... X 5
Erzabt-Klotz-Str. .... X 9
Gstättengasse .... X 12
Kaiserschützenstr. .... V 20
Lindhofstr. .... V 22
Mirabellplatz .... V 26
Nonntaler Hauptstr. .... X 29
Nußdorfer Straße .... X 31
Rainerstraße V
Schießstrattstr. .... V 33
Schwatzstr. .... V 34
Späthgasse .... X 37

Salzburger Barockmuseum . V M³

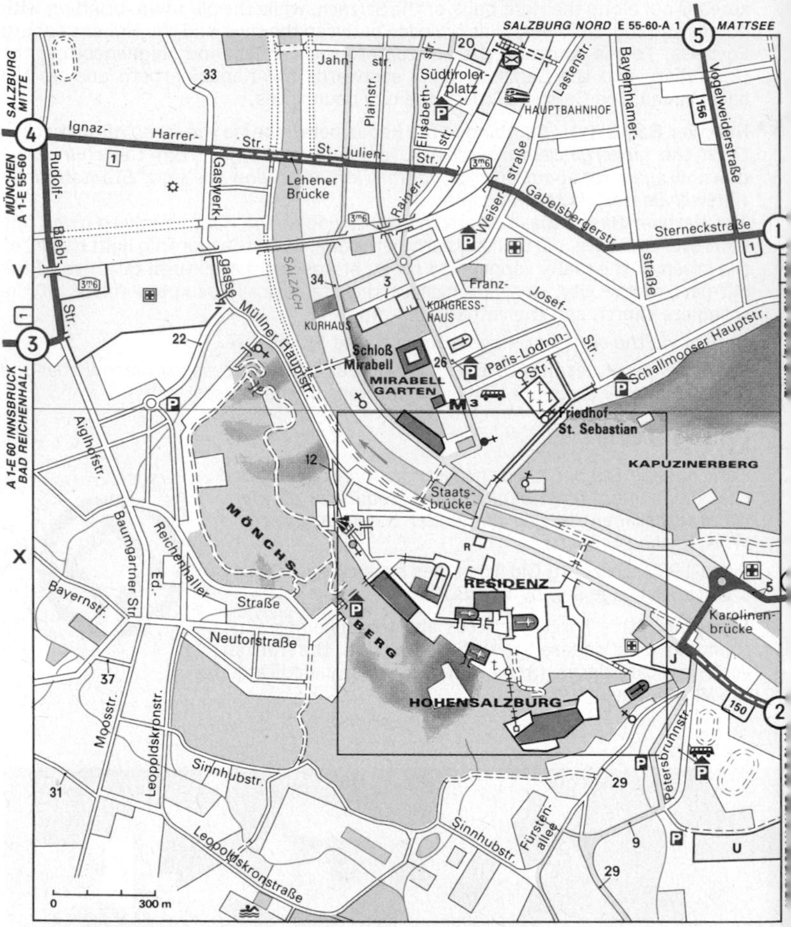

★ **Dom** (**Z**) – The cathedral, which was built from 1614 to 1655, is a huge construction in which the Baroque style shows through late Italian Renaissance features.

The west front, flanked by two symmetrical towers, is of light-coloured Salzburg marble. The pediment between the two towers, dominated by the statue of Christ, is adorned with the coats of arms of archbishops Markus Sittikus and Paris Lodron, flanked by statues of Moses and Elijah.

Below them are the figures of the four Evangelists and in front of the main door are statues of St Rupert, St Virgil, St Peter and St Paul. The modern bronze doors (1957-58) in relief have been designed on the theme of Faith *(left)* by Toni Schneider-Manzell, Hope *(right)* by Ewald Mataré and Charity *(centre)* by Giacomo Manzù.

The interior is impressive in both size and richness of its marble, stucco and paintings. Mozart was baptized in the Romanesque baptismal font in 1756.

The **crypt** was completely remodelled after traces of the Romanesque cathedral had been uncovered (look at the plan of the succession of different buildings on the same spot on the pavement beneath the central rotunda, from the episcopacy of St Virgil in the 8C). The tombs of the prince-archbishops and a Romanesque Crucifix may be seen in the crypt.

Dommuseum ⏲ – Featured here is the cathedral treasure and the archbishops' gallery of "art and wonders" (Kunst- und Wunderkammer) presented as it was in the 17C. The museum also houses religious art from the Middle Ages to the present from the presbyteries of the Salzburg archbishopric.

In the Kapitelplatz is the Kapitelschwemme, a drinking trough for the horses of members of the chapter. The trough, built in 1732 by Archbishop Leopold Anton Firmian, is in the form of a monumental fountain.

From the square a street leads uphill to the station of the **Hohensalzburg funicular** ⏲.

★★ **Hohensalzburg** (Z) – The former stronghold of the prince-archbishops stands on a block of Dolomite rock, about 120m/400ft above the Salzach. The castle was begun in 1077 by Archbishop Gebhard, who was an ally of the Pope and wished to secure a safe retreat from the threats of the princes of South Germany who were supporting the Emperor in the war between Church and empire. The castle was frequently enlarged and remodelled, becoming a comfortable residence by the addition of state rooms. The archbishops often resided there until the end of the 15C, reinforcing it considerably by the addition of towers, bastions for cannon and barbicans and the construction of magazines and arms depots.

At the exit from the upper station, turn left to the panoramic terrace from which stairs and a postern lead into the fortress. Go past the guided tours office and a little way downhill, bearing right along the lists and round the fortified nucleus of the inner castle until you come out in a square opposite the south wall of the **St. Georgskirche**, which is decorated with two beautiful marble reliefs: a group of statuary in red Salzburg marble of Archbishop Leonhard von Keutschach (1495-1519) between two priests, and above it a Crucifixion.

The door to the right of the church leads to the terrace of the **Kuenburgbastei** from where there is a good **view**★★ of the old town, particularly its domes and belfries.

Return to the square (at the end of the tour take the steps "Abgang zur Stadt" at the east end to return into town) and go straight ahead through the castle by the vaulted "Feuergang" passage which is equipped with cannon.

Castle and Museum ⌚ – From the Reck watchtower there is a **panorama**★★, which is particularly interesting towards the Tennengebirge and the Salzburg Alps (south). In the castle is a hand-operated barrel organ dating from 1502. It plays melodies by Mozart and Haydn as well as the original 1502 chorale.

The state rooms, formerly the archbishops' apartments, were fitted out by **Leonhard von Keutschach** and have kept their original decorations in the form of walls adorned with Gothic woodcarvings, doors fitted with complicated ironwork and coffered ceilings with gilded studs. In the Gilded Room is a monumental porcelain stove, dating from 1501, the work of a local potter. It is decorated with flowers and fruit, scenes from the Bible and the coats of arms and portraits of sovereigns of the period.

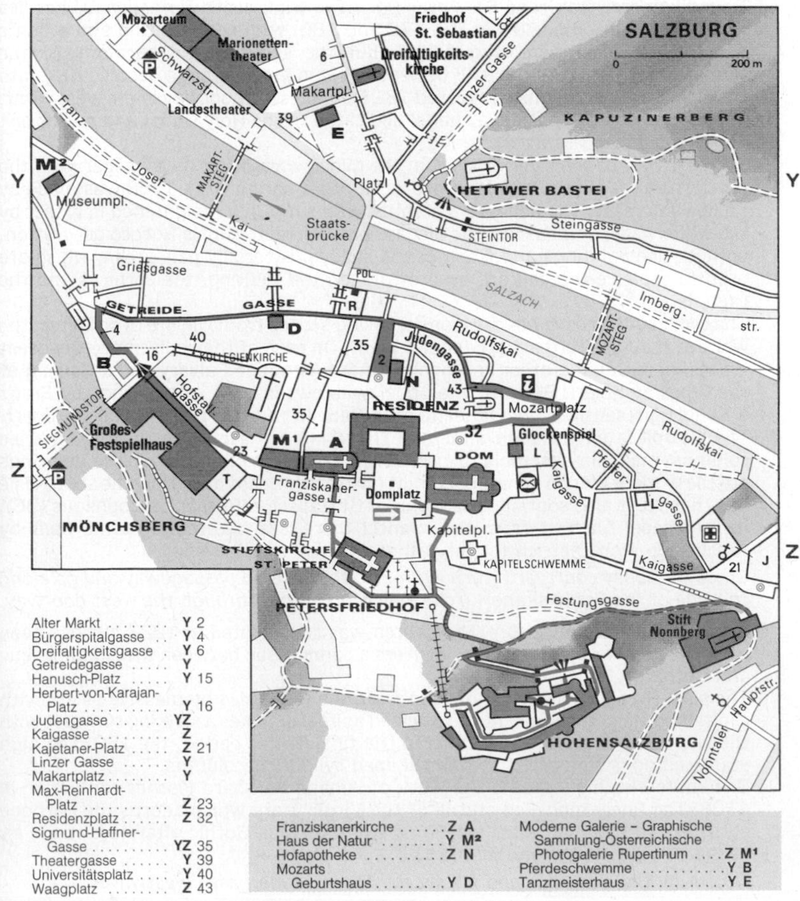

The Hall of Justice has a coffered ceiling on which the beams are adorned with shields bearing the arms of the province and the dioceses or abbeys under the archbishop and those of the dignitaries of his court. The hall also has four red-marble columns with twisted barrels bearing the coat of arms (a turnip) of Leonhard von Keutschach.
An interesting **museum★** (Burgmuseum) may also be visited. Apart from records – plans and prints – showing the development of the town throughout the history of the Salzburg archbishopric, this museum contains a remarkable series of medieval works of art (arms, armorial bearings etc).

Go back down the ramps and follow the path on the right to Nonnberg convent.

Stift Nonnberg (Z) – This Benedictine convent was founded around 700 by St Rupert, whose niece, St Erentrud, was its first abbess. It is the oldest convent in the German-speaking world.
The **Stiftskirche**, enclosed by its churchyard, is in Late Gothic style and dates from the end of the 15C. The main doorway was built between 1497 and 1499; it incorporates the older Romanesque tympanum with its figures of the Virgin Mary flanked by John the Baptist and St Erentrud on one side and by an angel and kneeling nun on the other. The high altar is adorned by a fine carved and gilded altarpiece; in the central section is a Virgin and Child attended by St Rupert and St Virgil, while the wings depict scenes from the Passion. The vast crypt contains the tomb of St Erentrud. The highly compartmentalized vaulting rests on 18 columns.
In the **Johanneskapelle** there is a Gothic altarpiece of 1498, attributed to Veit Stoß, with a lively central section showing the Nativity.

Go down to the lower station of the funicular via the Festungsgasse, then into the Petersfriedhof immediately on the left.

★★ **Petersfriedhof** (Z) – This touching cemetery, which evokes the past history of the town, abuts on the vertical rock wall of the Mönchsberg, in which catacombs were hollowed out. Wrought-iron grilles under Baroque arcades enclose the chapels where several generations of the patrician families of Salzburg lie. The 15C Margaretenkapelle is a delicate construction dating from the end of the Gothic period.

★★ **Benediktinerstiftskirche St. Peter** (Z) – The triple-aisled Romanesque basilica was drastically remodelled in the 17C and 18C, with new vaulting and a dome above the transept crossing added, but the serenity and harmony of the Romanesque structure can still be sensed behind the Baroque decor. Entry into the building is via the much restored 13C Romanesque doorway in the west front. Immediately on the right is a chapel dedicated to the Holy Ghost and on the left another dedicated to St Wolfgang.
The best view of the interior is from the gilded **wrought-iron grille★** separating the porch from the nave. This elaborate work of art dating from 1768 was made by Philip Hinterseer. The building's architectural simplicity, heightened in effect by the white walls, emphasizes the elegance of Benedikt Zöpf's Rococo decoration, with its fine paintings and fresh pastel shades, especially pale green, which are used to enhance the delicate stuccowork on the vaulting, the cornices and the capitals.
The ceiling of the nave has frescoes showing scenes from the life of St Peter, the work of the Augsburg artist, Johann Weiß. On each of the walls above the great arches, note, among other compositions, an Ascent to Calvary and a Raising of the Cross by Solari. Beneath the upper windows is a set of paintings by Franz X König representing *(right)* the life of St Benedict and *(left)* the life of St Rupert. The altarpiece on the high altar and those in the nave, with their red-marble columns, make an ensemble of great richness. Most of the altarpiece paintings are the work of Martin Johann Schmidt ("Kremser Schmidt"). Only the south aisle has chapels. It also contains the tomb of St Rupert, a Roman sarcophagus (3C). In the chapel furthest from the chancel there is a fine marble tomb built by Archbishop Wolf Dietrich for his father, Werner von Raitenau.

Cross the abbey courtyard, turn right into the covered passageway and go along the side of the Franziskanerkirche which is entered through the west doorway.

★ **Franziskanerkirche** (Z A) – The church was consecrated in 1223 but has been remodelled several times since. It offers a comparison between the Romanesque and Gothic styles.
The plain Romanesque nave, divided from the side aisles by massive pillars with capitals adorned with foliage and stylized animals, makes a striking contrast with the well lit chancel which dates from the final Gothic period, the 15C. The high star vaulting is supported by palm-shaped cylindrical columns.
The impressive high altar is the work of Johann Bernhard Fischer von Erlach in 1708. The finely modelled statue of the Virgin Mary which adorns the Baroque altarpiece of the high altar was formerly part of a Gothic altarpiece made by Michael Pacher at the end of the 15C.

Go out by the side door and follow the Franziskanergasse westwards.

Moderne Galerie - Graphische Sammlung - Österreichische Photogalerie Rupertinum ⓥ (**Z M**[1]) - This museum is located in a 17C town house and contains a contemporary art collection. Temporary exhibitions illustrate the avant-garde movements.

North of Max-Reinhardt-Platz stands the massive Baroque Kollegienkirche (University Church), the work of architect Johann Bernhard Fischer von Erlach. Continue west past the Festspielhaus (Festival Hall).

From the Herbert-von-Karajan-Platz (**36**) there is a tunnel (the Siegmundstor), about 135m/150yd long, which was made in 1767 under the Mönchsberg hill. Look back for a fine view of the Hohensalzburg Fortress and the church of St. Peter.

Pferdeschwemme (**Y B**) - This monumental horse trough was built about 1700. It was reserved for the horses in the archbishops' stables and is adorned with a sculptured group, the *Horsebreaker* by Mandl, and frescoes depicting fiery steeds.

★★ **Haus der Natur** ⓥ (**Y M**[2]) - *Allow at least 2hr for the natural history museum's 80 rooms.* This well-presented exhibition includes a number of lively displays on various aspects of the natural world. Particularly interesting sections are those on dinosaurs, the world of the sea with its large display of sharks, the world of outer space, people, pets, human and animal characters in myth and fable, giant rock crystals, the aquarium and the reptile house.

★ **Getreidegasse** (**Y**) - This is one of the main streets of old Salzburg. Like the rest of the Old Town, which, being crowded between the Mönchsberg and the Salzach, could expand only vertically, it is narrow and lined with five- and six-storey houses.

A lively shopping street, it is adorned with many wrought-iron signs which provide a picturesque touch, while the houses with their carved window frames lend the street a certain elegance.

Bohnacker/ÖSTERREICH WERBUNG

Getreidegasse

Mozarts Geburtshaus ⓥ (**Y D**) - *Getreidegasse 9.* Leopold Mozart lived on the third floor from 1747 to 1773. It was there that Wolfgang was born on 27 January 1756.

In this flat, where Mozart composed many works of his youth, numerous mementoes of his life can be seen, such as his violins, including the violin he used as a child. His harpsichord, his piano and musical manuscripts are on display, as well as a selection of portraits and letters.

A "bourgeois interior at the time of Mozart" has been installed in the house. The first and second floors house a display on the theatre with models of stage sets and literature on Mozart's operas.

Particularly passionate Mozart fans may also like to visit the Tanzmeisterhaus *(see below)*.

Continue along the Getreidegasse past the town hall (Rathaus, **R**) on the left and on the right the Alter Markt (Old Market Square), with a fountain to St Florian and a curious **Hofapotheke** (**YZ N**), a chemist's shop with its Rococo interior.

Judengasse (**YZ**) - This street is in the middle of the former Jewish Ghetto. It is narrow and picturesque and, like the Getreidegasse, adorned with wrought-iron signs. At no 4, note a sculptured group in stone representing the Virgin of Maria Plain *(see Excursions below)*.

Through the Waagplatz make for the Mozartplatz; on the north side, instead of roofs and belfries, rises the wooded spur of the Kapuzinerberg.

Residenzplatz (**Z 32**) - Until the 16C there was a cemetery on this site. Prince-archbishop Wolf Dietrich created the present square when he had his cathedral built. It was adorned in the 17C with a fine fountain (group of horses, a Triton and Atlantes). The square is bounded on the south by the cathedral and to the west by the Residenz. On the east is the **Glockenspiel** (**Z**), a carillon of 35 bells cast in Antwerp at the end of the 17C and set up in Salzburg in 1705.

★★ **Residenz** (**Z**) – The present buildings, which were modified in 1595 on the initiative of Prince-archbishop Wolf Dietrich, took the place of a building which had been the residence of the prince-archbishops since the middle of the 11C. The northwest wing is late 18C.
In the Conference Hall the young Mozart conducted many concerts before the guests of the prince-archbishop. A door in one of the rooms gives an unexpected view down into the Franziskanerkirche. It was in this palace that Emperor Franz Joseph received Napoleon III in 1867, and the German emperor, Kaiser Wilhelm I, in 1871.

Residenzgalerie ⓥ – The gallery houses a collection in true princely tradition of important European paintings from the 16C to the 19C. A highlight of the collection is the 17C Dutch painting, which includes works by great masters such as Rembrandt, Rubens and Brueghel. The valuable exhibition, which occupies 15 state rooms, is rounded off with a display of 19C masterpieces.

★ **Mirabellgarten** (**V**) – Little is left of the Altenau mansion built at the beginning of the 17C by Prince-archbishop Wolf Dietrich for Salome Alt *(see Historical Notes above)* and given the name "Mirabell" by Markus Sittikus. It was remodelled by the architect Johann Lukas von Hildebrandt in the following century to form part of the great ensemble known as Schloß Mirabell. It was badly damaged by fire in 1818 and subsequently rebuilt in a much more sober style. Today it houses the offices of the city administration.
Of the original building, the monumental **marble staircase**★★ with its sculptures by Raphael Donner still stands, together with the richly decorated Marmorsaal (Hall of Marble), all gilt and coloured stucco, now used for wedding ceremonies and chamber concerts.
The gardens were laid out in 1690 by Fischer von Erlach. With their abundance of flowers, statues and groups of sculpture adorning the pools, they are a favourite place in which to relax. From a terrace there is a fine view over the gardens themselves towards the old fortifications and the Hohensalzburg.
The buildings of the old orangery have been restored and enclose a pretty courtyard with colourful flowerbeds. The south wing houses a small museum of Baroque art.

★ **Salzburger Barockmuseum** ⓥ (**M**[3]) – Designs for frescoes, paintings and sculptures and a collection of master sketches form the contents of this attractive little museum which sets out to give a general view of 17C and 18C European art.

Tanzmeisterhaus (Mozart-Wohnhaus) ⓥ (**Y E**) – *Makartplatz 8. Tour with audio-guide.* The Tanzmeisterhaus, which was the Mozart family home from 1773 to 1787, was partially destroyed by bombs in 1944, but was rebuilt in 1994-95.
Mozart, who lived in the house until 1780, composed a number of his works here. The museum displays literature on the Mozart family and their contemporary environment as well as a collection of historical keyboard instruments. The visit ends with two video shows on Mozart's travels from 1762 to 1791 (about 25min) and the life of his family (about 30min), illustrated with passages of music.
The house also contains a **Mozart-Ton- und Filmmuseum** ⓥ, with a collection of audio and video clips from 1896 to the present. Visitors can choose a clip and then listen to it or watch it using the archive's equipment.

Friedhof St. Sebastian (**VX**) – Only the doorway in the Rococo style (1752), surmounted by a bust of the patron saint, remains of the original church of St. Sebastian, which was destroyed by fire in 1818 and subsequently rebuilt. Behind a wrought-iron grille is the tomb of **Paracelsus**, a doctor and philosopher of the Renaissance who died in Salzburg in 1541.
Adjacent to the north side of the church are cloisters whose arches shelter funerary monuments and surround a shaded cemetery which in about 1600 was made into the likeness of an Italian *campo santo.* In the centre stands the curious tomb of Wolf Dietrich; the interior is lined with porcelain in many colours. In the central lane of the cemetery are the tombs of Mozart's wife and father.

Dreifaltigkeitskirche (**Y**) – This church was built from 1694 to 1699 by the great architect Fischer von Erlach.
The oval dome and the interior are in the Baroque style. As in the Karlskirche in Vienna, the originality and daring of this dome make it a perfect framework for the frescoes by Rottmayr.

Stiegl's Brauwelt ⓥ – *West of the city centre. Bräuhausstraße 9. From the centre, take Neutor-, Moos- and Nußdorfer Straße (**X 31**). Bräuhausstraße is the fourth turning on the left.* The exhibition in the old malthouse of one of Salzburg's largest breweries covers the whole world of beer, obviously with the emphasis on Austria and Salzburg: ingredients, comparison of beer production around the world, advertising. The display is very interesting, and has interactive sections. It ends with a tasting session in the brewing room.

SALZBURG

Street	Grid
Bürglsteinstr.	U 5
Eberhard-Fugger-Str.	T 7
Gaisbergstr.	T 10
Georg-Nikolaus-von-Nissen-Str.	U 13
Grazer Bundesstr.	T 14
Hellbrunner Brücke	U 16
Innsbrucker Bundesstr.	U 17
Itzlinger Hauptstr.	T 19
Kleßheimer Allee	T 22
Maxglaner Hauptstr.	U 24
Minnesheimstr.	T 25
Münchner Bundesstr.	T 27
Nonntaler Hauptstr.	U 29
Plainbergweg	T 31
Siezenheimer Str.	T 34
Sterneckstr.	T 38
Vogelweiderstr.	T 42

EXCURSIONS

★★ **Gaisbergstraße** - *13km/8mi. Leave Salzburg on ①, B 158 towards St. Gilgen. After about 4km/2:5mi turn right along the road towards Gaisberg, along a well-laid road (maximum gradient, 1 in 8), which passes through woods, past meadows and is even hewn out of the rock in some places.*

Park the car at the end of the road by the plateau below the Gaisberg summit. There is a **view**★ of Salzburg, the Salzach gap and the Salzburg Alps. Follow the path between the guesthouses, past the transmitting station, and a few minutes walk will bring you to the cross that marks the summit, at an altitude of 1 288m/4 226ft: **panorama**★ of the mountains of the Salzkammergut and the Dachstein massif.

★ **Schloß Hellbrunn** ⓥ **(U)** - The castle, once the summer residence of Archbishop Markus Sittikus, was built between 1612 and 1615 in the spirit of the great Italian villas of the Veneto.

The banquet hall, with its *trompe-l'œil* painting, and the high, domed Octagon or music room are most interesting. A tour of the attractive gardens and fountains is full of surprises: fountains and caves are adorned with human figures, a "mechanical theatre" has 113 figures which are set in motion by the action of water to the music of an organ, and fountains suddenly shower the unwary visitor. Close by the castle is a zoo, the **Tiergarten Hellbrunn** ⓥ *(access via the Schloßpark or main entrance in Hellbrunner Allee)*. It has generously proportioned outdoor enclosures, a tropical house, an aquarium and a children's zoo.

★ **Volkskundemuseum** ⓥ - *In the Monatsschlößl in the Schloßpark*. The hunting lodge built for Archbishop Markus Sittikus in 1615 now houses a collection on regional folklore with some outstanding exhibits. The display, which ranges from touchingly simple to extremely sophisticated, occupies three floors and covers traditional customs, costume, popular religion and way of life in Salzburg province.

★ **Untersberg** ⏲ – *12km/7.5mi plus 1hr there and back, including 15min by cable-car. Leave Salzburg on ② towards Berchtesgaden. Just after the major St. Leonhard crossroads, bear right onto the road leading to the lower cable-car station.*
At a height of 1 853m/6 079ft, there is a splendid **panorama** of the Salzburg basin, the Salzburg Alps (Watzmann, Steinernes Meer, Staufen), the Wilder Kaiser and the Dachstein.

Schloß Leopoldskron (**U**) – Mirrored in its tranquil lake, complete with ducks and swans, Leopoldskron was built in 1744 as a summer residence for Prince-archbishop Leopold Anton Firmian by Father Bernhard Stuart, a Benedictine monk from the Scottish St James' Convent at Regensburg, who was also Professor of Mathematics at Salzburg University. It was acquired in 1918 for cultural and artistic purposes by Max Rêinhardt, one of the founders of the Salzburg Festival. Its charming setting, its car-free lakeside walk, its modern swimming pool and other recreational facilities make Leopoldskron a pleasant place to relax in, especially in summer.

The Trapp Family

Rodgers and Hammerstein's Broadway musical *The Sound of Music* (1959, made into a film in 1965 with Julie Andrews) was based on the true story of the Von Trapp family. The young novice Maria Kutschera (1905-87) became governess to widower Baron Georg von Trapp's seven children and finally married the baron himself. She formed a family choir with the children in the mid-1930s. In 1938, they fled Nazi rule in Austria and emigrated to the USA, where they were able to earn a living with their musical activities.
Settings used for the film in Salzburg include the Benedictine Nonnberg Abbey. the Hohensalzburg Fortress, Schloß Mirabell and the Mirabell garden, the Felsenreitschule, where the family sing their farewell song, and Schloß Leopoldskron, where the front facing the lake is used as Baron Trapp's house, and in whose music pavilion the love scene takes place.

Maria Plain (**T**) – *After crossing Plain bridge, turn right onto Plainbergweg, the road which ends at the church of Maria Plain. Park the car by "Plainwirt" inn.*
The church, built from 1671 to 1674 crowning a bluff, has a squat façade framed by two towers. The interior is ornate: the altars in the chancel and the side chapels are adorned with altarpieces, and the pulpit, organ, confessionals and chancel screen were made in the late 17C in an exuberant Rococo style.

Mattsee – *23km/14mi. Leave Salzburg on ⑤ and Itzlinger Hauptstraße. Follow the road through Bergheim, Lengfelden and Elixhausen.*
This pleasant summer holiday resort is the main community in the area of the Trumer lakes (Obertrumer See, Mattsee, Grabensee). It offers a variety of leisure activities, and also, for cultural interest, the **Stift Mattsee**, an abbey founded here in 777. The 14C abbey church features Baroque interior decor and a huge 18C tower; the cloisters house 14C to 19C tombstones; and the priory contains an abbey museum and cellar.

SALZBURGER SPORTWELT AMADÉ**

Salzburg

Michelin map 926 folds 20 and 33

The vast **ski area** covers a distance of almost 30km/18.5mi between the Tennen range and the Radstädter Tauern. It comprises a group of just under a dozen small resorts, which however offer a countless range of downhill and cross-country skiing opportunities to holders of a joint ski pass.
Overall, no fewer than 120 ski lifts give access to 320km/199mi of piste in the area. In practice however, due to the distances between the individual resorts and the lack of skiable links between some of the peaks, it is difficult to explore the entire area on skis. Furthermore, snow cover in the valley is generally only average, because of the relatively low altitude (around 800m/2 625ft). Since there are also no Alpine peaks, none of the ski slopes have a drop in altitude of more than 1 000m/3 300ft. Consequently, despite the area it covers, Sportwelt Amadé is most suitable for those seeking a comfortable, relaxed skiing holiday, rather than thrills, on a variety of ski runs in a pleasant wooded setting.

Two smaller networks of slopes stand out in particular within the overall ski area. First of all Zauchensee, Flachauwinkl and Kleinarl (88km/55mi of piste in total) and secondly Flachau, Wagrain and Alpendorf. Each of these areas can be explored in a single day. The most interesting places are mentioned below.
For cross-country skiers, Radstadt (65km/40mi of track), Filzmoos (35km/22mi) and Flachau (40km/25mi) are particularly recommended.

✻ **Zauchensee** - Alt 1 361m/4 465ft. Zauchensee is by far the highest-lying resort in the Salzburg Sportwelt Amadé and consequently offers the best snow cover in the ski area as a whole. This small winter sports resort is especially popular with keen downhill skiers, who are able to indulge their passion here in a beautiful **low-altitude mountain setting**★ with ski runs of varying degrees of difficulty. Those wishing to sample an authentic village atmosphere and a more extensive range of leisure facilities should visit the charming little village of Altenmarkt im Pongau (Gothic church), which lies in the valley at an altitude of 840m/2 756ft.

★★ **Schwarzwand-Seilbahn** - Alt 2 100m/6 890ft. *For skiers only.* The cable-car leads to the foot of the Schwarzkopf, from where there is a magnificent **panorama**★★ of the Tennengebirge range, the Dachstein and the Radstädter Tauern.

★ **Rauchkopfhütte mountain lodge** - Alt 1 890m/6 201ft. *Travel up on the chair-lift.* **Panorama**★ of the Dachstein, the Radstädter Tauern and the entire area around Zauchensee.

Flachauwinkl - The pistes are on two slopes, with the A 10 motorway running between them. They are connected by a small train, pulled by a tractor.

★★ **Roßkopf** - Alt 1 929m/6 329ft. *Travel up on the* **Flachau cable-car** ⓥ. At the top of the cable-car ride there is a remarkable **view**★ to the right over Modermandl and Faulkogel to the south.
Then take the chair-lift up to the Roßkopf. It is well worth climbing up to the peak itself, which only takes a few minutes, to enjoy the **panorama**★★ over the ski areas of Zauchensee and Flachau and over the Dachstein, the Radstädter Tauern and the Hohe Tauern.
Note that blue piste 21, which runs from the cable-car mountain station down into the valley, can also be tackled on foot, making a long, pleasant **walk**★, for which sticks and waterproof climbing boots are required. The only particularly steep stretch is the final kilometre on the main downhill piste.

Kleinarl - Alt 1 014m/3 327ft. This attractive village, which enjoys plenty of sun, lies at the foot of a rocky massif with a highly varied relief. The ski pistes on the southern slopes offer comfortable runs for fairly good skiers.

★★ **Mooskopf** ⓥ - *Take the Kleinarl chair-lift and then the Bubble-Shuttle chair-lift. The peak itself can be reached on foot in just a few minutes.* From the peak a splendid **panorama**★★ opens up over the limestone massifs of the Tennengebirge range and the Dachstein to the north, the impressive Ennskraxn massif and the Glingspitze peak to the south, and further to the west over the Hohe Tauern with the Großglockner, Hocharn, Ankogel group and Hochalmspitze peak in the background.

✻ **Wagrain** - Alt 838m/2 749ft. The holiday resort of Wagrain has the best accommodation and the most generous network of ski lifts in the entire area. It has acquired a certain fame by being the home of the factory of the largest Austrian ski manufacturer, Atomic.
Wagrain is centrally located within Sportwelt Amadé, but unfortunately suffers, as does its neighbour Flachau, from unreliable snow cover. The busy pistes follow easy routes through dense forest.

★ **Koglalm** - Alt 1 878m/6 161ft. **Panorama**★ over Wagrain, Flachau and Kleinarl with the Tennengebirge range, the Dachstein and the Niedere Tauern in the background. From here, good skiers in the winter and walkers in the summer are able to reach the **Saukarkopf**, where a broader **panorama**★★ opens up. A small ski lift and good snow cover invite skiers to make the most of the pistes here.

SALZKAMMERGUT★★★

Oberösterreich, Salzburg and Steiermark

Michelin map 926 folds 20 and 21

Salt, a traditional emblem of good health and a source of riches, has given the Salzkammergut its name and, until recently, exceptional economic importance. In the 20C tourism has helped restore the prosperity of this former salt area of which the long-established spa resort of Bad Ischl is the centre.

A total of some 76 lakes, together with numerous mountains including the massive Dachstein and Totes Gebirge ranges, explain why the area has become a popular tourist destination.

Starting from Salzburg it is possible to tour the Salzkammergut in four days, by following, in succession, itineraries 1, 2, 3 on day one, and itinerary 4 on days two, three and four.

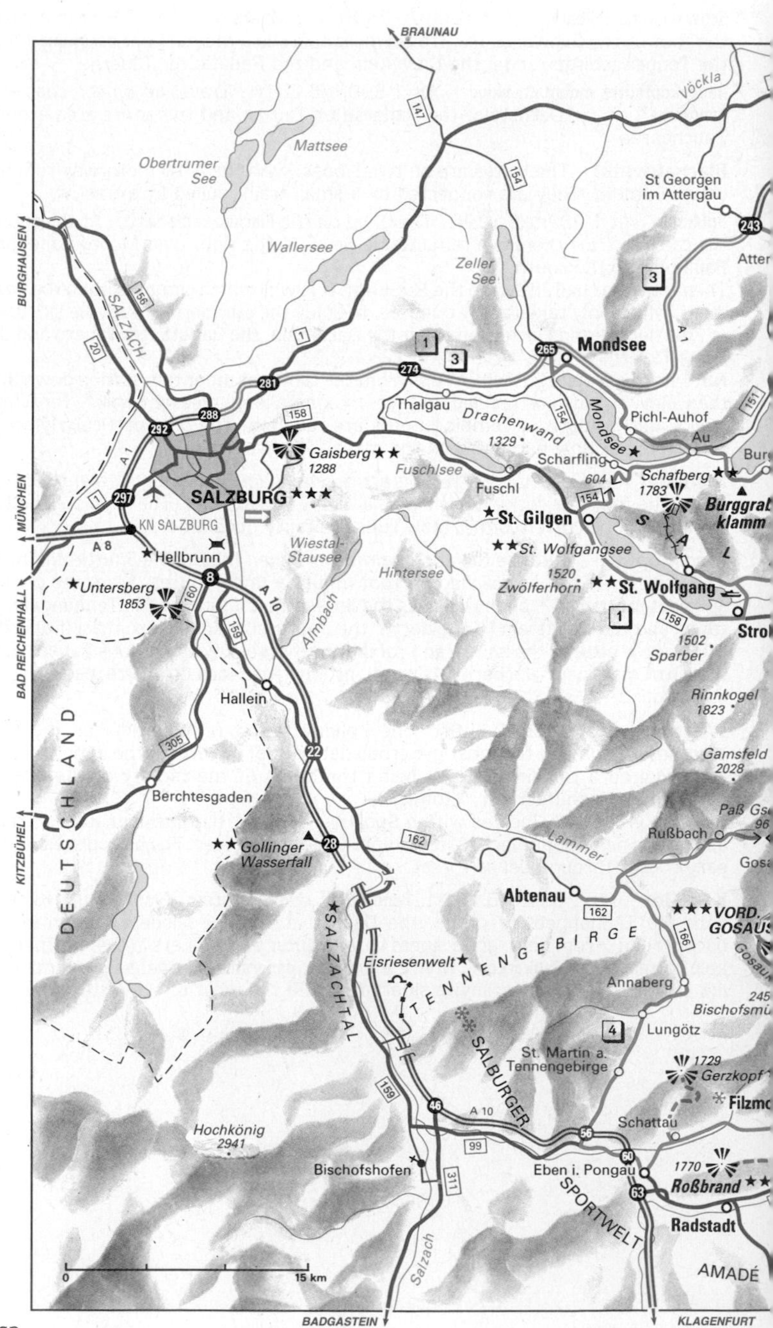

★★ TOUR OF THE LAKES

1 From Salzburg to Bad Ischl *84km/52mi*

Owing to the low pass (alt 608m/1 995ft) carrying the road over the wooded ridge between Scharfling and St. Gilgen, the route is able to take in both the Mondsee and the lake of St. Wolfgang.

★★★ **Salzburg** - *See SALZBURG.*

Leave Salzburg on ⑤, then take the A 1 motorway to the Mondsee exit.

Between Salzburg and Mondsee, the motorway above the little Thalgau Valley, is slightly raised and affords open views of the Drachenwand cliffs beyond which, in the middle distance, stands the Schafberg spur. The lake of **Mondsee**★ at last appears below the Schafberg.

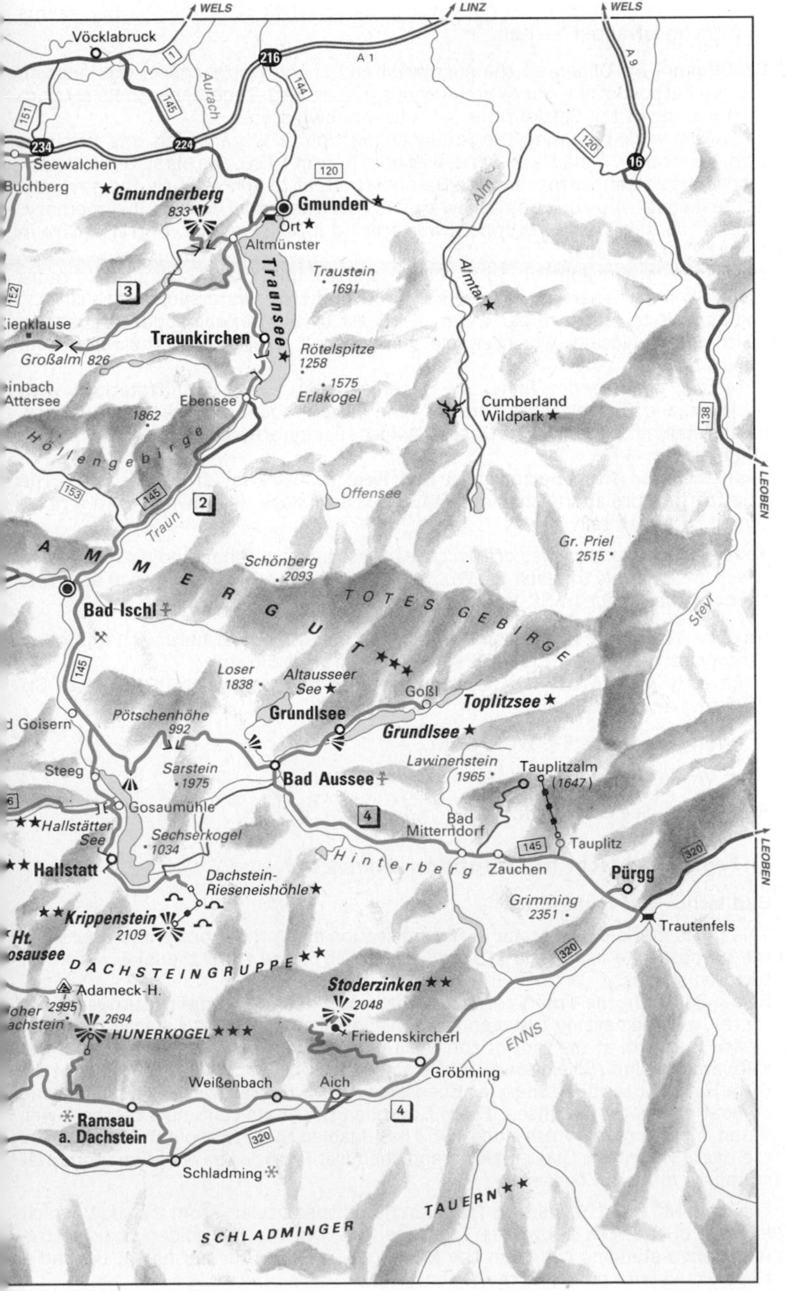

Mondsee - *See MONDSEE.*

The north shore of the Mondsee, which is calm and welcoming at first, becomes a little more severe beyond the Pichl promontory, where the road climbs over a wooded rise.

Burggrabenklamm - *5km/3mi from Au along the road beside the Attersee at the foot of the Schafberg slopes, leave the car in the Gasthaus Zum Jägerwirt car park; 30min on foot there and back. Unprotected walk on rocks which are slippery after rain.* Exploration of a ravine as far as a waterfall.

The south shore of the lake of Mondsee between Au and Scharfling is framed by the lower cliffs of the Schafberg; the road passes through sections cut into the overhanging rock and through short tunnels.
The crossing of the pass connecting Scharfling and St. Gilgen is remarkable for the **panoramic section★★** which bends in a curve above St. Gilgen *(car park)*. Beyond the slender bulbous-domed village bell-tower, the **Wolfgangsee★★** Lake stretches towards the Rinnkogel massif of which a characteristic peak, the Sparber, seems to form an advanced bastion.

★ **St. Gilgen** - St. Gilgen, at the northwest end of the Wolfgangsee, was once an eastern outpost of the prince-archbishops of Salzburg. Together with its setting, it forms one of the Salzkammergut's best-known scenes.
It is worthwhile repeating the family connection of Mozart with this favoured land: his mother, Anna Maria Pertl, was born here in 1720, and his sister, Nannerl, settled here after her marriage to Baron Berchtold zu Sonnenburg, the governor of the district. A plaque on the law courts (Bezirksgericht) recalls this memory, while a fountain (Mozartbrunnen) was erected in 1927 on the central square in front of the Rathaus.
St. Gilgen is a delightful sight for anyone coming from Salzburg, or more especially from Scharfling. The lake attracts numerous watersports enthusiasts, and appeals to sailors in particular, not least because of the sudden squalls to which it is subjected, which enable them to test their skill to the full during regattas.
A regular boat service links St. Gilgen's landing-stage (Schiffstation) with St. Wolfgang, Strobl and a total of nine places around the lake. The veteran paddle-steamer *Kaiser Franz Joseph*, which inaugurated the service in 1873, is still in use.
Soon the road from Salzburg to Bad Ischl draws away from the lake. The Schafberg, more approachable on this southern slope, is crowned with a hotel served by a rack railway.

To the left a road branches off which leads to the Gschwendt landing-stage from which it is possible to reach St. Wolfgang by boat. Leave the main road at Strobl to make the detour to St. Wolfgang.

Strobl - The pretty village square, the church and the lakeshore with its flower gardens form a quietly graceful scene when traffic allows.
From early May to late Oct there is a regular boat service from Strobl to St. Wolfgang and St. Gilgen.

★★ **St. Wolfgang** - *See ST. WOLFGANG.*

Take the direct road to Bad Ischl, avoiding Strobl.

‡ **Bad Ischl** - *See Bad ISCHL.*

2 From Bad Ischl to Gmunden *34km/21mi*

‡ **Bad Ischl** - *See Bad ISCHL.*

This run is marked by a scenic cliff road section along the shore of the **Traunsee★**, the deepest lake in Austria (191m/527ft). Cliffs rise from the lake waters in tortured shapes.
Below Bad Ischl the Traun corridor, which was one of the great European salt routes, unwinds evenly between the Höllengebirge and Totes Gebirge foothills. Beside the road, at the foot of the west slope, a track follows the course of the saltwater conduit *(Soleleitung)*, which since the 17C has brought the salt waters from Hallstatt to the refinery at Ebensee, whence the salt was at one time sent by boat across the Traunsee. From Gmunden the boats continued on the lower Traun, along a reach which since 1552 has enabled them to avoid the last falls of the river (Traunfall). Glass-making and chemical factories have set an industrial stamp on modern Ebensee.

The **cliff road★** from Ebensee to Traunkirchen is spectacular. From the road, which is hewn in the rock above the Traunsee, one can see the golden peak of the Rötelspitze standing out from the Erlakogel, and then further north, beyond a slope pitted with quarries, the Traunstein.

S. Vannint/VIENNASLIDE

Corpus Christi Festival at Traunkirchen

Traunkirchen – On its promontory **site★**, Traunkirchen enjoys a variety of views over the Traunsee, particularly to the south, where the setting is steep and wild. It is a popular stopping place for visitors exploring the Salzkammergut.

Pfarrkirche – On the northern flank of the rock, the parish church is surrounded by a terraced graveyard overlooking the lake. There are views of the Erlakogel and of the mighty peak of the Traunstein. The building originally belonged to a convent, later occupied by the Jesuits in the 17C and 18C. In 1632 they rebuilt the church in its present form, and in the same year the first of the annual **Corpus Christi festivals** was held on the waters of the lake.
The church has splendid Baroque furnishings, particularly the **Fisherman's Pulpit★**, made in the form of the Disciples' fishing boat, complete with dripping nets, while on the sounding-board is a legendary episode from the life of St Francis Xavier, who introduced Christianity to Japan. In the course of his voyage, the saint was shipwrecked and lost his crucifix, which is shown here being returned to him by a lobster.

Floating Corpus Christi Festival

Since 1632 a procession whose reputation reaches far beyond the borders of Upper Austria has been held on the lake here every year in celebration of the feast of Corpus Christi. In days gone by, boats called "Trauner" which were used for shipping salt were pressed into service for the procession. Nowadays, these have given way to the rather less romantic motor boat.

Altmünster – Altmünster has a Late Gothic hall-church with sumptuous decoration and a stone high altar dating from 1518.

The charming Schloß Ort welcomes travellers to Gmunden.

★ **Gmunden** – *See GMUNDEN.*

3 From Gmunden to Salzburg *117km/73mi*

The route, which links the three lakes, the Traunsee, the Attersee and the Mondsee, crosses attractive countryside as in the upper Aurach Valley or occasionally open countryside as in the Mondsee hollow.

★ **Gmunden** – *See GMUNDEN.*

From Gmunden take the Bad Ischl road to Altmünster.

Altmünster – *See 2 above.*

★ **Gmundnerberg** – *See GMUNDEN: Excursions.*

The road leaves the banks of the Traunsee to enter a tranquil hilly region dotted with brilliantly whitewashed farmhouses and clumps of huge lime trees. After skirting the hamlet of Großalm to the right the road burrows into the forest which lies within sight of the northern escarpments of the Höllengebirge to reach a pass at an altitude of 826m/2 710ft.

The descent down the Attersee slope, which is at first very steep, becomes interesting only on reaching the **panoramic section**★ from Kienklause to Steinbach, where the road runs along a bare slope which plunges directly into the lake.

Steinbach am Attersee – It was here that the composer **Gustav Mahler** spent his holidays and worked in his "Komponierhäuschen" (composing shed) on some of his great compositions.

The road runs like a quayside along the **Attersee**★ (or Kammersee), the largest lake in the Austrian Alps *(fishing, boating)*, bordered to the south by the last cliff-like slopes of the Schafberg. The west shore of the lake, between the villages of Seewalchen and Attersee, unfolds through a region of charming sun-drenched hills where orchards flourish. Only the cliffs of the Höllengebirge, rising up on the east shore lend a note of harshness to the scene. To get a good view of the whole lake, stop at the viewpoint *(bench)* beside the Buchberg Chapel.

Attersee – This well-known holiday resort has a pilgrimage church, Mariae Himmelfahrt, with fine Baroque furnishings, including works by Meinrad Guggenbichler.

Leave the lake at Attersee and take the motorway towards Salzburg.

The road down towards Mondsee offers a **panorama**★ of the mountains which frame the lake (Drachenwand, Schafberg) and the Salzkammergut Alps.

Mondsee – *See MONDSEE.*

Continue on the motorway to Salzburg.

★★★ **Salzburg** – *See SALZBURG.*

★★ TOUR AROUND THE DACHSTEIN

4 Leaving from Bad Ischl *267km/166mi*

Day one: Bad Ischl, Hallstatt, Krippenstein, Gosauseen
Day two: Filzmoos, Roßbrand, Hunerkogel, Ramsau
Day three: Stoderzinken, Bad Aussee, Bad Ischl

♆ **Bad Ischl** – *See Bad ISCHL.*

Branching off from the Pötschenhöhe route south of Bad Goisern, the road to Bad Ischl at Hallstatt follows the floor of the Traun Valley, which is planted with orchards. At Steeg, the road starts along the west shore of the **Hallstätter See**★★, on whose deep-blue waters boats with lofty prows can be seen sailing. At the Gosaumühle fork, continue along the lakeside at the foot of a steep slope. Across the water is the Sechserkogel promontory, a spur of the Sarstein. The **view**★ opens out onto the town of Hallstatt grouped below its church; the amphitheatre of Obertraun also appears.

Enter the tunnel to by-pass Hallstatt, leave the car at the viewing terrace which at one point makes a break in the tunnels, and walk into town.

★★ **Hallstatt** – *See HALLSTATT.*

★★ **Ascent to the Krippenstein** – *Detour south from Hallstatt (6km/4mi) and ascent: 2hr 30min (viewpoint only) to 4hr (viewpoint and caves) of cable-car and walking – see DACHSTEIN.*

After visiting Hallstatt, continue through the tunnel and on emerging turn round to take the tunnel for south-north traffic only. At Gosaumühle turn left.

After passing under the saltwater aqueduct *(Soleleitung)* the road enters the mountains along the Gosaubach. When the valley widens again, the magnificent crest of the Gosaukamm, bristling with peaks, unfolds on the left above the Gosau basin. Here two almost identical churches are a reminder that Protestant communities have been able to survive in this part of Upper Austria.

Turn towards the lake of Gosau and leave the car at one of the car parks at the end of the road.

★★★ **Gosauseen** – *See GOSAUSEEN.*

Return to Gosau; turn left onto the Gschütt pass road.

On the west slope of the pass, the road drops among parklands to the Rußbach hollow, where large peasants' houses with little belfries recall those of the Tyrol; it then crosses the Abtenau depression at the foot of the Tennengebirge.

Abtenau - This little holiday resort (*Abtenau* - "the abbey meadow") at the foot of the enormous Kogel is popular in the summer and a good departure point for hikes and excursions. Especially to be recommended is the drive to St. Wolfgang along the **Postalmstraße** *(toll payable)*, which offers fine views. The Postalm is the largest area of Alpine meadows in Austria, and the second largest high-lying plateau in Europe. The Gothic church, with its twin aisles, a former place of pilgrimage, is interesting as much for its graceful outline as for its furnishings (statues of St George and St Florian). The beautifully built priest's house is worthy of the patronage of the abbey of St. Peter at Salzburg.

Return east; turn right to Annaberg, the **"Salzburg Dolomites"** *road.*

The furrow of the Upper Lammer, separating the Tennengebirge and Dachstein massifs, begins with a romantic gorge. The most remarkable views of the journey are oriented to the east, especially in the Annaberg-Lungötz section. This is in the direction of the Gosaukamm which is distinguished here by the cleft peak aptly named Bischofsmütze - bishop's mitre. The pass at St. Martin leads into the Fritztal, a tributary valley of the Salzach (views westwards towards Hochkönig).

★★ **From Eben im Pongau to Gröbming** - *One day. See DACHSTEIN.*

The road follows the Enns Valley. To the right there appears the massive bulk of Trautenfels Castle.

Schloß Trautenfels ⏲ - A fortress called Neuhaus, built on a mountain ridge overlooking the Enns Valley, is first recorded in 1261. The governor of the province of Styria, Siegmund Friedrich von Trauttmannsdorff, converted the fortress to a Baroque country palace in 1664 and renamed it Trautenfels. All that now remains of the interior decor is a number of stucco ceilings with valuable **frescoes** painted by Carpoforo Tencalla and some marquetry doors.
The castle houses a museum of local natural history and folklore, a department of the Steiermärkisches Landesmuseum Joanneum in Graz.

At the Trautenfels crossroads, leave the Enns Valley and take road no 145.

The road through the Styrian Salzkammergut massif rises quickly into a ravine carved by the Grimming at the foot of the scaly cliffs of Großer Grimming. To the right the white village of Pürgg dominates the Enns Valley.

Pürgg - *Leave the car at the entrance to the village.* Art-lovers should go up to the bluff on which the **Johanneskapelle** stands. The church decoration is typical of a country church of about the year 1200. The **Romanesque frescoes** uncovered and restored (the last time in 1959) depict, in the nave, the Annunciation, the Birth of Christ and its Announcement to the Shepherds, a fabulous fight between cats and mice and the Wise and Foolish Virgins. Figures seen on the triumphal arch are Christ Giving His Blessing, Cain and Abel and the church donors. On the chancel dome the Mystic Lamb is surrounded by the four Apostles, who are symbolically supported by the four sections of the world (on the pendentives). The crucifix on the altar is also Romanesque and was carved in c 1220.
The parish church dedicated to St George dates from 1130 and is built on the mountain slope in such a way that both the entrances through the façade and at gallery level are on ground level.
The road goes through a narrow stretch of the Grimming-Bach Valley into a dip known as the Hinterberg Plateau. In the foreground the magnificent chiselled walls of the Grimming face the slab-like shapes of the Lawinenstein. This crest masks the Alpine combe pastures of the **Tauplitzalm** which is popular with skiers in winter because of the mountain road beginning at Zauchen and a cable-car which travels up from the village of **Tauplitz** (winter sports resort).

Bad Mitterndorf - This place is known not only as a spa but as a winter sports resort. The local museum shows a remarkable collection of masks worn for the Nikolospiel, a traditional play for St Nicholas' Day.

Through a ravine of the Traun the road approaches Bad Aussee.

⚕ **Bad Aussee** - *See Bad AUSSEE.*

★ **Grundlsee and Toplitzsee**★ - *Both lakes are described under Bad AUSSEE: Excursions.*

The Pötschenhöhe (alt 992m/3 255ft) road provides a shortcut avoiding the great loop of the Traun, partly drowned by the Hallstatt Lake. The east slope of the pass from Bad Aussee forms a small **crest**★★ with a panoramic view. The pincer-shaped precipitous promontories of the Loser and the Trisselwand jut out from the petrified surface of the Totes Gebirge. Opposite stands the Sarstein. The west slope of the Pötschenhöhe begins in the pleasant Bad Goisern basin. The last bend, in which there is a space for cars to stop, makes a **viewpoint**★ overlooking the waters of the Hallstatt Lake. The lake turns to penetrate the amphitheatre hollowed out by the Traun at the foot of the Dachstein cliffs.

At Bad Goisern turn right onto road no 145 to Bad Ischl.

ST. ANTON AM ARLBERG**

Tirol

Population 2 400

Michelin map 926 fold 28 – Local map see ARLBERGGEBIET – Alt 1 304m/4 278ft

St. Anton is something of a shrine for lovers of the sport of skiing. In 1907 Hannes Schneider, pioneer of the Arlberg school of downhill skiing technique, gave skiing instruction for the first time on the surrounding mountain slopes. From the 1920s onwards, winter sports became extremely popular in St. Anton, made possible thanks to the good transport communications (St. Anton has been accessible by express train from Vienna or Paris, via the Arlberg tunnel, since 1885) and the extensive skiing area. Today, St. Anton is one of the largest winter sports resorts in the Northern Alps, with accommodation for 8 000 tourists.

The resort lies in a deeply incised valley and features modern architecture. Those in search of peace and quiet or of unspoilt nature will feel more at home in the nearby village of St. Jakob or at **St. Christoph**, which lies at an altitude of 1 793m/5 883ft close to the pass.

Nevertheless, St. Anton attracts numerous families, who enjoy its youthful, sporty atmosphere. No other ski slopes in Austria have as much to offer good skiers, and after a hard day's skiing, the boutiques, bars and restaurants in the pedestrian zone are an ideal place to unwind. St. Anton is also equipped with an ice stadium (skating and curling), several swimming pools, tennis and squash courts.

Summer brings a degree of calm to the resort, although the Arlbergstraße does attract much tourist traffic. Summer visitors are drawn by a 17 000m²/20 332sq yd leisure park, with its many and varied facilities (mini-golf, table-tennis, angling, children's recreation ground). There are 90km/56mi of trails for hikers, in particular in the Moostal Valley.

*** **Arlberg ski area** – An Arlberg ski pass gives skiers access to the pistes of **Lech*****, **Zürs**** *(see ZÜRS: take the bus there)* and Stuben, besides those at St. Anton. The 500km²/193sq mi ski area, which lies at an altitude of 1 300-2 650m/4 250-8 700ft, has 260km/162mi of marked-out and 190km/118mi of unmarked pistes, which are accessed by a total of 86 ski lifts.

Elsewhere in Europe, only the ski slopes of the Trois Vallées (Courchevel, Méribel, Les Ménuires, Val Thorens) and Tignes-Val d'Isère in France and St. Moritz, Zermatt and Verbier in Switzerland, are able to offer similar or comparable skiing facilities.

The area around St. Anton is equipped with 40 ski lifts. It is especially suitable for experienced skiers, who can ski down the many steep, undulating pistes from the Schindler Spitze, Kapall and Pfannenkopf peaks. Less proficient skiers are also catered for, however, with a number of suitable pistes on the Galzig, Gampen and Gampberg slopes.

Arlberg-Kandahar-Haus – This is a museum on the history of skiing and the development of tourism in the Arlberg area.

Y. Rontoux

Arlberg ski slopes seen from the Valluga ridge

VIEWPOINTS

★★★ **Valluga** ⏲ – Alt 2 811m/9 222ft. *About 2hr 30min there and back. If possible, take binoculars. There are mountain restaurants in the first and second sections of the cable-car ride.*
First take the Galzig cable-car. From the mountain station, which lies at an altitude of 2 185m/7 169ft, there is a wonderful **view**★★ over the ski slopes, from the Schindlerspitze peak to St. Anton, and to the south over the Verwall range. Then take the cable-car Valluga I to the Valluga ridge (alt 2 650m/8 695ft). The **panorama**★★ from here is very impressive, but you need to travel up to the peak itself on the little Vallugaspitze cable-car to enjoy a full **360° panorama**★★★ *(climb up on foot to the upper viewing terrace).*
To the south the view encompasses the Rätikon (Sulzfluh, Zimba, Madrisahorn), the Montafontal Valley (Hochjoch), the Silvretta group and the Bernina (Switzerland) behind the Verwall range and the Samnaun. To the southeast lie the high peaks of the Ötztal (Weißkugel, Wildspitze) and Stubai Alps. The Lechtal Alps (Rote Wand, Omeshorn, Kriegerhorn and Rüfikopf) tower to the north, and in the distance, to the northeast, you can see the Zugspitze.
The various peaks can be made out easily with binoculars.

★★ **Kapall** ⏲ – Alt 2 326m/7 592ft. *About 1hr there and back. Ride up on the Kandahar funicular railway or the Gampen chair-lift, then take the Kapall chair-lift.*
You will arrive at the foot of the rocky Weißschrofenspitze peak. There is a very beautiful **panorama**★★ to the south over the whole St. Anton Valley as far as the hamlet of Pettneu. The view stretches to the Swiss Alps, the Rätikon (Drei Türme) and the Verwall range. There is a beautiful view straight ahead over the Moostal Valley.

★ **Rendl cable-car** ⏲ – Alt 2 030m/7 632ft. *30min there and back. Sit facing backwards.* During the trip there are several **general views**★ to be enjoyed of St. Anton and its ski slopes from Valluga to the Kapall. From the cable-car mountain station *(mountain inn)* the view sweeps southwards to the beautiful Moostal Valley, which is enclosed by the Kuchenspitze peak, the Küchlspitze peak and their glaciers.
Skiers take a T-bar lift up to the Gampberg (alt 2 407m/7 897ft), and at the top it is only a short distance to the hill on which the last cable-car support stands. From here there is a broad **panorama**★ of the Verwall range and of the Hochkarspitze peak in particular.

Stift ST. FLORIAN★★

Oberösterreich

Michelin map 926 fold 9 – 18km/11mi southeast of Linz

The abbey of St. Florian, the largest in Upper Austria and an eminent cultural centre, has been occupied, since the 11C by Augustinian canons. The present buildings are in the purest Baroque style, since the monastery was entirely rebuilt (1686-1751) under the direction, first of Carlo Antonio Carlone, then of Jakob Prandtauer. The latter was also the architect of Hohenbrunn, the palatial edifice built nearby for one of the abbey's provosts.

HISTORICAL NOTES

The Legend of St Florian – Florian was head of the Roman administration in the Noricum province. He was converted to Christianity, martyred in 304 near the camp of Lauriacum and thrown into the Enns. It was near the site of his grave that the monastery which bears his name was later built. His death by drowning caused him to be invoked against flooding and also against fire, often with the prayer, "Good St Florian, spare my house and rather burn my neighbour's". There is, therefore, hardly a church in Austria without a statue of this saintly protector, in which he figures as a Roman legionary holding a sprinkler or a pail to put out the flames.

TOUR ⏲

The west façade, which is 214m/702ft long, is surmounted by three towers. The doorway (Stiftstor) leading into the abbey's inner courtyard (Stiftshof) is particularly elegant, with two superimposed balconies, carved columns and statues.
A remarkable sculptured fountain, the Eagle Fountain (Adlerbrunnen), and a wrought-iron well-head, dating from 1603, adorn the wide inner courtyard.

Anton Bruckner at St. Florian

Anton Bruckner, recognized as Austria's greatest 19C composer of church music, was born in 1824 at Ansfelden, a little village near St. Florian. His father, a local schoolmaster, died when Bruckner was 13. The boy was taken into the choir school at the monastery, where he was introduced to the major works in the repertoire of religious music.
Bruckner trained as a teacher, and after two posts as an assistant teacher, far from the abbey where he felt his real ties were, he managed to win an appointment as teacher at the monastery in 1845, and, to his great joy, he was also appointed its organist. It was at St. Florian that Bruckner made the decision to devote himself to music. He began a course of study on counterpoint under Simon Sechter. In 1856 he was called to Linz as cathedral organist, where he composed a number of masterpieces including his three masses and two of his nine symphonies, and then to Vienna as a professor at the Conservatory. Despite his increasing fame, Bruckner's thoughts kept returning to the abbey at St. Florian, and it was there that he expressed a wish to be buried, beneath the organ which had helped him on the way to success as a composer and performer.

Bibliothek (Library) – The fine allegorical paintings on the library ceiling, by Bartolomäus Altomonte, represent the union of religion and science. Marquetry in walnut, encrusted with gold, sets off the valuable early texts, manuscripts and over 140 000 books.

Marmorsaal – The marble hall was dedicated to Prince Eugene of Savoy as a tribute to the leading part he played, as a captain, in the defence of the Austrian Empire against the Turks. It was used as a concert hall and is adorned with frescoes and pictures. The paintings on the ceiling *(Victory over the Turks)* are by Martin Altomonte.

★★★ **Altdorfer Galerie** – The most valuable pictures in the abbey collection are by **Albrecht Altdorfer** (1480-1538), master of the Danubian School, who distinguished himself not only as a painter but as a steel and wood engraver and architect.
The 14 pictures on the altar to St Sebastian, painted in 1518 for the Gothic church of the abbey, form the world's most important collection of Altdorfer's work.
The panels depicting the martyrdom of St Sebastian, and the eight pictures evoking scenes of the Passion, are striking for the feeling in the characters of Christ, the Virgin, Judas and Caiaphas. The background of foliage in shadow lends power to the dramatic scenes.
In his devotion to landscape, Altdorfer resembled his contemporary Dürer, and was by several centuries a forerunner of the Romantics. The most attractive aspects of his work are the balanced composition and rich, warm colour.

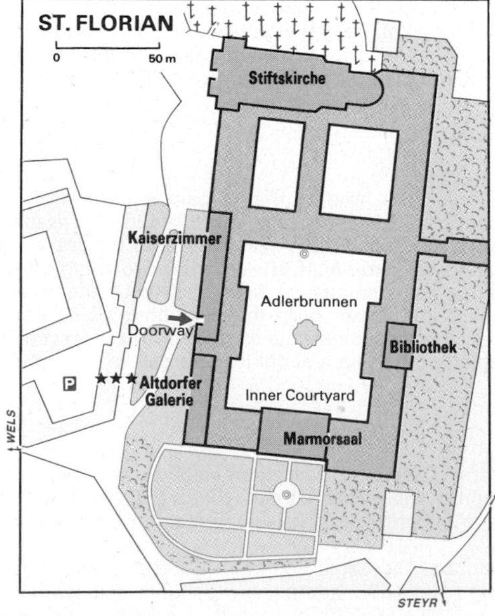

Kaiserzimmer (Imperial Apartments) – The Imperial apartments are reached by the magnificent grand staircase, which rises through two storeys; the balustrades are adorned with statues and the walls and ceilings embellished with stucco and frescoes. Until 1782 the apartments received such illustrious visitors as Pope Pius VI, emperors and princes.
Amid a succession of halls and state rooms note the Faistenberger room, the bedrooms of the Emperor and Empress, the reception room and a room known as the "Gobelins" room; they contain rich furniture and interesting stuccowork, frescoes and pictures.

H. W. Partaj /BILDAGENTUR BUENOS DIAS

St. Florian Abbey

Stiftsbasilika – The Baroque basilica was built to replace the old Gothic church from 1686 under the direction of Carlo Antonio Carlone. Carlo's brother Bartolomeo was responsible for the stuccowork. The fresco adorning the whole of the ceiling, almost 5 000m²/53 800sq ft, was executed by painters Johann Anton Gumpp and Melchior Steidl from Munich. The great organ was built by Franz Xaver Chrisman (1770-74). It now has more than 103 stops and 7 836 pipes. It was called after Anton Bruckner, who worked here as organist and composer and was buried in the crypt beneath the organ in accordance with his wishes.

There is a 20min recital given on the organ mid May to mid Oct, daily (except Sat) at 2.30pm. Further details available from the abbey porter.

ST. JOHANN IN TIROL*

Tirol

Population 7 800

Michelin map 926 fold 19 – Local map see KAISERGEBIRGE – Alt 670m/2 198ft

Its location at the intersection of several valleys makes St. Johann a lively place. The wide bowl of the valley – quite a suntrap – is enclosed by the Wilder Kaiser and Kitzbüheler Horn peaks. The market town, which grew up on the site of a scattered village, boasts a number of beautiful Baroque houses with façades decorated with painted, sometimes *trompe-l'œil*, scenes, which are typical of the Tyrolean region and never fail to charm visitors.
St. Johann has established itself as a popular tourist resort, capable of accommodating 5 000 visitors, which offers a wide variety of leisure facilities during the summer, catering for a range of visitors – from seekers of peace and quiet, to ramblers, to amateur mountaineers. But it is as an international winter sports resort that St. Johann has really made a name for itself in recent years, offering a corresponding range of facilities.

* **Ski slopes** Downhill ski slopes are concentrated on the north face of the Kitzbüheler Horn. The pistes at Harschbichl, which go up to an altitude of 1 700m/5 600ft, are well-equipped with ten ski tows, five chair-lifts and two cable-cars, which can transport 19 000 people per hour. Out of the 60km/37mi of pistes, 28km/17mi are served by artificial snow machines if necessary.
The facilities for **cross-country skiing** are equally impressive. There are 74km/46mi of tracks, including two of 16km/10mi in length which are classified as difficult, so all are catered for. In association with some of the neighbouring resorts, such as Oberndorf, Going-Ellmau, Kirchdorf-Erpfendorf and Waidring, there are almost 200km/124mi of cross-country ski tracks to be explored!

Pfarrkirche – This Baroque building, designed by the architect Abraham Millauer, dates from 1723-28. Its well lit interior is remarkable for its paintings; the six decorating the vaults are by **Simon Benedikt Faistenberger**, a student of Rottmayr. All the altar paintings are by the same artist, Jacob Zanusi (1679-1742), court painter at Salzburg.

Antoniuskapelle – *In Bahnhofstraße, about 200m/220yd past the parish church to the right.* The fresco on the cupola (1803, renovated in 1921) of this rotunda built between 1669 and 1674 contains a panoramic representation of St. Johann in the early 19C.

★ **Spitalskirche zum hl. Nikolaus in der Weitau** – *See Kaisergebirge* 1.

Abtei ST. LAMBRECHT

Steiermark

Michelin map 926 fold 35

The Benedictine abbey of St. Lambrecht lies over 1 000m/3 300ft above sea level in a tributary valley leading off from the Neumarkter Sattel gap. The first record of a church of "St Lambert in the Woods" dates from 1066. Next to this church, the Carinthian ducal family, the Eppensteins, built a family convent in the last decades of the 11C. This foundation was finally granted the status of an abbey by Duke Heinrich III of Carinthia in 1103. The first large Romanesque abbey church, a basilica with twin west towers consecrated in 1160, was replaced in 1327 to 1421 by the present building, a High Gothic triple-aisled hall-church. The abbey buildings were built in 1640 following the designs of abbey master builder Domenico Sciassia. The 17C building had a south wing, with a doorway flanked by statues, added to it in 1730 to close off the outer courtyard on the side of the market square.
The abbey was dissolved in 1786 by Joseph II, but was able to move back into the buildings when the foundation was re-established by Emperor Franz II in 1802.

TOUR

Enter the abbey through the great south doorway. To the right stretches the impressive west façade of the abbey building, 135m/443ft in length, with its harmonious arrangement of plastered walls broken up by marble window jambs. The medieval façade of the west tower was transformed into the Baroque style by Domenico Sciassia. Opposite the west façade, the abbey courtyard is closed off by a bastion adorned with statues by Johann Matthias Leitner in 1746. In the middle of the bastion, an open staircase leads to the Gothic **Peterskirche**. Behind the church stand the remains of the castle. To the north, the abbey courtyard is closed off by the Granarium (1625), the west end of which is adjoined by further ancillary buildings. In the cemetery to the north of the abbey church stands a simple Romanesque **ossuary** (12C).

Benedictine abbey of St. Lambrecht

Stiftskirche – The elaborate marble doorway, built to a design by Sciassia, opens into the narthex, which houses the 14C Lettner crucifix in a Baroque framework. The abbey church itself is an impressive Gothic hall-church with medieval frescoes on the vault above the chancel and on the walls of the nave. The beautiful interior decor is Early Baroque. The enormous **high altar★**, 16m/52ft in height, dates from 1632 and was built after designs by Valentin Khautt. The side altars and the choir stalls are the work of Neumarkt sculptor Christoph Paumgartner. The sculpted decoration of the altar to St Emmeramus at the front on the right, the statues of the church Elders on the organ gallery, and the Madonna in the narthex are the work of famous sculptor Michael Hönell. The pulpit, richly decorated with figures, and the Mariazell altar in a side chapel are showpieces from the late 18C.

Castle ruins – To the northeast of the abbey stand a square tower and a small chapel, the remains of a castle built in the early 15C, apparently on the site of an older fortress, perhaps that of Count Marward von Eppenstein.

ST. PAUL IM LAVANTTAL★

Kärnten

Michelin map 926 fold 36 – Alt 400m/1 312ft

The abbey of St. Paul, founded in 1091, half-hidden in the trees and slightly above the wide lower Lavant Valley, has always been occupied by Benedictines. Its church is one of the finest examples of Romanesque architecture to be seen in Austria.

Stiftskirche (Abbey church) ⏲ – *To reach the church by car leave St. Paul by the Lavamünd road. At the top of the climb enter the walls through a monumental doorway (the "Hofrichtertor").* The church, construction of which was begun in 1180, ends in a flat chevet from which three rounded apses jut out, their great blind arcades, chequered friezes and cornices above blind arcades composing a very pure Romanesque decoration. The south doorway features an image of the Adoration of the Magi, and the west door one of Christ in Majesty.
Inside, the **Romanesque frescoes** behind the altar and the fresco on the north wall of the transept, depicting a pair of donors with saints (15C), are particularly interesting.

Stiftsgebäude (Abbey buildings) ⏲ – The west wing houses a considerable collection of works of art: a numismatic collection of some 30 000 items, objets d'art, silverwork, porcelain, woodcarvings, Romanesque chasubles, and valuable pieces such as Rudolf of Swabia's imperial cross (also called the Adelaide cross, 11C). There is also a superb display of paintings (works by Rubens, Rembrandt, Van Dyck) and drawings (Dürer, Rembrandt, Troger).
The abbey library contains an equally fine collection of some 180 000 volumes, including 4 000 manuscripts, Austria's oldest book (5C) and the world's oldest printed book from Johannes Gutenberg's workshop (mid 15C).

ST. PÖLTEN★

L Niederösterreich

Population 50 000

Michelin map 926 fold 11 – Alt 271m/889ft

St. Pölten, which was founded by the Romans in AD 1, is the most recently established provincial capital in Austria. The earliest monastery in Lower Austria was established here after 791, so still during the Carolingian era. This monastery was dedicated to St Hippolytus, from which the name St. Pölten is derived.

Baroque city – During the Baroque period, the city flourished. Master builders such as **Jakob Prandtauer** (who lived in St. Pölten from 1692 to his death in 1726), Josef and Franz **Munggenast**, and also famous painters such as Daniel Gran, Paul Troger and Bartolomäus Altomonte, lived and worked here. Evidence of their creativity is found at every turn, so that a stroll around the city centre is something of an intensive course in Baroque art.

Provincial capital – On 10 July 1986 the state Parliament of Lower Austria, the true heart of Austria, whose first written mention dates back to 996 and which had been without a capital city since 1922 (the area was administered from Vienna), voted unanimously to make St. Pölten its provincial capital. As the largest city in the province, a major traffic junction and also an industrial location, St. Pölten seemed entirely predestined for this role.

TRAVELLERS' ADDRESSES

Tourist information

Tourist information of all kinds available from **Touristeninformation** (Rathausplatz 1), ☏ 0 27 42/3 33 28 10, Fax 0 27 42/3 33 28 19. Information on St. Pölten is available on the Internet at *www.st-poelten.gv.at*. The local **Calendar of events** on the city and its surroundings comes out monthly between May and October and can be obtained from the tourist office and hotels.

City tours

The tourist office organises walking tours of the old town (lasting about 1hr 30min) and city tours (lasting about 1hr). For further details and reservations call ☏ 0 27 42/3 33 28 11. Otherwise, it is possible to hire a headset and recorded commentary for a cost of 20S, in order to discover St. Pölten at your own pace (tour lasts about 1hr 30min).

Between Apr and Oct the "**City-Express**" (red) operates in the city centre (Thur to Sat every half hour, free of charge), to enable visitors to travel in comfort between their exploratory walks around town. This tour is also a good way of getting an initial overview of the old town of St. Pölten.

Riemerplatz is the beginning and end of the "**Landhaus-Express**" (blue), which operates a shuttle service between the old town and the government district (spring to Dec, otherwise the same operating details as the City-Express). For more precise information, contact the tourist office.

Public transport

The city-bus operates in the city centre on a total of nine lines. Tickets can be bought from the bus drivers, and so can bus timetables at a cost of 15S. A single-trip ticket costs 18S (valid for 1hr; allows change of vehicle and of direction of travel). Multiple-trip tickets cost 80S and are valid for six single trips. A weekly ticket costs 90S. Timetable and price details can be obtained by calling ☏ 0 27 42/25 23 60. After 8.40pm, a taxi service (Sammel-Taxis) operates, ☏ 0 27 42/25 35 45.

Inner city car parks

Multi-storey or underground car parks are to be found in Eybnerstraße, on Dr.-Karl-Renner-Promenade, in Bräuhausgasse, on Roßmarkt, on Rathausplatz and in the government district. In the short-stay car parking zones (signposted) parking is free between noon and 1pm. Otherwise, the fee is 5S for 30min. The maximum time cars may be parked for is 3hrs.

Post offices

The city centre post office (Wiener Straße 12) is open Mon-Fri 8am-noon and 2-6pm. The main post office (Hauptpostamt) at Bahnhofsplatz 1a is open Mon-Fri 7am-8pm and Sat 7am-1pm.

Shopping

The main axes of the pedestrian shopping zone are formed by Kremser Gasse and Wiener Straße. There is a wide variety of shops here, catering to every taste.

Entertainment

Theater der Landeshauptstadt – Rathausplatz 11, ☏ 0 27 42/35 20 26 19. Theatre, musicals, operettas, children's theatre. Closed for a summer break in July and August.

Bühne im Hof – Linzer Straße 18, ☏ 0 27 42/35 22 91. Cabaret, dance, concerts.

Festspielhaus – Franz-Schubert-Platz, ☏ 0 27 42/20 10. Wide range of entertainment on offer: concerts of classical music, folk music, jazz, pop, rock, opera, operettas, musicals, ballet, folk dancing.

Kultur Gasthof Figl – Ratzersdorf, Hauptplatz, ☏ 0 27 42/25 74 02. Inn with cabaret.

Cinemas

The **Hollywood Megaplex** (☏ 0 27 42/28 80; Engelbert-Laimer-Straße 1 on the right of the Traisen) offers eight cinema screens and various options for eating out or other entertainment under a single roof.

Eating out

Galerie – Fuhrmannsgasse 1, ☎ 0 27 42/35 13 05. Top quality restaurant, considered the best in town.

Parzer & Reibenwein – Riemerplatz 1, ☎ 0 27 42/35 30 17 30. Restaurant with stylish decor in a 12C building (Baroque façade, arcaded courtyard).

Gasthof Winkler – Mühlweg 64, ☎ 0 27 42/36 49 44. Menu varies with the seasons, idyllic garden for clientele.

Zum Gwercher – In Stattersdorf (right of the Traisen, southeast of city centre), Schiffmannstraße 98, ☎ 0 27 42/23 05 90. Welcoming restaurant with a large garden inside the courtyard. International selection of wines and cigars.

Cafés and bars

Kaffee-Konditorei Amler – Brunngasse 4-6. Traditional coffee house.

Café Punschkrapferl – Domgasse 8. More than 80 pastries to choose from and, as if that were not enough, ice cream and a salad bar.

Zum Rothen Krebs – Kremser Gasse 18. Modern daytime bar with a library corner, where visitors feel as if they have been transported to some grand mansion.

Winzig ("Little", Kremser Gasse 25) and **Riesig** ("Large", Wiener Straße 24) are two bars, which despite their names are both relatively small, where a pleasant evening can be spent over a light meal or a drink or two (beer or wine).

Mitt'n Drin – Wiener Straße 10. Visitors barely need to set foot over the threshold to be in the thick of things. Good for a quick drink to recharge the batteries.

Drunter & Drüber – Kugelgasse 6. Bar with comfortable sofa corner and garden. During the colder months, there is also live music ranging from rock to blues.

Narrenkastl – Wiener Straße 33. Small bar with a platform overlooked by the figure of a dwarf. During summer, the pretty courtyard is where most of the action takes place.

Salzamt – Linzer Straße 18. Bar atmosphere beneath a fine vaulted ceiling.

Cabrio – Linzer Straße 30. Local bar serving beer to a youthful set, with plenty of greenery adorning the premises (not all of it real, however).

Flieger-Bräu – Ferstlergasse 9. House-brewed naturally dark beer. Rustic local bar, where flying is the main theme of the decor (as the name suggests).

Dates for your diary

Meisterkonzerte: Dec to Apr. Concerts of classical music in the Stadtsaal and Festspielhaus.

St. Pöltner Festwochen: early May to early June. Concerts, plays, cabaret.

Film am Dom: early June. The "Cinema Paradiso" association presents a discriminating programme of open-air cinema on the Domplatz.

Hauptstadtfest: second Fri in July. Music, cabaret, children's entertainment at various venues in the city centre. Fireworks display.

Sonnenblumenfest: July. "Sunflower Festival": musical and culinary delicacies on offer on the Rathausplatz.

Film-Festival: one-month film festival between late July and early Sept. Films and food from all over the world on the Rathausplatz.

St. Pöltner Seefest: Aug. Ballet, concerts, children's entertainment by the Ratzersdorfer Lake.

Musica Sacra: late Sept to early Oct. Performances of international church music in the cathedral and the abbey churches of Herzogenburg and Lilienfeld.

More precise details about dates and other information is available from the tourist office on ☎ 0 27 42/35 33 54.

SIGHTS

Rathausplatz – In the centre of the square, which is bordered by beautiful patrician houses, stands the massive **Trinity Column**, created between 1767 and 1782 by Andreas Gruber. The column is made of marble, and the associated fountain arrangement is made of sandstone. It shows St Hippolytus, St Florian (recognisable by his attribute of a burning house), St Sebastian (arrow) and St Leopold (model of a church).

Herzberger/ÖSTERREICH WERBUNG

Rathaus tower and Trinity Column, St. Pölten

Rathaus - The town hall was built in the 16C by connecting two existing Gothic houses. The Renaissance portals also date from the time of its construction. In 1727 Josef Munggenast, the pupil of Jakob Prandtauer, built the Baroque façade. The tower has become the emblem of St. Pölten.

Patrician houses - To the left of the Rathaus stands the **Schuberthaus**, in which the composer stayed in 1821, holding "Schubertiade" musical evenings. The building dates from the 16C. The Baroque façade is attributed to Jakob Prandtauer, who is also thought to have planned the **Montecuccoli-Palais** *(Rathausplatz 5)*. The **Theater der Landeshauptstadt**, built in 1820 by Josef Schwerdfeger and converted in 1893, has a neo-Classical façade.

Franziskanerkirche - The slightly sweeping façade lends a lively quality to the church, built between 1757 and 1779 on the narrow north side of the Rathausplatz. The wall, which is concave in the central axis, is divided by flat pilasters. The beautiful statues in niches of St Joseph (above), St Theresa and the Prophet Elias are the work of an unknown master. The double vaulted interior is beautifully balanced, with its Rococo pulpit, the exuberant high altar by Andreas Gruber and the four side paintings by Martin Johann Schmidt, and Kremser Schmidt.

Karmeliterinnenkirche - Also known as the Prandtauer Church after its builder, this church, which was built in 1707, stands to the right of the Rathaus on the south side of the Rathausplatz. It served as a model for the Franziskanerkirche. Its elegant interior houses a high altar created in 1712 by Johann Lukas von Hildebrandt for the castle chapel at Aschach in Upper Austria, for which Georg Johann Schmidt painted the work in the pediment in 1721. The main altarpiece (Crucifixion scene) is attributed to the Spanish painter Ribera (1588-1652).
A local museum, the **Stadtmuseum** ⌚, is housed in the former Carmelite nunnery (Prandtauerstraße 2), attached to the church. Among other things, it contains a gallery displaying local Jugendstil works.

★ **Institut der Englischen Fräulein** - *From Prandtauerstraße turn left onto Linzer Straße (no 11).* You cannot miss the sumptuous **façade**★ which was begun by Jakob Prandtauer, and which is thought to have been extended in 1767-69 by Josef Munggenast's son Mathias.
The main colours are white and pink, against which the black of the wrought-iron window grilles makes a striking contrast. Four portals, richly decorated with scrolls and busts of angels, divide up the long building. A particularly unusual feature of the façade is its three tabernacle-style niches. At the level of the ground floor, these contain a group of figures between columns, with above them a single figure in a wall niche. The figures depicted are, from right to left, St Katharine of Alexandria with St Ignatius above her; a guardian angel with child, with the Virgin Mary "Immaculata" above; and finally St Anne with the Virgin Mary, with St Joseph above them. This iconography illustrates the vocation of the institute, which was dedicated to the welfare and education of young people. Schools are still housed here.
The Baroque **Institutskirche** *(request entry at the gate)* consists of two unequally sized rooms, the smaller of which was designed by Jakob Prandtauer. On its 20m/66ft high cupola is a magnificent fresco entitled *Revelation of the Incarnation of Christ* by Paul Troger. The main room boasts a ceiling fresco by Bartolomäus Altomonte with scenes from the life of the Virgin Mary.

CATHEDRAL DISTRICT

★ **Dom Mariä Himmelfahrt** - From the Domplatz, the cathedral building appears almost totally lacking in any decoration. Only the two figures (St Hippolytus on the left, St Augustine on the right) and the Baroque spire alleviate the building's otherwise austere appearance. The core of the cathedral originates from 1150 and the 13C, and the building was modified several times in the 16C and 17C. The splendid Baroque decoration of the interior comes as all the more of a surprise after the sobriety of the exterior.

★ **Interior** - The soft tones of the stucco marble and paintings, the sheen of the liberally applied gilding, the inlaid work, combine to create an unusually warm red-gold colour effect, which the eye first of all takes in as a whole and only then breaks down into detail. It is difficult to believe that this work of art was contemptuously dismissed in the 19C as a "sign of the reckless energy" of the Baroque period.
The conversion of the cathedral interior to the Baroque style began in 1722 under Jakob Prandtauer and was completed in 1735 under Josef Munggenast. The high altar painting was executed by Tobias Pock in 1658; it depicts the Assumption of the Virgin Mary. The splendid **choir stalls**★ with their elaborately carved wooden decoration were executed in 1722 by Peter Widerin, who was also responsible for the organ case. Other artists from St. Pölten were involved in the creation of the beautiful pulpit and the confessionals.
The ceiling frescoes and the 10 large **wall-paintings**★, which depict scenes from the life of Christ, are the work of Thomas Friedrich Gedon and clearly show the influence of Daniel Gran.
During the cathedral's conversion to the Baroque style, the side aisles underwent an interesting transformation, with every second bay being topped by a cupola with a high lantern. The other domes were adorned with frescoes. The first two in the south and north side aisles (from the chancel) are the work of Bartolomäus Altomonte, the others, originally by Daniel Gran, were restored in 1949-50 by HA Brunner. Daniel Gran also painted the altarpieces in the side altars.

Bistumsgebäude - The former Canons' Chapter stands on the north side of the cathedral (access through the side aisle of the cathedral). It is a large, early Baroque ensemble arranged on five floors. The cloisters are adjoined to the north by the fountain courtyard; the east gallery features an ornate **wrought-iron gate**★, which leads to a beautiful staircase designed by Josef Munggenast.

★ **Diözesan-Museum** ⏲ - *On the upper floor of the cloister courtyard.* This museum houses religious works of art from the Romanesque period to the present, in particular Gothic altarpieces and sculptures, and works by leading Austrian Baroque artists. The crowning glory of the visit, which also includes the Bishops' Oratorium, is unquestionably the sumptuous library, the **Stiftsbibliothek**★, with sculptures attributed to Peter Widerin and frescoes by Daniel Gran and Paul Troger. These depict the four faculties: theology, philosophy, medicine and law.

ADDITIONAL SIGHTS

Riemerplatz - Rathausgasse leads to Riemerplatz with its beautiful houses, some of the basic structures of which date back to the Middle Ages, and which were given Baroque façades in the 18C, for example at no 1 Riemerplatz, believed to have been worked on by Josef Munggenast. Nos 3 and 4 are attributed to his son Mathias.

★ **Herrenplatz** - Take Wiener Straße towards the Traisen (note some remarkable Baroque façades) to reach this square with a Marian column in its centre and surrounded by buildings immortalizing all the Baroque artists who were active in St. Pölten. An outstanding example is the house at no 2, which features a front gable bearing a relief sculpture based on the designs of Austria's foremost Baroque sculptor, Georg Raphael Donner. It depicts *Darkness being driven out by Light.*

There is an important example of a Jugendstil building at Kremser Gasse 41. The **"Stöhrhaus"** was built in 1899 by Joseph Maria Olbrich, creator of the Vienna Secession building.

GOVERNMENT AND CULTURAL DISTRICT

As the new seat of the Lower Austrian government, St. Pölten has built a new government district to the east of the old town by the Traisen. The place of work was transferred to the elegant new state parliament building and the more functional administrative offices in May 1997. A single shopping street (Landhaus-Boulevard) and the modern cultural district have also been set up in the area. The **Festspielhaus** (concert hall) was designed by Klaus Kada and the **Shed-Ausstellungshalle** (exhibition gallery) by Hans Hollein. The vertical focal point of the cultural complex is the **Klangturm** ⓥ ("Sound tower"), designed by the mastermind behind the entire project, Ernst Hoffmann. The tower (which has a viewing terrace) houses temporary exhibitions (mostly interactive) of artistic installations experimenting with sound. The new Lower Austrian regional museum, also designed by Hans Hollein, is scheduled to open in 2002.

EXCURSIONS

Schloß Pottenbrunn – *In Pottenbrunn. 5km/3mi north of St. Pölten, via Wiener Straße and Ratzersdorfer Straße.* The old moated castle acquired its present Italian style Renaissance appearance when it was converted in the 16C. Especially characteristic are the overhanging arcaded galleries running round the tower and main building. A bulbous Baroque roof caps the tower.

★ **Stift Herzogenburg** ⓥ – *12km/7.5mi north of St. Pölten.* The Augustinian canons' monastery at Herzogenburg, founded at the beginning of the 12C by Bishop Ulrich of Passau, has enjoyed a prosperity to which the collections of works of art and manuscripts bear witness. The church and monastery buildings were virtually rebuilt in the Baroque style in the 18C.

Church – Franz Munggenast was in charge of the building of the church. The tower is crowned with the most unusual motif of a cushion bearing a replica of a ducal headdress, attributed to Fischer von Erlach. Inside the church, the frescoes and the altarpieces on the side altars are the work of Bartolomäus Altomonte. The picture on the high altar, painted by Daniel Gran, depicts the Virgin and Child in the centre, flanked by the patron saints of the monastery, St George and St Stephen.

Monastic buildings – These buildings were designed by Jakob Prandtauer who oversaw construction work until his death in 1726. The central section of the east wing, the work of Fischer von Erlach, is of particular interest. The vaulting of the main hall (Festsaal) is adorned with a huge allegorical composition by Altomonte to the glory of the prince-bishops of Passau.
Decorated with pictures, frescoes and *grisailles* (paintings in tones of grey), the **library** contains more than 80 000 works.
One room, displaying Gothic art, contains a collection of 16C **panel paintings**★, belonging to the Danubian School, among which are four panels by Jörg Breu representing scenes from the Passion on the outside and the Life of the Virgin on the inside.

Kirchstetten – *15km/9mi east.* This village was for many years the summer retreat of the poet **WH Auden** (1907-73), who now lies buried here.

ST. VEIT AN DER GLAN

Kärnten

Population 12 020

Michelin map 926 fold 35 – Alt 476m/1 562ft

St. Veit was the seat of the dukes of Carinthia until 1518, when the role of regional capital passed to Klagenfurt. The well preserved town wall, the picturesque narrow streets, the two town squares with their beautiful houses and arcaded courtyards all contribute to the charming appearance of this town. Modern architecture has left it s mark on St. Veit in recent years: the centre of the old town, on Herzog-Bernhard-Platz, is home to Austria's longest glazed arcade. Another unforgettable sight is Ernst Fuchs's **Kunsthotel** *(Prof.-Ernst-Fuchs-Platz 1)* with its brightly coloured façade blithely defying all conventions (1 100m²/11 800sq ft of Tiffany glass).

On the hills round St. Veit stand an unusually large number of castles – no less than 15 in a radius of about 10km/6mi. These provide many excursions and walks for tourists.

SIGHTS

★ **Hauptplatz** – Between spring and autumn the centre of town is transformed into a **sea of flowers**, making a beautiful sight. Unsurprising, then, that St. Veit was awarded a prize for its flowers in 1998.
The mainly three-storey houses give the square a very uniform character, which the narrow side streets leading off it do nothing to detract from. Of the three structures which distinguish the square, the most interesting, apart from the traditional memorial column to the plague erected in 1715, is the fountain called the **Schüsselbrunnen**; its basin is believed to have come from the forum of the Roman city of Virunum *(see MARIA SAAL)*. The small bronze statue (1566) surmounting it, the "Schüsselbrunnbartele" representing a grotesque figure in 16C miner's costume, is the town mascot. In the west half of the square stands the

St. Veit Information

Kunsthotel, St. Veit

Walther-von-der-Vogelweide fountain, dating from 1676 with a bronze statue made in 1960 depicting this most famous of the German troubadours, or Minnesänger, who once worked at the Court of St. Veit.

★ **Rathaus** – This elegant building was built during the Late Gothic period, as indicated by the ogee-arched gateway and cast metal panel from 1468, but was given a grand pilastered **stucco façade**★ in 1754, the work of Joseph Pittner. The central panel is adorned with an exuberant Baroque figure of Justice. On the pediment is the double-headed eagle of the Holy Roman Empire, embossed, in the centre, with the statue of St Veit. The gateway, which has retained its Gothic arch and a Gothic vaulted passage, leads to the stylish **Renaissance courtyard**★, one of the finest of its kind in Carinthia. The arcades are decorated with sgraffiti. The great hall, or **Rathaussaal**★, is on the first floor, beneath a fairly shallow Gothic vault lavishly decorated with delicate stucco lacework in the 18C by Joseph Pittner.
The **Bezirkshauptmannschaft** (seat of local government) closes off the Hauptplatz to the west. The building was erected in 1780 and with its marble gateway it embodies the transition from Baroque to the more sober neo-Classicism. To the east stands **Carinthia-Haus**, serving as gateway to the lower square. The imposing three-storey building essentially dates from the Middle Ages; the distinctive portal structure was added in the mid 16C.

Verkehrsmuseum – *Hauptplatz 9.* This small but unusually informative museum began life as a railway museum. It now covers a variety of means of transport and communication (Austrian railways, motoring, post and telecommunications). There is a fine model railway with 200m/220yd of tracks.

Stadtpfarrkirche – This triple-aisle pillared basilica dedicated to St Veit was built in the early 13C. In the 15C, a ribbed vault and the chapel of St Bernhard were added. The Late Baroque high altar, the altar of the Holy Cross (in the middle of the nave) and the chancel are the work of St. Veit master wood-carver Johann Pacher. The frescoes on the north chancel wall date from 1406; they were discovered behind the altar to St Florian in 1959.
To the south of the church, in the middle of the old churchyard, stands the circular Romanesque **ossuary**, erected in the 12C or 13C. Next to the doorway is a fragment of some rare Carolingian interlaced stonework (c 900).

EXCURSIONS

★ **Schloß Frauenstein** – *5km/3mi plus 30min on foot there and back. Very narrow country roads (passing impossible). Leave St. Veit via Obermühlbach (northwest) and then about 1 500m/1mi beyond the village take the second road on the right.*
This well preserved 16C castle makes a picturesque ensemble with its towers, turrets and roofs of unequal height. Take a look at the pretty, arcaded courtyard.

★ **St. Veit hill country** – *Round tour of 25km/16mi – about 2hr. Leave St. Veit on the road to Brückl.*
It is not long before the fortress of Hochosterwitz comes into sight, on the right, on the top of a rock, round which winds a fortified access ramp.

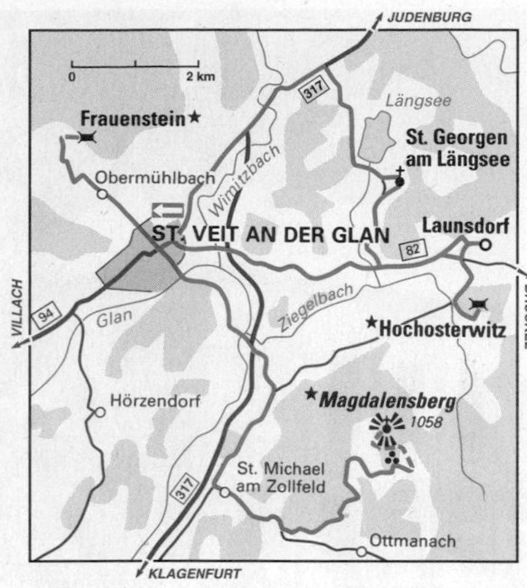

About 400m/435yd beyond a level crossing turn right. In the hamlet, at the foot of the rock, turn left up the road to the castle.

★ **Burg Hochosterwitz** – *See Burg HOCHOSTERWITZ.*

Turn back, then follow the direct road to Launsdorf, straight ahead.

Launsdorf – All periods since the Romanesque have left their mark on this appealingly unsymmetrical country church. In the tiny Gothic chancel is a gracious little 15C figure of the Virgin Mary with a pomegranate. The south side chapel contains an unusual tabernacle made of painted wood with a sliding door.

Return towards St. Veit but bear right to St. Georgen. After 1 300m/about 1mi turn right off the by-pass to enter St. Georgen.

St. Georgen am Längsee – The former abbey for Benedictine noble ladies and oldest surviving convent in Carinthia has kept its original design. A large quadrilateral of buildings encloses a church transformed into the Baroque style about 1720. The inner court is imposing, with large façades pierced by rounded arches. Facing the main door of the church is the Renaissance north gallery (1546) topped with graceful arcatures (ornamental miniature arcading). The building is now used as a training and cultural centre, hotel and restaurant.

After skirting the little lake of Längsee (right), turn left onto the main road to return to St. Veit.

★ **Magdalensberg** – *15km/9mi – about 2hr. Leave St. Veit on the road to Klagenfurt.* After 7km/4mi turn left onto an uphill road on the flank of the Magdalensberg, within view of the Klagenfurt basin and the Karawanken mountain barrier.

The road ends at the **Magdalensberg excavations** (Ausgrabungen) ⏲ which have exposed traces of an early Roman town, built on the remains of a pre-Roman settlement. In the period around the birth of Christ this was the political and economic centre of the eastern Alps. An **archeological park** has been set up with various exhibitions about this town.

Walk *(45min there and back)* up to the top of the mountain (alt 1 058m/3 470ft), where there is a Gothic pilgrims' chapel dedicated to St Helen and St Mary Magdalene, which houses a beautiful hinged panelled altarpiece (pre-1502) from the woodcarving workshops at St. Veit. There is a majestic **panorama**★ of the wooded Saualpe range, the Klagenfurt basin, the Karawanken and the great semi-mountainous area known as the Nockgebiet, to the northwest. Among the nearest heights is the Ulrichsberg (west) with Celtic temple ruins.

ST. WOLFGANG★★

Oberösterreich

Population 2 790

Michelin map 926 fold 20 – Local map see SALZKAMMERGUT – Alt 549m/1 801ft

An invasion of visitors is no novelty for St. Wolfgang which stands beside a lake of the same name. It has been a place of pilgrimage since the 12C, and its church is enriched by magnificent works of art. This tradition explains, perhaps, why local life has not been upset by the modern influx of tourists, who come to see the original of the "White Horse Inn", and the beautiful landscape and magnificent **lake**★★ praised in the operetta of that name *(Weißes Rößl)*. The charm of St. Wolfgang is most strongly felt in the less busy periods either side of the main summer season and during the winter.

Access – Parking in St. Wolfgang can be difficult in summer. There are two car parks: at the entrance to the village and at the Schafberg station, 1km/0.5mi beyond the church. In the high season a pleasant alternative is to arrive by **boat** ⏲; frequent services operate from Strobl and St. Gilgen and call in at Schafberg and the centre of St. Wolfgang.

CHURCH (PFARRKIRCHE)

This church was the successor to the chapel of a hermitage built, according to tradition, by St Wolfgang, Bishop of Regensburg (canonized 1052), who came to seek solitude on the shores of the "Abersee". The present structure dates from the second half of the 15C. Its site on a rocky spur and the need to accommodate as many pilgrims as possible have given rise to its irregular plan. It abuts on to the elegant structure of the 16C priory, which at one time was served by the Benedictines of Mondsee. The outer cloisters, lined with arcades which yield bird's-eye views of the lake, complete the charming character of the **site**★★.

Enter the church through the south door.

★★ **Michael-Pacher-Altar** – This masterpiece (1481), showing rare unity in composition and considered to be an outstanding example of Gothic art, was commissioned for the high altar by an abbot of Mondsee and made at Bruneck (Brunico) in South Tyrol, in the master's studio. Subjects for the various scenes were supplied to Pacher by the local bishop, Cardinal Nikolaus Cusanus, famous theologian and humanist of his time. It is certain that the carving of the central panel (Coronation of the Virgin) and the complementary paintings with gilded backgrounds on the shutters showing scenes from the life of the Virgin Mary, are by Michael Pacher himself. An explanation is available on how the various positions of the shutters were arranged to follow the liturgy.

Pacher reveals himself to be a master of perspective and of detail in this work. On the 12m/39ft high altarpiece both form and expression are reproduced with consummate expertise.

★ **Schwanthaler-Doppelaltar** – This Baroque masterpiece was created by Thomas Schwanthaler in 1675-76. On the left panel of this double-panelled altarpiece, executed in black and gold and placed in the middle of the nave, the Holy Family is depicted on their pilgrimage to Jerusalem. On the right panel is the figure of St Wolfgang. This exceptionally lively composition depicts more than 100 figures full of life and energy.

It is said that Thomas Schwanthaler dissuaded the abbot of Mondsee from replacing Pacher's altarpiece with his own during the conversion of the church to the Baroque style, but there is no evidence to corroborate this story. Modern visitors have the unusual chance here of visiting a village church and viewing two masterpieces which were created for it at an interval of 200 years.

Altar by Michel Pacher, St. Wolfgang

A family of artists

The **Schwanthaler family**, from Ried im Innkreis, produced no less than 21 artists in a period of 250 years, the majority of whom were sculptors. A 19C descendant, Ludwig Ritter von Schwanthaler, Court Sculptor to King Ludwig I of Bavaria, was responsible for the sculpted figure of Bavaria on the Theresienwiese in Munich.

A third great artist was active at St. Wolfgang: the Mondsee master **Meinrad Guggenbichler**, to whom the three altars on the north side of the church, including the majestic Rosenkranzaltar, and the pulpit are attributed. His *Man of Sorrows* is particularly heart-rending.
Close by the church is the famous **Weißes Rößl** (White Horse Inn).

EXCURSION

★★ **Schafberg** ⌚ – *About 4hr there and back, including 2hr by rack railway and 30min on foot.* From the terminus, make for the hotel on the summit (alt 1 783m/ 5 850ft), a few metres from the impressive precipice on the north face. It is said that from here one can count 13 lakes in the Salzkammergut; the most visible are the lakes of Mondsee, Attersee and St. Wolfgang. In the background, in succession, are the Höllengebirge, the Totes Gebirge, the Dachstein with its glaciers, the Tennengebirge, the Hochkönig, which can be recognized by its large patch of snow, the Steinernes Meer, the Berchtesgaden Alps and the Loferer Steinberge.

SCHÄRDING★

Oberösterreich

Population 5 640

Michelin map 926 fold 7 – Alt 318m/1 043ft

First mentioned in 804 as a farmstead within the domain of Passau Cathedral, Schärding received its town charter in 1316. The Wittelsbach family, to whom the town belonged almost without a break from 1248 to 1779, built a castle and fortifications here, of which only the gateway, the outer ward and the moat remain. The favourable position on the Inn allowed trade to flourish in salt and wood, in tuff and marble, and even in wine. In 1779 Schärding with the rest of the Innviertel was ceded by Bavaria to Austria.

R. Chéret/MICHELIN

Silberzeile, Schärding

SIGHTS

Stadtplatz – The main square is divided into upper and lower sections (Oberer and Unterer Stadtplatz) by a row of buildings called a Grätzel running across it, and presents a remarkable combination of elements, dominated by the tower of the nearby Stadtpfarrkirche. To the east the upper square is closed off by the Linzer Tor (Linz Gate), while the Rathaus (town hall) marks the beginning of the lower square, in the centre of which stands the St.-Georgs-Brunnen (St George's Fountain) of 1607 with its wrought-iron grille. The end of the square narrows and the ground falls away as one reaches the **Wassertor** (Water Gate), which bears a painting of St Florian on the town side. High water marks provide evidence of disastrous flooding by the Inn.

★ **Silberzeile** – This row of houses running northeast in the upper Stadtplatz, dating from the 16C to the 19C, is Schärding's showpiece. The name ("Silver Row") recalls the rich merchants who lived here and wanted to display their wealth. Neat, gently curving Late Baroque gables surmount the colourfully rendered house fronts, creating a scene of remarkable homogeneity. At the rear the houses have simple pointed gables (as can be seen from the Seilergraben).

Stadtpfarrkirche – The parish church is away from the main square, an unusual feature in the Inn-Salzach area. The Late Baroque structure, completed in 1724 and dedicated to St George, had to be restored in the early 19C after a bombardment by the Napoleonic army. The fine proportions give the well-lit nave a lofty dignity, emphasized by the columns extending upwards more than one storey. The side altar on the left has a panel by Michael Rottmayr (Christ appearing to St Theresa) of about 1690.

Innlände – It is worth taking a stroll along this promenade by the river, as the town can be seen from a different and no less attractive perspective. The landing-stage for the river steamers is here, and on the other side of the river the monastery of Neuhaus can be made out.

SCHLADMINGER TAUERN★★

Steiermark

Michelin map 926 folds 21, 33 and 34

This mountain chain is surrounded to the west by the Radstädter Tauern and to the east by the Wölzer Tauern. It stretches for 40km/25mi and towers over the broad **Ennstal**. On the other side of this valley, opposite and parallel to the Schladminger Tauern, is the majestic **Dachstein massif★★** *(see DACHSTEIN)*.

The contrast between these two mountain chains is surprising. Whereas the Dachstein has the appearance of a fortress with its limestone rocks, steep jagged cliffs and the essentially barren landscape which is its distinguishing feature, the Schladminger Tauern are made up mainly of crystalline rocks and are characterised by long, densely wooded and easily accessible valleys, in which there are numerous lakes and rivers.

It is precisely these varied landscapes that lend the Ennstal its special attraction, which was further enhanced by the growth in popularity of winter sports in the 1960s. It was then that the outlying sections of the Schladminger Tauern with their smooth slopes were equipped with the appropriate infrastructure and thus became an important ski area. Above these foothills of moderate height (peaks of around 1 850 to 2 000m/6 070 to 6 560ft), the heart of the chain consists of an Alpine area which towers above the valley, in places, by more than 2 000m/6 560ft. The most famous peaks, from east to west, are the Hochwildstelle (alt 2 747m/9 012ft), the Hochstein (alt 2 545m/8 350ft), the **Hochgolling** (alt 2 863m/9 393ft) and the Steirische Kalkspitze (2 459m/8 067ft). Here, the hiker has access to wide-open, unspoilt areas with spectacular views, but only after a long and arduous climb.

The Ennstal is the optimum starting point for exploring the Schladminger Tauern and has become, over the years, a large centre for tourism with plenty of hotel and leisure facilities.

DACHSTEIN-TAUERN SKI AREA

In order to be able to offer holidaymakers the largest possible hinterland, the resorts scattered between the Schladminger Tauern and the Dachstein have joined forces and issue a joint ski pass. The area comprises 78 lifts, 140km/87mi of downhill ski-runs and 350km/217mi of off-piste slopes.

The **downhill ski runs**❄ are mainly concentrated on the Schladminger Tauern and consist of five areas: the **Reiteralm** (alt 800-1 860m/2 625-6 102ft) above Pichl; the **Hochwurzen** (745-1 850m/2 444-6 069ft) above Rohrmoos; the **Planai** (745-1 894m/2 444-6 213ft) above Schladming; the **Hauser Kaibling** (752-2 015m/

2 467-6 611ft) above Haus; and the **Gaisterbergalm** (680-1 976m/2 231-6 483ft) above Pruggern, as well as three smaller areas: Fageralm, Stoderzinken and the Dachstein glacier.

The four main ski areas – Hauser Kaibling, Planai, Hochwurzen and Reiteralm – have been connected to each other since 1998. Buses also operate between them, as before. The Dachstein-Tauern region is suitable, above all, for moderately good skiers, who will find suitable pistes on each massif, but less so for those who like open spaces and large differences in altitude. Good skiers, however, can try out their skills on the "east slope" of the Hauser Kaibling and on the World Cup piste on the Planai. The pistes along the Weitmoos ski lift to Schladming and the Rohrmoos II chair-lift are suitable for beginners.

The snow cover is good as a rule, but the moderate altitude can pose problems. The snow on the lower pistes, which are equipped with artificial snow cannon, is hard and icy at times and is therefore not suitable for inexperienced skiers.

For cross-country skiers, the Schladminger Tauern provide 60km/37mi of cross-country ski tracks all round Rohrmoos in beautiful, sunny surroundings, and a further 28km/17mi around Schladming. Cross-country skiers should spend their holidays on the **plateau** of **Ramsau am Dachstein**✻ *(see DACHSTEIN)*: the internationally renowned **cross-country ski area**✻✻✻ there is distinguished by a particularly enchanting setting.

✻ **Schladming** – Alt 745m/2 444ft. The regular World Cup downhill races arranged on the Planai slopes since 1973 have given Schladming plenty of publicity as a ski resort. Après-ski entertainment is also provided for, with generous sports facilities (themed swimming pool, indoor tennis courts etc). Schladming is an ideal destination for golfers, too, for whom there is a demanding 18-hole course at Oberhaus. In summer, the pedestrian zone is a joy to stroll around.

Other holiday resorts in the valley include **Rohrmoos**, Pichl, **Haus** (with a pretty Baroque church) and Pruggern.

However, many holidaymakers prefer the sunny plateau of **Ramsau**✻ *(see DACHSTEIN)*, in order to enjoy the unspoilt countryside and enchanting setting of the Dachstein.

VIEWPOINTS

★★★ **Hunerkogel** – Alt 2 694m/8 836ft. Wonderful view across the whole Schladminger Tauern chain. *See DACHSTEIN.*

★★ **Roßbrand** – Alt 1 770m/5 807ft. *1hr there and back by car (28km/17mi west of Schladming) followed by 20min there and back on foot.* Splendid view over the Enns Valley with the Dachstein on one side and the Schladminger Tauern on the other. *See DACHSTEIN.*

★★ **Planai** ⌚ – Alt 1 906m/6 253ft. *1hr there and back from Schladming. Take the cable-car up, in two stages (sit facing the back). Also accessible via a small mountain (toll) road.*

The view from the mountain station at an altitude of 1 825m/5 987ft is rather limited. Climb up on foot *(15min)* to the summit marked with a cross, from where there is a wonderful **panorama**★★. In winter, skiers can make the journey via the Burgstallalm piste and also the chair-lift of the same name.

To the south, the Schladminger Tauern (Höchstein, Hochgolling, Steirische Kalkspitze) and behind them, further to the west, the Radstädter Tauern (Mosermandl) and the Hohe Tauern (Großglockner) can be seen. To the north tower the Hochkönig, the Steinernes Meer, the Tennengebirge, the Dachstein and the Totes Gebirge peaks.

Hikers can climb up to the **Krahbergzinken** (alt 2 134m/7 001ft) in 2hr 30min *(there and back)*. An easy nature trail takes you round the summit of the Planai in 45min.

★★ **Hochwurzen** ⌚ – Alt 1 849m/6 066ft. *30min there and back. Accessible from Rohrmoos by cable-car. Climb to the summit up a flight of steps.*

Remarkable **panorama**★★ of the Dachstein opposite. View of Schladming. Walk as far as the terrace of the mountain inn, from where it is possible to see the heart of the Schladminger Tauern massif with the Hochgolling and Steirische Kalkspitze summits.

★ **Hauser Kaibling** ⌚ – Alt 1 870m/6 135ft. *At least 45min there and back. Accessible from Haus by means of the Hauser Kaibling cable-car and also the Quattralpina chair-lift. If these are closed, take the Schladminger Tauern cable-car.*

View★ across the Planai area and the Sonntagerhöhe. To the northeast looms the Stoderzinken and, behind it and to the right, the Großer Priel (Totes Gebirge). To the north, the Dachstein stretches as far as the Bischofsmütze.

Skiers should not fail to take the lift to the summit and then climb, in a few minutes, to the actual top of the Hauser Kaibling (marked by a cross). Wonderful **panorama**★★, above all of the Hochstein. The view stretches as far as the Großglockner.

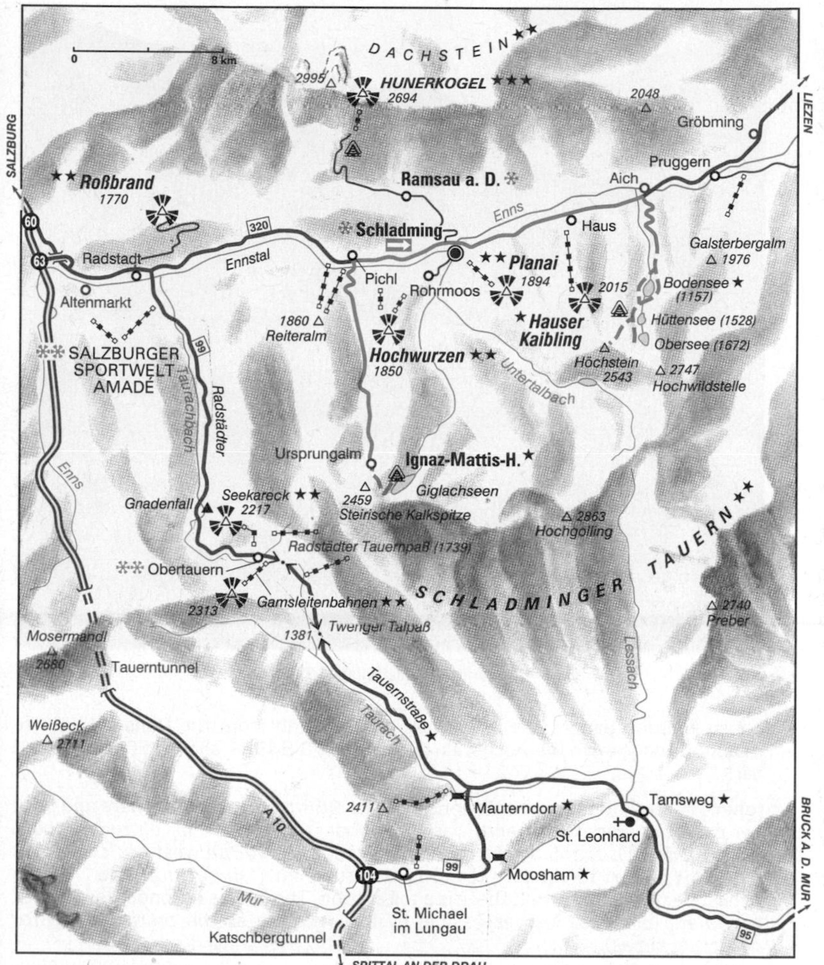

HIKES

The villages scattered throughout the Ennstal, and especially Schladming, are ideal starting points for **walks and hikes**★★ in the relatively low-lying surrounding mountain ranges. A magnificent panorama can be enjoyed from a number of summits (Höchstein, Hochgolling), but because of the long climb involved, it is necessary to plan an overnight stay at the mountain lodge. A number of easily accessible excursions are described below, which we would recommend, above all, for holidaymakers who are staying in the region for a longish period, rather than for tourists who are only making a brief stay.

★ **Dreiseen circuit** – *45min drive for the round trip (17km/11mi east of Schladming). 45min easy walk as far as the sparkling Bodensee Lake. For the full circuit round the three lakes, allow for a 4hr round trip involving some quite taxing walking; the trip leads through a nature reserve. Drive on E 651 towards Liezen then turn right, level with Aich, and continue on a small toll road towards the Bodensee.*

From the car park, a broad trail leads *(15min)* to the **Bodensee**★, which is dominated by a beautiful waterfall. The walk round the lake *(just under 30min)* is a pleasant one. There is an inn on the shore of the lake.

People who like hiking and who have sturdy footwear can walk along the western edge *(to the right)* to the far end of the lake and then take 1hr or so to climb an arduous trail up to the Hans-Wödl-Hütte mountain lodge (alt 1 528m/5 013ft) on the shores of the **Hüttensee**, a lake lying in an idyllic **setting**★. A beautiful spruce forest and two waterfalls, which plunge down from the rocky foothills of the Hochwildstelle and the Hochstein, form the backdrop.

In 45min, the trail takes you through luxuriant vegetation as far as the **Obersee** (alt 1 672m/5 485ft), a crystal-clear, shallow expanse of water. Climb down to the Bodensee again and this time walk along its eastern edge.

Y. Bontoux

Bodensee, Schladminger Tauern

Those keen on panoramic views may like to climb from the Hans-Wödl-Hütte mountain lodge up to the Hochstein (alt 2 543m/8 343ft), allowing 6hr there and back.

★ **Ignaz-Mattis-Hütte mountain lodge** – Alt 1 986m/6 516ft. *1hr there and back by car and 3hr there and back on foot (difference in altitude: about 500m/1 640ft).* Travel by car to Pichl-Preunegg *(5km/3mi west of Schladming on E 651).* Turn to the left towards Ursprungalm *(14km/9mi).* **View★** of the Dachstein. After 6km/4mi, there is a toll station. The road is no longer tarmacked but is still drivable. Also accessible by bus *(enquire at the tourist office for departure times).*
From the car park at the end of the road, the picturesque hamlet of Ursprungalm at the foot of the **Steirische Kalkspitze** (alt 2 459m/8 067ft) can be reached in a few minutes. Walk past the houses on the left-hand trail. After an hour's walk, the Giglachsee-Hütte mountain lodge comes in sight. Turn off to the left and carry on for another 20min to the Ignaz-Mattis-Hütte mountain lodge. From the footpath, there are a number of **views★** of the two **Giglach** lakes, set amid beautiful unspoilt countryside. Climb down from the lodge to the lower lake, walk along on the other side as far as the Giglachsee-Hütte mountain lodge and then return to the car park on the same footpath that you climbed up.

Stift SCHLÄGL★

Oberösterreich

Michelin map 926 fold 8

The abbey of Schlägl, founded at the foot of the Bohemian Forest by a ministerial of the Bishop of Passau, is one of the forest clearance monasteries and as such has an appropriate name, since it could be derived from "Slage" meaning a clearing; hence the crossed hammers (Schlägel) in the abbey's coat of arms.
Cistercians from Upper Franconia made the first attempt at founding a monastery between 1202 and 1204, about 3km/2mi from the present site, but this came to nothing. A group of Premonstratensians from Osterhofen in Lower Bavaria were however successful when they settled in 1218 on the left bank of the Großer Mühl. The community suffered various vicissitudes over the centuries (seven instances of fire), but escaped secularization under Joseph II. In the 19C, under Abbot Dominik Lebschy, it even experienced a time of great prosperity, as evidenced by the purchase of many works of art and the building of the library.
The abbey now has its own brewery, an abbey cellar with a restaurant and a seminar centre.

TOUR ⏲

Stiftskirche (Abbey church) – Above the well proportioned doorway of 1654 made of red and white marble stands a Madonna in glory as patroness of the monastery, together with cherubs and coats of arms in cartouches. Passing through a narthex, one enters the interior divided by rectangular pillars into three aisles, which have retained their Gothic character despite the Baroque stuccowork. The church may not be very large, but the unusual height of the nave and in particular the monumental flight of steps leading up into the choir (below which is the crypt) make a deep impression. The **furnishings**★, in which shades of brown and gold predominate, are Baroque in style. The pulpit is the work of the South Tyrolean sculptor Johann Worath, completed in 1647 with representations of the twelve Apostles and John the Baptist in shell-like recesses. The high altar with the Assumption of the Virgin Mary, as well as the side altars, date from 1721 to 1740. The richly carved choir stalls lining the chancel walls were completed in c 1735. A skilfully crafted chancel railing by Hans Walz in 1635 closes off the chancel area. The great **organ** in the west gallery was made by the Passau organ builder Andreas Putz and is a superb example of 17C South German organ building. The case is by the sculptor Georg Obermayr, also from Passau.

Frühgotischer Kreuzgang (early Gothic cloisters) – Note the tombstones of former abbots and an exhibition on the history and present activities of the order.

Turmkapelle (Tower chapel) – Only revealed in 1988, it probably dates from about 1410 and is a rare example of simulation in Gothic architecture.

Krypta (Crypt) – The Romanesque crypt, with its octagonal central pillar, is the oldest room in the abbey complex, dating from about 1250. A round arch leads through to the **Gothic crypt**, which was laid out later.

Bildergalerie (Picture gallery) – This was set up in 1898 to house part of the abbey's important **collection of paintings**★, the main items of interest are the Late Gothic panels and winged altarpieces. Unusually for an abbey, the portrait gallery contains a collection of portraits of former monks (after 1802).

Stiftsbibliothek (Abbey library) – The neo-Baroque library was completed in 1852 and contains over 60 000 volumes. It is modelled on the abbey library in St. Florian. A small number of manuscripts and incunabula are on view in display cases.

Meierhof des Stiftes (Old dairy yard) – Collection of local rural implements from the Upper Mühlviertel region.

EXCURSION

★ **Moldaublick** – *17km/11mi. First go to Aigen im Mühlkreis, and from there to Ulrichsberg; shortly after this place take the road to the right for Moldaublick.* The route passes through pretty and very peaceful countryside. The observation tower is 24m/79ft high with 137 steps, and gives a wonderful **view** into the Czech Republic and of the Moldau (Vltava), which is dammed at this point.

Tour of the SCHNEEBERG★

Niederösterreich

Michelin map 926 folds 24 and 25

The limestone bastions of the Raxalpe and the Schneeberg are separated by the deep Schwarza Valley (called the Höllental or "Hell Valley" along its central section). Since the completion of the Semmering railway in the mid 19C, this region has been within easy reach of Vienna, and the mountains are much frequented by Viennese hill walkers and touring enthusiasts in summer and by skiers from the capital as soon as the first snows whiten the ski runs of their summits in winter.

★FROM NEUNKIRCHEN TO SEMMERING *102km/63mi*

The route described below includes some very steep (up and down) and narrow stretches of road, particularly towards the end between Hirschwang and Semmering.

Neunkirchen – North of the Hauptplatz with its Trinity Column, the massive chancel belonging to the parish church of Mariä Himmelfahrt (mid 12C-16C, Baroque interior) towers above the surrounding rooftops. The town's frontier site meant that the church was designed as a defensive installation; it was even originally surrounded by a moat.

In Neunkirchen, turn off B 17 onto B 26 towards Puchberg.

From **Ternitz** a pleasant road, sometimes under trees, runs up the delightful Sierning Valley. At the exit to the Ternitz outpost of Sieding, the imposing fortress of Stixenstein comes into view above the road.

A little before Puchberg rocky cliffs become increasingly numerous on either side of the road.

Puchberg am Schneeberg – This pleasant mountain air health resort, with idyllic spa gardens laid out around a lake, is gathered at the foot of a hill on which the village church (rebuilt after the original was destroyed in the Second World War) and a 12C ruined castle stand. From Puchberg station, a mountain **rack-railway** ⏲ runs visitors up the Schneeberg.

★ **Ascent of the Schneeberg** – *Using the Schneeberg railway and then an easy walk to the summit (about 3hr on foot there and back; for the entire trip depending on train times allow between half to a whole day). The walk is suitable also for young children, but you may need to allow more time.*

The old-fashioned steam engine or modern, vibrantly patterned train takes visitors up to the upper station (1 795m/5 889ft) next to Hochschneeberg mountain refuge (rooms available, restaurant) and a memorial church to Empress Elisabeth (1899-1901). A panoramic table by the upper station is the starting point for a "Wander-Autobahn" ("hiking-motorway" – a very well maintained footpath with further "service stations") leading via the Fischer refuge (2 048m/6 719ft) to the **Klosterwappen** spur (2 076m/6 811ft), the Schneeberg's highest point, with a directional radio station beneath the cross marking the summit (**view**★ of the Raxalpe beyond the Höllental).

A few yards above the Fischer refuge, to the north, stands a small stone monument, marking the Kaiserstein (2 061m/6 762ft, **view**★ on a clear day as far as Vienna and the Neusiedler See). Those who walk as far as this viewpoint will be able to take the Schneeberg train back down into the valley with the uplifting thought that they have conquered two 2 000m/6 500ft high summits in a single day.

Leave Puchberg on B 26 towards Wiener Neustadt and at the exit to town turn left towards Waldegg.

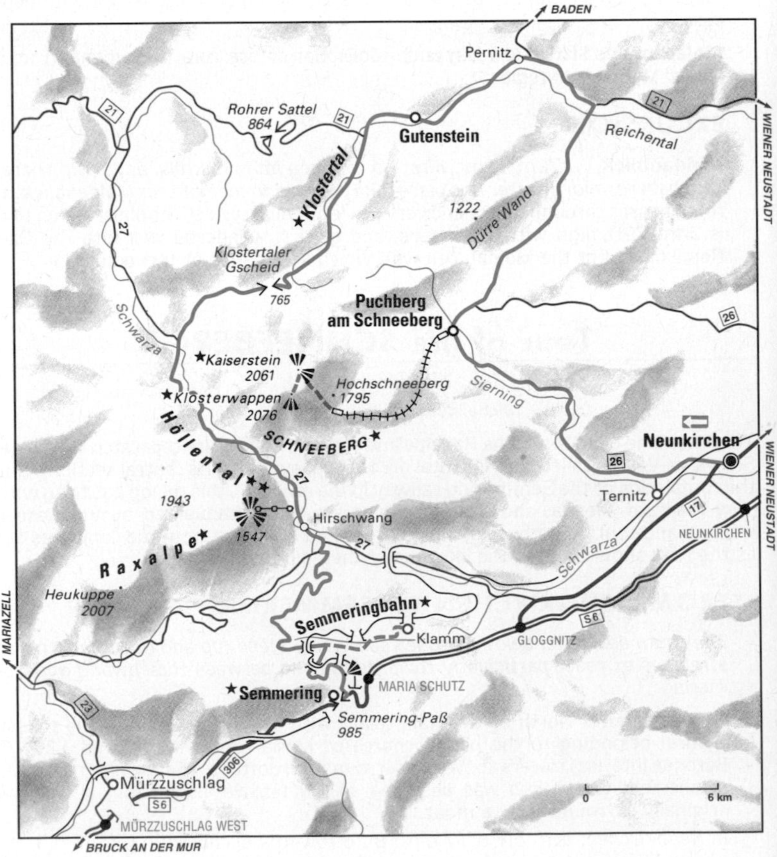

The road winds among fir trees, following the course of the Miesenbach which in places still seems totally untouched by human hand. It passes several sawmills (as it will do later on in the tour), indicating an important source of local income. To the left of the road are the wooded slopes of the "Dürre Wand" (arid wall).

In Reichental turn left onto B 26 towards Gutenstein.

The road follows the railway. After the industrial town of **Pernitz** comes the relatively broad and green floor of the Piesting Valley, stretching as far as Gutenstein.

Gutenstein – In the 19C Gutenstein was a popular summer holiday resort, attracting artists such as Lenau, Brahms and Waldmüller. In memory of the Austrian actor and playwright **Ferdinand Raimund**, who committed suicide here in 1836, fearing that he had caught rabies from a dog, and who is buried in the town graveyard, the market town hosts the annual Raimundspiele (open-air theatre performances during the summer). A further cultural highlight is the "Cartusiana" summer festival of classical music (concerts).

Wallfahrtskirche Mariahilfberg – *In the centre of Gutenstein, turn left just before the church towards Mariahilfberg. About 3km/2mi along a delightful stretch of road (very narrow, numerous hairpin bends, gradient at times 1 in 8) there is a car park. Short walk from here to the pilgrimage church.* A convent of the Servite Order, in charge of looking after pilgrims, is attached to the Baroque pilgrimage church (completed in 1724). The pilgrimage dates back to 1661, and various Habsburg emperors are among those to have taken part in it. In the left side aisle of the church, next to the entrance, is the altarpiece of the condemned soul with a striking depiction of an angel coming to the rescue of a soul burning in Purgatory.

2km/1.2mi beyond Gutenstein turn left into the Klostertal.

★ **Klostertal** – *About 16km/10mi.* This valley is only sparsely populated and long sections of it are almost completely unspoiled: a lush green idyll. For the most part, the valley floor is quite broad, but it narrows considerably towards the end, and an increasing number of passages between steep cliffs herald the Höllental, into which you turn left at the end of the Klostertal.

★★ **Höllental** – *About 14km/8.5mi.* Höllental, or Hell Valley, is the name given to the gap cut by the River Schwarza between the two limestone massifs of the Schneeberg and the Raxalpe. Initially there is quite a contrast between the delightful Klostertal and the harsher Wildbach Valley, where the green water gushes over the boulders and gravel of the deeply embedded riverbed. It is not long before this rugged environment works its charm on the onlooker, however, as the road switches from one bank to the other. The valley becomes even narrower and is enclosed between magnificent, often quite sheer, cliffs, to which pine trees cling precariously.

At the entrance to Hirschwang, the valley station of the Rax cable-car is to the right of the road.

★ **Raxalpe** – This steep-sided limestone massif has become a regular climbing centre, from where numerous climbs and mountain tours can be undertaken. From the upper station of the **Rax cable-car** ⌚ at an altitude of 1 547m/5 075ft (ascent takes about 10min) there are a number of options for a hike *(between 10-16.5km/6-10mi in length)*, sold as "Hüttenhüpfen auf der Raxalpe" ("Hut-hopping on the Raxalpe") by the Reichenau tourist office. These bring you to several charming **viewpoints**★ over the Schneeberg and Höllental to the north, and Semmering, its surroundings and east Styria to the south.

At the exit to Hirschwang turn right towards Prein. 500m/550yd further on turn left towards Gloggnitz (there is also a green signpost to "Gasthof-Pension Hecher"). After another 300m/330yd turn right towards Semmering (another signpost to the same inn).

The road leaves the Schwarza Valley, and with many bends cuts across a picturesque, rugged Semmering region with wooded spurs and ravines. 2.5km/1.5mi after the Semmering turning, Schloß Rothschild (late 19C, information panel) comes into view to the left in the valley below. As the road drops **down to Breitenstein**★ *(gradient of up to 1 in 4)* it passes one or two quite threatening-looking cliffs and outcrops of rock, giving the first glimpses of the superbly engineered viaducts of the **Semmering railway**★ *(see box)*, whose tracks cross the road more than once.

Shortly after the signpost indicating "Semmering" turn left towards "Haltestelle Wolfsbergkogel". After a couple of hundred yards turn left again and follow the wooden "Aussichtswarte Doppelreiterkogel" signs. Park the car and take the marked path to the look-out point (about 10min on foot).

From the **Doppelreiterkogel look-out point**★★ there is perhaps the finest view of the Semmering railway, which cuts a particularly fine route at this point, with numerous viaducts and tunnels. To the left of Breitenstein station towers the mighty Pollos cliff-face with the Raxalpe range behind it.

Semmering railway

There were already rail links between Vienna and Gloggnitz, and between Mürzzuschlag and Bruck an der Mur. It was only over the Semmering range that horse-drawn carts were still used. In order to complete the final gap in the southern railway network, the Venetian engineer Carlo di Ghega (1802-60; later knighted and known as **Carl Ritter von Ghega**) was invited to take over the Semmering railway project. Between 1848 and 1854, up to 20 000 workers, mainly of Italian or Slavonic descent, were employed during peak periods on the track of Europe's first standard-gauge mountain railway (some 1 000 of them died in accidents or from epidemics during construction). On the 41km/25mi stretch between Gloggnitz and Mürzzuschlag (21km/13mi above ground) the train passes through 15 tunnels, crosses 16 viaducts and more than 100 smaller bridges and, as the difference in altitude of 480m negotiated during this section suggests, must have a gradient of between 1 in 5 or 1 in 4 for about 60% of its length. In spite of the tremendous feats of construction - 1.4 million m^3/49 million cu ft of rock alone had to be blasted - the railway blends harmoniously into the beautiful landscape around Semmering. After the inauguration of the railway line by Emperor Franz Joseph and Empress Elisabeth the region experienced a spectacular growth in popularity as a summer retreat for the Viennese. For example, for the Whitsun break in 1857 55 000 people travelled from Vienna to Mürzzuschlag in only two days. Originally, steam engines trundled over the Semmering range at 6kph/4mph, but after the line was electrified in 1956 speeds increased to 60kph/37mph.
In 1999, the "Ghega railway" and the surrounding countryside were officially declared a world heritage site by UNESCO.

Retrace your steps and follow the signposts to "Hochstraße/Südbahnstraße" to get to Semmering town centre.

★ **Semmering** - This climatic mountain spa and winter sports centre, built on terraces between 985m/3 231ft and 1 291m/4 235ft, enjoys a privileged position. After construction of the Semmering railway, the town experienced a real economic boom as a result of the influx of visitors from Vienna. This is evident from the numerous smart villas and hotels, very fancy indeed in some cases, that were built, between 1850 and 1910 for the most part. The resort does not suffer from the cold fogs of the valleys and has an exceptionally sunny climate, which helps to make it one of the greatest centres of attraction in Lower Austria.

Archiv Zwick/ÖSTERREICH WERBUNG

The Semmering railway

★ **Bahnwanderweg** *The departure for this walk along the railway is Semmering station. Near a memorial to the railway builder Carl Ritter von Ghega is a diesel engine containing information panels on the story of the railway's construction. The section of the walk described below leads as far as the station at Klamm 15.5km/10mi away (allow at least 5hr). Return on the Semmering railway. Good sturdy walking shoes are essential, as there are some steep sections. Information on the Semmering railway timetable and the entire walk (23km/14mi) is available from the Semmering tourist office.*
Follow the path indicated by yellow signs ("Bahnwanderweg") to the left behind the station.
The path follows a mainly shady route through breathtaking countryside, often very close to the Semmering railway constructions, to the regular accompaniment of the trains. The highlight of the walk is the **Doppelreiterkogel lookout point**★★ *(see above)* about 2.5km/1.5mi after Semmering station. After Breitenstein *(about 9.5km/6mi)* the landscape takes on softer contours and mountain pastures alternate with woodland. The end of the path is Klamm, marked by a ruined fortress (skirt the fortress past the gate to the right to reach a good viewpoint on a rocky spur: to the left is the 640m/700yd bridge spanning the valley at Schottwein). From the station in Klamm, you can make out the Baroque pilgrimage church of **Maria Schutz** on the other side of the valley. The return to Semmering by train is in itself a remarkable experience, allowing visitors to review their walk in reverse order. The railway goes through nine tunnels and crosses seven viaducts. After about 15min the train arrives at Semmering, its passengers no doubt fully appreciating the comfort of rail travel after their tiring walk.

SCHWAZ★

Tirol

Population 12 500
Michelin map 926 fold 17 – Alt 538m/1 765ft

From the 15C to the 16C when its **silver and copper mines** were in full production, Schwaz was the largest town in the Tyrol, after Innsbruck. The town was well cared for by the emperor and the financial powers of the period, especially the Fugger family of Augsburg. The degree of prosperity it enjoyed is attested today by the unusual size and the decoration of its most representative buildings, all erected between 1450 and 1520.
This extravagant period also survives in popular tradition, according to which the miners of the past could make the paving of Schwaz ring with the silver nails in their boots.

★ PFARRKIRCHE (PARISH CHURCH)

The plain church façade, topped with a pinnacled gable, stands at the end of Franz-Josef-Straße. Under a huge roof, covered with 15 000 copper tiles, it shelters four aisles and two parallel chancels, restored in 1912 to their Gothic style of the 15C, with network vaulting. The main south aisle and its chancel were reserved for the miners' corporation, as certain tombs indicate.
The organ-loft shows particularly elaborate Gothic decoration in the vaulting supporting it and in its balustrade. The Baroque organ-case is quite sumptuous. In the main part of the church, there are traces of the Gothic furnishings: the octagonal font of 1470 and, against the pillar separating the two chancels, a Christ with a very intense expression. The finest piece of religious sculpture is the **altar of St Anne** in the south side aisle. Its Baroque altarpiece (1733), honouring the patron saints of Austria, St George and St Florian, frames a fine group of the early 16C: the Holy Family between St Elizabeth on the right and St Ursula on the left. The gardens climbing up the slope to the south are graced by two fine **cloister walks**★ with pointed vaults.

ADDITIONAL SIGHTS

Franziskanerkirche – The Gothic church was finished in 1515. In the layout of its three naves it was in accordance with the strict building rules imposed by the Order. Its conversion to the Baroque style in 1736 destroyed neither its pleasant proportions nor its good lighting. The capitals on the tall marble columns, reduced to simple rings, have a decorative function. The Renaissance **stalls**★ (1618) are the work of a local master craftsman.

Kreuzgang (Cloisters) – *Entrance through the door of the monastery on the south side of the church.* The cloisters are pure Gothic in style. They contain important remains of wall paintings representing scenes from the Passion (1519-26), attributed to a brother who came from Swabia. Charming designs of foliage, fruit and birds have adorned the vaulting since the beginning of the 17C. The community of Schwaz is symbolized by various shields: craftsmen and miners' guilds, as well as wealthy shareholders are shown. Emperor Maximilian is represented by the arms of his hereditary states.

★ **Silberbergwerk (Silver mine)** ⌚ – *Alte Landstraße 3a.* It is well worth taking the time to visit this display mine *(constant temperature of 13°C/55°F. Warm clothing and strong shoes recommended).* A pit railway takes visitors 800m/0.5mi into the Sigmund gallery, which was created about 500 years ago when Schwaz was the largest silver mining centre in the world and 11 000 miners dug out the precious metal. Then steps give access to a labyrinth of galleries, while the techniques of mining and excavation of shafts are graphically explained.

Schloß Freundsberg ⌚ – The square keep gives the castle a defiant appearance as it sits picturesquely on its knoll, with a commanding **view**★ of the Inn Valley and the town. The castle was built at the beginning of the 12C by the Ritter von Freundsberg, in whose family's possession it remained for over 300 years until it was acquired and then mortgaged by Sigmund der Münzreiche. The church may be viewed, and also the **Museum der Stadt Schwaz** (Schwaz Town Museum) in the tower.

EXCURSION

★ **Schloß Tratzberg** ⌚ – *5km/3mi. Leave Schwaz on the road to Stans.* Standing half way up its slope, this castle is the result of two distinct phases of building. Its severe exterior, still late medieval in appearance, dates from around 1500; other elements, like the painted arcades, were added some 60 years later in Renaissance style. The castle was used as a hunting lodge by Emperor Maximilian and the Fuggers, the powerful merchant dynasty from Augsburg, who had interests in Schwaz and in the silver mine.

A short walk brings visitors from the car park to the castle gate. There is a recorded description of the castle's history (in seven languages). The castle's roof is covered in larch shingles. Inside, there is still some original furniture, as well as pictures and weapons. The ceiling of the royal chamber (Königinzimmer) of 1569 is a magnificent timber construction, held together without a single nail. The Habsburg Room is also of interest; it contains a 46m/151ft long wall-painting (dating probably from 1508) which depicts 148 of Emperor Maximilian's ancestors in the form of a family tree. At the same time as guided tours for adults, there are special children's guided tours (minimum age four years) available in the form of fairy stories.

Rohracker/ÖSTERREICH WERBUNG

Schloß Tratzberg

Abtei SECKAU

Steiermark

Michelin map 926 south east of fold 22 – 11km/7mi north of Knittelfeld

The abbey at Seckau, founded in 1140, was run by Augustinian canons, and from 1218 was also a diocesan seat, until its dissolution by Joseph II in 1782. The bishop of Styria, who now resides at Graz, nonetheless still has the official title "Graz-Seckau". In 1883, Benedictine monks from Beuron Abbey came and took over the abbey at Seckau, thus preventing it from falling into ruin.
The extensive abbey complex, whose corner towers lend it a somewhat military air, stands majestically at the foot of the Seckau Alps (Niedere Tauern).

★ BASILICA ⏲

The body of the church, which dates from about 1150, was built with alternating piers and columns topped with huge square capitals with little decoration, in accordance with the Romanesque German tradition. The rich network vaulting of the main nave – originally roofed with timber – was added in the 15C, and the transept and changes in the chancel were introduced in the 19C, under the Benedictines.
A simple but moving **Crucifixion** is especially captivating; the figure of Christ Crucified dates from 1260, while those of Mary and Joseph probably date from earlier, c 1200.
Three chapels, of differing periods and arrangements, spring from the north aisle. They are interesting for their works of art. The first one, the **Engelkapelle** (Angel's Chapel), contains frescoes by Herbert Boeckl in 1960 depicting the Revelation of St John.

Gnadenkapelle – Over the tabernacle in the chapel of Grace is a 12C alabaster of Venetian origin, representing the Virgin and Child. This is the jewel of the Seckau Treasury and the oldest Marian image venerated in Austria.

Bischofskapelle – The **altarpiece**★★ of the high altar (1489) in the Episcopal chapel, celebrates the Coronation of the Virgin. In a circular framework, which is itself most unusual, the artist has represented the three Persons of the Holy Trinity with identical features, in strict conformity with the orthodox definition, three persons in one god. Stand back a little to see with what talent the sculptor has mastered so difficult a subject, for the slightest error of taste in this group of three heads on one body would have been fatal.

Mausoleum of Karl II – The Mausoleum of Archduke Karl II stands in the chapel which forms a prolongation of the north side aisle. Together they form a decorative scheme which is regarded as a specimen of the transition from Late Renaissance to Baroque art. As it was carried out by two Italians between 1587 and 1612, it also marks the beginning of the penetration of transalpine taste into Austria. This influence, which appeared in a dazzling fashion rather later in the mausoleum in Graz of Ferdinand II (the son of Archduke Karl), was naturally felt first in Styria.

SEEFELD IN TIROL❄❄

Tirol

Population 2 800

Michelin map 926 fold 16 – Local map see SEEFELDER SATTELSTRASSEN

Alt 1 180m/3 871ft

Seefeld lies on a broad mountain plateau, well exposed to the sun, with thick surrounding forest cover and a good view of the rocky ridges of the Hohe Munde, Wettersteingebirge and Karwendel range. It has become one of the most popular cross-country ski resorts in the Alps.
In the 1930s, Seefeld was already making a name for itself worldwide with the help of local skier Toni Seelos, who had mastered slalom like no other and who made a tremendous contribution to the technique of skiing. The village only really began to develop for tourism in the 1950s and 1960s, however, and its reputation grew even more after it had been the venue for the Nordic skiing events of the 1964 and 1976 Winter Olympic Games as well as for the World Skiing Championships of 1985.
The sophisticated ski resort boasts elegant hotels and restaurants, and a variety of excellent leisure facilities, including a large entertainment and congress centre, a modern swimming pool with water slides and a sauna etc, two ice rinks (with a skating school), numerous curling rinks, two riding centres, eight indoor tennis

courts, an indoor golf course and a casino. In summer these are augmented by an 18-hole golf course and 20 open-air tennis courts. Other options include paragliding, white water rafting and mountain biking.
But the principal charm of this resort lies in the refreshing landscape which surrounds it, which lends itself to walking at any time of year. Seefeld can offer, incredibly enough, 60km/37mi of excellently maintained footpaths in winter and 250km/155mi in the summer *(maps and guides available from the tourist office)*. The best walk is that up to the **Reither Spitze**★ *(see below)*. For those who prefer a less taxing walk, there is the circuit linking the lakes of Wildmoossee, Lottensee and Mösersee *(3hr walk from the Seekirchl Chapel)*. The last two of these lakes have water only when the snows are melting.

Ski slopes Seefeld boasts one of the largest **cross-country ski areas**❄❄❄ in the Alps, with 250km/155mi of tracks, and was the venue for the cross country skiing in the 1964 and 1976 Winter Olympics. Good snow cover is usually guaranteed from Christmas to March.
For downhill skiers, the resort has 25 ski lifts and a ski school (about 100 instructors), offering lessons in both kinds of skiing and in snowboarding. The slopes, parts of which are covered with artificial snow, are divided into two areas, each of which requires a separate ski pass. A chair-lift leads from near the Seekirchl up to the **Geschwandtkopf** summit (alt 1 500m/4 921ft). The most interesting slopes are to be found on the **Seefelder Joch** and more especially the **Härmelekopf**. The area is ideally suited to beginners or those who prefer gentle skiing.

SIGHTS

Pfarrkirche St. Oswald – This Gothic church was erected, with the generosity of the princes of the Tyrol, in the 15C, to perpetuate the worship of a miraculous host, which had been an object of pilgrimage since 1384 and was kept until 1949 in the high chapel of the Holy Blood.
The tympanum of the south door represents, on the right, the martyrdom of St Oswald of England, the patron saint of the church, and, on the left, the miracle of the host.
Inside there is network vaulting with slender ribs characteristic of the Late Gothic style. In the chancel, the mural paintings of the 15C (legend of St Oswald, the Passion, legend of St Mary Magdalene) have been restored. On the right, a picture (1502) of the Late Gothic period depicts the miracle of the host.

The Miraculous Host

The **Golden Chronicle of Hohenschwangau** records the miraculous event. One day, at the conclusion of Mass, the knight Oswald Milser and his armed followers surrounded the priest. His head covered and brandishing his sword, the arrogant nobleman insisted that his rank gave him the right to eat the same special wafer as the priest himself. Forced to comply, the man of God offered it to Milser. Suddenly the ground opened up beneath the feet of the sacrilegious knight. His whole body shaking with fear, he was only just able to cling to the altar, where his fingers left their mark as if in wax. The priest retrieved the wafer and the ground became firm again, though shortly afterwards the wafer turned blood-red.

Seekirchl – This chapel, which houses a miraculous cross of 1510, stands at the south end of the village and was built in 1632. It has a ground plan in the form of a rotunda which is most unusual for the Tyrol. The lovely building makes a charming sight silhouetted against the backdrop of the mountains.

EXCURSIONS

★★ **Seefelder Joch** ⌚ – Alt 2 074m/6 804ft. *Take the funicular up to the Roßhütte mountain refuge (alt 1 800m/5 906ft). Then take the Seefelderjochbahn.* From the mountain station, it takes a few minutes to reach the cross at the summit, from where there is a beautiful **panorama**★★. To the east are the Karwendel mountains, and to the north lies the Scharnitz pass road. To the northwest towers the long-drawn-out rocky ridge of the Wetterstein range, with the Zugspitze plateau at its edge. To the west, the view covers Seefeld and the broad Inn Valley behind it, framed by the Hohe Munde (Mieminger Gebirge) and Rietzer Grießkogel.
Even in winter, it is possible to walk from the Roßhütte down into the valley. Sturdy, waterproof shoes are, however, essential.

R. Chéret/MICHELIN

The Seekirchl, Seefeld

★★ **Hike to Reither Spitze** – Alt 2 374m/7 789ft. *For experienced hikers only.* From the Seefelder Joch, follow the ridge path to the Seefelder Spitze (alt 2 221m/7 287ft), then take the path down to the Reither Scharte. This eventually brings you to the Reither Spitze, from where there is a magnificent **panorama★★** as far as the Ziller Valley and the Stubai Alps. Climb down to the Nördlinger Hütte, and then walk on to the Hämelekopf cable-car station. Either walk the final part of the circuit down towards Reither Alm, or take the cable-car.

SEEFELDER SATTELSTRASSEN★★

Tirol and Bayern (Germany)

Michelin map 926 folds 16, 17 and 30

The Seefelder Sattel, or Seefeld Saddle, high above the Inn Valley and the Scharnitz ravine, makes a broad breach in the Northern Limestone Alps along the Munich-Innsbruck axis. The road is of great tourist interest but international traffic uses the lengthier, though less mountainous, motorway route following the Inn Valley.

★ZIRLERBERG

1 From Innsbruck to Mittenwald (Germany) *38km/24mi*

★★ **Innsbruck** – *See INNSBRUCK. Leave town on B 171.*

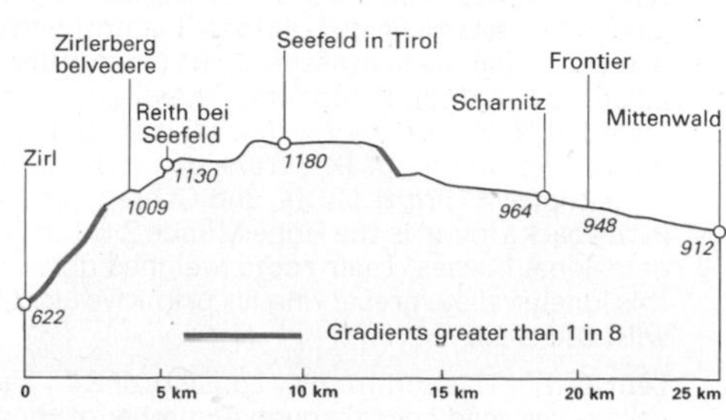

Between Innsbruck and Zirl the road, following the floor of the Inn Valley, runs beneath the steep slopes of the **Martinswand** (right) opposite the tributary valley of Sellrain. This promontory marks the traditional boundary between the upper and lower Inn Valley and provided the setting for an episode dear to the hearts of the Tyrolese: Emperor Maximilian is said to have fallen down the cliff in the excitement of the hunt and been saved from a perilous plight by an angel, appearing in the guise of a peasant.

Rather than driving into Zirl, turn right towards Seefeld.

On the other side of the road to the right are the Baroque Kalvarienbergkirche (1803-05) and the ruined fortress of Fragenstein outlined above Zirl. The well known **Zirlerberg★** slope covers the 500m/1 640ft difference in altitude between Zirl and Reith bei Seefeld. It was as steep as 1 in 4 in places before improvement - it is 1 in 7 - and it is said that every weekend spectators posted themselves at vantage points on the look-out for accidents. The only hairpin bend is now an organized **viewpoint★**, with a car park and restaurant (Rasthaus Zirlerberg), which has a great view of the "saw-teeth" of the Kalkkögel to the south of Zirl. Higher up in line with the road, to the right in the foreground, is the surprisingly smooth hump of the **Hohe Munde** with the other Mieminger Gebirge peaks to the left.

★ **Reith bei Seefeld** - The church stands in a charming **setting★** facing the small Roskogel range and the jagged crests of the Kalkkögel, which lie south of the Inn Valley.

★★ **Seefeld in Tirol** - *See SEEFELD IN TIROL.*

PlayCastle Tirol ⏲ - Wondering where to take the children if it's raining? Wonder no longer - this "adventure castle" north of Seefeld was opened in 1999 and is right by the main road (no 177, heading towards Scharnitz, Garmisch). In the PlayCastle itself, reminiscent of a massive toy shop, children will find a variety of entertainment including dolls, video games, a bouncy castle and even their own "Caribbean world", where they can splash about in water and build sandcastles to their heart's content (take swimming costumes with you). The **FunDome** offers the young and young-at-heart a broad spectrum of sports and recreation: airpark, tracks for skateboarding and rollerblading, hockey, climbing wall etc. Equipment can be hired for a fee or bought on site (or you can bring your own). In the **iWERKS-Erlebniskino**, visitors are shaken to their shoes as they experience the thrills and spills on screen in a less vicarious way than in standard cinemas. It's nail-biting stuff! Fast-food and drinks are on sale, so that visitors' every need is catered for. From the PlayCastle car park, the **view★** embraces, from left to right, the grey pyramid of the Hohe Munde summit (2 662m/8 734ft) peeking out of the pine forests on its lower slopes, the **Wetterstein** ridge (except for the Zugspitze), the Ahrnspitze (2 196m/7 205ft) and the first peaks of the Karwendel.
The road drops to the floor of a valley leading to the Isar and reaches the mouth of the Scharnitz ravine, gateway to Bavaria; a few miles over the border is Mittenwald.

★ **Mittenwald** - This violin-making community on the old trade route linking Augsburg with Verona is a popular tourist destination. The fine painted **houses★★** along the high street and the town's ideal location as a starting point for numerous excursions explain Mittenwald's popularity. Indeed, Goethe described it as a "living picture-book". A memorial at the foot of the church serves as a reminder that in 1684 local townsman Matthias Klotz introduced the craft of violin making to the village Mittenwald, thereby ensuring a prime position for the town in the world of music. Klotz had lived in Italy and had learned his craft from the master violin maker Amati. This tradition survives today in the form of a dozen violin makers, a technical school and the local museum, the **Geigenbau- und Heimatmuseum.**

★★ LEUTASCH VALLEY

2 From Mittenwald (Germany) to Telfs *32km/20mi*

This route combines a run through the Leutasch Valley and a visit to Mösern, one of the most attractive viewpoints in the upper Inn Valley.

★ **Mittenwald** - *See above.*

South of Mittenwald the road comes out of the Isar Valley and immediately climbs above the **Leutasch Gorge** (Leutaschklamm) within view of the Karwendel range.
After crossing the Leutascher Ache (beautiful view of this mountain stream to the left of the bridge), it runs into the grassy combe of Unterleutasch, majestically bounded on the left by the Ahrnspitze, and on the right by the rock walls of the Wettersteinwand (peaks from front to back: Wetterstein 2 298m/7 540ft, Öfelekopf 2 475m/8 120ft, and Gehrenspitze 2 377m/7 799ft; the fourth peak in the background is the Hohe Munde 2 662m/8 734ft). A few roofed crosses and occasional houses, their roofs weighed down with big stones, are dotted about this lonely valley, preserving its primitive air. Ahead, the Hohe Munde rises in line with the road.

Leutasch - This community consists of 24 village segments, strung out along the valley. The road goes through a number of them, and in Gasse forks left towards Seefeld. At the junction, there is another splendid view of the majestic Hohe Munde to the right.
From Gasse to Seefeld the road cuts a sinuous route through wooded countryside.

★★ **Seefeld in Tirol** - *See SEEFELD IN TIROL.*

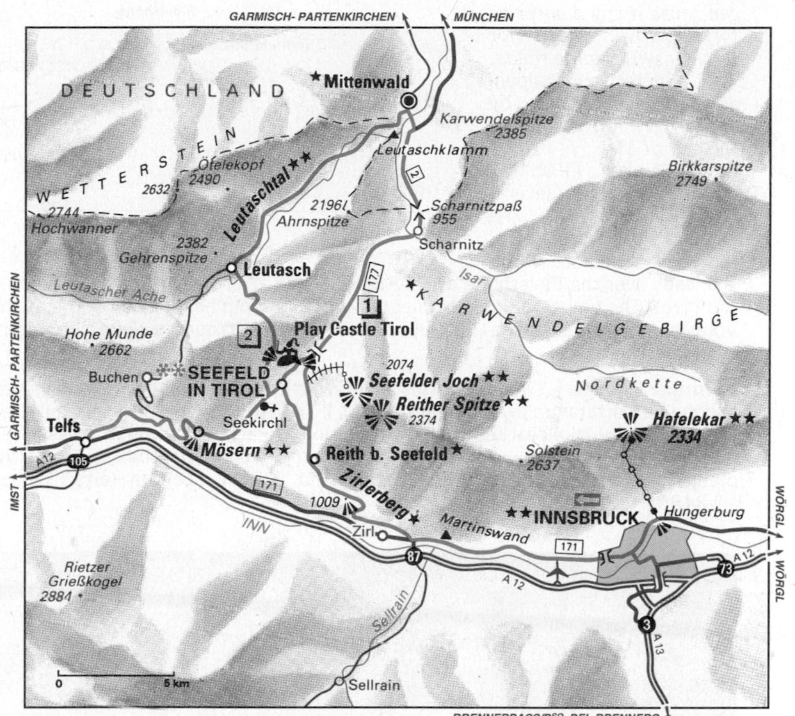

A charming rotunda chapel **(Seekircherl)** marks the beginning of a short valley which climbs up (5km/3mi) to Mösern 600m/2 000ft above the Inn Valley.

Mösern - This is a superbly sited village above the Inn Valley. Albrecht Dürer also liked it, and he used the surrounding landscape as the background to his self-portrait of 1498 (now in the Prado at Madrid). What better place for a picnic! *At the exit to the village towards Telfs, there are parking spaces to the left of the road just below the Inntaler Hof hotel.* The **view**★★ is particularly fine. Upstream the Inn can be seen winding along the floor of the Telfs furrow and then slipping into a tangle of crests among which, on the horizon, the Hoher Riffler (alt 3 168m/10 394ft) stands flecked with snow. Further to the right, the green terrace of the Mieming Plateau (Mieminger Hochland) can be seen at the foot of the Mieming range, which ends at the great dome of the Hohe Munde. South of the valley rise the Sellrain mountains and, in the middle distance, the jagged crests of the Kalkkögel *(far left)*.
After Mösern, the road drops quickly down into the Inn Valley in a series of hairpin bends.

Telfs - This market town, first recorded in 1175, has quite an urban character. The local museum (Fasnacht- und Heimatmuseum) contains costumes and masks from the **Telfser Schleicherlaufen** which takes place every five years *(see Calendar of events)*.

SILVRETTA-HOCHALPENSTRASSE★★

Vorarlberg und Tirol

Michelin map 926 folds 27 and 28 – Local map see ARLBERGGEBIET

The Silvretta-Hochalpenstraße links the Ill Valley (**Montafon**★, *see entry*) with the Trisanna Valley (Paznaun Valley) via the Bielerhöhe pass (2 036m/6 680ft). The rugged mountainous character of this high-lying pass is mitigated by the shimmering green-blue waters of the reservoirs.

FROM PARTENEN TO LANDECK *73km/45mi.*

Including the hike to the Hoher Rad, allow at least one day. Gaschurn/Partenen, Galtür or Ischgl are ideal places to find lodging in the evening.
Parking overnight (for example, in a camping van) anywhere along the Silvretta-Hochalpenstraße road is forbidden. The road is barred to trailers and caravans. There are 30 narrow bends to negotiate on the road on the western slope, which

can cause many a surprise for the driver who is not familiar with Alpine roads. The Silvretta-Hochalpenstraße is usually blocked by snow from November to the ènd of May.

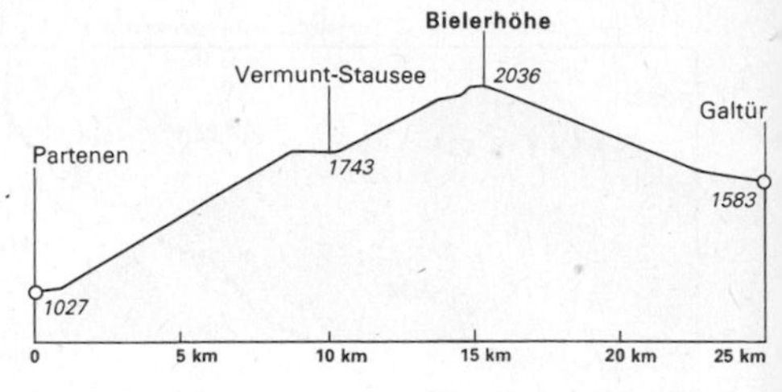

From **Partenen** (1 051m/3 448ft), where several power stations use the water of the Silvretta area, the road begins to climb and leads over the Bielerhöhe at 2 031m/6 664ft after Galtür into Paznaun and the Tyrol. The breathtaking road negotiates 32 hairpin bends, past some of the Vorarlberg's highest peaks (Piz Buin 3 312m/10 867ft) and the deep blue waters of Alpine reservoirs.

Vermunt-Stausee – This lake forms an intermediate reservoir between Partenen and the Silvrettatal Valley, at an altitude of 1 743m/5 718ft. The water collected in this artificial lake reaches the power station at Partenen through pressurized pipelines. The **view**★ towards the wild Kromertal Valley stretches as far as the mountain ridges of the Großer Litzner and Großer Seehorn (alt 3 124m/10 249ft).

Vermunt reservoir

While the road winds upwards to the mountain pass, which has been polished smooth by glaciers, the Silvretta dam and mountain summit come gradually into view above the upper lake.

Bielerhöhe – The **Silvretta-Stausee**★, at 2 036m/6 680ft above sea-level, blends superbly into the **Alpine landscape**★★. People are glad to take a break here, and mountaineers and those on ski tours use the large hotels as a starting point for their trips around the Silvretta mountains. Motor boat trips are available on the lake, the highest in Europe with such a service.
The reservoir is the principal component of the power station at Ill. The water collected by the dam reaches the Rodund power station below Schruns in the Montafon region via a number of intermediary reservoirs, and then flows freely on its way again from that point.
A walk along the dam (432m/1 417ft long and 80m/262ft high) gives a remarkable **view**★ of the surrounding mountains. The countryside can best be explored on a walk round the lake.

★★ **Walk round the Silvretta-Stausee** – *An easy hike (about 1hr 45min).* Walk first along the east shore of the lake at the foot of the dark, pointed pyramid of the Hohes Rad. The route is bordered by several waterfalls and numerous Alpine rose bushes. The return path leads along the west shore, towering above which is the Lobspitze. On this trip there are a number of splendid **views**★★ of the Schattenspitze peak to the south, the Klostertal Valley with the Tällispitze and Sonntagspitze peaks to the southwest, the Hochmaderer to the west and the Vallüla massif to the north.

★★★ **Ascent to the Hohes Rad** – *Park in the car park at the east end of the lake. The hike (allow 5hr 30min not including breaks and with a climb to the Hohes Rad of over 800m/2 625ft) is suitable for experienced walkers. Waterproof climbing boots and warm, knee-high socks are essential. The outstanding beauty and diversity of the landscape are ample reward for the exertion. Those with less stamina should content themselves with the footpath to the Wiesbadener Hütte mountain lodge (allow 4hr 15min there and back).*

It takes about 45min to walk the length of the entire lake. The footpath then leads uphill through the Ochsental Valley alongside the gushing waters of the Jil, which is fed by numerous waterfalls and brooks. To the right, the splendid valley is enclosed by an impressive reddish wall of rock. Gradually, all the peaks in the area come into view (the Kleine Schattenspitze, the Kleiner Egghörner, the Schattenspitze, the Schneeglocken with a small glacier and the Silvrettahorn). Most eye-catching of all, however, is the glacial cirque which closes off the valley.

From the **Wiesbadener Hütte** mountain lodge (alt 2 443m/8 015ft), there is a wonderful **view**★★ of the highest peak in the Silvretta group, the **Piz Buin** (alt 3 312m/10 866ft), which is flanked by the Vermunt glacier (on the left) and the Oschsental glacier (on the right).

Next comes a 1hr 30min climb to the Radsattel. Turn left past the mountain lodge and follow the **Edmund-Lorenz-Weg trail** which climbs steeply at first but then leads straight ahead without too noticeable a slope. From this trail, there are a number of particularly beautiful **views**★★ of the entire valley. The trail leads down to a small lake (alt 2 532m/8 307ft), shimmering in amazing shades of colour from orange to green and lying in a splendid setting at the foot of the Rauherkopf glacier. From this point, the trail leads uphill, with one or two steep bends, as far as the **Radsattel** (alt 2 652m/8 701ft), which forms the boundary between Vorarlberg and the Tyrol. There is a superb **panorama**★★, to the west, of the Großer Litzner and all the glaciers already mentioned. To the east lies the Bieltal Valley, which likewise has a glacier towering above it.

The footpath climbs slightly as it leads along the foot of the rocky foothills of the Hohes Rad, before crossing numerous glacial snowfields and then leading over a slight incline until, after 45min, it comes to the **Radschulter**★★ (alt 2 697m/8 843ft). About 100m/110yd before the pass, the Radsee, with its partially ice-covered waters tinged a dark green, comes into sight beneath the Madlener Spitze peak. From the pass, there is an impressive **view**★★ of the Bieltal and Rauerkopf glaciers, which tower upwards out of a rocky, almost lunar landscape.

Experienced hikers, who have a good head for heights and are not too tired by this stage, may like to climb up to the left to the **Hohes Rad**★★★ summit (alt 2 934m/9 626ft). The rocky trail makes this quite a demanding detour, for which you should allow about 1hr 30min there and back, but at the end of it, a **360° panorama** of the Silvretta range and reservoir will make you forget all your exertions.

Y. Bontoux

Piz Buin peak and glacial cirque

The walk down from the Radschulter takes 1hr 30min. The very steep **route**★★ leading between two rock walls is covered by a thick layer of snow well into August. After the rocks have been left behind, the landscape suddenly becomes green. To the east, the Madlener Spitze peak with its glacier can be seen and (opposite) to the north, the Kleinvermunttal Valley, dominated by the mighty Vallüla massif.
For the last part of the walk, the trail is covered with splendid alpine roses and yellow gentians, and provides a number of magnificent **views**★★ of the Silvretta reservoir with the Hochmaderer in the background.

Return to the car.

On the Tyrolean side of the Bielerhöhe, the pastoral valley of Kleinvermunt, in which cattle can be seen grazing, provides a number of views of the Lobspitze and Madlenerspitze peaks.

Turn left. After 5km/3mi, the road reaches the **Kops-Stausee**★ (alt 1 809m/5 935ft), flanked by the Ballunspitze to the south, the Versalspitze to the west and the Fluhspitzen peaks to the north. Return to the main road and drive on to Galtür.

Galtür - Alt 1 584m/5 197ft. This pretty village on the slopes of the Ballunspitze, which can accommodate 3 400 visitors, provides a small but interesting ski area above the Kops reservoir. A total of 11 ski lifts lead to 40km/25mi of pistes covering all degrees of difficulty. With 45km/28mi of cross-country tracks and good snow cover, it also has plenty to offer cross-country skiers.

Between Galtür and Ischgl, in the upper Paznaun Valley, the forest cover becomes more dense, and stands of larch can be distinguished from the surrounding trees by their lighter colour.

❄❄ **Ischgl** - *See ISCHGL.*

The Trisanna Valley now narrows still further and becomes increasingly picturesque and rugged. Villages lie high up on mountain plateaux or on mountain ledges. The road leads alongside the mountain torrent, through fairly dense forest. After a long drive, the appearance of the Burg Wiesberg heralds the famous **Trisanna bridge**★.
Towering in the background are the mighty mountain ridges of the Parseierspitze (alt 3 036m/9 961ft), the highest peak of the Limestone Alps in the north of Austria.

Landeck - *See ARLBERGGEBIET* 1.

SÖLDEN❄❄

Tirol

Population 3 056

Michelin map 926 fold 29 - Local map see ÖTZTAL - Alt 1 377m/4 518ft

With an area of 468km²/181sq mi, only 1km²/0.4sq mi of which is inhabited, and surrounded by more than 90 summits of over 3 000m/10 000ft, Sölden is the largest municipality in Austria. This old Tyrolean village has developed into an important winter sports and summer holiday resort and constitutes the tourist centre of the **Ötz Valley**★★ *(see ÖTZTAL)*. Sölden lies strung out along a deeply incised, wooded valley, with the Gaislachkogl towering over it.
The little village of **Hochsölden** (alt 2 090m/6 857ft) occupies a beautiful mountain plateau site and offers excellent snow cover and extensive views.
Sölden owes its popularity to the quality of its après-ski entertainment. It offers a wide range of sports facilities (a leisure centre, offering about 30 different types of sport, with a "water-world" swimming pool plus sauna, and tennis courts), but the winter sports resort is distinguished, above all, by the lively atmosphere of its cafés, bars and clubs, which ensure that holidaymakers in Sölden can continue partying at full steam until well into the night.

Ski slopes (1 377-3 260m/4 518-10 696ft) - The Ötztal Arena Sölden has 36 ski lifts, 30 artificial snow machines and 108km/67mi of pistes (45km/28mi blue, 45km/28mi red and 18km/11mi black), which means it is generally possible to ski down the valley until spring. Two long descents are particularly worth recommending: that leading from the Gaislachkogl to the valley station of the Stabele chair-lift (**view**★ over the Ötztaler glacier road), and that linking the Hainbachjoch with Sölden. Less experienced skiers should use the piste (above Hochsölden) leading along the route taken by the Silberbrünnl chair-lift, followed by the broad trail through the woods from Gaislachalm. At the Gaislachkogel-Giggijoch cable-car there are free car parks with up to 1 000 spaces. Those not in cars can take advantage of the free ski bus system.

The **Ötztaler Gletscherstraße**★★, one of the highest roads in the east Alps (highest point: 2 822m/9 258ft), or the Alps' first and only "Glacier ski swing" (in operation since 1998 after expansion of the Schwarzkogl ski area) give access to another ski area (29km/18mi of piste and 10 ski lifts) in a beautiful Alpine landscape on the Rettenbachfern and Tiefenbachfern glaciers.
There is also the possibility of driving to nearby Vent and, in particular, to **Hochgurgl-Obergurgl**❄, where there are further downhill ski runs. *However, the Sölden ski pass is not valid here.*
Cross-country skiers have 8km/5mi of cross-country tracks available to them in Sölden, 8km/5mi in Zwieselstein and 3km/1.9mi in Vent.

VIEWPOINTS

★★ **Gaislachkogl** ⏲ - Alt 3 058m/10 033ft. *1hr round trip. Sturdy footwear is required for walking on the summit. Ascent via a double-cable circulating cable-car.*
During the first section, there is a view of the locality, which is dominated by the Söldenkogel and the Rotkogel. From the mountain station of the second stage the cross at the summit can be reached on foot in a few minutes.
From here there is a splendid **panorama**★★ of the peaks and glaciers of the Ötztal Alps. In particular, the Wildspitze (alt 3 774m/12 378ft) can be seen to the southwest, following the line of the cable-car. Towering up to the right of it are the Pitztal peaks (the Watzespitze and Hohe Geige). To the left, are the Weißkugel (alt 3 736m/12 254ft), the Fineilspitze (alt 3 514m/11 529ft), the Similaun (alt 3 602m/11 815ft) and the Großer Ramolkogel (alt 3 551m/11 647ft), all of which have at least one glacier. The ski area of Hochgurgl lies to the south at the foot of the Kirchenkogel and, in the distance, the Dolomites. To the east, the view stretches as far as the Stubai Alps, the second highest mountain of which is the Zuckerhütl (alt 3 511m/11 520ft).

Giggijochbahn ⏲ - Walk round the terrace of the mountain station, from where there is a beautiful **view** of the Sölden ski slopes, from the Gaislachkogl to the Hainbachjoch which, at 2 727m/8 947ft above sea-level, is the highest peak in the Hochsölden ski area. It is flanked by the Roßkirpl on the left and by the Breitlehner on the right. To the east lie the Söldenkogel, the Rotkogel and the Gurgler Tal Valley.

EXCURSIONS

★★ Ventertal

This beautiful long valley is surrounded by glaciers on all sides and provides wonderful opportunities for hiking.

★ **Road from Zwieselstein to Rofen** - *16km/10mi.* The road leads through a delightful wooded area and, 6km/4mi further on, passes through the hamlet of Heiligenkreuz, in which there is a chapel with a pretty, onion-domed tower.
After a further 7km/4mi, the road reaches **Vent** (alt 1 900m/6 234ft), the only holiday resort in the valley. In winter, Vent is an unpretentious winter sports location which nevertheless has remarkably good snow cover and offers good skiers the challenge of steep slopes. It has 15km/9mi of piste at altitudes of between 1 900m/6 234ft and 2 680m/8 793ft, and four ski lifts. In summer, the number of holidaymakers is substantially greater since the opportunities for trips into the high mountains are simply inexhaustible. After Vent, the valley splits into two parts on either side of the imposing Talleitspitze peak (alt 3 406m/11 174ft). The **Rofental** Valley, which is situated on the right, runs alongside the **Wildspitze** (alt 3 774m/12 378ft) and the **Hochvernagtspitze** (alt 3 535m/11 598ft) peaks before being blocked by the **Weißkugel** (alt 3 736m/12 254ft); the **Niedertal** Valley on the left of the Talleitspitze peak runs along at the foot of the Ramolkogel (alt 3 551m/11 647ft) and the Schalfkogel (alt 3 537m/11 604ft). It ends in the glacial basin of the **Similaun** (alt 3 602m/11 815ft). All these peaks cause the amateur mountaineer's heart to beat faster since they are, after all, the goal of legendary mountain expeditions.
A road leads as far as **Rofen**, the highest-lying permanently inhabited hamlet in Austria (alt 2 014m/6 608ft). The climb to Rofen *(1hr 30min there and back)* makes a pleasant walk for a family: follow the road and cross the mountain torrent on a small suspension bridge. A good footpath, bordered by ledges, leads back to Vent. It offers picturesque views of the valley floor.

★ **Wildspitze-Sesselbahn** ⏲ - *Leave the car in Vent at the chair-lift (there is a charge for the car park). 10min travelling time.* From the mountain station (alt 2 356m/7 730ft), there is a beautiful **view**★ of the ski area, the Talleitspitze peak and in particular, in the background, the glaciers which surround the Ramolkogel and the Schalfkogel.

A number of hikes starting from the mountain station of the chair-lift are suggested below. Fit, experienced hikers may like to climb up to the Wildes Mannle or walk to the Vernagthütte mountain lodge. Less experienced hikers should opt for walking to the Breslauer Hütte mountain lodge.

★★★ **Wildes Mannle** – *Climbing boots are essential, and binoculars are recommended. This hike is for hikers with good levels of stamina: 3hr on foot and a 670m/2 198ft difference in altitude, going straight there and back. The complete circuit described below, which includes a climb to the Breslauer Hütte mountain lodge via the Rofensteig footpath, is recommended only to experienced hikers, since it involves a number of extremely steep, vertiginous passages. Allow about 4hr – difference in altitude 800m/2 625ft.*

Walk from the mountain station of the chair-lift towards the Breslauer Hütte mountain lodge. After a 30min walk, turn off to the right *(waymarker)* onto a narrower trail. The view becomes more and more breathtaking during the climb. Look out for the markers and "WM" indications. Towards the end, the path gets very steep and rocky, but does not present any real difficulties.

From the peak (alt 3 023m/9 918ft), which is marked with a cross, there is a splendid **panorama**★★★ of about 15 glaciers belonging to the Ötztal Alps, the most impressive and closest of which is the Rofenkar glacier, covering a difference in altitude of 1 000m/3 300ft on the slopes of the Wildspitze. Chamois are often to be seen in this region. To the west, notice the Breslauer Hütte lodge at the foot of a rocky amphitheatre which is easy to make out because of its reddish colour. A detour to this mountain lodge is a pleasant extension of this hike. Those with a poor head for heights should first follow the same trail as on the way there and then turn off towards the right *(waymarked on the rocks)*. Experienced hikers can take a walk of about 15min across the ridge of the Wildes Mannle as far as a metal sign *(towards Breslauer Hütte via Rofenkarsteig)*. But on the way, be sure to pay attention to the markers *(stone cairns)*. At the sign, turn off onto a steep, narrow trail which leads down to the foot of the Rofenkar glacier *(ropes have been fitted in a number of the trickier passages)*.

The path then leads over a narrow ridge to give beautiful **views**★★ of the glacial cirque. Very soon afterwards, turn off to the right *(waymarked "BH" on a rock)* and reach the Rofenbach brook which is crossed in two stages, the last on wooden planks. Then follow the brook for about 10m/11yd without attempting to climb the slippery rock walls, before regaining the path, which leads up to the Breslauer Hütte mountain lodge. From here, there is a splendid **panorama**★★ *(see below)*. The climb down *(1hr)* to the chair-lift which will take you back to Vent is easy.

★★ **Breslauer Hütte** – Alt 2 844m/9 331ft. *A really easy hike, starting from the mountain station of the chair-lift. 2hr 30min on foot there and back, and a difference in altitude of 500m/1 640ft.*

From the hut, there is a very beautiful **panorama**★★ across the Wildspitze and the ridges of the Wildes Mannle to the north, the glaciers above the Niedertal Valley to the east and the Kreuzspitze peak and its glaciers to the south.

★★ **Hike to the Vernagthütte** – *This splendid circuit is highly recommended for hikers with stamina. Take the Wildspitze chair-lift (outward journey only) early in the morning and walk to the Breslauer Hütte mountain lodge in 1hr 30min. Then allow 5hr walk, with almost no uphill sections, but with a drop in altitude of 1 000m/3 300ft.*

From the Breslauer Hütte mountain lodge, the footpath leads straight across the mountainside. After walking for about 30min, you will reach the Mitterbach brook, which is fed by a glacier on the Wildspitze. This is most easily crossed at a spot where wooden planks have been laid across it further downhill. Return to the footpath.

A little further on, the path leads along a second rocky amphitheatre (Platteikar) and, after a sharp bend to the right, finally reaches a small lake. From here there is a splendid **view**★★, straight ahead and towards the northwest, of the Vernagthütte mountain lodge which lies 250m/820ft above the valley floor in a gigantic glacial cirque. Stretching out to the right is the Großer Vernagtfern glacier, above which towers the Hochvernagtspitze peak. Rearing up to the left are the Guslarfern glacier and the Fluchtkogel. The **view** to the south is also interesting, taking in the Hochjochfern glacier tongue, which runs down the right flank of the Fineilspitze peak.

The path leads down into the valley below the Vernagthütte mountain lodge. The climb to this lodge *(allow an extra 50min there and back)* is of particular interest to amateur mountaineers, since the lodge is a good starting point for mountaineering expeditions. Those preferring to keep the whole hike a reasonable length should leave out this climb and begin the long trek down to Vent along the banks of the Vernagtbach *(2hr 45min)*. Along the route are the waterfalls of the Platteibach, Mitterbach and Rofenbach, which was crossed further upstream. In Rofen, rather than following the tarmacked road, cross the brook on a suspension bridge, and take the good footpath leading to Vent.

SPITAL AM PYHRN

Oberösterreich

Population 2 290

Michelin map 926 fold 22 – Alt 647m/2 123ft

Spital is the halting place on the ancient road over the Pyhrn pass (alt 945m/3 100ft) which connects the Steyr and Enns valleys, and, through them, Linz and Graz. Its old collegiate church is in an unusually unified Baroque style.

★ CHURCH (EHEMALIGE STIFTSKIRCHE)

The collegiate church, built from 1714 to 1730, has a harmonious façade framed by two towers, their height all the more striking by being articulated by three projecting cornices.

The interior of the main building gives an impression of fullness enhanced by the harmonious addition of decorative features to the architecture. When Master Schmidt of Krems had finished the paintings on the altarpieces of the side altars, about 1780, no further embellishment in the taste of that time was given to the church.

In the chancel, Bartolomäus Altomonte (1693-1783) painted a remarkable decoration of colonnades in *trompe-l'œil*, opening at the centre on the scene of the Assumption of the Virgin. This **fresco**★ (1740) culminates in the dome with a representation of the Celestial Court.

SPITTAL AN DER DRAU

Kärnten

Population 14 770

Michelin map 926 fold 33 – Alt 554m/1 818ft

The charming city of Spittal an der Drau lies in a valley at the confluence of the Lieser and the Drava (Drau), at the foot of the Goldeck peak. The tempting waters of Millstätter See are not far away. The city's strategic position on a major trade route between Germany and Venice enabled it to flourish over the centuries as an economic and cultural centre. Nowadays, it is still one of Upper Carinthia's main communications intersections.

★ **Schloß Porcia** – This four-square structure was begun in 1527; it is framed by corner turrets and is one of the most important specimens of an Italian-style palace on Austrian soil. It was built for Gabriel Salamanca, a brilliant financier who was General Treasurer to the Archduke Ferdinand until 1526. From 1662 to 1918 the palace was the residence of the princes of Porcia, a noble family from northeast Italy (Friuli Venezia Giulia). The park and arcaded courtyard are open to the public all the time.

★ **Arcaded courtyard** – The three-storey arcaded courtyard in the Italian manner features typical Renaissance ornamentation in the form of antique medallions, balustrade pillars, door frames etc. On the south side the coat of arms of the

Trumier/ÖSTERREICH WERBUNG

Schloß Porcia

Porcia family are in pride of place: six golden lilies on a blue background. Note the splendid 16C wrought-iron **gates**★ separating the stairs from the upper galleries. Theatre performances are held in the courtyard in summer.

★★ **Museum für Volkskultur** (Museum of Popular Culture) ⏱ – *On the upper floors of the palace.* This museum covers popular tradition of Upper Carinthia in almost overwhelming detail in 47 displays on different themes. These range from traditional religious beliefs and customs to gold, garnet and arsenic mining, to the work of coopers and potters. There is a reconstruction of a primary school classroom from the turn of the 19C-20C, as well as a grocer's shop and Carinthian farm interior. Since there are 20 000 exhibits, it is extremely practical that visitors can look up information about items on computer.

Goldeckbahn ⏱ – The 4km/2.5mi cable-car leads in two sections up to an altitude of 2 050m/6 726ft, spanning an increase in altitude of 1 500m/4 922ft. From the upper station there is a fine **view**★ of Spittal, the surrounding mountains and Millstätter Lake.

EXCURSION

Teurnia Excavations (Ausgrabungen). – *5km/3mi northwest. At St. Peter in Holz, 4.5km/2.5mi from Spittal, turn off left from the road to Lienz.*
At a bend in the old roadway stand the two isolated buildings which house the **museum** ⏱ of the Teurnia excavations.
Excavations have uncovered the remains of the Roman city of Teurnia, in the shape of two residential terraces, the forum, a bathing house and a temple to the Celtic god Grannus. In the 5C and 6C, Teurnia was a fortified provincial town and episcopal seat. The diocesan church, with its guesthouse (Hospitium) and two graveyards outside the city walls, dates from this period. Next to the present museum stands the Friedhofskirche, in which a side chapel is decorated with a large **mosaic floor**★ (5C) featuring animal motifs.

STAINZ

Steiermark

Population 2 000

Michelin map 926 fold 36 – 25km/16mi southwest of Graz

Local map see STEIRISCHE WEINSTRASSE – Alt 377m/1 237ft

Lying in the valley and watched over by its ancient abbey, the town of Stainz gives many hints of its past opulence, which was based on the wine trade. It still boasts a number of old houses with smart façades, particularly in the main square, which date from the period of prosperity in the 16C and 17C.
At the northern entrance to the town, the magnificent buildings of the ancient abbey of the Augustinian canons provide a fine setting for the Baroque parish church. In the 18C, at the time of Austria's secularization, the abbey lost its religious function. It was declared a castle and in 1840 was bought by Archduke Johann.

Schloß – Arcaded galleries embellish the two courtyards of the castle; within the walls stand a church and an ethnographic museum.

Church ⏱ – The church, which dates from 1229 and was rebuilt in 1686, has a broad nave which is painted in gleaming white and lined by side chapels. Only the vault has been decorated – with painted medallions within a stucco composition. The masterly elevation of the high altar (1695) is articulated by columns supporting the pediment and entablature. At the centre is a work by Hans Adam Weißenkircher, who was also responsible for the paintings in the Room of the Planets (Planetensaal) in Schloß Eggenberg.
The two west towers of the original Early Gothic church survive. The church's layout can be explained by the fact that when the church was rebuilt in the Baroque style, it was reoriented like the abbey of Rein *(see GRAZ: Excursions)*. The church is dedicated to St Catherine and has been the local parish church since its secularization in 1785.

★ **Museum** ⏱ – *Entrance on the right in the passage to the first courtyard.* This section of the Joanneum Landesmuseum occupies two floors and contains objects, illustrations, photographs and documents on the subject of Styria's agricultural traditions and local crafts. Items of particular interest include the collection of model equipment from the "Royal and Imperial Agricultural Society" dating from the mid 19C, collected on the orders of Archduke Johann, as well as examples of "popular technology", such as hand-operated threshing machines and the "Schmeißwachl", a machine for threshing corn. There is a large collection of everyday ceramic ware and traditional country furniture. A press for producing pumpkin seed oil recalls a process practiced for centuries in southern Styria; this **Kernöl** is still considered a great delicacy.
The museum also exhibits two original **panelled rooms** from the years 1568 and 1596, and a so-called "Seitenstübel" (side room) from a west Styrian farmhouse, complete with a painted ceiling (1796).

Stift STAMS★★

Tirol

Michelin map 926 north of fold 29

The Cistercian abbey of Stams was founded in 1273, in the upper Inn valley, by Elizabeth of Bavaria, the widow of Emperor Konrad IV, who later married Count Meinhard II - the pioneer of Tyrolean unity. She built the abbey in memory of her son by her first marriage, Konradin, the last of the Hohenstaufen line, who was tortured and beheaded at Naples by order of Charles of Anjou. The majestic architectural ensemble, made even more striking since the end of the 17C by the two residential towers, is purely Baroque in style. Stams also has a famous ski school, housed for many years in a conventual annexe, where young hopefuls study and improve their skiing at the same time.

TOUR ⓥ

Leave the car on the shady esplanade at the foot of the pretty 14C village church, with Rococo decoration. Ticket office is in the arch of the abbey gateway.

★★ **Stiftskirche** - The present building results from the remodelling in the Baroque style in 1732 of a Romanesque nave without a transept, which was vaulted only in the 17C. The small apses behind the high altar have kept their original appearance but the aisles have been replaced by six side chapels.

Near the entrance, on the right, is the famous **Rose Grille**★. This screen, a masterpiece in ironwork dating from 1716, closes the passage leading to the Heiligblutkapelle (Chapel of the Holy Blood) outside.

A balustrade in the nave surrounds the open crypt, where 12 naive gilded wood statues of the princes of the Tyrol are reminders that Stams is the burial place of this dynasty.

The showpiece of the furnishings is the **high altar**★ (1613), whose altarpiece represents the Tree of Life in the form of interlacing boughs supporting 84 carved figures of saints surrounding the Virgin Mary. On either side of the altar, Adam and Eve represent the beginnings of mankind; at the crown, Christ on the Cross represents the mystery of the supernatural. The work is by **Bartholomäus Steinle**. In the monks' chancel a grille marks the tomb of Duke Friedrich the Penniless *(see INNSBRUCK: Goldenes Dachl)*.

★ **Bernardisaal** - The Bernardi Hall is reached from the porter's lodge by an oval shaped **grand staircase** with a fine wrought-iron balustrade. The hall of state, whose ceiling opens in the centre onto a balustraded gallery, is decorated with paintings (1722) recalling outstanding episodes in the life of St Bernard.

If you have time, it is worth taking a look at the **museum**, which displays selected items from the abbey's collections.

Y. Bontoux

Stams Abbey

STEIRISCHES THERMENLAND

Michelin map 926 folds 37 and 38

The **Styrian spa region** comprises the five spa towns of Bad Waltersdorf, Blumau, Loipersdorf, Bad Gleichenberg and Bad Radkersburg in the southeast corner of Styria. However, the region has more to offer than mineral water. It is one of Austria's most fertile belts of land, as illustrated by the numerous vineyards, orchards and fields of pumpkins and cereal crops.
The following is a brief summary of the main tourist sights on offer in the Styrian spa region.

BLUMAU

About 7km/4mi north of Fürstenfeld.

The thermal springs and hotel complex at Blumau was designed by Viennese architect **Friedensreich Hundertwasser**. About half the complex eventually planned has been completed to date, with a bed capacity of 600. Hundertwasser's distinctive architectural style with its imaginative use of colour and shape is to be found in the small spa village. The houses seem to be growing out of the ground. Instead of tiled roofs, there are lawns and shrubs on top of the buildings, where it is possible to walk about. A fairy-tale landscape has been created here, in which people, architecture and nature are intended to harmonise with each other. Correspondingly, a range of relaxation and health cures with holistic treatments (music therapy, treatments from the Far East) is on offer.
Access to the spa complex is open to hotel or day guests at the spa, or to those participating in a **guided tour** ⏲ *(about 45min)*. After viewing a model of the whole complex, the tour smuggles you through a small part of the buildings and grounds. For hygienic reasons, tour visitors cannot enter the spa area itself. Afterwards, there is the chance to walk around the grounds in peace and let the architecture take its effect *(start from the "eye-slit" houses)*.

★ RIEGERSBURG ⏲

On Bundesstraße 66, 10km/6mi north of Feldbach.

Riegersburg, proudly standing above the village that shares its name on the remains of a volcano nearly 482m/1 581ft high, is one of the most imposing strongholds to have guarded the eastern frontiers of Austria through the ages. From whatever direction one approaches, Riegersburg's bold **site**★ comes as a surprise. The village lies 100m/330ft below the castle clinging half way up the sheer slope. First the Celts, then the Romans, appreciated the value of this defensive position and dug in there whenever danger threatened from the east. The castle, built in the 12C, successfully withstood the onslaught of the Hungarians and the Turks. The 3km/2mi of ramparts and 11 bastions made it virtually impregnable. Since 1822, the castle has belonged to the royal family of Liechtenstein and now houses a museum on witches and an exhibition on the family history of its royal owners. However, the castle's interest lies more in the wonderful **views**★ of the Styrian countryside that it offers, than in its layout and interior decor.

⚕ Bad GLEICHENBERG

On Bundesstraße 66, 11km/7mi south of Feldbach.

The spa of Bad Gleichenberg, not far from the Hungarian and Slovenian frontiers, is famous for its medicinal springs and its mild climate.
In 1834, the Count of Wickenburg, from the Rhineland like his contemporary Metternich, was introduced to the healing properties of the Gleichenberg springs. Being a shrewd businessman as well as the local governor, he did not need long to transform the town into an elegant spa resort. By the end of the 19C, Bad Gleichenberg was the favourite Austrian spa among the aristocracy.
The town still boasts some beautiful **Biedermeier style villas and hotels**, and is set amid countryside more reminiscent of a landscaped garden. A large 20ha/50 acre spa park adds to this effect.
The spa is frequented by sufferers from a variety of complaints, such as diseases of the heart, lungs and circulatory tract, stomach or digestive problems, rheumatism or eczema. However, it is not only the sick who appreciate the pleasant atmosphere here; after Graz and Mariazell, Bad Gleichenberg is the most popular holiday destination in Styria.

Styrassic Park ⏲ – *West of the town centre. Take B 66 and follow the signposts.* Watch out, the dinosaurs are on the loose! A 5ha/12 acre forest park has been filled with more than 60 life-size model dinosaurs (made of steel and concrete).

"Wait 'til the ranger sees that...!" - A Diplodocus in Styrassic Park

Try walking underneath the enormous Brachiosaurus, but beware of the terrifying Tyrannosaurus Rex (Spielberg sends his regards)! The tour of the park is organised chronologically, under scientific supervision from the University of Berlin. Display panels give brief explanations on the chronology, fossil discoveries and dimensions of each species. Definitely not only for children.

★ Bad RADKERSBURG

On Bundesstraße 69, 26km/16mi south of Bad Gleichenberg just before the Slovenian border.

Since its foundation (first officially recorded in 1182), Radkersburg has been one of the leading trading centres in Styria. Timber, iron and salt, transported down the Mur on rafts, were traded for farm produce such as wine and honey from the southeast. Most importantly, the town had the right of prior purchase on wine. During the wars against the Turks, Radkersburg was an important bastion, with the result that it was named as an Imperial stronghold at the Augsburg Diet in 1582. The well-preserved **ring of fortifications**, with moats, six bastions and towers all still virtually intact, dates from this period. Numerous mansions and merchants' houses with beautiful stone doorways and courtyards give an indication of the town's former wealth. Italian master builders have left their mark on Radkersburg, with the result that the town centre still exudes a certain Mediterranean style.

Radkersburg was pronounced a spa town on the strength of its springs rich in calcium and bicarbonate. The main illnesses treated here are those affecting the nerves and the urinary tract.

Walk around town

Hauptplatz – In the middle of the main square with its beautiful houses stands the **Pest-und Mariensäule**, a column dedicated to the Virgin Mary which commemorates the town's deliverance from the plague in 1680. In 1766, four statues of "plague-healing" saints were added to it (St Anthony, St Sebastian, St Roch and St Francis). The Late Gothic (bottom section) octagonal **town hall tower** with its onion dome on the west side of the square has become the emblem of the town. Continue further west to reach the **arcaded courtyard** of Palais Herberstdorff, to the left through a glass door at the end of Dechantgasse.

Stadtpfarrkirche – The Late Gothic triple-naved, pillared basilica (14C-16C) was built onto a fortified tower from the town wall. In 1830, the vaulting above the central nave was modified, and its pointed barrel vault contrasts with the delicate ribbed vaulting above the side aisles.

Turn into Radkersburg's main street, the Langgasse, and continue north as far as Tabor-Platz with a column to St Florian. This square gives access to the **old arsenal** (Altes Zeughaus). A covered alleyway leads to a fine two-storey arcaded courtyard. The arsenal now houses the cultural and historical heritage of the town and its surroundings (regional museum).

Take Emmenstraße and Bindergasse back to the Hauptplatz. Go through Our Lady's Gateway (Frauentor) by the tourist office to get to the **Frauenplatz**, an idyllic little square which is home to the Late Baroque Frauenkirche.

STEIRISCHE WEINSTRASSE★

Michelin map 926 folds 36 and 37

The **Styrian vineyard trail** is some considerable distance from the major tourist centres and provides the visitor with an opportunity to discover traditional Austria, a tranquil unaltered world in the midst of outstandingly beautiful, picturesque countryside dotted with traditional bars (**Buschenschenken**) where people meet over a glass of wine and listen to music played on the accordion. The people of Graz are very fond of making Sunday outings to these bars, particularly in autumn when the vines are mature and at their most brilliantly coloured.

The great majority (80%) of Styrian vines produce white wine. Welschriesling, a dry white wine, alone accounts for 22% of the land planted, while 10% of the vines are Weißburgunder, whose grapes produce a sweet, fruity white and are the first to ripen; 8% are Müller-Thurgau. Zweigelt may be the most important of the reds, but **Schilcher**, a rosé, is better known; the region southwest of Graz where the Schilcher vine is grown is the starting point of the tour.

TOUR STARTING FROM GRAZ *180km/112mi*

Leave Graz on Bundesstraße 70 (**AX**). *Take either the motorway as far as Steinberg or Bundesstraße 70 to Krottendorf, and then follow signs to Stainz.*

1 Schilcher Trail

The Schilcher hills back on to the lower foothills of the Koralpe range, sometimes almost overlapping them. Here the vines are grown on patches of land that are sometimes so steeply inclined that harvesting by machine is impossible. Only south-facing slopes are planted, and one should leave the road to admire the mosaic of the vineyards as they follow the slightest twists and turns of the land.

Schilcher

Schilcher has not always been known by this name. It is only since 1976 that this has been the official name of wine made from the Blauer Wildbacher grape variety. Records show that this late-ripening, acidic grape (a distinction is made between the late blue and sloe varieties of Wildbacher), with its characteristic flavour and pretty "onion-skin" colour, has been cultivated in west Styria since as early as 1580. Schilcher vineyards cover about 80ha/198 acres.

Grape-pickers' cottages

Grape-pickers ("Weinzierle") traditionally had no property of their own, but lived in small cottages owned by the vineyard owner for whom they worked. This "Winzerei", the grape-picker's cottage typical of west Styria, would have a small garden attached to it, and would consist of two rooms, a kitchen and a front veranda. A separate wooden hut would be used to store coal and fodder. There are still one or two examples in the region of cellar outhouses, in which a pressing room was built above the cellar.

On leaving the motorway, the road immediately begins to climb, providing charming **views**★★ (left) of the plain of Graz, the undulating hills northwest of the town and, further in the distance, Mount Schöckl (1 445m/4 741ft) with its flat summit. Chestnut trees soon come into view, just as the vines begin to withdraw from the immediate roadside.

Gundersdorf – At the entrance to the village, there is *(right)* a strange wooden stake with a four-bladed propeller on the top *(Klapotetz)*. This is a familiar sight in the vineyards of Styria as its noise scares away the birds during the period from June to harvest time. In the distance, also to the right, can be seen the peaks of Reinischkogel (alt 1 463m/4 800ft), a local downhill ski resort. The local speciality is Schilcher wine, which can in some cases be bought directly from the producer.

Beyond Gundersdorf, a typical vine-growing village, there is a kind of hinterland which has been shielded from latter-day standardization and has preserved its old rural dwellings and traditions. The wooden farmhouses, which stand alone or grouped together in small villages, look like so many doll's houses with their tiny windows adorned with brightly coloured shutters.

After Gundersdorf turn right, then left towards Langegg and Greisdorf.

GEORG MIKES

Styrian vineyard landscape with the local version of a scarecrow ("Klapotetz")

Langegg - Thirsty travellers can choose from a number of traditional inns *(Buschenschenken)* in this village: the simple wooden-roofed summer houses or terraces attached to wine-growers' houses are a real local institution. Wine may be consumed with **Verackertbrot**, black bread with chopped, spiced bacon, or perhaps with a **Brettljause**, cold meats served on a wooden platter.
From Langegg there is a delightful **view**★★ of the Mur Valley, Mount Schökl (northeast) and the vine-clad hills of Sausal (southeast).
The road between Greisdorf and Marhof runs through maize fields: it is this cereal that is used to make a local speciality, **Sterz**, which is a kind of polenta and constitutes the staple diet of peasants in the area.

Turn left at Marhof and follow the signs to Stainz.

Stainz - *See STAINZ.*

The landscape is undulating and full of charm, with many pleasant walks.

Bad Gams ob Frauental - The village takes the first word of its name (*Bad* means bath) from its chalybeate springs. The region is, however, also well known in Styria for its traditional pottery; there is a potter's workshop on the outskirts of Furth, a town close to Bad Gams.
The road from Bad Gams to Deutschlandsberg descends into a plain encircled by forests.

Deutschlandsberg - This town at the foot of the Koralpe near the Slovene border takes its name from the fortified castle of Landsberg. The prefix *"deutsch"* was not added until the 19C, because of its location on German-speaking territory. Deutschlandsberg is famous throughout Styria for its lively and colourful Corpus Christi celebrations in which each processional altar is magnificently bedecked with flowers.
From time immemorial wine has been made here, benefiting from the favourable climate with its 280 days of sunshine; Deutschlandsberg is now the centre for the production of **Schilcher** wine.
To the north of the town stands the castle of Wildbach, where Schubert is supposed to have composed his famous Lied *The Trout.*

Castle ruins - *Cross the elongated main square with its brightly painted façades and follow the signs marked "Burghotel" on the right.*
Deutschlandsberg has managed to preserve the keep from a 12C castle until the present. Around it, a castle has been reconstructed and now makes quite a picture perched on a hill of vines, one of the last spurs of the Koralpe.

From the car park, the starting point for walks in the surrounding countryside, there is a fine **view**★ of the surrounding plain.

Rejoin the road from Stainz; continue south in the direction of St. Andrä-Leibnitz via St. Martin; to reach St. Andrä, turn left onto the valley road which joins up with the Sausal Vineyard Trail.

2 Sausal Hills

St. Andrä is the point of entry to the Sausal hills which rise to 670m/2 198ft above sea-level and cover a clearly defined area of fascinating character. The wine most frequently produced in these parts is **Rheinriesling**, a distinguished, semi-sparkling white with an excellent bouquet.

The road winds its way from hill to hill through the overhanging foliage. From time to time there are splendid views down over the plain of Graz (north), the Koralpe range (northwest) and Slovenia (south).

★ **Kitzeck** – The high situation (564m/1 850ft) of the village, which is set on a ridge in a quasi-mountainous landscape, provides an almost **panoramic view**★★ over a sea of hills (east). It is the highest wine-growing village in Europe, well known for its mild yet sunny climate.

The **Wine Museum** (Weinmuseum) ⏲, which occupies an old wine-grower's house (1726), complete with the main room *(Stube)*, contains articles and tools, handed down from generation to generation of wine-growers, which were associated with the many aspects of vine cultivation; a reconstruction of a device for smoke curing, an old press and a wagon for transporting barrels recall age-old systems of working now replaced by modern techniques.

Drive down towards Fresing, on the edge of the Sausal district. Continue to Klein Klein.

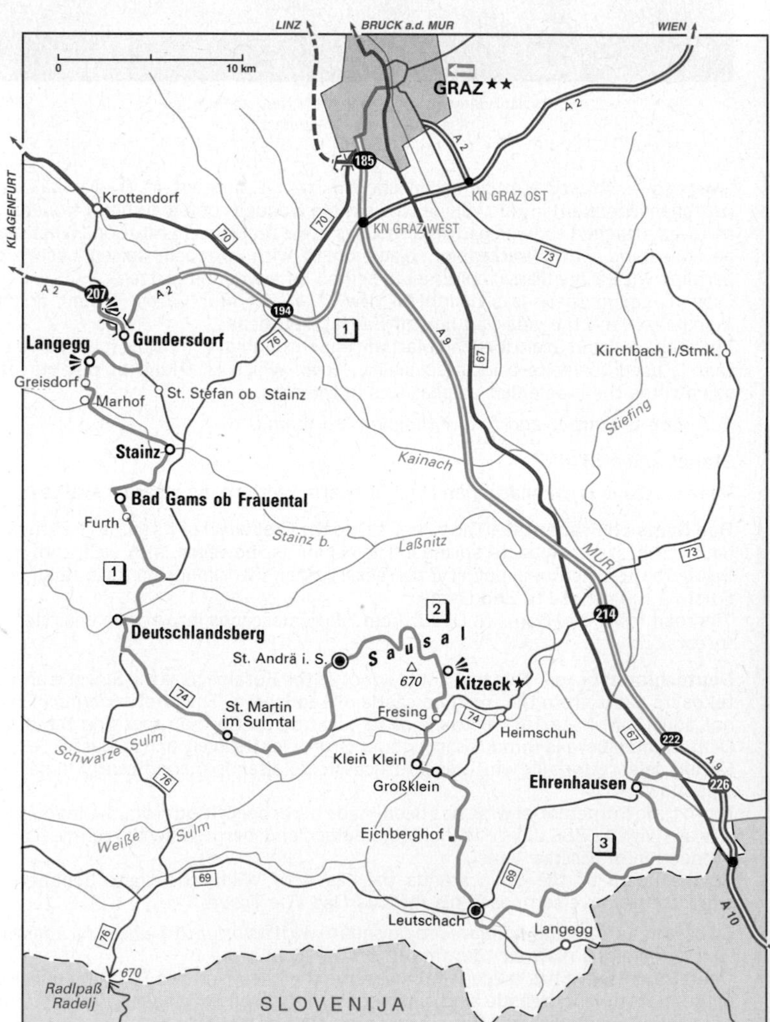

A sharp eye will detect, particularly in **Klein Klein**, splendid storks' nests, securely constructed on chimney-stacks and occupied between Easter and September.

Celtic tombs dating from the 6C-4C BC have been discovered under some tumuli in the forest near **Großklein**, indicating early human occupation of the district. The finds are kept in Schloß Eggenberg.

In Großklein turn left towards Heimschuch; shortly afterwards, turn right to Eichberghof to the south.

The road meanders through wild and hilly country, past the peaks of hills where small south-facing vineyards alternate with fields of maize and wooded areas.

Leaving the Eichberghof Restaurant on the right, follow signs to Leutschach in the south.

3 South Styrian Route

On either side of the road near **Leutschach** the fields are full of hops growing up the characteristic tall hop poles.

In Leutschach turn left in front of the church (green road sign: Südsteirische Weinstraße - South Styrian Wine Route). On leaving Leutschach take the road to Langegg following the Wine Route signs.

This is the most southerly wine-growing area in Austria, where, for several miles, the wine route forms the frontier with Slovenia. This region is nowadays known as the **Styrian Tuscany** on account of its sunny climate and its similarity to the Tuscan countryside in Italy.

A forest of conifers gives way to rows of vines which cover the hills with their gentle contours, like waves frozen in the mist. This is the very heart of Welschriesling and Samling country. The road continues among picturesque small hillocks, offering splendid, almost panoramic, **views**★. To the south, at no great distance, are the Slovenian hills. Frequent signs indicate those stretches of road which form the frontier.

Ehrenhausen - Near the Slovenian frontier, a wooded bluff overlooking the south bank of the Mur and the village of Ehrenhausen was chosen by the Eggenberg princes as the site of a castle and a mausoleum. The **Pfarrkirche** on the main square has a fine bell-tower with a particularly elaborate roof. The building was remodelled in Baroque style in 1752 and given a Rococo interior.

★ **Mausoleum** ⓥ - This curious funerary monument shelters the tomb of Ruprecht of Eggenberg, who distinguished himself as a general in the struggle with the Turks at the end of the 16C and won several significant victories with his troops. The building was completed in 1640 but the interior decor was not added until 1681-91, the work being entrusted to pupils of Johann Fischer von Erlach.

The interior is striking for the number of stuccoes on the central dome. The great commander lies in the crypt, accompanied by his successor, Wolfgang von Eggenberg.

Castle - The castle, standing near the square keep has preserved an elegant courtyard with Renaissance arcades in three tiers and an old well.

Take the motorway back to Graz.

STEYR★

Oberösterreich

Population 43 000

Michelin map 426 fold 22 - Alt 310m/1 017ft

Steyr had a glorious past, becoming, for a time, a rival to Vienna. It is now Upper Austria's third largest town (after Linz and Wels) and still an important economic centre. The picturesque old town, which has preserved its character and charm, clusters at the confluence of the Enns and the Steyr. On the edge of town, international firms such as BMW, MAN, SKF (Swedish ball-bearing manufacturer) and GMF (manufacturing engineering and machine construction) have set up in business.

OLD TOWN

★ **Stadtplatz (Y)** - The Stadtplatz, which is a street in the form of a square, is lined with fine Late Gothic and Renaissance houses with projecting first floors. In the middle is a 17C fountain, the **Leopoldibrunnen (A)**. Two of the buildings in particular, the **Rathaus (R)** and the **Bummerlhaus** (no 32), are of outstanding interest. The Rathaus, built in the Rococo style from 1765 to 1771, has a narrow façade surmounted by a tower; the Bummerlhaus is a fine mansion in the Gothic style, with a gable and the characteristic first-floor overhang.

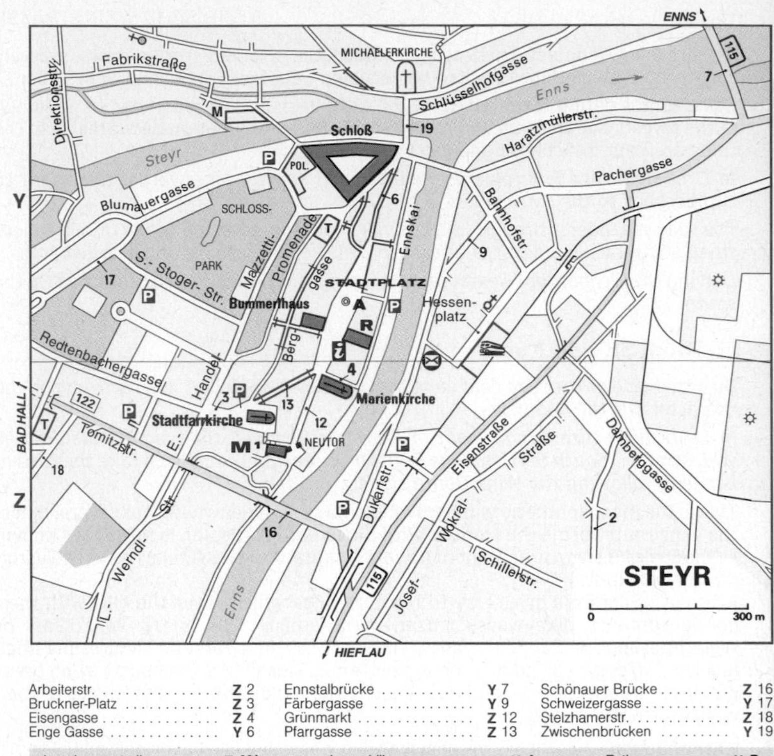

Arbeiterstr.	Z 2	Ennstalbrücke	Y 7	Schönauer Brücke	Z 16
Bruckner-Platz	Z 3	Färbergasse	Y 9	Schweizergasse	Y 17
Eisengasse	Z 4	Grünmarkt	Z 12	Stelzhamerstr.	Z 18
Enge Gasse	Y 6	Pfarrgasse	Z 13	Zwischenbrücken	Y 19

Innerbergerstadl .... Z M¹	Leopoldibrunnen .... Y A	Rathaus .... Y R

Many of these houses have remarkable courtyards: no 9 has a Renaissance court, with fine pillars supporting two tiers of arcades on which Virginia creeper grows; no 11 has arcades adorned with sgraffiti *(see GMÜND Niederösterreich)* and a wooden loggia; nos 36/38 are two houses sharing a Late Gothic arcaded courtyard and tower with floral Renaissance decoration.

Marienkirche (**Z**) – The former Dominican church is flanked on the north side by the **Eisengasse** (**Z 4**), a picturesque alley going down to the Enns.
The interior Baroque decoration includes a high altar overloaded with gilding, a Virgin and Child of 1704, pictures framed in stucco and a Rococo pulpit.
South of the Stadtplatz is the **Innerbergerstadl** (**Z M**), a 17C granary turned into a local museum. Together with a town gate (the Neutor) and a house flanked with a turret built on brackets, it forms a charming picture.

Go round the Innerbergerstadl to the right and make for the parish church along an alley ending in a stairway.

Stadtpfarrkirche (**Z**) – The Gothic church was built in the mid 15C by Hans Puxbaum, the architect of the Stephansdom in Vienna, which it resembles both in plan and elevation. This master was also responsible for the **tabernacle**★, with its delicate tracery, and the tripartite chancel baldaquin opposite. The font is adorned with 16C low-relief sculptures.

Schloß (**Y**) – *At the confluence of the Steyr and the Enns.* Records mention a fortress on this spot as early as the end of the first millennium. This castle, which was built in the Baroque style in 1666, was given its present appearance by Passau architect Domenico d'Angeli after a fire in 1727. The oldest part of the building is the keep, or Römerturm.

EXCURSIONS

★ **Stift Seitenstetten** ⊙ – *19.5km/12mi to the east on Bundesstraße 122.* This Benedictine abbey (still very active today with its famous grammar school) was founded in 1112. Only the apse and the side walls of the Ritterkapelle (Knights' Chapel) remain from this early period.

Stiftskirche (Abbey church) – The three-aisled Early Gothic basilica dates from around 1300 and was converted to the Baroque style between 1670 and 1706, with rich stucco decoration and frescoes. The high altar is dominated by an Assumption of the Virgin Mary, a major work by Johann Karl Reslfeld of Garsten.

Stiftsgebäude (Abbey buildings) – They are substantially based on designs by Josef Munggenast. Above the festive **abbey staircase** is a ceiling fresco by Bartolomäus Altomonte, while that in the **Marmorsaal** (Marble Hall) representing The Alliance between Religion and Worldly Wisdom is by **Paul Troger**. The 12 paintings by the **Kremser Schmidt** in the Maturasaal are particularly fine, while the Mineralienkabinett (Cabinet of Minerals) with its Rococo cabinets is more intimate in character. The abbey's **art collection**★ is also of interest, with paintings by the Kremser Schmidt and Paul Troger (Stiftsgalerie).

The gallery and the bookcases of the two-storey **library**★ are made of walnut and contrast delightfully with the exclusively white leather bindings of the books.

A beautiful wrought-iron gate of 1780 gives access to the restored **Hofgarten** (formal garden), which is well worth visiting.

Bad Hall – *19km/12mi west of Steyr.* Iodized springs, which are among the most concentrated in Central Europe, and up-to-date equipment for the treatment of diseases of the eyes, heart, and circulatory disorders, make Bad Hall a much sought-after spa resort. The spa park, with paths bordered with fine trees and lawns adorned with clumps of flowers, blends in harmoniously with the rest of the town. Generous sports facilities (golf, tennis, thermal baths) add to the resort's appeal.

Pfarrkirchen – *1km/0.5mi southwest of Bad Hall.* The **parish church**★ ⌚ in this village is one of the most attractive of its kind in Austria and belongs to the abbey at Kremsmünster. The modification of its interior decoration in a charming Rococo style was carried out around 1744. The frescoes on the vaulting, enhanced by delicate stuccowork, make a picture of great harmony glorifying the mystery of the Holy Blood. The pulpit, the organ-loft and the high altar are richly adorned with painting, cherubs and statues. They are well proportioned and fit perfectly into the magnificent ensemble.

R. Chéret/MICHELIN

Ceiling fresco in the Marble Hall, Stift Seitenstetten

STUBACHTAL★★★

Salzburg

Michelin map 926 fold 32

The Stubachtal, a valley about 20km/12mi long, is one of the most beautiful Alpine regions in Austria. A well-built scenic road leads from Uttendorf (alt 804m/2 638ft) to Enzingerboden (alt 1 480m/4 856ft). From this point, the Weißsee-Gletscherbahn cable-car takes skiers in the winter and walkers in the summer to several mountain lakes and a magnificent glacial massif at the boundary to the Hohe Tauern National Park.

★★ **Uttendorf to Enzingerboden road** – *17.5km/11mi. The trip begins in Uttendorf, 6km/4mi east of Mittersill on B 168. The road provides a view of the Steinkarlhöhe range and then leads through a beautiful spruce forest. There is a car park behind the reservoir at the foot of the cable railway. This is the starting point for climbing the Kalser Tauern.*

★★★ **Kalser Tauern** – *2hr 30min there and back, 1hr of which is on foot.*

Cable-car – *25min ascent.* The first stage of the climb passes over luxuriant vegetation (Alpine roses) with a view of the Grüner See at the foot of the Kitzkarkogel. To the left, you can look over the Totenkopf and the lower Riffel glacier. The Rudolfshütte mountain lodge is situated at the mountain station (alt 2 315m/7 595ft). There is a splendid **view**★★ of the Weißsee Lake and the nearby **Sonnblick glacier** (alt 3 088m/10 131ft). A 10min walk brings you to the chair-lift lower down.

Medelzkopf chair-lift – Alt 2 564m/8 412ft. *15min ascent.* The route leads through a majestic Alpine massif and offers a magnificent **panorama**★★★. At the halfway point, you can look back and see the **Tauernmoos Lake and dam**, with the Kleiner Eiser towering above them. On arrival at the top, the **Johannisberg** (alt 3 453m/11 329ft), enthroned in the centre of the massif, and further to the right the **Eiskögele**, which stands out boldly from the icicles of the Odenwinkl glacier, are the most impressive features of the landscape.

Walk to the Kalser Tauern pass – *45min return. Sturdy footwear needed.* A path, waymarked in red and white, leads through the rocks. Apart from its geological interest, the pass has a beautiful **view**★ of the lake and the Dorfertal Valley.

STUBAITAL★★

Tirol

Michelin map 926 folds 29 and 30

Local map see INNSBRUCK: Tour of the Mittelgebirge

The Stubai Valley is one of the most popular destinations in the vicinity of Innsbruck to go for day trips. In summer, it is an ideal starting point for hiking expeditions, and it also provides one of the largest all-year ski areas in Europe.

★ FROM INNSBRUCK TO MUTTERBERGALM *44km/27mi*

Leave Innsbruck via the Brenner-Bundesstraße. After crossing the Europa bridge turn off into the Stubai Valley at Schönberg. It is also possible to take the Brenner motorway (toll).

On entering the valley, you will soon see, facing you, the enormous glacial massif of the **Zuckerhütl** (alt 3 511m/11 520ft). The well-built road runs past the Stubai Valley's five resorts: first **Schönberg**, then **Mieders**, with **Telfes** on a sunny terrace opposite. The locality of **Fulpmes** specializes in the manufacture of mountaineering equipment and tools. The most famous metalworkers in the North Tyrol used to work here in days gone by. **Neustift** is the fifth of the valley's main holiday resorts, dominated by the striking silhouette of the 18C Pfarrkirche (parish church) built by Franz de Paula Penz; its high altar merges with the side altars to form a single picture.

Over the last 7km/4mi of the journey, the gradient becomes ever steeper and the landscape more rugged. The road finally leaves the wood and arrives at Mutterbergalm (alt 1 728m/5 669ft) at the foot of the rocky cirque which forms the beginning of the valley.

★★ STUBAI GLACIER (STUBAIER GLETSCHER)

This all-year ski area offers ski enthusiasts downhill slopes of varying degrees of difficulty covering a total distance of 53km/33mi. The area's attraction lies in its outstanding snow cover and the speedy transportation of winter sports enthusiasts around the site. Snow-boarders and skiers can ply their sport at the same time as each other on this extensive ski area between 2 300m/7 546ft and 3 200m/10 499ft. Good skiers will appreciate the 10km/6mi long **Wilde Gruben** descent, which leads down to Mutterberg through splendid, unspoilt **countryside**★★.

A 4.5km/3mi long cross-country course at an altitude of 2 600m/8 530ft (starting from the Gamsgarten cable-car) is available to cross-country skiers.
The skiing season generally begins in October and ends at the beginning of July on the highest pistes.
The most important viewpoints, which can be reached by lift or on foot, are indicated below *(take warm clothing, sunglasses and thick-soled, waterproof footwear).*

★★ **Eisgrat** - Alt 2 900m/9 514ft. A cable-car in two stages leads to the glacial cirque and the foot of the Stubaier Wildspitze peak (alt 3 340m/10 958ft) and Schaufelspitze peak (alt 3 333m/10 935ft). Forbidding **Alpine landscape**★★. Walk round the restaurant to see the lower part of the valley, which is dominated by the Ruderhofspitze peak and the Habicht.

★★ **Jochdohle** - Trip starting from the Eisgrat. Hikers take the waymarked footpath over the Schaufelfern glacier, which follows the ski piste *(climbing the 250m/820ft difference in altitude takes about 1hr; do not leave the footpath; it is possible to hire the appropriate mountaineering equipment at the sports shop in Eisgrat).*
Skiers travel down to the Gamsgarten restaurant and then take the Eisjoch six-seat chair-lift which leads to a small pass (alt 3 170m/10 400ft); **view**★ of the Ötztal Alps. Continue by means of the tiny Windachfern ski tow. Finally, you will reach the Jochdohle, where the highest restaurant in Austria is situated (alt 3 150m/10 335ft).
There is a rewarding **panorama**★★ across the Swiss Alps, the Arlberg and, in particular, the Ötztal Alps, the Ortler in the south Tyrol and, further to the east, the glaciers of the Zillertal Valley.
Ski down further on the other slope to the right of the Gaiskarfern ski tow and take the Pfaffengrat double chair-lift to Fernauferner. After completing two thirds of the piste you will see, on the right-hand side and slightly higher up, a place from which is it easily possible to reach the ridges (about 100m/110yd from the piste). A signpost indicates the way to the Hildesheimer Hütte mountain lodge. Breathtaking **view**★★★ of a landscape of jagged peaks and glaciers, dominated by the impressive Zuckerhütl (alt 3 511m/11 520ft).

★★ **Daunferner** - Skiers can reach the glacier (alt 3 160m/10 367ft) by means of the Daunfern ski tow, the Wildspitz double chair-lift and the Rotadl four-seat chair-lift. Impressive **view**★★ over the rocky cliffs which frame the glacier from the Stubaier Wildspitze peak to the Ruderhofspitze peak.

TAMSWEG★

Salzburg

Population 6 000

Michelin map 926 fold 34 - Alt 1 024m/3 360ft

The best view of the town, dominated by the great pilgrimage church of St Leonard standing alone in the forest on the valley slope, is from the approach via the Mauterndorf road.
Tamsweg is the capital of the Lungau and fosters many old traditions: according to a custom reminiscent of that of Flanders, processions take place every summer *(see Calendar of events)*, headed by a gigantic dummy representing Samson, accompanied by two dwarfs.

SIGHTS

Marktplatz - The regular design of this square, lined with pretty houses, lends distinction to Tamsweg. The **Rathaus** (town hall), in a building dating from the 16C, features corner turrets and closely resembles the style of country mansions commonly found in the Salzburg region. Opposite, stands the old **Schloß Kuenburg** built from several houses between 1742 and 1745 following a fire and now housing offices and a cultural centre.
The delicate stuccowork in the **Dekanatspfarrkirche** is the work of Johann Cajetan d'Androy from Graz. Further off is the old hospice of St Barbara, which now houses the **Lungauer Heimatmuseum** (exhibits include artefacts from excavations of Roman sites).

St. Leonhardkirche - *Drive south from Tamsweg over the bridge over the River Mur (the Murau road). Cross the railway and park at the start of the road (right) which climbs directly up to the church; keep further right onto a footpath which is less steep.*
There is a good view of Tamsweg and of the deeply jagged ridges of the Tauern. The 15C church of St Leonard has kept its Early Gothic plan and design - tall light windows, network vaulting etc. Some of its **stained glass**, which dates from the

period when the building was erected, is among the finest in Austria. Note also, immediately to the left on entering (near the gallery), the window of the Tree of Life in which the Virgin of the Annunciation is presented at the foot of the tree, which spreads out on either side, and at its tip forms the arms of the Cross. The "**gold window**" *(Goldfenster)*, on the right of the chancel, is very well known: in a flamboyant architectural setting, it depicts, upwards from the base, the arms of Salzburg borne by two cherubs, St Virgil and St Rupert standing on either side of the donor prelate, and the Holy Trinity figuratively represented as the Throne of Grace - the Holy Father presenting Christ - between St Peter and St Paul. South of the high altar, the small altar to St Leonard is surmounted by a statuette of the saint held in the branches of a juniper tree. The discovery of the statuette is the basis of the pilgrimage.

TULLN

Niederösterreich

Population 14 650

Michelin map 926 fold 11 - Local map see DONAUTAL - Alt 180m/591ft

Tulln grew up on the site of the Roman camp of Comagenae, founded here in the 1C AD on the very edge of the Roman Empire and surrendered in the 5C. Between 1042 and 1113, the town was the residence of the Babenberg dynasty, predecessors of the Habsburgs, and was thus the capital of Austria until replaced in that role by Klosterneuburg, then by Vienna which became the royal seat in 1156. Tulln's most famous local figure is the painter Egon Schiele, who was born on 12 June 1890 the son of Tulln stationmaster on the first floor of the station building.
The town's favourable site on the banks of the Danube meant that it has always been an important trade centre. Tulln now hosts trade fairs (including the international gardeners' trade fair) and is an important industrial town (sugar production).

SIGHTS

Egon-Schiele-Museum ⏲ - *Donaulände 28*. The old local prison now houses an exhibition on the life and work of Tulln-born painter Egon Schiele (1890-1918). On the first and second floors is a small collection of originals (drawings, lithographs, watercolours, a few oil paintings), mainly from Schiele's early work (1905-08), and works by contemporaries of his.

Salzturm - On the banks of the Danube level with Nibelungengasse stands a fortified tower from the west side of the Roman cavalry garrison in Tulln that has survived almost unchanged in shape and height. The "**Römerturm**" was built under Emperor Diocletian (AD 284-305). In the Middle Ages it was used as an arsenal and from the early 19C as a salt store, which explains why the locals now call it the "salt tower".

Pfarrkirche St. Stefan - *Wiener Straße*. This originally Romanesque basilica from the 12C was transformed in the 15C into the Gothic style and then remodelled in the Baroque style in the 18C.
The Romanesque doorway in the west façade, framed between two Baroque towers, is adorned with busts of the 12 Apostles and surmounted by a double-headed eagle, the symbol of the Holy Roman Empire, holding two Turks' heads in its talons. The Turks represent the terrible danger of invasion which threatened Austria in the 16C and 17C. In front of the doorway are statues of St John of Nepomuk (left) and St Charles Borromeo (right).
The nave and chancel have ogive vaulting and are strikingly large. The 1786 altarpiece represents the stoning of St Stephen.

★ **Karner** - Level with the chevet of the parish church stands one of the finest **funerary chapels** (ossuaries) in Austria. It is known as the chapel of the Three Kings and was built about 1245. Its outside shape is that of an 11-sided polygon, to which an oven-vaulted apse is attached. Each face of the polygon is adorned with arches and richly decorated capitals; under one of the arches (right of the doorway) is a statue said to be of the donor (but this is a subject of debate). The **doorway**★★ itself is decorated with palm-leaf capitals and geometrical motifs. The interior of the chapel is roofed with a dome adorned with Romanesque mural paintings. The frescoes were however drastically restored in 1874 in the 19C style. From the side opposite and facing the entrance, looking back towards the doorway, you can see the old ossuary beneath the chapel.

Minoritenkirche - *Minoritenplatz*. This Baroque building constructed in 1739 was dedicated to St John of Nepomuk. Inside, to the left of the high altar, there is a glimpse of the sacristy with a magnificent inlaid cabinet dating from the 18C.

M. Hertlein/MICHELIN

Minoritenkloster and Minoritenkirche, Tulln

★ **Minoritenkloster** ⓥ – *Between the Minoritenkirche and the banks of the Danube.* The origins of the monastery date back to the 13C. It was dissolved in 1807 and subsequently used as a military school, barracks and residence. Since the building was renovated between 1990 and 1994, it has hosted various administrative bodies, not to mention at least six museums and exhibitions.
Basement. **Subterranean Tulln**: excavations beneath the monastery and archeological discoveries from Tulln. **Region on the move**: exhibition on the origins and evolution of Tulln.
Ground floor. **Lower Austrian Fire Brigade Museum**: collection of historic fire engines in the courtyard. Lively presentation of the past and present of fire-fighting. **Limes museum**: explanations and artefacts on the Roman presence in the province of Noricum, which extended with the Danube as its north border from Passau almost as far as Vienna (military and everyday life etc).
1st floor. **Local museum** (town and region).
3rd floor. Austrian Sugar Museum: information on sugar production, including reproductions of equipment in an 1830 sugar factory, with a comparison to modern standards.

West of the main square at the junction between Buchinger Straße and Nußallee is a fine **Jugendstil building** (villa built in 1902 for former Austrian Minister of Agriculture Rudolf Buchinger), that is an absolute must for anyone strolling around Tulln.

TURRACHERHÖHE

Kärnten und Steiermark

Michelin map 926 fold 34 – Alt 1 763m/4 812ft

This small mountain resort has sprung up around the Turracher See Lake close to the Turrach pass, which serves as the border between Styria and Carinthia. It is a well appointed all-year holiday resort; in summer there is boating and hiking and in winter skiing on slopes that rise from 1 400m/4 605ft to 2 240m/7 637ft. The road between Predlitz and the resort at Turracherhöhe passes through a landscape of sturdy forests and Alpine pastures. For a period from the early years of the 17C, the village of Turrach was a mining centre with an ironworks which belonged to the princes of Schwarzenberg, resident at Murau. The first **Bessemer converter** to be installed in Western Europe began operating here in 1863: it was used to decarbonize cast iron by forcing pressurized air through the metal.
The speed of technical change and the pace of international competition caused the tall furnaces to be abandoned; the last fire died in 1909. Although most of the ironworks have now disappeared, there still stands beside the road near the church the delightful old administration building with its ornamental façade and pilasters, the last remnant of the valley's industrial traditions.

VIENNA***

See WIEN

VILLACH*

Kärnten

Population 54 640

Michelin map 926 fold 34 – Local map see WÖRTHER SEE – Alt 501m/1 644ft

Villach, Austria's "gateway to the south", to both Italy and Slovenia, is a major road and railway junction at which the international lines between Vienna and Venice and between Salzburg and Belgrade intersect. The town's favourable site on the banks of the Drava (Drau) must also have appealed to the ancient Celts and Romans, if archeological evidence of settlement here and in the surrounding area during the Hallstatt and Roman periods is anything to go by. Records mention a bridge *(pons)* Uillah, from which the town takes its name, in the 9C.

A significant event in the town's history was Heinrich II's gift of it to his newly founded bishopric of Bamberg (Bavaria) in 1007. This was to shape the town's fortunes for the next 752 years, until Maria Theresa bought Villach back in 1759. Frequently referred to as the "secret capital" of Carinthia, Villach is the province's second largest town and the economic and cultural hub of the region. The way the municipality's boundaries have been drawn up means that it stretches as far as the Faaker and Ossiach lakes, so that it also caters for a variety of sports and leisure activities. Finally, there are the thermal baths with their mineral springs which have also made Villach a certain reputation as a spa resort.

Carinthian Summer – There is a music festival held in Villach and Ossiach every July and August, which offers a wide variety of musical entertainment including chamber music, ballet, puppet shows and opera.

SIGHTS

★ **Old town** – The old town of Villach is delimited to the north and east by the Drava. The **Hauptplatz** which straddles it, a square dating from the 12C, is surrounded by a number of houses which essentially date from the 14C to 16C. These include the Paracelsushof *(Hauptplatz 18)*, named after the great physician, who spent his youth in Villach; and the old Khevenhüllers' house, now the Hotel Post, with its splendid Renaissance oriel, where Emperor Karl V lived for seven weeks in 1552.

Markowitsch/ÖSTERREICH WERBUNG

Villach – the all year round destination

The most interesting feature to look out for is the beautiful arcaded courtyards – there are some particularly good examples in the Widmannsgasse.

Hauptstadtpfarrkirche St. Jakob – The simplicity of the exterior of this triple-aisled hall-church makes the complexity of the stellar and ribbed vaulting inside all the more pleasant a surprise. Besides the high altar with its magnificent sculptures, beneath a baldaquin, note the stone pulpit dating from 1555. There are also several 15C-18C **tombstones★** on the inside and outside of the south wall. In summer it is possible to climb up the free-standing church tower and admire the view.

★ **Museum der Stadt Villach** ⓥ – *Widmanngasse 38.* Many centuries of architectural styles have left their mark on this grand building. With its arcaded courtyard, it forms a fine backdrop for the local historical collections. The cobblestone surface in the entrance hall is the last of its kind in Villach. The two Gothic panel paintings by **Master Thomas of Villach** are of great importance to the town. They depict Domitian, Duke of Carinthia, and Matthew the Apostle. They were probably painted in c 1500 and demonstrate this master's exceptionally delicate brush strokes. Other interesting items include the death plaque of head of provincial government Christoph Khevenhüller, who died in 1557, and the large iron chests from the 16C-19C that were used as fire-proof storage places for valuables.

Relief von Kärnten ⓥ – *In the Schillerpark, Peraustraße.* This immense relief model is on a scale of approximately 1:10 000 – about 6in to 1mi (vertical exaggeration x 2). By studying this tourists can familiarize themselves with the general character of the countryside, often difficult to determine on the spot.

Wallfahrtskirche Heiligenkreuz – *Follow Peraustraße as far as the junction with Ossiacher Zeile.* This Late Gothic church building with its striking twin-towered façade stands on the south bank of the Drava. The unusual ground plan, which seems unable to decide between length and central space, allocates more space to the transept crossing and chancel than to the actual nave, which is reduced to one and a half bays. The richly decorated high altar with the Crucifixion scene, the Lamentation altarpiece in the north and the extremely rare depiction of the Thief on Christ's Right in the south transept, along with the pulpit which dates from the church's original construction, all contribute to the overall harmony of the church interior. The excellent paintings beneath the organ gallery depict Christ driving the Moneychangers from the Temple.
From the north nave, an oval room links the church with the Chapel of Mercy. Both rooms are beautifully painted.

Villacher Fahrzeugmuseum ⓥ – *Draupromenade 12. It is worth buying the short museum guide, in order to learn about the technical details of the vehicles on display.* This small museum is devoted to means of transport manufactured after 1950 and manages to display a maximum number of exhibits in a very small space. The collection of bicycles is particularly good.

Warmbad – *South of town.* Every day, 24 million l/over 5 million gal of therapeutic spring water bubbles up daily from the six warm springs (29°C/84°F). When Villach was part of the French Illyrian Provinces between 1809 and 1813, Napoleon nursed plans to develop it into a spa resort of world renown. These came to nothing, but the modern spa at Villach has all the facilities one would expect to find at a well maintained health resort.

EXCURSION

★ **Villacher Alpenstraße** – *16.5km/10mi.* This modern mountain road is well laid out along the wooded mountainsides and later along the cliff-like edge of the Dobratsch; many viewpoints have been constructed overlooking the deep Gail Valley, facing the jagged crests of the Julian Alps to the south. From car park P4 there is a very good view of the "Schütt", a rocky chaos created by a landslide in 1348.

★ **Alpengarten** ⓥ – *Access from car park P6.* This Alpine garden devoted to the flora of the southern Alps should not be missed. It covers an area of 10 000m²/11 960sq yd and is home to 900 types of Alpine plant, with explanatory panels.

On reaching the end of the roadway (alt 1 732m/5 682ft) take the **chair-lift** ⓥ to the plateau at 1 957m/6 421ft and then climb on foot to the top of the **Dobratsch★★** (alt 2 167m/7 107ft). This isolated peak offers a famous **panorama** of the Karawanken, the Carinthian lakes, the Julian Alps and the Tauern *(about 2hr 30min there and back from the end of the road, of which 10min are spent in the chair-lift and 2hr walking).*

Burgruine Landskron – *From St. Andrä via a steep toll road.* The castle, which in the Middle Ages was one of the strongholds of the Habsburgs in Carinthia, passed in the middle of the 16C to the Khevenhüller family who rebuilt it.

Bartholomäus Khevenhüller, who also owned the castle of Velden *(see WÖRTHER SEE)*, had the castle fitted out in sumptuous style. His period of residence was a high point for Landskron. During the Thirty Years War, however, decline set in. Landskron Castle was taken away from the Khevenhüllers, who supported the Reformation, as part of the measures taken in Austria against the Protestants, and the fortress subsequently changed hands frequently. From the terrace (café-restaurant) there is a wide **view**★ of the Villach basin, the Karawanken and Ossiacher See.

★ **Eagle flight demonstration** ⓥ – Falconers from the bird of prey station set up in Burg Landskron put on a spectacular flight demonstration. In a performance lasting about 1hr, spectators experience at sometimes very close range the breathtaking feats of various birds of prey in flight (kites, falcons, eagles).
Half way up the toll road leading to the Landskron ruins is the **Affenberg**, where a colony of Japanese macacos (type of monkey) lives in the open countryside. *Visits are only possible as part of a guided tour.*

★ **Ossiacher Lake** – *See OSSIACHER SEE.*

VÖCKLABRUCK

Oberösterreich

Population 12 000

Michelin map 926 folds 20 and 21 – Alt 430m/1410ft

Vöcklabruck bestrides the old main road halfway between Salzburg and Linz. The first record of a bridge built here over the River Vöckla dates from 1134, and a century later, in 1246, the town was granted its charter. It was fortified in the early 14C.
The place is still a busy market town and educational centre for the surrounding countryside with a number of schools and colleges (agriculture, commerce and technology). It benefits too from its proximity to the Salzkammergut to the south, Austria's best-known tourist area. Nearby are the lakes of Attersee and Traunsee with their own range of attractions.

SIGHTS

Stadtplatz – As is frequently the case in Austria, the town square is simply a widening of the main road. Much older buildings are concealed by the Baroque façades lining the square. No 14 has an arcaded courtyard very much in the Italian style. The square is closed at either end by two towers. One of them, the **Unterer Stadtturm** (Lower Tower), is decorated with the arms of the various possessions of Burgundy as well as those of the Habsburgs, a reminder that **Emperor Maximilian I**, who owned a house in the town, was married to Mary, daughter of Charles the Bold of Burgundy.

Dörflkirche St. Ägidius ⓥ – *Leave the town via the Unterer Stadtturm and cross the river; the church is just over the bridge on the right.*
This elegant building is the successor to a much earlier church, first consecrated in 1143. It was built in 1688 by the architect **Carlo Antonio Carlone** and decorated by Giovanni Battista Carlone. It was restored to its former Baroque splendour in 1980.

VORAU

Steiermark

Population 1 503

Michelin map 926 south of fold 24 – Alt 660m/2 165ft

On a solitary hillock in Joglland the abbey of Vorau, founded in 1163, belongs to Augustinian canons, who still minister to the needs of 11 nearby parishes.

SIGHTS

Stift (Abbey) – Within the main gateway, the monastery buildings are laid out to a strict plan. The western façade of the church, decorated with fine stuccowork and flanked by two towers, is placed between two symmetrical wings.

Stiftskirche – The abbey church was entirely rebuilt in 1660, following the designs of a Swiss architect, Domenico Sciassia, and in 1700 to 1705 the interior was adorned, rather excessively, with gilt, stucco and paintings. The high altar is particularly elaborate.

Freilichtmuseum ⓥ – Not far off from the abbey is an open-air museum with a collection of traditional rural buildings – including a house, a mill, a sawmill, a press... – giving a glimpse of the life of the area as it was lived in the past.

WAIDHOFEN AN DER THAYA

Niederösterreich

Population 5 650

Michelin map 926 fold 10 – Alt 510m/1 673ft

Waidhofen is situated on the left bank of the River Thaya in attractive rural surroundings of farmland and forest. The town grew up from a fortified settlement, first recorded in 1171, which occupied a triangular site in a field. The parish church stands on the highest point, while the town fortress was built on the lowest ground, to the east.

SIGHTS

Altstadt – In the old town, the north promenade with the powder tower and the south promenade with a partially preserved defence tower are all that remain of the original fortified town wall. There are some interesting old houses along Wienerstraße (no 14, the Heimathaus), Böhmgasse and Pfarrgasse.

Hauptplatz – In the centre of the town square stands the **Rathaus**, a beautiful example of an essentially Gothic town hall, which owes its stepped gables to the Renaissance, however. The ridge turret was added in 1721. The **Dreifaltigkeitssäule** column was put up in 1709, unusually enough not in fulfilment of a vow, but to protect the town from plague, fire and war.

R. Chéret/MICHELIN

Church, Waidhofen an der Thaya

Pfarrkirche – The church's exterior, although finely proportioned, gives no hint of the interest of the interior decorations, which date from Baroque times. The vault of the nave is decorated with frescoes and surrounded by stuccowork; the pastel tones are dominated by gold and violet. These are the work of Josef Michael Daysinger and depict scenes from the life of Mary. The magnificent **high altar** (1721) fills the chancel with its lofty columns. The beautifully carved **stalls** feature a double-headed eagle on the upper part, to symbolize the church's function in an Imperial parish. The pulpit and the organ gallery contribute to the harmony of the whole. To the right of the chancel a 17C chapel contains a Virgin and Child (1440), which is charming, despite the stiffness of the pose. The Late Gothic relief on the altar (1510) dedicated to relief from the plague unusually substitutes St Nicolas and the Virgin Mary with Child for two of the 14 "auxiliary saints" it depicts.

Östliches WEINVIERTEL

Michelin map 926 folds 12 and 13

The route described below is an invitation to explore Austria's **eastern vineyard country**, a region that is still somewhat off the beaten tourist track. Its position on the border of the former Eastern Block and in the shadow of the great metropolis of Vienna to the southwest means that the countryside has remained relatively unspoiled. Nonetheless, this delightful region has many a treasure to offer visitors. Since this is a wine-producing region, visitors should naturally make sure that they sample some of the excellent local wines in one of the region's charming *Kellergassen* (roads just outside wine-growing villages lined with rows of tiny wine cellars with winepressing rooms).

FROM GÄNSERNDORF TO POYSDORF *62km/39mi*

Take care, as there are numerous unmarked railway crossings along this drive!

The route begins at the edge of the wine-growing area in the district capital of **Gänserndorf** *(26km/16mi northeast of Vienna; reached via Bundesstraße 8).*

Safari- und Abenteuerpark Gänserndorf ⏲ – *4km/2.5mi south of Gänserndorf, towards Orth an der Donau.* It is hard to imagine a safari park practically at the gates of Vienna, but here it is. At Gänserndorf **safari park**, visitors can feed ostriches and gnus from their car, or drive at walking pace past a pride of lions. There is a 6km/4mi tour *(allow about 45min)*, that visitors can follow either in their own car *(at their own risk; open-top cars and motorbikes are not admitted)* or in the "Safari bus", through enclosures of tigers, lions, zebra, elephants, antelopes and more. Children especially will be delighted at seeing gangling giraffes and cheeky ostriches at such close quarters. Next to the safari park is an **adventure park**, with a traditional zoo, home to some extremely rare Bengal tigers, family shows (several times a day), and other entertainment *(some of which costs extra)* such as camel rides, children's zoo, trampolining – all guaranteed to make tiny hearts beat faster.

From Gänserndorf drive on towards Prottes.

Along the road from Gänserndorf to Prottes are numerous pumps, extracting oil or gas from the ground in endless up and down motion. Their original shape has resulted in their being labelled locally as "the bobbing or nodding horses of the oilfields". In **Prottes**, where oil has been produced since 1949, there is a trail, the **Erdöl-Erdgas-Lehrpfad**, which gives more information about this singular feature of the southern Weinviertel. The footpath covers a distance of 4km/2.5mi through charming countryside *(departure from the Erdöl-Erdgasmuseum in the village, then follow the red and white markings)*, past display panels with background information and numerous original pieces of machinery connected with the extraction of this raw material (oil detection probes, mobile drilling gear, production derricks etc).

Drive on via Matzen towards Groß-Schweinbarth. Vineyards and fields of sunflowers embody the friendlier side of the Weinviertel, which is a very fertile region thanks to its loess soil.

Niederösterreichisches Museum für Volkskultur ⏲ – *In* **Groß-Schweinbarth.** *Right by B 220; from Prottes keep left heading towards Gänserndorf.* This museum of traditional regional culture (complete with wine section) has found the perfect home in Groß-Schweinbarth's old dairy farm, once the farm for the neighbouring castle. Displays include traditional costume from the various regions of Lower Austria, furniture and crockery, and a broad range of items on the topics of local customs, religious practices and craftwork. The history and role of the dairy farm is also explained. The pretty courtyard contains a collection of historic vehicles and agricultural machinery.

Take B 220 towards Pirawarth. At the exit to Groß-Schweinbarth turn right towards Hohenruppersdorf. From there head towards Zistersdorf and then to Niedersulz.

"Eing'richt"

This painstaking craft in which tiny scenes, mainly on religious themes (such as the Crucifixion), are patiently crafted – often from very simple materials – and then inserted *("eingerichtet")* into bottles used to keep many a farming family occupied on long winter evenings. A small collection of this naive art form is on display in the Lower Austrian museum of popular culture.

★ **Weinviertler Museumsdorf** ⓥ – *In* **Niedersulz**. More than 60 items from the Weinviertel which for one reason or another could not be kept at their original location have been reconstructed in an open-air museum. The museum site has been planted with flora typical of the region which have been allowed to grow as they would in a natural setting. The realistic layout of houses around a village square, complete with church, inn, presbytery and even graveyard, creates the impression of walking around a village whose inhabitants are all out working in the fields but who could be back at any moment. The houses contain authentic typical furnishings or exhibitions on rural life. The "living farm" on the museum site is worked as for real and contains traditional domestic and farm animals. The south Moravian courtyard ("Südmährerhof") by the museum entrance documents the agricultural, regional and popular traditions of south Moravia. The museum also runs a comprehensive programme of events (details available from the museum).

M. Hertlein/MICHELIN

The "living farm" at the Weinviertler Museumsdorf

Drive on through Obersulz and Schrick towards **Mistelbach**. *In Lanzendorf, shortly before reaching the district capital, turn left and follow the brown signposts to "Schloß Asparn/Zaya – Museum für Urgeschichte".*

Asparn an der Zaya – This town at the foothills of the Leiser Berge boasts a fine ensemble of historic buildings in a very small area: the Baroque Minorite convent (dating from the18C and now housing a museum on wine-growing and the local region on the ground floor, with a colourful collection of exhibits reflecting local culture); the elegant parish and convent church of St Pancras and St Francis; and the castle.

Museum für Urgeschichte ⓥ – *In the castle.* The exhibition in this prehistory museum (tour begins on the 2nd floor with a diagram of the earth's evolution in the stairwell) illustrates the evolution of humankind and of human culture from their earliest days to the beginning of the Christian calendar (includes a room with reproductions of cave paintings from Altamira, Lascaux etc). The **open-air museum**★ behind the castle is a particular highlight, with reconstructions of prehistoric dwellings from the Paleolithic Age to New Iron Age (25 000 BC to 2C AD) that visitors can enter.

A little tip for any incurable romantics: in Ladendorf (8km/5mi south of Asparn) there is a 2km/1mi long four-row avenue of lime trees leading off from the police station which was planted back in the 18C. It is the perfect place to go for a walk, preferably à deux.

From Asparn drive on towards Hörersdorf and then turn left onto Bundesstraße 46 to Laa an der Thaya.

Burgruine Staatz – *At the Laa-Poysdorf crossroads, carry straight on, following the signposts to "Ruine". Park the car by the Musikerheim and continue on foot along the path that follows the fortified wall.* The castle ruins can be seen from miles off (seen from a distance they are strongly reminiscent of Tuscany), standing on the relatively low Staatzer Berg (331m/1 086ft). However, their exposed site means that there is a magnificent **view**★★ from here of the Weinviertel and the Carpathian mountains to the northeast.

Carry on to Poysdorf.

Shortly before reaching this town, the road passes the **pilgrimage church of Maria Bründl** in an idyllic setting shaded by trees to the left of the road. This was built between 1740 and 1751 following the designs of Italian master builder Donato Felice d'Allio, who also designed the abbey church at Klosterneuburg *(see entry)*.

Poysdorf – The "wine town of Austria", whose vineyards are mainly used for the production of sparkling wine *(Sekt)*, still has numerous picturesque *Kellergassen* within town limits. Particularly fine examples of these streets of wine cellars are to be found in Bürsting *(via Singergasse from the tourist office)* and Berggasse *(below the parish church)*. A circular footpath on the theme of *Kellergassen (allow 1hr; leaves from the Stadtmuseum, follow the beige-white markers)* also leads through some of the delightful vineyards on the edge of town. From May to October, daily, under the slogan *"offener Keller"*, the wine-growers take it in turns to throw their premises open to the public and show people round, as well as offering the chance to partake in wine-tasting sessions with a commentary.

WELS

Oberösterreich

Population 60 000

Michelin map 926 fold 21 – Alt 317m/1 040ft

Situated at the junction of ancient trade routes, the small Celtic settlement of Vilabis evolved into the Roman town of Ovilava. Under Hadrian, it was raised to the status of city, while Caracalla made it a Roman colony. By this time, Wels was an important supply centre behind Limes and capital of the Roman province of Noricum. Wherever excavations are carried out inside the boundaries of the town, they uncover yet more evidence of its Roman past. This has resulted in a particularly rich local museum collection. The most important exhibits in the Stadtmuseum are the marvellous **Wels Venus** and the **Wels Genius**.

Wels is now an important towns for trade and trade fairs, but has nonetheless managed to preserve its lovely historic town centre over the centuries.

OLD WELS

Start in Polheimerstraße.

Beyond the **Ledererturm** (Leather Tower) (**A**), built in the 13C, is the elongated **Stadtplatz★** (**AB**) with its flower-bedecked fountain. There are no Roman remains but the quality and variety of the old buildings of the medieval area around the Stadtplatz make it one of the most evocative of its kind in Upper Austria.

No 62-63, once the property of Kremsmünster Abbey, has an imposing Baroque façade.

Go into the arcaded courtyard of no 63.

This courtyard gives a view of the Wasserturm, the water tower built in 1577 to feed the town's fountains.

Go out of the far end of the courtyard and along the stream to the left.

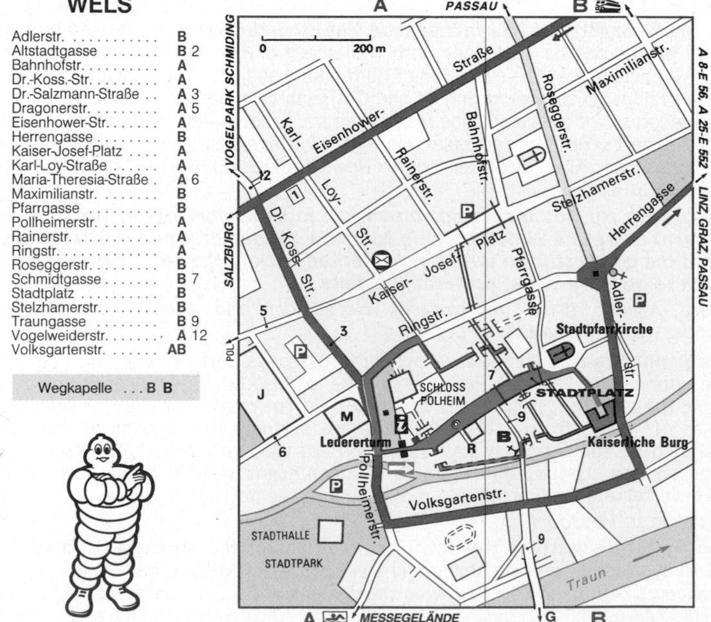

In Traungasse (**B 9**) note the little oratory on the left (**B B**), dedicated to St John of Nepomuk; it shelters a fine statue of the saint. Altstadtgasse (**B 2**) runs along remains of the medieval walls. Opposite the west entrance to the Kaiserliche Burg is the Revenue building, given its present Baroque façade in 1684.

Burg Wels ⓥ (**B**) – Emperor Maximilian I, the "last knight", died here in 1519. The restored Imperial castle now houses four **museum collections**: the history of the town, with a remarkable display of Biedermeier items; agriculture, arranged on the theme of the "farmer's year"; the Austrian museum of bakery, the only one of its kind; and the museum of displaced persons.

Return to Stadtplatz and the parish church.

Stadtpfarrkirche (**B**) – Behind the high altar in the Gothic chancel are some fine 14C stained-glass windows. Beneath the tower, a beautiful late-12C **Romanesque porch** has been grafted on.

A number of buildings in the Stadtplatz are worthy of attention: the Rathaus (no 1) has a Baroque façade with stuccowork and an attic storey topped by four stone urns; there is a Jugendstil façade at no 10; the 1570 paintwork is still intact on the house (no 24) where Salome Alt, mistress of Wolf Dietrich, Prince-archbishop of Salzburg, lived; Biedermeier style (no 49); a lively example of Rococo (no 52); a 16C courtyard (no 34) leads to the Schmidtgasse (**B 7**). To the north of town stands Schloß Polheim (**A**), dating from the 13C and originally the residence of the counts of Polheim, a local noble family.

On the northwest side of Polheimerstraße is the somewhat pompous façade of the **Stadtmuseum** (**A M**), built 1900-02.

Vogelpark Schmiding

A resident of Schmiding bird reserve

EXCURSION

★ **Vogelpark Schmiding** ⓥ **(Bird Reserve)** – *7km/4mi north of Wels (in Krengelbach).* This 85 000m²/915 000sq ft bird reserve with a zoological garden, biotopes and a 3.5km/2mi circular path is home to 2 000 animals and birds (350 species). There is a tropical house and a walk-in aviary with birds of prey. Besides birds, the reserve is home to antelopes, gazelles, kangaroos, reptiles and monkeys.

WIEN***

[L] VIENNA

Population 1 539 848
Michelin map 926 folds 3, 4 and 12
Local maps see DONAUTAL and WIENERWALD
Alt 156m/512ft
Hotels and restaurants: see The Red Guide Europe
For longer visits to the city, consult The Green Guide VIENNA

Vienna was the residence of the Imperial court for six centuries and is indelibly stamped with the seal of the Habsburg dynasty. Even now as capital of the Republic of Austria, Vienna has retained its incomparable grandeur and considerable prestige as one of Europe's most important artistic centres.

In 1967 Vienna was elected the permanent headquarters of OPEC (Organization of Petroleum Exporting Countries). In 1979 thanks to the opening of the Vienna International Centre, the "UNO-City" (**BR**), outside the city centre, it was possible to accommodate several UNO organisations here: the International Atomic Energy Agency (IAEA), the United Nations Industrial Development Organization (UNIDO), the Office for Drug Control and Crime Prevention (ODCCP) and the Office for Outer Space Affairs (OOSA). Austria is now the third UN capital after New York City and Geneva.

For many, the name Vienna evokes the rhythm of the waltz or the shape of the Prater's Giant Wheel. The city's global renown, however, is due above all to its historic buildings, to the magnificent art collections accumulated by the Habsburgs, to its excellent museums, to the musical tradition preserved by the Opera and Vienna's famous choirs and orchestras, and to the elegance of the shops which line its grand avenues.

Michaelertor, entrance to the Hofburg

TRAVELLERS' ADDRESSES

Tourist information

Tourist information for motorists – There are tourist information points for motorists on the outskirts of Vienna. **To the north**: Floridsdorfer Brücke, "Donauinsel" exit (open 1 May-late Sept daily 9am-7pm). **To the south** on motorway A 2, "Zentrum" exit (open July-Sept 8am-10pm, week before Easter-late June and Oct 9am-7pm). **To the west** on motorway A 1, Wien/Auhof service station (open Apr-Oct 8am-10pm, Nov-Mar 10am-6pm, Nov 10am-6pm).

For those arriving by rail – There are tourist information points at the **Westbahnhof** (open Apr-Oct 7am-10pm) and at the **Südbahnhof** (open May-Oct 6.30am-10pm; Nov-Apr 6.30am-9pm).

For those arriving by air – The tourist information centre at Wien-Schwechat airport is open daily 8.30am-9pm, ☎ 01/70 07 3 28 75.

City centre – Tourist information centre in the city centre: Am Albertinaplatz 1, 1. Bezirk, open daily 9am-7pm, ☎ 01/21 11 40.

Enquiries by post – Write to: Wiener Tourismusverband, Obere Augartenstraße 40, A-1025 Wien, Austria.

Information on Vienna on the **Internet** is available from the following Web sites: *info.wien.at* (specifically: tourist information) and *www.magwien.gv.at* (City of Vienna). For tips on where to go consult *www.servus-in-wien.at.*

The City of Vienna monthly cultural **calendar of events** is available from the tourist office (from the 15th of the previous month).

There is a weekly calendar of events called **wienside** specifically aimed at young people which comes out every Thur with tips on where to party, exhibitions and other events. Since it also contains cinema programmes, anyone on a visit to Vienna should get hold of a copy: available free from local "in" bars, cinemas, bars, nightclubs etc.

"Wien-Karte"

This ticket is valid for three days and is available from many hotels, tourist information centres, various ticket sales and information offices belonging to the Viennese transport authorities (Wiener Linien; for example, Stephansplatz, Karlsplatz, Westbahnhof) or from abroad by credit card payment from ☎ 00 43/1/7 98 44 00 28. The ticket gives unlimited free travel on the city's public transport (underground/subway (U-Bahn), bus, tram – but not on night buses) for 72hr (from when it is first validated), as well as reductions on entrance to about 150 museums, on purchases in certain department stores, in cafés, wine bars and restaurants. Full details are included in the coupon booklet that comes with the ticket. The Wien-Karte costs 210S *(at the time of going to press).*

City tours

City bus tours

Vienna Sightseeing Tours, Stelzhamergasse 4/11, 3. Bezirk, ☎ 01/71 24 68 30. City tour with the "Vienna Line Hop on Hop off". This operates hourly between 13 stops (for example, Staatsoper, Heldenplatz, Prater) from 9.30am to 6.10pm. Commentaries in English and German. Cost of a ticket valid for two days is 250S, available from any hotel in Vienna, or any travel agency in Austria as well as abroad.

Cityrama, Börsegasse 1, 1. Bezirk, ☎ 01/53 41 30. City tours daily at 9.30am and 2.30pm with a guided tour of Schloß Schönbrunn. Takes about 3hr 30min. Tour costs 400S per person (including pick-up from hotel).

Robin Reisen-Stattwerkstatt, Kolingasse 6, 9. Bezirk, ☎ 01/3 17 33 84. City tour entitled "Dream and Reality" focussing on Jugendstil and "Red Vienna" (1920s social-democrat housing projects). Departures: Tues and Thur at 1pm, Sat at 10am, sometimes also at 2pm. Takes about 3hr. Tour costs 330S. Booking necessary.

Round tour in an old-fashioned tram – Early May-early Oct, Sat and Sun and public holidays at 11.30am and 1pm. On Sun and public holidays the "Oldtimer" tram also runs at 9.30am. Departure from Karlsplatz. Takes about 1hr. Tickets available from "Wiener Linien" information office at Karlsplatz U-Bahn station. ☎ 01/7 90 94 40 26.

Diejun/ÖSTERREICH WERBUNG

Horse-drawn carriage

City tour by horse-drawn carriage – The horse-drawn carriage stands are located on Albertinaplatz behind the Staatsoper as well as on Heldenplatz and Stephansplatz.

Vienna on foot – The city of Vienna organises themed walks around town, such as Musical Capital of the World, Jugendstil, Unadulterated Habsburgs, The Viennese Coffee-house, Old Houses and Quiet Courtyards, Underground Vienna. Takes about 90min. Monthly programme available from the tourist office at Albertinaplatz 1.

City tour with a difference "On the Trail of the Third Man" – This tour naturally takes place underground in the Viennese sewer system: greetings from Orson Welles's classic film "The Third Man". The tour (which takes about 25min) leaves from opposite the Café Museum (**JS**) in the Esperantopark (cross Friedrichstraße, ticket office in metal container). During heavy rain, tours understandably do not take place; only children older than 12 years old are admitted; sturdy closed-in footwear is recommended; tour participants should have a good command of German. If all these criteria are met, this tour is a lively and interesting experience, full of all kinds of surprises. Advance booking and information from MA 30 – WienKanal, A-1030 Wien, Friedrichstraße/Esperantopark, ☎ 01/5 85 64 55.

Cycle tours – Cyclists in Vienna have some 700km/435mi of cycle paths at their disposal. Those arriving in Vienna by train can hire bicycles from the following stations: West- and Südbahnhof, Wien Nord and Florisdorf, and Franz-Josefs-Bahnhof. These can be returned at any station with luggage check-in facilities. Further cycle hire outlets can be found on the Donauinsel or at the Hundertwasserhaus (cost from about 40S per hour with some form of identification such as a passport left as a security).

"Pedal Power" cycle tours through Vienna are offered in various languages May-Sept daily at 10am; takes about 3hr; 280S (180S with your own bicycle); further details from ☎ 01/7 29 72 34.

The brochure entitled **Tips für Radfahrer**, available free from tourist offices, gives full details of the above.

Boat tours – DDSG Blue Danube Schiffahrt GmbH offers boat tours on the Danube Apr-late Oct; for example a Hundertwasser tour on the *Vindobona* (departure from Schwedenplatz, takes 1hr 30min). Details from DDSG Blue Danube Schiffahrt GmbH, Friedrichstraße 7, A-1010 Wien, ☎ 01/58 88 00, Fax 01/58 88 04 40.

Air tours – Vienna Aircraft Handling, Hangar 3, A-1300 Flughafen Wien-Schwechat, ☎ 01/70 07 2 22 04, Fax 01/70 07 2 24 64 offers airborne circuits (30min) in a CESSNA 210 (single-engine plane). Recommended price: 1 100S per person.

Public transport

Viennese transport authorities, Wiener Linien, operate services in the central zones of the Vienna city area (all districts) and are linked with the east Austrian transport authority (Verkehrsverbund Ost-Region, VOR). Written enquiries and requests for information by telephone can be addressed to either organisation:

Wiener Linien, Erdbergstraße 202, A-1031 Wien, ☏ 01/79 09 105.
Verkehrsverbund Ost-Region, Neubaugasse 1, A-1070 Wien, information hotline ☏ 08 10/22 23 24.
Further details on public transport in Vienna are to be found on the Internet at the relevant Web site *(www.wienerlinien.co.at or www.vor.at)*.

Tourists in Vienna are advised to pay a visit in person to one of the **information and ticket offices** in the following U-Bahn stations: Stephansplatz, Schwedenplatz, Karlsplatz, Landstraße/Wien-Mitte, Westbahnhof, Spittelau, Schottentor, Reumannplatz, Philadelphiabrücke, Hietzing, Florisdorf or Kagran. *To find your way around: a map of the U-Bahn network is included on the city map published by the Vienna tourist office and available from most hotels, among other places.* These outlets can also supply timetables for Vienna's transport system or the more comprehensive timetable book, as well as selling tickets (runabout or magnetic strip tickets).

Tickets – Tickets are valid for travel on the underground/subway (U-Bahn), tram, high-speed rail (Schnellbahn) and bus. Single tickets can be validated using ticket machines on the transport in question or in U-Bahn stations. It is cheaper, however, to buy tickets in advance from ticket offices or an authorised tobacconist's (Tabaktrafik). Tickets that are well-suited to the needs of tourists include the **24**- (60S) and **72**- (150S) **hour runabout ticket** or the **8-day ticket** (300S; this allows the bearer unlimited travel within Vienna city centre limits per strip validated, on the date it was validated). The **"Wiener Einkaufskarte"** (Viennese shopper's ticket) offers another interesting deal: for 50S you can make unlimited trips in the city centre for one day (between Mon and Sat) 8am-8pm.
Of course, there is always the option of the "Wien-Karte" *(see above)*, which allows three days of unlimited travel on Viennese public transport.

Night line – When normal city transport finishes running for the day (after about 12.30am until about 4.30am), 22 night bus lines operate in the city centre every 30min, for which special rates apply (runabout tickets are not valid on these night buses; single ticket 15S; tickets available from ticket machines on the bus or as strip tickets bought in advance – 45S for four trips). Further details and a map of the night line services are available from indicated Vienna transport authority ticket offices.

Inner city car parks

Vienna old town and the surrounding districts (Bezirke 1-9 and 20) are **fee-paying short-stay parking zones**. However, these are only signposted as such at the entrance to each district concerned (no further indication is given in the streets themselves – a paid-up parking ticket is obligatory from the minute you park). In commercial streets, parking regulations may vary, for example concerning how long you may park, in which case these will be specifically indicated. Pre-paid parking tickets can be bought from most authorised tobacconists (Tabaktrafiken) and banks, stations and from Vienna transport authority (Wiener Linien) ticket offices. Visitors who have booked a hotel on advance are advised to telephone before they arrive and confirm where they may leave their car (a day parking ticket may be available from reception).

The most practical solution to the difficulty of parking in the city centre is offered by numerous multi-storey or underground **car parks**, which are open daily 24hr/24hr. In the 1. Bezirk these are the following underground car parks: Am Morzinplatz (Franz-Josefs-Kai), Rathauspark (Ring/Stadiongasse), Operngarage (Kärtner Straße 51), Am Hof, Beethovenplatz 3, Cobdengasse 2. An overview of car parks in Vienna can be requested from the tourist office (☏ 01/21 11 42 22) or found on the Internet *(www.wkw.at/garagen)*.

Post offices

The second and third digit in Viennese **post codes** denote the district (Bezirk) in question, thus 1070 denotes the 7. Bezirk, Vienna.

The main post offices are open daily 24hr/24hr:
Hauptpostamt, Fleischmarkt 19, 1. Bezirk, ☏ 01/51 50 90
Post am Westbahnhof, Mariahilfer Straße 132, 15. Bezirk, ☏ 01/89 11 50
Post am Franz-Josef-Bahnhof, Althahnstraße 10, 9. Bezirk, ☏ 01/3 19 14 70

Shopping

Most department stores and specialist boutiques are located in the pedestrian zones in Kärntner Straße, Graben, Kohlmarkt, Naglergasse, Tuchlauben, Stephansplatz, part of Krugerstraße and Franz-Josefs-Kai, Wolfengasse, Seitenstettengasse, Rabensteig, Griechengasse, Ballgasse and Vienna's main shopping street – **Mariahilfer Straße**.

H. Wiesenhofer/ÖSTERREICH WERBUNG

Augarten porcelain workshop

Souvenirs

Augarten GmbH, Stock-im-Eisen-Platz 3-4, 1. Bezirk. In Schloß Augarten, 2. Bezirk. Sales outlet for the famous porcelain manufacturer, whose origins date back to 1717.

Backhausen, Kärntner Straße 33, 1. Bezirk. This textile factory sells furnishing materials, curtains and silk scarves with Jugendstil designs.

Frimmel, Freisingergasse 1, 1. Bezirk. This is *the* shop for buttons, which used to supply the Imperial court.

J. & L. Lobmeyr, Kärntner Straße 26, 1. Bezirk. A glassware specialist which used to supply the Imperial court, and which is famous for its extremely fragile and delicate "Musselinglas".

Maria Stransky, Hofburg. Burgpassage 2, 1. Bezirk. This is the home of typical Viennese petit point embroidery.

Piatnik, Kandlgasse 33, 7. Bezirk. This establishment founded at the end of the 19C sells such beautiful playing cards that they can almost rank as works of art.

Schau Schau Brillen, Rotenturmstraße 11, 1. Bezirk. Spectacles in the strangest shapes are the speciality here, signed by Peter Kozich. One of his clients is no less a figure than Elton John.

Food markets

Naschmarkt, Linke Wienzeile/Kettenbrückengasse. 4. and 6. Bezirk. This is divided into the **Naschmarkt** proper (fruit and vegetables): Mon-Fri 6am-6.30pm, Sat 6am-5pm, and the **Bauernmarkt** (farm produce): Mon-Thur 6am-noon, Fri 6am-1pm, Sat 6am-5pm.

Markt auf der Freyung, 1. Bezirk, May-Nov Tues and Thur 10am-6.30pm.

Flea markets

Naschmarkt: Linke Wienzeile. 4. and 6. Bezirk. The flea market is located at the south end of the Naschmarkt: Sat 6am-6pm.

Art and antiques markets

Kunst- und Antikmarkt am Donaukanal (art and antiques market on the promenade along the banks of the Danube on the old town side by the Marienbrücke, 1. Bezirk): May-Sept Sat 2-8pm, Sun 10am-8pm.

Am Hof (1. Bezirk): Mar-Christmas Fri and Sat 10am-8pm.

Kunst- und Handwerksmarkt im Heiligenkreuzerhof (art and crafts market, Schönlaterngasse, 1. Bezirk): every first weekend in the month, in Dec every weekend.

Christmas markets

Christkindlmarkt Rathausplatz mid Nov-Christmas
Weihnachtsmarkt am Spittelberg late Nov-Christmas
Altwiener Christkindlmarkt Freyung late Nov-Christmas
Kultur- und Weihnachtsmarkt in front of Schloß Schönbrunn late Nov-Christmas
Kunsthandwerksmarkt in front of Karlskirche late Nov-Christmas

Entertainment

Theatre

Burgtheater, Dr.-Karl-Lueger-Ring 2, 1. Bezirk. ☎ 01/5 14 44 44 40. A European theatre offering the entire range of theatrical repertoire. Tickets sold in advance from the 20th of the month preceding the month in question, for the whole calendar month. Written applications for tickets should be addressed at least 10 days in advance of the date in question to the Servicecenter Burgtheater, Hanuschgasse 3, A-1010 Wien (Fax 01/5 14 44 41 47). Tickets can be ordered by telephone (payment by credit card) daily 10am-9pm from ☎ 01/51 31 513. For performances that are not sold out, tickets can be obtained at 50% of their original price from 1hr before the performance starts from the "Abendkasse" (☎ 01/51 44 44 44 0). Other theatres linked with the Burgtheater are the **Akademietheater** (Lisztstraße 1, 3. Bezirk, ☎ 01/51 44 44 740) and the **Kasino** (Schwarzenbergplatz 1, 3. Bezirk, ☎ 01/51 44 44 830).

Theater in der Josefstadt, Josefstädter Straße 24, 8. Bezirk. ☎ 01/42 70 03 00. Venue for theatrical productions since 1788, where such famous Austrian names as Nestroy and Raimund made their debut: both classic and modern theatre.

Volkstheater, Neustiftgasse 1, 7. Bezirk, ☎ 01/524 72 63. Broad spectrum of plays from the classics to the avant-garde.

gruppe 80, Gumpendorfer Straße 67, 6. Bezirk, ☎ 01/586 52 22. Predominantly Austrian plays from the classics to contemporary drama.

Schauspielhaus, Porzellangasse 19, 9. Bezirk, ☎ 01/3 17 01 01. Young, unconventional theatre.

Komödie am Kai, Franz-Josefs-Kai 29, 1. Bezirk, ☎ 01/533 24 34. Popular comedies from all over the world for a pleasant evening.

English Theatre, Josefsgasse 12, 8. Bezirk, ☎ 01/40 21 26 00. English-language theatre productions from both Britain and America have been staged here since 1963 (classics, comedies, guest performances by solo artists).

Musical venues

Staatsoper (Herbert-von-Karajan-Platz, 1. Bezirk) and **Volksoper** (Währinger Straße 78, 9. Bezirk) - *the* opera venues of the Austrian capital. Tickets go on sale one month before the performance date. Written applications for tickets must be submitted at least three weeks before the performance to the Österreichischer Bundestheaterverband, Bestellbüro, Hanuschgasse 3, A-1010 Wien. Tickets can be ordered by telephone (payment by credit card) from ☎ 01/5 13 15 13. Remainder tickets can be purchased from the Bundestheater ticket offices, Hanuschgasse 3, ☎ 01/51 44 29 60 or from the Volksoper itself (Mon-Fri 8am-6pm, Sat, Sun and public holidays 9am-noon). For programme details call ☎ 01/15 18 (recorded message).

Neue Oper Wien: The independent opera group, which stages only a few productions per year, has dedicated itself to premieres and 20C works that have some relevance to current affairs and that concern humanitarian and social-political matters. Information on the programme and performances from ☎ 01/5 97 30 37 or on the Internet at Web site *(www.neueoperwien.music.at)*.

Musikverein: Vienna's association for friends of music (Bösendorferstr. 12, A-1010 Wien, ☎ 01/5 05 81 90, Fax 01/5 05 81 94) puts on about 500 concerts of classical music per year. Tickets go on sale about three weeks before the concert date, Mon-Fri 9am-7.30pm, Sat 9am-5pm. For programme details call ☎ 01/5 05 13 63 (recorded message).

Concerts by the Vienna Boys' Choir (Wiener Sängerknaben): The Vienna Boys' Choir perform from Apr-June and Sept-Oct Fri at 4pm in the Brahms Room at the Musikvereins. Tickets (390-550S) are on sale in hotels and from Reisebüro Mondial (travel agent's), Faulmanngasse 4, A-1040 Wien, ☎ 01/58 80 41 41, Fax 01/5 87 12 68, e-mail: *ticket@mondial.at*

Sung Masses in the Burgkapelle at the Hofburg on Sundays and 25 Dec (with the Vienna Boys' Choir and members of the chorus and orchestra of the Vienna State Opera): These begin at 9.15am. Seats cost 60 to 340S; there is no charge for standing room. Orders must be placed in writing (please do not enclose either cash or cheques) at least 10 weeks in advance to: Hofmusikkapelle, Hofburg, A-1010 Wien, Fax 01/5 33 99 27 75. Collection and payment of pre-ordered tickets is on Fri 11am-1pm and 3-5pm or on Sun from 8.15-8.45am in the Burgkapelle. Availability permitting, tickets for seats for a particular Sun are sold at the Burgkapelle Tageskasse from 3-5pm on the immediately preceding Fri.

Wiener Konzerthaus, Lothringerstraße 20, 3. Bezirk, ☎ 01/7 12 12 11. Orchestra and soloists from all over the world as well as performances by the concert house's resident company.

Top-quality **musical productions** are presented by Vereinigte Bühnen Wien GmbH (Linke Wienzeile 6, A-1060 Wien, ☎ 01/58 83 02 00, Web site: *www.musicalvienna.at*), which incorporates three venues:
Theater an der Wien, Linke Wienzeile 6, 6. Bezirk.
Raimund-Theater, Wallgasse 18-20, 6. Bezirk.
Ronacher, Seilerstätte 9, 1. Bezirk.

WUK, Währinger Straße 59, 9. Bezirk, ☎ 01/4 01 21 10. Self-administered "**W**erkstätten- **u**nd **K**ulturhaus" (workshops and cultural centre): music, dance, concerts, readings and exhibitions.

Szene Wien, Hauffgasse 26, 11. Bezirk, ☎ 01/74 93 341. Live concerts by advertised bands, world music.

Planet Music, Adalbert-Stifter-Straße 73, 20. Bezirk, ☎ 01/3 32 46 41. Venue for all sorts of musical varieties - hip-hop, pop through Blues, reggae, jazz to rock and heavy metal. There are also events specially for children and families.

Ticket reservations - The following organisation also deals with ticket reservations from abroad, principally for musicals and classical music: **Vienna Ticket Service**, Börsegasse 1, A-1010 Wien, ☎ 01/5 34 17 75 (Mon-Fri 9am-5pm, Fax 01/5 34 17 26). For rock and pop concerts, contact **Österreich Ticket**, Kärtner Straße 19, (1. Bezirk, Kaufhaus Steffel, 3. Stock), A-1010 Wien, ☎ 01/96 0 96 (Mon to Sat 9am-9pm, Sun 10am-9pm).

Other venues

Orpheum, Steigenteschgasse 94b, 22. Bezirk, ☎ 01/481 17 17. Entertainment venue (with adjoining inn - ☎ 01/2 03 12 54), in which cabaret, music and readings are on offer.

Kulisse, Rosensteingasse 39, 17. Bezirk, ☎ 01/485 38 70. Musicals, cabaret, children's theatre and its own inn (☎ 01/4 85 44 02).

Wiener Metropol, Hernalser Hauptstraße 55, 17. Bezirk, ☎ 01/40 777 40. Venue for concerts (ballads and songs, world music), cabaret and home-produced musical productions.

Vindobona, Wallensteinplatz, 20. Bezirk, ☎ 01/3 32 42 31. *The* place to go for cabaret; Sat and Sun children's theatre. There is also a restaurant close at hand so that visitors will be well taken care of all evening.

Miscellaneous

Spanische Reitschule: Ticket reservations for performances (gala performances, 80min, seats 250-900S, standing room 200S; classic displays of riding skills to music, 60min, 250S) should be addressed as far in advance as possible to the Spanische Reitschule, Hofburg, A-1010 Wien, Fax 01/53 50 186, e-mail: *office@srs.at*, or alternatively to authorised Vienna theatre ticket offices or travel agencies (there will be a supplementary charge of at least 22% in this case). Reservations are not necessary for morning training sessions ("Training der Lipizzaner"). Tickets (100S) for this can be bought on the same day at the entrance to the Spanische Reitschule (Hofburg, Josefsplatz).
A folder in several languages is available from the Vienna tourist office giving details of precise dates and terms and conditions.

Casino Wien, Palais Esterházy, Kärntner Straße 41, 1. Bezirk, ☎ 01/5 12 48 36.

Cinemas

The following are only a small selection, away from the mainstream, of the numerous cinemas that there are in Vienna. For the current cinema programme and additional addresses, consult *wienside*, the weekly calendar of events available from cinemas, local "in" bars etc or the daily press.

Österreichisches Filmarchiv, Obere Augartenstraße 1, 2. Bezirk, ☎ 01/2 16 13 00. Classics from the history of film.
Schikaneder Kino, Margarethenstraße 24, 4. Bezirk, ☎ 01/5 85 28 67. Small-screen, committed mainly to recent arts films.
Votiv Kino, Währinger Straße 12, 9. Bezirk, ☎ 01/3 17 35 71. Preview cinema.
Imax-Filmtheater (next to the Technisches Museum, **AZ**), Mariahilfer Straße 212, 14. Bezirk, ☎ 01/8 94 01 01; info hotline: 01/15 47.

(Especially English-language) films in their original versions are shown at:
Burg, Opernring 19, 1. Bezirk, ☎ 01/5 87 84 06. In summer, but also on most weekends throughout the year, Carol Reed's **The Third Man** is screened here.
English Cinema Haydn, Mariahilfer Straße 57, 6. Bezirk, ☎ 01/5 87 22 62.
American Flotten Center, Mariahilfer Straße 85-87, 6. Bezirk, ☎ 01/5 86 51 52.

Where to stay

The following lists of hotels and restaurants make a distinction between three categories: "Budget" includes addresses that are within the means of even modest budgets. "Our selection" regroups hotels or restaurants which offer a slightly higher level of comfort at correspondingly higher prices. "Treat yourself!" denotes really outstanding establishments - a taste of luxury that it would probably not be possible to afford every day.

BUDGET

Pension Franz – Währinger Str. 12, 9. Bezirk, ☎ 01/34 36 37, Fax 01/34 36 37 23. Family guesthouse with decor in the style of the turn of the 19C-20C. 24 rooms. Single room from 590S.

Pension Pertschy – Habsburgergasse 5, 1. Bezirk, ☎ 01/53 44 90, Fax 01/5 34 49 49. Family guesthouse in a 250 year old Baroque palace with Louis XV style furniture. 47 rooms. Single room from 700S.

Zur Wiener Staatsoper – Krugerstr. 11, 1. Bezirk, ☎ 01/5 13 12 74, Fax 01/51 31 27 41 5. Grand Viennese town house, small friendly hotel, with rooms furnished with period furniture. 22 rooms. Single room from 900S.

Kaiserpark Schönbrunn – Grünbergstr. 11, 12. Bezirk, ☎ 01/81 38 61 00, Fax 01/8 13 81 83. City hotel right next to Schloß Schönbrunn. 45 rooms. Single room from 900S.

Park-Villa – Hasenauerstr. 12, 19. Bezirk, ☎ 01/3 19 10 05, Fax 01/3 19 10 05 41. Jugendstil building dating from 1888, tasteful rooms, pleasant area to stay. 21 rooms. Single room from 950S.

Landhaus Fuhrgassl-Huber – Rathstr. 24, 19. Bezirk, ☎ 01/4 40 30 33, Fax 01/4 40 27 14. Country house in the middle of the Heurige district, furnished with period and rustic furniture; quiet rooms facing the garden. 22 rooms. Single room from 960S.

OUR SELECTION

Theater-Hotel in der Josefstadt – Josefstädter Str. 22, 8. Bezirk, ☎ 01/4 05 36 48, Fax 01/4 05 14 06. Modernised inner city hotel near the Ringstraße. 54 rooms. Single room from 1 250S.

Am Stephansplatz – Stephansplatz 9, 1. Bezirk, ☎ 01/53 40 50, Fax 01/53 40 57 10. Located directly opposite the Stephansdom; rooms at the front have a view of the cathedral. 60 rooms. Single room from 1 330S.

Dorint Rogner Hotel Biedermeier im Sünnhof – Landstraßer Hauptstr. 28, 3. Bezirk, ☎ 01/71 67 10, Fax 01/71 67 15 03. Biedermeier style room decor. 203 rooms. Single room from 1 550S.

König von Ungarn – Schulerstr. 10, 1. Bezirk, ☎ 01/51 58 40, Fax 01/51 58 48. Comfortable little hotel redolent of Vienna in the old days. 33 rooms. Single room from 1 610S.

TREAT YOURSELF!

Sacher – Philharmonikerstr. 4, 1. Bezirk, ☎ 01/5 14 56, Fax 01/51 45 68 10. Vienna's classic Grand Hotel – and home of the world-renowned Sachertorte. 108 rooms. Single room from 2 500S.

Im Palais Schwarzenberg – Schwarzenbergplatz 9, 3. Bezirk, ☎ 01/7 98 45 15, Fax 01/7 98 47 14. Former royal palace from the 18C, novel decor with some antiques, 7.5ha/18.5 acre private park. 44 rooms. Single room from 3 000S.

Eating out

BUDGET

Figlmüller – Wollzeile 5, 1. Bezirk, ☎ 01/5 12 61 77, main dishes starting at 80S. One of several local eateries serving the famous Wiener Schnitzel.

Pfudl – Bäckerstr. 22, 1. Bezirk, ☎ 01/5 12 67 05, main dishes starting at 85S. Ranks among the inns that have become a Viennese institution.

Haas & Haas – Stephansplatz 4, 1. Bezirk, ☎ 01/5 13 19 16, main dishes starting at 95S. One of the most popular local restaurants in the immediate vicinity of the cathedral; in the evening the cathedral garden is a pleasant place to sit.

OUR SELECTION

Fadinger – Wipplingerstr. 29, 1. Bezirk, ☎ 01/5 33 43 41, main dishes starting at 120S. A simple bar at the front, with a more sophisticated restaurant at the back, serving interesting modern Viennese dishes.

Eckel – Sieveringer Str. 46, 19. Bezirk, ☎ 01/3 20 32 18, main dishes starting at 130S. Cosy rustic restaurant with an elegant side room.

Hedrich – Stubenring 2, 1. Bezirk, ☎ 01/5 12 95 88, main dishes starting at 165S. Simple restaurant, calling itself a fast-food restaurant, but which in reality offers an interesting regional menu at a very reasonable price.

Vikerl's Lokal – Würffelgasse 4, 15. Bezirk, ☎ 01/8 94 34 30, main dishes starting at 165S. Really comfortable little local restaurant with wooden panelling where Viennese nouvelle cuisine is on the menu.

Hietzinger Bräu - Auhofstr. 1, 13. Bezirk, ☎ 01/87 77 08 70, main dishes starting at 170S. The classic restaurant for Viennese Tafelspitz (boiled beef and vegetable stew) and other beef dishes.

K & K Restaurant Piaristenkeller - Piaristengasse 45, 8. Bezirk (below the Piaristenkirche), ☎ 01/406 01 93, main dishes starting at 175S. In a 300 year old vaulted cellar where traditional Viennese dishes are served, there is the additional option of visiting two museums - the Kaiser-Franz-Joseph Hat Museum (souvenir photos are available, of visitors taking part in the "Old-style Viennese Hat Parade") and the K & K Weinschatzkammer (treasure trove of four centuries of wines from the Imperial wine cellars). For further details, consult the Internet *(www.piaristenkeller.com)*.

Plachutta - Wollzeile 38, 1. Bezirk, ☎ 01/5 12 15 77, main dishes starting at 185S. Restaurant dedicated to the Viennese beef tradition.

Salut - Wildpretmarkt 3, 1. Bezirk, ☎ 01/5 33 13 22, main dishes starting at 185S. Small friendly restaurant in several welcoming rooms in the city centre.

Hauswirth - Otto-Bauer-Gasse 20, 6. Bezirk, ☎ 01/5 87 12 61, main dishes starting at 190S. Typical Viennese restaurant with a pretty garden in the courtyard.

Cantinetta Antinori - Jasomirgottstr. 3, 1. Bezirk, ☎ 01/5 33 77 22, main dishes starting at 200S. *The* Italian restaurant in the 1.Bezirk.

Windows of Vienna - Wienerbergstr. 7, 10. Bezirk, ☎ 01/6 07 94 80, main dishes starting at 200S. Restaurant on the 22nd floor of a business centre, with an excellent view of Vienna and its surroundings.

Mraz & Sohn - Wallensteinstr. 59, 20. Bezirk, ☎ 01/3 30 45 94, main dishes starting at 240S. Modern restaurant, in which a father and son team produce some outstanding results.

TREAT YOURSELF!

Steirereck - Rasumofskygasse 2, 3. Bezirk, ☎ 01/7 13 31 68, lunchtime menu from 395S, evening main dishes starting at 320S. Located near the Hundertwasserhaus. Arguably the best food in Vienna, with a substantial wine cellar which it is possible to have a look round.

Heurige (Wine taverns)

Mayer am Pfarrplatz - Pfarrplatz 2, 19. Bezirk, ☎ 01/32 24 16. Wine tavern-buffet. Comfortable local tavern with a beautiful garden.

Altes Presshaus - Cobenzlgasse 15, 19. Bezirk, ☎ 01/3 20 02 03. Wine tavern-buffet. The oldest Heuriger in Grinzing (house dates from 1527), parts of the vaulted cellar are very old, as are the winepresses it contains.

Buschenschank Wolff - Rathstr. 46, 19. Bezirk, ☎ 01/4 40 23 35. Wine tavern-buffet. Typical wine tavern in cosy rooms with an extensive, magnificently maintained garden.

Fuhrgassl-Huber - Neustift am Wald 68, 19. Bezirk, ☎ 01/4 40 14 05. Wine tavern-buffet. Earthy rustic atmosphere spread over several rooms with Viennese "Schramml-Musik" (popular music played on violin, accordion and guitar).

Cafés, bars and nightclubs

Coffee-houses - The coffee house is a Viennese institution, and visitors should therefore make sure that they try out one of the numerous speciality coffees, with perhaps an accompanying slice of cake, in at least one such establishment.

Central, Herrengasse 14, 1. Bezirk, ☎ 01/5 33 37 63 26. Specialities are the "Mazagran" (iced coffee with rum) and "Pharisäer" (hot coffee with rum and whipped cream). Piano music between 4pm and 7pm (Mon-Sat 8am-10pm; July and Aug only to 8pm).

Hawelka, Dorotheergasse 6, 1. Bezirk, ☎ 01/5 12 82 30. Specialities include "Buchteln" (pastry filled with plum jam), served only after 10pm (Wed-Mon 8am-2am, Sun and public holidays 4pm-2am; closed on Tues).

Imperial, Kärntner Ring 16, 1. Bezirk, ☎ 01/50 11 03 89. Both Sigmund Freud and Anton Bruckner were regular clients at this coffee house which opened in 1873 (daily 7am-11pm).

Landtmann, Dr.-Karl-Lueger-Ring 4, 1. Bezirk, ☎ 01/5 32 06 21. Near the Parlament, Rathaus and Burgtheater, this café is a popular meeting place, which also boasts a beautiful summer terrace (daily 8am-midnight).

Café Museum, Friedrichstraße 6, 1. Bezirk, ☎ 01/5 86 52 902. Coffee house designed by Adolf Loos in the late 19C near the Secession building (daily 8am-midnight).

Kalmar/ÖSTERREICH WERBUNG

Café Central

Sacher, Philharmonikerstraße 4, 1. Bezirk, ☎ 01/5 14 56 0. The legendary *Sachertorte* is on sale here, an absolute must on the Viennese cake list (daily 8am-midnight).

Im KunstHaus, Weissgerberlände 14, 3. Bezirk, ☎ 01/7 12 04 97. Superb garden and inside room almost overgrown with plants – a coffee house with a difference (daily 10am-midnight).

Confectionery and patisserie

Altmann und Kühne, Graben 30, 1. Bezirk, ☎ 01/5 33 09 27. Fantastically packed confectionery.

Central, Herrengasse 17, 1. Bezirk, ☎ 01/535 99 05. This patisserie shop sells the **Imperialtorte**, rival to the Sachertorte, in five different packages (guaranteed to last four weeks).

Demel, Kohlmarkt 14, 1. Bezirk, ☎ 01/53 51 71 70. The prices are high, but you get something special for your money.

Lehmann, Graben 12, 1. Bezirk, ☎ 01/5 12 18 15. Apfelstrudel to die for.

Bars

The "**Bermuda triangle**" of the Viennese bar scene is located in the 1. Bezirk around the Ruprechtskirche and Rudolfsplatz (**KPR**). There is something to cater to every taste here. Just dive right in ...

Flanagans Irish Pub, Schwarzenbergstraße 1-3, 1. Bezirk, ☎ 01/5 13 73 78. The stone floor comes from an Irish chapel, and the bar has spent a century of its life in Ireland. Open Thur-Sat 11am-4am, Sun-Wed 11am-2am.

Kolar-Beisl, Kleeblattgasse 5, 1. Bezirk, ☎ 01/5 33 52 25. Open daily 5pm-2am.

Krah Krah, Rabensteig 8, 1. Bezirk, ☎ 01/5 33 81 93. Open daily 11am-2am. Popular local bar offering more than 50 varieties of beer.

Loos-Bar, Kärntner Straße 10, 1. Bezirk, ☎ 01/5 12 32 83. Open daily 6pm-4am. Small, but to be recommended, and not only because it was designed by Adolf Loos.

Panigl, Schönlaterngasse 11, 1. Bezirk, ☎ 01/5 13 17 16. Open 4pm-4am. Small Italian wine bar.

Philosoph, Judengasse 11, 1. Bezirk, ☎ 01/5 35 45 32. Open Sun-Wed 6pm-2am, Thur-Sat until 4am. Good music.

Planter's Club, Zelinkagasse 4, 1. Bezirk, ☎ 01/5 33 33 93. Open 5pm-4am. Those wishing to spend the evening in this chic, Colonial style bar room must be prepared to queue for quite some time to get in.

Reiss, Marco-d'Aviano-Gasse 1, 1. Bezirk, ☎ 01/5 12 71 98. Open Sun-Wed 11am-2am, Thur, Fri 11am-3am, Sat 10am-3am. Champagne-set hang-out with interior design by architects' office Coop Himmelblau.

Zum Basilisken, Schönlaterngasse 3-5, 1. Bezirk, ☎ 01/5 13 31 23. Open daily noon-2am, Fri and Sat until 4am.

Zum Bettelstudent, Johannesgasse 12, 1. Bezirk, ☎ 01/5 13 20 44. Open 10am-2am, Fri, Sat until 3am.

Jazz

Jazzland, Franz-Josefs-Kai 29, 1. Bezirk, ☎ 01/5 33 25 75. International groups appear in this vaulted jazz cellar beneath the Ruprechtskirche. Great atmosphere. Music from 9pm.

Miles Smiles, Lange Gasse 51, 8. Bezirk, ☎ 01/4 05 95 17. Not only for fans of Miles Davis.
Jazzclub Porgy & Bess, Riemergasse 11, 1. Bezirk, ☎ 01/50 37 009. Concerts by Austrian and international jazz musicians, live music every day.
Otto, Altmannsdorfer Straße 101, 12. Bezirk, ☎ 01/8 04 76 50. Oct-Apr Sun at 11.30am pre-lunch drinks with jazz.

Nightclubs

P1, Diskothek. Rotgasse 9, 1. Bezirk. House, techno, soul.
Havanna Club, Krugerstraße 8, 1. Bezirk, ☎ 01/5 13 32 25. Latin-American music: DJ and dance courses.
U4, Diskothek. Schönbrunner Straße 222, 12. Bezirk. Techno, Dance Floor.
B72, Hernalser Gürtel-Bogen 72, between 8. and 17 Bezirk, ☎ 01/4 09 21 28. Live music and DJs.

On the banks of the blue Danube

Donauinsel (Neue Donau) – *Linie 1, U-Bahn-Station: Donauinsel.* A total of 42km/26mi of beach, with cycle, surfboard and boat hire outlets, and a rich selection of local bars and restaurants on the "**Copa Cagrana**" (after the Viennese suburb of Kagran, with apologies to Rio) on the river banks attract not only the Viennese – this is a great place to escape the heat of the city and really chill out.

Donauinsel

Alte Donau – *Linie 1, U-Bahn-Station: Alte Donau.* The Viennese also come here to enjoy themselves in summer. The old branch of the Danube offers meadows, beaches and numerous bar-restaurants in which you can while away a pleasant evening on the banks of the Danube.

Dates for your diary

Wiener Eistraum – Jan-Mar. Ice-skating in front of the Rathaus.

Wiener Festwochen – May-June. Avant-garde festival of theatre, music and art.

Donauinselfest – Late June. Free open-air concerts which lure thousands to the Donauinsel.

Im-Puls-Tanzfestival – July-Aug. International dance performances which you can watch, or in which you can take part, in the museum district.

KlangBogen – July-Aug. Wide range of musical events at various venues around town. ☎ 01/40 00 84 10

Filmfestival am Rathausplatz – July-Aug. Free open-air video shows on a giant screen with recordings of classical music, in front of the Vienna Rathaus.

Viennale – Oct. International film festival. Details: *www.viennale.or.at.*

Wiener Ballsaison – Nov-Ash Wednesday. Viennese Ball Season, the highlight of which is of course the world renowned Vienna Opera Ball.

HISTORICAL NOTES

From Antiquity to the Babenbergs - Since ancient times, the Vienna basin has been a crossroads of European significance, commanding the neighbouring lands: Bohemia, Moravia, the Hungarian plain and the Alps.
The Romans established their camp at Vindobona facing the territory of the Germanic tribes. It is here that Marcus Aurelius is supposed to have died, and here - according to the Song of the Nibelungen - that Attila and Kriemhilde celebrated their wedding. Later, when the Babenberg family assumed control of the Eastern Marches, its representatives adopted in succession, as residences, Pöchlarn, Melk, Tulln and Leopoldsberg before settling in Vienna. In 1155, Heinrich II Jasomirgott installed his ducal court in the city at a place called Am Hof. The eminence arising from its official function enabled Vienna also to expand as a market town.
Under one of his successors, Leopold the Glorious, Vienna became the capital of the duchy and was guarded by massive walls with six fortified gateways and 19 towers. In the centre stood the Romanesque church of St Stephen (it became the bishop's seat only in 1469). By the time Frederick the Warrior, last of the Babenbergs, died in 1246, Vienna had become, after Cologne, the most important city on German-speaking territory. Its growth, from then on, was linked with the fortunes of the Habsburgs, who reigned over Austria from 1273 to 1918.

The plague and the Turks - In 1678, just after the celebrations in Vienna for the birth of a son to Emperor Leopold I, a terrifying sickness made its appearance. Corpses lay in heaps in the streets or were thrown into the Danube. All who could, fled the capital. Only a few notables, headed by Prince Schwarzenberg, decided to fight the plague. Drastic measures of hygiene enabled them to stop the epidemic, which died out a year after its first appearance.
In 1682 the first column to commemorate the deliverance from this plague was erected in the Graben, but another threat, exceptionally grave, loomed on the frontiers of the Empire.

The Turks - An army 300 000 strong, under the command of Grand Vizier Kara-Mustapha, crossed the Danube at Belgrade, heading for Vienna, Prague and the Rhine. Following the green standard of the Prophet was a motley horde of Turks, Slavs, Bosnians, Tartars and even Hungarian rebels.
Although the fate of the Empire and the Christian world was at stake, Leopold had much trouble in organizing resistance. He could not count on the support of Louis XIV, who was pursuing a policy of weakening the Austrian royal house and playing the Turkish card. Of all the monarchs of Western Europe, only Sobieski, the King of Poland, who felt himself to be directly threatened, concluded a pact of mutual assistance with the Emperor.
On 14 July 1683 the Grand Vizier lay siege to Vienna (it had previously been besieged by the Turks in 1529). The town was abandoned by the Emperor and the court and defended only by 24 000 men under **Ernst Rüdiger Count of Starhemberg**. For nearly two months the beleaguered city resisted all attacks. Duke Charles of Lorraine was urged by the Emperor to organize a relief force. King John III Sobieski crossed the river at Tulln and Krems at the head of 80 000 Austrians, Poles, Saxons, Bavarians, Swabians and Franconians on 10 September. The following night he camped on the hill at Kahlenberg and on the 11th deployed his army in the Wienerwald. On 12 September the Turks, caught between two forces, took flight in a general panic.
The famous victory of the Kahlenberg had repercussions throughout Europe. From that time on, the western sovereigns recognized the pre-eminence of the Emperor, who had saved Christendom. The Turkish menace disappeared, broken by Prince Eugene, one of the most famous generals of his time. There followed for the Austrian Empire a long period of prosperity, distinguished by the reign of Maria Theresa.

The Congress of Vienna - When Napoleon's empire collapsed in March 1814, Vienna supplanted Paris as the centre of Europe. It became the scene of the international congress which was to settle the fate of victors and vanquished. For a year, outside the working sessions of its committees, the Congress of Vienna furnished a pretext for splendid festivities, of which the echoes can still be heard. Here the crowned heads - the Emperor of Austria, Franz I, the young and handsome Czar Alexander I, the King of Prussia, Friedrich-Wilhelm, the King of Württemberg, and many princes and archdukes - made up a brilliant court. Diplomats added their prestige: Lord Castlereagh for Great Britain; Nesselrode for Russia; Wilhelm Humboldt for Prussia; Talleyrand for France; Metternich for Austria.
Receptions and balls were held at the embassies, in the state rooms at the Hofburg, and in the Great Gallery at the Schönbrunn Palace. *"Le Congrès ne marche pas, il danse"* (The Congress is not working, it is dancing), said the old Prince de Ligne maliciously. The remark became famous. More than any other city, Vienna could offer choice entertainment to its guests: art collections of rare quality, theatre, opera, concerts of chamber music. Ludwig van Beethoven himself conducted a gala concert and his opera *Fidelio* was received with enthusiasm.

Metternich

The career of Klemens Lothar Wenzel, Prince of Metternich-Winneburg, began in 1806, when he was appointed Ambassador in Paris and had every opportunity to observe Napoleon I. In 1809 Metternich was given the heavy burden of directing the foreign policy of his country. It was then that he proposed a *rapprochement* with France and succeeded in making this alliance a reality by negotiating the marriage of Napoleon and Archduchess Marie-Louise. With remarkable diplomatic insight he made Austria a buffer state between the Russian and French empires, a third force which might restore the balance of Europe.
This policy enabled Metternich to act as mediator at the Congress of Vienna and to have a moderating influence which made Austria, till 1848, defender of order in Europe.

Although Czar Alexander I made himself conspicuous by the brilliance of his receptions and by his libertinism, and though Prince Talleyrand succeeded, by his cleverness and a long experience of European affairs, in acquiring for himself a privileged position among the participating states while defending the rights of minorities, the central figure of the Congress remained Prince Metternich, the Austrian Minister of Foreign Affairs.

A "Belle Époque" – After the Napoleonic Wars, the Congress of Vienna began a carefree period that the Austrians call **Vormärz**, Pre-March, because it ended with the revolutionary events of March 1848. Wine, women and song – also dancing – seem to have been the chief interests of the Viennese, who lived at that time in a fever of pleasure.
Under the benign dictatorship of Metternich, the idyllic Vienna of the **Biedermeier** consumed mokka, chocolate and pastries at cafés like Hugelmann's, near the Danube, on the road to the Prater. On holidays the Viennese went out among the wine shops *(Heurige)* of the Danube and Vienna Woods, where they would relax over pitchers of young wine, listening to impromptu poets, violinists and zither players. Anything was an excuse for idling: the parade of beasts being led to the abattoir, the menageries, the boatmen, the changing of the guard to Schubert's dreamy music. People would also meet to hear Schubert's Lieder, which were in the repertory of every woman singer in Vienna. The violins sobbed in the Schottenfeld quarter. At the Apollo, a dance hall which could hold 4 000 people and had the biggest floor in Europe, 28 meeting rooms and 13 kitchens formed annexes to the establishment.

Growth of Vienna – After the disappearance of the Turkish menace, a new face had been given to the capital, marked by the influence of Baroque architecture.
Princely palaces, winter residences and churches sprang up, including the Schwarzenberg Palace (Prince Eugene's mansion) on the Belvedere hill and the Karlskirche. The buildings overflowed the narrow limits of the 17C city walls. New quarters developed and extensive suburbs were established without a definite plan.
Death took Joseph II, "the enlightened despot", by surprise, while he was preparing to transform the whole of Vienna. The difficult period of the Napoleonic Wars did not facilitate the implementation of grandiose projects and the city had to await the reign of **Franz Joseph** (1848-1916) for the large-scale planning and building that made Vienna what it is today.

The Ring – In 1857 the Emperor signed the decree ordering the removal of the bastions and the formation of a belt of boulevards round the old town. The creation of the "Ring" was to turn the capital into a huge building site. Famous architects and artists, from Austria and abroad, contributed to this great project, which was rivalled only by the transformation of Paris by Baron Haussmann several years later. The great new boulevard is lined by Vienna's most important public buildings as well as by the numerous grand tenement blocks characteristic of the city.

The Gürtel – In 1890, the outer boroughs were incorporated into Vienna and the second ring of fortifications razed, making space for an outer circular road, known as the "Gürtel" (Girdle or Belt).

VIENNA, CAPITAL OF MUSIC

Venerable traditions – St Peter's in Salzburg may have been the cradle of sacred music in the German-speaking world but, by the 12C, Vienna under the Babenbergs had become an important centre of secular music. Many Minnesänger came here, achieving corporate recognition at the end of the 13C. At the end of the Middle Ages, Maximilian I moved his dazzling court choir here from Innsbruck, confirming Vienna's status as a musical capital. The choir became an institution, much admired in the 15C and still arousing the enthusiasm of today's audiences under the name of **"Hofkapelle"**.

The great days of Viennese music – The 18C was dominated by the figure of **Haydn**, the initiator of Classicism in Vienna.
The princely palaces became veritable musical workshops, places for great performers and composers to meet. Haydn's *The Seasons* is intimately linked to the Schwarzenberg Palace, while **Mozart** discovered the works of Bach and Handel in the house of Maria Theresa's doctor's son, and **Beethoven** and **Gluck** were guests at the Lobkowitz Palace. With the encouragement of Joseph II, the number of theatres multiplied, helping to bring music within reach of the middle classes.
Around 1825 the musical soirées known as "**Schubertiades**" began, at which Schubert interpreted Lieder for a circle of friends and which ended in dancing.
After the revolution of 1848, music societies proliferated, promoting high standards of concert performance and of musical education. The most illustrious of these societies was the "Friends of Music" which numbered the German composer **Brahms** among its conductors. Brahms enjoyed unparallelled prestige, but **Bruckner**, "God's troubadour", who had left his native Linz to become court organist, found his sacred masterpieces to be beyond the comprehension of the Viennese public. **Mahler** used his 10 years in Vienna as Kapellmeister to undertake the reforms which helped give birth to a new musical era.
By the end of the century music was no longer the prerogative of high society and there was hardly a household in the city which failed to meet at least once a week to make music.

The force of destiny (1770-1827) – There are few other artists who have been more captivated and inspired by the romantic countryside around Vienna than **Ludwig van Beethoven**. He adored this kind of landscape, indeed he confided to the painter Anton Schindler, accompanying him on a walk from Heiligenstadt to Grinzing, that it was here that he thought of the motifs in the brookside scene in the Pastoral Symphony (no 6).
Irresistibly drawn to the musical metropolis, Beethoven arrived in Vienna at the age of 20. He enchanted the city with his ability as a pianist. It was in Vienna and the picturesque villages now engulfed in its suburbs that he created the works which revolutionized the language of music: the Eroica Symphony, the opera *Fidelio*, the Fifth Symphony, and ending in that great "Ode to Joy", the monumental Ninth Symphony, which the master, by now stone-deaf, conducted (though in fact the orchestra had to be conducted by an understudy). Deafness had in fact, afflicted him from the age of 30 and led to the deep despair evident in the *Heiligenstadt Testimonies*.

Johann Strauss

Wiesenhofer/ÖSTERREICH WERBUNG

The triumph of the Viennese Waltz – The sensation of the Congress of Vienna was the **waltz**. This vigorous and light-hearted dance kept the city on its toes throughout the 19C, particularly from 1820 onward, when fashioned by the talented and prolific **Strauss** dynasty.
Polished, refined, and made a genre in its own right by **Joseph Lanner** and Johann Strauss the Elder, the waltz was to dominate the dance floor under **Johann Strauss the Younger**, whose tributes to the great city like *Vienna Blood*, *Tales from the Vienna Woods*, were more than amply rewarded by their enthusiastic reception by the

Rock me Amadeus

Two hundred years after Mozart, another Austrian musician of a different kind won world-wide fame. This time it was Hans Hölzl from Vienna, in his eccentric stage persona of **Falco**, who not only won over the European hit parade with his single "Rock me Amadeus", referring to Salzburg's wonder child, but also managed to top the American charts with it for four weeks. This was an outstanding performance for a German-language pop song. With his characteristic combination of speech-song and catchy tunes Falco is the only Austrian pop star to have made it big on the world stage. Killed in a motor accident in the Dominican Republic in 1998, Falco was buried in an "honorary grave" awarded by the City of Vienna in the Zentralfriedhof in recognition of his talent (unlike his illustrious predecessor).

Viennese. Strangely enough, the *Blue Danube* waltz was more successful in Paris than on the banks of the river itself. The ballrooms of Vienna were kept supplied with musicians from among the 300 or so managed by the younger Strauss and his brothers Joseph and Eduard.
Today, the statue of Strauss the Younger in Vienna's Stadtpark, which is copied in the souvenir shops, has become one of the city's emblems.

The "New School" of Vienna – This is the name given to the movement founded by the Viennese **Arnold Schoenberg**, promoter of a veritable musical revolution whose effects would make themselves felt throughout the century.
Originally self-taught, Schoenberg became the pupil of the opera composer Alexander Zemlinsky (1871-1942). His first works, like the *Gurrelieder*, still have affinities with the post-Romantic style. They were soon followed by works like the First String Quartet (1905), then by the Second Quartet in whose last two movements the boundaries of tonality are left behind. In 1912 his *Pierrot Lunaire*, a melodrama in 21 sections for narrator and five instruments, brought him international recognition. Schoenberg's theories of 12-tone composition are set out in his *Treatise on Harmony* in which he established new relationships between sounds freed from traditional harmonic conventions.
Schoenberg was a born teacher and exercised a profound influence on a number of pupils including Webern and Berg, both Viennese. Of the three composers, it was Webern who went furthest away from classical tonality, while Berg enjoyed the greatest public success with his operas *Wozzeck* and *Lulu*.

Viennese ball season

During the winter in Vienna, one ball follows close on another. The famous Emperor's Ball is held on New Year's Eve, reawakening the elegance and splendour of the former Imperial court at the Hofburg. During Carnival time (Fasching), the various associations and professional guilds put on about 300 balls, many in magnificent surroundings (Rathaus, Hofburg, Musikverein), including the Floral Ball, organized by gardeners and florists, the Rudolfina-Redoute Masked Ball, and the balls of the Viennese Coffee-Houses, the Vienna Philharmonic Orchestra and the Technicians' Circle. Doctors and lawyers each have a ball, and so do hunters and firemen.

The ball to end all balls in terms of sheer elegance is the **Opera Ball**, held in February at the Staatsoper. This event draws the rich and famous from Austria and abroad, and is *the* High Society event of the year. The ball is opened by ballet dancers from the Vienna State Opera and a committee of young ladies and gentlemen dancing a Polonaise with fans.

Pratt-Pries/DIAF

Opera Ball, Vienna

LIFE IN VIENNA

The coffee house, a Viennese institution – Among the baggage abandoned by the fleeing Turks in 1683 was a great quantity of coffee beans. The dark-coloured beverage was to become so popular that it even gave its name to the establishments in which it was consumed.
In the 19C the coffee house became the place for people to meet and to read the newspapers, an indispensable part of middle class as well as of intellectual life. Many writers like Schnitzler would spend the whole day in their favourite coffee-house, using it as their study.

H. A. Jahr/VIENNASLIDE

Sampling new wine in one of Vienna's Heurigen

The modern coffee house scene – The city's coffee houses fill up as the working day ends. Discreetly attired waiters serve the traditional glass of water at the same time as the coffee, which is available in bewildering variety *(see above)*. It can be drunk accompanied by cakes and pastries of equally astounding variety.
Once the customer's coffee is finished, the waiter collects the cup and brings another glass of water. He will also keep the customer supplied with newspapers and magazines. It is not unusual for customers to stay for hours without repeating their order; savouring the passing moment in a leisurely way is an essential part of the Viennese temperament.

Wine bars, inns and taverns – Vienna's restaurants welcome the visitor into their friendly ambience to enjoy dishes from all the countries which once made up Austria's empire, often served to a musical accompaniment. A convivial atmosphere can be enjoyed in a **Keller**, not unlike a German beer hall, where snacks and cold meals are downed with a glass of beer or wine.
Some establishments (Gasthäuser, Weinhäuser) offering good home cooking are known as **Beisel**. Similar are the taverns *(Weinstuben)* where the Viennese congregate once the working day is over. Then there are the famous wine pubs called **Heurige**, where, by special dispensation, the new wine is served; these cheerful places are to be found in the wine-growing villages on the edge of the city like Grinzing, Nussdorf, Sievering and Gumpoldskirchen. Usually run by the wine-growers themselves, who while not licensed to run a bar nonetheless have special dispensation to sell their young wine, and they can be recognized by the pine branch hung up above the entrance. In cosy rooms or leafy courtyards, customers sample the grower's new wine *(Heuriger)*, accompanied perhaps by a snack or simple meal in the restaurant that is usually part of the premises, in an utterly Viennese atmosphere enlivened by **Schrammelmusik** (played by a pair of violins, an accordion or clarinet plus a guitar).

EXPLORING VIENNA

★ **Tour of the Ring** – *By car or tram (circular routes nos 1 and 2). Start at the Stubenring (**LR**) to the east, near the Danube.*
The Ring is particularly attractive at night when the main buildings are floodlit, but it is interesting at any time of day as a preliminary to exploring the historic centre of the city.

Guide to Coffee, Viennese style

Listed below are some descriptions of the more commonly served types of Viennese coffee, among the 30 or so preparations which are available:

Barth/ÖSTERREICH WERBUNG

Großer/kleinerSchwarzer - large/small cup of black coffee

Großer/kleiner Brauner - large/small cup of black coffee with a dash of milk

Verlängerter Schwarzer/ Brauner - "Schwarzer"/ "Brauner" diluted with water

Einspänner - black coffee served in a glass with whipped cream-*(Schlagobers)*

Fiaker - black coffee in a glass with a tot of rum

Franziskaner - coffee mixed with chocolate chips

Kaffee verkehrt - coffee with more milk than coffee

Kaisermelange - coffee with egg yolk and alcohol

Kapuziner - black coffee with a small blob of whipped cream

Konsul - mocca diluted with cold water

Mazagran - iced coffee with rum

Melange - milky coffee (can be served with whipped cream)

Türkischer Kaffee - strong coffee prepared in a small copper coffee pot,served hot in tiny cups

Verlängerter - mocca diluted with hot water
A further tip: never ask for a cup of coffee (eine Tasse Kaffee) in Vienna - it is *"eine Schale Kaffee"* (literally, a bowl of coffee). Depending on how high a milk content you would like, coffee can be ordered "Braun", or even "Gold".

★ **Postsparkasse (LR)** - On the right stands this important Jugendstil (Art Nouveau) building designed at the very start of the 20C by Otto Wagner. *Description of the interior on p 370.*

★★ **Österreichisches Museum für angewandte Kunst (LR)** - To the left is this monumental building designed in Florentine Renaissance style, its stone and brick façade articulated by round-headed bays and twin windows. *Description of the interior on p 374.*

Stadtpark (KLRS) - To the south of the museum and flanking the River Wien stretches the attractively landscaped City Park, laid out in 1862; it is famous for its statues of musicians, Franz Schubert, Anton Bruckner, Franz Lehar, Robert Stolz and, above all, the memorial to Johann Strauss.

★★ **Oper (JS)** - Just after the Schwarzenbergplatz (**KS**), which leads to the Belvedere palaces further south, stands Austria's national opera house *(right)* with its elegant arcades. In French Renaissance style, this was the first of the great public edifices to be erected along the Ring. The main façade was all that was left standing when the building burnt down in 1945 *(see p 370)*.

Burggarten (JRS) - Between the Ring and the Hofburg, the palace gardens, first laid out in the 19C, were once the preserve of the Imperial Court. Since 1919 they have been open to the public. At the entrance stands a statue to Goethe, and there are other memorials to Franz Joseph, Franz I (on horseback) and Mozart.

Neue Burg (JR) - The Neue Burg is the most recent wing of the Hofburg. Its semicircular colonnade opening out on to the Heldenplatz (Heroes' Square) is part only of a great building project that was fated never to be completed; another, identical edifice was to have been built to the northwest of the square, turning it, together with the Marienplatz, into a vast "Imperial Forum". The Neue Burg was completed only just before the outbreak of the First World War and the disappearance of the monarchy led to the abandonment of the grandiose scheme. The building now houses a number of museums *(see p 344)*.

Maria-Theresien-Platz (HRS) – The square takes its name from the monument erected in 1888 to the glory of the great empress. At her feet are equestrian statues of her generals, Daun, Laudon, Traun, Khevenhüller; other figures represent the statesmen who served her grand designs, like her Chancellor, Kaunitz, Count Mercy-Argenteau and Prince Liechtenstein, as well as the great composers of her reign, Gluck, Haydn and Mozart.
Facing each other across the square are two symmetrical domed buildings, constructed between 1872 and 1891 in the official architectural style of the Ring (Ringstraßenstil) to house the imperial collections: to the southeast the **Kunsthistorisches Museum★★★** *(see p 360)*, to the northwest the **Naturhistorisches Museum★** *(see p 375)*.
Bounding the square to the southwest is the 18C façade of the Messepalast, designed by Fischer von Erlach as the Imperial stables and now the city's Fairs and Exhibition building.

★ **Volksgarten (HR)** – This quiet park with its pools and statues, a favourite place for a stroll, is one of the most pleasant public open spaces along the Ring. An exotic note is struck by the "Temple of Theseus", a copy of the so-called Theseion in Athens. The rose garden is famous and the park's formally clipped trees frame attractive views outwards.

Parlament (HR) – Opposite the Volksgarten next to the law courts stands Austria's seat of government (1873-83) with its elegant Grecian façade. This was intended by its architect, Theophil von Hansen, as a symbolic reference to Greece as the "cradle of democracy".

Neues Rathaus ⏱ **(HR)** – The neo-Gothic city hall building is linked to the Ring by attractive gardens. The tower is topped by the famous "Rathausmann" carrying the city flag. Summer concerts are held in the arcaded courtyard.
Reception rooms, council chambers and the huge banqueting hall are open to the public. As is usual in German-speaking countries, in the basement is a vast restaurant, the "Rathauskeller". Opposite the Rathaus is the elegant façade of the Burgtheater.

★ **Burgtheater** ⏱ **(HR)** – Opened in 1888, this theatre replaced the Hofburgtheater (Court Theatre) on the Michaelerplatz founded in 1741 under Maria Theresa. Gottfried Semper was responsible for the Renaissance façade, while Carl Hasenauer designed the neo-Baroque interior. The Burgtheater was for long considered the most important German-language theatre, and an engagement here was, and still is, the summit of an acting career. The theatre was much criticized for its lack of comfort, but this was improved when the serious war damage was repaired. It is possible to view the interior (only with a guided tour), and admire some early work by Gustav Klimt, who painted the **ceiling frescoes★** together with his brother Ernst and Franz Matsch.

Universität (HP) – On the north side of the Rathausplatz stands the university building designed by Heinrich von Ferstel in the style of the Italian Renaissance, housing the oldest German-language university after that in Prague. Beyond it, on the left, as the Ring makes its final bend, is the Votivkirche.

Votivkirche (HP) – Two tall spires flank the west door of this neo-Gothic church, completed in 1879. Its name commemorates Franz Joseph's escape from an assassination attempt early in 1853. His brother Archduke Maximilian, later Emperor of Mexico, had the church built to a design by Heinrich von Ferstel. Note the so-called Antwerp Altar in the right-hand chapel beyond the transept, and in the baptistery the tomb of Count Salm from 1530, with its **reclining figure★**.
After passing the **Börse** (Stock Exchange – **JP**) on the right, the tour ends by the Donaukanal at the Franz-Josefs-Kai.

City viewpoints – There are two splendid viewpoints in the hills overlooking the city from the northwest, the **Kahlenberg★** and the **Leopoldsberg★★** *(see p 377)* **(BX)**. The **Donauturm** ⏱ **(CX)** (Danube Tower) was built on the north bank of the river in 1964. From its two revolving restaurants or its viewing terraces 150m/nearly 500ft above the Donaupark there is a far-ranging **view★★** over the city and its surroundings. There is a similar **panoramic view★** from the **Riesenrad★★** (Great Wheel) in the Prater *(see p 374)* **(GU)**.

★★★ HOFBURG: a city within a city

The Imperial palace, winter residence of the Habsburgs, was progressively enlarged during the centuries. The nucleus, built in the 13C, was a quadrilateral bristling with towers round a courtyard which came to be known as the Schweizerhof (Swiss Court) from the 18C.
The presence of successive additions by sovereigns anxious to enlarge and beautify their residence explains the juxtaposition of different styles.
The castle chapel, Burgkapelle, was erected in the mid 15C; the Amalienburg and the Stallburg in the 16C; the Leopoldinischer Trakt (the apartments in the main wing, which overlook the inner Burgplatz and Heldenplatz courtyards, once Maria

Theresa's apartments and now the official office of the Federal President) in the 17C; the Reichskanzleitrakt (Imperial Chancellery), the Spanische Reitschule and the Nationalbibliothek (National Library) in the 18C; and in the 19C and 20C, the Neue Burg, whose completion just before 1914 marked the end of the structural history of the Hofburg.

Exterior

The architecture, which is austere and full of majesty, provides remarkable vistas of the intervening courts or the surrounding monuments.

★ **Michaelerplatz wing** – The designs for this complex were essentially prepared by JE Fischer von Erlach, but were not executed until 1892-93. The semicircular façade giving on to the Michaelerplatz is decorated with two monumental fountains, adorned with statues; above this façade rises the dome which roofs the rotunda. The main arches are closed by bronze gilded grilles. The magnificent gateway, the **Michaelertor**★, flanked by figures from the Hercules legends, gives access to the octagonal rotunda beneath the famous **Michaelerkuppel**★, one of the most elegant domes in Vienna. It is an inspiration to stand inside the rotunda and look back, through a wrought-iron lattice, at the steeple of the Michaelerkirche. The square known as "In der Burg", in the centre of which stands the monument to Emperor Franz II, is reached through this rotunda. From the courtyard the **Schweizertor**★, a fine Renaissance gateway bearing coats of arms and inscriptions, leads to the **Schweizerhof**, in which we find, on the right, the stairs leading up to the Burgkapelle.

★ **Josefsplatz** – Arched passageways lead into this square, regarded as Vienna's finest because of its ideal proportions. It owes its name to the fine equestrian statue of Joseph II, the base of which is adorned with low-relief sculptures in bronze. The pediments of the buildings round it are surmounted by groups of sculpture.
One side of this square is formed by the early-18C **Österreichische Nationalbibliothek** by Fischer von Erlach.

Return to the Heldenplatz.

Neue Burg – The new Imperial palace, which was erected between 1881 and 1913 in the Italian Renaissance style, was intended by the architects to be complemented by a similar wing on the northwest side but this was never constructed. This building presents a concave façade to the view from the **Heldenplatz**★ which is bounded on the northwest, beyond the shady Volksgarten, by the steeple of the Neues Rathaus. Here stand the memorials, in the form of equestrian statues, of Prince Eugene of Savoy and Archduke Karl, both by the sculptor Anton Dominik Fernkorn.
On the southwest side is the monumental gateway (1824), the Äußeres Burgtor, which leads to the Ring. Since 1934 it has served as a war memorial (Heldendenkmal).

Neue Burg from Heldenplatz

Interior: souvenirs of the Habsburgs

★★★ **Schatzkammer** ⏱ – In the treasury are displayed the insignia of Habsburg power, as well as mementoes and holy relics collected by the family. A visit to the treasury is one of the highlights of any trip to Vienna.
The **Secular Treasure** *(Rooms 1 to 8 and 9 to 16)* contains in fact some items of religious significance, including several dazzling pieces, as does the **Ecclesiastical Treasure** in Rooms I to V. Listed below are the most important exhibits, which should not be missed on any account:

Room 1 – The regalia of the archdukes of Austria used in coronation ceremonies for the Crown Lands corresponding to modern Austria. Orb and sceptre (Prague, 14C). Ducal mantle (Vienna, 1764).

Room 2 – The prize exhibit is the **Imperial crown of Rudolf II★**, made in Prague by Jan Vermeyen from Antwerp (early 17C), with matching orb and sceptre by Andreas Osenbruck (Prague 1615). Also notable is the **bronze bust of Rudolf II** by Adriaen de Vries (1607).

Room 3 – Coronation mantle (1830) and ceremonial robes. Insignia of various Orders.

Room 4 – Coronation regalia of Ferdinand I.

Room 9 – **Insignia and crown jewels of the Holy Roman Empire**. They were last used at the coronation of Franz II in 1792.

Room 5 – **Cradle of the King of Rome★** made of silver gilt. **Portrait of Marie Louise★**.

Room 6 – Christening robes and other effects; keys to the coffins in the Kaisergruft *(see below)*.

Room 7 – **Crown of Stephan Bocskay★**. Jewellery, emerald vessel (2 680 carat).

Room 8 – **Agate bowl★** (4C). Narwhal horn measuring 2.43m/8ft.

Room I – **Miniature replica of the Mariensäule★** (Column carrying the Virgin Mary), which formerly stood on the square Am Hof. It is decorated with 3 700 precious stones.

Room II – Reliquary cross of King Ludwig I of Hungary (c 1370). Stephen's bursa (end of the 11C).

Room III – Small ebony temple with an ivory figure of Christ by Christoph Angermair; Florentine crucifix by Giambologna (about 1590).

Room IV – Reliquary altars from Milan (1660-1680); altar furniture in Dresden china.

Room V – 18C and 19C works of art including 22 bust reliquaries, some in solid silver.

Room 10 – Ceremonial robes of the Norman kings, including the **Coronation mantle★★** of Roger II of Sicily (Palermo, 1133); ceremonial sword of Friedrich II.

3BIS/MICHELIN

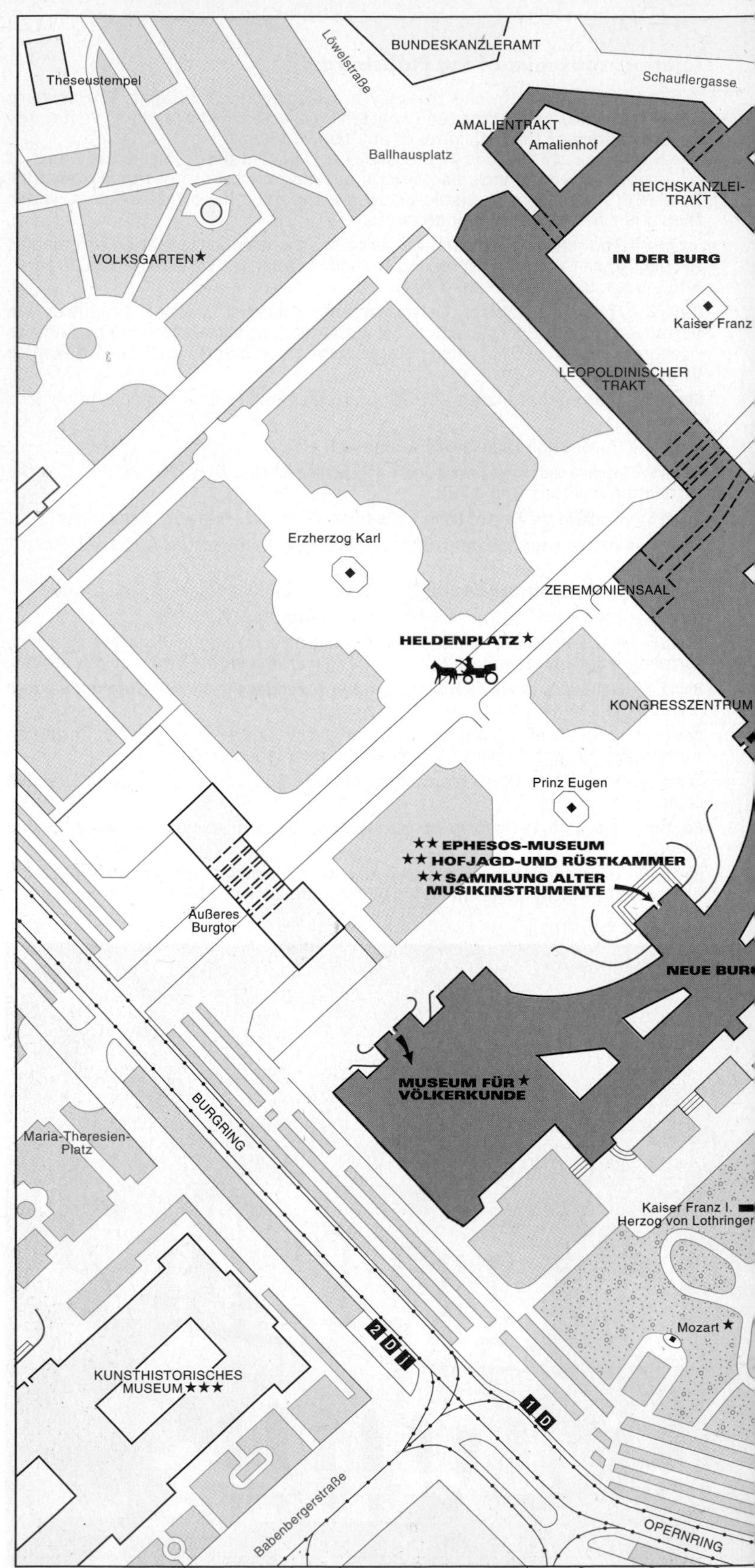

BUNDESKANZLERAMT
Theseustempel
Löwelstraße
Schauflergasse
AMALIENTRAKT
Amalienhof
Ballhausplatz
REICHSKANZLEI-
TRAKT
VOLKSGARTEN★
IN DER BURG
Kaiser Franz
LEOPOLDINISCHER
TRAKT
Erzherzog Karl
ZEREMONIENSAAL
HELDENPLATZ★
KONGRESSZENTRUM
Prinz Eugen
★★ EPHESOS-MUSEUM
★★ HOFJAGD-UND RÜSTKAMMER
★★ SAMMLUNG ALTER
MUSIKINSTRUMENTE
Äußeres
Burgtor
NEUE BUR
MUSEUM FÜR★
VÖLKERKUNDE
BURGRING
Maria-Theresien-
Platz
Kaiser Franz I.
Herzog von Lothringen
Mozart★
2 D J
KUNSTHISTORISCHES
MUSEUM★★★
1 D
Babenbergerstraße
OPERNRING

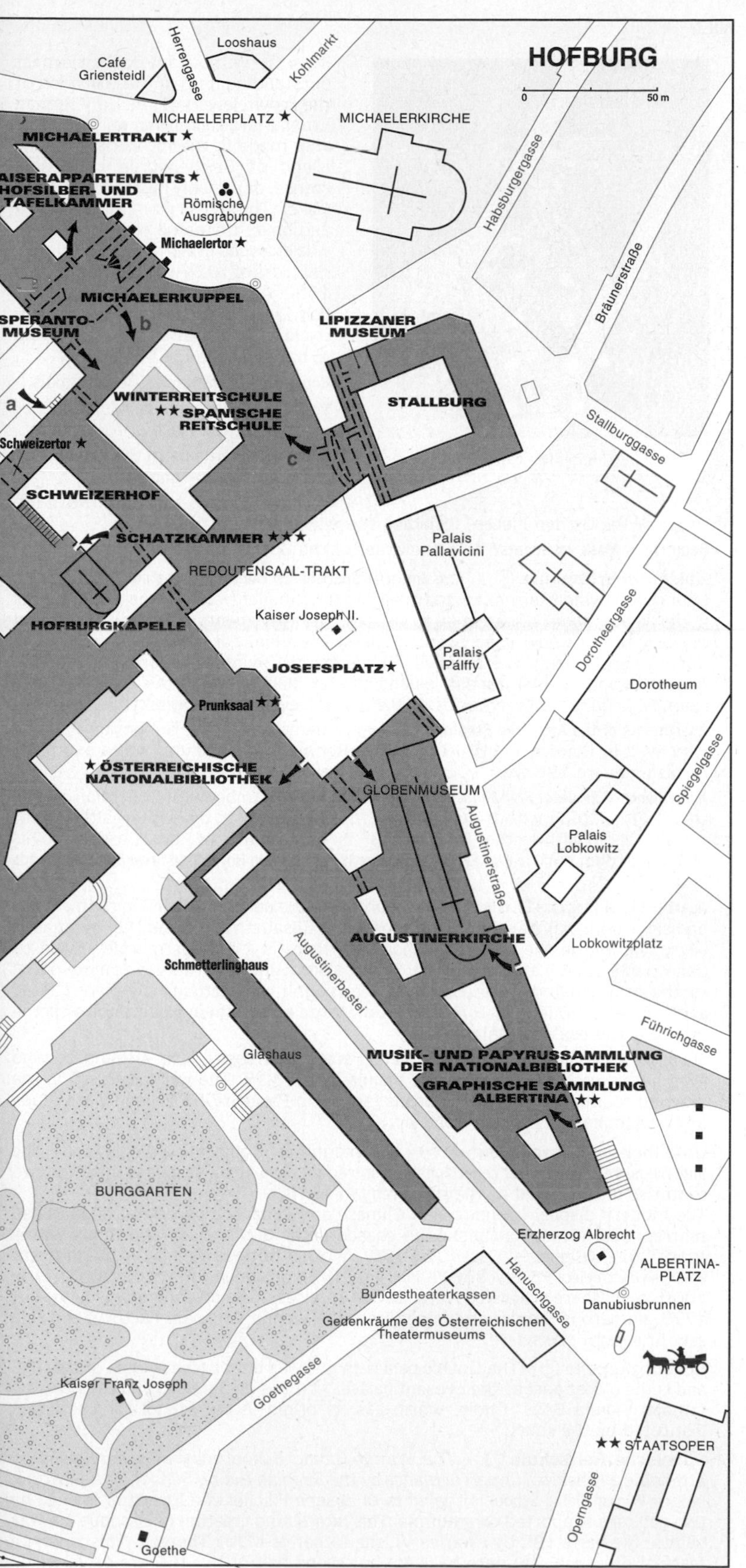
HOFBURG
0
50 m
Looshaus
Café Griensteidl
Herrengasse
Kohlmarkt
MICHAELERPLATZ ★
MICHAELERKIRCHE
MICHAELERTRAKT ★
AISERAPPARTEMENTS ★
HOFSILBER- UND TAFELKAMMER
Römische Ausgrabungen
Michaelertor ★
Habsburgergasse
Bräunerstraße
MICHAELERKUPPEL
SPERANTO-MUSEUM
b
LIPIZZANER MUSEUM
STALLBURG
WINTERREITSCHULE
★★ SPANISCHE REITSCHULE
a
Schweizertor ★
c
Stallburggasse
SCHWEIZERHOF
SCHATZKAMMER ★★★
Palais Pallavicini
REDOUTENSAAL-TRAKT
HOFBURGKAPELLE
Kaiser Joseph II.
Dorotheergasse
Palais Pálffy
JOSEFSPLATZ ★
Dorotheum
Prunksaal ★★
★ ÖSTERREICHISCHE NATIONALBIBLIOTHEK
GLOBENMUSEUM
Spiegelgasse
Augustinerstraße
Palais Lobkowitz
AUGUSTINERKIRCHE
Lobkowitzplatz
Schmetterlinghaus
Augustinerbastei
Führichgasse
Glashaus
MUSIK- UND PAPYRUSSAMMLUNG DER NATIONALBIBLIOTHEK
GRAPHISCHE SAMMLUNG ALBERTINA ★★
BURGGARTEN
Erzherzog Albrecht
ALBERTINA-PLATZ
Hanuschgasse
Bundestheaterkassen
Danubiusbrunnen
Gedenkräume des Österreichischen Theatermuseums
Kaiser Franz Joseph
Goethegasse
★★ STAATSOPER
Operngasse
Goethe

Imperial crown

Room 11 – Without any doubt the most outstanding item in the collection of the crown jewels of the Holy Roman Empire is the **Imperial crown**★★★, probably made in the monastery on the island of Reichenau in Lake Constance, or possibly in Milan, for Otto I (962). The arch is from a later period and bears the name of Konrad, who was crowned in Rome in 1027. Imperial cross of 1024 with a base added in 1352. An astonishing reliquary is the **Holy Lance**★★ (8C), while the **Imperial sword**★ (sheath from the 11C) is said to have belonged to St Maurice.

Room 12 – Reliquaries, jewel boxes.

Room 13 – Robes and heraldic coats of arms from the Duchy of Burgundy.

Room 14 – Items from the treasure of the dukes of Burgundy.

Room 15 – Items associated with the Order of the Golden Fleece, including the **potence**★★ (mid 15C).

Room 16 – **Mass vestments**★★ of the Order of the Golden Fleece.

★ **Kaiserappartements** ⓥ – The **Imperial apartments** occupy the first floor of the Chancellery wing (Reichskanzleitrakt) and the Amalientrakt. Of the 2 600 rooms in the palace, about 20 are open to visitors. The apartments of Maria Theresa and of Joseph II are now used by the Federal President for official purposes. The Imperial apartments are reached via the **Imperial staircase**. Luxurious furniture, Aubusson and Flemish tapestries and crystal chandeliers (in the large audience chamber) conjure up memories of the historic events that occurred here.

Apartments of the Archduke Stephen – They are named after the Hungarian Palatine who lived in them from 1848 to 1867. Rooms are entirely in white and gold, furnishings are 19C with 16C and 17C Brussels tapestries.

Apartments of Emperor Franz Joseph – Grand audience chamber with Bohemian crystal chandeliers; study with a portrait of Empress Elisabeth by Winterhalter; great drawing room with further fine **portraits**★ by Winterhalter of Franz Joseph and his wife (charming portrait of **Empress Elisabeth of Austria in Royal Gala Dress with Diamonds in her Hair**).

Apartments of Empress Elisabeth – The bedroom was also used as a living room; in the dressing-room may be seen the rings on which Elisabeth performed her gymnastic exercises, and in the large drawing room there is a famous marble statue by Canova of Elisa Bonaparte (1816). The small drawing room serves as a memorial to the assassinated Empress, with the magnificent **portrait**★ by Georg Raab showing her as Queen of Hungary. In the large anteroom are paintings of some of Maria Theresa's 16 children.

Alexander's apartments – These are named after the Russian czar Alexander I who lived here during the Congress of Vienna in 1814-15. The **wall tapestries**★ in the drawing room are from the Gobelins factory in Paris (1772-76) and were made after cartoons by François Boucher.

★ **Hofsilber- und Tafelkammer** ⓥ – The magnificent objects on display from the **Imperial porcelain and silver collection** were in regular use at the Imperial table for two centuries until the fall of the monarchy in 1918.
The modern display includes 18C Chinese and Japanese porcelain, huge gilded centrepieces, ewers and dishes in chased silver gilt, and an enormous **vermeil service**★ for 140 guests *(Cases 126-130)*. Another famous item is the magnificent **Milanese centrepiece**★★ of 1838 *(Cases 138-142)*, designed for a table 30m/nearly 100ft long. There are also several Sèvres services, including the green service of 1776, numerous Empire-style ones from the Vienna Porcelain Factory, and fine sets of crystal glassware.

Hofburgkapelle ⓥ – The Gothic palace chapel was built in the middle of the 15C and is the oldest part of the present palace. At mass on Sundays you can hear the famous Vienna Boys' Choir, which has its origin in the school for choristers instituted by the court.

★★ **Spanische Reitschule** ⓥ – *The Winter Riding School may only be viewed by attending a rehearsal or performance by the Spanish Riding School.* The all-white, indoor **Winter Riding School** is the work of Joseph Fischer von Erlach; it is lined by two galleries supported on columns. This interesting creation of Baroque art was built in the early 18C by Charles VI, the father of Maria Theresa. This is where feats of dressage that date back to the second half of the 16C are performed.

ONAT

The Spanish Riding School

The riders wear brown tailcoats, white buckskin breeches, riding boots and cocked hats. The Lipizzaner stallions *(see Piber under PACK- und STUBALPEN-STRASSE)* are white, with gleaming coats, their tails and manes are plaited with gold ribbons; they perform with great accuracy changes of pace, passage, and especially at the end of the programme, the school quadrille with a group of horses.
The **training** session (Morgenarbeit) although less spectacular (without music or chandeliers) shows the horses performing difficult jumps, steps and other movements.

Stallburg - *Entrance: Reitschulgasse 2.* Separated from the indoor riding school by a glazed-in passageway, the Stallburg is composed of three floors of galleries, surrounding a Renaissance courtyard, decorated with a wrought-iron well. The ground floor was transformed by Maximilian II into stables for the horses of his guard. It is still used as a stable for the Lipizzaner stallions of the Spanische Reitschule.

Lipizzaner-Museum ⓥ - *In the Stallburg.* Genealogical tables, uniforms, harness and audio-visual displays give a comprehensive account of the history and present of this world-famous breed of horses. At the end of the tour, visitors can take a look at some of the stalls through a thick glass screen.

★ **Österreichische Nationalbibliothek** ⓥ - The building is the work of Joseph Emanuel Fischer von Erlach (early 18C). The core of the collection is formed by the Imperial library, established in the 14C.
The **Prunksaal**★★ (Great Hall), a masterpiece of architecture and Baroque decoration with **ceiling frescoes** by **Daniel Gran** in the oval dome and statues by the Strudel brothers, holds Prince Eugene of Savoy's magnificent library. It also hosts special exhibitions of items from this library and elsewhere.

★★ **Kaisergruft** ⓥ - *Entrance to the left of the Kapuzinerkirche.* For more than three centuries the vaults of the Kapuzinerkirche have been the burial place of the Imperial family. The church was built from 1622 to 1632.
In a niche on the façade of the church stands a statue of the Capuchin Marco d'Aviano, Papal Legate with the army of Charles of Lorraine, who brought about the unification of the leaders of the Christian armies in the battle to win freedom from the Turks in 1683. The morning after the battle was successfully won, he celebrated Mass on the Kahlenberg hill.
The remains of 12 emperors, 16 empresses and more than 100 archdukes are buried in these vaults; their hearts are in the Augustinian church and their entrails in the catacombs of the Stephansdom. Here lay the bronze coffin of the King of Rome, Duke of Reichstadt, son of Napoleon I and Marie-Louise, before it was transferred to Paris in December 1940. Of the 139 coffins here (37 of which are walled in), only one does not belong to the Habsburg family: it is that of Countess Fuchs, who brought up Maria Theresa and whom the latter held in such esteem that she granted her this signal honour.
In the Karlsgruft (Charles's vault) are the sarcophagi of Leopold I and Joseph I by Johann Lukas von Hildebrandt, also the **sarcophagus of Charles VI** decorated with coats of arms and an allegorical figure of Austria mourning, a masterwork by Balthasar Ferdinand Moll. Empress Maria Theresa and her husband, Francis of

WIEN

Adalbert-Stiffer-Str.	CX	3	Döblinger Hauptstr.	BXY	21	Freudenauer Hafenstr.	CDZ	37
Altmannsdorfer Str.	AZ	6	Donaustadtstr.	CXY	24	Grenzackerstr.	CZ	45
Breitenfurter Str.	AZ	16	Erdbergstraße	CY	30	Grinzinger Allee	BX	48
			Erzherzog-Karl-Str.	CY	31	Grinzinger Str.	BX	49
			Floridsdorfer Brücke	CX	36			

Lorraine, lie in a beautiful **double sarcophagus★★**, also by Moll. The tin coffin lid is in the form of a magnificent bed on which the Imperial couple is lying, turned symbolically towards an angel who is about to sound his trumpet for the day of judgement. In front stands the coffin of their son, Joseph II.

The sarcophagus of Emperor **Franz Joseph**, his wife Empress **Elisabeth**, and their son Archduke Rudolf are in a separate room, built in 1908-09. The bodies of the heir to the Imperial throne, Archduke Franz Ferdinand, and his wife, both murdered by an assassin in Sarajevo in 1914, are laid to rest at Schloß

Hietzinger Kai	AZ	60
Hirschstettner Str.	CX	63
Hohe Warte	BX	64
Meidlinger Hauptstr.	BZ	83
Raxstraße	BZ	93
Schlachthausgasse	CY	99
Speisinger Str.	AZ	109
Veitingergasse	AZ	126
Wienerbergstr.	BZ	134

Eroicahaus	E
Weinbaumuseum	M¹
Technisches Museum	M²
Wiener Straßenbahnmuseum★	M³

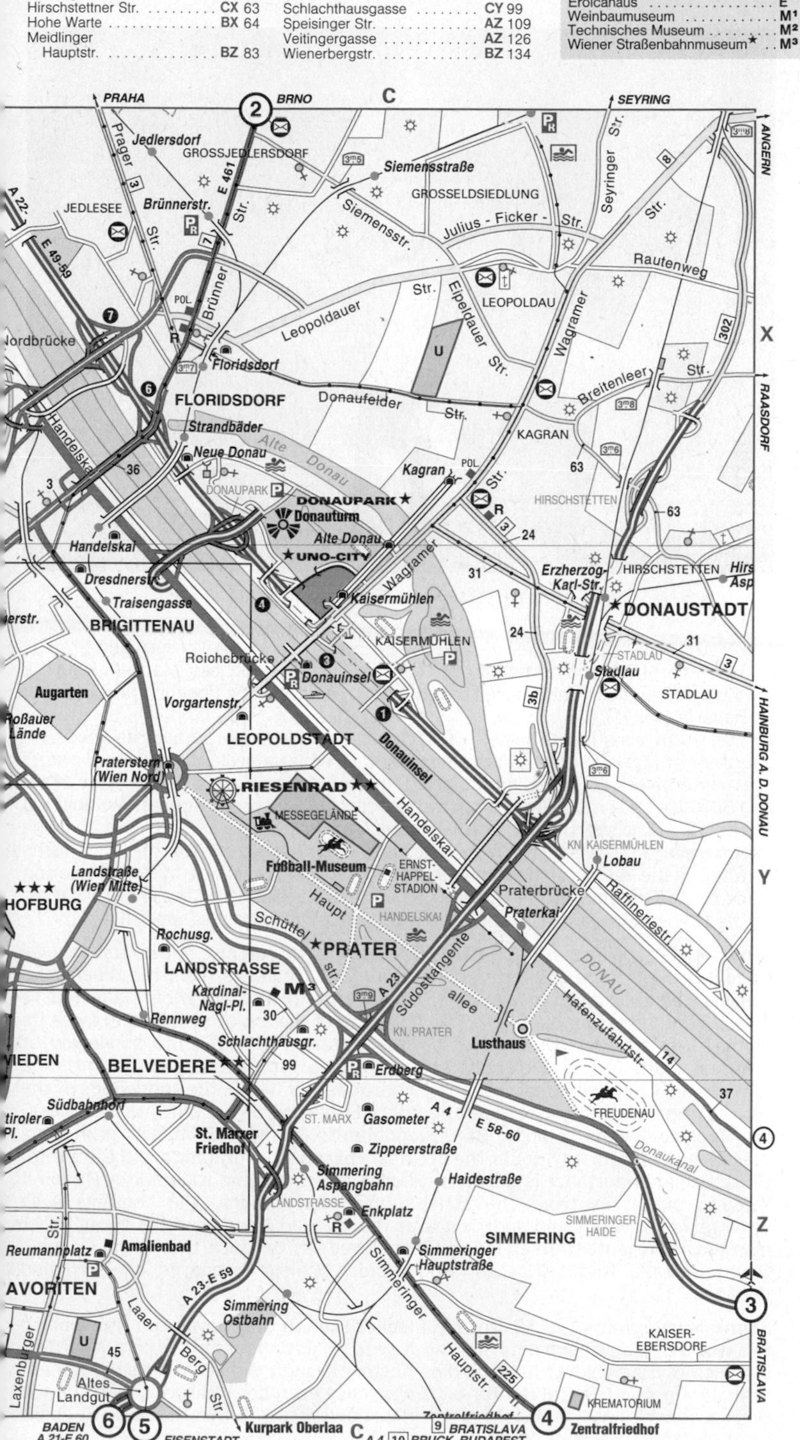

Artstetten. The so-called Neue Gruft, or new vault, built in 1961, contains the sarcophagi of **Marie-Louise**, Empress of France, and **Maximilian of Mexico**. The last Habsburg emperor, Charles VI, is still buried on Madeira, but his wife, Empress Zita, was buried in the chapel of the Imperial vault in 1989.

Augustinerkirche – Built during the first half of the 14C in the enclosure of the Hofburg, this was the church of the court. In 1784 the Baroque interior decoration was removed and the building thus regained its original Gothic aspect.

H. A. Jahn/VIENNASLIDE

Tomb of Archduchess Maria Christina, Augustinerkirche

Many court marriages were celebrated in this church: Maria Theresa and Francis of Lorraine (1736); the marriages by proxy of Archduchess Marie-Antoinette (1770), of Napoleon and Marie Louise (1810) and of Franz Joseph and Elisabeth of Bavaria (1854).
In the south aisle is the **tomb**★ of Archduchess Maria Christina, the favourite daughter of Maria Theresa. This mausoleum of white marble is considered one of the masterpieces of the Italian sculptor Canova, who worked in Vienna from 1805 to 1809. Under a medallion, a portrait of the Archduchess, figures symbolizing Virtue and Christian Love are depicted advancing towards the tomb. The **Loretokapelle** ⌚ *(access by the right side aisle)* holds in its **crypt** (Herzgruft) 54 urns containing the hearts of the Habsburgs. The Georgskapelle nearby was a meeting place for the knights of the Order of St George, and later for those of the Order of the Golden Fleece. It contains the cenotaph of Emperor Leopold II.

★★ **Albertina** ⌚ – *The parent gallery is closed until further notice for renovation. However, there are temporary exhibitions of works from the Albertina's considerable collections in the exhibition galleries at Akademiehof, Makartgasse 3 (near the Secession building).* The Albertina collection of graphic art owes its name to its founder, Duke **Albert of Saxe-Teschen** (1738-1822), a son-in-law of Empress Maria Theresa, through his marriage to Archduchess Maria Christina *(see above)*. To his personal collection were added, in 1920, the engravings of the former Imperial library assembled by Prince Eugene of Savoy. With about 45 000 drawings and watercolours, 35 000 publications and 1.5 million prints the Albertina is without any doubt the greatest collection of graphic art in the world. Of particular importance is the **Dürer collection**, which was put together by Rudolf II through purchases from the artist's heirs and others, and contains such well-known drawings and engravings as the *Praying Hands* and the *Hare*. Other masters represented are Baldung Grien, Bruegel, Cranach the Elder, Chagall, Goya, Holbein, Klimt, Picasso, Rembrandt, Schiele, Leonardo da Vinci and Watteau.

Schmetterlinghaus ⌚ – Visitors will feel as though they have been transported to a world of magic upon entering the Jugendstil glasshouse in the palace garden, in which myriad colourful butterflies flutter through the air in an environment reminiscent of a tropical rainforest. Some have even been known to land on the tip of a visitor's nose. Mind where you step, however, as there are busy little quails scuttling around at ground level.

★★ **Hofjagd- und Rustkammer** ⌚ – *Neue Burg, entrance from the Heldenplatz.* This exceptionally rich collection of arms and armour was created in the 15C from the collections of the archdukes Ernst of Styria (1377-1424) and Ferdinand of the Tyrol (1527-95), and then merged in 1806 with the Imperial Court weaponry collection.
The filigree work and elaborate decoration on the ceremonial harnesses, helmets and saddles that were made for kings and emperors at the same time reflect European history. The fine quality and tremendous variety of exhibits makes this one of the best collections of its kind in the world.

★★ **Sammlung alter Musikinstrumente** ⓥ – *Neue Burg, entrance from the Heldenplatz. It is a good idea to hire headsets from the ticket office.* This collection goes back to the 16C when Archduke Ferdinand of the Tyrol filled his "Kunstkammer" in Schloß Ambras near Innsbruck with old musical instruments. It was later augmented with the items from Castello Catajo near Padua. This gives this collection of Renaissance instruments its unique historical significance. Of particular historical and artistic interest are a **rebec**★, or early bowed instrument, made from a single piece of wood (an animal's feeding trough) with a picture of Venus on the base (Venice 15C, Room IX); a **harpsichord**★ (Venice 1559); a **cittern**★★ made in Brescia in 1574; a **reed-organ**★ from Innsbruck (before 1569, Room X). In Room XIII six magnificent, partly gilded **trumpets**★ (Vienna 1741 and 1746), and in Room XVIII a **piano**★ (Vienna 1867) made by **Ludwig Bösendorfer** for the Paris World Exhibition, with ornate inlaid work, attract one's attention.

★★ **Ephesos Museum** ⓥ – *Neue Burg, access from the Heldenplatz.* Austrian archeologists working on the important site at Ephesus in Turkey have unearthed many significant items, and finds from the excavations in Samothrace on the Aegean augment the display. Some of the most important exhibits are in the stairway, fragments of the Altarpiece of Artemis; in the mezzanine, the **Frieze of the Parthian Monument**★★ (c AD 170) in honour of Emperor Lucius Verus. The marble frieze (40m/131ft long) shows the adoption of Marcus Aurelius, battle scenes from the wars with the Parthians, and the consecration and apotheosis of Lucius Verus. On the upper floor are the impressive **Athlete of Ephesus**★★ and the **Boy with the goose**★.

★ **Museum für Völkerkunde** ⓥ – *Neue Burg, access from the Heldenplatz.* The ethnological museum includes a Japanese section with a complete Samurai horseman's suit of armour from the 17C. On the mezzanine level, there is a well documented exhibition on Polynesia, with some items belonging to Captain James Cook. The section for early American civilizations has some very interesting items from Mexico, which made their way to Austria in the 16C. One of the most important exhibits in this section is the unique **Aztec feather headdress**★★.

★★ OLD VIENNA *Start from the Stephansplatz* (**KR 115**)

Between the cathedral and the Danube canal lies the heart of Old Vienna – its houses, hotels and long narrow streets, which in spite of reconstruction still evoke a special atmosphere.

★★★ **Stephansdom** ⓥ (**KR**) – Vienna's cathedral is its most potent symbol. The great Austrian writer Adalbert Stifter said of it: "As you go around a corner, the cathedral comes suddenly into view. Like a mountain, it is simple and wonderful; its sheer beauty lifts the spirit...". With its vast roof (exactly twice the height of its walls) of variegated and glittering tiles and its mighty south tower (the famous **Steffl** without which the city would lose part of its soul), this is a building without parallel.

Historical notes – On the site of the present building originally stood a Romanesque basilica consecrated in 1147. This church was badly damaged by the great fire of Vienna in 1258, with only the west front with the **Riesentor**★★ (Giants' Doorway – *see Introduction: ABC of architecture*) and the **Heidentürme** (Towers of the Heathens), terminating in their unusual small spires, remaining today. The first Gothic building was begun in 1304, and the Stephansdom as we now know it was built over the next two centuries.

In 1359 Duke Rudolf IV of Habsburg, wishing to adapt the building to the new Gothic taste, laid the foundation stone of the present three-aisled nave, which was consecrated in 1446. In 1469, in response to the request of Emperor Frederick II, the Pope declared Vienna the seat of a bishopric and St. Stephan became a cathedral.

Damaged during the Turkish siege of 1683, the cathedral suffered renewed and serious damage in 1945, when flying sparks from burning houses opposite the west front set fire to the framework of the north tower. It was swiftly restored to its former beauty after the war (1952).

Exterior – The small size of the Stephansplatz, centre of the medieval city, accentuates the great size of the cathedral, whose one complete steeple, the **Stefansturm**★★★ or "Steffl", rises like an arrow to the height of 136.7m/449ft (Salisbury Cathedral 123m/404ft). The north steeple is still incomplete and will probably remain unfinished for ever. It was given its Renaissance roof in 1579. Here hangs the great 21.3t bell known as the **Pummerin** (the largest bell in Austria), which is rung only on special occasions and to ring in the New Year. The bronze bell was cast in 1711 from 180 Turkish cannon captured in 1683, and hung originally in the south steeple. It was shattered in 1945, and a new Pummerin bell was cast from the remains in 1951.

The Romanesque west door, the **Riesentor**★★, is crowded with statues: Christ in Majesty on the tympanum, the Apostles in the recessed arches. The decoration is intricately carved.

WIEN

Alserbachstraße . . . . EFT 4
Billrothstraße . . . . ET 12
Erdberger Lände . . . . GU 28
Favoritenstraße . . . . FV 34
Gregor-Mendel-Str. . . . . ET 43
Hasenauerstr. . . . . ET 54
Heiligenstädter Lände . . . . FT 57
Heiligenstädter Str. . . . . FT 58
Kundmanngasse . . . . GU 71
Lange Gasse . . . . EU 75
Neubaugasse . . . . EU 86
Spitalgasse . . . . EU 11
Spittelauer Lände . . . . FT 11
Weißgerberlände . . . . GU 12
Wiedner Gürtel . . . . FV 13
Zieglergasse . . . . EU 13

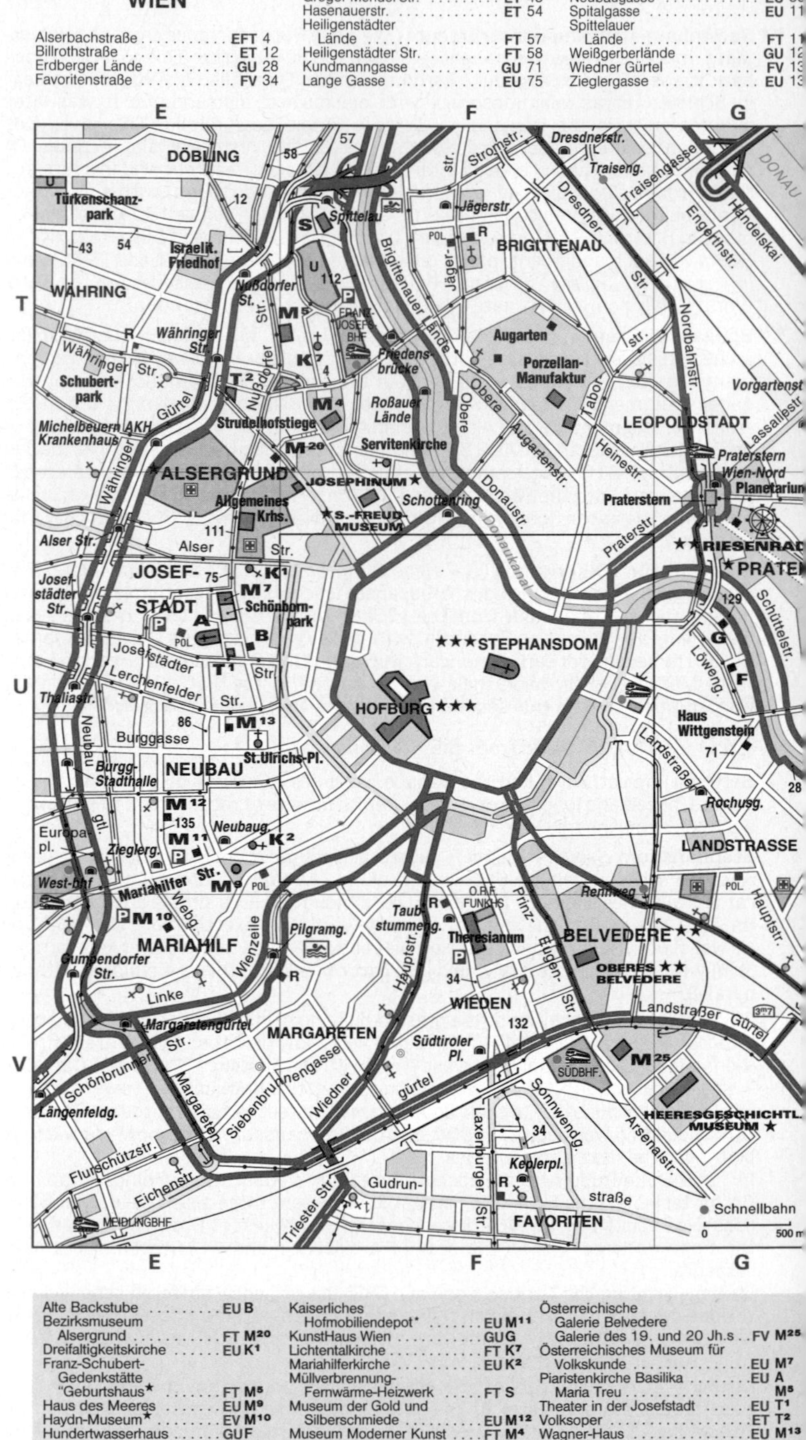

Alte Backstube . . . . EU B
Bezirksmuseum Alsergrund . . . . FT M20
Dreifaltigkeitskirche . . . . . . EU K1
Franz-Schubert-Gedenkstätte "Geburtshaus"★ . . . . FT M5
Haus des Meeres . . . . EU M9
Haydn-Museum★ . . . . EV M10
Hundertwasserhaus . . . . . . GU F
Kaiserliches Hofmobiliendepot★ . . . . EU M11
KunstHaus Wien . . . . GU G
Lichtentalkirche . . . . FT K7
Mariahilferkirche . . . . EU K2
Müllverbrennung-Fernwärme-Heizwerk . . . . . FT S
Museum der Gold und Silberschmiede . . . . EU M12
Museum Moderner Kunst . . . . FT M4
Österreichische Galerie Belvedere Galerie des 19. und 20 Jh.s . . FV M25
Österreichisches Museum für Volkskunde . . . . EU M7
Piaristenkirche Basilika Maria Treu . . . . EU A M5
Theater in der Josefstadt . . . . . EU T1
Volksoper . . . . ET T2
Wagner-Haus . . . . EU M13

Go round the cathedral anticlockwise; at its southwest corner stands the copy of a Gothic lantern of the dead, from the old cemetery of St. Stephan (now the Stephansplatz). In the square, tiles outline the plan of the chapel of St Mary Magdalene which served as a charnel house.

Along the south side of the cathedral are tombstones (recalling the former cemetery) and sculptures, and on the south side of the chancel scenes depicting the Visitation and Christ in the Garden of Olives. On the wall of the axial chapel there is an early-15C bust popularly known as the Christ with Toothache.

On the northeast chancel wall the chapel of rest near the Capistrano Pulpit marks the spot where, on 6 December 1791, Mozart's mortal remains were given absolution.

Enter the cathedral through the Giants' Doorway.

Interior – Clearly inspired by the traditional Germanic hall-church, the long nave (107m/352ft) gives an impression of great majesty. It is ingeniously linked to the three-aisled chancel.

The magnificent carved stone **pulpit**★★★ dates from c 1480 and is a masterpiece of Austrian Gothic art. The artist, who has never been conclusively identified, has portrayed himself, under the ramp, holding his sculptor's tools and looking out of a half-open window (so he is known as the "Fenstergucker"). All round are busts of the four Doctors of the Latin Church: St Augustine, St Ambrose, St Gregory the Great and St Jerome. The boldness of its carving and the vigorous attitudes struck by its figures place it among the finest and most sophisticated works of the Flamboyant Gothic style.

H.A. Jahn/VIENNASLIDE

Pulpit, Stephansdom

The left apsidal chapel, known as the Frauenchor, contains a beautiful altarpiece decorated with carved wood, painted and gilded, known as the **Wiener Neustadt altarpiece**★. Carried out in the first half of the 15C, it shows a group of figures sculpted in the round on the wooden base; on the central panel are the Virgin and Child flanked by St Barbara and St Catherine and, up above, the Coronation of the Virgin Mary. In the chancel the altarpiece on the high altar represents the stoning of St Stephen.

The right apsidal chapel, the Apostelchor, preserves a remarkable **tomb**★★ of Emperor Friedrich III, made of red Salzburg marble by Nikolaus Gerhart of Leyden at the end of the 15C. The artist has illustrated the struggle between Good and Evil, symbolizing the evil spirits in the form of animals trying to enter the tomb to trouble the sleep of the Emperor, while the good spirits, represented by local personages, stop them.

Catacombs ⓥ – In the catacombs are urns containing the organs of the emperors of Austria, and chapels established since 1945.

Cathedral towers ⓥ – The south tower (Hochturm) can be climbed to a height of 73m/240ft, while the platform of the north tower (which houses the Pummerin bell) 60m/197ft above ground is reached by lift. In fine weather there are good **views**★★ over the city, the Kahlenberg heights and the Danube plain to the east.

★ **Dom- und Diözesanmuseum** ⓥ (**KR M**[19]) – *Stephansplatz 6.* This museum, installed in the 14C former Zwettler Hof, displays a fine collection of painting and sculpture alongside the cathedral's most precious treasures, thus rounding off a visit to the Stephansdom in ideal fashion.

Cross Stephansplatz to Singerstraße.

Deutschordenskirche (**KR E**) – *Singerstraße 7.* This church was built by the Teutonic Order, a German hospitaller order founded in the Holy Land in 1190 for German pilgrims (it became a military order in 1198 and was consecrated in 1395).

The church, a 14C Gothic building, remodelled in the Baroque style, contains a beautiful 16C Flemish **altarpiece**★ at the high altar, which is made of gilded and carved wood, with painted panels.

WIEN

Babenbergerstr. . . . . HJS
Bäckerstraße . . . . KR 9
Bauernmarkt . . . . KR 10
Bognergasse . . . . JR 13
Bräunerstraße . . . . JR 15
Dominikanerbastei . . . . KR 22
Dorotheergasse . . . . JR 25
Dr.-Ignaz-Seipel-Pl. . . . . KR 27
Falkestraße . . . . KLR 33
Friedrichstraße . . . . JS 38
Georg-Coch-Pl. . . . . LR 40
Getreidemarkt . . . . HJS 42
Graben . . . . JR
Griechengasse . . . . KR 46
Gutenberggasse . . . . HS 51
Heiligenkreuzer Hof . . . . KR 55
Himmelpfortgasse . . . . KR 61
Judengasse . . . . KR 66
Judenplatz . . . . JR 67
Kärntner Straße . . . . JRS
Kettenbrückengasse . . . . HS 69
Kohlmarkt . . . . JR 70
Landstraßer Hauptstr. . . . . LR 73
Lichtensteg . . . . KR 78
Löwelstraße . . . . HR 79
Marc-Aurel-Str. . . . . KPR 81
Mariahilfer Str. . . . . HS
Mölkerbastei . . . . HP 84
Naglergasse . . . . JR 85
Neuer Markt . . . . JR 87
Neustiftgasse . . . . HR 88
Oppolzergasse . . . . HR 89
Philharmonikerstr. . . . . JS 90
Plankengasse . . . . JR 91
Renngasse . . . . JPR 94
Rotenturmstr. . . . . KR

Salvatorgasse .... JKR 96
Schauflergasse .... JR 98
Schönlaterngasse .... KR 100
Schottengasse .... HJP 102
Schreyvogelgasse .... HR 103
Schulhof .... JR 105
Schwertgasse .... JP 106
Seitzergasse .... JR 107
Sonnenfelsgasse .... KR 108
Spittelberggasse .... HS 114
Stephansplatz .... KR 115
Stock-im-Eisen-Platz ...... JR 116
Tegetthoffstr. .... JR 117
Tiefer Graben .... JPR 120

Tuchlauben .... JR 123
Uraniastraße .... LR 124
Weiskirchnerstr. .... LR 130
Wollzeile .... KR

Albertina im Akademiehof .... JS M[23]
Akademie der Wissenschaften .... KR N
Ausstellung "Der Österr. Freiheitskampf" .... JPR M[21]
Böhmische Hofkanzlei .... JR H
Dom- und Diözesanmuseum★ · KR M[19]
Gedenkräume des Österr. Theatermuseums .... JS M[22]

Kirche "zu den neun Chören der Engel" .... JR K[8]
Kunstforum
Salvatorkapelle .... JR K[4]
Malteserkirche .... JR K[6]
Palais Ferstel .... JR P[2]
Palais Harrach .... JR P[3]
Palais Lobkowitz .... JR P[5]
Puppen- und Spielzeug-Museum .... JR M[16]
Uhrenmuseum der Stadt Wien★ .... JR M[17]
Ursulinenkirche und Kloster .. KR M[18]

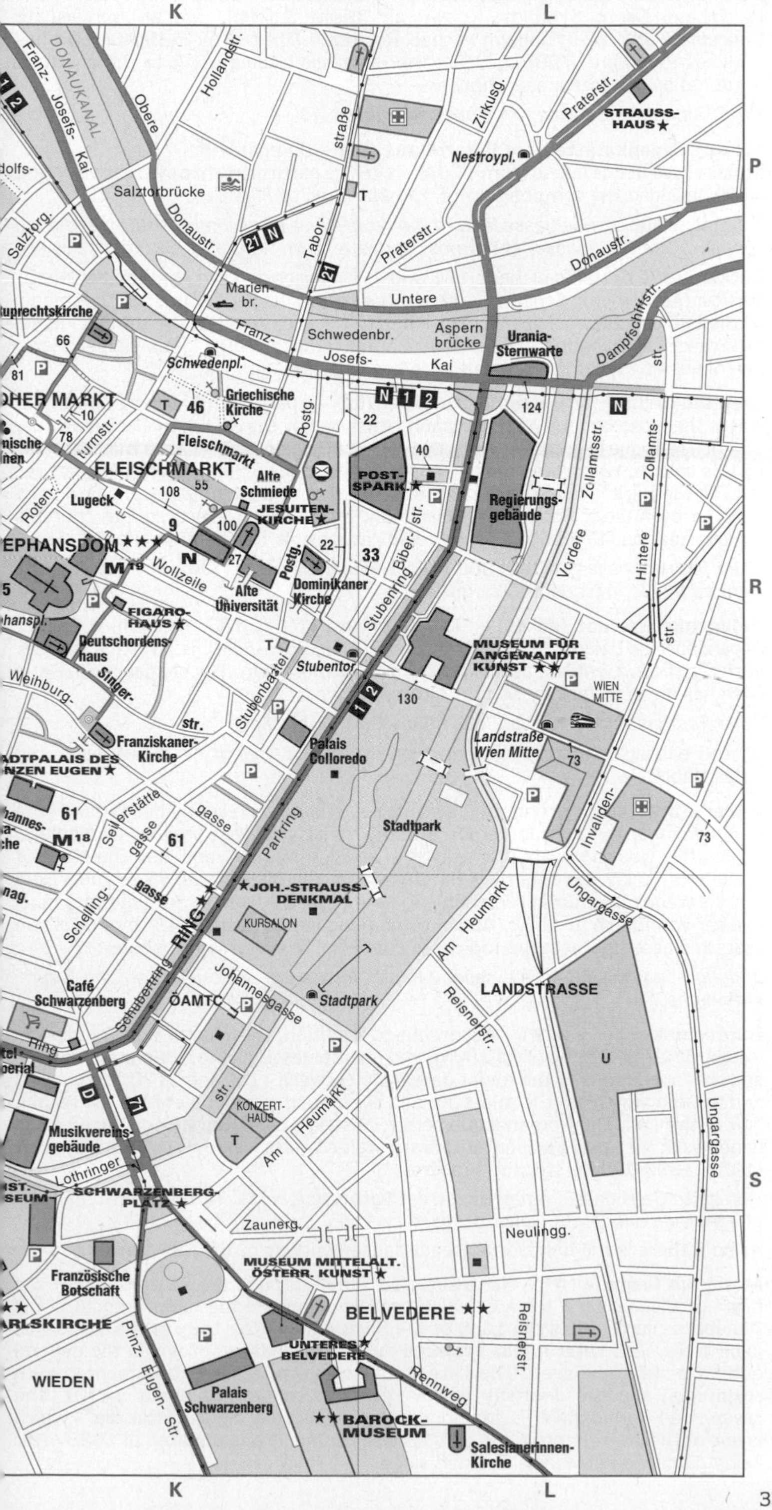

★ **Treasure of the Teutonic Order** ⓥ – The history of the Order is shown (in seals, coins etc). Its wealth accumulated over the centuries is impressive: robes and mementoes of Heads of the Order, such as a **chain of the Order**★ (c 1500, Room 1), sacred vessels, silverware, arms decorated with gold and precious stones, and also clocks, including a **longcase clock**★ carried by Hercules (about 1620, Room 3).

Franziskanerkirche (KR) – The interior of this church was transformed in the Baroque taste in the 18C. On one of the right hand altars is a painting of St Francis by Johann Georg Schmidt, known as **"Wiener Schmidt"**, and an Immaculate Conception of 1722 by Johann Michael Rottmayr. The nearby **Franziskanerplatz** has a Moses fountain (1798) and, like the Ballgasse leading off it to the south, is bordered by picturesque old houses.

From Singerstraße turn right onto Blutgasse (**13**).

★ **Mozart-Gedenkstätte** ⓥ **or Figarohaus (KR)** – *Domgasse 5.*
Mozart lived in this house from 1784 to 1787, a particularly happy creative period which included the composition of *The Marriage of Figaro.*

Domgasse and Strobelgasse lead to the Wollzeile, a busy commercial street in old Vienna. Take Essiggasse (**40**) *almost opposite, turn right onto Bäckerstraße* (**9**).

Bäckerstraße contains elegant 16C and 17C houses and the **Akademie der Wissenschaften** (Academy of Sciences – **KR N**), the former university built in the middle of the 18C to plans by Jean-Nicolas Jadot, the French architect brought to Vienna by Francis of Lorraine. The Jesuit Church stands in Dr Ignaz Seipel Platz, surrounded by quiet houses and little covered passageways.

★ **Jesuitenkirche** ⓥ **or Universitätskirche (KR)** – Apart from Salzburg Cathedral, this is the most famous Austrian church inspired by the church of Gesù in Rome. The rich Baroque decoration from the early 18C completely altered the character of this church, which was built in the Early Baroque style. Interesting features include the **pulpit**★, inlaid with mother-of-pearl, and the *trompe-l'œil* painting of a dome by Andrea Pozzo, the Jesuit lay brother who executed the church's transformation (1703-05) and was also responsible for the high altar.

Take Sonnenfelsgasse (**108**) *and then Schönlaterngasse* (**100**); *both streets are flanked by picturesque 16C houses.*

Heiligenkreuzerhof (KR 55) – The courtyard of this 18C mansion, a former dependence of Heiligenkreuz Abbey *(see HEILIGENKREUZ)*, is a retreat popular with artists and writers, seeking a peaceful atmosphere. The chapel of St. Bernhard has an altarpiece by Martin Altomonte.

Take Postgasse (**97**) *to the Fleischmarkt (Meat Market).*

At the entrance to the Griechengasse is one of the city's oldest inns, the Griechenbeisel.

Hoher Markt (KR) – Interesting remains have relatively recently been found here of Vindobona, the Roman Legion's Camp which preceded Vienna. In medieval times, this was the heart of the city, the "High Market" and also the place of execution. Today the square is dominated by the **fountain** known as the Virgin Mary's Wedding fountain (Vermählungsbrunnen), the work of Joseph Emmanuel Fischer von Erlach in 1732. At no 10 is a Jugendstil **clock** (1913) by Franz von Matsch where figures in period dress come to life every day at noon.

Judengasse (**KR 66**), *where second-hand clothes are sold, leads to the Ruprechtskirche.*

Ruprechtskirche ⓥ **(KPR)** – According to tradition, this church was founded in 740 by St Virgil, Bishop of Salzburg, and is the oldest building in Vienna. The nave and the foundations of the tower date from between 1130 and 1170, the chancel and the doorway from the mid 13C, and the church was completed in the second half of the 15C. The Romanesque belfry, Austria's oldest surviving stained-glass windows in the apse, and contemporary stained-glass windows by Lydia Roppolt (1953, 1992-93) are striking features.

Return to Sterngasse, a narrow street with some steps. Turn left onto Fischerstiege, then onto right Salvatorgasse.

At no 5 there is the handsome Renaissance doorway of the Salvatorkapelle.

★ **Maria am Gestade (JP)** – *Salvatorgasse; enter through the south door.* At the heart of Vienna, on a terrace which used to dominate the main branch of the Danube, a church called Our Lady of the River Bank or Our Lady of the Steps was built in the 12C. Later it was replaced by a Gothic edifice, of which the general outline is still to be seen. The Late Gothic western façade is ornamented with sculptures, and the doorway is covered by a canopy (of about 1410). The seven-sided Gothic tower is surmounted by a delicately pierced **stone cap**★, which is one of the loveliest products of Viennese Gothic. It was replaced in 1688 after being damaged during the Turkish siege.

In the interior, the chancel has interesting stained-glass windows, and elegant statues on the pillars of the nave.

Walk down Schwertgasse (**106**) - Interesting Baroque doorway at no 3.

In Wipplingerstraße, facing each other, are two handsome Baroque buildings: on the left the **Altes Rathaus** (**JR**), the former town hall of Vienna from the 14C to 19C - in the courtyard is the **fountain of Andromeda**★ (1741) by Raphael Donner - on the right is the old **Böhmische Hofkanzlei** (Chancellery of Bohemia - **JR H**) with its outstanding façade by Johann Bernhard Fischer von Erlach (1708-14). Skirt the chancellery to the Judenplatz (**JR 67**), the heart of the Viennese ghetto in the Middle Ages, then follow the narrow Parisergasse to the Am Hof Church.

★ **Uhrenmuseum der Stadt Wien** ⏱ (**JR M**[17]) - *Schulhof 2.* The way clocks have changed technically and in appearance from the 15C onwards is reflected in a display over three floors. The collection covers all types of clock from the sundial to the electronic clock, not forgetting the cuckoo clock. Note the amazing **astronomical clock**★ (1769) by David a Sancto Cajetano.

Am Hof (**JR**) - This square, on the site of the Roman military camp, is decorated by a bronze column to the Virgin Mary (Mariensäule, 1667). It was here that Franz II, on 6 August 1806, announced the renunciation of the German Imperial Crown, thus ending the Holy Roman Empire.

Take Bognergasse (**16**) *to the Graben.*

★ **Peterskirche** ⏱ (**JR**) - This beautiful church, which is acclaimed as the most splendid of all the Baroque churches of the capital with its frescoes and gilded stuccowork, was built from 1702 to 1708 by Johann-Lukas von Hildebrandt, among others, to replace a three-aisled Romanesque church, which was itself a replacement of the first place of worship in Vienna, a 4C building in the camp of Vindobona. The nave is topped by an oval cupola ornamented with a fresco representing the Assumption attributed to Michael Rottmayr (1714). The **interior furnishings**★ are sumptuous down to the last detail. The magnificent high altar is the design of Antonio Galli-Bibiena, and the altar painting by Martin Altomonte.

H. Wiesenhofer/ÖSTERREICH WERBUNG

The Graben with the Plague Column, Vienna

★★ **Pestsäule** (**JR**) - The High Baroque, richly decorated plague column, dominating the elegant Graben, was erected in 1693 in fulfilment of an oath made during the disastrous plague epidemic of 1679 by Emperor Leopold I, who is shown kneeling in prayer.

Turn right onto Spiegelgasse to the Donner fountain.

★ **Donnerbrunnen** (**JR X**) - *Neuer Markt* (**JR 87**). The fountain was built by Georg Raphaël Donner from 1737 to 1739.
The central statue, representing Providence, is surrounded by cherubs and fish spouting water. The statues (copies in bronze) round the fountain personify the rivers Traun, Ybbs, Enns and Morava (March), symbols of the four provinces nearest to the capital. The original statues in lead are in the museum of Baroque art in the Lower Belvedere *(see p 366).*

Return to Stephansplatz via Kärntnerstraße.

★★★ KUNSTHISTORISCHES MUSEUM (MUSEUM OF FINE ARTS) ⏲ (HS)

The collections of art in this museum, patiently assembled by the art-loving Habsburgs, are among the most important as well as the largest in the world. Their star attraction is without any doubt the Picture Gallery, a really princely collection. It still has one peculiarity however: the unsystematic way the collections are put together, and this is the fundamental difference between it and the famous English and German museums.

The sections – There are five collections in the Kunsthistorisches Museum, displayed over some 4km/2.5mi of galleries: the Egyptian and Oriental Collection on the mezzanine level (right wing) from Gallery I to Gallery IX; the Greek, Etruscan and Roman Antiquities and Objets d'Art Collection on the mezzanine level (right wing) from Gallery X to Gallery XVIII; Objets d'Art on the mezzanine level (left wing) from Gallery XIX to Gallery XXXVI; the Picture Gallery on the first floor, with Flemish, Dutch and German painting from Gallery IX to Gallery XV and from Room 14 to Room 24 (left wing), and Italian, French and Spanish painting from Gallery I to Gallery VIII and from Room 1 to Room 13 (right wing); the Coins and Medals Collection on the second floor from Gallery I to Gallery III.
In Gallery VIII on the first floor interesting special exhibitions are mounted on particular topics, admission to which is included in the price of the ticket for the museum.

As is often the case in large museums, some exhibits may be missing because they are being restored, because they have been sent to another exhibition or simply because they have been replaced by another item. Our selection cannot take into account such changes. So some of the works described here may not be on show or may be displayed in a different place at the time of your visit.

★★ Egyptian and Oriental Collection

Mezzanine level, to the right, Galleries I-IX

Gallery I – Late period mortuary cult: Sarcophagus of Nes-Shu-Tefnut (c 300 BC); ***Papyrus stalk columns***★ (18th dynasty).

Gallery II – Pre- and early history of Egypt, Nubia, the Hyskos and South Arabia.

Gallery III – Animal cult: statuettes, mummies and literature; ichneumon (6C-4C BC), relief in green slate.

Gallery IV – Papyri: Book of the Dead of Chonsu-Mes (c 1000 BC). Seals.

Gallery V – Late period sculptures: Statue of Hor-En-Ta-Bat (4C BC); statue of Gem-Nef-Hor-Bak (4C BC); bronzes.

Gallery VI – Everyday culture: clothing, toiletries, jewellery, crafts, furniture, food religious artefacts.

Gallery VIA – Old Kingdom: Tomb Chapel of Ka-Ni-Nisut (5th dynasty).

Gallery VII – Middle and New Kingdom sculptures: Hippopotamus (12th dynasty); ***Sebek-em-sauf***★★ statue (13th dynasty); ***King Thutmosis III***★★★ (18th dynasty).

Gallery VIII – Old Kingdom sculptures: ***Reserve Head***★★ (4th dynasty); statue of Snefru-Nofer (5th dynasty).

Gallery IX – Works of art from various periods.

★★ Collection of Greek, Etruscan and Roman Antiquities

Mezzanine level, to the right, Galleries X-XVIII

Gallery X – Greek and Roman sculptures: ***Youth from Magdalensburg***★ (16C copy), ***Amazon sarcophagus***★ (4C BC), ***Portrait of Aristotle***★ (Roman copy).

Gallery XI – Greek and Roman sculptures: Mithras relief, Sphinx with four faces (2C).

Gallery XII – Greek bronzes: Hercules (4C BC), ***Head of Zeus***★ (1C BC).

Gallery XIII – Etruria: bronze helmets, amphorae, Athena Rocca d'Aspromonte.

Gallery XIV – Greek pottery: ***Duris bowl***★, Tanagra figures, ***Ptolemaic cameos***★.

Gallery XV – Rome: collection of cameos, ***Gemma Augustea***★★★, ***Gemma Claudia***★ (1C), busts of emperors.

Gallery XVI – Late period: sculptures and jewellery.

Gallery XVII – Early Christian art; art from the period of mass migration.

Gallery XVIII – Art from the period of mass migration: ***Gold treasure of Nagyszentmiklós***★ (9C).

★★ Objets d'art

Mezzanine level, to the left, Galleries XIX-XXXVI

The Habsburgs' passion for collecting precious objects is legendary, and the quantity and variety of collections that they built up over the centuries as discerning connoisseurs of art defies belief. The collections of Archduke Ferdinand II from Schloß Ambras near Innsbruck, of Rudolf II in Prague and of Archduke Leopold Wilhelm in Vienna, as well as the contents of the Imperial Treasury, were combined in 1891 and now constitute a collection without equal anywhere in the world in the quality and variety of its exhibits.

A number of the particularly interesting items mentioned here are in galleries that are currently closed; for these no gallery number is given. Neither the listing of the works nor the tour of the galleries is in chronological order.

German Renaissance, Mannerism and Baroque – Gilded silver goblets from Nuremberg (c 1510) show how much table silverware changed between the Late Gothic period and the Early Renaissance. The ***equestrian statue of King Joseph I***★★ is a masterpiece in ivory by Matthias Steinl (Vienna 1693). The bust of ***Emperor Leopold I***★ by Paul Strudel is one of a series of six portrait busts of monarchs. The gold-enamelled bezoar goblet (c 1600) by Jan Vermeyen is a work of great artistry (bezoars are stones from the stomachs of animals such as llamas and antelopes). Adriaen de Vries was responsible for the ***bust of Emperor Rudolf II***★★, the great patron of art among the Habsburgs. A magnificent silver dish of 1605 by Christoph Jamnitzer bears a representation of the Triumphal Procession of Amor (Gallery XXIV). Outstanding among the items made of natural materials are the ***Seychelle nut jug***★ (1602) by Anton Schweinberger and an ostrich-egg goblet decorated with coral by Clement Kicklinger (Gallery XXIV).

French Mannerism and Baroque – The bust of ***Archduchess Marie-Antoinette***★ by Jean-Baptiste Lemoyne shows her at the age of 15 (Gallery XX). Several enamel pieces from Limoges are displayed in the glass cases (mid 16C). The golden "Mercury goblet" is partly enamelled and set with emeralds and rubies (Gallery XXIV).

Italian Renaissance and Mannerism – The bust of ***Isabella of Aragon***★★ by Francesco Laurana dates from 1488. The partly enamelled gold ***saliera***★★ (salt cellar) by Benvenuto Cellini was made in Paris for King François I between 1540 and 1543. The ***small house altar with Christ and the Samaritan woman***★ is a typical Florentine work of 1600.

Saliera (salt cellar) by Benvenuto Cellini

Kunsthistorisches Museum

Middle Ages – The ***Griffon ewer***★ (first quarter 12C) is made of nielloed and gilded bronze decorated with silver. The Wilten chalice (c 1160) is of partly gilded silver. The Poseidon cameo in onyx (beginning of 13C) comes from Southern Italy, while the graceful Krumau Madonna (c 1400) is from Bohemia.

The first floor is reached from the upper ground floor by ascending a magnificent **stairway**★, on whose half-landing stands the marble sculpture ***Theseus defeats the Centaur***★ by Antonio Canova. The ceiling fresco represents the *Apotheosis of the Renaissance* and was painted by the Hungarian artist Mihàly von Munkácsy.

★★★ Picture Gallery

Rather than trying the reader's patience with an exhaustive list of works, we have limited ourselves to particularly exceptional works which really should be viewed. The aim is to pick out the highlights of this remarkable art collection, which might be missed given the profusion of works on display.

Gallery IX – Michael Coxcie: *Original Sin* and *The Expulsion from the Garden of Eden* (c 1550); works by Hans Vredeman de Vries and Frans Floris.

Room 14 – Jan van Eyck: ***Cardinal Niccolò Albergati***★★ (c 1435) and The Goldsmith Jan de Leeuw; Jean Fouquet: ***The Ferrara Court Jester Gonella***★ (c 1440); Hugo van der Goes: ***Diptych with the Fall of Man and Salvation***★★ (c 1470); Rogier van der Weyden: ***Crucifixion Triptych***★ (c 1440); Hieronymus Bosch: *Christ bearing the Cross*; Joachim Patenier: *Baptism of Christ*.

KUNSTHISTORISCHES MUSEUM (First floor)

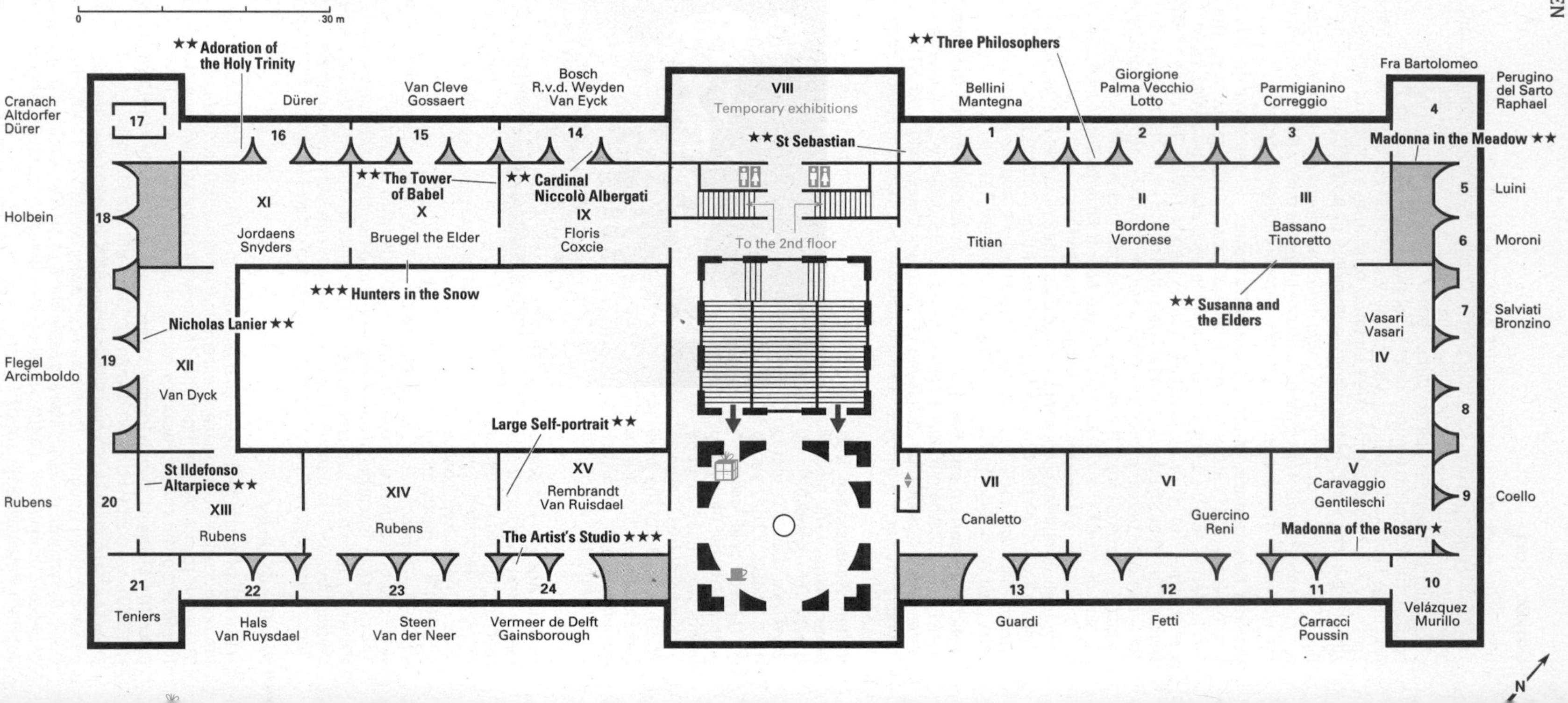

0
30 m

★★ Adoration of the Holy Trinity
★★ Three Philosophers
Cranach
Altdorfer
Dürer
17
Dürer
16
Van Cleve
Gossaert
15
Bosch
R.v.d. Weyden
Van Eyck
14
VIII
Temporary exhibitions
★★ St Sebastian
Bellini
Mantegna
1
Giorgione
Palma Vecchio
Lotto
2
Parmigianino
Correggio
3
Fra Bartolomeo
4
Perugino
del Sarto
Raphael
Madonna in the Meadow ★★
★★ The Tower of Babel
★★ Cardinal Niccolò Albergati
Holbein
18
XI
Jordaens
Snyders
X
Bruegel the Elder
IX
Floris
Coxcie
To the 2nd floor
I
Titian
II
Bordone
Veronese
III
Bassano
Tintoretto
5
Luini
6
Moroni
★★★ Hunters in the Snow
Nicholas Lanier ★★
★★ Susanna and the Elders
7
Salviati
Bronzino
Vasari
Vasari
IV
Flegel
Arcimboldo
19
XII
Van Dyck
8
Large Self-portrait ★★
St Ildefonso Altarpiece ★★
Rubens
20
XIII
Rubens
XIV
Rubens
XV
Rembrandt
Van Ruisdael
The Artist's Studio ★★★
VII
Canaletto
VI
Guercino
Reni
V
Caravaggio
Gentileschi
Madonna of the Rosary ★
9
Coello
21
Teniers
22
Hals
Van Ruysdael
23
Steen
Van der Neer
24
Vermeer de Delft
Gainsborough
13
Guardi
12
Fetti
11
Carracci
Poussin
10
Velázquez
Murillo
N

Room 15 – Joos van Cleve: ***Lucretia***★; Jan Gossaert: *St Luke painting the Madonna* (c 1520).

Gallery X – The collection of paintings contained in this room is unique: 14 of the total of 45 surviving all over the world by **Pieter Bruegel the Elder**. These include: ***Christ bearing the Cross***★ (1564), ***The Tower of Babel***★★, ***Children's Games***★★ (1560), ***The Battle between Carnival and Lent***★★ (1559), ***Peasant Dance***★ (1568-69), and ***Peasant Wedding***★. The undoubted masterpiece is ***Hunters in the Snow***★★★ (1565), which is one of six pictures illustrating the seasons; three of the five that survive are in this museum.

Gallery XI – Jacob Jordaens: *The Bean King's Feast (Twelfth Night)* (c 1640-45); Frans Snyders: *The Fish Market* (c 1620-30).

Room 16 – Albrecht Dürer: ***Young Venetian Woman*** (1505), *The Martyrdom of the Ten Thousand Christians* (1508, with a self portrait of Dürer in the centre of the painting), the ***Adoration of the Holy Trinity***★★ (1511) and *Mary with the reclining Child* (1512).

Room 17 – Albrecht Dürer: portrait of ***Emperor Maximilian I***★ (1519); Martin Schongauer: ***The Holy Family***★ (c 1480-90); Lucas Cranach the Elder: ***The Crucifixion of Christ***★ (c 1500-01) and ***Judith with the Head of Holofernes***★ (c 1530). Albrecht Altdorfer: ***The Birth of Christ***★ (c 1520-25).

Room 18 – Hans Holbein the Younger: ***Jane Seymour***★ (c 1536-37).

Room 19 – Giuseppe Arcimboldo: ***Fire***★★ (1566); Georg Flegel: ***Still Life of Dessert with a Bunch of Flowers***★ (1632).

Gallery XII – Devoted exclusively to paintings by Anthony van Dyck, including ***Nicolas Lanier***★★ (1632) and ***Venus in Vulcan's Forge***★.

Room 20 – This room and the following two galleries are given over to paintings by Peter Paul Rubens: *Young Girl with Fan* (c 1612-14).

Gallery XIII – ***Self-portrait*** (c 1638-40), ***Hélène Fourment with Fur Cloak***★★ (c 1636-38), ***St Ildefonso Altarpiece***★★ (c 1630-32).

Gallery XIV – *Vincenzo II, Gonzaga* (c 1604-05), *Medusa's Head* (c 1617-18).

Room 21 – David Teniers the Younger: ***Archduke Leopold Wilhelm in his Picture Gallery in Brussels***★ (c 1651).

Archduke Leopold Wilhelm in his Picture Gallery in Brussels by David Teniers the Younger

Room 22 – Salomon van Ruysdael: *Landscape with a Wooden Fence and Cloudy Sky* (1631).

Room 23 – Aert van der Neer: *Riverscape with Boats by Moonlight* (c 1665-1709).

Room 24 – Thomas Gainsborough: *Suffolk Landscape* (c 1748); Jan Vermeer: ***The Artist's Studio***★★★ (c 1665-66).

Gallery XV – Jacob van Ruisdael: *The Great Wood* (c 1655-60); Rembrandt: *The Artist's Mother as Hannah the Prophetess* and *The Artist's Son Titus van Rijn reading*, as well as the very interesting pair of paintings ***Small Self-portrait***★ (c 1657) and ***Large Self-portrait***★★ (1652).

Gallery I – Titian: *The Gipsy Madonna* (c 1510), *The Madonna with the Cherries* (c 1516-17), ***Young Woman with a Fur***★ (c 1535) and ***Ecce Homo***★ (1543).

Room 1 – Andrea Mantegna: ***St Sebastian***★ (c 1457-59); Giovanni Bellini: *Young Woman at her Toilette* (1515).

Room 2 – Giorgione: *Laura* (1506) and the ***Three Philosophers***★★ (c 1508-09); Lorenzo Lotto: ***Portrait of a Young Boy in front of a White Curtain***★ (c 1508).

Gallery II – Veronese: the *Anointment of David* (c 1555) and the *Adoration of the Magi* (c 1580-88).

Gallery III – Tintoretto: *Lorenzo Soranzo* (1553) and ***Susanna and the Elders***★★ (c 1555).

Room 3 – Correggio: *Abduction of Ganymede* (c 1530); Parmigianino: *Self-portrait in a Convex Mirror* (c 1523-24).

Room 4 – Perugino: *The Baptism of Christ* (c 1498-1500); Andrea del Sarto: *The Mourning of Christ* (c 1519-20); Raphael: the ***Madonna in the Meadow***★★ (1505-06).

Room 5 – Bernardino Luini: *Salome with the Head of St John the Baptist* (c 1525-30).

Room 7 – Bronzino: the *Holy Family with St Anne and the young St John the Baptist* (c 1540).

Room 10 – Velázquez: ***Portraits of the Infanta***★. Murillo: *St Michael* (c 1665-68).

Room 11 – Annibale Caracci: ***Pietà***★ (c 1603).

Gallery V – Caravaggio: ***David with the Head of Goliath***★ (1606-07) and ***Madonna of the Rosary***★ (c 1606-07).

Gallery VI – Guercino: ***Return of the Prodigal Son***★ (c 1619); Giordano: ***Archangel Michael and the Rebellious Angels***★ (c 1660-65).

Gallery VII – Hyacinthe Rigaud: *Count Ludwig Philipp Wenzel Sinzendorf* (1728); Canaletto: ***Vienna from the Belvedere***★ (c 1758-61).

Collection of Coins **(Münzkabinett)**

Second floor, to the left.

This section of the museum holds a collection of some 700 000 items, making it one of the largest numismatic collections in the world. Besides collections of medals, decorations and insignia, there is also an account of the evolution of money from coins to notes. The coin collection includes Ferdinand II of Tyrol's 16C portrait collection, incorporating more than 1 000 pictures no larger than a postcard.

★★ BELVEDERE ⏲

The two palaces of the Belvedere were built by the architect Lukas von Hildebrandt for **Prince Eugene of Savoy** (1663-1736), and are seen as major works of Baroque architecture.

The Unteres (Lower) Belvedere was built in 1716 as the Prince's summer residence, while the Oberes (Upper) Belvedere intended for the festivities given by the Prince was completed in 1722. At this time the Duke of Marlborough was enjoying Blenheim Palace (1705, northwest of Oxford), a national gift from the English Parliament for the victory at Blenheim he had shared with Prince Eugene. Both Belvedere palaces now house the **Österreichische Galerie Belvedere** (gallery of 19C and 20C art in the Oberes Belvedere, and Museum of Baroque Art and of Medieval Art in the Unteres Belvedere).

Prince Eugene of Savoy (1663-1736)

Eugene of Savoy, son of the Count of Soissons and Olympia Mancini, a niece of Cardinal Mazarin, joined the French army under Louis XIV. When he was refused the command of a regiment, he resigned his commission and entered into the service of Leopold I. At the age of 20, he joined the relieving army under the command of the Polish king Jan Sobieski, which in 1683 freed Vienna from the Turkish siege.

The soldier who had been spurned by Louis XIV achieved great fame when the Austrian army under his command defeated the Turks in the Battle of Zenta (1697). Prince Eugene, the "saviour of Christendom" and a field marshal at the age of 25, became Joseph I's confidant and political adviser and senior minister under Charles VI. He had the satisfaction of concluding the Treaty of Rastatt with Louis XIV in 1714, as the great general was now also an influential statesman.

The Prince was showered with honours and money and had two magnificent residences built, a town palace for the winter in the Himmelpfortgasse (now occupied by the Ministry of Finance), and as his summer seat, the Belvedere.

★★ Oberes Belvedere (FV)

See Introduction: ABC of architecture.

The main façade faces south, and in several sections of it the projecting central part has a splendid main doorway. *(The entrance to the palace today is through the ground floor on the north side.)* To the right of the vestibule, the **Sala Terrena★** with its four figures of Atlas by Lorenzo Mattielli, is a room with frescoes by Carlo Carlone. The first floor is reached by ascending the grand staircase, where an enormous room in red marble fills the whole height of the central section of the building. It was here on 15 May 1955 that the State Treaty was signed which put an end to the occupation of the country by the Allied Powers.

Today the palace houses a picture gallery with the main emphasis on Austrian art.

★★ **Galerie des 19. und 20. Jahrhunderts** ⓥ **(M[25] - section of the Österreichische Galerie Belvedere)** - The galleries contain a large number of works which reflect the broad trends in Austrian and international painting in the last two centuries.

Ground floor - Special exhibitions.

1st floor - As one crosses from the staircase to the Marmorsaal (Marble Hall), the section on "Historicism, Realism and Impressionism" is on the left, and on the right is the section "Art at the Turn of the Century". Chronologically, the tour begins on the left.

Alongside works of the French Impressionists such as Monet and Renoir, it is the works of Austrian artists that claim our attention: Hans Makart ***(Lady at the Spinet★, The Five Senses★)***, Anton Romako ***(Empress Elisabeth★★, Mathilde Stern★)***, Gustav Klimt ***(The Kiss★★, The Bride★★)*** and Egon Schiele ***(Death and the Maiden★★, Four Trees★★)***.

The Kiss by Gustav Klimt

2nd floor - From the top of the staircase, the sections "Classicism" and "Romanticism" are on the right and "Biedermeier" on the left. In addition to historical paintings, works by Moritz von Schwind ***(Party Game★)***, Ferdinand Georg Waldmüller, Caspar David Friedrich *(Rocky Landscape in the Elbsandsteingebirge)* and Friedrich von Amerling ***(Girl in a Straw Hat★)*** are displayed.

Bundesgarten Belvedere ⓥ - The garden was laid out in the French style at the beginning of the 18C by Dominique Girard, a pupil of Le Nôtre, whose speciality was waterworks and fountains. As was often the case in those days, there are esoteric allusions: the upper part of the garden represents Olympus, the central part Parnassus and the lower part the domain of the Four Elements. From the highest point there is a wonderful **view★** over the garden and the city.

Go down to the Unteres Belvedere via the avenue on the right-hand side of the gardens.

★ Unteres Belvedere (KLS)

The Lower Belvedere is built at an angle to the Rennweg (the street), with a court of honour in front of it entered through an impressive gateway bearing the cross of Savoy in its gable. The long building has a well-proportioned façade on the garden side, which owes its elegance and style to the use of pilasters and sculpted decoration for the central section and the corner pavilions. The sumptuous former apartments of the Prince make an ideal setting for the display of 18C Austrian painting and sculpture.

★★ **Barockmuseum (Section of the Österreichische Galerie Belvedere)** ⌚ – Paintings and sculptures are displayed in various rooms, underlining the wealth of variety of the Baroque period by being displayed according to themes such as "Baroque Man", "Man and Destiny", "Everyday life and Festivals", "Power and Powerlessness of Religion". Major painters of this period included **Paul Troger**, in sober or ceremonial mood, and **Franz Anton Maulbertsch**, the "Viennese Tiepolo" who tended more to excess.
The magnificent **Marble Room**★ features a ceiling fresco by Martin Altomonte, depicting the The Apotheosis of Prince Eugene. Visitors can also admire the original **Mehlmarkt fountain**★★ by **Georg Raphael Donner** (1693-1741), a copy of which stands on the Neuer Markt.
In the **Grotesque Room**★, named after the motifs of the stuccowork which adorns its walls, there are, besides the wonderfully luminous wall-paintings by Jonas Drentwett, the marvellous **heads**★ by **Franz Xaver Messerschmidt**, who also executed the figures of Maria Theresa and François of Lorraine in the marble gallery. This gallery is home to the famous Herculanean Women.
At the end of the gallery is the dazzling **Gold Room**★★ with its mirrors and gilded carved woodwork, in which **Balthasar Permoser's** impressive marble sculpture of ***The Apotheosis of Prince Eugene***★ (1718-21) is reflected many times over. The sculptor included a figure representing himself at the feet of the prince.
Of the many paintings the following are outstanding: ***Christ on the Mount of Olives***★ by Paul Troger (c 1750), ***Napoleon on the St Bernard Pass***★ by Jacques Louis David (1801) and ***View of Laxenburg***★ by Johann Christian Brand (1758).

★ **Museum mittelalterlicher österreichischer Kunst (Section of the Österreichische Galerie Belvedere)** ⌚ – The museum is housed in the Orangery adjoining the Unteres Belvedere. The works are mostly from the Gothic period, or to be more precise the religious art of the Viennese, Lower Austrian and Styrian schools from the end of the 14C to the beginning of the 16C.
The following is a small selection of the works which will doubtless be on view again when the museum reopens: the *Romanesque crucifix* from Stummerberg in the Tyrol (c 1160); ***Christ's Crucifixion***★ by Conrad Laib (1449); the ***Mourning of Christ***★ by the Master of the Viennese Schottenaltar (c 1469); several works by the Tyrolean painter and sculptor Michael Pacher; the ***Legend of Susanna***★ by the Carinthian painter Urban Görtschacher; and *The Visitation* and *The Virgin Mary going up to the Temple* (c 1515) by **Marx Reichlich**.

★★★ SCHLOSS SCHÖNBRUNN (AZ)

U-Bahn – U-4 (green line): Schönbrunn or Hietzing stop.

Three centuries ago, the site of Schönbrunn was covered by a vast forest, a favoured hunting ground of the Habsburgs. In 1569 they acquired a wooded estate which had once belonged to a mill. Emperor Matthias is credited with the discovery, at the beginning of the 17C, of the Schöner Brunnen (Beautiful Fountain) which has given its name to this area of the city. The quarter has a fine view over most of Vienna and, beyond it, to the vine-clad hills and the Kahlenberg. In 1683 the imposing hunting lodge was destroyed by the Turks.
Ten years later, architect Johann Bernhard Fischer von Erlach in his role as architecture tutor to Emperor Leopold I's oldest son, later Joseph I, drew up the plans for an extensive palace complex. In this way he won the commission from the Emperor to build the Imperial family's summer residence, which was begun in 1695.
On the death of Charles VI, who was not particularly interested in Schönbrunn, his daughter Maria Theresa took the palace on and had it modified to its present form, after the plans of Nicolaus Pacassi, from 1743 to 1749. The park was laid out by French landscape architect Jean Trehet and later modified by Johann Ferdinand Hetzendorf of Hohenberg, who also had the Neptune fountain, Roman ruin, Obelisk and Gloriette built.
In 1996, Schloß Schönbrunn was declared a world heritage site by UNESCO.

Historical notes

Many historical memories are linked with the palace and the park. During the reign of Maria Theresa, Schönbrunn was the summer residence of the court. Marie-Antoinette, the future Queen of France, spent her childhood there. It was in the hall of mirrors that Mozart, at the age of six, astonished the Empress and her courtiers with his amazing talents. Later on, his work *Don Giovanni* was played in the palace's little theatre. In 1805 and 1809 Napoleon I set up his headquarters in Schönbrunn. In 1815, during the Congress of Vienna, the Great Gallery was the scene of many magnificent receptions.
It was at Schönbrunn that Emperor Franz Joseph was born and where he died and it was in this palace that Karl I, last of the Habsburgs, signed the Declaration of Renunciation on 11 November 1918.

★★ Tour of the Palace

The main part of the building lies behind a façade 180m/550ft long which has little of the flowing line characteristic of Viennese Baroque at its height in the time of Fischer von Erlach, but is a fine example of a classically restrained Baroque. The harmony of the whole construction is maintained by the ochre colour of the buildings, known as Schönbrunn Yellow, which is heightened by the green of the window frames.
From the façade, giving on to the park, there is a fine **view**★★ of the Gloriette, an elegant gazebo on a small rise which now houses a café-restaurant.
At present, a total of 40 rooms out of the 1 440 that make up the palace are open to visitors.
The palace is a triumph of the Rococo style of the 18C – red, white and gold. The detailed elegance of the stuccowork, framing ceilings and frescoes with their scrolled whorls, the crystal chandeliers, the richly ornamented faience stoves, and the priceless tapestries and furniture give these apartments an exceptional air of magnificence.
The **apartments of Emperor Franz Joseph and Empress Elisabeth** are followed by the **ceremonial rooms** consisting of three rooms decorated by the Austrian painter Josef Rosa, two **Chinese chambers**★, one adorned with lacquerwork, the other with porcelain. These chambers lie on either side of the Little Gallery, which communicates through an arcade to the Great Gallery *(see below)* and the Great Ceremonial Hall with its beautiful portrait of Maria Theresa by Meytens.
The **Maria Theresa apartments** are among the most luxurious in the palace. They include the Blue Salon, hung with Chinese tapestry, in which the negotiations were held which led to Karl I, last of the Habsburgs, signing the Declaration of Renunciation on 11 November 1918; the **Vieux-Lacque Room**★, with black oriental lacquered panelling framing remarkable miniatures; the Napoleon Room, decorated with Brussels tapestry (this was the Emperor's bedchamber where, on 22 July 1832, his son, the Duke of Reichstadt, died at the age of 21); and the **Millionenzimmer**★ (so called because its costly decoration) with its South American rosewood panelling framing Indo-Persian miniatures painted upon paper.

Trumler/Schloß SchönbrunnK. u. BetriebsgesmbH/Archiv Schönbrunn

Great Gallery

After crossing a last suite of apartments visitors reach the **Great Gallery**★★★, adorned with gilded stucco-work and paintings. This is where the delegates to the 1814-15 Congress of Vienna did actually dance, giving rise to de Ligne's famous remark. Since summer 1999, the Schönbrunn palace theatre is open to the public between mid July and mid September.

★★ **Schloßpark** – Modified between 1772 and 1780 after plans by the Viennese Court Architect, Ferdinand of Hohenberg, the park is a remarkable creation of Baroque art, mixed with both Rococo and a taste for Antiquity. Arbours, veritable cradles of greenery, and vast formal beds of flowers serve as settings for charming groups of allegorical statues and gracious fountains.

Shaded walks lead to the fountain of Neptune (Neptunbrunnen), the Roman ruin (Römische Ruine), and to the **Tiergarten**★, a Baroque-style zoo laid out in 1752 by Francis of Lorraine, Maria Theresa's husband. These are the oldest zoological gardens in the world.

The **Palmenhaus**★ is the European continent's largest glass and metal hothouse building, built between 1880 and 1882. It houses some 4 000 plants from all over the world in separate sections with different climate conditions, from mountain plants found in the Himalayas to tropical rainforest vegetation.

★★ **Gloriette** – On its mound rising above the park, this elegant colonnaded structure resembling a triumphal arch is crowned above its central section by a stone baldaquin surmounted by the Imperial eagle. It was built to commemorate the victory of Maria Theresa's troops over the Prussians at the Battle of Kolin in 1757 (Seven Years War). From the **roof terrace** (access via the east wing of the Gloriette) there is a fine view of Schönbrunn and the west of Vienna. The café gives people a chance to recover from their efforts of scaling the dizzy Gloriette heights.

★ **Wagenburg** – The **coach house** contains a very interesting collection of coaches, dating from the early 18C to the 20C, which belonged to the court.
Included are those of Marie Louise, Napoleon, Franz Joseph and Elisabeth, the **phaeton of the King of Rome**★, sumptuous harnesses and pelmets, and the gilded and ornate **Imperial coach**★★ of Emperor Franz Stephan (Francis of Lorraine), Maria Theresa's husband, which was pulled by eight white horses.

JUGENDSTIL BUILDINGS

Rejecting the academic architecture of the Ring, the architects of the Vienna Secession designed several buildings to show their theories in practice. Though few in number, they nevertheless mark an important stage in the development of modern European architecture.

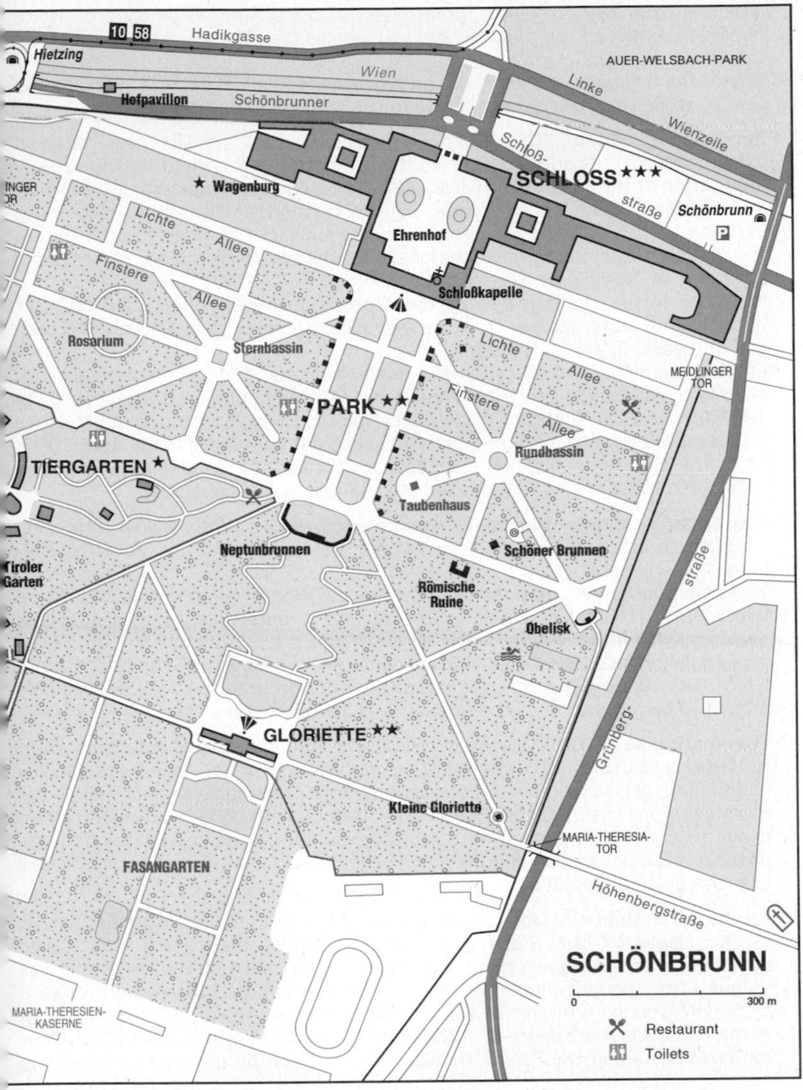

★ **Wagner-Pavillons** (JS) – *Karlsplatz*. Otto Wagner's two highly original Viennese Jugendstil pavilions, designed in 1899 to house the entrances to the Vienna Underground, face each other to the north of the Karlskirche. The extraordinary combination of glass, dazzling white marble and green-painted metalwork, topped with a corrugated copper roof, was a highly original form of construction, which the architect then decorated with gold reliefs and floral motifs. Wagner saw the construction of the metropolitan railway (which was built under his

GEORG MIKES

Wagner-Pavillon, Karlsplatz

direction from 1894 to 1900), predecessor of the U-bahn, as an opportunity to improve the face of the modern city, and applied his genius to the design of the most minor details.

One of the buildings still serves as an entrance to the U-Bahn and an exhibition centre, while the other houses a café in the summer months.

★★ **Secessionsgebäude** ⓥ **(JS)** – The Secession building in Vienna has been run as an exhibition hall for contemporary art from Austria and abroad by the artists' association of the same name since 1898. This Jugendstil masterpiece was built by **Joseph Maria Olbrich**, one of Wagner's pupils. It stands at the parting of the ways between Historicism and Modernism. It was built as a "temple to art", but on completion its architecture, revolutionary for the age, earned it the rather harsh nickname of "temple to tree-frogs".

Its sober forms are crowned by the famous openwork globe of 3 000 gilt wrought-iron laurel leaves. Over the entrance stands in gold letters: "To each period its art, to art its freedom".

In the basement is to be found the **Beethoven Frieze**★★★, a monumental work painted by **Gustav Klimt** on the theme of the Ninth Symphony. It was created in 1902 for the 14th exhibition of the Secession. The 34m/111ft long mural series was removed from the premises in 1903, and did not return home until 1986, after the Secession building had been restored. The magnificent frieze is considered to be one of the masterpieces of Viennese Jugendstil.

★ **Otto Wagner Linke Wienzeile Apartments (HJS)** – **Otto Wagner** originally intended to create a kind of Imperial Way linking Schönbrunn with the Hofburg.

This ambitious project never came to fruition but Wagner nevertheless built these two blocks of flats in 1899 illustrating the architectural principles of the Secession. No 40 is known as the **Majolica House** (Majolikahaus); the otherwise sober building faced in ceramic tiles appears to have been invaded by floral motifs which flow vigorously across the façade. The gilt decoration of no 38 is equally original. The decoration of the interior is in a similar style.

★ **Postsparkasse** ⓥ **(LR)** – Otto Wagner built the **Post Office Savings Bank** from 1904 to 1906 and from 1910 to 1912, using the the most modern materials (aluminium, glass bricks) and construction methods available at the time. So the marble plaques covering the façade were fixed on with bolts, whose aluminium heads provided at the same time a decorative element. Wagner was also in charge of the interior decoration and fittings. In the cashiers' hall, his use of space was to prove ground breaking.

★★ **Kirche am Steinhof** ⓥ **(AS)** – Built between 1904 and 1907 by Wagner to serve as the chapel of the Steinhof mental institution, the church was placed symbolically at the highest point of the leafy hill occupied by the asylum. It was Vienna's first modern church. Its marble sheathing conceals the straightforward brick construction underneath which made it possible to complete the building in the relatively short space of three years (in contrast to the 12 necessary for the buildings along the Ring). The use of tiles, fixed by means of deliberately exposed metal rivets, was a response to the new architectural ideology, with its priorities of speed of assembly and the basing of ornament on constructional features.

Interior – Wagner carried through his scheme for the design of the interior against all opposition, insisting on its functional, rather than its aesthetic qualities. Thus the stoups containing holy water were designed to avoid contamination, the floor sloping towards the altar means that the celebrant can be seen from anywhere in the church, all parts of the building are easily accessible for maintenance purposes and the three entrances facilitated the separation of men and women. The central building in which space is used to a maximum, and its plain functionality is softened to some extent by the white-gold wall covering. The large side **stained-glass windows**★ with their typically linear Jugendstil figures are an impressive sight.

MUSICAL MEMORIES

A number of great musicians have left their mark on Vienna, musical capital of Europe from the late 18C to the early 20C.

★★ **Staatsoper** ⓥ **(JS)** – Begun in 1861 and formally opened in 1869 by Emperor Franz Joseph II with a performance of Mozart's *Don Giovanni*, the opera house was the first of the great public edifices to be completed along the Ring. One of the great opera houses of the world, it was rebuilt after wartime damage and reopened in 1955 to the accompaniment of much pomp and circumstance.

Technology in the service of opera

The lighting, air conditioning and machinery of the opera uses about 9 000kWh per day. Three hundred people are employed, 100 of them involved in the continuous changes of costume and scenery. The larger items of scenery have to be stored at the Arsenal, 4km/2.5mi away. The vans transporting the scenery have their own entrance behind the building and the scenery is moved into place behind the stage by means of special lifts 22m/72ft high. The huge stage (50m/164ft deep, 45m/148ft high) is designed to cope with the needs of today's productions, with an array of the latest machinery including hydraulic winches, lifts, cranes and a 45t turntable.

A symbolic institution – With its unchallengeable international reputation, the home of Austria's national opera has counted among its directors such outstanding figures as Gustav Mahler, Richard Strauss, Karl Böhm, Herbert von Karajan, Lorin Maazel, and Claudio Abbado. Players in the famous **Vienna Philharmonic** (Wiener Philharmoniker) are recruited from the members of the Staatsoper orchestra. The orchestra needs four rehearsal rooms to be able to guarantee a performance schedule which changes every day. The season lasts from 1 September to 30 June, during which time a cosmopolitan crowd enjoys a total of about 300 performances within these hallowed walls.

Tour – The standard tour of areas which would normally be accessible to opera-goers is supplemented by a visit to the stage and backstage. First visitors see the **interval rooms**. Then there is the Gustav Mahler room decorated with modern tapestries illustrating scenes from Mozart's *Magic Flute*. Decor in the **foyer**★ is by the painter Moritz von Schwind. The **tea room**, formerly for the exclusive use of the Imperial family, was one of the few parts of the building to be spared by the fire of 1945, together with the magnificent **grand staircase**★. Completing this sophisticated setting is the horseshoe-shaped main auditorium with its 2 280 seats.

★ **Haydn-Museum** ⌚ (**EV M**[10]) – *Haydngasse 19.* The house where the composer wrote the oratorios *The Creation* (1798) and *The Seasons* (1801) is now a museum, whose exhibits illustrate the context of the music and in particular the places that were important in Haydn's life.

★ **Franz-Schubert-Gedenkstätte** ⌚ **or Geburtshaus** (**ET M**[5]) – The house in which Schubert was born on 31 January 1797 and where he spent the first four years of his life (subsequently he lived at no 4 Säulengasse) has been restored to its original modest state as a memorial to the composer. There is a museum on the first floor.

★ **Mozart-Gedenkstätte or Figarohaus** (**KR**) – *See p 358.*

Palais Lobkowitz (**JR P**[5]) – Also known as the Palais Dietrichstein, this was built between 1685 and 1687 to the plans of Giovanni Pietro Tencula. From 1709 to1711 JB Fischer von Erlach endowed it with an attic storey bordered by statues as well as a grand doorway. In 1804 Beethoven conducted the premiere of his *Eroica Symphony* in the palace's great hall (Eroica-Saal).

Zentralfriedhof ⌚ (**CZ**) – *Via* ④. In this huge cemetery (3km²/1.1sq mi) are the graves of many famous people from the worlds of politics and art. Beethoven, Brahms, Gluck, Schubert and Hugo Wolf all lie in the "Musicians' Corner" (Plot 32A), alongside the Viennese masters of operetta and the waltz: Johann Strauss the Elder and the Younger, Josef Lanner, Karl Millöcker, Franz von Suppé. The monument to Mozart is simply a memorial.
In Plot 32C lie Arnold Schoenberg, Franz Werfel and Curd Jürgens, and in 14A are Theophil von Hansen and Hans Makart, while Antonio Salieri and Adolf Loos are to be found in Plot 0.
A plan of the cemetery is available from the attendant at the second (main) entrance gateway.

St. Marxer Friedhof (**CZ**) – Mozart was buried here on 6 December 1791 in a pauper's grave. His mortal remains have never been found.

ADDITIONAL SIGHTS

Within the Ring

Herrengasse (**JR**) – A pleasant busy street, linking the Freyung with the Michaelerplatz, the Herrengasse (Lords' Street) recalls its aristocratic past. It was also an important administrative centre: at no 13, on the site of an earlier 16C building of which the chapel and a Renaissance doorway in the courtyard remain, stands the former Landhaus (government building) for Lower Austria, from where the Revolution of 1848 began. It was built from 1837 to 1848 by Alois Pichl. At no 9 is the Palais Mollard-Clary, built in 1689 and modified in 1760; and at no 7, the old Modena-Palais, with a 19C façade, which now houses the Austrian Ministry of the Interior.

Michaelerkirche (**JR**) – This church, at an angle opposite the semicircular façade of the Hofburg overlooking the Michaelerplatz, began life as a Romanesque building (nave, transept, right side of the chancel) but the exterior reveals a mixture of styles: neo-Classical façade (1792), tower (1340) with a 16C spire. The group of figures on the high altar (1781) represents the **Fall of the Angels**★, and was completed in 1781, the last religious work of Baroque style executed in Vienna. In the north transept is the tomb of the Italian Baroque poet, Metastasio (brief information panel to the right near the chapel of the Holy Cross), the official author of operas during the reign of Maria Theresa. *The Mount of Olives*, a magnificent coloured stone sculpture, dating from 1494, stands against the outside of the south wall of the church (access via the passage at no 6 Michaelerplatz).

★ **Jüdisches Museum der Stadt Wien** ⏲ (**JR**) – The Adelspalais Eskeles in Dorotheergasse (no 11) dates back to the 15C; it was once the site of a foundation of Augustinian canons. After a turbulent history, the building now (since 1993) houses the **Jewish museum**: religious and ceremonial objects, documents, paintings and drawings on the history of Vienna's and Austria's large Jewish community. Temporary exhibitions.

Minoritenkirche ⏲ (**JR**) – The Minorite church was begun in the first half of the 14C. The chevet is flanked by an octagonal tower and the right side by an elegant ribbed gallery. Since 1784, the church has been the "Italian national church" by Imperial decree, and still serves Vienna's Italian community. On the north wall there is a huge mosaic copied from *The Last Supper* by Leonardo da Vinci and executed by Roman artist Giacomo Raffaelli on the orders of Napoleon I.

Annakirche (**KR**) – In c 1750 this church acquired its present shape and decoration of marbles, stucco, gilding and murals. The painted decor is the work of famous Baroque painter Daniel Gran (altarpiece and ceiling fresco). There is a fine wooden carving (1505) thought to be by Veit Stoss, depicting St Anne with the Madonna and Child.

Palais Kinsky (**JR**) – The palace, which was built in 1716 by Johann-Lukas von Hildebrandt for Count Daun, is one of the most remarkable secular buildings of the Baroque period. The **façade**★ is richly decorated with armorial bearings, statues, pilasters and sculptured motifs. The doorway and balconies are highly ornate.

Alte Ursulinenklosterapotheke ⏲ (**KR M**[18]) – Part of the Austrian Folk Art Museum, this early-18C Ursuline convent **dispensary** houses a collection of religious folk art.

Beyond the Ring

★★ **Karlskirche** (**KS**) – The church, which is dedicated to St Charles Borromeo, was built from 1716 to 1737 to plans by Johann-Bernhard Fischer von Erlach, following a vow made by Emperor Charles VI during the plague of 1713. It is an extraordinary mixture of styles and architectural features which combine to form a harmonious whole, a **synthesis of the arts**★★.

Exterior – It is said that the inspiration to combine Trajan's Column, a Roman portico and a Baroque cupola came to Fischer von Erlach on the Pincian Hill in Rome. Two columns, modelled on Trajan's Column and ornamented with low-relief sculptures illustrating the life of St Charles Borromeo, flank a portico reminiscent of a temple façade. This central unit is itself flanked by two squat towers with windows in the lower floors.

Interior – In the absence of a nave, the attention is drawn to the huge oval **dome**★★ decorated with frescoes by Johann Michael Rottmayr. All the characteristics of the Baroque are present: an accumulation of ornament, dynamic statuary, indirect lighting of the main altar, effects of perspective. Huge pilasters divide the walls into panels – symmetry and harmony preside over the interior; the chancel relates to the pulpit and portal; two chapels face one another, flanked by two smaller ones. The sole use of pink marble for decoration has a unifying effect. In the centre of the pool in front of the church is a monumental bronze by **Henry Moore**.

3BIS/MICHELIN

Dome of the Karlskirche, Vienna

★ **Historisches Museum der Stadt Wien** ⏲ (**KS**) – *Karlsplatz 8.*
This museum illustrates the history of the city of Vienna with maps and views of the city's evolution – including the **circular plan of Vienna**★ (1545) by Augustin Hirschvogel from Nuremberg – and artefacts from various periods in its history. These include items found on the site of the Roman military camp, medieval stained-glass windows and statues of royalty from the cathedral, booty taken from the Turks after the second siege of Vienna in 1683, porcelain and glassware from Viennese workshops and crafts from the Wiener Werkstätte etc. Added to these are the reconstructed interiors of the ***Pompeian Room***★ (c 1800) from the Palais Caprara-Geymüller, author Franz Grillparzer's Biedermeier style living room, and Adolf Loos's dining room and snug (1903). These give an insight into the evolution of domestic living conditions and reflect the artistic creativity of their respective ages. There are also some outstanding paintings in the museum's collections, ranging from Gothic (altarpieces) to Baroque (Maulbertsch, Rottmayr, Troger), Biedermeier (Amerling, Waldmüller) and works from the period around 1900 (including ***Love***★ and *Emilie Flöge* by Gustav Klimt, and ***Self-portrait with Splayed fingers***★★, 1911, and *Blind Mother* by Egon Schiele).

Österreichisches Museum für Volkskunde ⏲ (**EU M**[7]) – The **Austrian folk life and culture museum** is housed in the old Schönborn Palace built by Johann Lukas von Hildebrandt at the beginning of the 18C. The museum exhibits collections on the popular culture of Austria and its neighbouring countries. The new layout of the presentation on the ground floor gives an overview of the museum's outstanding collection of popular art. The objects date mainly from the 17C to 19C and reflect aspects of everyday life in days gone by: building, domestic life, work and religious faith, poverty and the pride of rural communities.
The first floor hosts special exhibitions on folk art and traditions.

★ **Prater** (**CY-GU**) – This immense green space, which extends between the two arms of the Danube, was a hunting reserve under Emperor Maximilian II. The benevolent Emperor, Joseph II, opened the Prater to the public in 1766. With its cafés, where people could sing and dance, the Prater was extremely popular during the heyday of the Viennese waltz. It won worldwide renown when it was featured in the film *The Third Man*; more recently scenes were shot here for the 15th James Bond film.

H. A. Jahn/VIENNASLIDE

Prater Giant Wheel

One part of the Prater (the "Wurstelprater") is a fairground. The **Riesenrad**★★ **(Giant Wheel** ⓥ) (diameter 61m/ 200ft), constructed by the Englishman Walter Basset in 1897, has become one of the capital's most famous landmarks. It gives a breathtaking **view**★ of the city.
Adjoining the Wurstelprater is a vast sports ground: Krieau trotting course, indoor cycling stadium, Ernst-Happel stadium, Freudenau galloping course. At the end of the main avenue leading out from the star-shaped crossroads in the Prater stands the Lusthaus, a summer mansion built between 1781 and 1783, which is now a café.

★★ **Akademie der bildenden Künste – Gemäldegalerie** ⓥ **(JS) (Picture Gallery, Academy of Fine Arts)** – This outstanding collection of paintings is housed in a building (built between 1872 and 1876) by Theophil Hansen in the neo-Renaissance style. Although there are numerous works here of considerable artistic and historical importance, they are all outshone by the extraordinary ***Triptych of the Last Judgement***★★★ by **Hieronymus Bosch** (1460-1516), a terrifying work in which monsters are shown with other horrible phenomena symbolizing the sins and suffering of mankind.
Further highlights of the collection include: ***Lucretia***★★ by Lucas Cranach the Elder, ***Boys playing dice***★ by Bartolomé Esteban Murillo, a ***Self-portrait***★ (c 1615) by Anthony van Dyck aged 16 years, ***Portrait of a young Woman***★★ (1632) by Rembrandt, ***Portrait of a Family from Delft***★ (c 1658) by Pieter de Hooch. Among the star attractions of the 18C collection of paintings are the eight ***Views of Venice***★ by Francesco Guardi, and you should not miss the well-known ***Still-life with Flowers and Fruit***★ (1703) by Rachel Ruysch.

★★ **Österreichisches Museum für angewandte Kunst** ⓥ **(LR)** – The **Austrian museum of applied arts** (MAK for short) is housed in a neo-Renaissance building designed by Heinrich von Ferstel and completed in 1871. It was completely transformed and reorganized in 1993 using a remarkable **display concept**★★. With a collection totalling way in excess of 200 000 items, thought had to be devoted to new ways of presenting aspects of the applied arts to visitors in an interesting way. Consequently, the new display presents only the most original, typical or informative exhibits, and the layout of certain rooms was entrusted to artists themselves: the displays of Baroque, Rococo and Classical furniture were set out by **Donald Judd**; the outstanding collection of lace and glassware by Franz Graf; Empire and Biedermeier exhibits by Jenny Holzer; 20C applied arts by Manfred Wakolbinger. A surprise is in store in the display on Historicism and Jugendstil, which Barbara Bloom has reduced to Michael Thonet's famous bentwood chairs (Bugholzmöbel)... and nothing else!
Of the numerous exhibits the following can be picked out by way of example: **Romanesque, Gothic and Renaissance: liturgical vestments**★ (c 1260) from the Benedictine monastery of Göss in Styria; **tabletop**★★ of painted cherrywood, made at the end of the 15C in Swabia.

Österreichisches Museum für angewandte Kunst, Vienna

Museum für angewandte Kunst, Wien

Baroque, Rococo and Classicism: marquetry panels★ (1779) made by David Roentgen; **table centrepiece** from Zwettl Abbey consisting of 60 small porcelain figures.
Empire and Biedermeier: an amazing **cherrywood secretaire**★ made in Vienna in 1825.
Historicism and Jugendstil: the centrepiece here is the famous **Thonet chair**★.
Oriental items: the **collection of carpets and rugs**★★ is one of the finest in the world.
Jugendstil and Art Deco: glass objects and furniture by Josef Hoffmann, Charles Rennie Mackintosh, Koloman Moser and Henry van de Velde. The focal point is provided by the **drawings**★★ which Gustav Klimt prepared from 1905 to 1909 for the Palais Stoclet in Brussels.
Wiener Werkstätte: the **collection of the Wiener Werkstätte**★★, the famous arts and crafts workshop, is an absolute must for any Jugendstil and Art Deco enthusiast.

★ **Naturhistorisches Museum** ⏱ (**HR**) – The collections of the Natural History Museum go back to Franz I, and are therefore older than the museum itself, which was opened in 1889.

Mezzanine – The **Mineralogy section**★★ has some remarkable specimens, including a piece of quartz crystal 1m/3ft 3in long from Madagascar, a topaz from Brazil weighing 117kg/257lb and the famous **"bouquet of jewels"**★ (1760), which was given by Maria Theresa to her husband.
In the Prehistory section there is the famous 25 000 year old **Venus of Willendorf**★, as well as remarkable finds from the **Hallstatt graves** and a dinosaur room.

Upper floor – The Zoology section has an outstanding collection of stuffed birds, including some that are extinct such as the moa and the dronte, and numerous stuffed animals, including mammals from moles to kangaroos and elks, reptiles such as the fearsome Indian Ghavial, a river-dwelling crocodile found only on the Indian subcontinent, and countless freshwater fish and seawater fauna.

Kurpark Oberlaa (**CZ**) – *Southeast of the plan.* South of the city this park has been used in the 20C as a backdrop for numerous Austrian feature films. After being laid out anew, the park hosted the 1974 Vienna International Horticultural Show. Visitors will appreciate the peace and tranquillity offered by the variety of paths lined with beautiful flowerbeds and fountains. Near the restaurant is a fine **view** of the surrounding countryside. The Oberlaa thermal baths on the edge of the park are supplied by a hot sulphur spring (54°C/129°F).

Palais Schwarzenberg (**KS**) – The two great Viennese architects of the Baroque period, Johann Lukas von Hildebrandt and Johann-Bernhard Fischer von Erlach, collaborated in the design of this palace (1697-1723), part of which is now a hotel. The façade giving onto the forecourt, ie facing the **Schwarzenbergplatz**★, is broken up with a row of huge pilasters.

Naschmarkt (**HJS**) – *Linke Wienzeile.* The fruit and vegetable stalls of the market make a colourful picture, full of local atmosphere.
Opposite the market is the historic Theater an der Wien (Theatre by the Wien, referring to the river). The city's Saturday **flea market** *(Flohmarkt)* takes place on the prolongation of the Naschmarkt.

Piaristenkirche Basilika Maria Treu ⌚ (**EU A**) – *On Jodok-Fink-Platz*. The church stands in the centre of the Josephstadt district. Its beautiful transitional Baroque-Classical façade faces the Jodok-Fink-Platz, known more familiarly as the Piaristenplatz. The interiors of the two great cupolas are decorated with famous frescoes by Franz Anton Maulbertsch (1752).

Salesianerinnenkirche (**LS**) – This church with its magnificent doorway and its 48m/157ft high dome is the work of the Italian architect Donato Felice d'Allio and was built between 1717 and 1730. The façade was completed by Fischer von Erlach.

Ch. Bastin et J. Evrard

Hundertwasserhaus

Hundertwasserhaus (**GU F**) – *Löwengasse/Kegelgasse*.

The Viennese artist, **Friedensreich Hundertwasser**, used this block of flats to express his ideas for reconciling human needs with the environment. Completed in 1984, his colourful, highly unusual building avoids the monotony of conventional mass housing by using a variety of motifs (arcaded loggias, galleries, statues etc), an extraordinary range of materials (glass, brick, rendering etc), and the terraced roof garden.

KunstHausWien ⌚(**GU G**) – *Untere Weißgerberstraße 13*. The museum is designed by Hundertwasser and one part also displays his works, which are deeply concerned with the man-environment relationship *(see above)*.
The other part of the building is used to house temporary exhibitions.

Museum moderner Kunst Stiftung Ludwig ⌚ (**DT M**[13]) – *Scheduled to remain open until the end of 2000, then in autumn 2001 the exhibition will reopen on Museumsplatz in the museum district*. The museum is housed in the **Palais Liechtenstein**, the old summer palace of Prince Johann Adam Andreas of Liechtenstein, ruler of the tiny sovereign state and a great patron of the arts. The palace, which still belongs to the royal family of Liechtenstein, was completed in 1700, and retains its **Baroque character** in both the layout of the buildings and the interior decor, especially that of the magnificent marble room on the first floor. The **collection of modern art** covers a good cross-section of international 20C art. The various artistic movements are each consigned their own display gallery: works by Jawlensky and Kokoschka represent Expressionism; Fernand Léger, among others, stands for Cubism; Max Ernst and René Magritte for Surrealism; Arman for Nouveau Réalisme; and Robert Rauschenberg and Andy Warhol for Pop Art. Examples of international painting of the 1980s and 1990s include works by Georg Baselitz, Jörg Immendorf and Ernesto Tatafiore. One gallery is devoted to "Wiener Aktionismus" (Hermann Nitsch, Günter Brus and Arnulf Rainer).
Further exhibition galleries belonging to the museum are located in the **20er Haus** *(Arsenalstraße 1, which is also moving to Museumsplatz in 2001)*. There are temporary exhibitions on the ground floor. On the first floor the internationally oriented exhibition places the emphasis on Concept Art, Minimal Art and Land Art from 1960 to the present. A **sculpture garden** contains works by Giacometti, Moore and Wotruba.

★ **Heeresgeschichtliches Museum** ⌚ (**GV**) – The **army museum** is housed in Vienna's earliest Historicist building designed by Theophil Hansen and Ludwig Förster. Its displays cover the history of the Habsburg monarchy from the late 16C to 1918, and Austria's progress from the fall of the monarchy to the Second Republic via the inter-war period and the Second World War, in five sections. Part of the museum is given over to the Austrian navy and its expeditions.

★ **Kaiserliches Hofmobiliendepot** ⓥ (**EU M**[11]) (Imperial court furniture store) – This collection of period furniture gives onlookers an impression of how things used to be "at home with the emperor". There is a fascinating variety of elegant exhibits, many of which reveal the Habsburgs' passion for foreign and exotic cultures: in the **Egyptian gallery** (at the entrance to the right of the ticket office); the **Habsburg room** (which reflects the births and deaths, celebrations, political events, religious and secular ceremonies of the family or individual members of it); or the **Laxenburg room** with its exquisite Renaissance furniture from Germany. On the second floor is the **Biedermeier** collection, reconstructions of bourgeois interiors put together in the 1920s using court furniture, and the repository itself, which is open to visitors. Here the warehouse's continued importance as storage immediately becomes apparent, for parts of the collection that are to be sent to other museums or exhibitions or used for Austrian state functions.

Court furniture

The court furniture inspectors were entrusted with transporting furniture, carpets, tapestries etc to the various premises used by the royal household, as well as looking after them and storing them. Until the early 19C only the Vienna Hofburg was left permanently furnished; all the Imperial summer residences and hunting lodges were furnished only for the duration of royal residency. At times it was necessary to prepare furniture to accommodate more than 1 000 people. For coronations and royal weddings (which could be as far away as Frankfurt, Florence or Venice) up to 100 heavily laden wagons would leave in advance of the royal party and fill the living and function rooms with furniture, tapestries, paintings and even indoor water closets. It was not until orders came from Franz II after 1808 that less frequently used palaces and residences were gradually left ready furnished.

Technisches Museum ⓥ (**AZ M**[2]) – The technical museum was founded in 1909 and was reopened in 1999 after extensive reorganisation. The exhibition has interactive sections and gives a comprehensive overview of the most varied aspects of technology and industry: history of science, tool manufacturing, mining, process engineering, heavy industry, energy etc. There are demonstration experiments on display in the basement, where visitors can get to the bottom of technical phenomena for themselves. This is an exhibition that will fascinate adults as well as children.

EXCURSIONS

Tour of the Kahlenberg Heights (AR)

*Round tour of 33km/21mi. Leave Vienna on the Heiligenstädter Straße (**BX**), the road to Klosterneuburg, which runs parallel with the railway. By Klosterneuburg-Kierling station turn left into the Stadtplatz and almost immediately left again where the road finally widens; cross the Kierlingbach rivulet and go uphill towards the abbey. Park in the Rathausplatz.*

★ **Klosterneuburg** – *See KLOSTERNEUBURG.*

Leopoldstraße leads south to the Weidlingbach Valley; cross Weidlinger Straße into Höhenstraße opposite.

The winding road rises between villas and then enters the woods, emerging with a **view** of Klosterneuburg Abbey.

★★ **Leopoldsberg** – This, the most easterly spur of the Wienerwald, overlooks the Danube from 423m/1 388ft. From the Burgplatz opposite the little church (Leopoldskirche) there is an extensive **view**★★ over the northern and eastern parts of the city and the plain of Wagram, the Leitha-Gebirge and the Wienerwald hills.

Return downhill; turn left onto Höhenstraße.

★ **Kahlenberg** – To the right of the Kahlenberg restaurant (483m/1 585ft), a terrace gives an attractive **view**★ over Vienna. The spires of the Stephansdom and the Ringturm stand out above the city. In the foreground are the vineyards of Grinzing and to the right the heights of the Wienerwald.

*Carry on along the Höhenstraße. Stop 500m/550yd beyond the left turn onto Cobenzigasse (**AX**).*

Level with the Cobenz café-restaurant there is an interesting **view** (left) of Vienna.

Continue on Höhenstraße as far as the Häuserl am Roan guesthouse.

From the car park there is a very fine view of the city of Vienna and the Wienerwald.

*Return towards the Kahlenberg; turn right into Cobenzlgasse (**AR 21**) down onto Grinzing.*

3BIS/MICHELIN

Grinzing

★ **Grinzing** – Grinzing is the best known of Vienna's village suburbs. Lying at the foot of the vine-clad slopes in the Döbling district, this little place with its pretty, low-lying houses and friendly atmosphere makes an idyllic scene, but its main attraction from the visitor's point of view is the large number of wine taverns, or Heurigen, to be found here, so that it becomes very busy in the evenings.

Heiligenstadt – Admirers of **Beethoven** will want to visit the central square of this old village (Pfarrplatz) to see the little 17C house (no 2 – now a wine tavern), where the musician lived for some months in 1817.
In Probusgasse stands the **Beethoven Testamenthaus** (no 6) ⊙, now a small museum, where the composer wrote his famous letter in 1802 called the *Testament of Heiligenstadt* when in despair over his deafness. The letter, addressed to his brother Carl, was never sent.

Return to Vienna along Hohe Warte (**BX 64**) *and Döblinger Hauptstraße* (**BXY 21**).

Marchfeld Schlösser

From Vienna to Marchegg – 58km/36mi. Michelin map 926 folds 12 and 13.

The Marchfeld, a gravel plain to the east of Vienna, is one of the most fertile regions in Austria. The Danube and the March, which forms the Slovakian border, have created water meadows that provide a habitat for many animals, so that this area is rich in game and regarded as ideal hunting country. Hence it is not surprising that patrician families who had performed great services to the nation were rewarded with country seats in the Marchfeld.

Leave Vienna heading east on B 3. After about 24km/15mi, the road reaches the first stop on this "castle route": Orth.

Orth an der Donau ⊙ – The history of this moated castle dates back to the 12C. The present building with four mighty corner towers dates from the 16C. At the end of the 17C, the sleek Baroque annex was added to the west wing where it was used as a hunting lodge by Crown Prince Rudolf *(see MAYERLING)*. The castle now houses a museum on angling, the River Danube, bee-keeping and local traditions.

Leave Orth on B 3 towards Wagram. Turn right in Pframa towards Eckartsau.

Eckartsau ⊙ – The castle was transformed into the Baroque style in c 1730, under the direction of Joseph Emanuel Fischer von Erlach (frescoes by Daniel Gran). The hunting lodge won renown as the final residence on Austrian soil of the Habsburg family after Karl I's abdication on 11 November 1918. On 23 March 1919, the Imperial family set off from here to their exile in Switzerland.

Sacher Torte

Frau Sacher, a leading personality in late 19C Vienna, fed the impoverished Austrian nobility in her famous restaurant long after they had ceased to pay. She was less generous with the recipe for her celebrated torte, but many have tried to equal her pastry prowess.

Preheat the oven to 165°C/325°F (thermostat 3).

Grate 180g/5-6oz semi-sweet chocolate.
Cream together until smooth 100g/half a cup sugar and 115g/half a cup butter.
Beat in 6 yolks, one at a time, until the mixture is light and fluffy.
Add the chocolate and 115g/half a cup dry bread crumbs, 30g/quarter cup of finely ground blanched almonds and a pinch of salt.
Beat the remaining egg whites until stiff but not dry, and fold them in gently.
Pour the mixture into an ungreased tin with a removable rim.
Bake for 50min to 1hr.
When the torte is cool, slice it horizontally through the middle (you may turn the top layer over so that the finished cake is flat on top) and spread 225g/1 cup apricot jam or preserve between the layers.
Cover with chocolate glaze.
For the genuine Viennese touch, heap on the *Schlag*!

From Eckartsau take B 3 back towards Kopfstetten and drive on to the junction with B 49. Turn left towards Marchegg. After about 2km/1mi the road arrives at Schloß Niederweiden.

Niederweiden ⏲ – Field Marshal Ernst Rüdiger von Starhemberg took over the domain in 1685, and commissioned Johann Bernhard Fischer von Erlach to build this Baroque hunting lodge in 1693. In 1726 it was acquired by Prince Eugen of Savoy before being finally taken over by Maria Theresa in 1755. It was at this time that Nicolaus Pacassi made the alterations that gave the palace its present form. Beneath the palace's slate mansard roof, only the oval **Great Hall★** painted in the Chinese manner provides evidence of the magnificence of the original decoration.

Leave B 49 and head towards Schloßhof.

Schloßhof ⏲ – In 1725 Prince Eugen bought the estate of Hof, on which stood at that time a fortified castle, and had it converted by Lukas von Hildebrandt between 1725 and 1729 into a huge Baroque palace. No fewer than 800 workers were involved, 300 of whom were gardeners. The gardens, in the French style and on a grand scale, were laid out with sculptures and fountains and divided up with terraces and ornate wrought-iron gates. Maria Theresa acquired Schloßhof together with Niederweiden, and had a further storey built on as well as furnishing it in magnificent style. After 200 years of continuous neglect, Schloßhof is now once again restored to its original splendour, with fine stuccowork and paintings. The masterly restoration of the **Sala terrena★** deserves particular praise.

Return to B 49 via Groißenbrunn and drive on to Marchegg.

Marchegg ⏲ – Although rebuilt in the 17C and 18C in the Baroque style, the origins of Schloß Marchegg are medieval and go back to the town citadel of the Bohemian king Przemysl Ottokar. The four-winged building belonged to the aristocratic Hungarian Pálffy-Erdöd family from 1629 to 1945. It now houses the **Niederösterreichisches Jagdmuseum** (Lower Austrian Hunting Museum). The view from the corner room of the northeastern wing of the **stork colony★★** in the water meadows behind the Schloß is unforgettable. Up to 50 pairs nest in the trees on the Austrian side of the March, although they cross the frontier to fetch their food from the Slovakian side. *A telescope is provided for observing the colony at the back of the palace.*

The white storks of Marchegg

White storks have been nesting in Marchegg for many years (always in the trees, rather than on roofs or towers like storks elsewhere), during which time a steady increase in the population has been recorded. They arrive here in spring after wintering in Africa, covering the 10 000km/6 200mi in their typical gliding flight. The female then lays three or four eggs in April, which the pair of storks take turns to incubate. The chicks are hatched after about a month, and have gained sufficient strength by the end of August (no easy task, given that for instance a three-week-old stork requires 500g/1lb of food daily) to undertake the long journey back to Africa. They stay there for two years, and only return to Europe in their third year, usually settling where they were born. The future of Marchegg's colony therefore seems assured.

WIENER NEUSTADT

Niederösterreich

Population 35 050

Michelin map 926 fold 25 - Alt 265m/869ft

The town was founded by Duke Leopold V of Babenberg in 1194 as a border fortress against Hungary. Part of the ransom paid for Richard the Lionheart is supposed to have been used to pay for this. Under Friedrich III, between 1440 and 1493, the town was an Imperial residence. In 1459, Maximilian I was born here, and here it is, far from the splendour of his mausoleum in Innsbruck, that he is in fact buried. A military academy still in existence was founded in Wiener Neustadt under Maria Theresa. The historic town centre, now an attractive pedestrian zone, still features the regular street layout of the Middle Ages, despite heavy damage suffered during the Second World War.

SIGHTS

Ehemalige Burg - The core of the former castle dates back to the 13C, but it was subject to numerous extensions and modifications. In 1751, Maria Theresa installed a military academy here, which is now recognized as the oldest of its kind in the world.

St. Georgskathedrale ⓥ - This was raised to the status of a cathedral as the church of the Chaplain General of the Austrian army. Its gable, which can be seen from the first courtyard, is covered with 107 carved coats of arms from the House of Habsburg - known as the "Wappenwand" (15C) - which frame the central window of the church and surround the statue of Friedrich III.

The Gothic hall-church, built during the reign of Friedrich III and completely restored after the Second World War, lies above the arched entrance. The Virgin on the north side altar and some stained-glass fragments (escutcheons), are the most outstanding remains of the original furnishings. Maximilian's mortal remains rest beneath the steps of the high altar.

Neuklosterkirche - *Ungargasse, near the Hauptplatz.* This Gothic abbey church, in which the chancel (first half of the 14C) is higher than the nave, has some magnificent Baroque altars. In the apse, inset into the wall behind the high altar, there is the beautiful **tomb**★ of Empress Eleanor of Portugal, the wife of Friedrich III, which was carved by Nikolaus Gerhart of Leyden in 1467.

Hauptplatz - On the south side of the town square stands the **Rathaus**, built in 1488, to which a tower with a rusticated stone façade was added in the 16C, and which was converted to the Late Classical style in 1834. The column dedicated to Mary was built in 1678.

The beautiful arcaded houses on the north side of the square date from the Gothic period.

Take the Böheimgasse to the Domplatz (cathedral square).

Dom - The Late Romanesque cathedral building had a Gothic transept and chancel added to it in the 14C. The **Brauttor**★, a doorway on the south side decorated with bands of lozenge and zigzag motifs, is a lovely example of Late Romanesque architecture. The height of the ceiling inside testifies to the importance of the cathedral during the reign of Friedrich III. The court gallery bears the motto A.E.I.O.U (*Austria Est Imperare Orbi Universo* - Austria rules the world). Friedrich was probably also the donor behind the 12 larger-than-life-size figures of the Apostles which adorn the pillars, the work of sculptor Lorenz Luch-

M. Hertlein/MICHELIN

Türkensturz, Seebenstein

sperger. The **high altar**, with its six Corinthian columns made of red marble, is magnificent without being overdone. The **pulpit** was created in 1609 by Johann Baptist Zelpi and features the statues of Doctors of the Latin Church St Augustine, St Ambrose, St Gregory and St Jerome.
On the north side of the cathedral square is the **Propstei** (Provost's House), which was the bishop's residence from 1469 to 1785. It has an ornate Baroque doorway with the coat of arms of Bishop Franz Anton, Count of Puchheim.

EXCURSION

Seebenstein – *17km/11mi south on A2 towards Graz.* This village in the Pitten Valley boasts two interesting buildings that can be seen from the A2 motorway some way off: the fortress of Seebenstein and the "Türkensturz" folly high above the valley.

Park the car in the car park by the local administrative offices. Take the path to the castle heading south. This leads to a shaded footpath up to the Türkensturz. After about 10min walk, take the left fork to the castle.

Burg Seebenstein ⌚ – This proud fortress dating back to the 11C houses a private collection of medieval art, including a fine Madonna by Würzburg sculptor Tilman Riemenschneider (c 1460-1531).

Return to the fork in the path and climb a well laid out path through the forest for about 45min.

Türkensturz – This "ruined" folly was built in 1825-26 by Prince Johann I of Liechtenstein, and its name harks back to a legendary event during the Turkish invasions of the 16C. It is a wonderful look-out point, with a view stretching west as far as the Raxalpe and imposing Schneeberg range.

WIENERWALD★

VIENNA WOODS – Niederösterreich

Michelin map 926 folds 12 and 24

The hills of the Vienna Woods form the northeastern spur of the Alps. This great green lung to the west of Vienna, which penetrates beyond the city boundary, gives the Austrian capital a rural feel. Vienna is in fact one of the few great cities in the world which has been able to retain something of the charm of village life within its city limits.
The Viennese associate "Wienerwald" with vine-covered hills and long walks through shady woods, which are pleasantly cool in the heat of summer. It also conjures up the sound of a zither in a remote country inn, or the musical landscapes of Beethoven's Pastoral Symphony. And then there is that famous Strauss waltz, *Tales from the Vienna Woods.*
If you are travelling by car, there is a good route with several sights along the way which also covers the part of the Vienna Woods favoured by Franz Schubert and his friends for their rural rambles.

TOUR OF THE VIENNA WOODS

Leave Vienna on Bundesstraße 12 and follow the sign "Perchtoldsdorf Zentrum". Turn right at the end of the Mühlgasse and then immediately left. Turn left again at the halt sign onto the Plättensttraße and follow the sign "Zentrum".

Perchtoldsdorf – In the centre of the market place stands the fine Pestsäule (plague column) of 1713, the work of Johann Bernhard Fischer von Erlach. The Late Gothic town hall (end of the 15C) contains the **Türkenmuseum** (Turkish Museum), which keeps alive the memory of the incursions of the Turks into Lower Austria. The massive fortified tower on the north side of the market place was built between 1450 and 1520.
In the porch of the Pfarrkirche (parish church) of St Augustine, a multi-coloured relief dating from 1449 and portraying the **Marientod★** (Death of the Virgin Mary) can be seen. The interior is dominated by a monumental high altar in the Baroque style dating from 1740, and adorned with the four patron saints of the crownlands (Styria, Carinthia, Upper Austria and Lower Austria).
To the west of the church are the remains of the Herzogsburg, a castle built between the 11C and the 15C.

In Perchtoldsdorf take Bundesstraße 13 in the direction of Vienna. After 1.3km/1mi turn onto the Kaltenleutgebnerstraße which becomes the Hauptstraße. After 11km/7mi turn left as for Sulz im Wienerwald. Pass through Sittendorf and (shortly before crossing the motorway) follow the sign saying "Naturpark Sparbach".

Naturpark Sparbach ⌚ – Lower Austria's oldest nature reserve has rambling footpaths and game enclosures which are home to fallow deer, moufflons etc. There is also a children's zoo and a pretty lake with a watermill. The reserve is particularly popular in the summer because it is pleasantly fresh when Vienna is sweltering under its pall of heat.

Cross the E 60/A 21 motorway and turn right onto Bundesstraße 11 in the direction of Gaaden, which leads through woods and valleys to the abbey of Heiligenkreuz.

★ **Stift Heiligenkreuz** – *See Stift HEILIGENKREUZ.*

Continue on Bundesstraße 11 in the direction of Alland. After 4km/2.5mi turn left for Mayerling.

Mayerling – *See MAYERLING.*

Turn left onto Bundesstraße 210 in the direction of Baden.

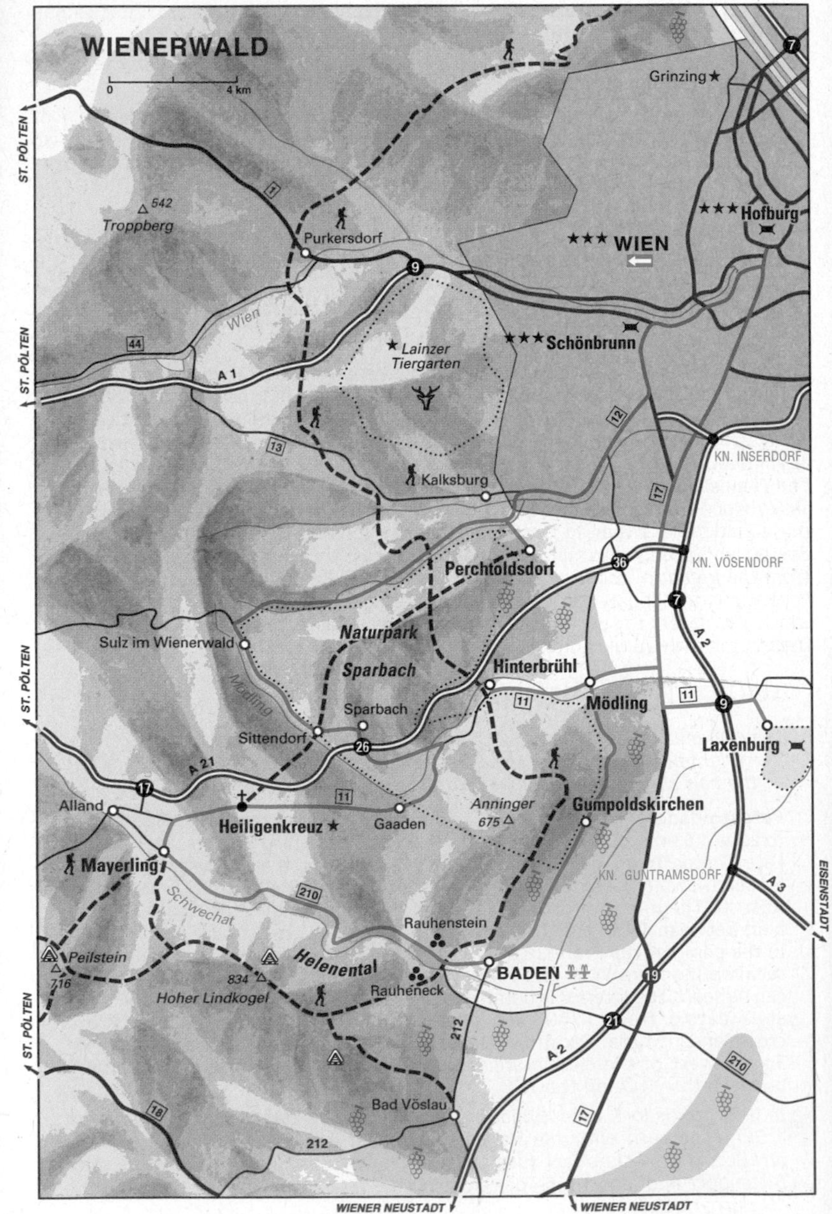

Helenental – The Schwechat winds its way through this valley, which features in many songs. Some 60km/37mi of waymarked paths make it a good area for getting out and about. Just before reaching Baden, there are the ruins of two once important castles, Rauhenstein (12C) on the left-hand slope and Rauheneck (11C) up on the right.

‡‡ **Baden** – *See BADEN.*

To get onto the Weinstraße (Wine Road) to Gumpoldskirchen and Mödling from the centre of Baden pass under the railway on the Kaiser-Franz-Joseph-Ring and then turn immediately left onto Bundesstraße 212. Continue under another bridge then turn right at the stop sign and immediately left for Gumpoldskirchen.

Gumpoldskirchen – This charming place at the foot of the 674m/2 211ft high Anninger has achieved great fame for its superb white wines. In the Kirchengasse it is the delightful Renaissance town hall that catches the eye. But to find out more about the wine, it is a good idea to take a walk through the vineyards (here called "Rieden"), where there are also boards providing information on the different grape varieties *(labelled "Weinwanderweg").*

The road passes through the vineyards and then drops down through many bends, giving a wonderful view towards Mödling and Vienna (even the Kahlenberg is visible in fine weather).

Mödling – This was a favourite haunt of three composers: Beethoven *(Hauptstraße 79, Achsenaugasse 6),* Schönberg and Webern. In the **Pfarrkirche St. Othmar** of 1523 the vaulting is supported by 12 columns representing the 12 Apostles. The circular charnel house, originally the Pantaleon chapel, dates from the second half of the 12C and has frescoes in its crypt. Mödling boasts Austria's oldest war memorial in the shape of the Husarentempel.

Go west on the Spitalmühlgasse which joins the Brühlerstraße following signs for the "Seegrotte" and E6/A21. After the football stadium turn right onto the Hauptstraße (following the signs), and after the bridge turn right again and park.

Hinterbrühl – There is something really unique to see here: the **Seegrotte**★ ⌚ (Lake Grotto) containing the largest underground lake in Europe with an area of 6ha/15 acres, which can be viewed from a motor boat. The lake was created in 1912, when 20 million l/4.4 million gal of water poured into the lower gallery of this former mine.

Return to Mödling on Bundesstraße 11. Pass through the town, and still on Bundesstraße 11 proceed along the Triester Straße towards Schwechat. The road crosses the E 59/A 2 motorway. Follow the signpost for Laxenburg.

Laxenburg – The former Imperial summer residence consists of three great houses and an extensive park.

Blauer Hof – *Schloßplatz.* It owes its name to its builder (the Dutchman Sebastian Bloe) rather than to its colour, as the rendering is yellow and not blue. It was here that Crown Prince Rudolf was born on 21 August 1858.
The **Pfarrkirche** (parish church) built between 1693 and 1699 at Leopold I's behest also stands on the Schloßplatz. The towers were added in 1722. The interior has an attractive pulpit in gilded wood and ceiling frescoes after a design by Johann Michael Rottmayr.

Park ⌚ – *Enter from the Hofstraße.* Emperor Joseph II had this 250ha/618 acre park laid out in the English style, to which Franz I added a lake.
Diagonally to the right of the entrance is the **Altes Schloß**, in which Karl VI signed the "Pragmatic Sanction" in 1713, making it possible for his daughter Maria Theresa to ascend the throne. On the island in the lake is the **Franzensburg**, a sham neo-Gothic castle built at the beginning of the 19C by Michael Riedl.

Return to Vienna on the E 59/A 2 motorway.

Stiftskirche WILHERING★★★

Oberösterreich

Michelin map 926 fold 8 – 8km/5mi west of Linz

The church and conventual buildings of the Cistercian abbey of Wilhering stand on the south bank of the Danube upstream from Linz. The abbey was originally a Romanesque building but over the centuries it was transformed into a masterpiece of Rococo art and today it is one of Austria's most striking examples of that style.

HISTORICAL NOTES

On 6 March 1733 the buildings of the abbey dating from the 12C and the church burned down. It was rumoured locally that the monks had themselves set fire to the buildings so that they could rebuild in the contemporary style. However, it was not long before the true culprit was found; a 12-year-old girl. She was condemned to death for her action but was later pardoned. The reconstruction of the abbey was begun in 1734, and work continued until 1748. The result was a building of exceptional beauty as anyone visiting the abbey today may testify. The most celebrated architects of the day, including Joseph Mathias Götz, Josef Munggenast and Johann Michael Prunner, submitted their drawings and plans in the hope of being awarded the commission. Against all expectation, a local craftsman called Johann Haslinger was preferred to his famous competitors.

TOUR

Abbey courtyard – The majestic yet sober main courtyard of the abbey is surrounded by monastery buildings arranged in a U shape; the open north side reveals some romantic outbuildings.

On the south side, a pedimented porch stands out from the central façade. The Baroque pomp of the courtyard is stamped with a characteristically Cistercian sense of measure and balance. The church façade, also white and pink, is subdivided by piers. The portal is the only visible remnant of the original Romanesque church.

Abbey church ⓥ – This church is considered to be one of the most outstanding examples of the Rococo style in the history of European architecture. It would be difficult to surpass this profusion of decoration, richness of colour, ingenuity of painting and sculpture and delicacy of stuccowork. The whole decor of the church evokes a timeless joy; the figures – both painted and sculpted – which float and gyrate in space seem to be caught up in heavenly bliss.

High altar – *See Introduction: ABC of architecture.* The high altar is designed round a painting of the Assumption of the Virgin Mary by **Martin Altomonte**. It was commissioned by the Abbot of Wilhering in 1737 when the painter, already in his eighties, enjoyed a great reputation. The painting illustrates the theological theme, chosen by the abbot for the decoration of the whole church, and inscribed in a scroll on the chancel vault: *'Assumpta est Maria in Caelum, gaudent angeli'* (Mary has ascended into heaven, the angels rejoice).

Less than a year later, Altomonte, who lived in Vienna, dispatched the painting by boat up the Danube contained in an enormous wooden case. He was paid the generous sum of 700 florins, the cost of buying about 50 cows at the time. During the next six years, Altomonte executed the paintings for the **side chapels**★★. These were to be his last compositions. When he learned about the huge programme of frescoes planned for the ceilings, he introduced his nephew and succeeded in having him chosen to do the work.

Frescoes – Bartolomäus Altomonte, who was unquestionably less talented than his uncle, nonetheless achieved a remarkable work of art at Wilhering, as he was responsible for painting more than 450m²/4 844sq ft of the ceiling (almost two-thirds of the total area).

The nave is decorated with an enormous painting of Mary, Queen of Heaven, surrounded by her court of saints and angels. Altomonte worked closely with stucco artists on this composition. The painted figures, gilt decoration of the surround and stucco angels all contribute to evoking an atmosphere of triumphant celebration.

Stucco – The stucco artist **Franz Joseph Holzinger** came from St. Florian with his students to spend three consecutive summers (1739-41) decorating the church. After an interruption caused by the aftermath of the Thirty Years War, their academic style was considered too rigid and too systematic and all their work was destroyed.

The abbot at once sent for some young stucco workers who had been trained in southern Germany. These young artists of the Rococo generation had turned their backs on the cumbersome, overbearing compositions of the Late Baroque period and had learnt how to apply stucco in moderation and with a delicacy hitherto associated with painting and gilding. It is this subtle harmony of all the decorative arts which makes Wilhering the undisputed Rococo masterpiece that is admired today.

The **cupola** above the transept crossing is the realm of *trompe-l'œil* and illusion. An erudite architectural composition, painted by the Italian Francesco Messenta, opens at the top on a glimpse of sky; the men chained to the Earth by their sins are protected by the Virgin Mary from divine wrath. To the right of the entrance to the monks' choir stands an imposing **pulpit**; it is easy to imagine thunderous sermons being declaimed from this explosion of black and white stucco and gold. The pulpit is a fine match for the **choir organ**, an elegant instrument constructed in 1746 by Nicolas Rumel of Linz, of which the composer Anton Bruckner was especially fond.

R. Chéret/MICHELIN

Detail, Wilhering Abbey Church

Great organ – The great organ is alive with exquisite detail. The part of the nave, which accommodates the organ, is itself a monumental work of art in which each element contributes to the overall effect: a magnificently worked iron gate; a discreetly elegant gallery which directs the gaze upward and beyond to the three banks of organ pipes. Overhead a clock marks the passing time and a purple curtain in *trompe-l'œil* hangs down from the vault, its heavy folds drawn back to reveal the theatrical scene. It is easy to imagine that, if the curtain were to rise, it would reveal artists putting the finishing touches to the stage set.

Cloisters – The cloisters may be visited through a door *(left)* from the narthex. A pre-Gothic 13C **doorway** leads into the old **chapter-house**; a series of fine 18C paintings depicts episodes in the life of St Bernard.

WÖRTHER SEE★

Kärnten

Michelin map 926 folds 34 and 35

The Wörther See, a lake stretching between Velden and Klagenfurt and over 17km/10mi long, receives little in the way of water from mountain streams and is therefore warm (24-28°C/75-82°F in summer), a fact which has encouraged the development of resorts such as Velden and Pörtschach, very popular with tourists from Germany. A screen of low hills sometimes hides the Karawanken, but a short stroll is generally enough to bring back into view the magnificent splendour of this mountain barrier which extends from Austria into Slovenia and Italy.

Villach is a good centre for visiting both the **Ossiacher See**★ and the **Gerlitzen**★★ *(for details of both, see OSSIACHER SEE).*

★ SOUTH SHORE OF THE LAKE

From Villach to Klagenfurt *76km/47mi*

At first the route runs through the Drava Valley, within sight of the Karawanken (on the way several wayside shrines called *Bildstöcke* can be seen). In Velden, instead of following the main road to the resorts of the Austrian Riviera, it takes the road along the south shore of the Wörther See *(narrow roads)*. Note the site of the Maria Wörth promontory and the panorama from the Pyramidenkogel.

★ **Villach** – *See VILLACH.*

From Villach take road no 84 as far as the east bank of the Gail.

Maria Gail – The core of this pilgrimage church is Romanesque, although it was transformed into the Gothic style in c 1450. On the walls inside are the remains of Late Romanesque frescoes from the second half of the 13C. The high altar contains a holy image of the Virgin Mary sheltering supplicants under her cloak, created in c 1600. The focal point of the church is a valuable Late Gothic **altarpiece**★★ (north wall) from the Villach woodcarving workshops (early 16C); its central panel depicts the Coronation of the Virgin. Besides one or two pieces of Late Gothic woodcarving inside, the church also features some interesting stone sculptures on the outside of its south wall, depicting a sort of Last Judgement scene. These sculptures probably date from just before 1300.

Further east, the road, which continues to climb, gives a wide general view of the Villach basin where the Gail and the Drava converge. Then the view embraces the beautiful sheet of water that is the **Faaker See** and the decapitated pyramid of the Mittagskogel, standing quite alone (alt 2 143m/ 7 031ft).
The route next descends to the Drava Valley; at the turn-off for the hamlet of St. Martin, stands a *Bildstock* consecrated to this saint, to the right of the roadside, depicting in naive fashion the dividing of the saint's cloak.

Wildpark Rosegg ⓥ – This wildlife park was laid out almost 200 years ago when the old castle at Rosegg was demolished. A great variety of animals can be seen, such as lynx, monkeys, wolves, deer, mouflons, bison, boar, eagles, falcons etc.
Next to the wildlife park is **Schloß Rosegg** ⓥ, home to a small waxworks museum.
Beyond the Rosegg bridge there are glimpses of the Karawanken range on the border between Austria and Slovenia.

★★ **Velden** – The elegant, long-established spa resort of Velden lies at the west end of the Wörther See. It is impossible to miss the yellow castle right on the banks of the river. This was built as a summer residence (Lustschloß) by the local prince, Bartholomäus Khevenhüller, between 1590 and 1603. It was rebuilt after a fire in 1893, but the 17C plan was retained, especially the Baroque fragment formed by the main doorway, surmounted with obelisks and bearing, on the pediment, the Khevenhüller family arms. It was at this time that the four hexagonal corner towers with their charming lantern roofs were added.
The lively promenade and grand villas lend this town the typical character of a chic seaside resort, further enhanced by its casino.

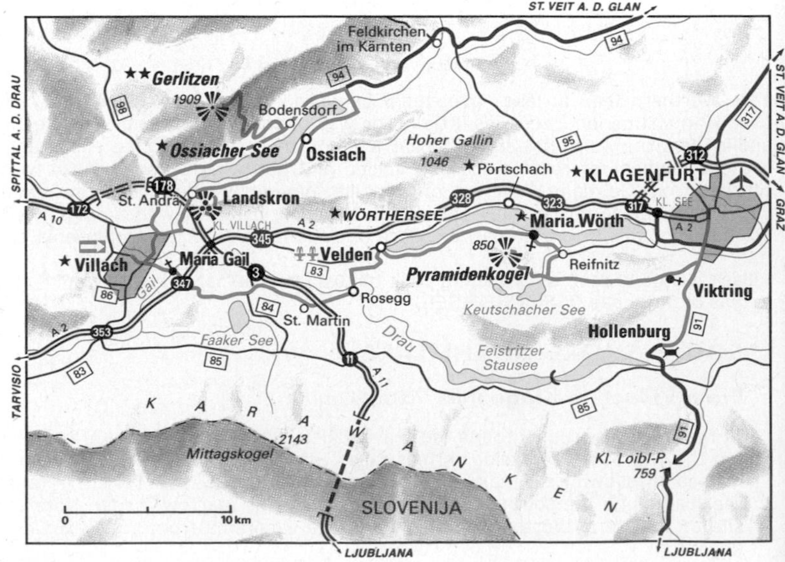

Velden on the Wörther See

★ **Maria Wörth** – The towers of the pilgrimage churches of Maria Wörth, in an idyllic setting on a promontory in the Wörther See, together with the round tower of the charnel house make a picturesque scene. Construction of the Gothic parish church went on from 1399 to 1540, although parts of the original Romanesque building were reused. The high altar of 1685 contains a Virgin Mary and Child Enthroned dating from the late 15C. The Imposing Altar of the Holy Cross with its early-16C crucifix and the pulpit of 1761 complete the interior decor. On the north wall of the chancel hangs a picture of the Madonna painted in 1469, which is a copy of the original in the church of Santa Maria del Popolo in Rome. The crypt is decorated with bright painted floral motifs (17C).

In the chancel of the **"Winterkirche"** are **Romanesque murals**★ from the late 11C, the oldest in Carinthia. Their style echoes Ottonian Romanesque, and they depict Christ in a mandorla (only the head is visible, as a stained-glass window with the Madonna in Glory was added in c 1420) with the 12 Apostles.

★ **Pyramidenkogel** – *Turn right in Reifnitz, and drive 8km/5mi to the Pyramidenkogel. Several parking spaces.* A 54m/177ft high **viewing tower** ⊙ crowns the summit (alt 850m/2 789ft). There is a fine **panoramic view**★★ over the great central valley of Carinthia, the Karawanken mountain barrier and, far to the west, the jagged Julian Alps (Slovenia and Italy). To the northeast lies the Ulrichsberg, looking like a sphinx emerging from the mass of hills. During the Celtic period this was one of the sacred mountains of Carinthia. In the foreground, the peninsula of Maria Wörth juts out into the waters of the lake. *In order to identify the individual peaks more easily, it is well worth buying a panoramic map.*

Viktring – *The entrance to the abbey is at the end of the main street of the village which runs north-south. The approach to the abbey is not very well signposted.* **Viktring Abbey**, founded by Bernard of Sponheim in 1142, is laid out round two vast courtyards with superimposed galleries. It was secularized in 1786.

The church, shortened in 1847, was the only example east of the Rhine to be modelled on the abbey of Fontenay in Burgundy. Thus at Viktring, one finds: the blind nave, with its broken cradle-vaulting extending to the crossing, the arched side aisles in transversal cradles buttressing the main nave, and the deep transepts with their square chapels.

The severity of the reformed Cistercian style was tempered by Gothic additions and alterations during the 14C. Ribbed vaulting was added above the chancel, and the flat chevet was replaced by a polygonal chancel with beautiful **stained-glass windows** (1380-90), which it is still possible to admire, although they are partially obscured by the Early Baroque high altar of 1622. In the 15C, the north transept was extended by a chapel dedicated to St Bernard with net ribbed vaulting. Some remarkable **ceiling frescoes**★ dating from c 1460 were recently uncovered in this chapel and have been restored.

Take road no 91 towards the Loibl pass.

Schloß Hollenburg – The massive Hollenburg fortress commands the Drava Valley, known at this point as the Rosental. The fortress dates from the 14C and 15C. *When the Loibl pass road begins to go downhill, turn off to the left into the road that leads to the castle. Park a little before the entrance to the fortified covered bridge.*

Although the exterior of the castle is relatively sober and bare of decoration, the **interior courtyard**★ with its Renaissance arcades and outside staircase exudes an almost Southern European exuberance. Above the doors and windows are paintings with inscriptions and mottoes. There is a good **view**★ of the Karawanken from the balcony.

Return to road no 91 to enter Klagenfurt from the south.

★ **Klagenfurt** – *See KLAGENFURT.*

ZELL AM SEE✻

Salzburg

Population 7 960

Michelin map 926 – South of fold 19 – Alt 757m/2 484ft

Zell am See enjoys a splendid location on the western shore of the lake named after it, and in the immediate vicinity of the Großglocknerstraße mountain road and the beautiful Kapruner and Glemm valleys (Saalbach). The peaks of the Hohe Tauern in the south, which are covered in glacial ice, the rugged rocks of the Steinernes Meer in the north and the soft Grasberge mountains define the landscape. The lively town has a wide variety of leisure facilities (swimming pool, ice-rink, 36-hole golf course and riding centre) and generous provision for accommodation. Anyone who values tranquillity above all else is well catered for in rural Thumersbach on the opposite side of the lake.

The town centre, with its beautifully laid-out pedestrian precinct, has managed to preserve its own character (Romanesque church, 16C town hall, local museum). In summer, Zell am See is the ideal starting point for hiking trips and excursions *(see below: Pinzgau walk).*

In winter, the Schmittenhöhe massif provides a pleasant **ski area**✻ with fairly gentle slopes at an altitude of between 760m/2 500ft and 2 000m/6 550ft. It consists of two areas (Sonnkogel and Hirschkogel) each of which is laid out in two sections. The

Zeller See

upper sections (above 1 400m/4 600ft) can generally guarantee good snow cover from Christmas to April. The long black-standard pistes, nos 1 and 2, which lead through a beautiful spruce forest, should not be missed.
In order to improve on what it can offer, Zell am See teamed up with **Kaprun**❄ *(see KAPRUN)*. The two towns offer a combined ski pass *(for a stay of at least two days)* for the **Europa-Sportregion** ski slopes, which has the advantage of combining two ski areas with a total of 150km/93mi of piste, which complement each other well.

Zeller See – During the Ice Age, the Saalach glacier dug the transverse breach at Zell and the Saalfelden basin at a soft point in the shale massif. When the ice melted, the offshore terminal moraines prevented the water from draining away into what is now the Saalach Valley. The water remained, so the Zeller See is not fed either by the Saalach or the Salzach. The lake is 4km/2.5mi long and 1.3km/0.8mi wide and has a depth of 69m/226ft in places. Although melt-water drains into it, the lake very quickly warms up to 23°C/73°F in summer. In winter, it generally remains frozen over until March.

Stadtpfarrkirche – Zell parish church, which dates from the 11C, has a beautiful façade in the Romanesque style. The interior bears the imprint of a number of periods, with a Romanesque nave, narthex and aisles in the Gothic style and Baroque ornamental elements. The interesting frescoes from the 16C to the right of the altar and under the diagonal ribs near the choir are worth a closer look.

★★ **Schmittenhöhe** ⏲ – Alt 1 965m/6 447ft. *2km/1.2mi and then a return trip of 1hr 30min, of which 15min is a journey by cable-car. Climb to the summit in a few minutes (orientation map).* Splendid all-round view of the bold limestone massifs (Wilder Kaiser, Loferer and Leoganger Steinberge, Dachstein) and the sparkling glacial peaks of the Hohe Tauern (Großvenediger, Sonnblick, Kitzsteinhorn, Großglockner, Wiesbachhorn).

★★ **Pinzgau walk** – *Allow a good day for this walk of about 6hr, which does not entail any major difficulties or differences in altitude, but which nevertheless demands a certain amount of stamina. A map with a scale of 1:50 000 is needed. Enquire at the tourist office about the departure times of the lifts and of the buses between Saalbach and Zell am See, so that you will be able to return to the departure point in the afternoon without any problems. Take the Schmittenhöhe cable-car very early in the morning (purchase the ticket that includes the descent to Saalbach by the Schattberg-Ost cable railway).*
The path, which can only be taken in dry weather, is among the most famous hikes in Austria. It lies at least 1 000m/3 300ft above the floor of the valley all the way, crosses just under a dozen passes and, on a number of occasions, provides a breathtaking **view**★★ of the surrounding mountains.
Walk down to the Ketting-Hütte mountain lodge and then straight ahead on a footpath which leads through the meadow parallel with the Hahnkopf ski lift. At the summit (alt 1 865m/6 119ft), go down towards the left and walk on along the slope on a narrow path.
Carry straight on at the Kessel pass (leave the track to the Maurerkogel behind on the right), until you reach the Rohrertörl pass (alt 1 918m/6 293ft) – after about 45min. From this point, there is a view over the Saalbach area and, in the background, over the rocky barrier of the Loferer Steinberge.
Walk on past the gap in the gorge and then turn right at the foot of the Hochkogel, and climb up to the Klinglertörl in the direction of Schattberg.
Climb down *(15min)* to the **Hackelberger Seen** (lakes), then take a bend towards the right and walk along Saalbachkogel and Stemmerkogel. At the Marxtenscharte gap, do not continue onto the path opposite, which leads directly to the Schattberg-West, but follow a track which leads round this summit on the right-hand side *(yellow-blue marking)*. After one last climb, you will finally reach the **Schattberg-Ost**★★ *(see SAALBACH-HINTERGLEMM)*.
Travel back by cable-car to Saalbach, and by bus to Zell am See.

ZILLERTAL★★

Tirol

Michelin map 926 folds 17, 18, 30 and 31

The Zillertal is among the most densely populated valleys and most important holiday destinations in the Tyrol. It covers a distance of about 60km/37mi from north to south and stretches from the Inn Valley to the Italian border.
The upper, wide part of the valley lies in easily accessible low mountain countryside. After Mayrhofen, the most important holiday resort in the region, it branches into four narrow valleys (Tuxertal, Zemmtal, Stilluppgrund and Zillergrund), which are delimited, to the south, by the giant crystalline massif of the Zillertal Alps. This mountain chain, with mighty glaciers extending over almost 40km/25mi, is dominated, above all, by the **Hochfeller** (alt 3 510m/11 516ft) and the **Großer Möseler** (alt 3 479m/11 414ft).

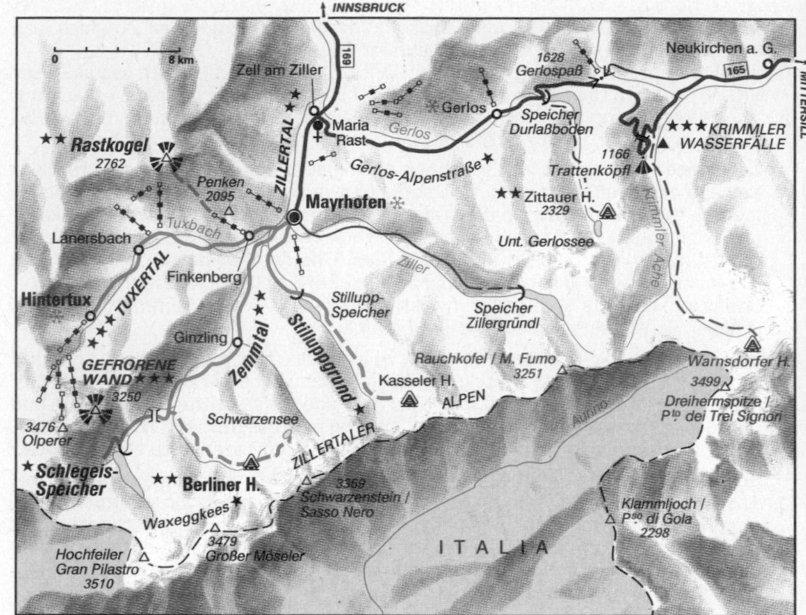

Even in the 19C, the Zillertal, with its unusual and varied landscape, was sought out by large numbers of hikers and mountain climbers.

In the 1920s, dams and reservoirs for generating hydroelectric power were constructed in the Zemmtal, Stilluppgrund and Zillergrund valleys as well as in the nearby Gerlostal.

But the growth in popularity of winter sports has also made a significant contribution to the valley's economic boom. It has unfortunately not been possible, because of the wayward relief of the region, to set up any integrated ski area. Instead, just under a dozen rather scattered massifs of modest size have been equipped with ski lifts. The more interesting sections include the **Tux glacier**✻, **Mayrhofen-Finkenberg**✻, **Gerlos**✻ and **Zell am Ziller**. Ski passes valid for at least four days cover all the massifs, between which there are bus connections. In view of the relatively long distances between the individual areas, however, there are only limited opportunities for switching between them in a single day. Also, because of the low altitude in the floor of the valley, good snow cover is not always guaranteed. The Zillertal Alps are therefore primarily suitable for a more relaxed style of downhill skiing.

MAJOR RESORTS IN THE LOWER VALLEY

Zell am Ziller – Alt 575m/1 886ft. The main town of the Zillertal clusters round its **church**★, which was built in 1782, on a daringly innovative octagonal ground plan. The enormous, lantern-crowned dome above the central section was painted by Franz Anton Zeiller (1716-93) from Reutte, the cousin of the famous Johann Jakob Zeiller *(see Oberes LECHTAL)*. Characters from the Old and New Testament are depicted, grouped around the Trinity, looking impressively majestic.

In May, the entire population of the valley gathers in Zell for the traditional "Gauderfest" festival which is celebrated with a procession, wrestling matches on the town green and the consumption of a 20° proof specially brewed beer (Gauderbier).

Zell am Ziller is not only an ideal winter sports resort for families (Zillertal Arena ski area – Zell, Gerlos, Königsleiten – with 115km/71mi of piste and 47 ski lifts), but also a popular summer holiday destination, as it is the starting point for many walking tours.

The **Gerlos-Alpenstraße**★ *(see GERLOS-ALPENSTRASSE)* which leads into the Hohe Tauern, also starts here.

✻ **Mayrhofen** – Alt 630m/2 067ft. Mayrhofen lies 7km/4mi up the valley from Zell am Ziller and is indisputably the main tourist centre of the region, with its extensive accommodation facilities (guest capacity of over 8 000 in hotels, boarding houses or holiday apartments), its many shops lining both sides of the main road and its excellent sports facilities (swimming pool and ice rink).

The village lies in the final flat, broad stretch of the Zillertal, in an ideal location at the foot of the four valleys of the upper reaches of the valley. For over 100 years it has been highly reputed as a centre for hikers and mountaineers. Peter

Habeler who, together with Reinhold Messner, succeeded in climbing Mount Everest for the first time without oxygen equipment, runs a school for mountaineers here.
Life takes on a particularly lively pace during summer because of the international holiday courses organized by the adult education college, which also ensure that the old customs of the region do not entirely pass into oblivion.
Skiing in winter mainly takes place on the **Penken massif** ⏲ at an altitude of up to 2 250m/7 382ft (76km/47mi of pistes, in conjunction with the neighbouring locality of Finkenberg) and on the Ahorn massif.

★★★ TUXERTAL

From Mayrhofen to Hintertux *19km/12mi*

After Mayrhofen, the valley narrows noticeably and becomes increasingly steeper. Pass through the localities of Finkenberg and Lanersbach at the foot of the Rastkogel massif. The valley broadens out again level with Juns and provides an unobstructed view of the Tux glacier at its head. The road ends in the small holiday resort of **Hintertux**✻ (alt 1 500m/4 921ft).

✻ **Ski slopes on the Tux glacier** – By virtue of its good snow cover and its large differences in altitude, this area is the most interesting for skiing in the entire Ziller Valley. Nineteen ski lifts lead to 86km/53mi of piste at altitudes of between 1 500m/4 900ft and 3 250m/10 650ft. In winter, really excellent snow cover is found only above the first section (alt 2 100m/6 890ft), and in summer, only in the fourth section (alt 3 050-3 250m/10 000-10 650ft). The pistes at the Kaserer lifts, above all, are suitable for moderately good skiers, while the bumpy slopes on either side of the Lärmstange chair-lifts provide good opportunities for experienced skiers.

★★★ **Gefrorene Wand** – Alt 3 250m/10 663ft. *3hr return trip. Ascent by means of two cable-cars and two chair-lifts. Thick-soled, water- and snowproof footwear, warm clothing and sunglasses are a must.*
From the second section onwards, the eye roves over the icicles of the Tux glacier and the rock face which connects Kleiner Kaserer and Armstange.
From the mountain station of the last chair-lift, the view is dominated by the pyramids of the **Olperer** (alt 3 476m/11 404ft) which towers above the gigantic Tux glacier. The barren Alpine setting contrasts with the green floor of the valley, which is dominated by Rastkogel and Kalkwandspitze. When visibility is good, it is possible to make out, to the north, the Kitzbühel Alps, the Karwendel mountains and the Zugspitzplatt. Walk 200m/220yd along the ski piste to a rocky peak in the shape of a bird's head.
There is a grand **panorama**★★★ over the Schlegeis-Stausee (a reservoir), which is dominated by the glacial cirque of the same name and flanked by the Hochfeiler and Großer Möseler. Further to the left, you can see the glaciers of Waxeggkees and Hornkees at the foot of the Tuxerkamm ridge, and also the Schwarzenstein. In the background it is possible to make out the Dolomites (to the south) and also the Stubai and Ötztal Alps (to the west).
From the chair-lift, it is possible to climb up to the Gefrorene Wandspitze peak, from where there is a beautiful all-round view. Anyone wishing to go hiking on a glacier can walk down to the third section *(about 20min)*.

★★ **Hike up the Rastkogel** – *5hr return trip on foot, difference in altitude of about 700m/2 300ft.* Travel up from Finkenberg (alt 840m/2 755ft), initially by cable-car, and then by chair-lift to the **Penken** ⏲ (alt 2 095m/6 873ft) *(buy a return ticket)*. From the mountain station, a track leads gradually up to the Wanglalm. The route then continues upwards to the Wanglspitze peak and past the mountain station of the chair-lift from Vorderlanersbach to the Rastkogel. There is a beautiful view over the valley at a number of points on the way. From the summit, there is a splendid **panorama**★★ over the Zillertal Alps. Note in particular the Lanersbach ski slopes, framed by the Grünbergspitze and Grüblspitze peaks, the Tuxer Hauptkamm ridge, and the Stillupptal (Tristnergipfel summit) and Floitental valleys.

★★ ZEMMTAL

★ From Mayrhofen to the Schlegeis-Speicher reservoir

23km/14mi – toll after 15km/9mi. Allow a whole day, if including the hike to the Berliner Hütte (mountain lodge). The road is open from May to October. The journey can be made by bus from the station at Mayrhofen.
Drive up the valley from Mayrhofen in the direction of Ginzling. Shortly after that point, a stretch of road only practicable in a car cuts its way through narrow, scenic **gorges**★. Anyone travelling in a larger vehicle or wishing to avoid difficult mountain stretches can drive to the left through a long tunnel which, although it makes the journey considerably easier, nevertheless also robs the excursion of a large part of its charm.

After 8km/5mi you will reach **Ginzling**, a peaceful village at the fork of the Floitengrundtal and Gungglta valleys. The journey continues to the Breitlahn car park, which is the start of the famous hike to the Berliner Hütte (mountain lodge). On the far side, our route continues on a single track **toll road**, on which traffic alternates through two long tunnels, as far as the Schlegeis-Speicher reservoir. From the final bends in the road, there is an impressive **view**★ of the 131m/430ft high dam and of the Hochfeiler (alt 3 509m/11 512ft).

★ **Schlegeis-Speicher reservoir** – This artificial lake is the largest in the area, with a capacity of 126.5 million m³/165.5 million cu yd. It lies in a splendid **setting**★ at the foot of the Hochsteller massif and the Schlegeis glacial cirque. The power station, which has four turbines, generates 284 million kWh annually and is linked to the other hydroelectric power stations in the Zillertal to create a generating capacity of over 610 million kWh per annum.

★★ **Hike to the Berliner Hütte** – *Park at the Breitlahn car park (alt 1 257m/4 124ft; charge for parking) by the toll station. Difference in altitude; 800m/2 625ft. 5hr 15min there and back on foot, with no technical difficulties, however the hike requires a certain amount of stamina.*

A large part of the route is covered on a beautiful footpath alongside a mountain torrent. It leads through woods and over Alpine pastures. A good hour's walk brings you to the **Grawandhütte** (mountain lodge) (alt 1 636m/5 367ft), from where you can enjoy a **view**★ of the impressive rock walls of the Großer Greiner and of the Schönbichl Horn with its small glacier, from which high waterfalls thunder down.

Leaving the lodge behind, the footpath gives numerous beautiful **views**★, along the way, of the valley floor, which is dominated by the Realspitze peak and Federbett glacier. On the climb up to the **Alpenrosenhütte**, the vegetation becomes increasingly sparse and the mountain torrent ever more tempestuous. Immediately after the lodge, the magnificent Waxegg glacial cirque, or **Waxeggkees**★, suddenly comes into view. After a further 30min you will finally arrive, up a steep path, at the Berliner Hütte, an imposing mountain hut dating from 1898. It lies amid magnificent **Alpine scenery**★★ dominated by the Großer Möseler, the Waxeggkees and the Hornkees.

Hikers with a particularly high level of stamina may like to carry on towards the **Schwarzensee Lake**. After only 30min, there is a beautiful **view**★ of the Schwarzenstein glacier, the Großer Mörchner and the Zsigmondy peak.

★ STILLUPPGRUND

From Mayrhofen to the Stillupptal waterfall inn

9km/6mi on a toll road. Journey by bus possible.

From Mayrhofen's Hauptstraße, turn off to the left after a small bridge, onto the Ahornbahnstraße. A steeply rising road snakes its way uphill. After passing through a dense wood, this road leads along the slope through small gorges. These are followed by narrow Alpine pastures, crammed in between mighty walls of rock.

The road leads to the far left end of the **Stilluppdamm** (alt 1 130m/3 707ft), from where there is a beautiful **view**★ across the lake. It continues through a tunnel as far as a pretty inn. After this, the road is blocked to traffic. The lake lies in the middle of a rugged, unspoilt **natural landscape**★ and is framed on both sides by a waterfall.

It is possible to travel by bus to the **Grüne-Wand-Hütte** (alt 1 438m/4 718ft) and to hike from that point to the **Kasseler Hütte** (alt 2 177m/7 142ft) in about 2hr.

ZÜRS❄❄

Vorarlberg

Population 130

Michelin map 926 fold 28 – Local map see ARLBERGGEBIET

Alt 1 716m/5 630ft

Until the end of the 19C, the barren erosion valley in which Zürs is now situated remained uninhabited throughout the winter. Because of the risk of avalanches, the route over the Flexenpaß was impassable and the snow cover reached a depth of more than 10m/33ft some years. In summer, the valley merely provided ordinary pasture lands, since the poor soil and the slopes made agricultural exploitation impossible. These initially unfavourable features of the locality (abundant snowfall, steep terrain without vegetation) finally became a decisive plus factor with the growth in popularity of winter sports. After the building of the road over the Flexenpaß, which was completed in 1900, the valley suddenly benefited from a lively influx of visitors. The first ski competitions were organized as early as 1906 for the local residents.

In the 1920s, the pioneers of modern skiing from the Lake Constance area met there. The first ski lifts in Austria were put into operation in the municipality of Zürs in 1937.
After the end of the Second World War, the Arlberg massif was soon regarded as one of the most beautiful ski areas in Europe. Like its neighbouring municipality of **Lech***** *(see LECH)*, Zürs consciously decided to limit its growth in an attempt to preserve the surrounding countryside. That is why the resort still consists, even nowadays, of an unpretentious group of about 20 hotels and boarding houses which blend in with the vast snowfields all around. Its 1 500 beds are generally occupied by a regular clientele to whom the sporting, lively and fashionable character of the place appeals.
Zürs is endowed with international stature thanks to the Arlberg ski pass, which is also valid for the pistes at Lech, Stuben and St. Anton. After a long day's skiing, holidaymakers can get together in the fitness centre (facilities for tennis and squash), the gourmet restaurants and, until the early hours, the famous Zürs discotheque.

SKI SLOPES

Although the ski area at Zürs is by no means vast, it is nevertheless of outstanding quality. Skiers glide along on the abundant, light snow as though on velvet and the pistes are remarkably well managed. The "Rüfikopf", "Family run" and "Muggengrat-Zürsersee" pistes are suitable for beginners, while moderately competent skiers prefer the "Palmen", "Steinmännle" and "Madloch-Zürsersee" pistes. The more proficient skiers can try out their skills on the magnificent **Muggengrat-Täli** piste and the unique run which leads down from the **Madlochjoch** to Lech, giving as an added extra a magnificent **view**★★ over the Lechtal Alps. Besides this, there are wonderful opportunities for off piste skiing alongside the Madloch and Muggengrat chair-lifts.
First and foremost, however, Zürs' location makes it the ideal starting point for excursions into the Arlberg area. The Lech snowfields are a perfect training ground for moderately good skiers, while particularly expert ones prefer to travel in the bus to St. Christoph or St. Anton in order to ski down the steep pistes of the Valluga there. The only drawbacks of the Arlberg district are the lack of skiable links between the individual areas and also the absence of high-altitude peaks.

VIEWPOINTS REACHABLE BY LIFT OR CABLE-CAR

★ **Trittkopf** ⓘ – Alt 2 423m/7 949ft. *Take the cable-car up to this viewpoint. Allow 20min there and back.* Beautiful **view** of Zürs and the surrounding area, towering above which are the mighty crags of Hasenfluh, Flexenspitze and Wildgrubenspitze. The Arlberg pass road can be seen to the south with, in the background, the Verwall group, the Rätikon and the Swiss Alps.

Wiesenhofer/ÖSTERREICH WERBUNG

Zürs am Arlberg

★ **Madlochjoch** - Alt 2 438m/7 999ft. *This viewpoint can be reached by skiers via the Seekopf and Madlochjoch chair-lifts.* View of the Schafberg from the mountain station. The Roggspitze peak and Valluga can be seen in the opposite direction.

★ **Muggengrat** - Alt 2 450m/8 038ft. *This viewpoint can be reached by skiers via the Seekopf and Muggengrat chair-lifts.* Scenic **Alpine landscape**★, from which the crags of Hasenfluh and Flexenspitze stand out in particular. The view stretches as far as the Verwall range to the south, and Lech and Oberlech at the foot of the Widderstein to the north.

Stift ZWETTL

Niederösterreich

Michelin map 926 fold 10 - 3km/2mi northeast of Zwettl

The great Cistercian abbey of Zwettl lies in a bend of the valley of the River Kamp, considered one of the most romantic in the Waldviertel. It was founded in 1137 by Hadmar I von Kuenring as a daughter establishment of Heiligenkreuz, the name being derived from the Slavonic word *"svetlá"* meaning clearing (in a wood). The Kuenring dynasty ruled over the Waldviertel for centuries, and hence also over the abbey, which flourished in the Middle Ages and again after the Counter Reformation. It even survived Joseph II's reforms and the Nazi period unscathed, so that today it still generates a vigorous spiritual and cultural life together with economic activity of great value to the region.

TOUR ⏲

★ **Stiftskirche (Abbey church)** - To the 14C Gothic church, built of granite from the Waldviertel, was added an elegant Baroque **west front**★★ in the 18C, which is decorated with larger-than-life-size statues in sandstone. The slender tower rising from it is 80m/262ft high and topped with an attractively curving roof and a lantern. **Matthias Steinl** and **Josef Munggenast** were responsible for the design, while the execution was handled by Josef Matthias Götz.
The Baroque also dominates in the interior, as hardly any of the original furnishings have survived. The rich decoration even distracts attention from the harmonious architecture of the chancel surrounded by its 14 side chapels. The **high altar**★ is fitted into this polygon and provides the majestic backdrop for a realistic representation of an oak tree, which recalls both the legend of the abbey's foundation - it is said to be built on the spot where an oak grew green leaves in winter - and also the Tree of Salvation, out of which arises Christ in Majesty. The Baroque **choir stalls**★ are richly inlaid and bear gilded vases and statues. The pulpit and choir organ face one another and form a stylistic unity with their bulbous forms. The altarpieces of the side altars are by Martin Altomonte, Paul Troger and Johann Georg Schmidt, the "Viennese Schmidt". Special mention should be made of the Late Gothic Bernhardi-Altar painted by an unknown master in about 1500.

★ **Kreuzgang** - Work on the **cloisters** began in 1204 and was completed in 1240. With its 330 columns on flat bases it is a fine example of the transitional style between Romanesque and Gothic. In the hexagonal *lavatorium*, or washing place, you are surrounded by small columns with crocketed or plain vase capitals.

Kapitelsaal - The **chapter-house** is the oldest part of the abbey, dating from after 1175. Vaulting ribs radiate from a massive central pillar, dividing the room into four bays. The length, width and height of the room are the same, symbolizing the perfection of the New Jerusalem.
The ancient **dormitory** is the oldest surviving Romanesque sleeping chamber.

EXCURSIONS

Schloß Rosenau ⏲ - *8km/5mi to the west.* Originally built in 1593 as a Renaissance castle, it was rebuilt in the first half of the 18C in the Baroque style after designs by Munggenast. Since for a short time there was a Freemasons' lodge here, which was dissolved under Joseph II, it was logical to install the **Österreichisches Freimaurermuseum** (Austrian Freemasonry Museum) in the rooms painted with the symbols of the Freemasons. It gives an excellent insight into the history of the movement. The **Pfarrkirche** (parish church) which is integrated into the building is a gem with a ceiling fresco attributed to Paul Troger. The castle now also houses a hotel and restaurant.

Burg Rappottenstein ⏲ - *12km/7.5mi to the south.* Rapoto von Kuenring built the castle between 1157 and 1176 on the Hohenstaufen model. The **site**★ on a rock high above the valley of the Kleiner Kamp, and the mighty defensive fortifications with five gates and six courtyards, give the impression of complete impregnabil-

Zwettl Abbey

ity. The core of the castle is Romanesque, even if there are later Gothic and Renaissance additions. Today it is still owned by the Abensperg-Traun family, who bought it in 1664. The archive room and the great hall contain remarkable **frescoes**★ from the 16C with scenes of courtly and bourgeois life. The five-sided chapel with stellar vaulting was consecrated in 1379 by the Bishop of Passau.

For more details on the castle's architecture, see Introduction: ABC of architecture.

Salzburg old town and Hohensalzburg

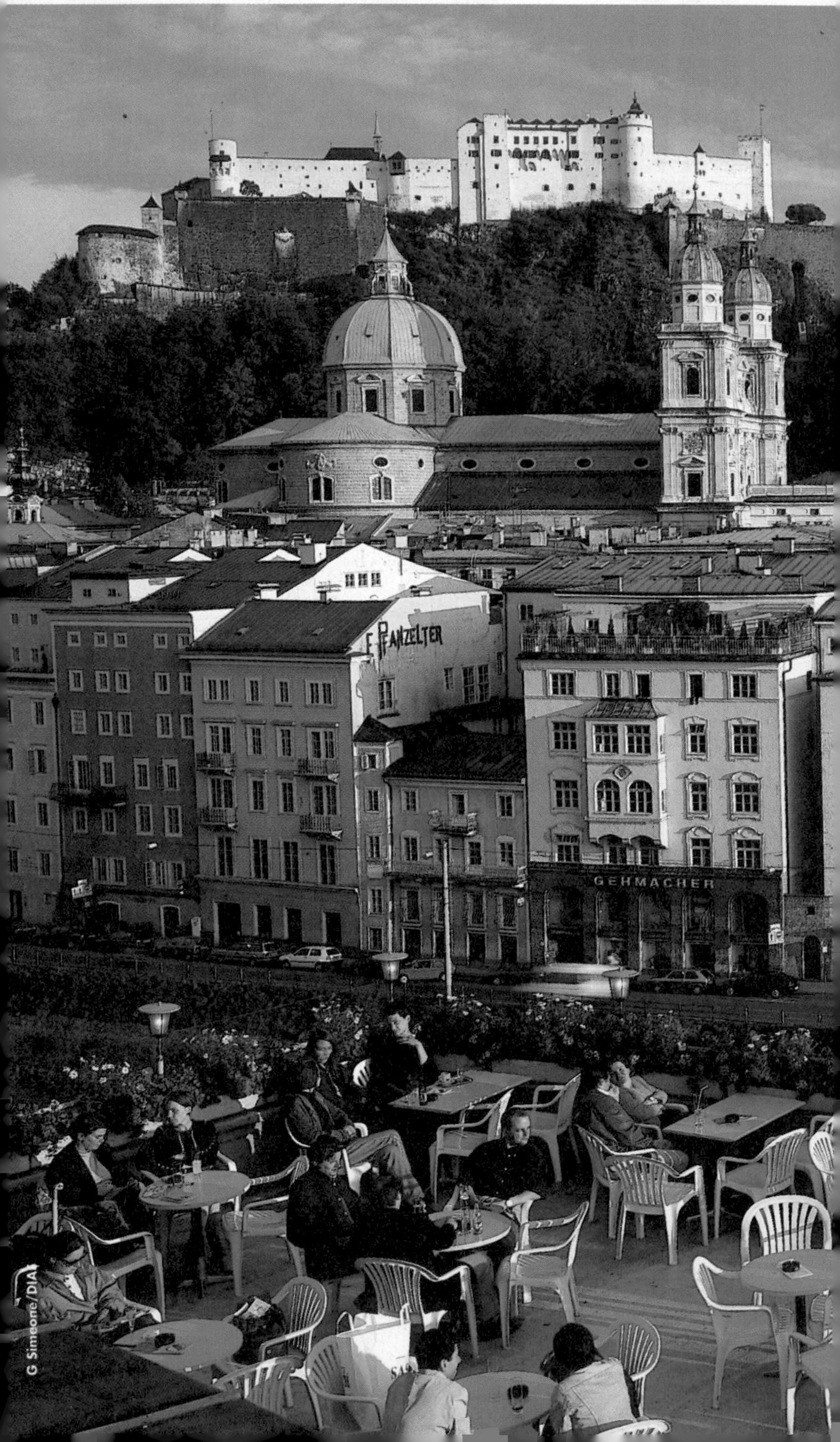

G Simeone/DIAF

Practical information

Organising your trip

The Austrian national tourist office offers information on a whole range of special deals for tourists and other practical details of interest to holidaymakers in Austria.

Austrian national tourist offices

Australia: 1st Floor, 36 Carrington Street, Sydney, NSW 2000, ☎ (2) 9299 3621.
Canada: 2 Bloor Street East, 3330 Toronto, ONT M4W 1A8, ☎ 416-967-3381.
Ireland: Merrion Hall, Strand Road, Sandymount, PO Box 2506, Dublin, ☎ (01) 283 0488.
UK: 14 Cork Street, London W1X 1PF, ☎ (020) 7629 6146, email: *tourism@austria.org.uk*.
USA: 11601 Wilshire Road, Suite 2480, Los Angeles CA 90025, ☎ 310-477-2038.
USA: PO Box 1142, New York, NY 10108-1142, ☎ 212-944-6880.

Web: *www.anto.com.*

Tourist offices of the Austrian provinces

Vienna: Wiener Tourismusband, Obere Augartenstraße 40, A-1025 Wien, ☎ 01/21 11 40, Fax 01/2 16 84 92.
Burgenland: Burgenland-Tourismus, Schloß Esterházy, A-7000 Eisenstadt, ☎ 0 26 82/6 33 84, Fax 0 26 82/6 33 84 20.
Carinthia: Kärnten Werbung GmbH, Casinoplatz 1, A-9220 Velden, ☎ 0 42 74/5 21 00, Fax 0 42 74/5 21 00 50.
Lower Austria: Niederösterreich Werbung GmbH, Fischhof 3/3, Postfach 10000, A-1010 Wien, ☎ 01/5 36 10 62 00, Fax 01/5 36 10 60 60.
Salzburg (province): Salzburger Land-Tourismus GmbH, Wiener Bundesstraße 23, Postfach 1, A-5300 Hallwang ☎ 06 62/66 88, Fax 06 62/66 88 66.
Styria: Steirische Tourismus GmbH, St.-Peter-Hauptstraße 243, A-8042 Graz-St. Peter, ☎ 03 16/40 03 00, Fax 03 16/40 03 10.
Tyrol: Tirol Werbung, Maria-Theresien-Straße 55, A-6010 Innsbruck, ☎ 05 12/5 32 00, Fax 05 12/5 32 03 00; Tirol-Information: ☎ 05 12/72 72, Fax 05 12/7 27 27.
Upper Austria: Landesverband für Tourismus in Oberösterreich, Schillerstraße 50, A-4010 Linz, ☎ 07 32/6 00 22 10, Fax 07 32/60 02 20.
Vorarlberg: Vorarlberg Tourismus, Bahnhofstraße 14/4, Postfach 302, A-6901 Bregenz, ☎ 0 55 74/42 52 50, Fax 0 55 74/42 52 55.

Local tourist information centres – These are indicated by the symbol **i** on the town plans in this guide. Addresses and telephone numbers are given in the Admission times and charges section. Further addresses and details can be obtained from the national or regional tourist offices.

Surfing? In Austria? ... try the Internet!

For a search engine specialising on Austria: *www.austronaut.at*

Official Austrian National Tourist Office Web site: *www.austria-tourism.at*

Further tourist information on Austria, including tips on food: *www.netwing.at/austria*

Accommodation is listed on: *www.tiscover.com* (also weather reports and general tourist information)

Find out more about Austrian mountains (resorts, refuges etc) at: *www.publish.at/trekking*

Details of current snow conditions in Austrian resorts: *www.lawine.at*

Austrian Railways has a web site at *www.oebb.at* and the two main Austrian airlines at *www.aua.at* (Austrian Airlines) and *www.laudaair.com* (Lauda-Air)

Michelin's online route planner can be consulted at: *www.michelin-travel.com*

When to go

Austria, two-thirds covered by mountains, is justly popular for its ski slopes in **winter**. The sweep of resorts, enjoyed equally by those just learning to ski as by the highly skilled, begins on the frontier around the Arlberg pass, itself famous in sporting history. The resources of the Tyrol, the most popular area, benefited considerably from the Winter Olympic Games held in Innsbruck in 1964 and 1976. The Salzburg region is also well developed for skiing, with major resorts such as the Sportwelt Amadé. Styria offers a variety of opportunities for skiers in the resorts of the Dachstein-Tauern and Schladming areas.

In the **spring** the longer days make it possible to ski at a high altitude, and add hiking to the holiday's activities. The season is also enlivened by carnival processions.

Summer is the time for enjoying Austria's mountain scenery to the full and making the most of the varied cultural events on offer. Welcoming Carinthia, with its warm-water lakes, attracts swimmers, water-skiing enthusiasts and anglers. Colder, but more romantic, are the picturesque lakes of the Salzkammergut. Mountaineers will choose the glaciers of the Ötztal or the Hohe Tauern, or the slopes of the Karwendel, the Kaisergebirge, the Dachstein or the Gesäuse.

Autumn, with the sun shining and a nip in the air, sheds a particularly beautiful light on the old stone buildings in the towns. This is a good season to discover the wealth of Austria's museums. The wooded valleys of Styria and Carinthia are a pleasure to explore on foot. Night falls swiftly, however. A journey through the vineyards of the Burgenland or Lower Austria, or along the Danube beneath the Wachau, is unforgettable at this time of year, which is marked in Vienna by the reopening of the theatrical and musical seasons (1 September and October respectively).

Pigneter/ÖSTERREICH WERBUNG

Other important things to remember

Health insurance – British citizens should apply to their local post office for an E111 form (application form included in the brochure Health Advice for Travellers available from the post office), which entitles the holder to emergency medical treatment for accidents or unexpected illness in EU countries. Non-EU residents should check that their private health insurance policy covers them for travel abroad, and if necessary take out supplementary medical insurance with specific overseas coverage. All prescription drugs should be clearly labelled, and we recommend that you carry a copy of the prescription with you.

Inoculation – From April to October there is some risk of contracting tick-borne encephalitis from infected ticks in grassy areas or undergrowth. Areas most at risk are below 1 000m/3 280ft, chiefly near rivers or on parts of the Danube river plains in Lower Austria, Carinthia, Styria and Burgenland. Vaccination is not absolutely necessary but recommended (for example for those planning on camping in such areas).

Telephone – The international dialling code for Austria is 43, so to call from abroad dial +43, then the local code (minus the first zero), then the correspondent's number.

To call abroad from Austria, dial 00, then the appropriate international dialling code (Australia: 61, Canada: 1, Eire: 353, New Zealand: 64, UK: 44, USA: 1), then the local code (minus the first zero), then the correspondent's number.

Telephone cards for public call boxes are on sale at Telekom Austria branches, in designated tobacconist's (Tabaktrafiken) and hotels.

Travelling to Austria

Formalities – Holders of a valid national passport from a member state of the European Union (even citizens of countries adhering to the Schengen Agreement, like Austria, are advised to bring some form of official identification with them), from the USA or from some Commonwealth countries (Australia, Canada, New Zealand) require no visa to enter Austria, and may remain there for up to 3 months (British citizens up to 6 months). Visitors of other nationalities should check with the **Austrian Embassy** whether they need a visa.

Austrian Embassy
18 Belgrave Mews West
London SW1X 8HU
UK
☎ (020) 7235 3731
Web: *www.austria.org.uk*

Austrian Embassy
15 Ailesbury Court
93 Ailesbury Road
Dublin 4
IRELAND
☎ (01) 269 4577

Austrian Embassy
3524 International Court NW
Washington DC 20008
USA
☎ 202-895-6700 or 202-895-6767
Web: *www.austria.org*

Austrian Embassy
12 Talbot Street
Forrest ACT 2603
Canberra NSW
AUSTRALIA
(Postal address: PO Box 3375, Manuka, ACT 2603)
☎ (26) 295 1533
Web: *www.austriaemb.org.au*

Customs regulations – Since Austria became a full member of the European Union in January 1995, EU nationals travelling in Austria are subject to EU regulations (citizens of countries adhering to the Schengen Agreement are in principle not subject to any customs restrictions when entering Austria, also part of the Schengen Agreement since 1998). Tourists are not charged duty on items brought into the country for their personal use. The UK Customs Office produces a leaflet on customs regulations and the full range of "duty free" allowances *(A Guide for Travellers)*; for details contact HM Customs and Excise (London Central office), Berkeley House, 304 Regents Park Road, London N3 2JY, ☎ (020) 7865 4400, Web site: *www.hmce-.gov.uk*). The US Customs Service (PO Box 7407, Washington, DC 20044, ☎ 202-927-5580) offers a free publication *Know Before You Go* for US residents. Further information can be obtained from the Austrian Customs Office in Vienna: ☎ 01/79 59 09.

Travel by air – Scheduled flights are provided by **Austrian Airlines** *(www.aua.com)* from London Heathrow (Austrian Airlines information line at Heathrow: ☎ (020) 8745 7114) to Vienna and on to Linz, Salzburg, Klagenfurt, Innsbruck and Graz; by **British Airways** *(www.british-airways.com)* from London Heathrow and London Gatwick to Vienna; by **Lauda Air** *(www.laudaair.com)* from London Gatwick and Manchester to Vienna and Salzburg; by **Aer Lingus** *(www.aerlingus.ie)* from Dublin to London for connecting flights to Vienna; and by **Lufthansa** *(www.lufthansa.com)* from Dublin to Munich (Germany). Contact your travel agent for details.

Travel by rail – From London Victoria via Dover and Ostend to Vienna (direct), Salzburg (change at Munich) or Innsbruck (change at Sargans). The Orient Express travels from Paris (which can be reached via the Channel Tunnel on Eurostar) through Germany to Salzburg and Vienna.
The Arlberg-Express provides a convenient rail link with the Tyrolean winter sports resorts, stopping at Feldkirch, Bludenz, Langen, St. Anton am Arlberg, Landeck, Imst, Ötztal and Innsbruck.
Details of motorail services can be obtained from DER Travel Service in London (18 Conduit Street, London W1R 9TD, ☎ (020) 7290 1111, Fax (020) 7629 7501, Web site: *www.dertravel.co.uk*), and further information on rail timetables and fares from local travel agents or rail companies. Austrian rail (Österreichische Bundesbahnen) Web site: *www.oebb.at*

Travel by road – Ostend to Vienna (1 238km/769mi) via Cologne, Nuremberg and Linz. Ostend to Salzburg (1 056km/656mi) and Ostend to Innsbruck (1 027km/638mi) via Stuttgart or Nuremberg and Munich. Calais to Bregenz (873km/542mi) via Rheims, Strasbourg and the Black Forest (long non-motorway sections). The shortest land route to Vienna (931km/578mi) involves the long sea crossing from Harwich to Hamburg, then travel via Berlin, Dresden and Prague (long non-motorway sections).
Michelin offers an online route planning service at: *www.michelin-travel.com* (fee-paying by credit card on a secure site (SSL) or by subscription).
Rail-drive services operate between Vienna and Villach (372km/231mi), Vienna and Salzburg (317km/197mi), Vienna and Innsbruck (572km/355mi), Vienna and Feldkirch (731km/454mi), Graz and Feldkirch (607km/377mi) and Villach and Feldkirch (466km/290mi). On certain days, rail-drive operates between Vienna and Schwarzach-St. Veit (385km/239mi), and Vienna and Lienz (476km/296mi). At weekends in summer, the rail-drive services operate into Italy, Slovenia, Croatia, Germany and Belgium. For further details, contact the central rail authorities in Vienna (☎ 01/05 17 17) or consult the Austrian rail Web site.
A rail-drive service also runs through the **Tauern tunnel** (Böckstein-Mallnitz, 8km/5mi). For further details, including fares (200S at the time of going to press) and timetables, contact the stations at Böckstein (☎ 0 64 34/26 63 0) or Mallnitz (☎ 0 47 84/60 03 83).

Travelling in Austria

Embassies and consulates

Australia
Embassy: Australian Embassy, 3rd floor Winterthur House, Mattiellistraße 2, A-1040 Wien, ☎ 01/512 85 80, Web site: *dima-vienna@dfat.gov.au.*

Ireland
Embassy: Embassy of Ireland, Hilton Center, Landstraßer Hauptstraße 2, A-1030 Wien, ☎ 01/715 42 46/7.

UK
Embassy: Royal British Embassy, Jaurèsgasse 12, A-1030 Wien, ☎ 01/7161 35151.

USA
Embassy: United States Embassy, Boltzmanngasse 16, A-1090 Wien, ☎ 01/31 339, Web site: *www.usembassy-vienna.at.*

Motoring information

Documents – It is necessary to have a valid driving licence (preferably an international driving licence), and third party insurance cover is compulsory. Drivers are advised to obtain the International Green Card from insurance companies.

Highway Code – Traffic in Austria drives on the right. Seat belts must be worn. Children under the age of 12 and less than 1.5m/4ft 11in in height must travel in appropriate and approved booster seats. It is compulsory to carry a first aid kit and emergency triangle. The blood alcohol limit is 0.5ml/g. The use of mobile telephones inside a moving vehicle is only permitted if you have a hands-free set.

Speed limits – 130kph/80mph on motorways/highways, 100kph/62mph on other roads, and 50kph/31mph in built-up areas (in Graz, generally only 30kph/18.5mph and 50kph/31mph on roads with right of way). Private cars towing a load in excess of 750kg/1 650lb must not exceed 100kph/62mph on motorways/highways, 80kph/50mph on other roads and 50kph/31mph in built-up areas.

Breakdown service – This is provided *(small charge for non-members)* by two Austrian automobile clubs:
ÖAMTC (Österreichischer Automobil-, Motorrad- und Touring Club, Schubertring 1-3, A-1010 Wien, ☎ 01/71 19 97), breakdown number ☎ 120;
and **ARBÖ** (Auto-, Motor- und Radfahrerbund Österreich, Mariahilfer Straße 180, A-1150 Wien, ☎ 01/89 12 10), breakdown number ☎ 123.

Motorway tolls (**Autobahngebühren**) – Since 1 January 1997, tolls have been levied on motorways, dual carriageways and urban highways in Austria. Motorists must buy a toll disc (vignette, or "Pickerl"), to be displayed in the centre or on the left of their windscreen (the discs are not valid if not displayed). Vignettes are available for one year (from December until the end of the January of the year after next, cost 550S), two months (150S) and ten days (70S, valid from a day of the motorist's choice). No extra vignettes are required for trailers/caravans; camper vans are charged the same as a car. Vignettes can be bought from Austrian motoring associations (ARBÖ, ÖAMTC), larger petrol stations, post offices and tobacconists' and at the border crossing points.

Additional tolls – These are levied on certain stretches of road not covered by the vignette:
★ **Arlberg-Straßentunnel** (information line ☎ 0 54 46/20 66 67; toll for car 130S);
★ **Brenner-Autobahn (motorway)** (☎ 05 12/52 01 20; total stretch 110S);
★ **Felbertauernstraße** (☎ 0 48 75/8 80 67; 140S);
★ **Gerlos-Alpenstraße** (☎ 06 62/8 73 67 30; 90S);
★ **Großglockner-Hochalpenstraße** (☎ 06 62/8 73 67 30; 350S);
★ **Karawankentunnel** (☎ 0 42 53/26 60; 90-135S);
★ **Pyhrn-Autobahn** (☎ 03 16/6 07 30; total stretch 180S);
Silvretta-Hochalpenstraße (☎ 0 55 58/83 07; 150S);
★ **Tauernautobahn** (☎ 06 62/62 05 11; total stretch 140S);
Timmelsjoch-Hochalpenstraße (☎ 05 12/58 19 70; one-way 85S);
Bahnverladung Tauernschleuse (Tauern tunnel rail-drive) (☎ 0 64 34/26 63 0 or 0 47 84/60 03 83; one-way 200S).
The tollroads marked ★ above offer a season ticket (Wertkarte) scheme for cars and motor cyclists. This ticket costs 800S and is valid for 18 months on the above stretches of road giving reductions of up to one third of normal toll rates. It can be bought from any toll point.
Failure to pay the toll is punished by a heavy fine or even court proceedings.

Traffic reports – These are given on the hour, after the news bulletin, on radio station Ö3. Information on traffic and road conditions is also available on the ÖAMTC's recorded message service ☎ 01/1 75 20.

Route planning – The **Michelin map** 926 (scale 1:400 000) covers the whole country and gives details of likely road closures in winter. The hikers' maps published by Freytag and Berndt are useful for more detailed exploration.

Car hire – Car-hire firms:

Avis	☎ 01/5 87 62 41
Budget	☎ 0 72 42/77 77 425
Europcar	☎ 01/7 40 50 40 00 or 0800 0800 800 (freephone from Austria)
Hertz	☎ 01/7 95 32
Sixt	☎ 01/5 03 66 16

Driving in winter – In snowy conditions winter tyres should be fitted, or chains if conditions are particularly severe. The ÖAMTC and ARBÖ have snow chain rental outlets in every Austrian province.

Winter closures – In winter the following passes and tollroads are closed:

Pass	**Linking**
Bielerhöhe	Partenen – Galtür
Furkajoch	Laterns – Damüls
Großglockner-Hochalpenstraße	Ferleiten – Heiligenblut
Hahntennjoch	Boden – Imst
Sölker Paß	Gröbming – Murau
Timmelsjoch	Obergurgl – St. Leonhard im Passeier Tal

Tollroad	**Toll point**
Breitlahner Schlegeis-Stausee	Ginzling/Mayrhofen
Maltatal-Hochalmstraße	Fallerhütte – Kölnbreinsperre
Silvretta-Hochalpenstraße	Galtür – Partenen
Sölden-Rettenbachstraße	Ötztaler Gletscher
Timmelsjochstraße	Gurgl

Caravans – Some mountain roads have gradients steeper than 20% (1 in 5), as well as very narrow stretches. Steep gradients are indicated on Michelin map 926, which also gives dates of likely road closures in winter. Stretches of road which seemingly present no particular difficulties (such as the approach roads to the Tauerntunnel) may be unsuitable for caravans because of the heavy volume of traffic they carry.
The table below indicates the most difficult stretches on the various access routes across the Alps (east to west).

Name of pass	Altitude (metres)	Route	Michelin map 926 fold no	★ road barred ● not recommended
Seefelder Sattel *(1)*	1 180	Innsbruck - Mittenwald	⑯	★
Rottenmanner Tauern	1 265	Oberes Murtal - Ennstal	㉒	●
Aflenzer Seeberg	1 254	Mariazell - Aflenz	㉓	●
Präbichl	1 227	Ennstal - Leoben	㉓	●
Bielerhöhe	2 036	Silvrettastraße	㉘	★
Hochtannbergpaß	1 679	Reutte - Dornbirn	㉘	●
Timmelsjoch *(2)*	2 474	Ötztal - Italy	㉙	★
Gerlospaß *(3)*	1 507	Zell am Ziller - Zell am See	㉛	★
Hochtor	2 505	Großglockner - Hochalpenstraße	㉜	★
Kartitsch-Sattel	1 529	Kötschach - Sillian	㉜	●
Radstädter Tauernpaß *(4)*	1 739	Radstadt - St. Michael im Lungau	㉝	●
Katschberg *(5)*	1 641	St. Michael im Lungau - Spittal an der Drau	㉞	●
Turracher Höhe	1 793	Murtal - Carinthian lakes	㉞	●
Loibltunnel	1 067	Klagenfurt - Slovenia	㉟	●
Gaberl-Sattel *(5)*	1 551	Direct link: Oberes Murtal - Graz	㊱	★★

(1) Easy access to Seefeld when heading from Mittenwald to Innsbruck.
(2) Access for caravans less than 3.4m/11ft high along the Ötztal as far as Untergurgl.
(3) Easy access to the Gerlos pass and to Gerlos heading east-west.
(4) We recommend taking the A 10 motorway.
(5) Inaccessible in winter; not recommended in summer.

Austrian Rail (ÖBB) Card

This rail card (1 290S) is valid for one year and entitles the holder to reductions of 50% on standard ÖBB rail fares (luggage and cycles are also up to half the price), as well as a range of additional advantages such as special discounts in hotels and car rental agencies. There are also special family rates available. The rail card ("Vorteilscard") is on sale at Austrian railway stations and travel agencies with ticket sales facilities and some mainline stations abroad. For further details call ☎ 01/9 30 00 3 64 57 or consult the Internet *(www.oebb.at)*.

Special rates

The following cities and regions offer special discount tickets covering a range of leisure and cultural activities, besides transport: Innsbruck ("Innsbruck Card", *see p 143*), Carinthia ("Kärnten Card", *see p 169*), Linz ("Linz City Ticket", *see p 193*), Salzburg ("Salzburg Card", *see p 247*), Salzburg region ("Salzburger Sommerjoker", *see p 247*) and Vienna ("Wien-Karte", *see p 327*).
The Lower Austrian ski slopes also offer a special discount ticket (**Niederösterreich-Winter-Vorteilscard**), giving 20% reduction on the cost of ski passes for the 21 Lower Austrian ski areas. This costs 1 600S and can be purchased from the ski pass sales offices. They work on a points system, and any points not used can be carried over to the following season. For further details call ☎ 0 26 64/ 25 39.

Steam engines and tourist trains

Steam engines and tourist trains operate in many regions all year round, but predominantly during the summer season. These offer a pleasant and relaxing way of discovering some of Austria's most beautiful natural regions. Further information is available from Erlebnis Bahn & Schiff Österreich, whose catalogue can be obtained from Urlaubsinformation Österreich, Margaretenstraße 1, A-1040 Wien, ☎ 01/5 87 20 00, or consult the Internet *(www.erlebnis-bahn-schiff.at)*.

Tourism for the handicapped

Special deals for wheelchair users and the visually impaired are summarised in the brochure *Tirol ohne Handicap*, which can be requested from the Austrian national tourist office or the Tyrolean tourist office. Information is also available on the Internet *(www.tiscover.com/handicap)*.
Another brochure gives details of rural guesthouses with special facilities for the handicapped *(Urlaub am behindertenfreundlichen Bauernhof)*. This is also available free of charge from the tourist office.

Other important general information

Currency – Until the introduction of the Euro in coin and note form in January 2002 and for a six-month transition period thereafter, the physical unit of currency in Austria is the Schilling (S), subdivided into 100 Groschen. Austrian notes are available to the value of 5 000, 1 000, 500, 100, 50 and 20 Schillings, and coins to the value of 500, 100, 50, 25, 20, 10 and 5 Schillings, and 50, 10 and 5 Groschen. The Euro was officially introduced in January 1999 and therefore appears on price labels etc.
Travellers' cheques and foreign currency can be changed into Austrian Schillings at banks, bureaux de change, and in some travel agencies and hotels. Credit cards such as Visa and MasterCard are generally accepted throughout Austria, although it is probably worth checking before making your purchases.
Banks are generally open 8am-12.30pm and 1.30-3pm on Mon, Tues, Wed and Fri, and 8am-12.30pm and 1.30-5.30pm on Thur. Banks are closed at weekends.

Post offices – Post offices (where currency can also be changed) are generally open Mon-Fri 8am-noon and 2-6pm. Cash-desks close at 5pm. A small number of post offices open on Sat 8am-10am. One or two main post offices in large towns and cities are open 24hr/24hr, and sometimes also at weekends, some even on Sundays.
Letters addressed to a destination in Austria should indicate the international abbreviation "A" in front of the post code.
Stamps can be bought from *Tabak-Trafik* outlets. At the time of going to press, the rate for a letter or post card from Austria to a EU destination is 7S.

Emergency telephone numbers
Fire: 122
Police: 133
Emergency calls: 140
Breakdown service: 120 or 123

Opening hours – Shops are allowed to open Mon-Fri 6am-7.30pm and Sat 6am-5pm. Obviously there is variation within these core hours. Shops in popular tourist areas and city centres often have special dispensation to remain open longer (Mon-Fri until 9pm, Sat until 6pm, in some stations and airports daily until 11pm).

Public holidays – 1 January (New Year), 6 January (Epiphany), Easter Monday, 1 May (State holiday), Ascension Day, Whit Monday, Corpus Christi, 15 August (Assumption of the BVM), 26 October (Austrian National Holiday), 1 November (All Souls'), 8 December (Immaculate Conception), 25 and 26 December (Christmas).

Accommodation

Hotels – Austria offers a great variety of hotel accommodation, with facilities for families, cyclists, tennis players, riders and golf players. Lists of hotels can be obtained from the Austrian national tourist office or from local and regional tourist information centres *(addresses listed on p 398)*.

The Red Guide Europe (for Vienna, Innsbruck and Salzburg) and **The Red Guide Deutschland** (for Salzburg and Bregenz) are revised annually and give a selection of hotels and restaurants based on inspectors' reports.

Farm holidays – These are popular in the Tyrol in particular, and they can often be combined with some sort of course (embroidery, sculpture, riding etc). Themed holiday accommodation on offer includes organic farms and healthy farm holidays. Details available from the Austrian national tourist office or from the Austrian farm holiday association Bundesverband Urlaub am Bauernhof in Österreich (Gabelsberger Straße 19, A-5020 Salzburg, ☏ 06 62/88 02 02, Fax 06 62/88 02 023, Web site: *www.farmholidays.com*).

Camping and caravaning – Lists of sites can be obtained from the Austrian national tourist office or from local tourist information centres. Information can also be obtained from the following Austrian camping and caravaning clubs: Camping- und Caravaningclub Austria (CCA), Mariahilfer Straße 180, A-1150 Wien, ☏ 01/89 12 12 22; and Österreichischer Campingclub (ÖCC), Schubertring 1-3, A-1010 Wien, ☏ 01/7 13 61 51.

Youth hostels – There are youth hostels in numerous locations throughout Austria, open to holders of an international youth hostelling membership card (which can be bought *in situ*). Booking is recommended. Addresses can be obtained from the Austrian national tourist office or the Austrian youth hostel association (Österreichischer Jugendherbergsverband, Schottenring 28, A-1010 Wien, ☏ 01/5 33 53 53, Web site: *www.oejhv.or.at*).

"Schlank & Schön in Österreich" – Health, beauty treatments, stress management and relaxation are the goals of the "Schlank & Schön" ("Slim and Beautiful") organisation. The catalogue is available from the Austrian national tourist office or directly from "Schlank & Schön in Österreich" (Hauptstraße 203, A-9210 Pörtschach, b 0 42 72/36 20 40, Web site: *www.tiscover.com/schlankundschoenhotels*).

Recreation

Map of places to stay

The map of places to stay below shows the principal Austrian holiday resorts (spas, winter sports and mountain resorts).

Casinos

There are casinos at Baden (near Vienna), Badgastein, Bregenz, Graz, Innsbruck, Kitzbühel, Kleinwalsertal, Linz, Salzburg, Seefeld in Tirol, Velden and Vienna. Further information is available from Casinos Austria AG (Dr.-Karl-Lueger-Ring 14, A-1015 Wien, ☎ 01/53 44 00, Web site: *www.casinos.at*).

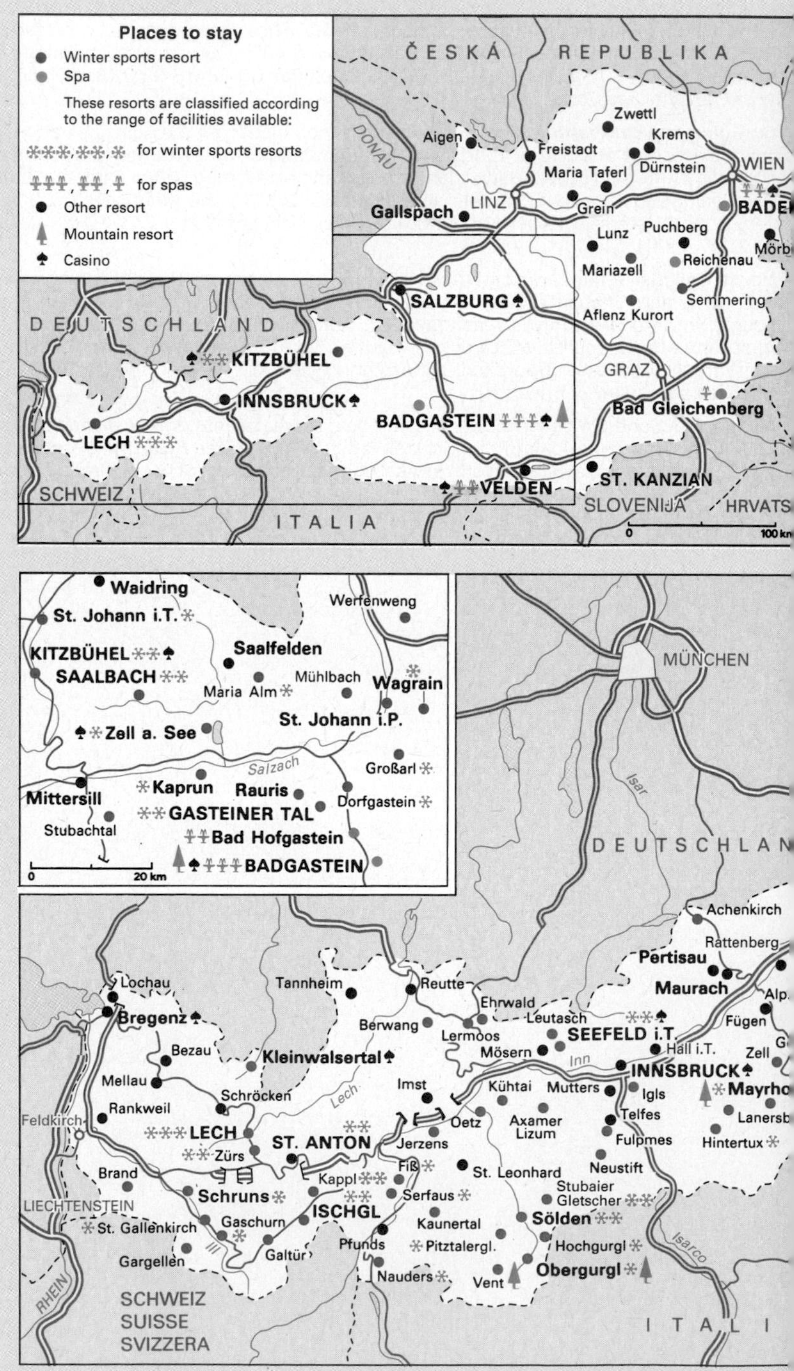

Spas

Austria has a wide selection of spa resorts equipped for the most varied treatment. In the skiing season many of these spa resorts (such as Badgastein) keep their thermal baths open.

Sulphur springs – These are used mainly to remedy ailments of the joints, muscles, the nervous system and skin troubles at resorts such as Baden whose thermal beach draws many Viennese and, in the Salzkammergut, at Bad Ischl and Bad Goisern.

Salt springs – Waters impregnated with sodium chloride (salt) from natural springs or "mother-waters", the residues of the refining of industrial salt, are exploited alongside the salt mines themselves. They are used in douches and baths and are good for gynecological and infantile diseases, and for inhaling, when they clear the bronchial tubes. To this group may be added the bicarbonate bearing waters, like those of Bad Gleichenberg in Styria, which are also recommended for drinking to treat the stomach, intestines and kidneys.

Iodized springs – These are invaluable for curing metabolic and circulatory disorders, and for vision and glandular troubles. They are particularly well represented by Bad Hall in Upper Austria. In addition to the true mineral springs, some hot springs such as those at Badgastein also have radioactive properties.

The Austrian national tourist office issues a brochure entitled *Von Körper, Geist und Seele empfohlen* listing establishments offering various treatments (spa, thermal baths, Kneipp etc) with a brief description of each health centre. Regional tourist offices can provide specialised lists of spa resorts in their area.
Further details can also be obtained from the Österreichischer Heilbäder- und Kurorteverband, Josefsplatz 6, A-1010 Wien, ☎ 01/512 19 04, Fax 01/512 86 39.

The Great Outdoors

National parks

Five national parks have been set up in Austria in which visitors can appreciate nature at its unspoiled best: rare flora and fauna, magnificent scenery, footpaths far from the beaten track etc.

Nationalpark Hohe Tauern (Carinthia, Salzburg province, Tyrol) – The park authorities offer excursions, slide shows and other events such as "children's days" or Alpine rambles. Contact:
Regionalverband Nationalpark Hohe Tauern, A-5722 Niedernsill, ☎ 0 65 48/84 170;

H. W. Partaj/BILDAGENTUR BUENOS DIAS

Reed banks by the Neusiedler See

Nationalparkverwaltung Kärnten, A-9843 Großkirchheim, ☎ 0 48 25/61 61 14; Nationalparkverwaltung Tirol, A-9971 Matrei in Osttirol, ☎ 0 48 75/51 610.

Nationalpark Neusiedler See–Seewinkel (Burgenland) – This is the only nature reserve of the steppes in central Europe. It offers guided excursions, tours in horse-drawn carts, on horse-back or by bicycle. A must for keen bird-watchers.
Contact:
Nationalpark Neusiedler See-Seewinkel, Informationszentrum, A–7142 Illmitz, ☎ 0 21 75/34 42.

Nationalpark Nockberge (Carinthia) – This national park lies between the Lieser Valley and the Turracher Höhe range, and is characterised by its gently undulating hills of crystalline rock ("Nocken"). It was designated a nature reserve to protect its eco-system.
Contact:
Nationalparkverwaltung Nockberge, A-9565 Ebene Reichenau 22, ☎ 0 42 75/66 50.

Nationalpark Kalkalpen (Upper Austria) – This park in the Pyhrn-Eisenwurzen region extends as far as the High Alps. It runs a varied programme of events for walkers of all levels of experience and fitness.
Contact:
Nationalpark-Infostelle Großraming, A-4463 Großraming, ☎ 0 72 54/84 14; Nationalpark-Infostelle Windischgarsten, A-4580 Windischgarsten, ☎ 0 75 62/61 37.

Nationalpark Thayatal (Lower Austria) – This cross-border park has been set up as a joint venture with the Czech Republic. The Thaya Valley cuts a deep incision into the ancient rock of the mountains, forming a breach.
Contact:
Amt der Niederösterreichischen Landesregierung, Abt. Naturschutz, A-3100 St. Pölten, ☎ 0 27 42/200 52 38.

Nationalpark Donau-Auen (Lower Austria) – This 11 000ha/27 200 acre park stretches from just east of Vienna to the Slovakian border and is home to a tremendous variety of flora and fauna, earning it the nickname of "Central Europe's rainforest". Its unique features can be discovered on foot or by boat.
Contact:
Nationalpark Donau-Auen, Fadenbachstraße 1, A-2304 Orth an der Donau, ☎ 0 22 12/34 50.

Nature parks

The 30 Austrian nature parks are also conservation areas, maintained by controlled land use designed to protect the environment. Further details are available from the Verband der Naturparke Österreichs (Albertastraße 10, A-8010 Graz, ☎ 03 16/31 88 48 99) or on the Internet *(www.naturparke.at)*.

Bird-watching

Burgenland: Neusiedler See; Seewinkel/Lange Lacke; veterinary care centre for storks and other birdlife at Parndorf (A-7111).
Carinthia: Eagle observation point from the castle ruins at Landskron; bird reserve on Großedlinger Lake (near Wolfsberg); Völkermarkter reservoir.
Lower Austria: Danube, March and Thaya river plains; Thaya Valley near Hardegg.
Salzburg (province): Pinzgau (between the Gastein and Habach valleys); Zeller See (south shore of the lake).
Styria: Mur reservoir (southern Styria).
Upper Austria: Danube plain in the Linz Valley; Schmiding bird reserve.

Angling

On the whole, two fishing permits are required: one valid for the whole province and the other a local, private one from the owner of the stretch of water. Further information from Fischwasser Österreichs, Congreß-Center, Hauptstraße 203, A-9210 Pörtschach, ☎ 0 42 72/36 20 30, which also issues a free brochure listing places to fish in Austria.

Water sports and boating on lakes

Austria boasts no fewer than 1 000 lakes, 200 of which are to be found in Carinthia alone. For information on water temperature for bathing: ☎ 01/15 28 (recorded message May-Oct) or ☎ 01/89 12 17 (ARBÖ information service).

From mid May to the end of September, there are regular passenger boat or ferry services on some of the larger lakes, such as the Achensee, the Attersee, Lake Constance, the Hallstätter See, the Ossiacher See, the Traunsee, the Wörthersee and the Wolfgangsee. Details are available from Erlebnis Bahn & Schiff Österreich, whose catalogue can be obtained from Urlaubsinformation Österreich, Margaretenstraße 1, A-1040 Wien, ☎ 1/ 5 87 20 00, or consult the Internet *(www.erlebnis-bahn-schiff.at)*.

In almost all cases, it is possible to row, sail, surf, water ski or quite simply swim in Austria's lakes. Further information on these possibilities is provided by the tourist offices of the lakeside communities.

R. Chéret/MICHELIN

Ossiacher See

Boat trips on the Danube - From early April to the end of October, boat trips on the Danube are organized by the companies DDSG Blue Danube, Ardagger and Wurm & Köck. Further details are available from DDSG Blue Danube Schiffahrt GmbH, Friedrichstraße 7, A-1010 Wien, ☎ 01/58 88 00; Donauschiffahrt Ardagger, A-3321 Ardagger 155, ☎ 0 74 79/6 46 40; and from Donauschiffahrt Wurm & Köck, Untere Donaulände 1, A-4020 Linz, ☎ 07 32/78 36 07, or Höllgasse 26, D-94032 Passau (Germany), ☎ +49/8 51/92 92 92.

White water sports and canyoning

Rafting is only permitted from 1 May to 31 October. Rafting and canyoning are prohibited in the Hohe Tauern national park.

Rivers on which it is possible to go rafting are:

- in **Carinthia**, the Gail, Gurk, Isel, Lieser and Möll;
- in **Lower Austria**, the Enns, March, Salza and Thaya;
- in the province of **Salzburg**, the Enns, Lammer, Mur, Saalach and Salzach;
- in **Styria**, the Enns and Salza;
- in the **Tyrol**, the Gerolsbach, Inn, Isel, Ötztaler and Tiroler Ache, Sanna and Ziller;
- in **Upper Austria**, the Enns, Steyr and Traun.

Further information is available from the Österreichischer Kanuverband, Giesereisstraße 8, A-5280 Braunau, ☎ 0 77 22/81 600, Fax 0 77 22/82 600.

Hang-gliding and paragliding

Venues for hang-gliding and paragliding include:

Carinthia - Bad Kleinkirchheim, Katschberg, Seeboden;
Salzburg - Dorfgastein, Golling-Werfenweng, Mattsee, Salzburg;
Styria - Graz, Gröbming, Ramsau am Dachstein;
Tyrol - Galtür, Hall, Kössen, Lienz, Neustift im Stubaital, Niederau, Seefeld;

Upper Austria – Hinterstoder, Leonstein, Linz, Spital am Pyhrn, Weyregg;

In the **Vorarlberg** region, paragliding is permitted from certain mountain summits and following prescribed routes only.
Further information is available from Österreichischer Aero-Club, Prinz-Eugen-Straße 12, A-1040 Wien, ☎ 01/50 51 02 80, Fax 1/5 05 79 23.

Golf

At the time of going to press, Austria boasts 108 golf courses nationwide: one 45-hole, two 36-hole; eight 27-hole; 59 18-hole and 38 9-hole. There are 121 golf clubs in Austria's nine provinces.
Further information is available from Österreichischer Golf-Verband, Haus des Sports, Prinz-Eugen-Straße 12, Haus des Sports, A-1040 Wien, ☎ 01/5 05 32 45 or on the Internet *(www.golf.at)*.

Cycling

Austria has over 10 000km/6 200mi of cycle paths to offer sightseers on two wheels. One of the most popular is the **Donauradweg**, a cycle path along the banks of the River Danube from Passau to Hainburg (305km/190mi). Details of the full range of cycle paths on offer are available from the Austrian national tourist office in the form of a brochure entitled *Radtouren in Österreich* (including an overview of hotels that cyclists might like to use en route).

Guides to these cycle paths can be obtained from "Radtouren in Österreich", c/o Salzburger Land, Postfach 1, A-5300 Hallwang, ☎ 06 62/66 88. Full details (brief descriptions of routes, useful addresses, documentation, accommodation) can also be found on the Internet *(www.radtouren.at)*.

Cycles can be transported by rail, or hired from some 50 Austrian railway stations. The brochure *Bahn & Rad* available from Austrian Rail (ÖBB) or the tourist office gives details.

Rambling

With a network of about 50 000km/31 100mi of waymarked footpaths, Austria is a hiker's paradise. Ten long-distance footpaths make it possible to explore the entire country on foot, if such is your wish. Three long-distance Euro-footpaths also cut across Austria.
Some villages who promote nature tourism have grouped together as the association of "Österreichische Wanderdörfer" (Austrian rambling villages), Unterwollaniger Straße 53, A-9500 Villach, ☎ 0 42 42/25 75 31, Internet *www.wanderdoerfer.at*. This association issues a brochure entitled *Faszination Wandern* (also available from the Austrian tourist authorities) with brief descriptions of hikes, places to stop for a rest and accommodation.

B. Lamm/VIENNASLIDE

Walking in the Dachstein range

Walking in the mountains – Austria boasts about 680 mountain peaks over 3 000m/10 000ft above sea level and 528 carefully managed mountain huts, offering mountain enthusiasts a wide variety of possibilities for walking and climbing slopes of every imaginable degree of difficulty.

For safety reasons alone, it is essential to plan the route of any mountain excursions very carefully in advance, and to ensure that you have the correct equipment and that you are in a good general state of fitness.

Mountain safety

The mountains, while spectacular, conceal very real dangers of their own, which can catch both inexperienced and experienced ramblers alike unawares. Avalanches, rock-falls, sudden changes in the weather, heavy mists, unstable terrain, the icy water of mountain streams and lakes, loss of orientation on the ground, mistaken judgement of distances – all these can represent great danger to mountaineers, skiers and ramblers. Mists and storms are difficult to anticipate and can manifest themselves unexpectedly even in high summer. At high altitudes, the snow cover remains into early July and snow banks often make north-facing slopes impassable.

You are advised never to set off alone or without having communicated your planned route and estimated time of return to a third party.

Lightning – In rocky countryside the arrival of lightning is often heralded by an electrostatic charge in the air (and one's hair). During storms you should not seek shelter on narrow ridges, or under overhanging rocks, just inside the entrance to caves or in clefts in the rock. You should also avoid standing under isolated trees or near metal objects (such as fences). Crampons and ice-axes should not be carried on your person. If possible, you should put at least 15m/49ft between yourself and any outcrop (such as a tree or a rock) and remain in a crouched position with your knees well drawn up to your chest and any exposed areas of skin (such as your hands) not touching any rock. During storms, the car is an excellent refuge, as it acts as a Faraday cage (electrostatic screen).

Mountain climbing

Mountain guides and climbing schools are to be found in the following areas:

Carinthia: Ferlach, Gmünd, Großkirchheim, Heiligenblut, Kolbnitz, Kötschach-Mauthen, Spittal an der Drau, Villach;
Lower Austria: Gloggnitz, Puchberg am Schneeberg;
Salzburg: Filzmoos, Kaprun, Maria Alm, Mauterndorf, Neukirchen, Salzburg;
Styria: Bad Aussee, Graz, Ramsau am Dachstein, Schladming;
Tyrol: Ehrwald, Ellmau, Fulpmes, Galtür, Going, Innsbruck, Kufstein, Landeck, Lanersbach, Mayrhofen, Nauders, Obergurgl, St. Anton, St. Johann, Sölden;
Upper Austria: Ebensee, Gosau am Dachstein, Grünau im Almtal, Gschwandt, Hallstatt, Hinterstoder, Linz, Mondsee, Spital am Pyhrn, Windischgarsten;
Vorarlberg: Bartholomäberg, Brand, Lech, Mittelberg, Vandans.

Further information is available from Verband Alpiner Vereine Österreichs, Bäckerstraße 16, A-1010 Wien, ☎ 01/5 12 54 88, Fax 01/51 25 48 84, or the Österreichischer Alpenverein, Wilhelm-Greil-Straße 15, A-6020 Innsbruck, ☎ 05 12/5 95 47, Fax 05 12/57 55 28.

Winter sports

Here are some statistics on winter sports facilities in Austria:
22 000km/13 700mi of ski slopes
147 cable-cars
2 708 ski tows
512 chair-lifts
16 000km/9 900mi of cross-country ski tracks
900 resorts with cross-country ski runs
292 resorts with snow-board runs
500 ski schools with 8 300 ski instructors
250 children's ski schools
500 natural toboggan runs
1 500 curling rinks
14 000km/8 700mi of footpaths cleared of snow

Austrian districts have set up numerous excellent ski areas equipped with an infrastructure designed to appeal to visitors. On request, the tourist offices of ski resorts will send out prospectuses with panoramic maps which clearly indicate the main ski areas.

Year-round skiing is possible at the following resorts:
- in **Carinthia**, Mölltaler Gletscher;
- in **Salzburg**, Kaprun/Kitzsteinhorn;
- in **Styria**, Ramsau/Dachstein;
- in the **Tyrol**, Hintertux/Tuxer Gletscher, Kaunertal, Stubaier Gletscher, Ötztal/Rettenbach-und Tiefenbachferner, Pitztal/Mittelbergferner.

Information on snow conditions:

ARBÖ, Mariahilfer Straße 180, A-1150 Wien, ☎ 01/89 12 17, or on the Internet (*www.lawine.at*).

All the winter sports resorts shown in the following table have ski schools.

WINTER SPORTS RESORTS*(1)*	No of fold on Michelin map 926	Altitude above sea-level of the resort in metres	Cable-cars	Chair-lifts and ski tows	total length in km of ski slopes	distance (in km) covered by cross-country ski runs	Skating rink	Indoor swimming pool	Horse-drawn sleigh rides	Summer skiing
Aflenz-Kurort St	㉓	765-1 810		8	20	18	⛸	1	x	
Altenmarkt/Zauchensee S	⑳	856-2 130	3	24	150	150		5	x	
Badgastein/Sportgastein S	㉝	1 083-2 686	6	25	175	31	⛸	10	x	
Berwang T	⑯	1 336-1 740		14	40	15	⛸	4	x	
Brand V	㉗	1 050-1 920		9	30	36	⛸	6	x	
Brixen im Thale/Westendorf T	⑱	800-1 827	1	12	32	18		1	x	
Dorfgastein S	㉝	835-2 033	3	19	80	20		1	x	
Ehrwald T	⑯	1 000-3 000	3	18	25	50	⛸	7	x	
Ellmau T	⑱	820-1 550	1	12	35	10	⛸	2	x	
Filzmoos S	⑳	1 057-1 645	1	15	32	34		6	x	
Flachau/Flachauwinkl S	⑳	925-1 980	7	45	60	150	⛸	6	x	
Fulpmes/Schlick 2000 T	㉚	960-2 260	2	7	20	15	⛸	8	x	
Galtür T	㉘	1 584-2 297		11	40	45	⛸	2		
Gargellen V	㉗	1 430-2 300		9	33			3		
Gaschurn/Partenen V	㉗	1 000-2 370	4	27	100	30	⛸	6		
Gerlos T	㉛	1 250-2 300		26	70	25		9	x	
Gosau O	⑳	766-1 800	2	35	65	45		2	x	
Großarl S	㉞	920-2 033	3	21	80	15		4		
Heiligenblut K	㉜	1 301-2 902	3	11	55	14	⛸	5		
Hermagor/Sonnenalpe/Naßfeld K	㉝	600-2 004	1	22	101	100	⛸	3	x	
Hofgastein (Bad) S	㉝	870-2 300	4	21	175	37	⛸	10	x	
Innsbruck/Igls T	㉚	575-2 256	3	7	25	25	⛸	15		
Ischgl T	㉘	1 377-2 872	5	36	200	48	⛸	11	x	
Kaprun S	㉜	800-3 029	5	22	50	15	⛸	10	x	⛷
Kaunertal T	㉙	1 273-3 160		8	25	15	⛸	2		⛷
Kirchberg in Tirol T	⑱	860-1 995	1	17	44	30	⛸	7	x	
Kitzbühel T	⑱	800-2 000	4	24	158	48	⛸	12	x	
Kleinarl S	㉝	1 014-1 980		11	120	20		2	x	
Kleinkirchheim (Bad) K	㉞	1 100-2 055	3	29	85	16	⛸	16	x	
Kleinwalsertal/Hirschegg Mittelberg Riezlern V	⑮	1 088-2 080	2	33	80	44	⛸	30	x	
Kössen T	⑱	600-1 700	1	10	25	83		1	x	
Kühtai T	㉙	2 020-2 520		10	40	15		3		
Lech/Oberlech V	㉘	1 450-2 444	5	29	110	19	⛸	15	x	
Lermoos T	⑯	1 004-2 250		19	29	61	⛸	10	x	
Leutasch T	⑯	1 130-1 605		4	9	150	⛸	8	x	
Lienz T	㉜	673-2 250	1	11	55	23	⛸	3		
Lofer S	⑲	639-1 747	2	12	30	50	⛸	6	x	

WINTER SPORTS RESORTS *(1)*	No of fold on Michelin map 926	Altitude above sea-level of the resort in metres	Cable-cars	Chair-lifts and ski tows	total length in km of ski slopes	distance (in km) covered by cross-country ski runs	Skating rink	Indoor swimming pool	Horse-drawn sleigh rides	Summer skiing
Mallnitz K	㉝	1 200-2 650	1	11	36	28	⛸	1	x	
Maria Alm S	⑲	800-2 000	2	33	70	30		8	x	
Mariazell St	㉓	785-1 267	1	6	11	70	⛸	1	x	
Matrei in Osttirol T	㉜	1 100-2 400		6	29	29	⛸	2	x	
Mayrhofen T	㉛	630-2 250	3	20	90	10	⛸	13	x	
Mitterndorf (Bad) St	㉑	812-1 965		21	25	95	⛸	1	x	
Mühlbach am Hochkönig S	⑳	853-1 826	1	22	160	12	⛸	2	x	
Nauders T	㉘	1 400-2 750	1	15	65	40	⛸	6	x	
Neukirchen am Großvenediger S	㉛	856-2 150	2	13	30	35	⛸	3	x	
Neustift/Hochstubai T	㉚	1 000-3 250	4	26	68	124	⛸	17	x	⛷
Obergurgl/Hochgurgl T	㉙	1 930-3 080	1	21	110	17	⛸	14		
Obertauern S	㉝	1 740-2 335	1	25	120	17		10	x	
Partenen V	⑳	1 100-2 370	5	27	100	30	⛸	6	x	
Radstadt S	⑳	856-1 677		10	17	150	⛸	3	x	
Ramsau am Dachstein St	㉑	1 100-2 700	1	20	40	155		5	x	⛷
Rauris S	㉜	950-2 200	1	9	25	43		4	x	
Saalbach-Hinterglemm S	⑲	1 003-2 100	9	50	180	10	⛸	20	x	
Saalfelden S	⑲	744-1 550		5	14	80	⛸	2	x	
St. Anton am Arlberg/St. Christoph T	㉘	1 304-2 810	4	37	260	19	⛸	8	x	
St. Gallenkirch/Gortipohl V	㉗	900-2 370	4	24	100	30		3		
St. Jakob in Defereggen T	㉛	1 389-2 520	1	8	35	26	⛸	2	x	
St. Johann im Pongau/Alpendorf S	⑳	650-1 850	2	26	19	25	⛸	5	x	
St. Johann in Tirol T	⑲	663-1 700	2	16	60	114	⛸	6	x	
St. Michael im Lungau S	㉞	1 075-2 360		11	60	65	⛸	7	x	
Schladming St	㉑	750-1 894	1	23	25	10	⛸	1	x	
Schruns/Tschagguns V	㉗	700-2 380	3	10	40	13	⛸	5	x	
Seefeld in Tirol T	⑯	1 200-2 100	3	18	25	170	⛸	32	x	
Semmering N	㉔	1 000-1 339		5	12	18	⛸	6	x	
Serfaus T	㉘	1 427-2 700	2	17	80	42	⛸	14	x	
Sölden/Hochsölden T	㉙	1 377-3 250	3	30	101	6	⛸	6		
Tauplitz/Tauplitzalm St	㉑	900-2 000		18	25	80		2	x	
Turrach/Turracherhöhe K/St	㉞	1 763-2 200		11	30	25	⛸	3	x	
Tuxertal/Lanersbach T	㉚	1 300-3 250	4	29	126	23	⛸	11	x	⛷
Wagrain S	⑳	900-2 014	6	42	150	35	⛸	3	x	
Werfenweng S	⑳	1 000-1 836		12	25	38		2	x	
Wildschönau T	⑱	828-1 903	2	25	42	30		4	x	
Zell am See S	⑲	758-1 969	6	27	70	40	⛸	15	x	
Zürs V	㉘	1 720-2 450	5	29	110	4		3		

(1) The letter following the name of the resort denotes the Land in which it is situated:

B Burgenland | **N** Niederösterreich | **S** Salzburg | **T** Tirol
K Kärnten | **O** Oberösterreich | **St** Steiermark | **V** Vorarlberg

Souvenirs

LOCAL CRAFTS

Those looking for good quality souvenirs in memory of their holiday should visit the **Heimatwerk**, an official outlet for the work of local artisans.

Burgenland - China (Stoob), basket-weaving (Piringsdorf and Weiden am See), jade jewellery and serpentine marble (Bernstein).

Carinthia - *Kärntner Heimatwerk*, Herrengasse 2, A-9020 Klagenfurt, ☎ 04 63/55 5 75. Costumes, ceramics, carved wooden boxes; wrought iron (Friesach).

Salzburg - *Salzburger Heimatwerk*, Residenzplatz 9, A-5010 Salzburg, ☎ 06 62/84 41 19. Pewter, china, regional costumes.

Styria - *Steirisches Heimatwerk*, Paulustorgasse 4, A-8010 Graz, ☎ 03 16/82 71 06. Printed linens, jewellery (Bad Aussee), carved wooden masks (Mitterndorf), painted pottery (Gams), *Loden* cloth (Ramsau and Mandling).

Tyrol - *Tiroler Heimatwerk*, Meraner Straße 2-4, A-6020 Innsbruck, ☎ 0 51 25/58 23 20. Wooden Christmas cribs, tablecloths and embroidered fabrics, wrought iron; majolica (Schwaz), cut and engraved glassware (Kufstein and Kramsach).

Upper Austria - *Oberösterreichisches Heimatwerk*, Landstraße 31, A-4020 Linz, ☎ 07 32/78 45 62. Painted glassware and painted wooden boxes: hand-woven linen (Haslach); leatherwork, candles (Braunau); wrought iron, steel-engravings (Steyr); china (Gmunden); headdresses and silver jewellery (Bad Ischl).

Vienna - Petit point, Augarten porcelain, embroidered blouses. Viennese bronze and enamel.

Vorarlberg - *Vorarlberger Heimatwerk*, Montfortstraße 4, A-6900 Bregenz, ☎ 0 55 74/4 23 25. Wooden articles, painted glassware, hand weaving; embroidery (Schwarzenberg and Lustenau); candles (Schruns).

Calendar of events

See also Introduction: Traditional Austria

Traditional folk festivals

6 January

Badgastein .... *Perchtenlauf:* carnival procession (every 4 years, next time 2002)

February

Imst .... *Bubenfasnacht:* carnival procession (every 4 years, next time 2002)

Imst .... *Schleicherlaufen:* carnival procession (every 4 years, next time 2004)

Telfs .... *Schleicherlaufen:* carnival procession (every 4 years, next time 2005)

Schleicherlaufen at Telfs

1st weekend in May

Zell im Zillertal .... *Gauderfest*: centuries-old traditional beer festival, including folk music and other traditional events, ☎ 0 52 82/22 81

Whit Monday

Freistritz an der Gail (west of Villach) map 926 fold 34 .... *Gailtaler Kufenstechen:* a joust using a barrel as target, followed by dancing

Corpus Christi (2nd Thursday after Whitsun)

Bischofshofen .... Procession with floral poles *(Prangstangen)*

Brixental in Tirol .... Procession on horseback

Gmunden .... Procession

Deutschlandsberg ...... Procession and carpet of flowers

Hallstatt, Traunkirchen . Processions on the lake

24 June

Zederhaus map 926 fold 18 .... *Prangstangentragen:* poles up to 8m/26ft long, decorated with flowers are carried to the church in a procession and left there until 15 August (the feast of the Assumption)

Prangstangen from Zederhaus

Moetschlmaier/ÖSTERREICH WERBUNG

August

Krakaudorf (early August), Murau (15 August) .... "Samson" processions

End September-early October

Burgenland and Lower Austria .... Wine harvest: processions, wine fountains, fireworks

End November or early December-Christmas

Nationwide .... Advent and Christmas markets

5 December

Bad Mitterndorf map 926 fold 21 .... *Nikolospiel:* street festival in honour of St Nicholas

27 December-15 January

Thaur (northeast of Innsbruck) map 926 fold 21 . Christmas nativity scenes are on display in people's houses, some of which are open to the public

Passion plays

End May

Erl (northeast of Kufstein) map 926 fold 18 .... Every 6 years (next time 2002)

May-October

Thiersee .... Every 6 years (next time 2005)

Festivals *(see also the Travellers' addresses sections under Graz, Innsbruck, Klagenfurt, Linz, Salburg, St. Pölten and Wien/Vienna)*

Holy Week

Salzburg .... Easter Festival

March-April

Graz .... Diagonale: Austrian film festival

May-June

Vienna .... Vienna Festival

May-September

Millstatt .... International music festival

June-July

Innsbruck .... Tanzsommer: summer dance festival

Krems und Wachau .... Danube festival, with a wide range of theatre, dance, music, arts etc, ☎ 0 22 36/21 2 12, *www-.donaufestival.at*

June-August

Wiesen map 926 fold 25	Open-air festivals (reggae, alternative rock, jazz, rock, reggae-Afro-Latin), ☎ 0 26 26/8 16 48

July-August

Ossiach/Villach	Carinthian Summer Festival
Klagenfurt	Musikforum Viktring
Innsbruck	Festival of ancient music, Schloß Ambras concerts
Petronell	Art Carnuntum: world theatre festival, ☎ 0 21 63/34 00
Vienna	Musikalischer KlangBogen

Mid July-end August

Mörbisch	Operetta festival (by Neusiedler See)

End July-end August

Bregenz	Lakeside festival
Salzburg	Salzburg Festival

September

Linz	Festival Ars Electronica
St. Anton am Arlberg	Film festival ("mountains, people, adventure"), ☎ 0 54 46/22 690

1st week in September

Mondsee	Mondsee festival of chamber music and literature, ☎ 0 62 32/35 44

2nd week in September

Eisenstadt	International Haydn Festival in Schloß Esterházy, ☎ 0 26 82/6 18 66

September and October

Linz	International Bruckner Festival
St. Pölten	Musica Sacra

October

Graz and its surroundings ...	Steirischer herbst: Styrian autumn festival

Further reading

A Brief Survey of Austrian History by R Rickett
Chronicle and Works (volume 2) *Haydn at Esterházy 1776-1790* by HO Robbins Landon
Exploring Rural Austria by G Beer
Fin de Siècle Vienna by CE Schorske
Mountain Walking in Austria by C Davies
Music and Musicians in Vienna by R Rickett
The Fall of the House of Habsburg by E Crankshaw
The Habsburg Monarchy 1809-1918 by AJP Taylor
The Kalkalpen Traverse by A Proctor
Unknown Austria (3 volumes) by B Whelpton
Vienna, the Image of a Culture in Decline by E Crankshaw

Literature

Aichinger, Ilse: *Die größere Hoffnung*
Bachmann, Ingeborg: *Malina, Die gestundete Zeit*
Bernhard, Thomas: *Das Kalkwerk (The Limeworks), Die Berühmten (The Famous), Holzfällen (Woodcutters), Heldenplatz (Heroes' Square)*
Freud, Sigmund: *Die Traumdeutung (The Interpretation of Dreams), Das Unbehagen in der Kultur (Civilization and its Discontents)*
Frischmuth, Barbara: *Die Schrift des Freundes*
Grillparzer, Franz: *Das Goldene Vließ (The Golden Fleece), König Ottokars Glück und Ende (King Ottocar, His Rise and Fall), Ein Bruderzwist in Habsburg (Family Strife in Habsburg)*
Handke, Peter: *Die Angst des Tormanns beim Elfmeter (The Goalie's Anxiety at the Penalty Kick), Die linkshändige Frau (The Left-Handed Woman), Publikumsbeschimpfung (Offending the Audience), Wunschloses Unglück (A Sorrow Beyond Dreams)*

Hofmannsthal, Hugo von: *Jedermann (Everyman), Das Salzburger große Welttheater, Der Rosenkavalier* **(libretto)**, *Chandos-Brief* **(essay)**, *Cristinas Heimreise (Christina's Journey Home), Der Turm (The Tower)*
Musil, Robert von: *Der Mann ohne Eigenschaften (The Man without Qualities), Die Verwirrungen des Zöglings Törleß*
Rilke, Rainer Maria: *Sonette an Orpheus (Sonnets to Orpheus), Duineser Elegien (Duino Elegies)*
Roth, Joseph: *Radetzkymarsch (Radetzky March), Kapuzinergruft (The Capuchin Tomb)*
Schnitzler, Arthur: *Liebelei (Playing with Love), Reigen (Merry-Go-Round), Leutnant Gustl (None But the Brave), Der Weg ins Freie (The Road to the Open)*
Stifter, Adalbert: *Der Nachsommer (Indian Summer), Bunte Steine (Colourful Stones)*
Zweig, Stefan: *Schachnovelle, Sternstunden der Menschheit (The Tide of Fortune), Ungeduld des Herzen (Beware of Pity)*

Admission times and charges

As admission times and charges are liable to alteration, the information below is given for guidance only. The information given applies to individual adults (not including special reductions for groups etc).

Every sight for which admission times and charges are listed is indicated by the symbol ⏲ in the alphabetical section of the guide. The information below is listed in the same order as the entries in the main body of the guide.

Churches do not admit visitors during services (other than to worship) and are usually closed between noon and 2pm. Admission times are given if the interior is of special interest. It is usual for visitors to make a donation, especially if accompanied by a keyholder of the church.

The telephone number, and in the case of larger towns the address, of the Tourist Information Centre is given to the right of the place name, and indicated by the symbol ℹ. These centres provide details of guided tours etc.

NB The feast of Corpus Christi is celebrated on the Thursday after Trinity Sunday (8th Sunday after Easter).

A

ADMONT
ℹ Rathaus, A-8911, ☎ 0 36 13/21 64

Stiftsbibliothek – Open Apr-Oct, daily 10am-1pm, 2-5pm; Christmas and school holidays 10am-noon. 60S. ☎ 0 36 13/2 31 26 01.

Museums – Closed for restoration until May 2002. ☎ 0 36 13/2 31 26 01.

Stift ALTENBURG

Stiftsgebäude – Guided tour (1hr) Easter Day-1 Nov, daily 10am-4pm. 60S. ☎ 0 29 82/34 51.

ARLBERGGEBIET

Lünersee cable-car – Operates end May-mid Oct, daily 8am-12.30pm, 1.10-4.50pm on the hour. 90S two-way trip. ☎ 0 55 59/5 14.

Schloß-Museum ARTSTETTEN

Erzherzog-Franz-Ferdinand-Museum – Open 1 Apr-1 Nov, daily 9am-5.30pm. 80S. ☎ 0 72 13/83 02 30.

Bad AUSSEE
ℹ Koloman-Wallisch-Platz, A-8990, ☎ 0 36 22/5 23 23

Ausseer Kammerhofmuseum – Open 15 June-30 Sept, daily 10am-noon, 3-6pm; Palm Sun-14 June, Oct, Tues 3.30-6pm, Fri 9.30am-noon, Sun 10am-noon. 40S (admission free 26 Oct). ☎ 0 36 22/5 25 11 21.

Motorboat excursions – Tour of 3 lakes (3hr) 13 May-8 Oct, daily 10.20am, 11.35am, 1.20pm and 2.25pm. 150S. ☎ 0 36 22/86 13.

Salzbergwerk (Altaussee) – Guided tour (1hr 30min) May-end Oct, daily 10am-4pm on the hour; 16-30 Apr, Oct, daily 10am, noon and 2pm; Nov-Easter, Thur 2.30pm. 150S. ☎ 0 61 34/84 00.

B

BADEN
ℹ Brusattiplatz 4, A-2500, ☎ 0 22 52/4 45 31 595

Beethoven-Gedenkstätte – Open Tues-Fri 4-6pm, Sat, Sun and public holidays 9am-11am, 4-6pm. Closed 1 Jan, 24, 25, 31 Dec. 30S. ☎ 0 22 52/86 80 02 30.

BRAUNAU
ℹ Stadtplatz 2, A-5280, ☎ 0 77 22/6 26 44

BREGENZ
ℹ Bahnhofstraße 14, A-6900, ☎ 0 55 74/4 95 90

Vorarlberger Landesmuseum – Open Tues-Sun 9am-noon, 2-5pm. Closed 1 Jan, 1 Nov, 25 Dec. 20S (admission free 26 Oct). ☎ 0 55 74/4 60 50.

Martinsturm – Open May-Oct, daily 9am-sunset; Nov-Apr, daily noon-5pm. 10S. ☎ 0 55 74/4 66 32.

Excursion

Pfänderbahn cable-car - Operates daily 9am-7pm every 30min (every 6min if busy). Closed 2nd and 3rd weeks in Nov. 125S two-way trip. ☎ 0 55 74/42 16 00.

Bird of prey flight displays - Displays May-3 Oct, daily 11am, 2.30pm. 48S. ☎ 06 63/05 30 40.

BREGENZERWALD

Dornbirn: Vorarlberger Naturschau - Open Tues-Sun 9am-noon, 2-5pm (July-mid Sept daily). 30S. ☎ 0 55 72/2 32 35.

Dornbirn: Rolls-Royce-Museum - Open Apr-Oct, Tues-Sun 10am-6pm; Nov-Mar, Tues-Sun 10am-5pm. 100S. ☎ 0 55 72/5 26 52.

Dornbirn: Rappenlochschlucht - Open mid Apr-late Oct. ☎ 0 55 72/2 21 88.

BRUCK AN DER MUR

ℹ Koloman-Wallisch-Platz 26, A-8601, ☎ 0 38 62/5 18 11

D

DACHSTEIN

Ascent of the Krippenstein - Cable-car operates May-mid Oct, Christmas-Easter, daily 8.40am-5pm every 15min. 260S two-way trip. ☎ 0 61 34/84 00.

Dachstein-Rieseneishöhle - Guided tour (1hr) May-mid Oct, daily 8.30am-4.30pm. 90S. ☎ 0 61 34/84 00.

Mammuthöhle - Guided tour (1hr) mid May-mid Oct, daily 9am-4pm. 90S. ☎ 0 61 34/84 00.

Koppenbrüllerhöhle - Guided tour (1hr) Apr-end Sept, daily 10am-4pm. 90S. ☎ 0 61 34/84 00.

Hunerkogel: Dachstein-Südwandbahn - Cable-car operates June-end Apr, daily 8.30am-4.50pm. 265S two-way trip. ☎ 0 36 87/8 12 41.

DONAUTAL (DANUBE VALLEY)

Burg Clam - Guided tour (45min) May-end Oct, daily 10am-5pm. 80S. ☎ 0 72 69/72 17.

Grein: Rokokotheater - Guided tour (20min) Apr-end Oct, daily 9am, 11am, 1.30pm and 4pm. 30S. ☎ 0 72 68/70 55.

Grein: Schiffahrtsmuseum - Open June-end Sept, Tues-Sun 10am-6pm; May, Oct, Tues-Sun 10am-noon, 1-5pm. 30S. ☎ 0 72 68/70 07.

Spitz: Pfarrkirche - Open Apr-Sept, daily 8am-7pm; Oct-Mar, daily 8am-5pm. ☎ 0 27 13/22 31.

Weißenkirchen: Wachaumuseum - Open Apr-end Oct, Tues-Sun 10am-5pm. 30S. ☎ 0 27 15/22 68.

DÜRNSTEIN

ℹ Rathaus, A-3601, ☎ 0 27 11/2 19

Pfarrkirche - Open Apr-end Oct, daily 9am (10am Sun)-6pm. 30S. ☎ 0 27 11/3 75.

E

Schloß EGGENBERG

State Apartments (Prunkräume) - Guided tour (45min) May-end Oct, Mon-Fri 10am-5pm, Sat-Sun 9am-5pm. 80S (admission free 26 Oct). ☎ 03 16/58 32 64.

Landesmuseum Joanneum, Graz

Strettweg Votive Chariot, Schloß Eggenberg

Abteilung für Vor- und Frühgeschichte – ♿ Open Feb-end Nov, daily 9am-5pm. 60S (admission free 26 Oct). ☎ 03 16/58 32 64 95 71.

EGGENBURG

ℹ Krahuletzplatz 1, A-3730, ☎ 0 29 84/34 00

Pfarrkirche St. Stephan – Church is kept locked. Keys obtainable from the presbytery daily during official hours. ☎ 0 29 84/35 69.

Krahuletz-Museum – Open Apr-Dec, daily 9am-5pm. 40S (admission free 26 Oct). ☎ 0 29 84/34 00.

Österreichisches Motorradmuseum – ♿ Open Mon-Fri 8am-4pm, Sat, Sun and public holidays 10am-5pm. Closed 21 Dec-5 Jan. 60S. ☎ 0 29 84/21 51.

EISENERZ

ℹ Freiheitsplatz 7, A-8790, ☎ 0 38 48/37 00

Erzberg: Opencast mines – Guided tour of exhibition mine (1hr 30min) May-end Oct, daily 10am-3pm. 160S. Trip on the Hauly truck: as for tours of the mine. Joint ticket for mine and truck: 270S. ☎ 0 38 48/32 00.

St. Oswald – Open Easter-end Nov, daily 8am-7pm. ☎ 0 38 48/22 67.

Stadtmuseum – Open May-Oct, Tues-Fri 9am-noon, 2-5pm, Sat 10am-noon, 2-5pm; Nov-Apr, Tues-Fri 9am-noon. 45S. ☎ 0 38 48/36 15.

EISENERZER ALPEN

Chair-lift up the Polster – Chair-lift operates daily 9am-5pm (9am-4pm in winter). Closed Easter-end May, Nov. 90S two-way trip. ☎ 0 38 49/6 06 00.

Vordernberg: Informationszentrum der Steirischen Eisenstraße – ♿ Open May-Oct, Mon-Sat 10am-4pm; Nov-Apr, Mon-Sat 9am-noon. ☎ 0 38 49/8 32.

EISENSTADT

ℹ Schloß Esterházy, A-7000, ☎ 0 26 82/6 33 84 15

Schloß Esterházy – Guided tour Apr-Oct, daily 9am-5pm on the hour; Nov-Mar, Mon-Fri 10am, 2pm. 60S. ☎ 0 26 82/7 19 31 12.

Haydn-Saal – Same admission times as Schloß Esterházy. 30S.

Haydn-Museum – Open Easter-end Oct, daily 9am-noon, 1-5pm. 30S (admission free 26 Oct). ☎ 0 26 82/6 26 52 29.

Österreichisches Jüdisches Museum – Open May-Oct, Tues-Sun 10am-5pm. 50S (admission free 26 Oct). ☎ 0 26 82/6 51 45.

Burgenländisches Landesmuseum – ♿ Open Tues-Sun 9am-noon, 1-5pm. Closed 1 Jan, 25, 26 Dec. 30S (admission free 26 Oct). ☎ 0 26 82/6 26 52.

Kalvarienberg and Bergkirche – Open Apr-end Oct, daily 9am-noon, 1-5pm. 30S. ☎ 0 26 82/6 26 38.

Excursion

Raiding: Liszts Geburtshaus – Open Easter-31 Oct, daily 9am-noon, 1-5pm. 20S. ☎ 0 26 19/72 20.

Höhlen EISRIESENWELT

Caves can only be visited as part of a guided tour (1hr 15min): July-Aug, daily 9am-4.30pm; May, June, Sept-26 Oct, daily 9am-3.30pm. 100S. ☎ 06 62/84 26 90 14.

Eisriesenwelt-Linie – Bus operates 29 Apr-26 Oct, daily 8.15am, 10.15am, 12.15pm and 2.15pm, or every 15min if busy. Journey time: 15min. 70S two-way trip. ☎ 0 64 68/52 93.

Cable-car – Operates July-Aug, daily 9am-6pm; May, June, Sept-26 Oct, daily 9am-5pm. 120S two-way trip. ☎ 06 62/84 26 90 14.

ENNS

ℹ Linzerstraße 1, A-4470, ☎ 0 72 23/83 26 10

Pfarrkirche St. Marien – Open Mon-Sat 7am-7pm (5pm Oct-Apr), Sun 8am-7pm (5pm Oct-Apr). Guided tours possible as part of a tour of the town or by appointment. ☎ 0 72 23/8 28 55.

Basilika St. Laurenz – ♿ Open daily 8am-7pm. Guided tour (1hr) mid Apr-mid Oct, daily 4pm. Parts of the church may be visited unaccompanied. Telephone in advance for guided tours. 30S. ☎ 0 72 23/8 74 12.

F

FELDKIRCH

ℹ Herrengasse 12, A-6800, ☎ 0 55 22/7 34 67

Domkirche St. Nikolaus – Open daily 8am-7pm. ☎ 0 55 22/7 22 32.

Schattenburg: Heimatmuseum – Open Tues-Sun 9am-noon, 1-5pm. 25S. ☎ 0 55 22/7 19 82.

FERNPASSSTRASSE

Ascent to the Zugspitze – Cable-car operates Whitsun-1 Nov, Christmas-1st week after Easter, daily 8.40am-4.40pm every 20min. Journey time: 10min. 430S (summer) or 385S (winter) two-way trip. ☎ 0 56 73/23 09.

Burg FORCHTENSTEIN

Fortress – Guided tour (1hr 15min) Apr-end Oct, daily 9am-4pm. 70S. ☎ 0 26 26/8 12 12.

FREISTADT

ℹ Hauptplatz 12, A-4240, ☎ 0 79 42/7 57 00

FRIESACH

ℹ Hauptplatz 1, A-9360, ☎ 0 42 68/43 00

Petersberg: Stadtmuseum – Open July-Aug, Tues-Sun 10am-5pm; 7 May-end June, Sept-8 Oct, Tues-Sun 1-5pm. 40S. ☎ 0 42 68/26 00.

FROHNLEITEN

ℹ Brückenkopf 1, A-8130, ☎ 0 31 26/23 74

G

GASTEINER TAL

ℹ Badgastein, Kaiser-Franz-Josef-Str. 27, A-5640 ☎ 0 64 34/2 53 10
ℹ Bad Hofgastein, Tauernplatz 1, A-5630 ☎ 0 64 32/71 10

Cable-car up to Schloßalm – Operates June-mid Oct, Dec-end Apr, daily 8am-4pm on the hour. 190S two-way trip. ☎ 0 64 32/64 55.

Chair-lift up the Stubnerkogel – Operates June-mid Oct, Dec-end Apr, daily 8.30am-4pm on the hour. 190S two-way trip. ☎ 0 64 32/64 55.

Tauerntunnel: train connections – Regular train service between Mallnitz and Böckstein: Mallnitz 28 May-1 Oct, hourly 6.10am-11.10pm; 2 Oct-9 June, hourly 6.10am-9.10pm; Böckstein 28 May-1 Oct, hourly 5.40am-10.40pm; 2 Oct-9 June, hourly 6.40am-9.40pm. Journey time: 12min. Price per car: 200S one-way, 320S two-way trip. ☎ 0 47 84/6 00.

Chair-lift up the Graukogel – Operates mid Dec-end Mar, daily 8.30am-4pm on the hour. 190S two-way trip. ☎ 0 64 34/64 55.

GERAS

ℹ Hauptstraße 16, A-2093, ☎ 0 29 12/70 50

Abbey – Guided tour (1hr) Easter-1 Nov, Tues-Sat 10am, 11am, 2pm and 3pm, Sun 2pm and 3pm. 60S. ☎ 0 29 12/9 45.

Markowitsch/ÖSTERREICH WERBUNG

Geras Abbey

GERLOS-ALPENSTRASSE

Krimmler Wasserfälle – The waterfalls can be visited from mid Apr-end Oct. 15S. ☎ 0 65 64/72 12.

GMÜND Kärnten

ℹ Rathaus, A-9853, ☎ 0 47 32/22 22

Porsche-Automuseum Helmut Pfeifhofer – Open mid May-mid Oct, daily 9am-6pm; mid Oct-mid May, daily 10am-4pm. 75S. ☎ 0 47 32/24 71.

GMÜND Niederösterreich

ℹ Weitraerstr. 44 A-3950 ☎ 0 28 52/5 32 12

Burg Heidenreichstein – Guided tour (50min) mid Apr-mid Oct, Tues-Sun 9am, 10am, 11am, 2pm, 3pm and 4pm. 60S. ☎ 0 28 62/5 22 68.

GMUNDEN

ℹ Am Graben 2, A-4810, ☎ 0 76 12/6 43 05

Lake cruises on the Traunsee – Trips on the paddle steamer "Gisela" July-Aug, Sat-Sun 2.30pm from Gmunden, and from other places if the weather is fine. Enquire at the lake cruise office. 190S. Traunseeschiffahrt, Rathausplatz, A-4810 Gmunden; ☎ 0 76 12/6 67 00.

Kammerhofmuseum – Open May-Oct, Mon-Sat 10am-noon, 2-5pm, Sun 10am-noon; Dec-mid Jan, daily 10am-noon, 2-5pm. Closed 24 Dec. 28S (admission free 26 Oct). ☎ 0 76 12/79 42 44.

Excursions

Scharnstein

Österreichisches Kriminalmuseum – Open May-mid Nov, Tues-Sun 10am-5pm. 60S. ☎ 0 76 15/25 50.

Reptilienzoo – Open May-mid Oct, Tues-Sun 9am-5pm, Sat-Sun 1-4pm. 60S. ☎ 0 76 16/81 46.

Cumberland Wildpark – ♿ Open Apr-Oct, daily 9am-6pm; Nov-Mar, Mon-Fri 11am-4pm, Sat-Sun 9am-4pm. 70S. ☎ 0 76 16/82 05.

Schloß GRAFENEGG

Open May-end Oct, Tues-Fri 10am-5pm, Sat-Sun 10am-6pm. 60S. ☎ 0 27 35/22 05 22.

Excursion

Schloß Gobelsburg – Open Mon-Fri 8am-5pm, Sat, Sun and public holidays 11am-5pm. Closed Sun from Nov to Apr. 30S. ☎ 0 27 34/2 42 20.

GRAZ

ℹ Kaiserfeldgasse 15, A-8011, ☎ 03 16/8 07 50

Zeughaus – Open Mar-end Oct, Tues-Sun 9am-5pm; Nov-6 Jan, Tues-Sun 10am-3pm. Closed 1 Jan, 1, 2 Nov, 24-26, 31 Dec. 60S (admission free 26 Oct). ☎ 03 16/82 87 96.

Mausoleum – Open May-Sept, Mon-Sat 11am-noon, 2-3pm; Oct-Apr entry 11am only. Closed public holidays. 10S. ☎ 03 16/82 16 83.

Stadtmuseum – ♿ Open 6 May-26 Oct, Mon-Sat 9am-7pm, Sun 9am-5pm; Jan-Dec 2001, Tues 10am-9pm, Wed-Sat 10am-6pm, Sun 10am-1pm. 50S. ☎ 03 16/82 25 80.

Funicular up to Schloßberg – Operates every 15min July-Aug, daily 8am-midnight; May-June, daily 8am-11pm; Apr, daily 9am-11pm; Sept, daily 9am-10pm; Oct-Mar, daily 10am-10pm. 20S. ☎ 03 16/88 74 50.

Steierisches Volkskundemuseum – Closed. Reopening scheduled for 2002. ☎ 03 16/83 04 16.

Mariahilf-Kirche: Minoritensaal – Open Mon-Fri 8am-6pm. Check beforehand. ☎ 03 16/71 31 70.

Alte Galerie des Steiermärkischen Landesmuseums Joanneum – Open Tues-Sun 10am-5pm. Closed 1 Jan, Easter Mon and Whit Mon, 24, 25, 31 Dec. 60S (admission free 26 Oct, 26 Nov). ☎ 03 16/80 17 97 70.

Excursion

Rein: Stiftskirche – Basilica and cloisters open daily 7am-8pm (7pm in winter). ☎ 0 31 24/5 16 21.

Schloß GREILLENSTEIN

Guided tour (40min) Apr-Oct, daily 9.30am-5pm. 70S. ☎ 0 29 89/80 80 21.

GROSSGLOCKNER-HOCHALPENSTRASSE

Museum Alpine Naturschau – Open May-Oct, daily 9am-5pm. Admission free. ☎ 06 62/8 73 67 30.

Pasterze glacier – "Gletscherbahn" (funicular) operates mid May-end Sept, daily 9am-4pm. 98S two-way trip. ☎ 0 48 24/25 02.

GURGLER TAL

Chair-lift up the Hohe Mut – Lifts operate July-end Sept, Dec-end Apr, daily 8.45am-4pm. 120S two-way trip. ☎ 0 52 56/62 74.

GURK
ℹ Dr. Schnerich Str. 12, A-9342 - ☎ 0 42 66/81 25 21

Cathedral

Interior – Open Apr-Oct, daily 9am-5pm; Nov-Mar, daily 10am-4pm. Guided tour (45min) 10.30am, 1.30pm and 3pm. 60S (cathedral and crypt). ☎ 0 42 66/82 36 12.

Fastenturch – Guided tour (20min) enquire about exact times. 40S. ☎ 0 42 66/82 36 12.

Crypt – Guided tour (15min) daily 10.30am, 1.30pm and 3pm. 60S (cathedral and crypt). ☎ 0 42 66/82 36 12.

Episcopal chapel – Guided tour (20min) enquire about exact times. 50S. ☎ 0 42 66/82 36 12.

Excursion

Straßburg: Schlo ß – Open May-26 Oct, daily 9am-5pm. 30S. ☎ 0 42 66/23 75.

HALL IN TIROL
ℹ Wallpachgasse 5, A-6060, ☎ 0 52 23/56 26 90

Burg Hasegg – Open daily 9am (10am in winter)-noon, 2-5pm. 50S (admission free 26 Oct). ☎ 0 52 23/5 62 69.

Stadtmuseum – Open 10 July-24 Sept, daily 11am-4pm. 25S. ☎ 0 52 23/5 62 69.

HALLSTATT
ℹ Seestr. 169, A-4830, ☎ 0 61 34/82 08

Prähistorisches Museum – Open May-Sept, daily 10am-6pm; Apr, Oct, daily 10am-4pm; Nov-Mar, Wed (but daily during Christmas holidays) 2-4pm. Closed 1 Jan. 50S (ticket includes admission to the Heimatmuseum). ☎ 0 61 34/82 80.

Salzbergwerk – Guided tour (1hr 15min) 29 Apr-24 Sept, daily 9am-4pm; 25 Sept-26 Oct, daily 9am-2.30pm. Temperature is 8°C/46°F inside the mine. 140S. ☎ 0 61 34/84 00.

Heimatmuseum – Open May-end Sept, daily 10am-6pm; Apr, Oct, daily 10am-4pm. 50S (ticket includes admission to the Prähistorisches Museum). ☎ 0 61 34/82 80.

HEILIGENBLUT
ℹ A-9844, ☎ 0 48 24/20 01 21

Church – Open daily 7am-6pm.

Schareck cable-car – Operates mid June-end Sept, mid Dec-mid Apr, daily 9am-4pm. 175S two-way trip. ☎ 0 48 24/22 88.

Stift HEILIGENKREUZ

Guided tour (45min) Mon-Sat 10am, 11am, 2pm, 3pm and 4pm, Sun 11am, 2pm, 3pm and 4pm. Closed Good Friday, 24 Dec. 65S. ☎ 0 22 58/87 03.

Schloß HERBERSTEIN

Schloß – Guided tour (50min) Mar-end Oct, daily 10am-4pm. 135S (ticket includes entry to the wildlife park). ☎ 0 31 76/8 82 50.

Tier- und Naturpark – Open Mar-Oct, daily 8am-6pm; Nov-Feb, daily 10am-4pm. 135S (ticket includes guided tour of the castle). ☎ 0 31 76/8 82 50.

Burg HOCHOSTERWITZ

♿ Open May-Sept, daily 8am-6pm; Apr, Oct, daily 9am-5pm. 70S. ☎ 0 42 13/20 10.

Schloß-Museum HOHENBRUNN

Jagd- und Fischereimuseum – Open Apr-end Oct, Tues-Sun 10am-noon, 1-5pm. 30S. ☎ 0 72 24/89 33.

HOHENTAUERNPASSSTRASSE

Oberzeiring: Silberbergwerk – Guided tour (50min) May-end Oct, daily 9.45am, 10am, 11am, 2pm, 3pm and 4pm. 60S. ☎ 0 35 71/28 11.

INNSBRUCK

Burggraben 3, A-6021, ☎ 05 12/5 98 50 or
Hauptbahnhof, ☎ 05 12/58 37 66

Hungerburg funicular – Operates July-Sept, daily 8.10am-6.10pm; Apr-June, Oct, daily 8.25am-5.10pm; Nov-Mar, daily 8.25am-5.10pm. 54S two-way trip. Closed two weeks in Apr and two weeks in Nov. ☎ 05 12/29 22 50.

Stadtturm – Open June-Aug, daily 10am-6pm; Sept-May, daily 10am-5pm. 30S (free admission 1 May, 26 Oct). ☎ 05 12/56 15 00.

Maximilianeum – Open May-Sept, daily 10am-6pm; Oct-Apr, daily 10am-12.30pm, 2-5pm. 50S. ☎ 05 12/58 11 11.

Dom zu St. Jakob – ♿ Open in summer, Mon-Sat 10.15am-6.30pm, Sun 12.30-6.30pm; in winter, daily 10.15am-7.30pm. ☎ 05 12/58 39 02.

Hofburg – ♿ Open daily 9am-5pm (last admission 4.30pm). Closed 15 Aug. 70S (free admission 26 Oct). ☎ 05 12/58 71 86.

Hofkirche – ♿ Open Mon-Sat 9am-5pm (5.30pm July-Aug), Sun and public holidays 9am-7pm. Closed 1 Jan, afternoon of Shrove Tues, Easter Day, Whit Sun, Corpus Christi, 1 Nov, 25 Dec. 30S (ticket includes admission to Silberne Kapelle). ☎ 05 12/58 43 02.

Silberne Kapelle – Can be viewed only as part of a visit to the Hofkirche. Same conditions apply. ☎ 05 12/58 43 02.

Tiroler Volkskunstmuseum – Open Mon-Sat 9am-5pm (5.30pm July-Aug), Sun 9am-noon. Closed 1 Jan, afternoon of Shrove Tues, Easter Day, Whit Sun, Corpus Christi, 1 Nov, 25 Dec. 60S. ☎ 05 12/58 43 02.

Tiroler Landesmuseum "Ferdinandeum" – ♿ Open May-Sept, daily 10am-5pm (also 7-9pm Thur); Oct-Apr, Mon-Sat 10am-noon, 2-5pm, Sun 10am-1pm. Closed 1 Jan, 25 Dec. 60S (free admission 26 Oct). ☎ 05 12/5 94 89.

Riesenrundgemälde – Open 1 Apr-30 Oct, daily 9am-5pm. 30S. ☎ 05 12/53 05 39 80.

Alpenzoo – Open daily 9am-6pm (5pm in winter). 70S; access by funicular free of charge if zoo ticket bought at lower station. ☎ 05 12/29 23 23.

Cable-car to the Hafelekar – Operates July-Sept, daily 1st trip up at 8.25am and last trip down at 5.30pm; Apr-June, Oct, daily 1st trip up at 8.40am and last trip down at 5pm; Nov-Mar, daily 1st trip up at 8.55am and last trip down at 4.30pm. Closed one week late Apr/early May and one week in Nov. 227S two-way trip. ☎ 05 12/29 05 20.

Wilten: Stiftskirche – Guided tour (1hr 30min) by appointment only. ☎ 05 12/58 30 48.

Wilten: Basilica – Open June-Oct, Mon-Fri 8.30am-5pm, Sat 8.30am-noon. ☎ 05 12/58 33 85.

Bergisel: Kaiserjägermuseum – Open Apr-end Oct, daily 9am-5pm. 35S. ☎ 05 12/56 16 49.

Schloß Ambras – Open daily 10am-5pm. Closed Nov, Tues Dec-end Mar and 1 May. 90S (admission free 26 Oct, 24 Dec). ☎ 05 12/34 84 46.

Volders: Church of St Charles Borromeo – Open daily 7am-7.15pm.

Wattens: Swarovski Kristallwelten – ♿ Open daily 9am-6pm. Closed 6-17 Nov, 1 Jan, 25 Dec. 75S. ☎ 0 52 24/51 08 00.

Igls: Patscherkofel cable-car – Operates end May-end Oct, daily 9am-noon, 12.45-4.30pm; end Nov-early Apr, daily 9am-4pm. 200S two-way trip. ☎ 05 12/37 72 34.

Trumler/ÖSTERREICH WERBUNG

Armoury at Schloß Ambras

ISCHGL

Pardatschgrat cable-car - Operates Dec-end Apr, daily 8.30am-4pm. 180S two-way trip. ☎ 0 54 44/6 06.

Bad ISCHGL

ℹ Bahnhofstr. 6, A-4820, ☎ 0 61 32/27 75 70

Kaiservilla - Guided tour (45min) May-mid Oct, daily 9-11.45am; 1-4.45pm. 125S. ☎ 0 61 32/2 32 41.

Marmorschlößl: Photomuseum - Open Apr-end Oct, daily 9.30am-5pm. 15S. ☎ 0 61 32/2 44 22.

KAISERGEBIRGE

Hohe Salve: Cable-car and chair-lift - Operate 27 May-22 Oct, 1 Dec-16 Apr, daily 8.30am-5pm. 105S two-way trip. ☎ 0 53 33/52 60.

KAPRUN

Kraftwerksgruppe Glockner-Kaprun - ♿ Open June-end Oct, daily 8am-5pm. 205S two-way trip (in 3 stages). ☎ 0 65 47/7 15 12 32 01.

Kitzsteinhorn - Cable-car and funicular operate daily 8am-4.30pm; funicular runs every 30min. ☎ 0 65 47/8 70 00.

KARWENDELGEBIRGE

Erfurter Hütte - Rofanbahn (cable-car) operates May-end Oct, mid Dec-Easter, daily 9am-5pm every 15min. 170S two-way trip. ☎ 0 52 43/52 92.

KAUNERTAL

Wiesejaggl-Sessellift - Chair-lift operates daily 8.30am-4pm. Journey time: 20min. 100S two-way trip. ☎ 0 54 75/29 20.

KITZBÜHEL

ℹ Hinterstadt 18, A-6370, ☎ 0 53 56/62 15 50

Museum Kitzbühel - Open Mon-Sat 10am-1pm (4pm July-Aug). 30S. ☎ 0 53 56/6 72 74.

Excursion

Cable-car up to the Kitzbüheler Horn - Operates mid May-end Oct and mid Dec-early Apr 8.30am-5pm. 180 S two-way trip. ☎ 0 53 56/6 28 57.

KLAGENFURT

ℹ Neuer Platz/Rathaus, A-9010, ☎ 04 63/53 72 23

Landhaus: Großer Wappensaal - Open Apr-end Sept, Mon-Fri 9am-12.30pm, 1-5pm. ☎ 04 63/53 63 05 40.

Landesmuseum - ♿ Open Tues-Sat 9am-4pm, Sun 10am-1pm. Closed Easter Mon and Whit Mon. 30S. ☎ 04 63/53 63 05 52.

Diözesanmuseum - Open mid June-mid Sept, Mon-Sat 10am-noon, 3-5pm; early-mid June, mid Sept-mid Oct, 10am-noon. 30S. ☎ 04 63/5 77 70 84.

Bergbaumuseum - ♿ Open Apr-end Oct, daily 9am-6pm. 50S. ☎ 04 63/51 12 52.

Excursions

Minimundus - ♿ Open July-Aug, daily 9am-7pm; May, June, Sept, daily 9am-6pm; Apr, Oct, daily 9am-5pm. 120S. ☎ 04 63/21 19 40.

Gustav-Mahler-Komponierhäuschen - Open May-Oct, daily 10am-4pm. 10S. ☎ 04 63/53 72 26.

KLEINWALSERTAL

ℹ Walserstraße 64, A-6992, ☎ 0 55 17/5 11 40 or
ℹ Oberstdorf, Marktplatz 7, D-87561, ☎ 0 83 22/70 00

Riezlern: Walsermuseum - Open Mon-Sat 2-5pm. Closed from one week after Easter until Whitsun, and 1 Nov-20 Dec. 4DM. ☎ 0 55 17/53 15 34 (from Austria), ☎ 0 83 29/53 15 34 (from Germany).

Hirschegg: Wintersportmuseum - Open Mon-Fri 8am-5.30pm. Free admission. ☎ 0 55 17/5 11 40 (from Austria), ☎ 0 83 29/5 11 40 (from Germany).

Trumler/ÖSTERREICH WERBUNG

Verdun Altarpiece (detail), Klosterneuburg

KLOSTERNEUBURG

In der Au, A-3400, ☎ 0 22 43/3 20 38

Abbey – Guided tour (1hr) daily 9am-noon, 1.30-4.30pm. Closed 25, 26 Dec. 70S. ☎ 0 22 43/41 12 12.

Stiftsmuseum – Open early May-mid Nov, Tues-Sun 10am-5pm. 60S. ☎ 0 22 43/41 11 54.

Sammlung Essl – ♿ Open Tues-Sun 10am-7pm (9pm Wed). Closed 1 Jan, 24, 25 Dec. 80S. ☎ 0 22 43/3 70 50.

KREMS und STEIN

Undstraße 6, A-3504, ☎ 0 27 32/8 26 76

Weinstadtmuseum – Open Mar-end Nov, Tues 9am-6pm, Wed-Sun 1-6pm. 50S (free admission 26 Oct). ☎ 0 27 32/80 15 67.

Excursion

Stift Göttweig – Open June-Sept, daily 9am-6pm; 21 Mar-end May, Oct-mid Nov, daily 10am-6pm. Closed Good Fri. 60S. ☎ 0 27 32/85 58 12 31.

KREMSMÜNSTER

Rathausplatz1, A-4550, ☎ 0 75 83/72 12

Abbey

Art collection – Guided tour (1hr) Easter-Oct, daily 10am, 11am, 2pm, 3pm and 4pm; Nov-Easter, Tues-Fri 10am and 2pm, Sat-Sun also 3.30pm. 60S. ☎ 0 75 83/5 27 51 51.

Natural science collection – Guided tour (1hr 30min) May-end Oct, daily 10am, 11am, 1pm, 2pm, 3pm and 4pm; Nov-Apr, Mon-Fri 11am and 2pm, Sat-Sun also 3.30pm. 65S (free admission 26 Oct). ☎ 0 75 83/5 27 51 51.

KUFSTEIN

Unterer Stadtplatz 8, A-6330, ☎ 0 53 72/6 22 07

Festung – ♿ Open Palm Sun-mid Nov, daily 9am-5pm; mid Dec-mid Mar, daily 11am-4pm. 130S. ☎ 0 53 72/60 23 50.

Heldenorgel – ♿ Organ recitals daily noon; July-Aug also 5pm. 10S. ☎ 0 53 72/60 23 50.

Excursion

Mariastein: Schloßmuseum – Currently open to visitors by appointment only. ☎ 0 53 32/5 64 85.

L

LAMBACH

Marktplatz 8, A-4650, ☎ 0 72 45/28 35 50

Stiftskirche – Guided tour (1hr 30min) Easter-end Oct, daily 2pm. 60S. ☎ 0 72 45/2 17 10.

LECH

A-6764, ☎ 0 55 83/2 16 10

Petersboden chair-lift – Operates end Nov-1 May, daily 9am-5pm; early July-10 Sept, daily 8.30am-4.30pm. 66S two-way trip. ☎ 0 55 83/2 16 10.

Rüfikopf cable-car – Operates end Nov-1 May, daily 9am-5pm; 18 June-24 Sept, daily 8.30am-noon, 1-5.30pm. 130S two-way trip. ☎ 0 55 83/2 16 10.

Oberes LECHTAL

Reutte: Heimatmuseum – Open early May-end Oct, Tues-Sun 10am-noon, 2-5pm. 20S. ☎ 0 56 72/7 23 04.

LEOBEN

ℹ Hauptplatz 12, A-8700, ☎ 0 38 42/4 40 18

Stadtpfarrkirche St. Xaver - Open daily 8am-7pm. ☎ 0 38 42/4 32 36.

Stift Göss - Open to visitors by appointment only. ☎ 0 38 42/2 21 48.

LIENZ

ℹ Europaplatz 1, A-9900, ☎ 0 48 52/6 52 65

Schloß Bruck and Regionalmuseum Osttirol - Open mid May-end Oct, daily 10am-6pm. 85S. ☎ 0 48 52/6 25 80.

Excursion

Anras: Pfleggerichtshaus - Open Mon-Fri 10am-noon, 2-4pm. Closed end Apr-mid May and early Nov-mid Dec. 50S. ☎ 0 48 46/65 95.

Stift LILIENFELD

Guided tour (1hr) 8am-noon and 2-6pm, Sun and public holidays afternoon only. 50S. ☎ 0 27 62/5 24 20.

LINZ

ℹ Hauptplatz 1, A-4010, ☎ 07 32/70 70 17 77

Pöstlingberg - A tram service links Linz-Urfahr (north bank) with the Pöstlingberg. Departure from Pöstlingberg station Mon-Sat 5.20am-8pm every 20min, Sun and public holidays 7.15am-8.20pm every 30min mornings and every 20min afternoons. 40S two-way trip. ☎ 07 32/78 01 75 45.

Alter Dom St. Ignatius - Open Mon-Sat 7am-7pm, Sun 7am-8pm. ☎ 07 32/77 08 66.

Minoritenkirche - Open May-Oct, daily 7am-4pm; Nov-Apr, daily 7am-11am.

Schloßmuseum - ♿ Open Tues-Fri 9am-6pm, Sat-Sun 10am-5pm. Closed 1 Jan, 24, 25, 31 Dec. 50S. ☎ 07 32/7 44 48 20.

Neue Galerie der Stadt Linz - Wolfgang-Gurlitt-Museum - ♿ Open June-Aug, Mon-Fri 10am-6pm (10pm Thur), Sat 10am-1pm; Sept-May, daily 10am-6pm (10pm Thur). 60S. ☎ 07 32/70 70 36 00.

Nordico - Museum der Stadt Linz - ♿ Open Mon-Fri 9am-6pm, Sat-Sun 2-5pm. 50S. ☎ 07 32/70 70 19 12.

Ars Electronica Center - ♿ Open Wed-Sun 10am-6pm. Closed 24, 25 Dec. 80S. ☎ 07 32/72 72 12.

Excursion

Kefermarkt: St. Wolfgangskirche - Open daily 8am-5pm. ☎ 0 79 47/62 03.

M

MALLNITZ

ℹ Hannoverstr. 11, A-9822, ☎ 0 47 84/5 22

Ankogelbahn - Operates 8 July-24 Sept, daily 8.30am-4.30pm every 30min. 200S two-way trip. ☎ 0 47 85/81 10.

MALTATAL

Kölnbreinsperre information centre - Open mid May-early Oct, daily from 7am. Free admission. ☎ 04 63/2 37 16.

MARIA SAAL

ℹ Am Platzl 7, A-9063, ☎ 0 42 23/22 14

Kärntner Freilichtmuseum - ♿ Open May-mid Oct, Tues-Sun 10am-6pm (last admission 5pm). 60S. ☎ 0 42 23/31 66.

MARIAZELL

ℹ Hauptplatz 13, A-8630, ☎ 0 38 82/23 66

Cable-car to Bürgeralpe - Operates Jan-Mar, daily 8am-5pm; Apr-June, Oct-Nov, daily 9am-5pm; July-Aug, daily 8.30am-5.30pm; Sept, daily 8.30am-5pm; Dec, daily 8am-4pm. Closed two weeks in Apr and Nov. 105S two-way trip. ☎ 0 38 82/25 55.

Schatzkammer der Basilika Mariazell - Open May-end Oct, Tues-Sat 10am-3pm, Sun 11am-4pm. 40S. ☎ 0 38 82/2 59 50.

Burg MAUTERNDORF

Lungauer Landschaftsmuseum - Open May-end Oct, daily 10am-5pm. 35S. ☎ 0 64 72/74 25.

MAUTHAUSEN

ℹ Heindlkai 13, A-4310, ☎ 0 72 38/22 43

Konzentrationslager - Open Apr-Sept, daily 8am-6pm; Feb-Mar, Oct-mid Dec, daily 8am-4pm (last admission 1hr before closing). 25S (admission free 1 May, 26 Oct, 1 Nov). ☎ 0 72 38/22 59.

MAYERLING

Chapel and memorial – Open Mon-Sat 9am-12.30pm, 1.30-6pm (5pm in winter), Sun 10am-12.30pm. 20S. ☎ 0 22 58/22 75.

Stift MELK

ℹ Rathausplatz 11, A-3390, ☎ 0 27 52/5 23 07

Open mid Apr-mid Nov, daily 9am-5pm (6pm May-Sept). Last admission 1hr before closing. Otherwise abbey can only be viewed as part of a guided tour at 11am and 2pm. No charge. ☎ 0 27 52/55 52 32.

Excursion

Schloß Schallaburg – ♿ Open May-Oct, Mon-Fri 9am-5pm, Sat-Sun 9am-6pm. 90S. ☎ 0 27 54/63 17.

R. Chéret/MICHELIN

Schloß Schallaburg

MILLSTATT

ℹ Rathaus, A-9872, ☎ 0 47 66/20 22

Abbey museum – ♿ Open June-end Sept, daily 9am-noon, 2-6pm. 30S. ☎ 06 76/4 60 64 13.

Kreuzgang – ♿ Open daily 9am-noon, 2-6pm. 30S. ☎ 06 76/4 60 64 13.

MONDSEE

ℹ Dr.-Franz-Müller-Str. 3, A-5310, ☎ 0 62 32/22 70

Heimat- und Pfahlbaumuseum – Open May-Sept, daily 10am-6pm; early-mid Oct, daily 10am-5pm; mid-end Oct, Sat-Sun and public holidays 10am-5pm. 40S. ☎ 0 62 32/22 70.

Freilichtmuseum Mondseer Rauchhaus – Open May-18 Sept, Tues-Sun, 10am-6pm; Apr Sat-Sun 10am-6pm; 19-29 Oct, Sat-Sun 10am-5pm. 30S. ☎ 0 62 32/22 70.

MONTAFON

Kristbergbahn – Operates 28 May-26 Oct, Dec-Apr, daily 7.50am-6.15pm. 125S two-way trip. ☎ 0 55 56/7 41 19.

Chair-lift up to Sennigrat – Operates early June-mid Oct, daily 8am-4.30pm; early Dec-end Apr, daily 8am-5pm. 194S two-way trip. ☎ 0 55 56/7 21 26.

Valisera cable-car – Operates early Dec-end Apr, daily 8.15am-3.30pm. 160S two-way trip. ☎ 0 55 57/6 30 00.

MURAU

ℹ Am Bahnhof, A-8850, ☎ 0 35 32/27 20

Excursion

Murtalbahn – Operates end June-early Sept, Tues 1.30pm from Murau and Wed 1pm from Tamsweg. 200S two-way trip. ☎ 0 35 32/22 33.

MURTAL

Österreichisches Freilichtmuseum – ♿ Open Apr-Oct, Tues-Sun 9am-5pm (last admission 4pm). 75S. ☎ 0 31 24/5 37 00.

Lurgrotte – Guided tour (1hr) Apr-Oct, daily 9am-4pm; Nov-Mar, by appointment only. 60S. ☎ 0 31 27/25 80.

N – O

NEUSIEDLER SEE

ℹ Rathaus, A-7071 Rust, ☎ 0 26 85/5 02

Neusiedl am See: Pannonisches Heimatmuseum – ♿ Guided tour (45min) May-Oct, Tues-Sat 2.30-6.30pm, Sun and public holidays 10am-noon, 2.30-6.30pm. Donations requested. ☎ 0 21 67/81 73.

Seebad Rust – ♿ Open May-mid Sept, daily 9am-7pm. 40S. ☎ 0 26 85/59 14.

Schloß Halbturn – ♿ Open May-end Oct, daily 10am-6pm (last admission 5pm). 70S. ☎ 0 21 72/85 77.

Frauenkirchen pilgrimage church – ♿ Open daily 7am-8pm. ☎ 0 21 72/22 24.

OBERNBERG AM INN

ℹ Marktplatz 1, A-4982, ☎ 0 77 58/36 00

OSSIACHER SEE

Gerlitzen chair-lift – Operates mid May-mid Oct, early Dec-mid Apr, daily 9am-4.30pm. Journey time: 25min. 180S two-way trip. ☎ 0 42 48/27 22.

Ossiach church – ♿ Open May-mid Oct, Mon-Sat 9.30am-5pm (closed noon-1.30pm July-Aug), Sun and public holidays 1.30-6pm. 20S. ☎ 0 42 43/22 80.

P

PACK- und STUBALPENSTRASSE

Gestüt Piber – ♿ Guided tour (1hr 10min) Mon before Easter-end Oct, daily 9am-10.15am, 2-3.15pm. 100S. ☎ 0 31 44/33 23.

PETRONELL-CARNUNTUM

ℹ Kirchengasse 57, A-2404, ☎ 0 21 63/22 28

Freilichtmuseum Petronell – ♿ Excavations and information centre open Apr-end Oct, Mon-Fri 9am-5pm, Sat-Sun 9am-6pm. 49S. ☎ 0 21 63/3 37 70.

Archäologisches Museum Carnuntinum – Open 16 Jan-17 Dec, Tues-Sun 10am-5pm. 60S. ☎ 0 21 63/3 37 70.

Excursion

Rohrau: Harrach'sche Gemäldegalerie – Open Easter-1 Nov, Tues-Sun 10am-5pm. ☎ 0 21 64/22 53.

Rohrau: Geburtshaus Joseph Haydns – Open Tues-Sun 10am-4pm. Closed 1 Jan, 24-26, 31 Dec. 20S (free admission 26 Oct). ☎ 0 21 64/22 68.

PITZTAL

Hinterer Brunnenkogel – Pitzexpress funicular railway operates daily 8.30am-4.30pm. Pitz-Panoramabahn cable-car operates daily 9am-3.15pm. Closed mid June-mid July. Combined ticket 280S two-way trip. ☎ 0 54 13/8 62 88.

Riffelsee cable-car – Operates mid June-early Oct, mid Dec-mid Apr, daily 8.30am-12.15pm, 1-4.30pm. 170S two-way trip. ☎ 0 54 13/8 62 88.

PÖLLAU

ℹ Schloß 1, A-8225, ☎ 0 33 35/42 10

R

RADSTÄDTER TAUERNSTRASSE

Schloß Moosham – Guided tour (1hr) Apr-Oct, daily 10am, 11am, 1pm, 2pm, 3pm and 4pm; Dec-Mar, daily 11am, 1pm and 2.30pm. 100S. ☎ 0 64 76/3 05.

RATTENBERG

ℹ Klostergasse 94, A-6240, ☎ 0 53 37/6 33 21

Augustinermuseum – Open 1 May-2nd Sun in Oct, daily 10am-5pm. 40S. ☎ 0 53 37/6 48 31.

Excursion

Freilichtmuseum Tiroler Bauernhöfe – Open mid Apr-end Oct, daily 9am-6pm (last admission 1hr before closing). 60S. ☎ 0 53 37/6 26 36.

RETZ

ℹ Hauptplatz 30, A-2070, ☎ 0 29 42/27 00

Retzer Erlebniskeller – Guided tour of wine cellars (1hr 30min) May-Oct, daily 10.30am, 2pm and 4pm; Mar, Apr, Nov, Dec, daily 2pm. Meet in the Hauptplatz in front of the Rathaus. 80S. ☎ 0 29 42/27 00.

Schloß RIEGERSBURG (Niederösterreich)

♿ Guided tour (30min) Apr-mid Nov, daily 9am-5pm; July-Aug, daily 9am-7pm. 90S. ☎ 0 29 16/4 00.

Excursion

Burg Hardegg - Open Apr-mid Nov, daily 9am-5pm; July-Aug, daily 9am-6pm. 72S. ☎ 0 29 16/4 00.

Schloß ROSENBURG

Guided tour (1hr) 1 Apr-1 Nov, daily 9am-5pm. 100S (joint ticket). ☎ 0 29 82/23 03.

S

SAALACHTAL

Salzburger Freilichtmuseum - ♿ Open Apr-Oct, Tues-Sun 9am-6pm. 70S. ☎ 06 62/85 00 11.

Wallfahrtskirche Maria Kirchental - ♿ Open daily 7am-7pm. ☎ 0 65 88/85 28.

Vorderkaserklamm - Accessible 7 May-26 Oct, daily 9am-6pm. 32S. ☎ 0 65 88/85 10.

Lamprechtshöhle - Open May-Oct, daily (except Thur in Nov-Apr) 9am-6pm. 38S. ☎ 0 65 82/83 43.

Seisenbergklamm - Open May-Oct, daily 8.30am-6.30pm. 27S. ☎ 0 65 82/8 35 24.

SAALBACH-HINTERGLEMM

ℹ A-5753, ☎ 0 65 41/68 00

Schattberg-Ost cable railway - Operates early June-early Oct, early Dec-mid Apr, daily 8.30am (9am in June)-4pm . 190S two-way trip. ☎ 0 65 41/6 27 10.

Zwölferkogel cable-car - Operates early June-early Oct, Dec-mid Apr, daily 9am-11.45am, 1-4.15pm. Journey time:13-18min. 170S two-way trip. ☎ 0 65 41/6 32 10.

SALZACHTAL

Liechtensteinklamm - Open mid May-mid Oct, daily 8am-5pm. 35S. ☎ 0 64 12/60 36.

Erlebnisburg Hohenwerfen - Open July-Aug, daily 9am-6pm; May, June, Sept, daily 9am-5pm; Apr, Oct, daily 9am-4.30pm. Flight demonstrations daily 11am and 3pm. 110S. ☎ 0 64 68/76 03.

Lammeröfen - Accessible May-end Oct, daily 9am-7pm. 22S. ☎ 0 62 44/84 42.

Salzbergwerk Dürrnberg - Guided tour (1hr 15min) Apr-Oct, daily 9am-5pm; Nov-Mar, daily 11am-3pm. 200S. ☎ 0 62 45/8 52 85 15.

M. Hertlein/MICHELIN

Flight demonstrations, Burg Hohenwerfen

SALZATAL

Wildalpen: Heimat-, Pfarr- und Wasserleitungsmuseum – Open 1 May-26 Oct, Mon-Fri 10am-noon, 1-3pm, Sun and public holidays 10am-noon. 30S. ☎ 0 36 36/45 10.

SALZBURG

Auerspergstraße 7, A-5020, ☎ 06 62/88 98 70

Salzburg Festival venues – Guided tour (1hr) Jan-19 Dec, daily 2pm. Meet at the entrance to the Kleines Festspielhaus. 70S. ☎ 06 62/84 90 97.

Lift up to Mönchsberg – Trip to the viewing terrace daily 9am-11pm (7pm Mon). 27S two-way trip. ☎ 06 62/44 80 62 85.

Dommuseum – ♿ Open end May-end Oct, Mon-Sat 10am-5pm, Sun 1-6pm. 60S. ☎ 06 62/8 04 71 27.

Hohensalzburg funicular – Operates May-Sept, daily 9am-9pm; Oct-Apr, daily 9am-5pm. Closed two weeks in Nov and Jan. 76S (includes entrance to the fortress). ☎ 06 62/84 26 82.

Hohensalzburg castle and museum – Open 15 June-14 Sept, daily 8.30am-7pm; 15 Mar-14 June, daily 9am-6pm; 15 Sept-14 Mar, daily 9am-5pm. 42S (castle), 84S (castle and interior). ☎ 06 62/84 24 30 11.

Moderne Galerie – Graphische Sammlung – Österr. Photogalerie Rupertinum – ♿ Open end July-end Sept, daily 10am-6pm (9pm Wed); Oct-end July, Tues-Sun 10am-5pm (9pm Wed). Closed 24, 25 Dec. 40S (60S end July-end Sept). ☎ 06 62/80 42 25 41.

Haus der Natur – Open, daily 9am-5pm. 55S. ☎ 06 62/84 26 53.

Mozarts Geburtshaus – Open July-Aug, daily 9am-7pm; Jan-June, Sept-Dec, daily 9am-6pm. 70S. ☎ 06 62/84 43 13.

Residenzgalerie – ♿ Open daily 10am-5pm. Closed Wed in Oct-Mar. 50S. ☎ 06 62/8 40 45 10.

Salzburger Barockmuseum – Open Tues-Sat 9am-noon, 2-5pm (9am-5pm July-Aug), Sun 10am-1pm. Closed 1 Jan, 24, 25 Dec. 40S (admission free 26 Oct). ☎ 06 62/87 74 32.

Tanzmeisterhaus (Mozart-Wohnhaus) – ♿ Open daily 9am-6pm (7pm July-Aug). 65S. ☎ 06 62/87 42 27 40.

Mozart-Ton- und Filmmuseum – ♿ Open Mon, Tues, Fri 9am-1pm, Wed, Thur 1-5pm. Free admission. ☎ 06 62/88 34 54.

Stiegl's Brauwelt – Open Wed-Sun 10am-5pm (last admission 4pm). 125S. ☎ 06 62/83 87 14 92.

Excursions

Schloß Hellbrunn – Guided tour (fountains: 35min, castle: 20min) July-Aug, daily 9am-10pm; May, June, Sept, daily 9am-5.30pm; Apr, Oct, daily 9am-4.30pm. 100S fountains and castle. ☎ 06 62/8 20 37 20.

Tiergarten Hellbrunn – Open end June-end Aug, Sun-Thur 8.30am-8pm, Fri-Sat 8.30am-10.30pm; May-June, 8.30am-6pm; Mar-Apr, 8.30am-5.30pm; Sept-Feb, 8.30am-5pm. Last admission 1hr before closing. 80S. ☎ 06 62/8 20 37 20.

Volkskundemuseum – Open July-Sept, daily 10am-6pm; Easter-end June, Oct, daily 9am-5pm. 20S. ☎ 06 62/8 41 13 40.

Cable-car to the Untersberg – Operates July-Sept, daily 8.30am-5.30pm; Mar-June, Oct, daily 9am-5pm; 20 Dec-end Feb, daily 10am-4pm. Closed two weeks in Apr, Nov-mid Dec. 225S two-way trip. ☎ 0 62 46/72 47 70.

SALZBURGER SPORTWELT AMADÉ

Flachau cable-car – Operates 1 Dec-25 Apr, daily 8.30am-4pm; 10 June-30 Sept, daily 9am-noon, 1-5pm. 136S two-way trip. ☎ 0 64 57/22 14.

Mooskopf – Chair-lift operates 15 Dec-20 Apr, daily 9am-4pm. 150S. ☎ 0 64 57/22 14.

SALZKAMMERGUT

Schloß Trautenfels – ♿ Open Palm Sun-end Oct, daily 9am-5pm. 60S. ☎ 0 36 82/2 22 33.

ST. ANTON AM ARLBERG

Arlberghaus, A-6580, ☎ 0 54 46/2 26 90

Valluga cable-car – Operates mid Dec-end Apr, early July-end Sept, daily 8.40am-4.15pm. 290S two-way trip. ☎ 0 54 46/2 35 20.

Kapall chair-lift – Operates Dec-end Apr, June-end Aug, daily 8.30am-4pm. 200S two-way trip. ☎ 0 54 46//2 35 20.

Rendl cable-car – Operates Jan-end Apr, daily 8.30am-4.10pm. 160S two-way trip. ☎ 0 54 46//2 35 20.

Stift ST. FLORIAN

Guided tour (1hr 30min) Easter-1 Nov, daily 10am, 11am, 2pm, 3pm and 4pm; otherwise by appointment only. 60S. ☎ 0 72 24/8 90 20.

ST. JOHANN IN TIROL

Poststr. 2, A-6380, ☎ 0 53 52/6 33 35

Abtei ST. LAMBRECHT

Abbey buildings - Guided tour (1hr 30min) mid May-mid Oct, Mon-Sat 10.45am and 2.30pm, Sun after the morning service and 2.30pm. 50S. ☎ 0 35 85/23 45.

ST. PAUL IM LAVANTTAL

Hauptstr. 10, A-9470, ☎ 0 43 57/20 17 22

Stiftskirche - ♿ Open daily 8am-5pm. ☎ 0 43 57/20 19 22.

Abbey buildings - Open May-Oct, daily 9am-5pm. 95S. ☎ 0 43 57/20 19 22.

ST. PÖLTEN

Rathausplatz 1, A-3100, ☎ 0 27 42/35 33 54

Stadtmuseum - Open Tues-Sat 10am-5pm. Closed 24 Dec-6 Jan. 20S. ☎ 0 27 42/3 33 26 43.

Diözesan-Museum - Open Apr-Oct, Tues-Fri 10am-noon, 2-5pm, Sat 10am-1pm, 1st Sun in the month 10am-noon. Closed public holidays. 30S (free admission 1st Sun in the month). ☎ 0 27 42/32 43 31.

Klangturm - ♿ Open 14 Apr-19 Nov, Tues-Fri 9am-6pm, Sat-Sun 10am-6pm. 40S. ☎ 0 27 42/2 01 72 28.

Excursion

Stift Herzogenburg - ♿ Guided tour (1hr) Apr-end Oct, daily 9am-11am, 1-5pm on the hour; otherwise by appointment only. 70S. ☎ 0 27 82/8 31 13.

ST. VEIT AN DER GLAN

Hauptplatz 1, A-9300, ☎ 0 42 12/55 55

Rathaussaal - ♿ Open Mon-Fri 7am-6pm. ☎ 0 42 12/5 55 56 68.

Verkehrsmuseum - Open May-mid Oct, daily 9am-noon, 2-6pm. 25S. ☎ 0 42 12/5 55 56 68.

Excursion

Magdalensberg excavations - Open May-mid Oct, daily 9am-7pm. 40S. ☎ 0 42 24/22 55.

ST. WOLFGANG

Kurdirektion, A-5360, ☎ 0 61 38/22 39

Boat service on the Wolfgangsee - Early May-end Oct. Landing stages at: Strobl, Geschwendt car park, St. Wolfgang (village and Schafberg station), Ried-Falkenstein, Ferienhort, Fürberg, St. Gilgen. ☎ 0 61 38/2 23 20.

Church - Open daily 8am-6pm. ☎ 0 61 38/23 21.

Excursion

Schafberg - Cog railway operates May-end Oct, daily every hour from 9.05am (8.05am July-Aug). 260S two-way trip. ☎ 0 61 38/2 23 20.

SCHLADMINGER TAUERN

Planai cable-car - Operates 11 June-22 Oct, Dec-1 May, daily 9am-5pm. 155S two-way trip. ☎ 0 36 87/2 20 42 13.

Hochwurzen cable-car - Operates early July-end Sept, Dec-Easter, daily 8.30am-5pm. 115S two-way trip. ☎ 0 36 87/2 20 42 13.

Hauser Kaibling cable-car - Operates Dec-Easter. 90S two-way trip. ☎ 0 36 86/30 30.

Stift SCHLÄGL

♿ Open 1 May-26 Oct, Tues-Sun 10am-noon, 1-5pm. Closed 1, 6 Jan, Easter Day, 25 Dec. 40S. ☎ 0 72 81/8 80 10.

Tour of the SCHNEEBERG

Reichenau, Hauptstraße 63, A-2651, ☎ 0 26 26/5 28 65
Semmering, Paßhöhe 248, A-2680, ☎ 0 26 64/2 53 91

Rack railway - Operates end Apr-end Oct. Ascent daily 9.50am and 11.55am (end June-early Sept also 8.50am); descent daily 2.40pm (end June-early Sept also 4.50pm). 290S two-way trip. ☎ 0 26 36/36 61.

Rax cable-car - Operates daily 8.30am-5pm every 30min. Closed two weeks in Nov. 198S. ☎ 0 26 66/5 24 97.

SCHWAZ

ℹ Schwaz-Pill, Franz-Josef-Straße 26, A-6130, ☎ 0 52 42/6 32 40

Silberbergwerk – Guided tour (1hr 30min) May-Oct, daily 8.30am-5pm; early-mid Nov, 26 Dec-end Apr, daily 9.30am-4pm. Visitors are provided with protective hats and jackets. Sturdy shoes are recommended. 150S. ☎ 0 52 42/7 23 72.

Schloß Freundsberg – Open mid Apr-mid Oct, Mon-Wed, Fri-Sun 10am-5pm. 30S (free admission Sun). ☎ 0 52 42/6 39 67.

Excursion

Schloß Tratzberg – ♿ Guided tour (1hr) 25 Mar-end Oct, daily 10am-4pm. 120S. ☎ 0 52 42/6 35 66 20.

Abtei SECKAU

Basilica – ♿ Open May-end Oct, daily 10am-5pm. ☎ 0 35 14/5 23 41 00.

SEEFELD IN TIROL

ℹ Rathaus 43, A-6100, ☎ 0 52 12/23 13

Funicular to Seefelder Joch – Operates June-end Oct, Dec-end Mar, daily 9am-5pm. 190S two-way trip. ☎ 0 52 12/2 41 60.

SEEFELDER SATTELSTRASSEN

PlayCastle Tirol – ♿ PlayCastle and Fun Dome open daily 10am-8pm (11pm Sun). 190S (joint ticket). ☎ 0 52 12/3 73 70.

SÖLDEN

Gaislachkogl cable-car – Operates mid June-mid Sept, end Dec-mid Apr, daily 9am-4pm. 230S two-way trip. ☎ 0 52 54/23 61.

Giggijochbahn – Cable-car operates mid Dec-end Apr, daily 9am-4pm. 135S two-way trip. ☎ 0 52 54/23 61.

Excursion

Ventertal: Wildspitze-Sesselbahn – Chair-lift operates mid June-end Sept, daily 8am-5.30pm; mid Dec-mid Apr, daily 9.30am-4pm. 95S two-way trip. ☎ 0 52 54/81 54.

SPITAL AM PYHRN

ℹ A-4582, ☎ 0 75 63/2 49

SPITTAL AN DER DRAU

ℹ Burgplatz 1, A-9800, ☎ 0 47 62/34 20

Museum für Volkskultur – ♿ Open 9 May-end Oct, daily 9am-6pm; 1 Nov-8 May, Mon-Thur 1-4pm. 45S. ☎ 0 47 62/28 90.

Goldeckbahn – Departure from Spittal: first trip up 9.30am, last trip down 5.40pm. Closed Easter Mon-9 June, 25 Sept-17 Dec. 195S two-way trip. ☎ 0 47 62/28 64 12.

Excursion

Museum Teurnia – Open May-mid Oct, Tues-Sun 9am-noon, 1-5pm. 30S. ☎ 0 47 62/3 38 07.

STAINZ

ℹ Erzherzog-Johann-Str. 3, A-8510, ☎ 0 34 63/45 18

Church – Open daily 8am-6pm. ☎ 0 34 63/22 37.

Castle Museum – Open Apr-end Oct, daily 9am-5pm. 60S (free admission 26 Oct). ☎ 0 34 63/2 77 20.

Stift STAMS

Guided tour (45min) Jan-Apr, Oct-Dec, Mon-Fri 9am, 10am, 11am, 2pm, 3pm and 4pm, Sat morning only, Sun (in Oct only) afternoon only; May, June, Sept, Mon-Fri 9am, 10am, 11am, 2pm, 3pm, 4pm and 5pm, Sat 9am, 10am, 11am, 2pm, 3pm and 4pm, Sun 1pm, 2pm, 3pm and 4pm; July-Aug, Mon-Fri 9am-11am, 1-5pm every 30min, Sat 9am-11am, 1-4.30pm every 30min, Sun 1-4.30pm every 30min. 40S. ☎ 0 52 63/5 69 72.

STEIRISCHES THERMENLAND

Blumau: Thermen- und Hotelanlage – ♿ Open daily 9am-5pm. 70S. ☎ 0 33 83/51 00 90 02.

Riegersburg – Open Apr-end Oct, daily 9am-5pm. 90S. ☎ 0 31 53/83 46.

Bad Gleichenberg: Styrassic Park – Open Apr-end Oct, daily 8am-6pm; Jan-Mar, daily 9am-4pm. 70S. ☎ 0 31 59/28 75 15.

STEIRISCHE WEINSTRASSE

Kitzeck wine museum – Open Apr-end Oct, Sat-Sun 10am-noon, 2-5pm. 30S. ☎ 0 34 56/35 00.

Ehrenhausen: Mausoleum – The church is kept locked. The key can be obtained from the parish office 8am-6pm or from the Marktgemeinde. ☎ 0 34 53/25 07.

STEYR

ℹ Stadtplatz 27, A-4400, ☎ 0 72 52/5 32 29

Stift Seitenstetten – Guided tour (1hr) Easter-1 Nov, daily 10am and 3pm. 70S. ☎ 0 74 77/4 23 00.

Pfarrkirchen: Parish church – Open daily 8am-5pm. ☎ 0 72 58/24 33.

T

M. Hertlein/MICHELIN

Petrol-driven fire engine (1913), Niederösterreichisches Feuerwehrmuseum, Minoritenkloster, Tulln

TAMSWEG

ℹ Kirchengasse 107, A-5580, ☎ 0 64 74/21 45

TULLN

ℹ Minoritenplatz 2, A-3430, ☎ 0 22 72/6 58 36

Egon-Schiele-Museum – Open Tues-Sun 9am-noon, 2-6pm (5pm Nov-Apr). 40S. ☎ 0 22 72/6 45 70.

Minoritenkloster – Open Wed-Fri 3-6pm, Sat 2-6pm, Sun 10am-6pm. 30S. ☎ 0 22 72/6 19 15.

TURRACHERHÖHE

ℹ A-8864, ☎ 0 42 75/83 92

V

VIENNA

See WIEN.

VILLACH

ℹ Rathausplatz 1, A-9500, ☎ 0 42 42/24 44 40

Museum der Stadt Villach – Open 2 May-31 Oct, Mon-Sat 10am-4.30pm. 35S. ☎ 0 42 42/2 05 35 00.

Relief von Kärnten – Open 2 May-31 Oct, Mon-Sat 10am-4.30pm. Closed public holidays. 25S. ☎ 0 42 42/2 05 35 50.

Villacher Fahrzeugmuseum – Open mid June-mid Sept, Mon-Sat 9am-5pm, Sun 10am-5pm; mid Sept-mid June, daily 10am-noon, 2-4pm. 60S. ☎ 0 42 42/2 55 30.

Excursion

Alpengarten – Open early June-end Aug, daily 9am-6pm. 20S. ☎ 06 63/9 14 29 53.

Chair-lift – Operates June-Sept, Dec-Mar, daily 9am-4pm. 80S two-way trip. ☎ 0 42 42/21 95 30.

Landskron: Eagle flight displays – Displays July-Aug, daily 11am, 3pm and 6pm; May, June, Sept, daily 11am and 3pm. 70S. ☎ 0 42 42/4 28 88.

VÖCKLABRUCK

ℹ Hinterstadt 14, A-4840, ☎ 0 76 72/2 66 44

Dörflkirche St. Ägidius – If the church is closed, apply to the presbytery. ☎ 0 76 72/7 26 08.

VORAU

ℹ Im Stift, A-8250, ☎ 0 33 37/35 04

Freilichtmuseum – Open Easter-end Oct, daily 10am (9am July-Aug)-5pm. 30S. ☎ 0 33 37/34 66.

WAIDHOFEN AN DER THAYA
ℹ Bahnhofstr. 2, A-3830, ☎ 0 28 42/5 15 00

Östliches WEINVIERTEL

Safari- und Abenteuerpark Gänserndorf - Open July-Aug, daily 9.30am-6.30pm; June, daily 9am-5.30pm; Apr, May, Sept, Oct, daily 9.30am-5.30pm. Last admission 2h before closing. Joint ticket for both parks, 1 adult in own car 193S. ☎ 0 22 82/70 26 10.

Groß-Schweinbarth: Niederösterreichisches Museum für Volkskultur - Open mid Apr-mid Nov, Tues-Sun 9am-5pm. ☎ 0 22 89/23 02.

Niedersulz: Weinviertler Museumsdorf - ♿ Open Palm Sun-1 Nov, Mon-Fri 10am-4pm, Sat-Sun 10am-6pm. 60S. ☎ 0 25 34/3 33.

Asparn an der Zaya: Museum für Urgeschichte - Open Apr-mid Nov, Tues-Sun 9am-5pm. 30S (free admission 26 Oct). ☎ 0 25 77/80 39.

WELS
ℹ Stadtplatz 55, A-4600, ☎ 0 72 42/4 34 95

Burg Wels - Open end Apr-early Nov daily 9am-6pm; otherwise Tues-Fri 10am-5pm, Sat 2-5pm, Sun 10am-noon and 2-5pm. Closed 1 Jan, Good Fri, Easter Sun, Whit Mon, 24, 25 and 31 Dec. 50S. ☎ 0 72 42/23 57 35.

Vogelpark Schmiding - Open mid Mar-mid Nov daily 9am-5pm. 120S. ☎ 0 72 49/4 62 72.

WIEN (VIENNA)
ℹ Am Albertinaplatz 1, A-1025, ☎ 01/21 11 40

Neues Rathaus - Guided tour (30min) Mon, Wed, Fri 1pm (except when council in session). Closed public holidays. Free admission. ☎ 01/5 25 50.

Burgtheater - Guided tour (1hr) Tues, Thur, Sat 9am and 3pm, Sun 11am and 3pm. 50S. ☎ 01/5 14 44 41 40.

Donauturm - Open daily 10am-midnight. Lift: 70S. ☎ 01/2 63 35 73.

Hofburg

Schatzkammer - ♿ Open, Mon, Wed-Sun. Closed 1 May, 13 June, 31 Dec. 100S. ☎ 01/5 33 79 31.

Kaiserappartements - ♿ Open daily 9am-4.30pm. 80S. ☎ 01/5 33 75 70.

Hofsilber- und Tafelkammer - Open daily 9am-5pm. 70S. ☎ 01/5 33 75 70.

Hofburgkapelle - Open Mon-Thur 11am-3pm, Fri 11am-1pm. 20S. ☎ 01/5 33 99 27.

Spanische Reitschule - Summer break July-Aug. For performances (reruns) Mar-Dec, Sun 10.45am; 31 May and 29 Sept 7pm. Apply in writing as far in advance as possible to: Spanische Reitschule (Hofburg, Michaelerplatz 1, A-1010 Wien - *do not send any money*) or to the theatre ticket or travel agencies. Advance booking is not necessary for the morning training sessions with musical accompaniment (Tues-Sun 10am-noon). Tickets are available on the same day at the entrance, Josefsplatz Tor 2. Performances: 250-900S, morning training sessions: 100S. ☎ 01/5 33 90 31.

Lipizzaner-Museum - Open daily 9am-6pm. 50S. ☎ 01/5 26 41 84 30.

Österreichische Nationalbibliothek - ♿ Open May-Oct, Mon-Wed, Fri, Sat 10am-4pm, Thur 10am-7pm, Sun 10am-2pm; Nov-Apr, Mon-Sat 10am-2pm. 60S (admission free 26 Oct). ☎ 01/53 41 04 64.

Kaisergruft - Open daily 9.30am-4pm. 40S. ☎ 01/5 12 68 53.

Augustinerkirche: Loretokapelle - Guided tour (15min) by appointment. 15S. ☎ 01/5 33 70 99.

Albertina - ♿ Open daily 10am-6pm. Closed 1 May, 24 Dec. 70S (admission free 26 Oct). ☎ 01/5 81 30 60 11.

Schmetterlinghaus - ♿ Open Apr-Oct, Mon-Fri 10am-5pm, Sat-Sun 10am-6.30pm; Nov-Mar, daily 10am-4pm. 70S. ☎ 01/5 33 85 70.

Hofjagd- und Rüstkammer - ♿ Open Mon, Wed-Sun 10am-6pm. Closed 1 May, 13 June, 25 Dec. 60S (admission free 26 Oct, 24 Dec). ☎ 01/52 52 44 84.

Sammlung alter Musikinstrumente - Same admission times as the Hofjagd- und Rüstkammer. 60S. ☎ 01/52 52 44 84.

Ephesos Museum - Same admission times as the Hofjagd- und Rüstkammer. 60S (admission free 26 Oct, 24 Dec). ☎ 01/52 52 44 84.

Museum für Völkerkunde - Open Mon, Wed-Sun 10am-4pm. Closed 1 Jan, Good Fri, 1 May, 1 Nov, 25 Dec. 50S. ☎ 01/5 34 30.

Stephansdom - ♿ Open Mon-Sat 6am-10pm, Sun 7am-10pm. Guided tour (30min) Mon-Sat 10.30am and 3pm, Sun 3pm. 40S. ☎ 01/5 15 52 37 67.

Catacombs - Guided tour (30min) Mon-Sat 10am-11.30am, 1.30-4.30pm every 30min, Sun 1.30-4.30pm every 30min. 40S. ☎ 01/5 15 52 37 67.

Cathedral towers – It is possible to climb the Hochturm on the south side of the cathedral, daily 9am-5.30pm. 30S. Nordturm (high-speed lift to "Pummerin" great bell): Apr-Oct, daily 9am-6pm (6.30pm July-Aug); Nov-Mar, daily 8.30am-5pm. 40S. ☎ 01/5 15 52 37 67.

Dom- und Diözesanmuseum – Open Tues-Sat 10am-5pm. 50S. ☎ 01/5 15 52 36 89.

Deutschordenskirche: Treasure of the Teutonic Order – Open Mon, Thur 10am-noon, Wed, Fri 3-5pm, Sat 10am-noon, 3-5pm. Closed public holidays. 50S. ☎ 01/5 12 10 65.

Mozart-Gedenkstätte or Figarohaus – Open Tues-Sun 9am-6pm. Closed 1 Jan, 1 May, 25 Dec. 25S (admission free Fri morning). ☎ 01/5 13 62 94.

Jesuitenkirche – ♿ Open Mon-Sat 7am-7pm, Sun and public holidays 8am-8pm. ☎ 01/5 12 52 32.

Ruprechtskirche – ♿ Open Mon-Fri 10am-1pm. Donation requested. ☎ 01/5 35 60 03.

Uhrenmuseum der Stadt Wien – Open Tues-Sun 9am-4.30pm. Closed 1 Jan, 1 May, 25 Dec. 50S. ☎ 01/5 33 22 65.

Peterskirche – Open daily 8am-6pm.

Kunsthistorisches Museum – ♿ Open Tues-Sun 10am-6pm (9pm Thur). Closed 1 May, 25 Dec. 100S (admission free 26 Oct, 25 Dec). ☎ 01/52 52 40.

Kunsthistorisches Museum

Hunters in the Snow by Bruegel the Elder

Belvedere

Galerie des 19. und 20. Jahrhunderts – ♿ Open Tues-Sun 10am-6pm (5pm in winter). 90S (admission free 26 Oct). ☎ 01/79 55 71 34.

Bundesgarten Belvedere – Open Apr-end July, daily 10am-6pm. 40S. ☎ 01/7 98 31 49.

Barockmuseum – ♿ Open Apr-Dec, Tues-Sun 10am-6pm; Jan-Mar, Tues-Sun 10am-5pm. Closed 1 Jan, Tues after Easter and Whitsun, 1 May, 1 Nov, 24, 25, 31 Dec (from 1pm). 90S. ☎ 01/79 55 71 78.

Museum mittelalterlicher österreichischer Kunst – ♿ Open Apr-Dec, Tues-Sun 10am-6pm; Jan-Mar, Tues-Sun 10am-5pm. Closed 1 Jan, Tues after Easter and Whitsun, 1 May, 1 Nov, 24, 25, 31 Dec. 90S. ☎ 01/79 55 71 34.

Schloß Schönbrunn

State apartments – ♿ Open Apr-Oct, daily 8.30am-5pm, Nov-Mar, daily 8.30am-4.30pm. 95S (Imperial Tour), 125S (Grand Tour), 150S (Grand Tour with guided tour). ☎ 01/81 11 32 39.

Tiergarten – ♿ Open May-Sept, daily 9am-6.30pm; Apr, daily 9am-6pm; Mar, Oct, daily 9am-5.30pm; Feb, daily 9am-5pm; Jan, Nov, Dec, daily 9am-4.30pm. 95S. ☎ 01/8 77 92 94.

Palmenhaus – Open May-Sept, daily 9.30am-5.30pm; Oct-Apr, daily 9.30am-4.30pm. 45S. ☎ 01/87 75 08 74 06.

Gloriette – Open mid Apr-mid Oct, daily 9am-5pm. 20S. ☎ 01/81 11 32 39.

Wagenburg – ♿ Open 1 Jan-9 Apr, 7 Nov-31 Dec, Tues-Sun 10am-4pm; 10 Apr-5 Nov, daily 10am-6pm. Closed 1 May, 25 Dec. 60S (admission free 26 Oct, 24 Dec). ☎ 01/8 77 32 44.

Secessionsgebäude – ♿ Open Tues-Sun 10am-6pm (8pm Thur). Closed 1 May, 1 Nov, 25 Dec. 60S. ☎ 01/5 87 53 07.

Postsparkasse – ♿ Hall open Mon-Fri 8am-3pm (5.30pm Thur). Guided tour by appointment only. Closed public holidays. 50S. ☎ 01/5 14 00 30 88.

Kirche am Steinhof – Guided tour (45min) Sat 3pm. 55S. ☎ 01/91 06 02 00 31.

Staatsoper – ♿ Guided tour (40min) July-Aug, daily 11am, 1pm, 2pm and 3pm; May-June, Sept-Oct, daily 1pm, 2pm and 3pm; Nov-Apr, daily 2pm and 3pm. Closed Good Fri, 24 Dec and during rehearsals (telephone in advance to check schedule). 60S. ☎ 01/5 14 44 26 13.

Haydn-Museum – Open Tues-Sun 9am-12.15pm, 1-4.30pm. 25S. ☎ 01/5 96 13 07.

Franz-Schubert-Gedenkstätte "Geburtshaus" – Open Tues-Sun 9am-12.15pm, 1-4.30pm. Closed 1 Jan, 1 May, 25 Dec. 25S (admission free Fri morning). ☎ 01/3 17 36 01.

Zentralfriedhof – ♿ Open May-Aug 7am-7pm; Mar, Apr, Sept and Oct 7am-6pm; Nov-Feb 8am-5pm. ☎ 01/7 60 41.

Jüdisches Museum der Stadt Wien – ♿ Open Mon-Fri, Sun 10am-6pm (8pm Thur). Closed Rosh Hashanah (New Year), Yom Kippur (Day of Atonement). 70S. ☎ 01/5 35 04 31.

Minoritenkirche – Open Apr-Oct, daily 8am-6pm; Nov-Mar, Mon-Sat 9am-5pm, Sun 8am-5pm. Donations requested. ☎ 01/5 33 41 62.

Alte Ursulinenklosterapotheke – ♿ Open Wed 10am-5pm, Sun 10am-1pm. Closed public holidays. 25S. ☎ 01/4 06 89 05 21.

Historisches Museum der Stadt Wien – ♿ Open Tues-Sun 9am-6pm. Closed 1 Jan, 1 May, 25 Dec. 50S (admission free Fri morning). ☎ 01/5 05 87 47.

Österreichisches Museum für Volkskunde – ♿ Open Tues-Sun 10am-5pm. Closed 1 Jan, Easter Day, 1 May, 1 Nov, 25 Dec. 45S (admission free 26 Oct, 26 Dec). ☎ 01/4 06 89 05 16.

Prater Giant Wheel – ♿ Operates May-Sept, daily 9am-midnight; Mar-Apr, Oct, daily 10am-10pm; Jan-Feb, Nov-Dec, daily 10am-6pm. 55S. ☎ 01/7 29 54 30.

Akademie der bildenden Künste – Gemäldegalerie – Open Tues-Sun 10am-4pm. 50S. ☎ 01/58 81 62 25.

Österreichisches Museum für angewandte Kunst (MAK) – ♿ Open Tues-Sun 10am-6pm (midnight Tues). Closed 1 Jan, 1 May, 1 Nov, 25 Dec. 30S (admission free 26 Oct, 24 Dec). ☎ 01/71 13 60.

Naturhistorisches Museum – ♿ Open Mon, Wed-Sun 9am-6.30pm (9pm Wed). Closed 1 Jan, 1 May, 1 Nov, 25 Dec. 50S (admission free 26 Oct, 24 Dec). ☎ 01/52 17 70.

Piaristenkirche Basilika Maria Treu – Can only be visited by appointment with the presbytery. ☎ 01/4 05 04 25 13.

KunstHausWien – ♿ Open daily 10am-7pm. 95S. ☎ 01/7 12 04 95.

KUNSTHAUSWIEN

KunstHausWien

Museum moderner Kunst Stiftung Ludwig – The Palais Liechtenstein and 20er Haus are closed due to the impending move. Reopening in the new premises in the museum district is scheduled for Dec 2001. ☎ 01/3 17 69 00.

Heeresgeschichtliches Museum – ♿ Open Mon-Thur, Sat-Sun 9am-5pm. Closed 1 Jan, Easter Day, 1 May, 1 Nov, 24, 25, 31 Dec. 70S (free admission 26 Oct). ☎ 01/79 56 16 00 02.

Kaiserliches Hofmobiliendepot – ♿ Open daily 9am-5pm. 90S. ☎ 01/5 24 42 40.

Technisches Museum – Open Mon-Sat 9am-6pm (8pm Thur), Sun 10am-6pm. Closed 1 Jan, 1 May, 1 Nov, 25, 26 Dec. 95S. ☎ 01/89 99 80.

Excursions

Heiligenstadt: Beethovens "Testamenthaus" – Open Mar-Dec, Tues, Thur, Sat-Sun 10am-noon, 1-4.30pm. Closed 1 Jan, 1 May, 25 Dec. 15S. ☎ 01/3 18 86 08.

Orth an der Donau: Schloß – Open mid Mar-mid Nov, Tues-Fri 9am-noon, 1-5pm, Sat-Sun 9am-5pm. 40S. ☎ 0 22 12/25 55.

Eckartsau: Schloß – Guided tour (1hr) Apr-Oct, Sat-Sun and public holidays 11am and 2pm. 60S. ☎ 0 22 14/22 40.

Niederweiden: Schloß – Open Palm Sun-1 Nov, Sat-Sun 10am-5pm. ☎ 0 22 14/28 03.

Schloßhof: Schloß – Open Palm Sun-1 Nov, Tues-Sun 10am-5pm. 70S. ☎ 0 22 85/65 80.

Marchegg: Schloß – Open 15 Mar-30 Nov, Tues-Sun 9am-noon, 1-5pm. 30S. ☎ 0 22 85/71 00 11.

WIENER NEUSTADT

ℹ Hauptplatz 1-3, A-2700, ☎ 0 26 22/37 34 68

St. Georgskathedrale – Guided tour (20min) Mon-Fri 8am-4pm, Sat 8am-3pm, Sun noon-5pm. Free admission. ☎ 0 26 22/3 81 20 91.

Excursion

Burg Seebenstein – Guided tour (50min) Easter-2nd Sun in Oct, Sat-Sun 10.30am, 2pm and 3pm. 50S. ☎ 0 26 27/4 70 17.

WIENERWALD

Naturpark Sparbach – Open Apr-Oct, daily 9am-6pm; Nov, Jan-Mar, Sat-Sun 10am-3pm (Nov), 10am-4pm (Jan), 10am-5pm (Feb), 10am-6pm (Mar). Closed and during bad weather. 20S. ☎ 0 22 37/76 11.

Hinterbrühl: Seegrotte – Guided tour (45min) Apr-Oct, daily 9am-noon, 1-5pm; Nov-Mar, Mon-Fri 9am-noon, 1-3pm, Sat-Sun 9am-noon, 1-3.30pm. 55S. ☎ 0 22 36/2 63 64.

Laxenburg: Park – Open daily 24hr/24hr. 16S. ☎ 0 22 36/71 22 60.

Stiftskirche WILHERING

Open Apr-Sept, daily 7am-6pm; Oct-Mar, daily 8am-4pm.

WÖRTHER SEE

Rosegg: Wildpark – Open July-Aug, daily 9am-6pm; Apr-June, Sept-Nov, daily 9am-5pm. 80S. ☎ 0 42 74/5 23 57.

Rosegg: Schloß – Open May-Oct, Tues-Sun 10am-6pm (also open on Mon July-Aug). 60S. ☎ 0 42 74/30 09.

Pyramidenkogel: Viewing tower – Open July-Aug, daily 9am-10pm; June, daily 9am-8pm; Apr, Sept-Oct, daily 10am-6pm; May, Sept, daily 9am-7pm. 60S. ☎ 0 42 73/24 43.

Z

ZELL AM SEE

ℹ Brucker Bundesstraße 3, A-5710, ☎ 0 65 42/7 70

Ascent to the Schmittenhöhe – Cable-car operates 20 May-22 Oct, mid Nov-mid Apr, 8.30am (9am 20 May-17 June)-5pm every 30min. 240S two-way trip. ☎ 0 65 42/78 90.

ZILLERTAL

Ascent to the Penken – Chair-lift operates mid May-mid Oct, early Dec-mid Apr, daily 9am-5pm. 160S two-way trip. ☎ 0 52 85/6 22 77.

ZÜRS

ℹ A-6763, ☎ 0 55 83/22 45

Trittkopf – Cable-car operates Dec-Apr, daily 8.30am-4pm. 130S two-way trip. ☎ 0 55 83/2 38 80.

Stift ZWETTL

ℹ Landstr. 10, A-3910, ☎ 0 28 22/5 22 33

Guided tour (1hr) July-Sept, Mon-Sat 10am, 11am, 2pm, 3pm and 4pm, Sun 11am, 2pm, 3pm and 4pm; May-June, Oct, Mon-Sat 10am, 11am, 2pm and 3pm, Sun 11am, 2pm and 3pm. 65S. ☎ 0 28 22/55 00.

Excursions

Schloß Rosenau – ♿ Open Apr-end Oct, daily 9am-5pm. 50S (free admission 26 Oct). ☎ 0 28 22/5 82 21 15.

Burg Rappottenstein – Guided tour (45min) May-end Sept, Tues-Sun 10am, 11am, 2pm, 3pm, 4pm and 5pm; Easter, mid-end Apr, Oct, Sat-Sun only. 70S. ☎ 0 28 28/82 50.

Index

Innsbruck .... Towns, sights and tourist regions
Steiermark .... Federal province *(Land)*
Berg, Alban .... People, historical events, artistic styles and subjectscovered in the text.

Individual sights (mountains, lakes, dams, abbeys castles etc) are indexed under their own names.

This index, like the other alphabetical lists in this guide, follows the normal German alphabetical order, where the vowels ä, ö and ü are classified under ae, oe and ue respectively, ß is classified under ss, and St. under Sankt (Saint).

A

B

C

D

H

I

J

N

P

R

S

T

U

V

W

Z